The History Of The First Discovery And Settlement Of Virginia

Joseph

Sabin's Reprints.

No. VI.

THE

HISTORY

OF THE

FIRST DISCOVERY AND SETTLEMENT

OF

VIRGINIA.

BY

WILLIAM STITH, A. M.

NEW YORK:

REPRINTED FOR JOSEPH SABIN.

1865.

TWO HUNDRED AND FIFTY COPIES PRINTED.

No.

ALVORD, PRINTER.

BIBLIOGRAPHICAL NOTICE.

THE Original Documents from which much of this valuable work was compiled having been lately deftroyed, and the work itfelf being fcarce, it is hoped its reprodu&ion will be an acceptable contribution to American Hiftory.

Two Editions of the work have been publifhed; the Firft, or Williamfburg Edition (of which this is a reprint), in 1747, and the London Reprint in 1753.

In the "Hiftorical Magazine," Vol. II., page 184, a writer, under the pfeudonym of B. FRANKLIN, defcribes what he confiders *Two* Williamfburg Editions, but which were, in reality, the Editions of 1747 and 1753, but probably having titles alike.

In the fame Magazine, Vol. V., page 350, D. P. S [MITH] attempts to point out the difference in the Editions, but falls into a double error: firft, in defcribing the *Fine Paper* Williamfburg Edition as correfponding with the London Edition in Type, Lines, Pages, and Ornaments; and fecond, in ftating that the "Poor Paper Williamfburg Edition" differs from the Fine Paper of the fame place and date.

As I have the *three* varieties now before me, I will endeavour to defcribe them.

The Firft, or Williamfburg Edition, of 1747, appears to have been printed on two varieties of paper, both the fame fize, and both *laid*, one being thicker than the other. The Signatures, Catchwords, Ornaments, &c., agreeing exa&ly with each other, and the error on page 104, which is printed 410, being alike in each.

Signature S is mifpaged. It fhould read 257 inftead of 247, and fo on to the end, adding 10 pages to the whole number (331) as they appear in this reprint.

The ſecond Edition has the following Title :—" The Hiſtory of the Firſt Diſcovery and Settlement of *Virginia*. By WILLIAM STITH, A. M., Preſident of the College of *William* and *Mary* in *Virginia*. *Tantæ molis erat * * * condere gentem.* Virg. *Virginia*, Printed : *London*, Reprinted for S. BIRT, in *Ave-Mary-Lane*. M.DCC.LIII."

The Number of Pages, Signatures, &c., is the ſame as in the Williamſburg Edition. The pagination runs on regularly up to page 304, then the *recto* of Signature X is paged 295, and ſo on till it terminates at page 331 (for 341) as in the other Edition.

,„The Paper and Types are the ſame as the Williamſburg Fine Paper, but in other reſpeĉts there are ſeveral variations.

On pages 1, 35, 101, 175, and 176, the Ornaments differ.

On pages 21 and 119, the London Edition has Signature marks not in the other.

On pages 33, 73, 82, 84, 86, 89, 98, 99, 131, 171, 178, 179, 206, 208, 214, 225, 233, 238, and 244, the Catchwords differ ; while Signature X appears to be preciſely the ſame in each Edition, and in my copy of the London Edition, the paper in *this* Signature differs from the reſt of the volume.

On page 308 of the Williamſburg Edition, there is a line acroſs the page, over the foot-note. This is omitted in the London Edition.

On page 2 of the Appendix, the capital J is in Roman— in the London Edition it is in Italic.

JOSEPH SABIN.

NEW YORK, 1865.

C.

THE
HISTORY
OF THE
Firſt DISCOVERY
AND
SETTLEMENT
OF
VIRGINIA:
BEING
An ESSAY towards a General
HISTORY of this COLONY.

By WILLIAM STITH, *A. M.*
Rector of *Henrico* Pariſh, and one of the Governors of
William and *Mary* COLLEGE.

Tantæ molis erat ***** *condere gentem.* Virg.

WILLIAMSBURG:
Printed by WILLIAM PARKS, M,DCC,XLVII.

2

THE

PREFACE.

I HERE *present the Reader with the first Part of my History of our own Country. When I had left my laborious Employment at the College, and began to enjoy a little Leisure, I could not think myself wholly discharged from the Service of the Publick. As therefore my late Uncle, Sir* John Randolph, *had purposed to write a Preface to our Laws, and therein to give an Historical Account of our Constitution and Government, but was prevented from prosecuting it to Effect, by his many and weighty Publick Employments, and by the vast Burthen of private Business from his Clients, I thought the History of* Virginia *would be no mean or unacceptable Undertaking. For such a Work, well performed, must naturally be a great Satisfaction, and even Ornament, to our Country. Besides which, I was farther induced by some other Reasons. It is now an hundred and forty Years, since the first Discovery and Settlement of* Virginia; *and as many useful Papers and Records, relating to our History, may probably be found at present, which will perhaps be lost hereafter, I conceived it high time, that something material should be attempted in it. For I need not say, how empty and unsatisfactory every thing, yet published upon the Subject, is; excepting the excellent but confused Materials, left us in Captain* Smith's *History.*

I speak not this with the Pride and Malevolence of an Author, that would raise his own Reputation by depreciating his Brother Writers; but it is a Censure most justly due to those, who have yet meddled with our History, and which I, for my own Part, owe them, for the Vexation and Disappointment I met with, in reading their Works. And I can farther declare with great Truth, that had any thing of Consequence been done in our History, I could most willingly have saved myself the Trouble, of conning over our old musty Records,

A 2

cords,

cords, and of *studying*, *connecting*, and *reconciling the jar-ring and disjointed Writings and Relations of different Men and different Parties*. However, I was sorry to see all our Hopes at an End by the Death of Sir John Randolph; and was unwilling the Design should be entirely abandoned, and that our History should still remain in its old Confusion and Uncertainty. I had also, by my Intimacy with that Gentle-man, had the Sight and Perusal of many excellent Materials in his Hands; and thought, I could not handsomely be denied the Use of any thing else to my Purpose, either in our publick Offices, or the Possession of private Gentlemen.

I may further add, that I at present enjoy a perfect Lei-sure and Retirement, and am not burthened with any publick Post or Office. So that such a Work will be a noble and ele-gant Entertainment for my vacant Hours, which it is not in my Power to employ, more to my own Satisfaction, or the Use and Benefit of my Country.

AS to my Helps in carrying on this Work, besides De Brye's Edition of Hariot's Treatise and With's Cuts and Maps, and besides casual Assistances from such Parts of Purchas, as I could procure, from Dr. Heylen, and other things in Print, the inquisitive Reader will easily perceive, how much of this Volume is founded on Captain Smith's Materials. They are large and good, and of unquestionable Authority, for what is related, whilst he staid in the Country. But they are how-ever, as I before observed, vastly confused and perplexed, and took me more Labour and Pains to digest them, than I at first expected. The latter Part of his History also, especially from Captain Argall's Government, is liable to some just Suspicion. Not that I question Captain Smith's Integrity; for I take him to have been a very honest Man, and a strenuous Lover of Truth. But being himself absent in those times upon other Projects, and having an Acquaintance and Friendship with Sir Thomas Smith and Captain Argall, he seems chiefly to have depended upon them and their Friends, for his Account of things. And particularly, his Account of Captain Argall's Government is expresly taken from himself, and from a Rela-tion of Mr. Rolfe's. Besides which, it is evident that his Mind was somewhat eagered by the Neglects shewn him, and by the Refusal of some just Reward for his many and great Services. So that he does not seem much inclined, to think well of the Company or their Proceedings. And such Prejudices and Partialities do silently and imperceptibly slide into the best and honestest Minds; and ought therefore to be carefully watched and guarded against by all Men, but especially by Historians. But from whatever Cause it proceeded, it is cer-tain, that he gave a very wrong Idea of Captain Argall and

his

his Government, and of the Reasons of the Dissolution of the Company, in which he has been implicitly followed by all our succeeding Historians. And I would not have the Reader surprised to find my Account of those Particulars, so very different from all others, yet in Print. For I assure him, there is not one Article, scarce a Word, in my Relation, which is not founded on the express Testimony, and the incontestible Authority, of our Records in the Capitol, and the Company's Journals.

FOR besides these printed Accounts, I have had the greatest most considerable Assistances from authentick Manuscripts. —
John Randolph's Collection of publick Papers, and the ...tol Records, have been of no little Use to me, and will be ...of greater Service and Consequence in the Prosecution of the Work. But I must confess myself most endebted, in this Part of my History, to a very full and fair Manuscript of the London *Company's Records, which was communicated to me by the late worthy President of our Council, the Honourable* William Byrd, *Esq; Neither could I well excuse myself, if I did not likewise acknowledge, with what Humanity and Politeness, that well bred Gentleman and Scholar, not only communicated those Manuscripts to me, but also threw open his Library (the best and most copious Collection of Books in our Part of* America) *and was himself even studious and sollicitous, to search out and give me, whatever might be useful to my Undertaking.*

AS these Records are a very curious and valuable Piece of the Antiquities of our Country, I shall give the Reader an Account of them, which I received, many Years ago, in Conversation with Col. Byrd *and Sir* John Randolph. *I had then no Thoughts of writing the History of* Virginia, *and therefore took less Notice, than I otherwise should have done. However, as I am perhaps the only Person now living, any thing acquainted with their History, it will not be improper to give it to the Reader, as I judge it highly worthy of his Knowledge.*

THESE Records are a Journal of the Company's Proceedings, from Day to Day; and are written in two large Folio Volumes, on a Kind of Elephant Paper, generally in a very fair and legible Hand. Each Page is subscribed by Edward Collingwood, *the Company's Secretary, thus; Com.* Collingwood, *which is, as I take it, Compared, Collingwood. Besides which, there is a Testification at the End of each Volume. At the End of the first, under the Hands of* Edward Waterhouse *and* Edward Collingwood, *Secretaries of the two Companies for* Virginia *and the* Somer-Islands, *that they had compared that with the Original Court-Book, and*
found

found it to be a true and perfect Copy of the same, except the Omiffion of one Court and Part of another. The second Volume is figned by the said Secretary Collingwood *and* Thomas Collet, *of the* Middle Temple, Gentleman, *teftifying the same thing, except in a few immaterial Points, where were wanted some Original Papers: These Volumes only contain the Company's Proceedings for a little above five Years, viz. from* April 28, 1619 *to* June 7, 1624; *including the whole Time of Sir* Edwin Sandys's *and the Earl of* Southampton's *Administration. However they are not a brief and summary Entry of the principal Points and Matters concluded upon, according to the common Methods of Courts, but give, at length, the chief Speeches, Reasons, and Debates, that happened in their Courts, during that time. And as it was a Period of vaft Conteft and Difpute, they often recur back to former Times and Tranfactions, and thereby give us a clear Idea and Account of the chief Matters and Proceedings of the Company, almoft from it's firft Inftitution and Foundation.*

THIS Copy was taken, by the Order, and for the Ufe, of the Earl of Southampton, *the Company's Treafurer at that time; who feeing, how things were going with the Company, had their Records thus carefully copied and compared, and authentically attefted. Whether his Lordfhip intended to ftand Suit with the King for the Rights and Privileges of the Company, or whether he did it only in Vindication of his own and the Company's Reputation, is uncertain. However they were carefully preferved in the Family; and as the Original Court-Books were taken from the Company by the King and Privy Council, and never again reftored to them, that I can find, but probably deftroyed or loft, this is perhaps the only Copy, now extant. After the Death of that Earl's Son, the Duke of* Southampton *(the worthy Partner in the Miniftry with the Earl of* Clarendon, *after the Reftoration) which happened in the Year* 1667, *the late Col.* Byrd's *Father, being then in* England, *purchafed them of his Executors, for fixty Guineas. And thus have they been handed down, to clear the Honour and Uprightnefs of the Actions of that Nobleman and the Company, and to the full Conviction of King* James's *arbitrary and oppreffive Proceedings againft them.*

I therefore hope, my Freedom with that King's Character, will need no Apology. For if more than a Century is not enough to un-folomonife that filly Monarch, I muft give up all my Notions of things. A King's Character, whilft he lives, is, and ought to be facred, becaufe his Authority depends upon it. But when his Authority, the Reafon of it's being facred, determines, the Inviolablenefs of his Character is alfo at an End. And I take it to be the main Part of the

Duty

The PREFACE. vii

Duty and Office of an Historian, to paint Men and Things in their true and lively Colours; and to do that Justice to the Vices and Follies of Princes and great Men, after their Death, which it is not safe or proper to do, whilst they are alive. And herein, as I judge, chiefly consist the Strength and Excellency of Tacitus and Suetonius. Their Stile and Manner are far inferior to Livy's, and the Writers of the Julian and Augustan Ages. But they have more than painted, and exposed alive to View, the greatest Train of Monsters, that ever disgraced a Throne, or did Dishonour to human Nature; and thereby have obtained to themselves a Rank, among the best and most valuable Writers. King James I. fell indeed far short of the Cæsar's superlative Wickedness and Supremacy in Vice. He was, at best, only very simple and injudicious, without any steady Principle of Justice and Honour; which was rendered the more odious and ridiculous, by his large and constant Pretensions to Wisdom and Virtue. And he had, in Truth, all the Forms of Wisdom; for ever erring very learnedly, with a wise Saw, or Latin Sentence, in his Mouth. For he had been bred up under Buchanan, one of the brightest Genius's and most accomplished Scholars of that Age, who had given him Greek and Latin in great Waste and Profusion, but it was not in his Power to give him good Sense. That is the Gift of God and Nature alone, and is not to be taught; and Greek and Latin without it, only cumber and overload a weak Head, and often render the Fool more abundantly foolish. I must therefore confess, that I have ever had, from my first Acquaintance with History, a most contemptible Opinion of this Monarch; which has perhaps been much heightened and increased, by my long studying and conning over the Materials of this History. For he appears, in his Dealings with the Company, to have acted with such mean Arts and Fraud, and such little Tricking, as highly misbecome Majesty. And I am much mistaken, if his arbitrary Proceedings and unjust Designs will appear from any Part of his History more fully, than from these Transactions with the Company and Colony; which have been thus far unknown to the English Historians, and will perhaps be still thought too insignificant for their Notice. However I hope, my speaking my Mind thus sincerely and impartially will give no Umbrage or Offence to any Man, or Party of Men. For I declare myself to be of no Party; but have laboured solely with a View, to find out and relate the Truth. And as for King James I. I think and speak of him, with the same Freedom and Indifferency, that I would think and speak of any other Man, long since dead; and therefore I have no way restrained my Stile, in freely exposing his weak and injurious Proceedings

IN

viii

The PREFACE.

IN the succeeding Parts of this History, I am afraid, I shall meet with much greater Difficulties, then I have yet encountered. For I must chiefly depend on such of our Records, as are still extant. Many of them doubtless perished in the State-house at James-Town, and by other Accidents; and those, which have survived the Flames and Injuries of Time, have been so carelesly kept, are so broken, interrupted, and deficient, have been so mangled by Moths and Worms, and lie in such a confused and jumbled State (at least the most ancient of them) being huddled together in single Leaves and Sheets in Books out of the Binding, that I foresee, it will cost me infinite Pains and Labour, to reduce and digest them into any tolerable Order, so as to form from them a just and connected Narration. And some of them have been lost, even since Mr. Hickman was Clerk of the Secretary's Office. For I cannot find, among the Papers in our Offices, some old Rolls, to which he refers. I have therefore been obliged, in a few Points, to depend upon the Fidelity of that Gentleman's Extracts out of our oldest Records, made for the Use of Sir John Randolph. But these things were so far from discouraging and rebuffing me, that they were rather an additional Spur to my Industry. For I thought it highly necessary, before they were entirely lost and destroyed, to apply them to their proper Use, the forming a good History. But as the House of Burgesses, in a late Session, upon my shewing their moldering and dangerous State to some of the Members, have justly taken them into their Consideration, and have ordered them to be reviewed and fairly transcribed, I doubt not, by their Assistance, and with the Help of the late Sir John Randolph's Papers, and such others, as are in the Hands of private Gentlemen in the Country, and will undoubtedly be readily communicated to further so noble and so useful a Design, to be able to collect and compose a tolerably regular and complete History of our Country.

Varina, Dec. 10, 1746.

THE

THE
HISTORY
OF
VIRGINIA.

BOOK I.

VERY Country hath it's Fables concerning it's Original, which give great Scope to light and fanciful Hiſtorians, but are uſually paſſed over with a ſlight Mention by the ſolid and judicious. The late Diſcovery of *America*, in hiſtorical and well-known Times, might, one would think, have exempted it from this common Fate of Nations. Yet ſuch is the Pride of ſome Men to ſeem of deep Reach and Inſight, and to ſtrike out things untouched and unthought of by others, and ſuch their prepoſterous Delight in groping after Truth in the Dark, and yet neglecting her in the clear and meridian Brightneſs of Day, that even this new World hath been endowed with it's fabulous Age, and old Tales revived, or new ones invented, to ſtretch it's Antiquities beyond *Columbus*, and the ſhort Date of two hundred and fifty Years. We are therefore told of one *Hanno*, a *Carthaginian* Captain, who made a Voyage to *America*. But in what Age he lived, or upon what Authority or Pretext the Story is grounded, I have not been yet able fully to diſcover. Even the monſtrous Legends of *Arthur*, *Malgo*,

and *Madock*, a *Welch* Prince, and of the Friar of *Lynne*,
who by his black Art tranfported himfelf to the Northern
Parts of *America*, have found Men weak enough to be
the Relators and Propagators of them.   *Plato*'s Fable alfo
of the *Atlantick* Iflands has been applied to this Subject;
and *Seneca* the Tragedian, who could never yet obtain from
the Criticks a firm Rank among the beft and moft approved
Claflicks, hath neverthelefs been acknowledged by the Hiftorians as a true Prophet, and fome Verfes of his quoted,
as containing a prediction of the future Difcovery and Settlement of *America*.   But as I have ever had an utter Contempt and Averfion for all fuch learned Trumpery, and
have often been difgufted and concerned to fee Authors,
otherwife of Judgment and Genius, carried by their Credulity too far into thofe dark and uncertain Tracts of
Time, I fhall leave thefe, with other Stories of the like
Nature, to their firft Authors or Inventors, and fhall apply
myfelf to give a plain and exact Hiftory of our Country,
ever regarding Truth as the firft requifite and principal Virtue in an Hiftorian, and relating nothing without a fufficient Warrant and Authority.

T H E *European* Nations had continued, through all Ages,
in the moft profound Ignorance of all the reft of the World,
except the beft Part of *Europe*, and the moft obvious and
adjacent Countries of *Afia* and *Africa*.   And although the
attractive Power of the Loadftone had been long known
and obferved, yet it's Poles, and the wonderful Qualities
and Inclination of the magnetical Needle, were ftill a Secret, till it feemed good to Divine Providence, that one
John Gioia, of *Amalfi* in the Kingdom of *Naples*, difcovered them about the Year 1300.   This important Difcovery lay long ufelefs, without any Application to Navigation; neither can we certainly fay, who firft turned it to
this great End.   However the Ufe of the Sea-Compafs
crept in by Degrees, and was undoubtedly the grand Inftrument and Foundation of all thefe later Difcoveries.

T H E *Portuguefe* was the firft Nation of *Europe*, that
engaged in maritime Expeditions, in order to explore and
difcover the unknown Parts of the World.   For Prince
Henry of *Portugal*, in the Year 1417, fent two fmall Barks
to make Difcoveries along the Coaft of *Africa*; which Beginning, having fome Succefs, was afterwards profecuted,
during the Life of that Prince, under his Aufpices and Direction.   After his Death, they ftill advanced by Degrees
in their Trade and Difcoveries, till at length in the Year
1486 they reached the Cape of *Good-Hope*.   But it was
1497, five Years after the Difcovery of *America*, before

Vafco

Vafco de Gama, by the Command, and in the Service, of *Emanuel,* King of *Portugal,* failed round that Cape to the *Eaft-Indies.*

Chriftopher Columbus, a *Genoefe* by Birth, a Perfon of great Knowledge and Experience in naval Affairs, of good Learning, and a comprehenfive Mind, and being alfo led perhaps by the late Difcoveries of the *Portuguefe,* was ftrongly poffeffed with a Notion of fome Lands to the Weftward, beyond the great *Atlantick* Ocean. He therefore firft offered his Service to his native Country, the Republick of *Genoa;* but being rejected as a whimfical and chimerical Man, he applied himfelf to King *John* II. of *Portugal, Henry* VII. of *England,* and to *Ferdinand* and *Ifabel,* King and Queen of *Caftile.* Many Years being fpent in fruitlefs Sollicitations, and after much Vexation and Difappointment, he was at laft entertained in the Service of the King and Queen of *Caftile,* and fent upon the Difcovery, which he happily effected the 11th of *October* 1492. After this, *Columbus,* being animated with a publick Spirit and a generous Principle of Glory, and the *Spaniards,* being as eagerly pufhed on by an infatiable Thirft of Gold, fo ardently purfued, and fo fuccefsfully improved this firft Difcovery, that they foon became Mafters of vaft Tracts of rich and fertile Country abounding in Gold, Silver, Pearls, Emeralds, and many other the moft precious and delicious Products of this Globe. The *Portuguefe* likewife, altho' fufficiently loaded and embarraffed with their vaft Acquifitions on the Coaft of *Africa* and in the *Eaft-Indies,* yet neverthelefs found the Means and Opportunity to make good their great Difcovery of *Brazil.* Neither were the *French* entirely idle; but they made many vigorous Efforts towards gaining a Share of the Riches and Territory of this new World.

T H E *Englifh* in the mean time, a maritime Nation, of great Bravery, and of a bold and adventurous Nature, lay quite negligent and fupine, and let flip all Opportunities in thofe early Times of acquiring fome rich and ufeful Provinces in *America.* For altho' they had in the Year 1497, under *Sebaftian Cabot,* made the Difcovery of *Newfoundland,* and of the main Continent of *America* from 38 to 68 Degrees of northern Latitude, yet they made no other Advantage of this Difcovery, but to fend out a few fifhing Barks in common with other Nations of *Europe.* At length Sir *Humphry Gilbert,* a Gentleman of great Reputation for his Skill in naval Affairs, and of a high and refolute Spirit, undertook to fettle a Colony in *Newfoundland,* a cold, barren, and unfruitful Soil, and moft unfriendly Clime. And

to this End, he obtained Letters patent from Queen *Eliza-*
beth, bearing Date the 11th of *June,* 1578.

T H E S E Letters patent granted "free Power and Li-
" berty to him, his Heirs and Affigns for ever, to dif-
" cover, find, fearch out, and view, all fuch remote,
" heathen, and barbarous Lands, Countries, or Territories,
" as were not actually poffeffed by any Chriftian Prince or
" People ; and thither to lead and carry with him, to travel
" thitherward, and there inhabit, fuch and fo many of her
" Majefty's Subjects, as would willingly accompany and
" join in the Enterprife.

" A N D that he fhould have, hold, occupy, and enjoy,
" to himfelf, his Heirs and Affigns, for ever, all fuch
" Lands, Countries, and Territories, fo to be difcovered
" or poffeffed, with the Rights, Royalties, and Jurifdic-
" tions, as well marine as other, within the faid Lands
" and Countries, or the Seas thereunto adjoining, with
" full Power to difpofe thereof to her Majefty's Subjects,
" and of any or every Part thereof, in Fee-fimple, or other-
" wife, according to the Laws of *England,* as nearly as
" conveniently might be ; paying to the Queen, her Heirs
" and Succeffors, for all Services, Duties, and Demands
" whatfoever, the Fifth Part of all the Ore of Gold and
" Silver, which fhould at any time there be gotten ;
" holding all the faid Lands and Countries of her Majef-
" ty, her Heirs, and Succeffors, by Homage, and by the
" Payment of the faid Fifth Part, before referved.

" M O R E O V E R granting to him, his Heirs and Affigns,
" for ever, Licence to encounter, expel, repel, and refift
" all Perfon or Perfons whatfoever, that fhould attempt
" to inhabit in the faid Countries, without his fpecial
" Licence and Liking, or within the Space of two Hun-
" dred Leagues of the Place, where he, his Heirs, or Af-
" figns, fhould, within Six Years next enfuing, make
" their Dwelling and Abode ; provided the faid Countries
" were not before planted or inhabited, within the aforefaid
" Limits, by the Subjects of any Chriftian Prince, in Amity
" with her Majefty. And giving and granting to him, his
" Heirs and Affigns, for ever, full Power and Authority,
" to take and furprife, by all manner of Means whatfo-
" ever, all and every Perfon and Perfons, with their Ships,
" Veffels, or other Goods and Furniture, that fhould be
" found trafficking within the Limits aforefaid, without
" the Licence of the faid Sir *Humphry,* his Heirs, or Af-
" figns ; the Subjects of the Queen's Realms and Domi-
" nions, and all other Perfons in Amity with her, being
" driven thither . by Force of Tempeft or Shipwreck, only
" excepted.   " A N D

" AND for uniting in more perfect League and Amity,
" such Lands and Countries with the Realms of *England*
" and *Ireland*, and for the better encouragement of thofe,
" who would engage in the Enterprife, the Queen grants
" and declares, that the faid Countries, fo to be poffeffed
" and inhabited, fhould from thenceforth be in the Alle-
" giance and Protection of her, her Heirs, and Succeffors;
" and farther grants to the faid Sir *Humphry*, his Heirs,
" and Affigns, and to every other Perfon or Perfons, to
" their, and every of their Heirs, that they, and every
" of them, that fhould thereafter be inhabiting in the faid
" Lands, Countries, and Territories, fhould and might
" have and enjoy all the Privileges of free Denizens, or
" Perfons native of *England*; any Law, Cuftom, or U-
" fage to the contrary notwithftanding.

" AND fhe farther grants to the faid Sir *Humphry*, his
" Heirs and Affigns, for ever, full Power and Authority,
" to correct, punifh, pardon, govern and rule, as well in
" Caufes capital or criminal, as civil, all fuch her Subjects
" or others, as fhould adventure themfelves in the faid
" Voyages, or fhould at any Time thereafter inhabit the
" faid Lands, Countries, or Territories, or fhould dwell
" within two hundred Leagues of the Place or Places,
" where the faid *Humphry*, his Heirs, or Affigns, or any
" of his or their Affociates, fhould inhabit within fix Years
" enfuing the Date thereof; with Power to conftitute fuch
" Statutes, Laws, and Ordinances, as fhould by him, the
" faid Sir *Humphry*, his Heirs, or Affigns, be devifed or
" eftablifhed, for the better Government of the faid Peo-
" ple: Provided always, that they fhould be, as near as
" conveniently might, agreeable to the Laws and Policy
" of *England*; and provided alfo, that they be not againft
" the true Chriftian Faith, profeffed in the Church of
" *England*, nor any way tend to withdraw the Subjects or
" People of thofe Lands or Places from the Allegiance of
" the Queen, her Heirs, or Succeffors.

" PROVIDED always, and fhe thereby declares to all
" Chriftian Kings, Princes, and States, that if the faid Sir
" *Humphry*, his Heirs, or Affigns, or any other by their
" Licence or Appointment, fhould at any Time or Times
" thereafter, rob or fpoil, by Sea or by Land, or do any
" Act of unjuft or unlawful Hoftility, to any of the Sub-
" jects of *England*, or of any other King, Prince, or State,
" in League or Amity with the Crown of *England*, that
" then, upon fuch Injury, or upon juft Complaint thereof,
" the Queen, her Heirs, or Succeffors, fhould make open
" Proclamation, within any of the Ports of *England* com-

B 3   " modious,

" modious, that the faid Sir *Humphry*, his Heirs, or Affigns,
" or any other, to whom thofe Letters patent might ex-
" tend, fhould, within the Term to be limited in the faid
" Proclamations, make full Reftitution and Satisfaction for
" all Injuries fo done : In Default whereof, it fhould be
" lawful for the Queen, her Heirs, or Succeffors, to put
" the faid Sir *Humphry*, his Heirs, or Affigns, with his or
" their Adherents, and all the Inhabitants of the faid Pla-
" ces, out of their Allegiance and Protection ; and that
" from fuch Time as they fhould be fo put out of the Pro-
" tection of the Crown of *England*, it fhould be free for all
" Princes and others, to purfue them with Hoftility, as
" being no longer Subjects of *England*, nor by the Queen,
" her Heirs, or Succeffors, any ways to be avowed, main-
" tained, or defended."

I N Confequence of thefe ample Powers and Privileges,
Sir *Humphry Gilbert*, with the Conjunction and Affiftance
of many other Gentlemen, prepared to put to Sea with a
noble Fleet.   But juft on the Point of Departure, upon fome
Difagreement and Diffention, he was deferted by his Affociates, and left with only a few of his firm and faithful
Friends.   With thefe, however, he ventured to Sea, but
having been expofed to fome Misfortunes, and loft a large
Ship of his Fleet, he was obliged to return without effecting
any thing.   Thefe expenfive and unfuccefsful Preparations
had fo impaired his Fortune, that it was 1583, before he
made any farther Attempt.   But then having fold his Eftate,
and being joined by divers Gentlemen of Fortune, he again
fet Sail with two Ships and three fmall Barks.   Coming before St. *John*'s Harbour in *Newfoundland*, he was refufed
Entrance by the fifhing Veffels within, to the Number of
thirty-fix Sail, of all Nations.   He therefore prepared to
make his Way good by Force of Arms ; but firft fent his
Boat in to inform them, that he had a Commiffion from
the Queen, to take Poffeffion of thofe Lands for the Crown
of *England*.   Queen *Elizabeth*'s Name was reverenced
through all *Europe*, and her Power and Authority at Sea, in
particular, much honoured and revered.   Thefe Fifhing-
Barks therefore readily fubmitted, and even made a Contribution of Provifions to fupply the Wants of this fmall
Fleet.

A F T E R this, Sir *Humphry* went afhore, being conducted by all the *Englifh* there ; and having caufed a Tent to
be fet up in View of the Bay and Veffels, being attended
by his Captains, Mafters, Gentlemen, and Soldiers, he
fummoned all the Merchants and Mafters, both *Englifh* and
Foreigners, to be prefent at his taking a formal and folemn
Poffeffion

Poffeffion of the Country. He then caufed his Commiffion to be openly read, and to be interpreted to thofe who were Strangers to the *Englifh* Tongue. By Virtue of this Commiffion, he declared, that he took Poffeffion of the Harbour of St. *John*'s, and of the Territory two hundred Leagues every way, and invefted her Majefty with the Title and Dignity thereof. And having had a Twig and a Turf of the Soil delivered to him, he entered Poffeffion alfo for himfelf, his Heirs, or Affigns, for ever. He further fignified to thofe prefent, and through them to all Men, that, from thenceforward, they fhould look upon thofe Territories as appertaining to the Queen of *England*, and upon himfelf, as authorifed by her Majefty to poffefs and enjoy them, with Power to ordain Laws, under which all People coming thither for the future, either to inhabit or to trade, fhould fubmit themfelves and be governed. And to exercife his Power and Jurifdiction, he enacted three Laws, immediately to take Place and be of Force ; and granted divers Parcels of Land, lying by the Sea Side, as well in the Harbour of St. *John*'s, as elfewhere.

AFTER fome Excurfions to fearch the Country, and the pretended Difcovery of a Silver Mine, with which Sir *Humphry* was much gulled and delighted, they fet Sail to the *Southward*, in order to explore and difcover the main Coaft of *America*. But falling among fome Shoals, and meeting with very bad and tempeftuous Weather, after having undergone much Danger and Fatigue, they refolved to return for *England*. Sir *Humphry*, the better to fearch the Coaft, and to run up into Creeks and Harbours, had gone on board a fmall Bark of ten Tons ; and could not afterwards be perfuaded to leave her in their Return homewards, till her Lights were fuddenly extinguifhed in the Night, at which Time fhe was fuppofed to fink, and was never after feen or heard of.

THE learned and valiant Mr. *Walter Ralegh* was half Brother to Sir *Humphry Gilbert* ; his Father having married Sir *Humphry*'s Mother, when a Widow, and had by her this his fourth and youngeft Son, with fome other Children. Led by this near Relation, and being alfo a Perfon of a noble and enterprifing Genius, he had been one of the principal Adventurers in this Undertaking of Sir *Humphry*, and had fitted out, entirely at his own Charge, the largeft Ship of his Fleet, called the *Ralegh* Bark. Some Authors fay, he went himfelf upon the Expedition, and commanded his own Ship in Perfon. But however that might be, it is certain, this Ship was, within a few Days, obliged to put back to *Plimouth*, greatly diftreffed by a violent and contagious Sick-

B 4   nefs

1584. neſs among her Company. But notwithſtanding this Diſ-
appointment, and the unhappy End of his raſh and unfortunate Brother, Mr. *Ralegh* was not diſcouraged; but being
moved with the Voyages and Relations of others, he ſtill
perſiſted in the Deſign of diſcovering and making a Settlement in *America.* He therefore obtained Letters patent
from Queen *Elizabeth*, of whom he was at that Time one
of the chief Favourites, bearing Date the 25th of *March*,
1584, for diſcovering and planting any ſuch Lands and
Countries, as were not already in the actual poſſeſſion of
any Chriſtian Nation. Theſe Letters patent are in *Hackluyt's* Collection of Voyages; but that Book is ſo very rare,
that our Country does not afford one Copy of it, at leaſt
that I could find out or procure. I have not therefore been
able to obtain a Sight of theſe Patents; but we are told,
that they were, *mutatis mutandis,* the very ſame with thoſe
granted to Sir *Humphry Gilbert*; of which I have therefore
before given a particular Extract.

ABOUT the ſame Time, the Queen granted Mr. *Ralegh*
another Patent, to licence the Vending of Wine throughout
the Kingdom; which was deſigned, as it has been ſuppoſed,
to enable him by the Profits, that would thence ariſe, to
ſuſtain the vaſt Charges which this Undertaking of a Colony would neceſſarily bring upon him. But yet the better
to ſtrengthen himſelf, and carry on the Affair, he perſuaded divers other Gentlemen and Merchants to join with
him; particularly his noble and gallant Kinſman, Sir *Richard Greenvil*, and Mr. *William Sanderſon*, who had married his Neice, and was much engaged among the Merchant
Adventurers of that Time; and was alſo one of the Queen's
Commiſſioners for the *Spaniſh* Prizes, and of Note for the
great Globes, which, by his Encouragement, were firſt
brought to Perfection. They therefore, with all convenient Speed, provided two ſmall Veſſels, and having plentifully furniſhed them with Neceſſaries, put them under the
Command of Captain *Philip Amidas,* and Captain *Arthur
Barlow*; which laſt was alſo a Land-Officer, and had ſerved
under Mr. *Ralegh* in the Wars of *Ireland*, with great Bravery and Honour. But Mr. *Ralegh*, being hindered by his
Employments, and too buſily engaged in his ambitious Pur-
ſuits at Court, did not come himſelf upon the Expedition,
as hath been generally, tho' erroneouſly, thought.

ON the 27th of *April*, 1584, theſe Adventurers ſet Sail
from the *Thames*; and having paſſed by the *Canaries* and
the *Weſt-Indies*, (a Circuit both needleſs and unhealthy,
but through the Inexperience of thoſe Times thought neceſſary) they fell in, on the 2d of *July*, with the Coaſt of
Florida.

Florida. For that was the Name which all this *Northern* Continent from Cape *Florida* then bore, there being yet no diftinct Settlements, which gave particular Names to the feveral Places along the Coaft. They were met at Sea with a moft delicate and delightful Smell; and foon after making the Land, they coafted it along for about an hundred and twenty Miles, without finding any convenient Harbour. The firft they faw, they entered with much Difficulty; and having returned Thanks to God, they went afhore to view the Country, and to take Poffeffion of it in the Queen's Name. The Place of their firft Landing was a low and fandy Beach; but it yielded fuch a wonderful Abundance of Grapes, as very much furprifed and delighted them. Every little Shrub was covered with them, and the Tops of the talleft Cedars were over-run and loaded with their Clufters.

T H E Y concluded, that the Place of their Landing was on the main Continent of *America*; but going up to the Top of a fmall Eminence at a little Diftance from the Shore, they perceived it to be an Ifland, of about twenty, or as Mr. *Hariot* judged, of fifteen Miles in Length, and fix in Breadth. This Ifland was called *Wococon*, and lay between Cape *Hatteras* and Cape *Fear*; and muft therefore be the Ifland of *Ocacock*, or at leaft fome of the other fmall Iflands along that Coaft. For it cannot be, by *With* and *Hariot*'s Plan, *Roanoke*, or any other of thofe which befet and ftop up the Mouth of *Albemarle* Sound, in *North-Carolina*, as has been commonly fuppofed. It was covered with tall and ftately Trees, Cedars, Pines, Cyprefs, Saffafras, and many others of excellent Smell and Quality; and abounded in Deer, Conies, and Wild-fowl, in incredible Numbers.

T H E Y faw none of the Natives, 'till the third Day after their Landing, when they fpied three in a Canoe. One of them went afhore, and waited without any Signs of Fear, till the *Englifh* rowed to him. He fpoke much to them in his own Language, and then went boldly aboard their Veffels. They gave him a Shirt, a Hat, Wine, and Meat, with which he was much pleafed. Having attentively viewed every thing, he went away; and within half an Hour he had loaded his Canoe with Fifh, which he brought and divided between the Ship and the Bark.

T H E next Day feveral Canoes came, and in one of them the King's Brother. His Name was *Granganameo*; the King was called *Wingina*, and the Country *Wingandacoa*. The King himfelf at that Time lay, at his chief Town, ill of the Wounds which he had lately received in a Battle. *Granganameo*, leaving his Canoes at fome Diftance, went

4

1584 to the Point of Land where the *English* had gone to the
Indian the Day before.   Having spread a Mat, he sat down
upon it; and when the *English* came to him well armed,
he shewed no Fear; but made Signs to them to sit down,
stroaking his own Head and Breast, and then theirs, to express his Love.   The Natives were a proper, well-proportioned People, very civil in their Behaviour, and highly respectful to *Granganameo*.   For none of them sat down, or
spoke a Word in his Presence, except four; on whom the
English also bestowed Presents.   But *Granganameo* took
them all from them, and made Signs, that every thing belonged to him.   After some small Traffick, he went away;
but returning in two Days, he eat and drank very merrily
with them.   Not long after, he brought his Wife and
Children on board.   They were of mean Stature, but well-
favoured, and very bashful and modest.   His Wife had a
Band of white Coral about her Forehead, and Bracelets of
Pearl in her Ears, hanging down to her Middle, of the
Bigness of large Pease.   As to the rest, they were decked
with red Copper, and such Ornaments, as are at present in
Fashion and Esteem among our *Indians.*

AFTER this, there came down, from all Parts, great
Numbers of People, with Leather, Coral, and divers Kinds
of Dyes.   But when *Granganameo* was present, none durst
trade but himself, and those, who wore red Copper on their
Heads, as he did.   He would have engaged a Bag of Pearl
for a Suit of Armour; but the *English* refused, as not regarding it, that they might thereby the better learn, where
it grew.   He was very just to his Promise, for they often
trusted him, and he never failed to come within his Day to
keep his Word.   He commonly sent the *English* every Day
a Brace of Bucks, Conies, Hares, and Fish; and sometimes
Melons, Walnuts, Cucumbers, Pease, and divers Kinds of
Roots.   And the *English*, to try the Strength and Goodness
of the Soil, put some of their Pease into the Ground, which
grew wonderfully, and were found in ten Days time fourteen Inches high.

AN Acquaintance being thus contracted by mutual Returns of Kindness and Beneficence, Captain *Amidas*, with
seven more, ventured up the River *Occam*, as they call it,
which must be *Pamptico* Sound.   The next Evening they
came to the Isle of *Roanoke*, at the Mouth of *Albemarle*
Sound, about seven Leagues, as they say, from the Harbour, where they first entered.   But this is a gross Mistake,
and must be an Error in the Copy.   For by the Scale in
With's Map, it cannot be less than thirty Leagues, from
Wococon to *Roanoke*.   On this Island they found a small
Town,

Town, confifting of nine Houfes; in one of which *Gran-*
ganameo lived.   He was abfent; but his Wife entertained
them with wonderful Courtefy and Kindnefs.   She made
fome of her People draw their Boat up, to prevent it's being injured by the Beating of the Surge ; fome fhe ordered
to bring them afhore on their Backs; and others, to carry
their Oars to the Houfe, for Fear of being ftole.   When
they came into the Houfe, fhe took off their Cloaths and
Stockings, and wafhed them, as likewife their Feet in warm
Water.   When their Dinner was ready, they were conducted into an inner Room (for there were five in the Houfe,
divided by Mats) where they found *Hominy**, boiled Venifon, and roafted Fifh ; and as a Defert, Melons, boiled
Roots, and Fruits of various Sorts.   While they were at
Meat, two or three of her Men came in with their Bows
and Arrows, which made the *Englifh* take to their Arms.
But fhe, perceiving their Diftruft, ordered their Bows and
Arrows to be broken, and themfelves to be beaten out of
the Gate.   In the Evening the *Englifh* returned to their
Boat ; and putting a little off from Shore, lay at Anchor.
At which fhe was much concerned, and brought their Supper, half boiled, Pots and all to the Shore Side ; and feeing
their Jealoufy, fhe ordered feveral Men, and thirty Women, to fit all Night upon the Shore, as a Guard ; and fent
five Mats to cover them from the Weather.   In fhort, fhe
omitted nothing, that the moft generous Hofpitality and
hearty Defire of pleafing could do, to entertain them.

    AND this was the fartheft Difcovery made upon this firft
Voyage, except fome confufed and uncertain Accounts of
the Country, which they gathered from the *Indians.*   They
returned to *England* about the Middle of *September,* carrying with them two of the Natives, *Manteo* and *Wanchefe* ;
and their Difcovery was fo welcome there, that the Queen
herfelf was pleafed to name the Country VIRGINIA, in
Memory of it's having been firft found out in the Reign of
a Virgin Queen.   Or as fome have been pleafed to glofs
and interpret it, becaufe it ftill feemed to retain the *Virgin*
Purity and Plenty of the firft Creation, and the People their
primitive Innocency of Life and Manners.   And foon after
their Return, Mr. *Ralegh* was elected, together with Sir
William Courtenay, Knight of the Shire for the County of
Devon.   On the 14th of *December,* he caufed a Bill to be
brought into the Houfe, to confirm his Patent for difcovering foreign Countries ; which being committed to Mr. Vice-
Chamberlain *Hatton,* Secretary *Walfingham,* Sir *Philip*
                                                      Sidney,

---

* A Food made of *Indian* Corn, or Maize, beaten and carefully hufked,
fomething like Furmety in *England*; and is an excellent Difh various Ways.

1584 *Sidney,* Sir *Francis Drake,* Sir *Richard Greenvil,* Sir *William Courtenay,* and others, it was in a few Days paſſed, after many Arguments and a Proviſo added.   And not long after, the Queen was pleaſed to Knight him, upon Occaſion, it is ' ſaid, of this grateful Diſcovery.   But Mr. *Oſborne,* an ingenious Obſerver on her Reign, ſays with Reſpeſt to Sir *Francis Vere,* a Man nobly deſcended, and Sir *Walter Ralegh,* exaſtly qualified, that they, with ſuch others, were ſet apart in her Judgment for military Services. Neither did ſhe ever raiſe them above Knighthood ; ſaying, when ſollicited to make *Vere* a Baron, That in his proper Sphere, and her Eſtimation, he was above it already.

1585.   T H E advantageous Accounts, which theſe firſt Adventurers gave of the Fertility, Pleaſantneſs, and Wholeſomeneſs of the Country, induced Sir *Richard Greenvil* himſelf to make a Voyage thither the next Year.   And he accordingly ſet out from *Plimouth* the 9th of *April,* with ſeven Ships.   Having made the uſual Circuit of the *Canaries* and *Weſt-Indies,* where they took two rich *Spaniſh* Prizes, and forced a profitable Trade, they fell in with the Continent of *America* near Cape *Fear,* and were in great Danger of being loſt upon it.   But having happily eſcaped, they came to an Anchor off the Iſland of *Wococon* the 26th of *May.* They immediately ſent to the Iſle of *Roanoke,* to *Wingina* the King ; and Mr. *Arundel* went to the Main, with *Manteo,* who proved throughout their whole Stay, very faithful and uſeful to them.   Soon after, the General, Sir *Richard Greenvil,* went himſelf to the Main, with a ſeleſt Body of Men ; and ranging about, diſcovered ſeveral *Indian* Towns. At one of them the *Indians* ſtole a Silver Cup ; for which they burnt their Town, and deſtroyed their Corn, and ſo returned to their Ships at *Wococon.*   At *Hatteras,* whither they went ſoon after, *Granganameo,* the King's Brother, came aboard the Admiral with *Manteo.*   This is the laſt Viſit he made to the *Engliſh* ; for ſometime this Year he died, and in him they loſt a ſincere and hearty Friend.

S I R *Richard Greenvil,* having only made that ſmall Excurſion on the Continent, returned to *England* this Summer.   In his Way home, he took another *Spaniſh* Prize, of three hundred Tons, richly laden, and with her arrived at *Plimouth* the 18th of *September.*   But he left behind him an hundred and eight Perſons, as a Colony, to keep Poſſeſſion of, and inhabit the Country.   Of theſe he conſtituted Mr. *Ralph Lane* Governor, a military Man of Note, who was afterwards Knighted, and applying himſelf to the Sea Service, was of eminent Command in the *Engliſh* Navy. With him remained Captain *Philip Amidas,* as Admiral,
one

one of the Commanders in Chief in the firft Adventure; Mr. *Thomas Hariot*; Captain *Stafford*; Mr. *Kendal*; with feveral others of Name in the Expedition.

THIS Colony chofe *Roanoke*, an Ifland at the Mouth of *Albemarle* Sound, for the Place of their Habitation; and their chief Employment was to reconnoitre and view the Country. Their fartheft Difcovery to the *Southward* was *Secotan*, an *Indian* Town, by their Reckoning, eighty Leagues from *Roanoke*, lying up between the Rivers *Pamp-ticoe* and *Neus*, in *North-Carolina*. To the *Northward* they went an hundred and thirty Miles to the *Chefapeakes*, a Nation of *Indians*, feated on a fmall River, to the *South* of our Bay, now called *Elfabeth* River, from whom, as thefe firft Difcoverers tell us, the Bay itfelf took its Name. But fome pretend to give another Derivation of this Word; and fay, that *Chefapeake* fignified, in the *Indian* Language, *The Mother of Waters*; implying, that it was the Parent and grand Refervoir of all the great Rivers within it. But this is a dark and uncertain Guefs; efpecially confidering the Unftablenefs and vaft Mutability of the *Indian* Tongues, and that no body at prefent can pretend to underftand their Language at that time. The beft Authority that I have met with for this Derivation, is what a Gentleman of Credit once affured me, that in a a very old *Spanifh* Map, which he had feen, our Bay was laid down under the Name of *Madre des Acquas*, or fome Expreffion to the like Purpofe. This Town of the *Chefapeakes*, we are told, for Pleafantnefs of Situation, for Temperature of Clime, Fertility of Soil, and Commodioufnefs to the Sea, was not to be excelled by any in the World. To the *Northweft*, thefe Difcoverers went up *Albemarle* Sound and *Chowan* River, an hundred and thirty Miles, to a Nation of *Indians* called the *Chawonocks*, inhabiting above the Fork of that River, where one Branch takes the Name of *Meherrin*, and the other of *Nottoway*.

THE King of the *Chawonocks*, whofe Name was *Menatonon*, was lame, but the moft fenfible and underftanding *Indian* they had met with. He amufed Mr. *Lane* and his Company with a Story of a Copper Mine, and of a Pearl Fifhery, which by the Defcription was fome where upon our Coaft, and with a ftrange Relation of the Head of the River *Moratuc*, now called *Roanoke*. This River was defcribed, as fpringing out of a Rock, fo nigh the Sea, that in high Winds the Surge beat over into the Spring. And the *Englifh* very fanguinely concluded this Sea to be either the Bay of *Mexico*, or the *South* Sea, or at leaft fome Arm that opened into it. Having their Heads filled with thefe

chimerical

1585. chimerical Fancies, they formed many Schemes, and undertook a very fatiguing and hazardous Voyage up that
River. And fo eager were they, and refolutely bent upon
this golden Difcovery, that they could not be perfuaded to
return, as long as they had one Pint of Corn a Man left,
and two Maftif Dogs, which being boiled with Saffafras
Leaves, might afford them fome Suftenance in their Way
back. But after fome Days fpent in vain, and having undergone much Mifery and Danger, they at laft returned, and
joyfully arrived at their old Habitation on *Roanoke* Ifland.

THE Death of *Granganameo* had caufed a great Alteration in the Affairs of the Colony. For whilft he lived, his
Credit with the King, joined to the Intereft of *Enfenore*,
their Father, had reftrained his Perfidy and Malice, and
kept him within Bounds. But upon the Death of *Granganameo*, he changed his Name from *Wingina* to *Pemiffapan*,
and became a fecret but bitter Enemy to the *Englifh*. To
his Machinations chiefly were owing the many Hardfhips
and Dangers, they had encountered in their laft Journey up
the River *Chowan*. For he had given fecret Intelligence to
thofe *Indians* of the coming of the *Englifh*; and had craf-
tily infituated Jealoufies into the *Indians* of the *Englifh*, and
into the *Englifh* of the *Indians*. But a Rumour being fpread,
that Mr. *Lane* and his Company were all either flain or
ftarved in this Journey, he began to act more openly. He
blafphemed the God of the *Englifh*, and endeavoured, by
all the Devices he could, to hurt and annoy them. And
Enfenore, his aged Father, the beft Friend the *Englifh* had
left after the Death of *Granganameo*, loft all his Credit to
affift or ferve them. But their Return foon after, and their
bringing the Son of *Menatonon*, their greateft King, Prifoner, joined to the Teftimonies of *Manteo*, and three other
Indians, that went with them, how little they valued any
People they met, or feared Hunger, Death, or any thing
elfe, reftrained his Devices for the prefent, and brought *Enfenore* again into Credit and Efteem.

1586.   SOON after, *Menatonon*, King of the *Chawonocks*, fent
a Prefent of Pearl to Mr. *Lane*; and *Okifco*, King of *Weo-
pomeoke*, (another powerful Nation, poffeffing all that
Country from *Albemarle* Sound and *Chowan* River, quite
to the *Chefapeakes* and our Bay) came himfelf, with twenty
four of his principal Men, to own Subjection to the Queen
of *England*. All which fo wrought on the Heart of *Wingina*, that by *Enfenore*'s Perfuafions, they came and made
Weirs for the *Englifh*, when they were ready to famifh,
and planted their Fields of Corn, which they intended to
abandon. But this good Intelligence was foon broke off by
the

the Death of *Enfenore*, which happened on the 20th of *A-* | 1586.
pril. For *Wingina*, under Pretence of folemnizing his Father's Funeral, had laid a Scheme of drawing together fixteen or eighteen hundred *Indians*, and of cutting off all the
Englifh at once. But his Defign took Wind, and was at
laft fully difcovered to Mr. *Lane* by his Prifoner *Skico*, King
Menatonon's Son. Then the *Englifh*, in their Turn, endeavoured to feize all the Canoes upon *Roanoke*, and thereby to have all the *Indians* in the Ifland at their Mercy. But
they took the Alarm, and after a fmall Skirmifh, in which
five or fix *Indians* were flain, the reft efcaped and fled into
the Woods. After this, neither Side cared much for trufting the other; and at laft, after much Tricking and Diffimulation on both Parts, *Wingina* was entrapped by the
Englifh, and flain, with eight of his chief Men. This is
the Account of that Action, as it is delivered by the Perfons concerned in it. But I find, that Mr. *Hariot*, who
was likewife upon the Spot, blames the Violence and Forwardnefs of the *Englifh*; and thinks, that the Caufes of
Sufpicion and Refentment had been better diffembled and
paffed over.

IN the Time of thefe Confufions and Broils with the *Indians*, Mr. *Lane* had been obliged, through Want of Provifions, to fend Captain *Stafford*, with twenty more, to
Croatan, on the *South* Part of Cape *Look-out*, to fhift for
themfelves, and to fee, if they could fpy any Sail pafs by
the Coaft. In like Manner he detached Mr. *Prideaux*,
with ten, to *Hatteras*, upon the fame Defign; and other
fmall Parties he fent to the Main, to live upon Roots and
Oyfters. Seven Days after the Death of *Wingina*, Captain *Stafford*, (who through the whole Voyage was very
vigilant and induftrious, and fpared no Labour or Danger,
to perform any ferious and important Service, committed to
him) fent Mr. *Lane* Word, that he defcried twenty three
Sail of Ships; and the next Day, he came himfelf with a
Letter from Sir *Francis Drake*. Sir *Francis* was then returning from an Expedition againft the *Spaniards* in the
Weft-Indies, where he had taken *Carthagena*, and the Capital City of *Hifpaniola*; and had burnt St. *Anthony*, and
St. *Helena*, on the Coaft of *Florida*; and done much other
Damage to the Enemy. He had Orders from the Queen
to vifit the Colony of *Virginia* in his Return, and to afford
them fuch Affiftance and Encouragement, as was proper.
He therefore offered to fupply their Wants, and to do any
thing elfe in his Power, towards their Relief and the Furtherance of the Undertaking; and after mature Deliberation, he appointed them a Ship of feventy Tons, with an .
hundred

1586. hundred Men, and four Months Provifions, befides two Barks and four fmall Boats, with able Mafters and fufficient Gangs. But juft as all was ready, there arofe fuch a Storm, as had like to have driven the whole Fleet afhore. Many Ships were forced out to Sea, among which was that lately given to the Colony, with all their Provifions and Company aboard.

THIS Accident did not difcourage the Admiral, but he allotted them another Ship of an hundred and feventy Tons, with all Provifions as before, to carry them to *England* the next *Auguft*, or when they fhould have made fuch Difco-veries as they thought fufficient. But their Harbour, which was very indifferent, would not receive a Ship of her Bur-then; and to lie in the open Road, expofed to the Winds and Sea, was very dangerous. And therefore, after Con-fultation, it was unanimoufly agreed, to defire the Admiral to take them home with him in his Fleet; for they had al-ready undergone much Mifery and Danger, and there ap-peared but little Hopes of Sir *Richard Greenvil's* Return. And fo this firft Attempt towards a Settlement became a-bortive, and they all arrived fafe at *Portfmouth* the latter End of *July*, 1586. But in his Way home, Sir *Francis Drake* touched on the Coaft of *New-England*; where he landed, and fpent two or three Days in trading with the Natives, and one of the *Indian* Kings came, and fubmitted himfelf to Queen *Elizabeth*.

UPON this Voyage, Sir *Walter Ralegh*, by the Queen's Advice and Directions, fent, at no fmall Expence, Mr. *John With*, a fkilful and ingenious Painter, to take the Si-tuation of the Country, and to paint, from the Life, the Figures and Habits of the Natives, their Way of Living, and their feveral Fafhions, Modes, and Superftitions; which he did with great Beauty and Exactnefs. There was one *Theodore de Bry*, who afterwards publifhed, in the Year 1624, the beautiful *Latin* Edition of Voyages, in fix Vo-lumes, *Folio*, a moft curious and valuable Work. He be-ing in *England* foon after, by the Means of the Rev. Mr. *Richard Hackluyt*, then of *Chrift's-Church*, in *Oxford*, who, *De Bry* tells us, had himfelf feen the Country, obtained from Mr. *With* a Sight of thefe Pieces, with Permiffion to take them off in Copper Plates. Thefe, being very lively and well done, he carried to *Frankfort*, on the *Maine*, where he publifhed a noble Edition of them, with *Latin* Explanations, out of *John Wechelius's* Prefs, in the Year 1590. And thefe are the Originals from which Mr. *Bever-ley's*, and the Cuts of many of our late Writers and Tra-vellers, have been chiefly imitated. And to fhew, that the

Inhabitants

Inhabitants of *England* were once as wild and barbarous as thefe of *Virginia*, Mr. *With* gave him the Figures of three of the *Piñs* and two of their Neighbours, that he had found delineated in an old *Englifh* Hiftory; which were accordingly publifhed with them, and was no mean or impolitic Device, to recommend the Profecution of the Enterprife to the *Englifh* Nation.

BUT befides this Painter, Sir *Walter* fent upon this Voyage a Domeftick of his, one Mr. *Thomas Hariot*, a Mathematician, and highly in his Patron's Intimacy and Friendfhip. He was a Man of Learning, and a very obferving and underftanding Perfon, and went chiefly to make Obfervations on the Situation of the Country, and to affift Mr. *With* in the Plan. After his Return, to obviate the clamorous and unjuft Reports of fome of the Company, he publifhed a fmall Treatife concerning the Country, divided into three Parts. The firft treats of fuch Commodities, as would be ufeful towards the Improvement of Commerce; the fecond, of thofe natural Produñs of the Earth, and of fuch Fifh, Fowl, and Beafts, as would contribute to the Suftenance of Man, and the Support of human Life; and the third, of the Trees and Timber, and other proper Materials for building Houfes, Ships, and the like. After which he fubjoins the following Account of the Doñrines and Manners of the Natives.

THEY believed, that there is one chief God, who hath exifted from all Eternity: That he created the World; but firft made other Gods of a principal Order, to be his Inftruments in the Creation and Government thereof: That next the Sun, Moon, and Stars were created, as petty Gods, and as Inftruments to thofe other Gods of a fuperior Order: That then the Waters were created, out of which were formed all Creatures: That a Woman was firft made; who, by the Congrefs of one of the Gods, conceived and brought forth Children; and that thence Mankind had their Beginning. They thought, the Gods were all of human Shape, and therefore reprefented them by Images, which they placed in their Temples; and they worfhipped, prayed, fung, danced, and made many Offerings to them. They held the Immortality of the Soul; which after Death, according to it's Works in the Flefh, was either carried up to the Tabernacles of the Gods, to eternal Happinefs; or elfe to *Popoguffo* (a great Pit at the furtheft Parts of the Earth, where the Sun fets) into perpetual Fire and Torment. And this Doñrine they fupported by the Authority of two Perfons, who, as they pretended, had rifen from the Dead.

THESE Opinions were thought to make but flight Impreffions on their *Weroances*, or Kings and Rulers; or upon their Priefts, and other Perfons of Figure among them. For that Chriftian Cuftom, for the Great and Eminent to free their Confciences from the Shackles of a Creed, and exempt their Actions from the unwieldy Clog of Religion and Morality, had reached even among thofe wild and favage Nations.   But thefe Doctrines had a great Influence on the common Sort.   They kept them in proper Subjection to their Rulers; and made them very follicitous to obtain the Blifs, and avoid the Torments of the next Life.

THEY were not however fo firm to their own Doctrines, but that they were very open to receive any Inftructions from the *Englifh*.   Their Compaffes, Perfpective Glaffes, Burning Glaffes, Clocks, Books, Writing, Guns, and other Inftruments and Inventions, fo exceeded their Capacities, and amazed them, that they thought them to be the Works of Gods rather than Men; or at leaft, that the Gods had taught the *Englifh*, how to make them. This caufed them to give great Credit to whatever they faid concerning God and Religion.   And *Wingina* himfelf would often be at Prayers with them; and when he was fick, which, he thought, proceeded from having offended the *Englifh* and their God, he would fend for fome of them, to pray, and be a Means to their God, of his living with him after Death; as alfo did many others.   And once, when their Corn was much hurt and withered with a long Drought, thinking it proceeded from fome Injury done the *Englifh*, they came to them in Flocks, and begged them to pray to their God to preferve their Corn, for which they promifed, when it was ripe, to give them a Part.

AND this high Opinion of the *Englifh* was greatly encreafed, by a marvellous Accident.   The Country was that Year afflicted with an epidemical Difeafe, which was obferved to fall upon none, but thofe Nations, which had endeavoured to injure or betray the *Englifh*.   This wrought many extravagant and fuperftitious Opinions, which were much confirmed by the Healthinefs of the *Englifh* Colony. Some thought it was the Work of the *Englifh* God; and others, that they themfelves fhot invifible Bullets from the Place, where they dwelt.   Others obferving, that the *Englifh* had no Women of their own, nor cared for any of theirs, thought they were not born of Women, but were Men of an ancient Generation, rifen again to Immortality; that there were more of them ftill in the Air, as yet invifible and without Bodies, who would afterwards come, and deftroy their Generation, and take their Places; and that thefe,

thefe, by the Entreaty, or out of Love to the *Englifh*, made the People die, as they did, by fhooting invifible Bullets into them. And their Phyficians, to cover their Ignorance, would make them believe, that they fucked out of the Bodies of the Sick Leaden Bullets in the Strings of Blood. In fhort, *Wingina* and others were fo firmly perfuaded, that it happened through their Means, that when any of their own Enemies had affronted or abufed the *Englifh*, they would defire them to make them die in the fame Manner. And altho' the *Englifh* remonftrated to them the Unrighteoufnefs of their Requeft, and how difagreeable it was to God; yet becaufe the Effect fell out foon after, they would come and return them Thanks in their Way; thinking, altho' they had denied them in Words, yet they had in Reality fully anfwered their Defire.

HE likewife tells us of the great Efteem and Veneration, in which the Natives held a Plant, which grew fpontaneoufly in the Country, and was by them called *Uppowoc*, but is now well known by the Name of *Tobacco*; derived, it is faid, from the Ifland of *Tobago*, one of the *Caribbees* in the *Weft-Indies*, where it grew in vaft Quantities. The Leaves of this they cured and dried, and then being rubbed into a Sort of Bran and Duft, they put it into Earthen Tubes, and drew the Smoke through the Mouth. They thought this Plant of fo great Worth and Virtue, that even the Gods themfelves were delighted with it. And therefore they fometimes made facred Fires, and inftead of a Sacrifice threw in this Duft; and when they were caught in a Tempeft, they would fprinkle it into the Air and Water. Upon all their new fifhing Nets they would caft fome of it; and when they had efcaped any remarkable Danger, they would throw fome of this Duft into the Air, with ftrange diftorted Geftures, fometimes ftriking the Earth with their Feet, in a Kind of Time and Meafure, fometimes clapping their Hands, and throwing them up on high, looking up to the Heavens, and uttering barbarous and diffonant Words.

MR. *Harriot* alfo, in paffing through their Towns, would fhew them the Bible, and explain the Contents: That in that Book was taught the true and only God, his Omnipotence, the Doctrine of Salvation by Jefus Chrift, and the other principal Heads of our Religion. But he was obliged to tell them, that there was no particular Virtue in the material Book itfelf, but only in the Doctrines, which it contained. For they paid their Kind of Adoration to the Book, by handling, hugging, and kiffing it, and by applying it to their Head and Breaft, and ftroking it over the other Parts of their Body. C 2

AND here, if it were an Imputation worthy of Notice,
I might tranfiently remark the great Injuftice, done to this
learned Mathematician and pious Scholar.   For as Sir *Walter Ralegh* was afperfed with holding atheiftical Principles,
fo it has been faid, that he imbibed them from this Mr.
Hariot, whom he retained in his Service with a handfome
Penfion, to teach him the mathematical Sciences at his leifure Hours.   But an orthodox Divine, Dr. *Richard Corbet,*
afterwards a Bifhop, tells us, that *Hariot*'s deep Mine was
without Drofs.   And Mr. *George Chapman,* another Contemporary, a grave and virtuous Author, fays, That his
Judgment and Knowledge in all Kinds were deep and in-
comparable, and as much to be admired, as his moft blame-
lefs Life, and the right facred Expence of his Time, were
to be honoured and reverenced.   To which might be added
other Teftimonies, which have been carefully colle&ed by
the diligent and induftrious Mr. *Oldys,* in his accurate Life
of Sir *Walter Ralegh,* lately prefixed to his Hiftory of the
World ; who likewife fhews, that the famous *French* Phi-
lofopher, *Defcartes,* borrowed much of his Light from this
excellent Mathematician ; and that the learned Dr. *Wallis*
gave the Preference to *Hariot*'s Improvements, before *Def-
carte*'s, altho' he had the Advantage of coming after, and
being affifted by him.

As to this groundlefs Afperfion, the Truth of it perhaps
was, that Sir *Walter* and Mr. *Hariot* were the firft, who
ventured to depart from the beaten Tra&t of the Schools,
and to throw off and combat fome hoary Follies and tra-
ditionary Errors, which had been riveted by Age, and rendered facred and inviolable in the Eyes of weak and preju-
diced Perfons.   Sir *Walter* is faid to have been firft led to
this, by the manifeft Dete&tion, from his own Experience,
of their erroneous Opinions concerning the *Torrid Zone* ;
and he intended to have proceeded farther in the Search after more folid and important Truths, 'till he was chid and
reftrained by the Queen, into whom fome Perfons had infufed a Notion, that fuch Do&trine was againft God.   And
this was fufficient Ground for Men, zealous without Knowledge, and ftifly orthodox, with a Charity ufual to fome fuch
in all Ages, to brand him with the odious Names of *Atheift*
and *Deift* ; altho' he was an eminent Affertor of God and
Providence, and has in many Parts of his Writings, efpecially in the Hiftory of the World, given ftronger Evidences
of his Chriftian Faith, than any of his Detra&tors ever did
of theirs.

MR. *Lane* and his Company carried home fome Tobacco, which, *Cambden* thinks, was the firft, that ever was
                                                            brought

brought to *England.* And Sir *Walter Ralegh,* a Man of
Gaiety and Fafhion, readily gave into it, and by his Intereft and Example, foon brought it into fuch Vogue at
Court, that many great Ladies, as well as Noblemen, made
no Scruple fomtimes to take a Pipe. We are not informed, whether the Queen made Ufe of it herfelf; but it is
certain, fhe gave great Countenance and Encouragement to
it, as a Vegetable of fingular Strength and Power, which
might therefore prove of Benefit to Mankind, and Advantage to the Nation. So far, as Mr. *Oldys* well obferves,
was this wife Princefs from the refined Tafte of her Succeffor, who held Tobacco in fuch Abomination, that he
not only refufed the Ufe of it himfelf, but endeavoured to
deftroy and fupprefs it among his Subjects, and would thereby have robbed the Crown of what has fince proved one of
its nobleft Jewels and moft confiderable Revenues, and the
Nation of a very advantageous and important Branch of
Trade.

SIR *Walter Ralegh*'s Tobacco-Box, with fome of his
Pipes, was lately extant, and laid up among the Rarities in
the *Mufeum* of that curious Antiquarian, the late Mr.
Ralph Thorefby, of *Leeds,* in *Yorkfhire.* There are alfo
fome humerous Stories ftill remembred, concerning his firft
Ufe of Tobacco; particularly his Wager with the Queen,
that he would determine exactly the Weight of the Smoke
which went off in a Pipe of Tobacco. This he did bv firft
weighing the Tobacco, and then carefully preferving and
weighing the Afhes; and the Queen readily granted, that
what was wanting in the prime Weight, muft be evapora-
ted in Smoke. And when fhe paid the Wager, fhe
faid pleafantly, that fhe had heard of many Labourers in
the Fire, that turned their Gold into Smoke, but *Ralegh*
was the firft, who had turned his Smoke into Gold. It is
alfo related, that a Country Servant of his, bringing him a
Tankard of Ale and Nutmeg into his Study, as he was in-
tently engaged at his Book, fmoaking a Pipe of Tobacco,
the Fellow was fo frightened at feeing the Smoke reek out
of his Mouth, that he threw the Ale into his Face, in order to extinguifh the Fire, and ran down Stairs, alarming
the Family, and crying out, His Mafter was on Fire, and
before they could get up, would be burnt to Afhes.

BUT whilft Mr. *Lane* and the Colony were in the above
mentioned Streights and Difficulties in *America,* Sir *Walter
Ralegh* was not idle at home. He provided a Ship of an
hundred Tons, and loaded her with Plenty of all things
neceffary for the Settlement; but it being *Eafter* before fhe
departed, Mr. *Lane* and his Company had fhipped themfelves

1586. felves for *England* in Sir *Francis Drake*'s Fleet, a few Days before her Arrival. Having therefore fpent fome Time in feeking them up the Country without Effect, they returned that Summer to *England*, with all their Provifion.

THOSE Authors who will have Sir *Walter Ralegh* to have been in *Virginia*, fay, that he came upon this Voyage : But the Conduct of it was fo weak and trifling, that I cannot be eafily induced to believe it agreeable to a Perfon of his Senfe and Refolution ; who, had he been there, would certainly have made fome vigorous Searches and Enquiries, and left fome ufeful Remarks on the Country, as he did in his Voyage to *Guiana*. Indeed it does not appear, that Sir *Walter* was ever in his Colony himfelf. The only Authority of Weight for it, that I have met with, is the Tranflation of Mr. *Hariot*'s Treatife, which mentions the Actions of thofe, *qui Generofum D.* Walterum Ralegh *in eam regionem comitati funt*. But this, I am inclined to think, muft be an Error of the Tranflator, who feems to have been a *Frenchman*, and might not therefore perfectly underftand our Language ; and I could never yet get a Sight of *Hariot*'s original Difcourfe, which was written in *Englifh*, but have been obliged to make Ufe of the *Latin* Tranflation, publifhed by *De Bry*, at *Frankfort*, 1590. But if Mr. *Hackluyt* ever was in *Virginia*, as we are exprefly told by *De Bry*, it muft have been, I think, either in this Voyage, or that immediately following by Sir *Richard Greenvil*, of which we have fuch brief and fummary Accounts. For it is not to be fuppofed, that a Perfon of his Figure and Confideration, would have been entirely paffed over in the full and particular Relations, that we have of all the other Voyages.

ABOUT a Fortnight after the Departure of this Ship, Sir *Richard Greenvil* arrived with three Ships more, well provided ; but he neither found that Ship, according to his Expectation, nor could hear any News of the Colony, which he himfelf had feated and left there the Year before. Therefore, after travelling in vain up and down to feek them, finding their Habitation abandoned, and being unwilling to lofe the Poffeffion of the Country, he landed fifty Men on the Ifland of *Roanoke*, plentifully furnifhed with all Provifions for two Years, and fo returned to *England*.

THESE unlucky Croffes and Accidents gave Occafion to many Perfons to difcant on their Proceedings, to the Difparagement of Sir *Richard Greenvil*. But their Cenfure was very unjuft. For to plant Colonies abroad, and to diffufe and propagate our Nation and our Trade, is certainly a moft princely and noble Enterprize, and highly worthy a
Perfon

Perfon of his eminent and illuftrious Family. And indeed he feems to have embarked in the Affair with great Hearti- nefs and Refolution, and to have hazarded and expofed his Perfon very freely in the Profecution of it. And it was upon Occafion of thefe Murmurs and Reports, that Mr. *Hariot* wrote and publifhed his Difcourfe, before mentioned.

THE next Year, three Ships were fent, under the Com- mand of Mr. *John White*, who was appointed Governor of the Colony, with twelve Affiftants, as a Council. To thefe Sir *Walter Ralegh* gave a Charter, and incorporated them by the Name of the Governor and Affiftants of the City of *Ralegh* in *Virginia*, with exprefs Directions to feat at *Che- fapeake*; which, however ufeful and important, they ne- verthelefs difobeyed and neglected. Having taken the old Route by the *Weft-Indies*, they had like to have been caft away upon *Cape-Fear*, through the Error or Defign of *Si- mon Ferdinando*. He had been with Captain *Amidas* in the firft Expedition; and being made Pilot in this, was fufpected of a Defign to ruin the whole Voyage. But being prevent- ed by the Vigilancy of Captain *Stafford*, they arrived all fafe at *Hatteras* the 22d of *July*.

THEY went immediately to *Roanoke*, to look for the fifty Men, left there by Sir *Richard Greenvil*, but they found nothing but the Bones of a Man; and where the Plantation had been, the Houfes were undeftroyed, but o- vergrown with Weeds, and the Fort defaced. They re- fitted the Houfes; and Mr. *George How*, one of the Coun- cil, ftragling abroad, was flain by the *Indians*. Soon after, Captain *Stafford*, with twenty Men, and *Manteo*, who, I believe, had been again in *England* this Voyage, went to *Croatan*, to enquire, if they could hear any News of the Colony. There they underftood, that Mr. *How* had been flain by fome of *Wingina*'s Men of *Daffamonpeake*; that the fifty, left the Year before, had been fuddenly fet upon by three hundred *Indians*, of *Secotan*, *Aquafcogoc*, and *Daf- famonpeake*; that after a fmall Skirmifh, in which one *En- glifhman* was flain, they retired to the Water Side, and hav- ing got their Boat, and taken up four of their Fellows ga- thering Crabs and Oyfters, they went to a fmall Ifland by *Hatteras*; that they ftaid there fome time, but after de- parted they knew not whither. And with this Account, Captain *Stafford* returned to the Fleet at *Hatteras*.

HOWEVER, Mr. *White* endeavoured to renew and keep up a good Underftanding with the feveral Nations of *Indians* on the Sea-Coaft. But finding his Offers of Friendfhip not much regarded, he refolved no longer to defer his Revenge on thofe of *Daffamonpeake*. This Nation was feated right

1587. oppofite to *Roanoke* Ifland, on the Main, in the Neck of Land, between the River now called *Allegator*, and the Narrows. About Midnight, Mr. *White* fet forward, with Captain *Stafford*, and twenty four Men, whereof *Manteo* was one, who was their Guide, and behaved himfelf as a moft faithful *Englifhman*. They landed by Break of Day, and having got beyond the Town, they affaulted fome *Indians* that were fitting by a Fire. One was fhot through, and they hoped to have been fully revenged, but were foon undeceived, and found that they were their Friends of *Croatan*, come to gather their Corn, becaufe they underftood, that the *Daffamonpeake Indians* had fled after the Death of Mr. *How*. *Manteo*, their Countryman, was grieved at the Miftake; but however, imputed it all to their own Folly. And fo having gathered what was ripe, and left the reft unfpoiled, they returned to *Roanoke*.

On the 13th of *Auguft*, *Manteo*, according to Command from Sir *Walter Ralegh*, was baptized, and ftiled Lord of *Roanoke* and *Daffamonpeake*, in Reward of his Fidelity. And on the 18th, the Governor's Daughter, Wife to *Ananias Dare*, one of the Council, was delivered of a Daughter, which, being the firft Child born there, was called *Virginia*. And foon after, there arofe a Difpute between the Governor and his Affiftants or Council, concerning a Perfon to be fent to *England* to follicit Supplies. All refufed, except one, who was thought very unequal to the Bufinefs. At laft, they unanimoufly pitched upon the Governor, as the fitteft Perfon; and having figned a Paper, teftifying his Unwillingnefs to leave the Colony, they at length prevailed upon him, with much Importunity, to undertake it. Leaving therefore above an hundred Perfons on one of the Iflands of *Hatteras*, to form a Plantation, he departed, and after many Croffes and Difficulties, got firft to *Ireland*, and from thence went to *England*.

At this time, the Nation was in great Commotion and Apprehenfion of the *Spanifh* Invafion and invincible *Armada*, as it was vainly called, and the Queen caufed frequent Councils to be held, by the oldeft and moft experienced Commanders at Sea; and alfo appointed a Council of War, of fuch Perfons as were in higheft Repute for military Skill and Knowledge, in order to put the Land Forces of the Kingdom in the beft Pofture of Defence. For this Purpofe were chofen the Lord *Grey*, Sir *Francis Knolles*, Sir *Thomas Leighton*, Sir *Walter Ralegh*, Sir *John Norris*, Sir *Richard Greenvil*, Sir *Richard Bingham*, Sir *Roger Williams*, and *Ralph Lane*, Efq; late Governor of *Virginia*, who were therefore all entirely taken up with thofe important Confultations.   How-

HOWEVER, having laid a Plan of Operations, and made proper Difpofitions for the Defence of the Nation, Sir *Walter* found Leifure to fit out a fmall Fleet for the Relief of the Colony, at *Biddeford*, early the next Year, which was put under the Command of Sir *Richard Greenvil*, and only waited for a fair Wind. But the Alarm of the vaft and formidable Armament, made by the King of *Spain*, encreafing, all Ships of Force, then in any Readinefs, received Orders from the State to ftay in their Harbours, for the Defence of their own Country; and Sir *Richard Greenvil* was perfonally commanded not to depart out of *Cornwall*, where Sir *Walter Ralegh* then was himfelf, muftering and training the Forces, and performing other Duties of his Office, as Lieutenant of that County. However, Governor *White* laboured fo ftrenuoufly with them, that he obtained two fmall Barks, and put to Sea from Biddeford, the 22d of *April*, 1588. But thefe Veffels, tho' of little Force, being more intent on a gainful Voyage, than the Relief of the Colony, ran in Chace of Prizes; till at laft, one of them, meeting with two Ships of War, was, after a bloody Fight, overcome, boarded, and rifled. In this maimed, ranfacked, and ragged Condition, fhe returned to *England* in a Month's Time; and in about three Weeks after, the other alfo returned, having perhaps tafted of the fame Fare, at leaft without performing her intended Voyage, to the Diftrefs, and as it proved, the utter Deftruction of the Colony in *Virginia*, and to the great Difpleafure of their Patron at home.

THESE Difappointments gave much Vexation to Sir *Walter Ralegh*, who had by this Time expended, as we are authenticly affured, not lefs than forty thoufand Pounds, upon the Enterprife. He had alfo, not long before, received, as a Reward for his great Services in the *Irifh* Wars, a very large Grant, out of the Earl of *Defmond*'s Lands there; the Terms of which he fairly and honeftly endeavoured to fulfil, by planting thofe Lands with *Englifh*, and made Ufe of none of the Arts and Frauds, which others of thofe Grantees were charged withal. So that this great Bounty of the Queen was at prefent rather a Burthen and Charge to him, than any real Profit or Advantage. Befides which, he was among the foremoft of the military Geniufes of that time, who were fired with the *Spanifh* Invafion, and profecuted the War againft them with great Coft and Induftry, and with an incredible Courage and Succefs. For all thefe Reafons, Sir *Walter Ralegh* made an Affignment, by Indenture, bearing Date the 7th of *March*, 1588-9, to *Thomas Smith*, (afterwards Sir *Thomas Smith*, and a Per-

fon

1589. fon of Note in the Sequel of this Hiftory) with other Merchants and Adventurers of *London*, and to Governor *White*, and other Gentlemen, for continuing the Plantation of *Virginia*. By this Indenture, he grants to the faid *Thomas Smith*, *John White*, and the reft, according to a Charter, formerly granted for the City of *Ralegh*, free Liberty to carry to *Virginia*, and there inhabit, fuch of her Majefty's Subjects, as would willingly accompany them; as alfo to them, their Heirs, or Affigns, free Trade and Traffick to and from *Virginia*, or any other Part of *America*, where the faid Sir *Walter*, his Heirs, or Affigns, did, or might claim any Intereft, Title, or Privilege. And he did farther, for their Encouragement, and for the common Utility, freely and liberally give them one hundred Pounds, to be employed for planting the Chriftian Religion in thofe barbarous and heathen Countries.

AND thus Sir *Walter Ralegh*, having difengaged himfelf for the prefent from this burthenfome and expenfive Affair, gave a Loofe to his martial Genius, and bent his whole Thoughts againft the *Spaniards*, which foon became the fixed and ruling Paffion of his Nature; as abafing the exorbitant Power of *France*, and preventing its ill Confequences on the Liberties of *Europe*, did, in later Times, engrofs all the Thoughts and Inclinations of King *William*, and was the principal Aim of moft of his Steps and Actions. And altho' this Comparifon may be thought very unequal with Relation to the Power and Dignity of the two Perfons, yet it will, I think, be found juft and exact with Refpect to their Inclinations and Defigns. For no Man of that Age was more deeply fenfible of the pernicious Confequences of the *Spanifh* Power and Aims, or was more eager and affiduous in fpeaking, writing, and acting againft them, than Sir *Walter Ralegh*.

1590. BUT thefe new Affignees were not fo diligent and careful of the Bufinefs, as they ought to have been. For it was a Year after, *March*, 1589-90, before any thing was undertaken by them for the Relief of the Colony. Then Mr. *White*, with three Ships, fet Sail from *Plimouth*; and paffing by the *Weft-Indies*, they ftaid fome time there, to perform fome Exploits, as they call them, which was to attack and plunder the *Spaniards*, among whom they got a confiderable Booty. On the 3d of *Auguft*, they fell in with fome low fandy Iflands, to the *Weftward* of *Wococon*. From thence they went to *Croatan*, and fo to *Hatteras*. There they defcried a Smoke, at the Place, where the Colony had been left three Years before. The next Morning, they difcharged fome Cannon, to give Notice of their Arrival; and

and having fitted out two Boats, Captain *Cooke* and Captain   1590.
Spicer went afhore, but found no Man, nor the Sign of
any, that had been there lately.   The next Day, they
prepared to go to *Roanoke*; but the Wind being hard
at North-Eaft, one of the Boats, in paffing a Bar, was half
filled with Water, and the other overfet.   Captain *Spicer*,
with fix more, were drowned; but four, who could fwim
a little, and did not truft themfelves to their Legs on the
Shoals, but kept in deep Water, were faved by the Care
and Dexterity of Captain *Cooke* in the other Boat.   This
Accident fo difcomfited the Sailors, that they could hardly
be prevailed upon to make any farther Search for the Colony.   But indeed, confidering the Shoals and Dangers, with
their Ignorance and Inexperience of the Coaft, which they
unfortunately happened upon in this their firft Attempt towards a Settlement, it is rather to be wondered, that they
met not with more Accidents and Misfortunes, than they
really did.

T H E Sailors being at length encouraged by the Forwardnefs and Readinefs of their Captains, two Boats more
were fitted out for *Hatteras*, with nineteen Men.   When
Mr. *White* left the Colony three Years before, they talked
of going fifty Miles up into the Main; and it had been
agreed between them, that if they left the Place, where
they then were, they fhould write the Name of the Place,
to which they went, on fome Tree, Door, or Poft; and
if they had been in any Diftrefs, they fhould fignify it, by
making a Crofs over it.   When they landed therefore, they
founded a Trumpet, but received no Anfwer; and going up
to the Fire, they found, it was nothing but the Grafs and
fome rotten Trees burning.   Then fearching up and down
the Ifland, they at laft found three fair *Roman* Letters
carved, C. R. O. but without any Sign of Diftrefs; and
looking farther, they faw C R O A T A N, carved in fair
Capital Letters on one of the chief Pofts, but ftill without
the Crofs, as a Sign of Diftrefs.   Their Houfes were taken
down; and an high Palifado built, after the Manner of a
Fort.   They likewife found, where their Goods had been
buried; but many of them had been dug up, and fcattered
about, and all were fpoiled; yet Mr. *White* knew and
diftinguifhed feveral of his own among them.   With this
joyful Difcovery, as they hoped, of where they were, they
returned to their Ships; but had like to have been caft
away by a violent Storm, that continued all that Night.

T H E next Morning, weighing Anchor for *Croatan*,
which was an *Indian* Town on the South Part of Cape
Look-out, one of their Cables broke, and carried off another

1590. ther Anchor with it. But letting go their third, the Ship went fo faft adrift, that fhe was very near ftranding. Dif-couraged with thefe Misfortunes, and having but one An-chor left, and their Provifions near fpent, they gave over all Thoughts of farther Search for the prefent, and deter-mined to go to the *Weft-Indies*, to winter and refrefh 'them-felves (chiefly perhaps with more *Spanifh* Plunder) and to return in the Spring, to feek their Countrymen. But the Vice-Admiral was obftinately bent upon going directly for *England*; and the Wind being contrary, the reft were obliged, within two Days, to make for the *Weftern-Iflands*, where they arrived the 23d of *September*, 1590, and met with many of the Queen's Ships, their own Confort, and divers others. But many fufpected, that private Intereft was the chief Occafion of their Failure in this Undertaking; and that the Riches, gotten from the *Spaniards* in the *Weft-Indies*, was the true Reafon of their Return, for which the Storm only furnifhed them with a colourable Pretext. However it is certain, that the Affignees made no farther Search, nor gave themfelves any other Trouble about the Matter; but thefe poor Souls were bafely deferted by them, and left a Prey to the barbarous Savages, neither were they ever feen or heard of afterwards.

1591. THE following Year 1591, Sir *Richard Greenvil* was fent, by the Queen, Vice-Admiral to the Lord *Thomas Howard*, with feven Ships of War, and a few other fmall Veffels, to intercept the *Spanifh* Plate-Fleet. At the *Azores*, this fmall Squadron was furprifed by fifty three capital Ships, purpofely fent from *Spain*; and Sir *Richard Greenvil*, who was unwilling to leave a great Part of his Men, then on Shore for Water and other Neceffaries, to the Infolence and Barbarity of the Iflanders, ftaid fo long in getting them off, that he was hemmed in between the Enemy's Fleet and the Ifland of *Flores*. In this dangerous Situation, he fcorned to fhew any Signs of Fear, or to owe his Safety to Flight; but he bravely bore down upon the Enemy, and endeavoured to break through them, in which Attempt he maintained a gallant and obftinate Fight, with the beft of the *Spanifh* Ships, for fifteen Hours together. He was at once laid aboard by the *St. Philip*, a Ship of fifteen hundred Tons and feventy eight large Pieces of Ordinance, and four other of the ftouteft Ships in the *Spanifh* Fleet, full of Men, in fome two hundred, in fome five hundred, and in others eight hundred Soldiers, befides Mariners; and he never had lefs than two large Galleons by his Side, which, from time to time, were relieved by frefh Ships, Men, and Ammu-nition. Yet he behaved himfelf with fuch uncommon Bra-very

very and Conduct, that he difabled fome, funk others, and
obliged them all to retire.   Neither did he ever leave the
Deck, tho' wounded in the Beginning of the clofe Fight,
till he received a dangerous Wound in the Body by a Mufket
Bullet.   When he went down to have it dreffed, he received another Shot in the Head, and his Surgeon was killed
by his Side.   By this time alfo moft of his braveft Men
were flain, his Ship much difabled, his Deck covered with
Dead, and Wounded, and fcattered Limbs, and his Powder
fpent to the very laft Barrel.   Yet in this Condition he ordered the Veffel to be funk, but it was prevented by the
reft of the Officers; tho' many of the Crew joined with
him, and the Mafter-Gunner, if he had not been reftrained, would have killed himfelf, fooner than fall into the
Hands of the *Spaniards.*   When the Ship, or rather
Wreck, was furrendered, Sir *Richard* was carried on board
the *Spanifh* Admiral, where he died within two Days,
highly admired by the very Enemy, for his extraordinary
Courage and Refolution.   And when he found the Pangs of
Death approach, he faid to the Officers, that ftood round
him, in the *Spanifh* Tongue: *Here die I*, Richard Greenvil, *with a joyful and quiet Mind, having ended my Life like
a true Soldier, that fought for his Country, Queen, Religion,
and Honour :* Thus fumming up, in fhort, all the generous
Motives, that fire the Breafts of the truly Brave and Great,
to exert themfelves beyond the common Pitch of Humanity.

A N D fuch was the gallant End of this noble Gentleman,
who, next to Sir *Walter Ralegh*, was the principal Perfon
concerned in this firft Adventure of *Virginia.*   He was a
Man eminently fitted to ferve his Country, in Peace or
War, by Land or Sea, and was fo deeply rooted in the Affection and Efteem of his illuftrious Kinfman, Sir *Walter
Ralegh*, that he honoured his Death with a particular Relation of the Action by his own excellent Pen, which he
caufed to be immediately printed the latter End of the fame
Year 1591, to obviate fome Afperfions, caft upon him by
fome of the *Spaniards.*   The reft of the *Englifh* Ships
having Sea-Room, fought bravely, and did every thing,
that could be expected from valiant Men, whilft they had
the Advantage of the Wind.   The Lord *Howard* was for
even hazarding the whole Fleet in the Refcue of Sir *Richard
Greenvil,* and for charging up to the Place, where he was
engaged.   But he was over-ruled by the other Officers,
whofe Prudence is commended even by Sir *Walter Ralegh* ;
altho' no Perfon can certainly fay, I think, what might
have been the Event, had fix Ships of War more befides
the

1591. the Privateers, fallen upon an Enemy, whom one Ship alone had for fo long a time kept in fuch warm Action. When the Night parted them from the Enemy, they all went off fafe, and in their Way home took feveral rich Prizes. Sir *Richard's* Ship too, the *Revenge*, of 500 Tons Burthen, and about 20 Iron Guns, made good her Name. For a few Days after fhe foundered at Sea, and drowned two hundred *Spaniards*, who had been put aboard to carry her to *Spain.*

BUT Sir *Walter Ralegh*, being, by the above-mentioned Affignment, eafed in fome Meafure of the Undertaking of *Virginia*, was foon engaged by his active and enterprifing Genius in other Adventures and Difcoveries. He contributed generoufly towards the Difcovery of the *North-Weft* Paffage, and other things of the like Nature. But having loft his Royal Miftrefs's Favour, by debauching one of her Maids of Honour, whom he afterwards married, he undertook in Perfon, in the Year 1595, the Voyage and Difcovery of *Guiana*, a rich Country up the River *Oronaque*, in *South America.* After his Return, he wrote a moft excellent Difcourfe upon his Expedition, in which his chief Aim was to engage the Queen and Nation in the Profecution of the Enterprife, and Settlement of the Country. But all his Reafons were overpowered by the Envy of fome great Men to his Perfon and Merit; and altho' he was reftored to the Queen's Favour, yet he could never get any thing done to Effect in this important and judicious Defign. However he never quitted it himfelf, but fent twice immediately after, to make farther Difcoveries, and to keep up the good Difpofitions of the Natives towards the *Englifh.* Even after his Fall, and when he was in the Tower, he found Means to continue this Defign; and his laft Voyage thither, after his Releafe, with the fatal Confequences of it, is too well known, to need a particular Relation here. Neither was he, notwithftanding the Affignment, negligent or forgetful of the Colony, which had been feated in *Virginia* upon his Account. For he fent five feveral Times, to fearch after, and relieve them; and laft he difpatched *Samuel Mace*, of *Weymouth*, in *March* 1602. But he, like all the reft, performed nothing, but returned with idle Stories and frivolous Allegations.

HOWEVER, thefe Efforts of Sir *Walter* were only intended to recover and bring off thofe poor People, and no ways in Profecution of his firft Defign of fettling a Colony. So that all Thoughts of *Virginia* were abandoned, and the Project lay dead for near twelve Years, when it was revived by Captain *Bartholomew Gofnold*, who undertook a Voyage thither, and fet Sail from *Dartmouth*, on

the

the twenty fixth of *March* 1602, in a fmall Bark, with
thirty two Men. He kept as far North as the Winds would
permit, and was the firft that came in a direct Courfe to
America.

On the 11th of *May*, being about the Latitude of forty
three, they made Land, on the Coaft of *New-England*, as
it hath been fince called. But as all this Continent bore
the Name of *Florida*, till the Difcovery of the *Englifh* in
1584, fo afterwards all that Tract of Country, from 34 to
45 Degrees of Northern Latitude, was called *Virginia*, till
from different Settlements it got different Names. The
Land was low; the Shore white Sand, and rocky, yet overgrown with fair and ftately Trees. Coming to an Anchor,
eight *Indians*, in a Shallop, with Maft and Sail, came boldly
on board them. By their Signs, and by the Shallop and
other things, which they had, they judged, that fome *Bif-
cayneers* had been fifhing there. But finding no good Harbour, they weighed, and ftood to the Southward into the
Sea. The next Morning, they found themfelves embayed
with a mighty Head-land; and going to the neighbouring
Hills, they perceived it to be Part of the Continent, almoft
environed with Iflands. Here, in a few Hours, they caught
more Cod, then they knew, what to do with; from whence
the Place obtained the Name of *Cape-Cod*. And they thence
alfo concluded, that a good Fifhery might be found there,
in the Months of *March*, *April*, and *May*.

Soon after they went to the Iflands, and anchored near
one of them. They found it four Miles in Compafs, without Houfe or Inhabitant. In it was a Lake, near a Mile in
Circuit; and the reft fo overgrown with Vines, which covered all the Trees and Bufhes, that they could fcarce pafs
through them. They likewife found Plenty of Strawber-
ries, Rafberries, Goofberries, and divers other Fruits in
Bloom, and therefore called the Ifland *Martha's Vineyard*.
They then vifited the reft of the Ifles, and found them replenifhed with the like Products. One they named *Elizabeth's Ifland*, in Honour to their ancient Sovereign, in which
they planted Wheat, Barley, Oats, and Peafe, which fprung
up nine Inches in fourteen Days. From hence they went
to the Main, where they ftood for fome time ravifhed at
the Beauty and Delicacy of the Country. But foon after
returning to *Elizabeth's Ifland*, they fpent three Weeks in
building a Houfe, in a fmall Ifland of about an Acre of
Ground, which ftood in the Midft of a large Lake of frefh
Water, about three Miles in Circumference.

They faw feveral of the Natives, with whom they
made mutual Prefents, and had fome fmall Traffick. They
were

1602. were of an excellent Conftitution of Body, active, ftrong, healthful, and very ingenious, as divers of their Joys teftified. The bafer Sort would fteal, but thofe of better Rank were very civil and juft. Not one of the *Englifh* was affected with any Sicknefs; but they rather grew more healthy and ftrong, notwithstanding their bad Diet and Lodging. Twelve had refolved to ftay; but, confidering how meanly they were provided, they were at laft all obliged to leave this Ifland, not without much Sorrow and Reluctancy, and arrived at *Exmouth* the 23d of *July*.

1603.   THE Beginning of the next Year, died that ever-memorable and glorious Princefs, Queen *Elizabeth*, and was fucceeded by King *James* VI. of *Scotland*. He was fcarce warm in his Throne, before, as a Prefage of his future weak and inglorious Reign, he confined Sir *Walter Ralegh* in the Tower, for a moft myfterious and inextricable Plot. This great Man, as he was the firft Undertaker and Mover of thefe Difcoveries, is ufually looked upon as the Founder and Father of our Country. And indeed we are proud to own for fuch, a Perfon of his diftinguifhed Merit and Parts, who was one of the brighteft Ornaments of his Age and Country, highly in the Favour and Efteem of Queen *Elizabeth*, and afterwards the Sacrifice of her mean and pufillanimous Succeffor. But yet it muft be confeffed, that his Adventurers touched but once, and then flightly, on our Country; but ftill kept on in the fame unfortunate Tract, on the fhoaly and importuous Coaft of *North-Carolina*. Altho' his Judgment foon diftinguifhed from the Accounts, he received, the Advantages of *Chefapeake* for feating his Capital City of *Ralegh*; and had his Orders been followed, it might perhaps have given a quite different Turn to the Affairs of the Colony. For it would not only have freed them from the Hazards and Difficulties, they encountered on that dangerous Coaft, and every where have fupplied them with fafe and convenient Harbours, but would have naturally led them to the Search and Difcovery of one of the moft commodious Countries perhaps in the World, for Shipping and Veffels.

THE fame Year 1603, by the Perfuafions of Mr. *Richard Hackluyt* (a curious and inquifitive Gentleman, and foon after a Prebend of *Weftminfter*, who publifhed the noted Collection of Voyages and Travels) the Mayor and Aldermen, with moft of the Merchants of *Briftol*, raifed a Stock of a thoufand Pounds, and fitted out two Veffels. But firft they obtained the Leave and Permiffion of Sir *Walter Ralegh*, as Proprietor of the Country, to make Difcoveries in *Virginia*. *Martin Pring* was made Captain,

an

an underftanding Gentleman and able Mariner; and *Robert*   1603.
Saltern, who had been with Captain *Gofnold* the Year before, was appointed his Affiftant and Pilot.   But as, for
the moft Part, they followed Captain *Gofnold's* Courfe,
their Difcoveries were nothing extraordinary or different
from his.

But another Bark was this Year fent from *London*, under the Command of Captain *Bartholomew Gilbert*, who
had likewife been with Captain *Gofnold*.   After fome fmall
Trade in the *Weft-Indies*, they fell in with the Coaft of
America in about 37 Degrees of Northern Latitude; and
fome Authors fay, they run up into *Chefapeake* Bay, where
the Captain, going afhore, was killed with four of his
Men.   This ftruck fuch a Damp and Difcouragement into
the reft, that they immediately weighed Anchor, and returned to *England*, without any further Attempt or Difcovery.

Two Years after, Captain *George Weymouth* was fent by   1605.
the Earl of *Southampton* and the Lord *Arundel* of *Warder*,
to make Difcoveries on the Coaft of *Virginia*.   He intended to the *Southward* of 39; but was forced by the Winds
farther *Northward*, and fell among fome Shoals in 41 Deg.
20 Min.   But having happily difengaged themfelves, on the
18th of *May* they made Land.   It appeared to be a main
high Land, but they found it an Ifland of fix Miles in
Compafs.   From thence they could difcern the Continent
and very high Mountains; and coafting among the Iflands,
adjoining to the Main, they found an excellent Harbour.
They dug a Garden the twenty fecond of *May*; and among
their Seeds, they fowed Barley and Peafe, which grew up
eight Inches in fixteen Days; altho' they judged the Mould
much inferior to what they found afterwards on the Main.
On the 30th of *May*, the Captain with thirteen more, went
to view and difcover the Continent; and having found a
fair River, running up into the Country, they returned
back to bring in the Ship.   What River this was, and
what Part of the *American* Coaft they fell upon, is difficult
to determine exactly.   For their neglecting to tell us what
Courfe they fteered, after they were difengaged from the
Shoals, renders it doubtful, whether they fell in with fome
Part of the *Maffachufet's* Bay; or rather farther *Southward*,
on the Coaft of *Rhode-Ifland*, *Naraganfet*, or *Connecticut*;
altho' I am moft inclined to believe, this River was either
that of *Naraganfet* or *Connecticut*; and the Ifland, what is
now called *Block-Ifland*.   However it is certain, that *Oldmixon*, (the Author of the Book, entitled, *The Britifh Em-
pire in America*) according to his ufual Cuftom, is here

1605. moſt egregiouſly bewildered and loſt. For after having,
injudiciouſly enough, determined the ſmall Iſland they firſt
made, of ſix Miles in Compaſs, to be *Long-Iſland*, on the
Coaſt of *New-York*, he immediately after, with ſtill greater Abſurdity and Groſneſs, calls this the River of *Powhatan*, now *James* River, to the *Southward*, as he ſays, of
the Bay of *Cheſapeake*.

WHEN Captain *Weymouth* returned aboard, he found,
that the *Indians* had contracted an Acquaintance with his
Crew; that they had had ſome ſmall Trade together; and
that there was much outward Shew of Kindneſs and Civility between them. For as the *Engliſh* intended to inhabit
their Country, and as it was the chief Deſign of the noble
Adventurers, who had ſent them, to propagate Chriſtianity
among thoſe barbarous People, they uſed them very kindly;
and exchanging Hoſtages, would ſometimes lie aſhore with
them, and they ſometimes aboard with the *Engliſh*. At
laſt they were very preſſing with the Captain, to go to the
Main, to trade with their Baſhabes, or chief Lord. He
accordingly manned his Boat with fourteen Hands, and attended them. But having plainly diſcovered their Treachery, and that it was only a Stratagem to cut them off,
he ſeiſed five, and ever afterwards treated them with great
Civility, but never more truſted them.

HAVING ſpent ſome time in ſounding all the Iſles,
Channels, and Inlets, and found four ſeveral Ways of bringing a Ship into the Bay, they at laſt ran theirs twenty ſix
Miles up the River. They found, it flowed eighteen Feet,
was a Mile wide forty Miles from the Mouth, had a bold
Channel from ſix to ten Fathom deep, and every half Mile
beautiful Coves and Harbours, ſome of them to contain an
hundred Sail of Veſſels. The Land was very rich, trend-
ing all along in an equal Plain, neither mountainous nor
rocky, but verged with a green Border of Graſs; and the
Woods were large and tall, and delightfully watered with
many freſh Springs and Rivulets. Leaving their Ship, they
went ſeven Miles higher than the ſalt Water flowed, and
then marched towards the Mountains. But the Weather
was ſo hot, and the Fatigue ſo great, that having erected
a Croſs, they willingly returned to their Ship. Soon after,
they ſailed for *England*, and arrived at *Dartmouth* the 18th
of *July*; carrying with them the five *Indians*, taken by
the Captain, whereof one was a Sagamo, or Commander,
and three others, Perſons of Figure and Diſtinction in their
own Country.

THE

THE

H I S T O R Y

OF

V I R G I N I A.

BOOK II.

CAPTAIN *Bartholomew Gofnold* had made a Voyage to the *Northern* Parts of *Virginia*, in the Year 1602, as hath been before related. He was fo wonderfully pleafed with the Pleafantnefs and Fertility of the Places he faw, that, after his Return to *England*, he made it his Bufinefs to follicit all his Friends and Acquaintance, to join with him in an Attempt to fettle fo delightful a Country. After fome Years fpent in vain, he at laft prevailed with Captain *John Smith*, Mr. *Edward-Maria Wingfield*, the Rev. Mr. *Robert Hunt*, and divers others, to join in the Undertaking. But fettling Colonies is an Enterprife of too great Burthen and Expence for a few private Perfons; and therefore, after many vain Projects, they applied themfelves to feveral of the Nobility, Gentry, and Merchants, and by their great Charge and Induftry, recommended their Scheme fo effectually to them, that they came into it very heartily.

AND firft, Letters patent were obtained from King *James* I. bearing Date the 10th of *April*, 1606, to Sir *Thomas Gates*, and Sir *George Somers*, Knights, *Richard Hackluyt*, Clerk, Prebendary of *Weftminfter*, *Edward-Maria Wingfield*, with others unnamed, for the *Southern* Colony; and to *Thomas Hanham*, and *Ralegh Gilbert*, Efqrs, *William Parker*, and *George Popham*, Gentlemen, and others

1606.

D 2 unnamed,

1606. unnamed, for the *Northern* Colony. By this Charter, all
that Tract of Country, from 34 to 45 Degrees of *North*
Latitude, which then went under the common Name of
Virginia, was divided into two Parts; called the First Colony and the Second. The First or *Southern* Colony was
designed for the City of *London*, and such as would adventure with them, to discover and chuse a Place of Settlement,
any where between the Degrees of 34 and 41. The Second or *Northern* Part, was appropriated to the Cities of
Bristol, Exeter, Plimouth, and the *Western* Parts of *England*, and all those, that would adventure and join with
them, to make their Choice, any where between the Degrees of 38 and 45; provided, there should be at least an
hundred Miles Distance between the two Colonies. For
each of them was to extend fifty Miles from the Place of
their first Habitation, each way along the Coast. But I
shall make no Abstract of this Charter, having caused it to
be printed at large in the Appendix, to which I refer the
Reader.

BUT besides this Charter, the King gave divers Articles,
Instructions, and Orders, under his Sign Manual, and the
Privy Seal of *England*, dated the 20th of *November*, 1606;
wherein he establishes and ordains a Council, under the
Name of the King's Council for *Virginia*. This consisted
of the following Persons; Sir *William Wade*, Lieutenant
of the Tower of *London*, Sir *Thomas Smith*, Sir *Walter
Cope*, Sir *George More*, Sir *Francis Popham*, Sir *Ferdinando
Gorges*, Sir *John Trevor*, Sir *Henry Montagu*, Recorder of
the City of *London*, and Sir *William Romney*, Knights;
John Dodderidge, Sollicitor General, and *Thomas Warr*,
Esqrs; *John Eldred*, of the City of *London*, *Thomas James*,
of *Bristol*, and *James Bagg*, of *Plimouth*, in the County of
Devon, Merchants. But these being soon found too few,
and by Reason of the Distance of their Habitations from
each other, difficult to be got together in any competent
Number, his Majesty, by an Ordinance dated the 9th of
March following, augmented this Council with Sir *Thomas
Challenor*, Sir *Henry Nevil*, Sir *Fulke Grevil*, Sir *John
Scot*, Sir *Robert Mansel*, Sir *Oliver Cromwell*, Sir *Morris
Berkeley*, Sir *Edward Michelborne*, Sir *Thomas Holcroft*, Sir
Thomas Smith, Clerk of the Privy Council, Sir *Robert Kil-
ligrew*, Sir *Herbert Croft*, Sir *George Copping*, Sir *Edwin
Sandys*, Sir *Thomas Roe*, and Sir *Anthony Palmer*, Knights,
nominated to him by and on the Behalf of the first Colony;
and with Sir *Edward Hungerford*, Sir *John Mallet*, Sir *John
Gilbert*, Sir *Thomas Freake*, Sir *Richard Hawkins*, and Sir
Bartholomew Mitchel, Knights; *Thomas Seamer, Bernard
Greenvil*,

Greenvil, and *Edward Rogers*, Efqrs ; and *Matthew Sutcliffe*, 1606.
·Doctor of Divinity, and afterwards Dean of *Exeter*, nominated to him by and on the Behalf of the fecond Colony.

IN this laft Inftrument, there was a Diftinction and Se-
peration made of the two Councils; but in the former of
the 20th of *November*, Sir *William Wade*, and the reft,
were conftituted his Majefty's Council for both Colonies,
" for all Matters that fhould happen in *Virginia*, or any the
" Territories of *America*, between 34 and 45 Degrees of
" *North* Latitude, according to the Purport and Tenor of
" the Letters patent: That they fhould have full Power
" and Authority, at the Pleafure, and in the Name of his
" Majefty, his Heirs, or Succeffors, to give Directions to
" the Councils, refident in *America*, for the good Govern-
" ment of the People there, and for the proper ordering
" and difpofing all Caufes within the fame, in Subftance
" as near to the Common Law of *England*, and the Equity
" thereof, as might be ; referving to his Majefty, his Heirs
" and Succeffors, a Power to increafe, alter, or change
" the faid Council, at their Will and Pleafure: And that
" this his Majefty's Council in *England*, fhould nominate
" and appoint the firft Members of the feveral Councils,
" to be refident in the Colonies.

" That the faid Councils, refident in the Colonies, or
" the major Part of them, fhould chufe one of their own
" Body, not being a Minifter of God's Word, to be Prefi-
" dent of the fame, and to continue in that Office by the
" Space of one whole Year, and no longer: And that it
" fhould be lawful for the major Part of the faid Councils,
" upon any juft Caufe, either of Abfence or otherwife, to
" remove the Prefident, or any other of the Council ; and
" in Cafe of Death or fuch Removal, to elect another into
" the vacant Place: Provided always, that the Number of
" each of the faid Councils fhould not exceed thirteen.

" That the faid Prefidents, Councils, and the Minifters,
" fhould provide, that the true Word and Service of God
" be preached, planted, and ufed, not only in the faid Co-
" lonies, but alfo, as much as might be, among the Sava-
" ges bordering upon them, according to the Rites and
" Doctrine of the Church of *England*.

" THAT they fhould not fuffer any to withdraw the
" People of the faid Colonies from the Allegiance of the
" King, his Heirs, or Succeffors ; but fhould caufe all
" Perfons fo offending, to be apprehended and imprifoned,
" till full and due Reformation, or if the Caufe fo required,
" fhould fend them to *England*, with all convenient Speed,
" there to receive condign Punifhment.

" That

" THAT all Lands, Tenements, and Hereditaments,
" fhould be had, inhabited, and enjoyed, within the faid
" Colonies, as the like Eftates are held and enjoyed, by
" the Laws in *England.*

" THAT Tumults, Rebellion, Confpiracy, Mutiny,
" and Sedition, together with Murder, Manflaughter, In-
" ceft, Rapes, and Adultery, committed within any of the
" Degrees aforefaid, (and no other Offences) fhould be
" punifhed by Death without Benefit of Clergy, except in
" Cafe of Manflaughter, to which Clergy fhould be allow-
" ed : And that the faid Prefidents and Councils, within
" their feveral Limits and Precincts, fhould have full Power
" and Authority, to hear and determine concerning the
" faid Offences, in Manner and Form following ; *viz.* by
" a Jury of twelve honeft and indifferent Perfons, returned
" by proper Officers, and fworn upon the Evangelifts,
" who fhould, according to the Evidence given, upon their
" Oath, and according to the Truth in their Confciences,
" convict or acquit the feveral Perfons fo accufed, and
" tried by them : That every Perfon who fhould volunta-
" rily confefs the faid Offences, or fhould ftand mute, and
" refufe to plead, or make direct Anfwer, fhould be, and
" be held as fully convicted of the fame, as if he had been
" found guilty by the Verdict of the twelve Jurors afore-
" faid : That the faid Prefidents and Councils, or the Ma-
" jor Part of them, within their feveral Precincts and Li-
" mits, fhould have full Power and Authority, to give
" Judgment of Death upon every fuch Offender, without
" Benefit of Clergy, except in Cafe of Manflaughter only :
" And that no Perfon, fo adjudged or condemned, fhould
" be reprieved, but by the Confent of the faid Prefident
" and Council, or the major Part of them ; nor fhould
" receive full Pardon, or be abfolutely difcharged from the
" faid Offences, but by the Pardon of the King, his Heirs,
" or Succeffors, under the Great Seal of *England :* And fi-
" nally, that all Perfons, offending as aforefaid, within
" the Degrees abovementioned, but out of the Precincts
" of their own Colony, fhould be tried and punifhed in
" their proper and refpective Colony.

" THAT the faid Prefidents and Councils, within their
" feveral Precincts and Limits, fhould have Power and Au-
" thority, to hear and determine all other Wrongs, Tref-
" paffes, and Mifdemeanors whatfoever ; and on fufficient
" Proof upon Oath, fhould refpectively punifh the Offen-
" ders, either by reafonable corporal Punifhment and Im-
" prifonment, or elfe by awarding fuch Damages, or other
" Satisfaction, to the Parties aggrieved, as to them, or the
                                                    " more

" more Part of them, fhould feem fit and convenient : And
" that the faid Prefidents and Councils fhould have Power
" to punifh all Manner of Excefs, through Drunkennefs
" or otherwife, and all loitering, idle, and vagrant Per-
" fons, within their refpective Precincts, according to their
" beft Difcretions, and with fuch convenient Punifhment,
" as they, or the moft Part of them, fhould think fit :
" That thefe judicial Proceedings fhould be made fumma-
" rily and verbally, without Writing, till they came to the
" Judgment or Sentence, which fhould be briefly regiftred
" into a Book, kept for that Purpofe, together with the
" Caufe, for which the faid Judgment or Sentence was
" given, fubfcribed by the faid Prefident and Council, or
" by fuch of them as gave the Judgment.

" T H A T for five Years, next after their landing on the
" Coaft of *Virginia*, the faid feveral Colonies, and every
" Perfon thereof, fhould trade altogether in one Stock, or in
" two or three Stocks at moft, and fhould bring all the Fruits
" of their Labours there, with all their Goods and Com-
" modities from *England* or elfewhere, into feveral Maga-
" zines or Storehoufes, for that Purpofe to be erected, in
" fuch Order, Manner, and Form, as the Councils of the
" refpective Colonies, or the more Part of them, fhould
" prefcribe and direct : That there fhould be annually cho-
" fen by the Prefident and Council of each Colony, or the
" major Part of them, one Perfon of their Colony, to be
" Treafurer or Cape-Merchant of the fame, to take Charge
" of, and to manage, all Goods and Wares, brought into,
" or delivered out of, the faid Magazines ; upon whofe
" Death, voluntary Refignation, or Removal for any juft
" and reafonable Caufe, it fhould be lawful for the faid
" Prefident and Council, to elect any other, or others, in
" his Room : That there fhould alfo be elected, by the
" faid Prefident and Council, two others (or more, if need
" be) Perfons of Difcretion ; the one to enter into a Book,
" kept for that Purpofe, all Goods, Wares, and Merchan-
" difes, brought into ; and the other, to charge, in a like
" Book, all taken out of the faid Magazines or Storehoufes ;
" which Clerks fhould continue in their Places, only at the
" Will of the Prefident and Council of their refpective Co-
" lony : And laftly, that every Perfon of each of the faid
" Colonies, fhould be furnifhed with Neceffaries out of the
" faid Magazines, for the Space of five Years, by the Ap-
" pointment, Direction, and Order, of the Prefident and
" Council of their refpective Colonies, or of the Cape-
" Merchant and two Clerks, or the major Part of them.

" THAT the Adventurers of the First Colony should
" chuse, out of themselves, one or more Companies, each
" consisting of three Persons at the least, to reside in or
" near *London*, or at such other Place or Places, as the
" Council for that Colony, for the time being, or the most
" Part of them, during the said five Years, should think
" fit: In the same Manner, that the Adventurers of the
" Second Colony should chuse the like Companies, to be
" resident at or near *Plimouth*, or at such one, two, or
" three other Places or Ports, as the Council for that Co-
" lony should think fit: And that these minor Companies
" should, from time to time, take Care and Charge of
" the Trade, and an Account of all the Goods, Wares,
" and Merchandises, that should be sent from *England* to
" their respective Colonies, and brought from the Colonies
" into *England*, and of all other Things, relating to the
" Affairs and Profits of their several Companies.

" THAT no Person should be admitted to abide or re-
" main in the said Colonies, but such as should take, not
" only the usual Oath of Obedience, but also the Oath,
" prescribed in the last Session of Parliament, holden at
" *Westminster* in the fourth Year of his Majesty's Reign,
" for due Obedience to the King, his Heirs, and Succes-
" sors.

(" THAT the Presidents and Councils of the said Colo-
" nies, or the major Part of them, should have Power to
" constitute, make, and ordain, from time to time, Laws,
" Ordinances, and Officers, for the better Order, Go-
" vernment, and Peace of their respective Colonies ; pro-
" vided nevertheless, that those Ordinances and Constitu-
" tions did not touch any Party in Life or Member : And
" that the said Laws and Ordinances should stand and con-
" tinue in full Force, till the same should be otherwise
" altered or made void by the King, his Heirs, or Suc-
" cessors, or by his Majesty's Council in *England* for *Vir-
" ginia*, or by their own Council, there resident : Provided
" always, that the said Alterations should stand with, and
" be in Substance consonant to, the Laws of *England*, or
" the Equity thereof.

" THAT all Persons should kindly treat the savage and
" heathen People in those Parts, and use all proper Means
" to draw them to the true Service and Knowledge of
" God, and that all just and charitable Courses should be
" taken with such of them, as would conform themselves
" to any good and sociable Traffick, thereby the sooner to
" bring them to the Knowledge of God, and the Obe-
" dience of the King, his Heirs, and Successors, under such
　　　　　　　　　　　　　　　　　　　" severe

" fevere Pains and Punifhments, as fhould be inflicted by
" the refpective Prefidents and Councils of the feveral Co-
" lonies.

" THAT as the faid Colonies fhould, from time to
" time, encreafe in Plantation, the King, his Heirs, and
" Succeffors, fhould ordain and give fuch Order, and fur-
" ther Inftructions, Laws, Conftitutions, and Ordinances,
" as by them fhould be thought fit and convenient: Pro-
" vided always, that they be fuch as might ftand with, and
" be confonant to the Laws of *England*, or the Equity
" thereof.

" AND laftly, that his Majefty's Council in *England*
" for *Virginia*, fhould take fuch Oath, as fhould be limit-
" ed and appointed by the Privy Council; and each Coun-
" fellor, refident in the Colonies, fhould take fuch Oath,
" as fhould be prefcribed by the King's Council in *England*
" for *Virginia*: And that thefe, as well as all future Or-
" ders and Inftructions of the King, his Heirs, or Succef-
" fors, fhould be tranfmitted over to the feveral Councils,
" refident in the faid Colonies, under the legal Seal of the
" King's Council in *England* for *Virginia*."

THESE Articles contain feveral Things of an extraordinary Nature; which Sir *John Randolph*, in the Sketch,
he has left of the Beginning of his Hiftory of *Virginia*, promifed afterwards to animadvert upon. I am no Lawyer,
and therefore fhall not prefume to enter deeply into the
Matter. I fhall only tranfiently remark, that, notwithftanding the frequent Repetition of the Laws of *England*,
and the Equity thereof, his Majefty feems, in fome things,
to have deviated grofly from them. He has certainly made
fufficient Provifion for his own defpotic Authority; and
has attributed an extravagant and illegal Power to the Prefidents and Councils. For he has placed the whole Legif-
lative Power folely in them, without any Reprefentative of
the People, contrary to a noted Maxim of the *Englifh*
Conftitution; That all Freemen are to be governed by Laws,
made with their own Confent, either in Perfon, or by their
Reprefentatives. He has alfo appointed Juries only in Cafes
of Life and Death; and has left all other Points, relating
to the Liberty and private Property of the Subject, wholly
to the Pleafure and Determination of the Prefidents and
Councils. He has indeed, agreeably to the Dictates of his
own Nature, been exprefs enough with Refpect to Rebellion, Confpiracy, and other Offences immediately againft
the Magiftrate; but then he has been very fparing in all
other criminal Matters. For altho' he has made Adultery
punifhable with Death, contrary to the Laws of *England*,

8   and

and contrary to a greater, the Law of the Gospel, in the
noted Determination of our B. Saviour, concerning the
Woman taken in Adultery; yet he has passed over all the
several Species of Robbery, Burglary, and Felony, with
other Crimes, capital by the Laws of *England*, and declared, that none, but those there specified, should be subject
to the Punishment of Death.

HOWEVER, furnished with these Powers and Authorities, the First or *Southern* Colony, which still retains the
Name of *Virginia*, was undertaken and begun by several
Nobleman, Knights, Gentlemen, Merchants and Citizens,
in and about *London*; and they chose Sir *Thomas Smith*,
a very eminent and wealthy Merchant of *London*, their
Treasurer, to have the chief Management of their Affairs,
and to summon and preside in all Meetings of the Council
and Company in *England*. He had been the chief of Sir
Walter Ralegh's Assignees, and was either now, or soon
after, Governor of the *East-India* Company; and had also
been sent, two Years before, his Majesty's Embassador to
the Emperor of *Russia*. And next, having provided two
Ships and a small Bark, they committed the Transporta-
tion of the Colony to Captain *Christopher Newport*, who
was esteemed a Mariner of Ability and Experience on the
American Coasts. For he had fourteen Years before, *Anno*
1592, with much Reputation and Honour, conducted an
Expedition against the *Spaniards* in the *West-Indies*; where,
with three Ships and a small Bark, he took several Prizes,
plundered and burnt some Towns, and got a considerable
Booty.

To him therefore, by an Instrument, bearing Date the
10th of *December* 1606, under the legal Seal of the Council, they gave Power to appoint all Captains, Soldiers, and
Mariners, and to have the sole Charge and Command of
the same, and of the whole Voyage, from the Date thereof, till they should land on the Coast of *Virginia*; and in
Case of his Death, the several Captains of the Ships and
Bark were ordered and impowered, to proceed and carry
them to the Coast of *Virginia* aforesaid. To Captain *Newport*, Capt. *Bartholomew Gosnold*, and Captain *John Ratcliffe*, they also delivered several Instruments, close sealed
with the Councils Seal, which they, the Survivors, or Sur-
vivor of them, should, within twenty four Hours after
their Arrival on the Coast of *Virginia*, and not before, open
and unseal, and publish the Names of the Persons, therein
set down, who should be declared and taken to be his Majesty's Council for that Colony: That the said Council
should immediately proceed to the Choice and Nomination
of

of a Prefident, who fhould have two Votes in all Matters of Controverfy and Queftion, where the Voices happened to be equal; and fhould have full Power and Authority, with the Advice of the reft of the Council, or the greater Part of them, to govern, rule, and command, all the Captains and Soldiers, with all other Perfons whatfoever of the faid Colony: And that the Prefident, immediately upon his Election, fhould, in the Prefence of the Council, and of twenty others of the principal Adventurers in the Voyage, to be by the Prefident and Council called thereto, take his Oath, according to a Form prefcribed, to bear true Allegiance to the King, and for the Performance of his Duty in the Place and Office of Prefident; after which he fhould adminifter the like Oath to each of the Council particularly. And finally, Captain *Newport* was commanded, with fuch a Number of Men, as fhould be affigned him by the Prefident and Council, to beftow two Months in the Search and Difcovery of the Rivers and Ports of the Country, and to give prefent Order for the lading the two Ships (the Bark being defigned to remain in the Country) with fuch principal Commodities and Merchandife, as could there be had and found, and to return with the faid Ships, full laden, bringing a particular Account of every thing, by the laft of *May* following, if God permit.

To thefe Orders the Council added other Inftructions, by way of Advice, concerning their ftrict Obfervation of the above-mentioned Ordinances by the King's Majefty, delivered to them under the Privy Seal; concerning the Choice of a Place, and the Manner of feating themfelves; the neceffary Orders and Methods of Difcovery; their Caution before, and Behaviour towards, the Natives; with various other Counfels and Directions for the better conducting themfelves and the Enterprife. And as the Council in *England* were ever follicitous and intent on the Difcovery of the *South-Sea*, as the certain and infallible Way to immenfe Riches, they were commanded, if they happened to difcover divers navigable Rivers, and among them any, that had two main Branches, if the Difference was not great, to make Choice of that, which tended moft towards the *North-Weft*; fince the other Sea, as they judged, would be fooneft found that Way. And they were to difcover, if they could, whether the River, on which they feated, fprung out of the Mountains or out of Lakes. For if it rofe from any Lake, it was likely, that the Paffage to the other Sea would be the more eafy, and that out of the fame Lake they might find fome other Stream, running the contrary Way, towards the *Eaft-India*, or *South-Sea*. And they con-

1606. concluded laftly and chiefly, that the Way to profper and obtain Succefs was to make themfelves all of one Mind, for their own and their Country's Good, and to ferve and fear God, the Giver of all Goodnefs, fince every Plantation, which he did not plant, would certainly be rooted out.

ALL thefe Orders and Inftructions being put into a Box, they fet Sail from *Blackwall* the 19th of *December* 1606; but were kept fix Weeks on the Coaft of *England* by contrary Winds. Even then they neglected the Council's laft falutary Advice, concerning Unity and Concord among themfelves. For they began to fall into fuch Factions and Difcords, as would have ruined the whole Voyage, had not Mr. *Hunt,* their Preacher, by his prudent Conduct and pious Exhortations, allayed their Fury and Diffenfion. That good Man, altho' he was fo fick and weak the whole Time, that few expected his Recovery, and had the additional Aggravation of being the principal Object of their Malice and Reproach, yet bore all with the utmoft Meeknefs and Patience. And he never betrayed the leaft feeming Defire to leave the Bufinefs, altho' his Habitation was but twenty Miles from the *Downs,* but preferred the Service of God and his Country, in fo good a Voyage, before all other private Refpects or Confiderations whatfoever.

1607. As foon as they got clear of the Coaft of *England,* they took the old Rout by the *Canaries,* where they watered. Here their Quarrels and Diffenfions grew fo high, that Captain *Smith* was feized and committed clofe Prifoner. It was fuggefted by Mr. *Wingfield* and fome others of the chief among them, who envied his Repute and Intereft with the Company, that he intended to murder the Council, ufurp the Government, and make himfelf King of *Virginia*; and this, they pretended, would be attefted and proved againft him by feveral of his Confederates, who were difperfed in all the three Ships. Upon thefe fcandalous Suggeftions, he was fufpected, and kept in clofe Confinement thirteen Weeks. From the *Canaries* they went to the *Weft-Indies*; where having traded with the Natives, and ftaid three Weeks to refrefh themfelves, they fteered away *Northward,* in Search of *Virginia.* The Mariners had paffed their Reckoning three Days, and yet found no Land; which fo difheartened the Company, that Captain *Ratcliffe,* Commander of the Bark, was urgent to bare up the Helm, and return for *England.* But a violent Storm, obliging them to hull it all Night under their bare Poles, drove them providentially, beyond all their Expectations, to their defired Port. For the next Day, being the 26th of *April* 1607, they

they made a Coaft, which none of them had ever feen. The firft Land, they defcried, they called *Cape-Henry*, in Honour to the Prince of *Wales*; as the Northern Cape was named *Cape-Charles*, after the Duke of *York*, King *James*'s fecond Son at that time, and afterwards King *Charles* I. of *England*. Thirty Men went afhore on *Cape-Henry*, to recreate and refrefh themfelves; but they were fuddenly affaulted by five Savages, who wounded two of them very dangeroufly.

WITHIN thefe Capes they found a Country, which, according to their own Defcription, might claim the Prerogative over the moft pleafant Places in the known World, for large and majeftic navigable Rivers, for beautiful Mountains, Hills, Plains, Vallies, Rivulets, and Brooks, gurgling down, and running moft pleafantly into a fair Bay, encompaffed on all Sides, except at the Mouth, with fruitful and delightfome Land. In the Bay and Rivers were many Iflands, both great and fmall, fome woody, others plain, but moft of them low and uninhabited. So that Heaven and Earth feemed never to have agreed better, to frame a Place for Man's commodious and delightful Habitation, were it fully cultivated and inhabited by induftrious People.

THE Night of their Arrival, the Box was opened, and the Orders for Government read. In them *Edward-Maria Wingfield*, *Bartholomew Gofnold*, *John Smith*, *Chriftopher Newport*, *John Ratcliffe*, *John Martin*, and *George Kendall*, were appointed of the Council. They were employed, till the 13th of *May*, in feeking a Place for their Settlement; and then they refolved on a *Peninfula*, on the North Side of the River *Powhatan*, about forty Miles from the Mouth. After which, Mr. *Wingfield* was chofen Prefident, the Council fworn, and an Oration made, why Captain *Smith* was not admitted of the Council, as the reft. But befides thefe Gentlemen and Mr. *Hunt*, their Chaplain, there came over another Perfon of very great Diftinction and Quality. This was the Honourable Mr. *George Percy*, of the ancient Family of the *Percies*, fo renowned in Story, and Brother to the Earl of *Northumberland*. Neither did his Actions here difgrace the Nobility of his Birth. For he juftly obtained the Reputation of being a Gentleman of great Honour, Courage, and Induftry. He feems to have come merely a Volunteer upon the Expedition, and bore no Poft or Office of Government; which might perhaps have proceeded from the Cloud, under which his Brother, the Earl of *Northumberland*, then lay. For on fome diftant Surmifes, and upon Account of

Edward-Maria Wingfield Prefident.

Mr.

1607.   Mr. *Percy*, his Kinfman, who was concerned in that Trea-
son, the Earl was fufpeded to have been privy to the
Edward- Gun-powder Plot; and was therefore thrown into the
Maria Tower, where he lay above twelve Years, was fined thirty
Wingfield thoufand Pounds *Sterling* in the *Star-Chamber*, and under-
Prefident. went much hard Ufage. And befides Mr. *Percy*, there
were *Anthony Gofnold*, Captain *Gabriel Archer*, *Nathaniel
Powel*, *Kellam Throgmorton*, *William Smithes*, *Richard
Frith*, and divers others of Note in this firft Plantation.
And Mr. *Thomas Studley* was eleded the firft Cape-Mer-
chant, or Treafurer, of the Colony.

HAVING pitched upon a Place to fettle, they called it
James-Town, in Honour of his Majefty then reigning, and
every Man fell to work. The Council contrive the Fort;
and of the reft, fome cut down and clear away the Trees,
to make a Place to pitch their Tents; fome get Clapboard,
to relade the Ships; whilft others were employed in making
Gardens and Nets, and providing other Neceffaries and
Conveniences. The *Indians* often vifited them kindly,
which was a great Satisfadion to them. For the Prefident's
Jealoufy would admit of no Exercife at Arms, nor any
other Fortification, but the Boughs of Trees caft together
in the Form of a half Moon, by the extraordinary Pains
and Diligence of Captain *Kendall*. And foon after *Newport* and *Smith*, with twenty others, were fent to difcover
the Head of the River *Powhatan*, which, from King *James*,
was afterwards called *James* River. They paffed by divers
fmall Habitations; and in fix Days arrived at a Town,
called *Powhatan*, confifting of about twelve Houfes, pleafantly feated on a Hill, on the North Side of the River,
with three fertile Ifles before it. This Place I judge to be
either Mrs. *Mayo*'s, or elfe *Marring*'s Plantation; and it
was the principal Seat, by Inheritance, of *Powhatan*, Emperor of the Country. To this Place they found the River
navigable; but within a Mile higher, by reafon of the
Rocks and Ifles, there was no Paffage for a fmall Boat; and
this they called the Falls. They were kindly treated by
the People in all Parts; but being returned to *James-Town*,
they found feventeen Men hurt, and a Boy flain, by the
Indians; and had not a Crofs-bar Shot from the Ships happened to ftrike a Bough from a Tree among them, which
frighted, and made them retire, the *Englifh* had been all
cut off, being fecurely at Work, and their Arms in dry
Fats. After this the Prefident permitted the Fort to be pa-
lifadoed, the Ordinance to be mounted, and the Men to
be armed and exercifed. For many and fudden were the
Affaults and Ambufcades of the *Indians*; and the *Englifh*,
by

by their diforderly ftraggling were often hurt, whilft they, | 1607.
by the Nimbleneſs of their Heels, eſcaped.

ALTHO' Captain *Newport* was named of the Council, *Edward-*
yet was he only hired for their Tranſportation, and was to *Maria Wingfield*
return with the Ships. The time of his Departure ap- *Preſident.*
proaching, Captain *Smith*'s Enemies pretended, out of
Tenderneſs and Compaſſion to him, to refer him to the
Council in *England*, to receive a Reprimand, rather than
by puſhing on their Accuſation, to endanger his Life, or
utterly deſtroy his Reputation. But he, being a Man of
high Spirit, and conſcious of his Innocency, ſcorned their
Charity, and defied their Malice; and behaved himſelf in
the whole Affair with ſuch Clearneſs and Prudence, that
all the Company perceived his Integrity, and their Envy and
Injuſtice. Infiſting therefore upon his Trial, the Perſons,
ſuborned to accuſe him, accuſed their Suborners; and altho' many Falſhoods were alledged againſt him, yet were
they all ſo plainly diſproved, that it raiſed a general Reſentment in the Hearts of the Audience againſt ſuch unjuſt
Commanders, and the Preſident was condemned to pay
him two hundred Pounds, in Reparation of the Injury.
In Conſequence hereof, all the Preſident's Effects were
ſeized in Part of Satisfaction; but *Smith* generouſly preſented them to the publick Store for the Uſe of the Colony.
Soon after their Heats and Animoſities were appeaſed by
the good Doctrine and Exhortations of Mr. *Hunt*, who
procured Captain *Smith* to be admitted of the Council; and
the next Day, they all received the Communion, in Confirmation of their Peace and Concord. The Day after,
being the 15th of *June*, the *Indians* voluntarily ſued for
Peace, and Captain *Newport* ſet Sail for *England*, leaving
an hundred Perſons behind him in *Virginia*.

THE Colony, being now left to their Fortunes, fell into
ſuch a violent Sickneſs, that within ten Days ſcarce ten a-
mong them could either go or ſtand. This was chiefly
owing to the Difference of their Diet. For whilſt the
Ships ſtaid, either by Way of Traffic, or for Money, or
Love, they got a daily Proportion of Biſcuit and other Proviſions from the Sailers, who always abounded even to
Luxury and Profuſion. But now they were all reduced to
the common Kettle; which contained the Allowance of
half a Pint of Wheat, and as much Barley, boiled with
Water, for a Man a Day. And this, having funked for
ſix and twenty Weeks in the Ship's Hold, contained nothing ſubſtantial, being only Bran, with as many Worms
as Grains. The Council in *England*, but eſpecially Sir
Thomas Smith, their Treaſurer, were juſtly charged with
much

much Cruelty and Inhumanity for thefe fcanty and ill-
conditioned Provifions ; which Management however con-
tinued, more or lefs, the whole time of that Gentleman's
Adminiftration of the Affairs of the Company and Colony.
This unwholefome Food, together with their continual
Toil and Labour in the Extremity of the Heat, carried off
fifty of the Company by *September* ; in which Number was
Captain *Gofnold*, the firft Mover and Projeƈtor of the whole
Bufinefs. The reft, that furvived by the Care of Captain
Smith, and the Skill and Diligence of Mr. *Thomas Wotton*,
their Surgeon-General, fubfifted on Crabs and Sturgeon,
till *September*.

BUT the Prefident, all this while, had felt neither Want
nor Sicknefs. For he had embezzled the public Oatmeal,
Sack, *Aqua-vitæ*, Beef, and Eggs, and had lived in great
Plenty and Elegance. Soon after, having projeƈted an
Efcape to *England* in the Bark, it raifed fuch Indignation
in the reft, that they depofed him, and eleƈted Captain
John Ratcliffe in his Room. *Kendall* was likewife at the
fame time difgraced, and removed from the Council, for
being concerned in thefe male Praƈtices of the Prefident.
And now, when all their Provifions were fpent, the Sturgeon gone, and no Profpeƈt of Relief from any Quarter
left, God wrought fo wonderful a Change in the Hearts of
the *Indians*, that they brought fuch Plenty of their Fruits
and Provifions, as no Man wanted.

Newport was gone, *Gofnold* dead, and *Wingfield* and
Kendall in Difgrace ; neither were their Places fupplied by
the Eleƈtion of any others, according to the Authority
given. So that the whole Government and Power of the
Council now refted in the new Prefident, *Martin*, and
Smith. But the Prefident and *Martin*, being little efteemed
or beloved, of weak Judgment in Dangers, and lefs Induftry in Peace, at firft very candidly and wifely permitted
every thing to *Smith*'s Management, who was peculiarly
fitted for conduƈting fuch an Enterprife, by a good Judgment, undaunted Courage, and an invincible Induftry and
Refolution. He immediately fet about the building of
James-Town ; and by good Words, fair Promifes, and his
own Example (himfelf always bearing the greateft Share
of the Labour and Fatigue) he pufhed on the Work with
fuch Vigor and Diligence, that he had, in a fhort time,
provided moft of them with Lodgings, negleƈting any for
himfelf. After which, finding the *Autumn* Superfluity of
the Savages begin to decreafe, he refolved to fearch the
Country for Trade. The Want of the Language and a
fufficient Power, with Cloathing for his Men and other
Ne-

Neceffaries, were infinite Impediments to this Defign, but   1607.
no Difcouragement to his bold and adventurous Spirit.
For with five or fix more, he went down the River, in a *J. Ratcliffe*
Shallop, to *Kicquotan*; where at firft they fcorned them, as *Prefident.*
poor famifhed Creatures, and would offer, in Derifion, a
Handful of Corn, or a Piece of Bread, for their Swords,
Mufkets, or Cloaths. But *Smith*, finding, that nothing
was to be had by Trade and Courtefy, ventured to exceed
his Commiffion, and entered upon fuch Meafures, as Neceffity and the Exigency of his Cafe required. And therefore, having difcharged his Mufkets among them, he ran
his Boat afhore; at which the *Indians* all fled into the
Woods. Then marching up to their Houfes, they faw
great Heaps of Corn. But *Smith* with much ado reftrained
his hungry Soldiers from immediately feizing it; expecting,
the Savages would return to affault them, as it foon after
happened. For fixty or feventy of them, fome painted black,
fome red, fome white, and fome party-coloured, iffued out of
the Woods, finging and dancing, and making a moft hide-
ous Noife, with their *Okée* borne before them. This was
an Idol, made of Skins, ftuffed with Mofs, and all painted
and hung with Chains and Copper. For there was no
Place in *Virginia* found fo barbarous and void of Humanity, in which they had not a Religion, Deer, Bows, and
Arrows. In this Savage Manner, being armed with Clubs,
Targets, Bows, and Arrows, they charged the *Englifh*,
who received them fo warmly with a fecond Volley of
Mufkets, loaded with Piftol Shot, that down fell their God,
and feveral of them lay fprawling on the Ground. The
reft fled again into the Woods, and foon after fent one of
their Priefts, to redeem their God and offer Peace. *Smith*
told him, if only fix would come unarmed, and load his
Boat with Corn, he would not only reftore their *Okée*, but
would be their Friend, and give them Beads, Copper, and
Hatchets befides. Which was agreed to, and performed to
the Satisfaction of both Parties. And then they brought
him Venifon, Turkies, Wildfowl, Bread, and whatever
elfe they had, finging and dancing in Sign of Friendfhip,
till he departed. And in his Return up the River, he difcovered the Town and Country of *Warrafqueake*.

AFTER his Return to *James-Town*, he made feveral
Journies by Land, and difcovered the People of *Chickahominy*. In one of thefe, *Wingfield* and *Kendall*, feeing
all things at random in *Smith*'s Abfence, and the Company's Scorn of the Prefident's Weaknefs and *Martin*'s
never-mending Sicknefs, took Advantage of the Occafion,
and combined with the Sailers and others, to regain their

former Authority, or at leaft to feize the Bark, which
Smith had fitted for a trading Voyage, and in her to efcape
and go for *England.* But *Smith,* returning unexpectedly,
with much Difficulty prevented their Defign. For he was
obliged to turn the Cannon of the Fort upon them, and fo
force them to ftay or fink in the River; which Action coft
the Life of Captain *Kendall.* And not long after, their
new Prefident *Ratcliffe* and Captain *Gabriel Archer* intended
to abandon the Country; but their Project was likewife
reftrained and fuppreffed by *Smith.* The *Spaniards* was never more greedy of Gold, than he was of Provifions; neither did the reft defire more eagerly to abandon the Country, than he to keep it. And therefore, having found
Plenty of Corn up the River *Chickahominy,* he went a trading Voyage thither, and was received by hundreds of *Indians,* who ftood in divers Places with Bafkets, expecting
his Coming. And now the Winter likewife coming on,
the Rivers were fo covered with Swans, Geefe, and Ducks,
that they daily feafted with good Bread, *Virginia* Peafe,
Pumpions, and Paffimmons, and with Fifh, Fowl, and divers Sorts of wild Beafts, as fat as they could well eat
them. So that none of their humourfome and tuftaffety
Sparks (as *Smith* calls them) were any longer difcontented,
or defirous to go to *England.*

BUT Captain *Smith*'s Activity and Induftry, in difcovering the Country, and providing for the Colony, could
not fcreen him from the vain Exceptions and Murmurs of
many Idlers at *James-Town.* He was cenfured by fome,
and even taxed by the Council, of being too remifs and
negligent in difcovering the Head of *Chickahominy* River.
And therefore foon after, with much Labour in cutting
away Trees and clearing a Paffage, he went up as far, as
his Barge could pafs. And then leaving her in a broad
Bay, beyond the Reach of the *Indians* Shot, he himfelf,
with two *Englifh* more, and two *Indians,* proceeded higher
up in a Canoe. When he left the Barge, he ordered, that
none fhould go afhore, till his Return. But he was not
long gone, before his diforderly and ungovernable Crew
difobeyed this Command, and thereby gave the *Indians* an
Opportunity of furprifing one *George Caffen*; and indeed
narrowly efcaped being all cut off to a Man. For *Opechancanough,* Brother to *Powhatan,* and King of *Pamunkey,*
a fubtle and favage Barbarian, was there with three hundred
Bowmen. And after having extorted from *Caffen,* which
Way his Captain was gone, he put him to Death in a moft
cruel and barbarous Manner, and then went in Purfuit of
Smith.

CAPTAIN

CAPTAIN *Smith* had got up twenty Miles higher, a- 1607.
mong the Swamps and Marſhes at the Head of the River;
and leaving the Canoe to the Care of *Robinſon* and *Emry*, *J. Ratcliffe*
his two Men, he himſelf was gone to kill ſome Proviſions. Preſident.
Opechancanough firſt happened on the two Men, aſleep, as
it was ſuppoſed, by the Fire; and ſhooting them full of Arrows, ſlew them. And then they traced the Captain; who,
finding himſelf beſet, bound an *Indian*, whom he had for
his Guide, to his Arm for a Buckler, and received their
Attack ſo ſmartly with his Fire-Arms, that he ſoon laid
three dead upon the Spot, and ſo wounded and galled divers
others, that none of them cared to approach him. He
himſelf received a ſlight Wound in the Thigh, and had
many Arrows ſticking in his Cloaths, but without any great
Hurt. Having the *Indians* thus at bay, he endeavoured to
ſheer off to his Canoe; but regarding them, as he went,
more than his Way, he ſuddenly ſlipped up to his Middle
into an oozy Creek. Altho' he was thus hampered, yet none
of them durſt come near him, till, being almoſt dead with
Cold, he threw away his Arms and ſurrendered. Then
drawing him out, they carried him to the Fire, where his
Men were ſlain, and carefully chafed his benumbed Limbs.
For this Winter, 1607, was extremely cold in *Virginia*,
as it was likewiſe remarkable for an extraordinary Froſt in
Europe.

WHEN *Smith* was a little recovered, he aſked for their
Captain, and being ſhewed *Opechancanough*, he preſented
him with a round Ivory double compaſs Dial. They wondered greatly at the playing of the Fly and Needle, which
they could ſee ſo plainly, and yet not touch, becauſe of the
Glaſs, that covered them. But when he explained by it
the Roundneſs of the Earth, the Skies, the Sphere of the
Sun, Moon, and Stars, with other ſurpriſing and unheard
of Doctrines to them, they all ſtood amazed. Yet within
an Hour after, they tied him to a Tree, and drew up in
Order to ſhoot him. But the King holding up the Compaſs in his Hand, they all laid down their Arms at once.
And then, with much Triumph, and in martial Order,
they conducted him to *Orapakes*, which was a hunting
Town and Seat, lying on the upper Part of *Chickahominy*
Swamp, on the *North* Side, belonging to, and much fre-
quented by *Powhatan* and the Imperial Family, on Account
of the Abundance of Game, it afforded. In their March,
they drew themſelves all up in File; and *Opechancanough*, being in the Midſt, had the *Engliſh* Swords and Muſkets
carried before him. Captain *Smith* came next, led by three
great Savages, holding him faſt by each Arm; and on either

E 2   Side

Side went fix in File, with their Arrows notched. When
they arrived at the Town, the Women and Children ftood
ftaring at a human Creature, fo unlike whatever they had
before feen; and the Soldiers, that had taken him, performed their military Exercife, throwing themfelves with
great Dexterity into their War-Dance, with ftrange Dif-
tortions and antic Poftures, finging and yelling out frightful and inharmonious Notes and Screeches. But they treated
Smith here very kindly, and feafted him with that Formality and Abundance, that he fufpe&ed, they intended to
fatten and to eat him. In the midft of thefe melancholy
Thoughts and Surmifes, one of them, in Return for fome
Beads and Toys, which *Smith* had given him at his firft
Arrival, brought him his Gown; which was of fingular
Service to him, and a very feafonable Defence againft the
exceffive Coldnefs of the Seafon.

BUT whilft his Mind was thus taken up with imaginary
Deaths, he had like to have met a real one. For a Man
came violently upon him, and would have flain him for
the Death of his Son, had he not been prevented by his
Guard. Whether this was one of thofe, that were wounded, when *Smith* was taken Prifoner, or whether he was
dying a natural Death, which they, through Ignorance
and Superftition, attributed to fome Sorcery in *Smith*, is
not eafy to be determined. However, they carried him
to recover the poor Man, breathing out his laft. *Smith*
told them, he had a Water at *James-Town*, that would do
it, if they would let him fetch it. But they had more Senfe
than to permit that, or to truft him out of their Hands.

THEY were now making the greateft Preparations they
could, to affault *James-Town*. To this End they defired
Smith's Advice and Affiftance; and, as a Reward, promifed
him Life, Liberty, Land, and Women. But he reprefented to them the extreme Danger and Difficulty of the Attempt; and defcribed the Springing of Mines, great Guns,
and other warlike Engines, in fuch a Manner, as exceedingly frighted and amazed them. And then he perfuaded
fome of them to go to *James-Town*, under Pretence of
fetching fome Toys; and in Part of a Table-Book, he informed them at the Fort, what was intended, and dire&ed
them, how to behave and affright the Meffengers, and without fail, to fend him fuch Things, as he wrote for. Within
three Days, the Meffengers returned, through as bitter
Weather as could be, for Froft and Snow; and were greatly aftonifhed themfelves, as well as all that heard it, how
Smith could divine, or the Paper fpeak. For all things
were delivered them, and had happened at *James-Town*, according as he foretold.   ALL

ALL Thoughts of an Attack upon *James-Town* being
therefore laid afide, they led *Smith* in Show and Triumph
about the Country. And firft they carried him to thofe,
that dwelt on *Youghtanund*, or as it is now called, *Pamun-*
key River. For the main River, which is fince named *York*
River, was then called *Pamunkey*; altho' the Country of
Pamunkey, over which *Opechancanough* was King, lay in
the Fork of the River, and his chief Seat was nearly, where
the *Pamunkey* Town now is. From the *Youghtanunds* they
led him to the *Mattaponies*, the *Piankatanks*, the *Nantaugh-*
tacunds, on *Rappahanock*, and the *Nominies*, on *Patowmack*
River. And having paffed him over all thofe Rivers, they
brought him back, through feveral other Nations, to *O-*
pechancanough's Habitation at *Pamunkey*; where, with frightful Howlings, and many ftrange and hellifh Ceremonies,
they conjured him three Days, to know, as they told him,
whether he intended them well or ill. After this, they
brought him a Bag of Gunpowder, which they judged to
be a Grain, fpringing out of the Earth, as other Grains
did; and therefore they carefully preferved it, intending to
plant it the next Spring, as they did their Corn. And then
he was invited, and feafted, in a fumptuous Manner, by
Opitchapan, fecond Brother to *Powhatan*, and next Heir to
all his Dominions. But here, as in all other Places, none
of them would touch a Morfel with him; altho' they
would feaft very merrily upon what he left. At laft they
conducted him to *Werowocomoco*, where *Powhatan*, the
Emperor, was. *Werowocomoco* lay on the *North* Side of
York River, in *Glocefter* County, nearly oppofite to the
Mouth of *Queen's* Creek, and about twenty five Miles below the Fork of the River. It was at that Time *Pow-*
hatan's principal Place of Refidence; altho' afterwards, not
admiring the near Neighbourhood of the *Englifh*, he retired
to *Orapakes*.

Powhatan himfelf was a tall, well-proportioned Man, of
a four Afpect, and of a very ftrong and hardy Conftitution
of Body. His proper Name was *Wahunfonacock*; and he
had that of *Powhatan*, from the Town fo called, near the
Falls of *James* River, which was the chief Seat and Metro-
polis of his hereditary Dominions; and he feems to have
removed to *Werowocomoco* for Conveniency, after he had
extended his Conquefts far *North*. For his hereditary
Countries were only *Powhatan*, *Arrohattock*, about twelve
Miles lower down, which hath fince been corrupted to
Haddihaddocks, *Appamatock*, *Youghtanund*, *Pamunkey*, and
Mattapony; to which may be added, *Werowocomoco*, and
Kifkiack, or as it hath fince been called, *Cheefecake*, be-

1607. tween *Williamſburg* and *York*. All the reſt were his Con-
queſts; and they were bounded on the *South* by *James* Ri-
J. Ratcliffe ver, with all its Branches, from the Mouth to the Falls,
Prefident. and ſo acroſs the Country, nearly as high as the Falls of
all the great Rivers, over *Patowmack* even to *Patuxen* in
Maryland. And ſome Nations alſo on the *Eaſtern* Shore,
owned Subjection to him. Theſe Dominions deſcended,
not to his Sons or Children, but firſt to his Brothers,
whereof he had three, *Opitchapan*, *Opechancanough*, and
Catataugh; and then to his Siſters, according to their Se-
niority; and after them to the Heirs male or female of the
eldeſt Siſter, and ſo of the reſt, but never to the Heirs of
the Males.

HE lived in great barbaric State and Magnificence.
He uſually had about his Perſon forty or fifty of the talleſt
Men, his Country afforded; which Guard was, after this
time, encreaſed to two hundred, on Account of the *Engliſh*. Every Night, upon the four Corners of his Houſe
were placed four Sentinels, each a flight Shot from the
other; and every half Hour, one from the main Guard
hollowed, ſhaking his Finger between his Lips, and every
Sentinel was obliged to anſwer from his Stand. If any failed,
an Officer was immediately ſent, who beat him extremely.
At all his ancient Inheritances, he had Houſes, ſome of
them thirty or forty Yards long; and at every Houſe, Proviſion for his Entertainment, according to the Seaſon. He
kept as many Women, as he pleaſed; and when he laid
down, one ſat at his Head, and another at his Feet; but
when he was up, one ſat on his right Hand, and another
on his left. And as he was weary of them, he beſtowed
them on ſuch of his Servants, as had moſt pleaſed him, or
beſt deſerved them at his Hands.

ALTHO' both himſelf and People were very barbarous,
and void of all Letters and Civility, yet was there ſuch a
Government among them, that the Magiſtrates for good
Command, and the People for due Subjection, excelled
many Places, that would be counted very civil. He had
under him above thirty inferior Kings or Werowances, who
had Power of Life and Death, but were bound to govern
according to the Cuſtoms of their Country. However, his
Will was, in all Caſes, their ſupreme Law, and muſt be
obeyed. They all knew their ſeveral Lands, Habitations,
and Limits to fiſh, fowl, or hunt in. But they held all of
their great Werowance, *Powhatan*; to whom they paid
Tribute of Skins, Beads, Copper, Pearl, Deer, Turkies,
wild Beaſts, and Corn. All his Subjects reverenced him,
not only as a King, but as half a God; and it was curious

to

to behold, with what Fear and Adoration they obeyed him. For at his Feet, they prefented whatever he commanded ; and a Frown of his Brow would make their greateft Spirits tremble. And indeed it was no Wonder ; for he was very terrible and tyrannous in punifhing fuch, as offended him, with Variety of Cruelty and the moft exquifite Torture.

W h e n *Smith* was prefented to him, he was about fixty Years of Age, fomething hoary, and of a favage Majefty and Grandeur. He fat before a Fire, upon a wooden Throne, like a Bedftead, clothed with a great Robe of Racoon Skins, and with a Coronet of Feathers about his Head. On either Hand, fat a young Wench, of about fixteen or eighteen Years of Age ; and along each Side of the Houfe, a Row of Men, and behind them, as many Women, painted and adorned in their beft Manner. When *Smith* entered, all the People gave a Shout ; and the Queen of *Appamatox* was appointed to bring him Water to wafh his Hands, and another brought a Bunch of Feathers, inftead of a Towel, to dry them. After that, having feafted him in their beft Manner, a long Confultation was held ; at the Conclufion of which, two great Stones were brought before *Powhatan*, and *Smith* was dragged to them, and his Head laid thereon, in order to have his Brains beat out with Clubs. But *Pocahontas*, the King's darling Daughter, when no Entreaty could prevail, got his Head into her Arms, and laid her own upon it, to fave his Life. Whereupon *Powhatan* was perfuaded to let him live, to make himfelf Hatchets, and her Bells, Beads, and Copper. For the King himfelf would make his own Robes, Shoes, Bows, Arrows, and Pots ; and would hunt, plant, and do every thing elfe, like the reft ; and therefore they thought him of all Occupations, as well as themfelves. And befides this furprifing Tendernefs and Affection of *Pocahontas*, who was at that Time about twelve or thirteen Years of Age, Captain *Smith* received many Services from *Nantaquaus*, the Emperor's Son. He was a Youth of the comelieft and moft manly Perfon, and of the higheft Spirit and Courage, of any in the Court of *Powhatan* ; and he embraced *Smith's* Intereft with much Warmth and Heartinefs, and did him many Acts of Friendfhip and Kindnefs.

T w o Days after, *Powhatan*, having difguifed himfelf in the moft frightful Manner, he could, caufed Captain *Smith* to be carried to a great Houfe in the Woods, and there to be left alone on a Mat by the Fire. Not long after, from behind a Mat, which divided the Houfe, was made the moft doleful Noife, he had ever heard ; and then *Powhatan*, with about two Hundred more, as frightful as himfelf,

felf,

felf, came to him, and told him, they were now Friends, and he fhould immediately go to *James-Town*, to fend him two great Guns and a Grindftone; for which he would give him the Country of *Capahowfick*, and ever after efteem him, as his Son *Nantaquaus*. Captain *Smith* put little Confidence in his Words, and expected every Minute, even till he got to *James-Town*, to be put to one Kind of Death or other. But *Powhatan* fent him off immediately, with twelve Guides; and having lodged that Night in the Woods, he arrived the next Morning early at the Fort.

AND thus Captain *Smith*, after feven Weeks Captivity, returned to *James-Town*, with the Advantage of being much improved in the Knowledge of the Country and their Language. He ufed his Guides with the utmoft Kindnefs; and fhewed *Rawhunt*, *Powhatan*'s trufty Servant, two Demi-Culverins and a Mill-ftone, to carry to their Mafter. Their Weight was fufficient to deter them from the Attempt; but when they faw him difcharge them, loaded with Stones, among the Boughs of a great Tree, hung with Icicles, the Terror of the Report, and the Ratling of the Boughs and Ice, fo frighted the poor Savages, that they ran away, half dead with Fear. But having regained fome Conference with them, he gave them fuch Toys for themfelves, and fent *Powhatan*, his Women, and Children, fuch Prefents, as gave a general fatisfaction.

AT *James-Town* every thing was in Confufion, and the ftrongeft were preparing once more to run away with the Bark. But *Smith*, with the Hazard of his Life, forced her the third time, to ftay or fink in the River. And the next Day, feveral combined with the Prefident, to put him to Death by the Levitical Law, for the Lives of *Robinfon* and *Emry*, whom, they faid, he had led to their End, and was confequently the Author of their Death. But he quickly took fuch Order with thofe Lawyers, that he laid them by the Heels, till he fent fome of them Prifoners to *England*. And then, by his Relation of the Plenty, he had feen among the Natives, efpecially at *Werowocomoco*, and of the State and Bounty of *Powhatan*, till then unknown, he very much appeafed their Fears, and revived their dead Spirits. And *Pocahontas*, with her Attendants, ever once in four or five Days, brought him fo much Provifion, as faved the Lives of many, who muft otherwife have perifhed with Hunger. Several others alfo of the Natives repaired daily to the Fort, with fuch Provifions, as fufficiently ferved them from Hand to Mouth. Part they always brought *Smith*, as Prefents from their Kings or *Pocahontas*; and he,

as

1607.

J. Ratcliffe Prefident.

as their Market-Clerk, fet the Price upon the reft. So much had he aftonifhed and enchanted thofe poor Souls, whilft their Prifoner, that they efteemed him, as a Demi-God, and were ready, at his Beck, to do, whatever he commanded. And the God, who created all things, they knew, he adored as his God, and would, in their Dif-courfe, call him the God of Captain *Smith*.

A N D this their high Opinion was much increafed by the Arrival of Captain *Newport*, whom *Smith*, among them, called his Father, nearly about the time, that he had fore-told. For the Treafurer and Council in *England* fent two Ships, the latter End of this Year, with a Supply of Pro-vifions, and an hundred and twenty Men. Thefe came, well furnifhed with all things, that could be imagined ne-ceffary, as Captain *Smith* tells us. But however, we muft always make fome Allowance in his Account of thefe things. For he was a very great Friend to Sir *Thomas Smith* ; and we fhall fee hereafter, from feveral authentic Papers, but efpecially from a Reprefentation of our General Affembly, among the Records in the *Capitol*, that that Officer was moft fcandaloufly negligent, if not corrupt, particularly in this Matter of Supplies. One of thefe Ships was com-manded by Captain *Newport*, the other by Captain *Francis Nelfon*, an honeft Man and expert Mariner. But fuch was the Lewardnefs of his Ship, that altho' he was within Sight of Cape *Henry*, yet by contrary Winds and ftormy Weather, he was driven off the Coaft, and forced to the *Weft-Indies*, to repair his Mafts, and to get a Recruit of Wood and Water. But before this, the Prefident and Council fo much envied *Smith*'s Efteem among the Natives, altho' they all equally participated of the good Effects of it, that to raife their Credit and Authority above his, they would give them four times as much for their Commodities, as he had appointed. And now, out of Joy for the Ar-rival of this firft Supply, and to gratify the Mariners, they gave them free Liberty to trade, as they pleafed. So that in a fhort time, what was before bought for an Ounce of Copper, could not be had for a Pound. To which Captain *Newport*'s profufe Prefents to *Powhatan* were added, and gave the finifhing Blow to their Trade. They ferved in-deed to entertain and keep up the high Idea of *Newport*'s Greatnefs, which *Smith* had raifed in *Powhatan*, and made him very defirous to fee him.

A C C O R D I N G L Y the Bark was prepared, and a great Coil there was at *James-Town* to fet him off. Captain *Smith* and Mr. *Matthew Scrivener*, a difcreet and under-ftanding Gentleman, newly arrived and admitted of the

10

Council,

Council, attended him with a Guard of thirty or forty
chofen Men. When they came to *Werowocomoco, New-*
port began to entertain many Fears and Sufpicions of Treachery. But *Smith*, with twenty Men, undertook to encounter the worft, that could happen; and going afhore,
was kindly conducted by two or three hundred *Indians* to
the Town. *Powhatan* ftrained himfelf, upon this Occafion, to the utmoft of his Greatnefs to entertain them, with
great Shouts of Joy, Orations, and Proteftations, and with
the moft fumptuous and plentiful Banquet, he could provide. He fat on a Bed of Mats, with a Pillow of Leather
embroidered with Pearl and white Beads; and was cloathed
in a Robe of Skins, as large as an *Irifh* Mantle. At his
Head and Feet, fat a handfome young Woman; and on
each Side the Houfe, twenty of his Concubines, with their
Heads and Shoulders painted red, and a great Chain of white
Beads about each of their Necks. Before them, fat his
chief Men, in the like Order; and above forty Platters of
fine Bread ftood in two Files, on each Side of the Door.
Four or five hundred People attended, as a Guard; and
Proclamation was made, that none, upon Pain of Death,
fhould prefume to do the *Englifh* any Wrong or Difcour-
tefy. And thus did *Smith* and he fpend the Day, in a kind
Renewal of their former Acquaintance, and in feafting,
and feeing them dance and fing, and play their other Feats
of Humour and Activity. And that Night, the *Englifh*
were quartered and lodged by *Powhatan*.

THE next Morning, *Newport* came afhore, and they
fpent three or four Days more in feafting, and dancing, and
trading. In all which time, *Powhatan* behaved himfelf with
fuch Loftinefs and State, and yet with fo much Difcretion,
that they could not forbear admiring his natural Parts and
Underftanding. Scorning to trade, as his Subjects did, he
told *Newport*, that he efteemed him a great *Werowance*,
as well as himfelf; that it was not agreeable to their Dignity to trade, in that pedling Manner, for Trifles; and
that therefore, if he would lay down all his Commodities
together, he would chufe, what he liked, and give him
their Value. *Smith*, who was their Interpreter, and knew
Powhatan's Difpofition, told the Company, his Intent was
only to cheat them. But *Newport*, thinking to out-brave
this ftately Barbarian in Oftentation and Greatnefs, and by
his Bounty to obtain from him, whatever he pleafed, accepted the Condition. And then *Powhatan*, having taken
what he liked, valued his Corn at fuch a Rate, that they
had not four Bufhels, for what they expected twenty Hogfheads. This bred fome Diftafte between the two *Englifh*
Captains;

Captains. But *Smith*, fmothering his Diflike before the   1607.
Savages, glanced feveral Trifles in the Eyes of *Powhatan*,
who foon fixed his Fancy on fome blue Beads. He was a *J. Ratcliffe*
long time importunate to have them; but *Smith* valued *Prefident.*
them fo much the higher, and told him, they were com-
pofed of a rare Subftance of the Colour of the Skies, and
were not to be worn by any, but the greateft Kings in the
World. This made him the more eager and mad for them;
fo that, for a Pound or two of blue Beads, he drew from
him two or three hundred Bufhels of Corn, and yet parted
in good Friendfhip. Upon this Voyage *Newport* gave
Powhatan a Boy, named *Thomas Savage*, whom he called
his Son; and *Powhatan* gave him *Namontack*, a Servant of
his, of a fhrewd and fubtle Capacity.

FROM *Werowocomoco* they went to *Pamunkey*, where
they were feafted in like Manner by *Opechancanough*.
Smith fitted him alfo, at the fame Rates, with blue Beads;
which, by this Means, grew into fuch Eftimation, that none
durft wear them, but their great Kings, or their Wives and
Children. At length weighing from thence, they returned
to *James-Town*; where this new Supply of Corn being
lodged with the reft, their Store-houfe was by fome Accident fired, and fo the Town, which, being thatched with
Reeds, burnt with that Fiercenefs and Violence, as foon
confumed their wooden Fortifications, with their Arms,
Apparel, and Bedding, and much private Goods and Provifion. The good Mr. *Hunt* loft all his Library, with every
thing elfe, that he had, except the Cloaths on his Back;
yet no one ever heard him murmur or repine at it.

NOTWITHSTANDING this unfortunate Accident,   1608.
they had yet a tolerable Stock of Oatmeal, Meal, and Corn,
had not the Ship loitered fourteen Weeks in the Country,
when fhe might as well have been gone in fourteen Days.
For they thereby helped to confume a great Part of the
Colony's Store, and near all the Provifions, fent to be landed. When they departed, they left them, what little they
thought proper to fpare; which they were glad to receive,
and make up an Account, highly commending their Care
and Providence, left they fhould difcourage the Council at
home from fending any more. Yet thofe Perfons, who
had either Money, fpare Cloaths, Credit for Bills of Ex-
change, Gold Rings, Furs, or any fuch valuable Commodities, were always welcome to this floating Tavern. Such
was their Neceffity and Misfortune, to be under the Lafh
of thofe vile Commanders, and to buy their own Provifions
at fifteen times the Value; fuffering them to feaft at their
Charge, whilft themfelves were obliged to faft, and yet

1608.   dare not repine, left they fhould incur the Cenfure of being
factious and feditious Perfons.   By thefe Means and Ma-
J. Ratcliffe   nagement, the Colony was rather burthened than relieved,
Prefident.   by the vaft Charge of this Ship; and being reduced to Meal
and Water, and expofed, by the Lofs of their Town, to
the moft bitter Cold and Froft, above half of them died.
Smith indeed and *Scrivener* endeavoured to correct all A-
bufes, and to put things into a better Pofture; but they
could do nothing to Effect, being overpowered by the Prefident and his Party, who had long before this laid afide
their Deference to *Smith*'s Judgment and Management.

ABOUT this time alfo, there fprung up a very troublefome Sect of Gold-finders, which was headed by Captain
Martin, and warmly embraced by *Newport*.   There was
no Thought, no Difcourfe, no Hope, and no Work, but
to dig Gold, wafh Gold, refine Gold, and load Gold.   And
notwithftanding Captain *Smith*'s warm and judicious Reprefentations, how abfurd it was, to neglect other things of
immediate Ufe and Neceffity, to load fuch a drunken Ship
with guilded Duft; yet was he over-ruled, and her Returns made in a Parcel of glittering Dirt, which is found
in various Parts of the Country, and which they very
fanguinely concluded to be Gold-Duft.   And in her they
fent home Mr. *Wingfield* and Captain *Archer*, to feek fome
better Place of Employment in *England*.   For they had
affumed many empty Titles of Offices here, as Admirals,
Recorders, Chronologers, Juftices of the Peace and of the
Courts of Plea, with other fuch idle and infignificant Pretenfions.

AND now *Martin* and the Prefident, carrying all things,
as they pleafed, by their Faction, lived in great Splendor
by the Sale of the Store's Commodities, as if they had been
their proper and hereditary Revenue.   And the Spring ap-
proaching, Captain *Smith* and Mr. *Scrivener* prepared Fields
for Corn, and applied themfelves to rebuild *James-Town*,
and repair the Church, Store-houfe, and Fortifications.
But whilft they were all bufily engaged at their feveral Labours, Captain *Nelfon*, who had been driven off the Coaft,
as was before faid, and as they all thought, loft, unexpectedly arrived, to their great Joy.   He had been very
careful and provident, and had fed his Company on what
he got at the *Weft-India* Iflands; fo that the Provifions
he now landed, joined to their former Store, were fufficient
to fupport them half a Year, according to their prefent
Allowance.   He himfelf alfo freely imparted, whatever he
had; and by his fair and generous Behaviour, he got the
Good-word and Love of the whole Colony.   And the Prefident,

1608.

J. Ratcliffe
Prefident.

fident, to fend fome good News by this Ship, ordered
Captain *Smith*, with fixty able Men, to difcover the Country of the ·*Monacan*, or as they were afterwards called, the
Manakin Indians; a Nation above the Falls of *James*-
River, not fubject to *Powhatan*, but profeft Enemies to
him and his Dominions.   For that ftrange Blood-thirftinefs,
and, as it were, judicial Infatuation, of warring againft
and exterminating each other, which at prefent infefts our
Indians, and has been the Caufe of the utter Extirpation of
moft of the Nations on this Continent, was even then rooted in their Nature, and may be obferved in the oldeft Accounts, that we have of them.   However as it was the
Time of planting Corn, and this Ship was to be difpatched,
Captain *Smith* thought thofe and other things more urgent
at that time, and therefore deferred the Difcovery, till he
could perform it with lefs Charge and more Leifure.

WHEN *Newport* left the Country, *Powhatan* prefented
him with twenty Turkies, and in return demanded twenty
Swords, which were immediately fent him.   Afterwards
he prefented Captain *Smith* with the like Number; but
having no Swords in Return, he was highly offended, and
ordered his People to take them by Stratagem or Force.
So that they became infufferably troublefome and infolent,
would furprife the *Englifh* at their Work, and feife their
Swords at the very Ports of *James-Town*.   The Prefident
and *Martin*, who now bore the Sway, would keep their
Houfes, or do any thing, rather than tranfgrefs a ftrict Command from *England*, not to offend them.   But at length
they happened to meddle with Captain *Smith*, who gave
them a rough Encounter, hunted them up and down the
Ifland, and feifed feven, whom he whipped and imprifoned.   By this and other fmart Proceedings, he brought them
to Submiffion; and they unanimoufly confeffed, that they
acted by *Powhatan*'s Direction, in order to get Swords from
the *Englifh*, to cut their own Throats; and they likewife
difcovered, how, where, and when, this Defign was to be
put in Execution; all which was confirmed by many con-
current Circumftances.   But *Powhatan*, finding, that things
went not according to his Defire and Intent, fent *Pocahontas* with Prefents, to excufe himfelf for the Injuries done by
fome of his ungovernable Captains; and he defired their
Liberty for this time, with Affurances of his Love and
Friendfhip for ever.   And *Smith* having given them a proper Correction, delivered them to *Pocahontas*; for whofe
Sake alone he pretended to fave their Lives, and give them
their Liberty.   Thus, without the Death of one Man, he
reftrained their Infolence, and brought them into fuch perfect

feĉt Fear and Obedience, that his very Name was fufficient to fright them; whereas before they had fometimes Peace and War twice in a Day, and feldom a Week paffed without fome Treachery or Ambufcade. But the peaceable Council were highly offended at thefe Proceedings, and expoftulated warmly with him for his Rafhnefs and Cruelty.

THERE had been a Difpute between *Martin* and *Smith*, whether this Ship fhould be laded with Cedar or Dirt. But her Freight being concluded to be Cedar, fhe was, by the Diligence of her Captain and *Smith*, quickly difpatched. In her Captain *Martin*, being always fickly and unferviceable, and having his Head full of the idle Whimfy of a Gold Mine, was moft willingly admitted to return to *England*. In thefe two Ships, befides Mr. *Scrivener*, came *Walter Ruffel*, Doĉtor of Phyfick, *Richard Fetherftone*, and fome others of Note. And whilft *Nelfon* and *Smith* were engaged in loading the Ship, Mr. *Scrivener* was neither idle nor flow in carrying on the Works of *James-Town*. But the Prefident's Prodigality and State went fo deep, and was fo fenfibly felt in their fmall Store, that he and *Smith* were obliged to bind him and his Parafites to the Rules of Proportion.

ON the fecond of *June* Captain *Nelfon* fell down the River, and was accompanied to the Capes by *Smith*, who, in an open Boat of about three Tons Burthen, together with Dr. *Ruffel* and thirteen more, was going to difcover *Chefapeake* Bay. Parting with the Ship at *Cape Henry*, they ftood over to thofe Iflands, which were then called, after him their firft Difcoverer, *Smith*'s *Iflands*. The firft People, they faw, were two grim and ftout *Indians* on *Cape Charles*, with long Poles, like Javelins, headed with Bone. They fternly demanded, what they were, and what they wanted; but grew afterwards more kind, and direĉted them to *Accomack*, the Habitation of their *Werowance*. This King treated them very kindly, and was the comlieft, moft proper, and civil *Indian*, they had met with. They fpoke the Language of *Powhatan*, and at that time lay under the Misfortune of a ftrange Mortality, which they attributed to a Miracle. Paffing on from thence, they coafted it along, and fearched every Inlet and Bay, that feemed proper for Harbours or Habitations; and many Harbours they found for fmall Veffels, but none fit to receive large Ships. Then fpying many Iflands out in the Bay, they bore up for them; but before they could reach them, there rofe fuch a Guft of Thunder, Lightning, Wind, and Rain, that with great Difficulty they efcaped being foundered. Thefe Iflands they named *Ruffel's Iflands*,

after

after Dr. *Ruſſel*; and they are the ſame with thoſe, now
called *Tanger Iſlands*.   Being in Want of Water, and finding none in theſe Iſlands, they were obliged to follow the *J. Ratcliffe*
next Eaſtern Channel, which brought them into the River *Preſident.*
Wighcocomoco, which is the River now called *Pokomoke*.
The Northern Point, at the Mouth, they called *Watkins*'s
Point, and a Hill, on the South of *Pokomoke* Bay, *Keel*'s
Hill, after two of the Company.   Running up the River,
the Natives at firſt threatened, with great Fury, to aſſault
them; but at laſt became very tractable and kind.   They
dug in ſeveral Places, and ſearched their Habitations, yet
could get but little Water, and that mere Puddle.   Yet
ſuch was their Diſtreſs two Days after, that they would
have refuſed a Quart full of Gold for a Pint of that Puddle.

DEPARTING from thence, they found on a high Point
of Land, which they called *Point Ployer*, a Pond of freſh
Water, but ſo exceedingly hot, that they ſuppoſed it to be
ſome Bath.   Then ſtanding over to ſome other Iſlands,
there aroſe ſuch another Thunder-Guſt, that their Maſt
and Sail was blown overboard, and ſuch mighty Waves
over-racked their Boat, that they could ſcarce, with much
Labour in bailing out the Water, keep her from ſinking.
Two Days they ſtaid among theſe Iſlands, and becauſe of
the Guſts and Storms, that then happened, they called the
Place *Limbo*; but they are the ſame, which have ſince been
named *Wats*'s *Iſlands*.   Having repaired the Loſs of their
Sail with their Shirts, they ſtood over again to the Eaſtern
Shore, and fell in with a pretty convenient River, then
called *Cuſcarawock*.   This is, what is laid down in our pre-
ſent Charts by the Name of *Wighcocomoco*, by whatever
Accident that Name hath ſhifted, in Proceſs of Time, from
Pokomoke River to this.   Here the Natives oppoſed them
very furiouſly; but leaving ſome Toys in their Huts, they
brought ſome of them over at laſt, to be very fond and
obliging.   On this River lived the Nations of *Sarapinagh*,
Nauſe, *Arſeck*, and *Nantaquack*, who were the beſt Merchants, and greateſt Traders of all the *Indians* of this
Country.   They had the fineſt Furs, and made large   †
Quantities of the beſt *Roanoke*; which was a Sort of white
Bead, that occaſioned as much Diſſenſion among thoſe
Barbarians, as Gold and Silver among Chriſtians.   They
told the *Engliſh* of, and highly extolled, a great Nation,
called the *Maſſawomecks*; in Search of whom they returned again, by *Limbo*, into the Bay.   And finding the Coaſt
of the Eaſtern Shore, nothing but ſhallow, broken Iſles,
and for the moſt Part without freſh Water, they ſtood away
from

1608.

J. Ratcliffe
Prefident.

from thence acrofs the Bay, bearing a little upwards, and fell in on the Weftern Side, above the Mouth of *Patuxen* River, againft fome high Clifts, which they called *Riccard*'s *Clifts*.   From hence they failed thirty Leagues farther Northward, without finding any Inhabitants.   The Coaft was all along well watered, but very mountainous and barren, except the Vallies, which were rich and fertile, but extremely thick wooded, and therefore abounded in Wolves, Bears, Deer, and other wild Beafts.   They paffed by many Coves and fmall Streams.   The firft they found navigable for a Ship, they called *Bolus River*, becaufe the Clay, in many Places under the Clifts, grew up in red and white Knobs, like Gum out of Trees, and they concluded it to be *Bole Armeniac* and *Terra Sigillata*.   This River, by it's Situation and Bearings, muft be the fame with *Patapfco* in *Maryland*.

And now Captain *Smith*'s Crew, who at firft feared nothing fo much as his too hafty Return, began to be very much foiled and fatigued.   They had laid twelve or fourteen Days in that open Boat, were often tired at the Oars, and their Bread was fpoiled and rotten with the Rain; fo that they were very importunate with him to return.   But he reminded them of the memorable Refolution of Sir *Ralph Lane*'s Company, in the Difcovery of the River *Moratuc*, who infifted on his going forward, as long as they had a Dog left, which, being boiled with Saffafras Leaves, would afford them a rich Repaft in their Return.   And he told them, what a Shame it would be, to oblige him to return, with fo much Provifion, as they then had, when they could fcarce fay, where they had been, or give any Account of what they were fent to difcover: That they could not deny, but he had fhared with them, in the worft of what was paft; and he was willing, to take to himfelf the worft Part of what was to come: That it was not likely, any thing worfe fhould befal them, than what had already happened; and that to return was as dangerous, as to proceed.   He therefore advifed them, to refume their loft Courage; for he was determined not to defift, till he had feen the *Maffawomecks*, found *Patowmack*, or traced the Head of the Bay.   But after this, they were detained by the Wind and Weather three Days; which added fuch a Difcouragement, that three or four fell fick, whofe Diffatiffaction and piteous Complaints at laft prevailed with him to return.

On the 16th of *June*, they fell in with the Mouth of *Patowmack*.   Their Fears being now gone, and Men recovered, they all agreed to take fome Pains in the Difcovery

of

of that feven-mile broad River.   For altho' *Smith* had been
carried over it in his Captivity, yet he knew it not again by
the Mouth.   For thirty Miles they found no Inhabitants ;
but afterwards were conducted, by two Savages, up a little
bayed Creek, towards *Nominy*, where they difcovered the
Woods laid with Ambufcades, to the Number of three or
four Thoufand *Indians*, ftrangely grimmed and difguifed,
and making a horrible fhouting and yelling.   They made
many Bravadoes, and *Smith* prepared, with as great feeming Willingnefs, to encounter them.   But commanding
fome Mufkets to be difcharged on Purpofe, the grazing of
the Bullets on the Water, together with the Report and
Eccho of the Woods, fo frighted and amazed them, that
they threw down their Arms, and became very kind and
hearty Friends.   They owned, they were commanded to
betray that Party of *Englifh*, by the Direction of *Powhatan*, who was defired fo to do, by fome difcontented
Perfons at *James-Town*, becaufe Captain *Smith* obliged them
to ftay in the Country againft their Will.   They afterwards
went up the River, as high as they could with their Boat ;
and were received in fome Places kindly, and in others in a
hoftile Manner.   Up a fmall River, then called *Quiyough*,
which I take to be *Patowmack* Creek, was a Mine like
Antimony.   In this the *Indians* dug, and wafhing away the
Drofs in a clear Brook, which ran by, they put up the Remainder in little Bags, and fold it all over the Country, to
deck their Bodies, Faces, and Idols ; which made them
look like Blackamores, dufted over with Silver.   *Newport*
had carried fome of thefe Bags home, and affured them,
that they were found, upon Trial, to contain half Silver.
Being therefore very eager after this Mine, they obtained
Guides from *Japazaws*, King of *Patowmack*, who lived at
the Mouth of that little River, and went up to it ; but all,
they got, proved of no Value.   Towards the Falls of *Patowmack*, they met feveral Parties of *Indians* in Canoes,
loaded with the Flefh of Bears, Deer, and other wild
Beafts, which they generoufly imparted to them ; and in
divers Places, they faw that Abundance of Fifh, lying with
their Heads above Water, that their Barge driving among
them, for Want of a Net, they attempted to catch them
with a frying Pan.   But they found that a bad Inftrument
to catch Fifh.

FROM *Patowmack* they fet Sail for *Rappahanock*, or as
it was by many called, *Toppahanock* River ; where the Captain intended to vifit his Captivity-Acquaintance.   But their
Boat, by Reafon of the Lownefs of the Tide, ran aground
on fome Shoals, at the Mouth of that River, where they

16c8.

J. Ratcliffe
Prefident.

1608.
J. *Ratcliffe*
Prefident.

fpied many Fifh, lurking in the Sedge. The Captain diverted himfelf by nailing them to the Ground with his Sword; and the reft betaking themfelves to the fame Sport, they took more Fifh in an Hour, than they could eat in a day. But Captain *Smith*, taking from his Sword a Fifh, like a Thornback, with a long Tail, in the Midft of which was a poifoned Sting, of two or three Inches Length, bearded like a Saw on each Side, fhe ftruck her Sting into his Wrift an Inch and a half. No Blood or Wound was feen, but only a little blue Spot; yet fuch was the Extremity of Pain, and his Hand, Arm, and Shoulder, were fo fwoln in four Hours Time, that they all, with much Sorrow, expected his Death, and prepared his Grave in an Ifland by, as he himfelf directed. But it pleafed God, by the Application of an Oil, which Dr. *Ruffel* had with him, his Torment was fo eafed and affwaged before Night, that to the great Joy of the Company, he eat of the Fifh for his Supper. And in Memory of this Accident, they called the Ifle *Stingray Ifland*, after the Name of the Fifh.

THEIR Provifions being near fpent, and being alfo deterred by this Misfortune, they fet Sail immediately for *James-Town*; and paffing by the Mouths of *Piankatank* and *Pamunkey* Rivers, they arrived the next Day at *Kicquotan*. From thence they proceeded up to *Warrafqueake*; where trimming their Barge with painted Streamers, and other fuch Devices, they were taken for a *Spanifh* Frigot at *James-Town*, where they arrived the 21ft of *July*. There they found the laft Supply of Men all fick; and of the reft, fome lame, fome bruifed, and all in a Tumult and Uproar againft the unreafonable Pride and Cruelty of the Prefident, whom they would as ftrangely have tormented with Revenge, had it not been for this feafonable Arrival of the Difcovery Barge. He had riotoufly confumed the Store, and had greatly harraffed and fatigued the People, in building an unneceffary Houfe of Pleafure for himfelf in the Woods. But their Fury was much appeafed, by the good News of this Difcovery, and by the Hopes, from fome miftaken Interpretation of the Savage's Account, that our Bay reached to the *South-Sea*, or fomewhere near it; but above all, by the depofing *Ratcliffe*, and Captain *Smith*'s taking the Government upon himfelf.

John Smith
Prefident.
Mat. Scrivener Vice-Prefident.

Smith fubftituted his good Friend Mr. *Scrivener*, who then lay exceeding ill of a Calenture, in the Prefidency; and having fettled all things to his own, and the People's Satisfaction, he ftaid but three Days at *James-Town*. For the 24th of *July*, he fet forward, with twelve Men, to finifh the Difcovery of the Bay. They were detained two

or

or three Days at *Kicquotan*, by contrary Winds, where
they were kindly entertained and feafted by the King, and
in Diverfion fired feveral Rockets, which greatly terrified
and aftonifhed the poor Savages. From thence they anchored, the firft Night, at *Stingray* Ifland; and the next
Day, crofling the Mouth of *Patowmack*, they hafted to
the River *Bolus.* A little beyond that, they found the Bay
divided into four Streams, all which they fearched, as far
as they could fail. Two of them they found inhabited, the
Rivers *Sufquefahanock,* and *Tockwogh,* fince called *Saffafras*
River. In crofling the Bay, they met feven or eight Canoes, full of *Maffawomecks,* a great and powerful Nation
of *Indians* inhabiting upon fome of the Lakes of *Canada,*
and the Original perhaps of thofe, at prefent known by the
Name of the *Senecas* or *Six Nations.* They were at that
Time profeft Enemies, and a great Terror, to the Nations
dwelling on the upper Part of our Bay, and had then been
at War with the *Tockwoghs.* After mutual Threats of Affault between them and the *Englifh,* they were at laft induced to go on board the Barge; and by interchangeable
Prefents becoming good Friends, they departed without
farther Intercourfe or Converfation.

THE next Day, entering the River *Tockwogh,* they were
invironed with a Fleet of Canoes, full of armed Men. But
coming to a Parley, and the *Tockwoghs* feeing the *Maffawomeck* Arms, which they had prefented to the *Englifh* the
Day before, and which the *Englifh* made them believe,
they had taken in War, they were foon reconciled, and
conducted them to their Town. It was pallifadoed round,
mantled with the Barks of Trees, had Scaffolds, like
Mounts, and was breafted very formally. The Men, Women, and Children did their utmoft to exprefs their Affection; and welcomed them with Songs, Dances, Fruits,
and Furs, and with whatever elfe they had. Here they
faw many Hatchets, Knives, and Pieces of Iron and Brafs,
which, they told them, they had from the *Sufquefahanocks,*
a mighty Nation, dwelling on the chief of the four Branches at the Head of the Bay, two Days Journey above the
Falls of that River. They prevailed with two *Tockwoghs*
to go and invite fome of the *Sufquefahanocks* to them. In
three or four Days, fixty of thofe gigantic People came
down, with Prefents of various Kinds; and the Wind being
two high for their Canoes, five of their chief Werowances
came boldly on board the *Englifh* Barge, and croffed the
Bay to *Tockwogh.*

THIS Nation of the *Sufquefahanocks* could mufter a-
bout fix Hundred fighting Men, and lived in pallifadoed

F 2   Towns,

Towns, to defend themfelves againft the *Maffawomecks,*
their mortal Enemies. They were very large, well-proportioned Men, and appeared like Giants to the *Englifh*
and other *Indians*; yet feemed of an honeft and fimple Difpofition, and were fcarcely reftrained from adoring the *En-*
glifh, as Gods. And their Language and Attire were very
fuitable to their Stature and Appearance. For their Language founded deep, and folemn, and hollow, like a Voice
in a Vault. Their Attire was the Skins of Bears and
Wolves, fo cut, that the Man's Head went through the
Neck, and the Ears of the Bear were faftened on his Shoulders, while the Nofe and Teeth hung dangling down upon
his Breaft. Behind was another Bear's Face fplit, with a
Paw hanging at the Nofe. And their Sleeves, coming down
to their Elbows, were the Necks of Bears, with their Arms
going through the Mouth, and Paws hanging to the Nofes.
One had the Head of a Wolf, hanging to a Chain, for a
Jewel; and his Tobacco Pipe was three Quarters of a Yard
long, carved with a Bird, a Deer, and other Devices at
the great End; which was fufficient to beat out a Man's
Brains. They meafured the Calf of the largeft Man's Leg,
and found it three Quarters of a Yard about, and all the
reft of his Limbs were in Proportion; fo that he feemed
the ftatlieft and moft goodly Perfonage, they had ever be-
held. His Arrows were five Quarters long, headed with
the Splinters of a white chryftal-like Stone, in Form of a
Heart, an Inch broad, and an Inch and half, or more, long.
Thefe he carried at his Back, in a Wolf's Skin for his Quiver, with his Bow in one Hand, and his Club in the other.

T H E Manner of the *Englifh* was daily to have Prayers
with a Pfalm; at which Solemnity thofe poor Barbarians
wonder   greatly. Prayers being done, the *Sufquefahanocks*
held   ultation; and then began in a very paffionate
M   to hold up their Hands to the Sun, with a moft
             Song. Then embracing Captain *Smith,* they be-
          to adore him in like Manner. He rebuked them for
      ; but they perfifted, till their Song was finifhed. After
which, with a ftrange furious Action, and a difmal Voice,
they began an Oration of their Love; which ended, they
covered him with a large painted Bear's Skin. One ftood
ready with a great Chain of white Beads, weighing fix or
feven Pounds, which he hung about his Neck. The others
had eighteen Mantles, made of divers Sorts of Skins fewed
together; all which, with many other Baubles, they laid at
his Feet, ftroaking their Hands about his Neck, for his Creation to be their Governor and Protector. They promifed
him Aids of Men and Victuals, and even offered all, that
they

they had, if he would ſtay with them, to defend and revenge them on the *Maſſawomecks.* But he was obliged to
leave them at *Tockwogh,* very ſorrowful for his Departure ;
yet promiſed to viſit them again the next Year. They
knew nothing of *Powhatan* and his Territories, but the
Name ; and they informed the *Engliſh,* that their Hatchets
and other Commodities came originally from the *French* of
Canada.

HAVING ſearched all the Rivers and Inlets, worth
Note, they paſſed down the Bay, naming all the remarkable Head-lands and Places after ſome of the Company or
their Friends. On the River *Patuxen* they found the People tractable and civil above all others. They, as well as
the *Patowmacks,* were very urgent with *Smith* to revenge
them on the *Maſſawomecks,* which he promiſed to do, but
was afterwards croſſed in his Purpoſe. For depending upon
the Aſſiſtance and Proviſions of thoſe two Nations, and of
the *Suſquefahanocks,* he was very willing to hazard his Perſon in the Expedition ; and therefore, after his Return, he
petitioned the Council for forty Men, to effect ſuch a Con-
queſt and Diſcovery. But the Council, envying his Induſtry and Succeſs, and deterred perhaps alſo by the Difficulty of the Undertaking, refuſed to riſque the Lives of ſo
many Men, in ſo long and ſo dangerous an Enterpriſe.

IN the Diſcovery of *Rappahanock* River, they were
kindly received and entertained by the People of *Moraughtacund.* Here they met with an old Friend and Acquaintance, one *Moſco,* a luſty *Indian* of *Wighcocomoco* on the
River *Patowmack.* They ſuppoſed him ſome *Frenchman's*
Son, becauſe, he had a thick, black, buſhy Beard, and the
Indians ſeldom have any at all. And he was not a little
proud of this, and to ſee ſo many of his Countrymen. He
was very officious and uſeful to the *Engliſh* ; and adviſed
them, by all Means not to paſs over to the *Rappahanocks,*
who would certainly kill them for being Friends with the
Moraughtacunds, who had lately ſtolen three of their
King's Women. But thinking, he only ſaid this to ſecure
their Trade to his Friends, they croſſed the River to the
Rappahanocks. There, under pretence of Trade, they were
invited up *Rappahanock* Creek, where they had laid an Am-
buſh ; and after a ſmart Skirmiſh, in which many *Indians*
were ſlain and wounded, the *Engliſh* came off Victors without the leaſt Hurt. Having driven them up into the Woods,
they ſeized three or four Canoes, full of Commodities,
which, with ſome Arrows, they had gathered up, they
preſented to *Moſco* for his Kindneſs. And he, on his Part,
received them in the moſt triumphant Manner, and in the

F 3   beſt

beft martial Order under Arms, that he could procure of
the *Moraughtacunds*.

T H E Y fpent the reft of the Day in fitting up their
Boat with a Breaft-work of *Maffawomeck* Targets, which
they had received from them, as Prefents, at the Head of
the Bay, and which had been of fingular Ufe in the Battle
with the *Rappahanocks*.   They were made of fmall Twigs,
woven together fo firmly with ftrings of wild Hemp and
Silk-grafs, that no Arrow could poffibly pierce them.   The
next Morning, they fet Sail up the River; and *Mofco* followed along the Shore, and at laft defired to go with them
in the Boat.   As they paffed by *Pifacack*, *Matchopeake*, and
Mecuppom, three Towns, fituate on the North Side of the
River, on high, white, clay Clifts, with a low Marfh over
againft them, and the River but narrow (the Place, where
the *Briftol* Works now are) thirty or forty *Rappahanocks*
had fo difguifed themfelves with Branches, that they took
them for little Bufhes, growing in the Sedge.   They faw
their Arrows often ftrike againft the Targets, and drop
into the River; and at laft *Mofco*, falling flat on his Face
in the Boat, cried out; *The Rappahanocks*.   They foon perceived them to be the Bufhes in the Sedge, which at the
firft Volley fell down.   And when they had paffed about
half a Mile further, they again fhewed themfelves, finging
and dancing very merrily.   But they were kindly treated
by the reft of the Nations to the Falls, and they even ufed
their utmoft Intereft with *Mofco*, to bring the *Englifh* to
them.   Between *Secobeck*, on the South, and *Maffawteck*,
on the North Side of the River, there was a fmall Ifland or
two, which made the River broader, than ordinary.   Here
Mr. *Richard Fetherftone*, one of their Company died; who,
from his firft coming to the Country, had behaved himfelf honeftly, valiantly, and induftrioufly.   They buried him in a little
Bay, which they then called *Fetherftone's Bay*, with a Volley
of their Arms.   But the reft of the laft Supply, who had, on
the Expedition, been miferably fick and harraffed with their
Seafoning, had by this time perfectly recovered their Health.

     T H E next Day, they failed up as high, as their Boat
could go, fetting up Croffes, and carving their Names on
the Trees; which they conftantly did at all the higheft
Places, they went to.   As they ranged about at the Falls,
the Sentinel faw an Arrow fall by him; and giving the A-
larm, they perceived about an hundred nimble *Indians*,
fkipping from Tree to Tree, and letting fly their Arrows as
faft, as they could.   But after half an Hour's Skirmifh, they
all vanifhed as fuddenly, as they came.   As the *Englifh* returned from the Purfuit, they found an *Indian*, lying as
dead,

dead, fhot in the Knee. *Mofco*, who had been of great
Service in the Battle, was as furious to beat out his
Brains, as ever Dog was againft a Bear. But protecting
him from his Rage, and carrying him to the Surgeon, who
attended to cure the Captain's Hurt of the Stingray, he
was within an Hour fo far recovered, that he both eat and
fpoke. He was Brother to the King of *Haffininga*, one
of the four Nations of the *Mannahocks*. Thefe were a People, dwelling above the Falls of *Rappahanock*, Neighbours to,
and in ftrict Friendfhip and Alliance with the *Manakins* a-
gainft *Powhatan* and his Territories. For the *Manakins*
were not confined to one Place or Town, as is vulgarly
thought, but fpread all that Country, from a fmall Diftance
above the Falls of *James* River up to the Mountains, in feveral Towns; and they were the Heads or Chiefs of the
League and Confederacy of the upland and mountain *Indians*
againft the Power and Tyranny of *Powhatan*. Thefe
Mannahocks, their Neighbours and Allies, lived on fmall
Streams, in a hilly Country, chiefly by hunting; and were
then come down to fifh at *Mohafkahod*, a fmall hunting
Town, on the North Side of the Falls of *Rappahanock*, and
the Boundary between them and the *Nantaughtacunds*, a
large Nation on the navigable River, below the Falls. The
Englifh afked their Prifoner; Why they had endeavoured
to deftroy them, who came to them in Peace, to feek their
Friendfhip. He anfwered, that they heard, the *Englifh*
were a People, come from under the World, to take their
World from them. Being afked; how many Worlds, he
knew, he faid, he knew none but that, which was under
the Sky, that covered him, and which confifted of the
Powhatans, the *Manakins*, and the *Maffawomecks*. And
he told them, that the laft dwelt on a great Water, had
many Boats, and fo many Men, that they warred on all
the World befides. After many other Queftions concerning the Country, efpecially beyond the great Mountains, to
which he could give no fatisfactory Anfwers, they prefented
him with fome Toys, and perfuaded him to go along with
them. But he preffed them much to ftay the coming of
the *Mannahock* Kings, who, for their good Ufage to him,
fhould be their Friends. And notwithftanding *Mofco*'s eager
Reprefentations to be gone, they refolved to ftay till Night,
preparing themfelves to entertain, whatever fhould come.

ALL this while the King of *Haffininga* was feeking the
reft, and held a long Confultation, what to do. When the
Englifh had weighed, and were gone, they followed them
all Night, yelling, and hollowing, and fhooting their Arrows,
and would come to no Terms or Difcourfe. But in the

1608.

*Matt. Scri-
vener* Vice-
Prefident.

1608.

Matt. Scri-
vener Vice-
Prefident.

Morning, being brought to a Parley, *Amoroleck*, the Prifoner, held a long Difcourfe with them. He told them, how
good the *Englifh* were, and how kindly they had ufed him ;
that they had a *Patowmack* with them, that loved them as
his Life, and would have flain him, had they not prevented
it ; and that he might have his Liberty, if they would be
Friends ; to which he advifed them by all means, fince to
do them any Hurt was impoffible. Upon this they all hung
their Bows and Quivers upon the Trees ; and one came
fwimming aboard with a Bow tied on his Head, and another with a Quiver of Arrows. Having prefented them to
the Captain, he ufed them very kindly, and told them, that
the other three Kings fhould do the fame, and then the
great King of his World fhould be their Friend. This was
no fooner demanded, than performed ; and fo going afhore
on a low morafs Point of Land, thofe four Kings came,
and received *Amoroleck*. And after many mutual Civilities
and Prefents, the *Englifh* departed, leaving four or five
hundred *Mannahocks*, finging, and dancing, and making
loud and barbarous Rejoicings.

In their Return down the River they vifited all their
Friends, who rejoiced much at their Victory over the *Mannahocks*. By their Intreaty, Captain *Smith* was induced to
make Peace with the *Rappahanocks* ; upon Condition, that
they fhould prefent him the King's Bow and Arrows, and
not offer to come armed, where he was ; and that they
fhould be Friends with the *Moraughtacunds*, his Friends,
and give their King's Son a Hoftage for the Performance.
Accordingly, the King's of *Nantaughtacund* and *Pifafack*
met the *Englifh* at the Place, where they firft fought.
There the King of *Rappahanock* prefented his Bow and Arrows, and performed all, they demanded, except the delivering his Son. For having no other, he faid, he could
not live without him ; and he offered in his Stead, to give
up the three Women, which the *Moraughtacunds* had
ftolen from him. This was accepted ; and the Women
being brought, Captain *Smith* prefented each of them with
a Chain of Beads. Then caufing the King of *Rappahanock*,
of *Moraughtacund*, and *Mofco* to ftand before him, he bid
the King of *Rappahanock* take her, he loved beft, *Moraughtacund* to chufe next, and to *Mofco* he gave the third.
And thus was the Peace concluded and celebrated with
feafting, finging, and dancing. And *Mofco*, to exprefs his
Love to the *Englifh*, changed his Name to *Uttafantafough*,
which fignified in their Language, *Stranger*, and was the
Name, by which they called the *Englifh*. And then all
the *Indians*, promifing to be always their Friends, and to
plant

1608.
Matt. Scri-
vener Vice-
Prefident.

plant Corn purpofely for them; and the *Englifh*, on their
Side, to provide Hatchets, Beads, and Copper for them;
they departed, giving them a Volley of their Fire-Arms,
which they returned with as loud Shouts and Cries, as their
Strengths could utter.

THAT Night they anchored in the River *Piankatank*,
and difcovered it, as high as it was navigable. But the
People were gone out to hunting, except a few old Men,
Women, and Children, that were tending their Corn. Of
thefe they obtained a Promife of Part, when they fhould
fetch it; as they had likewife done of all the Nations,
where-ever they had been. Going from thence to *Point
Comfort*, they where in a Bay on the South of the
Mouth of *York* River, then called *Gofnold's Bay*, furprifed,
in the Night, with fuch a fudden Guft of Thunder and
Rain, that they never expected more to fee *James-Town*.
But difcerning the Land by the Flafhes of Lightening, they
avoided fplitting on the Shore; till, by the Help of the
fame Light, they found *Point Comfort*, where they landed,
and refrefhed themfelves the reft of the Night.

HAVING difcovered fo many Nations at a Diftance,
they thought it highly proper and neceffary to know their
near Neighbours, the *Chefapeakes* and *Nandfamonds*, of
whom they had, as yet, only heard. Therefore fetting Sail
for the Southern Shore, they entered a narrow River, then
called *Chefapeake*, but now *Elfabeth*, on which the Town
of *Norfolk* ftands. It had a good Channel, but fome Shoals
about the Entrance. They failed up fix or feven Miles,
and faw two or three little Garden-plots with Houfes, and
the Shores overgrown with the largeft Pines, they had ever
feen in the Country. But neither feeing, nor hearing any
People, and the River being very narrow, they returned
back, and coafted the Shore towards *Nandfamond*, which
they found to be chiefly Oyfter-Banks. At the Mouth of
Nandfamond, they fpied fix or feven *Indians*, making their
Weirs, who prefently fled. But the *Englifh* went afhore,
and threw divers Toys, where they were working, and fo
departed. They were not gone far, before the *Indians* returned, and began to fing, and dance, and call them back.
One of them came voluntarily into their Boat, and invited
them up the River to his Houfe, which was in a little
Ifland, where (as well as on the main Land againft it) they
faw many and large Corn-fields. He treated them with
great Civility, and they in return, prefented him, his
Wife, and Children, with fuch Toys, as highly pleafed
them. By that time the others being come, invited them
higher up the River, under Pretence of going to their

Houfes likewife. But they foon found, that they only intended to decoy them up into the Narrows of the River, where the whole Nations of the *Nanfamonds* and *Chefapeakes* were in Ambufh to receive them. Having difcovered the Treachery, they made the beft of their Way down into the Open, amidft the Shot of three or four Hundred *Indians*, which they returned from their Mufkets with fuch Effe&, that they foon made them glad to take Shelter behind the Trees. Above an hundred Arrows ftuck in their Breaftwork of *Maffawomeck* Targets, and about the Boat, yet none was hurt. Only *Anthony Bagnall*, the Surgeon, was fhot in his Hat, and another in the Sleeve. Having gained the Open againft the Ifland, they feized on all their Canoes, and refolved, upon Confultation, to burn every thing on the Ifland at Night. In the mean while, they began to cut to Pieces their Canoes; at the Sight of which the *Indians* threw down their Arms, and fued for Peace; which the *Englifh* granted, on Condition, they would bring their King's Bow and Arrows, with a Chain of Pearl; and fhould, when they came back again, give them four hundred Bafkets of Corn. Otherwife they threatened, to break all their Canoes, to burn their Houfes and Corn, and to deftroy all, that they had. To thefe Conditions the *Indians* moft joyfully agreed; and flocking down in great Numbers with their Bafkets, they foon loaded the Boat with Corn, and fo parted good Friends.

A N D thus having viewed and reconnôitred all the Places on the Bay, one of the fineft perhaps and moft commodious Countries in the World, which Nature feems to have formed for one noble and complete Dominion, but which is fince unhappily divided by the large Grant to the Lord *Baltimore*, and having paffed about three thoufand Miles, according to their own Computation, in that fmall and open Boat, and in the Midft of many barbarous and favage Nations, they returned with Joy and Triumph to *James-Town*, where they arrived fafe the 7th of *September*, 1608. There they found Mr. *Scrivener*, and feveral others, well recovered; fome fick; many dead; the late Prefident a Prifoner for Mutiny; and the Corn, by Mr. *Scrivener's* honeft Diligence, gathered; but the Provifions in the Store much injured by the Rain.

B U T whilft Captain *Smith* and others were thus induftrioufly engaged in making good this Settlement, the Second or *Northern* Colony, granted by the Letters patent to the Town of *Plimouth* and others, was embraced and undertaken by feveral Perfons of Fortune and Diftin&ion, and particularly by Sir *John Popham*, Lord Chief-Juftice of *England*.

gland. He was a Gentlemen of one of the greatest Families in the *Weft of England*, but is memorable to all Posterity for his infamous Partiality and Injustice in the Trial of Sir *Walter Ralegh.* However, he was a Person, at that Time, of great Power and Interest, and in high Esteem with many for Wisdom and Virtue; and having procured Men and Money, he sent Captain *George Popham*, as President, Captain *Ralegh Gilbert*, as Admiral, and many other Gentlemen in several Posts and Offices, with an hundred Men, to possess and settle the Country. They set Sail from *Plimouth*, the last of *May*, 1607, and fell in with some Islands, then called *Monabigan*. From thence they proceeded to the Continent, and settled upon a very barren and rocky Coast, at the Mouth of *Sagadahock*, a large navigable River, which must be either the River *Saco* in *New-England*, or elfe St. *Juan* in *Acadia*. But that Winter was so extremely cold and frozen, that they could not range much about, nor search the Country; and their Provision was so scanty, that they were obliged to send all, except forty five of their Company back. Captain *Popham*, their President, died soon; and not long after, they were informed by the Ships that brought them Supplies, of the Death of the two principal Promoters and Supporters of the Undertaking, the Lord Chief-Justice *Popham*, and Sir *John Gilbert.* This last Gentleman, who was Brother, or perhaps rather Nephew, to the famous Sir *Humphry Gilbert*, before-mentioned, was chosen President of the Council for the *Northern* Colony. His Brother, Captain *Ralegh Gilbert*, Admiral of this Colony, succeeding to his Estate, was obliged to return to *England*, to enter upon his Inheritance, and take Care of his Affairs. And the rest also, being doubtful of proper Assistance and Encouragement, and having no Prospect in the Country, but of the most extreme Misery and Famine, all returned to *England* this Year 1608. And thus was this Plantation begun and ended in one Year; and that vast Grant, in which lay large Tracts of fine and noble Country, was stigmatized in the Grofs, and despised, as a cold, barren, mountainous, and rocky Desert.

ABOUT this Time also, Captain *Henry Hudson* discovered *Long-Island*, *New-York*, *Hudson's* River, and the Parts adjacent. As the *English* were busily employed in their own Discoveries and Settlements, he could hope for but little Advantage from his own Country; and therefore he applied himself to the States-General of the United Provinces, and fold this important Discovery to them. But this Sale was always excepted against by the *English*, as the Discovery was made by his Majesty's Commission, and the

Margin notes: 1608. *Mat. Scrivener Vice-President.*

Sale

1608. Sale paffed without the King's Confent, to whom, of Right, all new Lands and Difcoveries belong. However, the *Dutch*

Mat. Scri- crept in by Degrees, built new *Amfterdam*, and other Towns, *vener* Vice-ftrongly fortified themfelves, planted, and became a flourifh-Prefident. ing Colony.

DOCTOR *Whitgift*, Arch-Bifhop of *Canterbury*, a Man of a mild and gentle Difpofition, having died four Years before this, was fucceeded in that high Preferment by Dr. *Richard Bancroft*, a Perfon of a quite different Temper. He had very high Notions with Relation to the Government of both Church and State; and was accordingly a great Stickler for, and Promoter of, the King's abfolute Power, and failed not to take all Occafions, to oblige the Puritans to conform to the Church of *England*. This Prelate's Harfhnefs and Warmth caufed many of that People to take the Refolution this Year of fettling themfelves in *Virginia*, and fome were actually come off for that Purpofe. But the Archbifhop finding, that they were preparing in great Numbers to depart, obtained a Proclamation from the King, forbidding any to go, without his Majefty's exprefs Leave. And this was the more readily granted, as the Court mortally hated that Sect, and were now afraid, that they would become too numerous and too powerful in *Virginia*.

John Smith IN *Virginia*, on the 10th of *September*, by the Election of Prefident. the Council, and the Requeft of the Colony, Captain *Smith* was invefted with the Government; which, till then, he would by no Means accept, tho' often importuned to it. And now the building of *Ratcliffe's* Palace was ftopped, and Works of more immediate Ufe and Neceffity undertaken. The Church was repaired; the Store-houfe new covered; and a Place made ready for the Reception of the Supplies, they daily expected from *England*. The Fort was reduced into Form; the Order of the Watch was renewed; the Troops trained at each Setting of the Watch; and the whole Company every *Saturday* exercifed, in the Plain towards the *Weft*, which was prepared for that Purpofe, and called *Smithfield*; where fometimes above an hundred *Indians* would ftand in Amazement, to behold how a File would batter a Tree, where the Prefident had made them a Mark to fhoot at. And now being the Time of gathering Corn, and of Plenty among the *Indians*, the Boats were trimmed for Trade, and fent out under the Command of Lieutenant *Percy*. But in their Way, meeting Captain *Newport* with the fecond Supply, he brought them back to *James-Town*.

CAPTAIN *Newport* was in reality an empty, idle, interefted Man; very fearful and fufpicious in Times of Danger and Difficulty; but a very great and important Perfon

in

in his own Talk and Conceit. He had, by the Advantage of going to and fro, gained fo much upon the Ear and Confidence of the Council and Company in *England*, that whatever he propofed, was, for the moft part, concluded and refolved on. And upon this Voyage, he obtained a private Commiffion, not to return without a Lump of Gold, a Certainty of the *South-Sea*, or one of the loft Company, fent out by Sir *Walter Ralegh*. Befides, he brought an exprefs Command, to difcover the Country of the *Manakins*, with a Barge, for Conveniency of Carriage, to be taken into five Pieces, which they were to carry beyond the Falls, to convey them to the *South-Sea*. He likewife brought over a Crown for *Powhatan*, with Orders for his Coronation, and Prefents of a Bafon and Ewer, Bed, Bedftead, Cloaths, and other coftly Novelties ; which ftately Kind of Court had this bad Effeft, that it made him value himfelf too much, and overrate his Favour, which they had before much better for a plain Piece of Copper. In this Voyage came over many Perfons of Diftinftion ; Captain *Peter Wynne*, and Captain *Richard Waldo*, two old Soldiers and valiant Gentlemen, both appointed of the Council ; Mr. *Francis Weft*, Brother to the Lord Delawarr ; *Ralegh Crofhaw*, *John Ruffel*, *John Codrington*, *Daniel Tucker*, Mr. *Hunt*, *Thomas Foreft*, and others, to the Number of feventy Perfons. In this Ship likewife arrived Mrs. *Foreft*, and *Anne Burras*, her Maid, the firft *Englifhwomen* ever in this Country. And eight *Poles* and *Germans* were fent, to make Pitch, Tar, Glafs, Mills, and Soap-Afhes ; which, when the Country was replenifhed with People and Neceffaries, would have done exceedingly well, but in that their infant State, they were only a Burthen and Hindrance to the reft, who were fufficiently puzzled and employed to find Subfiftance for themfelves.

CAPTAIN *Smith*, whofe Mind was folid and provident, and plainly forefaw the ill Confequence of fpending that Time in thefe Projefts, which ought to be employed in the fpeedy Difpatch of the Ship, and in trading and laying in a Store of Provifions for the Year, was much mortified and perplexed with thefe Orders, and ftrenuoufly oppofed their Execution in Council. But *Newport* undertook to freight the Bark of twenty Tons with Corn, in going and returning from the *Manakins* ; and to obtain another Load for her of *Powhatan*, from *Werowocomoco*. He alfo promifed a large Proportion of Viftuals from the Ship ; which he was fo far from performing, that the Colony was obliged to fpare him three Hogfheads of Corn to viftual him homeward. In fhort, he reprefented *Smith*'s Oppofition, as a mere Device,

to hinder his Journey, that he might himfelf effect the Difcovery ; and he faid, that his Cruelty to the *Indians* might
well be a Means to hinder thefe Defigns, and to make them
feek Revenge.   *Smith*'s Opinion being therefore over-ruled
by the unanimous Voice of the Council, all other Works and
Defigns were laid afide, and an hundred and twenty chofen
Men appointed for *Newport*'s Guard on the Expedition.

BUT *Smith*, to clear himfelf of thefe Sufpicions, and to
fhew, that the *Indians* were not fo defperate, as was pretended by *Newport*, and how willing he was to affift, as
far as he could, undertook himfelf to carry their Meffage
to *Powhatan*, and to invite him to *James-Town* to receive
his Prefents.   And taking with him only Captain *Waldo*,
and three more, he went acrofs by Land, about twelve
Miles, to *Werowocomoco*, where he paffed the River in an
Indian Canoe.   *Powhatan*, being thirty Miles off, was immediately fent for ; and in the mean time, *Pocohontas* and
her Women entertained him with a ftrange Mafk and
barbarian Piece of Revelry, and feafted them with all the
favage Dainties, they could devife.   The next Day, *Powhatan* came, and *Smith* delivered his Meffage, together with
Namontack, his Servant, whom he had fent to *England*.
And he defired him to come to his Father *Newport*, to receive his Prefents, and to enter upon Meafures for their
effectual Revenge againft the *Manakins*.   To this that fubtle Barbarian anfwered : *That if their King had fent him any
Prefents, he alfo was a King, and that was his Land: That
he would ftay eight Days, to receive them: That* Newport
*ought to come to him, and not He to go to their Fort, which
was too foolifh a Bait to be taken: That as to the* Manakins,
*he could revenge his own Wrongs; and for any falt Water
beyond the Mountains,* he told him, *that all the Relations, they
had received from his People, were falfe.*   Whereupon he
began to draw Plots upon the Ground, according to his
Difcourfe, of all thofe Regions.   Many other complimen-
tal Difcourfes paffed between them ; and fo *Smith* returned
with this Anfwer to *James-Town*.

HEREUPON the Prefents were fent round by Water,
and the Captains went acrofs by Land, with a Guard of fifty
Men.   All being met at *Werowocomoco*, the next Day was
appointed for his Coronation.   Then the Prefents were
brought ; his Bafon and Ewer, Bed and Furniture, were
fet up ; and his Scarlet Cloak and Apparel, with much ado,
put on him, being perfuaded by *Namontack*, that they would
not hurt him.   But a great Coil and Trouble there was to
make him kneel, to receive his Crown.   He neither knew
the Majefty of a Crown, nor the Meaning of bending the
                                                    Knee,

Knee, which obliged them to ufe fo many Perfuafions, Examples, and Inftructions, as tired them all. At laft, by leaning hard on his Shoulders, he ftooped a little, and three, being ready with the Crown, put it on his Head; when, by the Warning of a Piftol, the Boats were prepared with fuch a Volley of Shot, that the King ftarted up in a horrible Fright, till he faw, all was well. Then recollecting himfelf, to return their Kindnefs, he gave his old Shoes and Mantle to Captain Newport; and finding him determined to difcover the *Manakins*, he did his utmoft to divert him from his Purpofe, and refufed to lend him either Men or Guides, except *Namontack*. And fo after fome flight Compliments on both Sides, in Requital for his Prefents, he gave *Newport* a Heap of Ears of Corn, which might contain feven or eight Bufhels, and as much more was purchafed in the Town, with which they returned to the Fort at *James-Town*.

IMMEDIATELY upon their Return, Captain *Newport*, with an hundred and twenty chofen Men, led by Captain *Waldo*, Lieutenant *Percy*, Captain *Wynne*, Mr. *Weft*, and Mr. *Scrivener*, fet forward for the Difcovery of the *Manakins*; leaving the Prefident at the Fort, with eighty or ninety weak and fickly Men, to load the Ship. Arriving at the Falls, they marched by Land about forty Miles, and found a very fair, fertile, well-watered Country. Two Towns of the *Manakins* they difcovered, fituate on the *South* Side of the River. The People ufed them neither well nor ill; yet for their Security, they took one of their petty Kings, and led him bound, to conduct them the Way. In their Return, they fpent fome Time in fearching for Mines, having with them one *William Callicut*, a Refiner, for that Purpofe. From the Cruft of Earth, which they dug, he perfuaded them, that he extracted fome fmall Quantity of Silver. With this poor Trial, they returned down the fame Path, they went, to the Falls; where the *Indians* feigned, that many Ships were come into the Bay, to kill the *Englifh* at *James-Town*. But as for their Corn, they had hid it in the Woods, and could by no Means be induced to trade. And being thus deluded and difappointed, they returned to *James-Town*, half fick, and all complaining, being fadly harraffed with Toil, Famine, and Difcontent.

No fooner were they landed, but the Prefident difperfed as many, as were able, fome to make Glafs, and others for Pitch, Tar, and Soap-Afhes. Leaving them at the Fort under the Councils Care and Overfight, he himfelf carried thirty about five Miles down the River, to learn to cut down Trees, make Clapboard, and lie in the Woods. Among thefe he chofe *Gabriel Beadle* and *John Ruffel*, two

fine

fine and proper Gentlemen of the laft Supply. Thefe
were, at firft, ftrange Diverfions for Men of Pleafure.
Yet they lodged, eat, and drank, worked or played, only
as the Prefident himfelf did; and all things were carried fo
pleafantly, that within a Week they became Mafters, and
thirty or forty of fuch voluntary Gentlemen, would have
done more in a Day than an hundred of the reft, who muft
be driven to it by Compulfion.   Being inured to Labour by
thefe means, they foon made it their Delight, to hear the
Trees thunder, as they fell; and afterwards became very
hardy, ufeful, and refolute Men, efpecially Mr. *Ruffel*.
But the Axes often bliftering their tender Fingers, they
would, at every third Stroke, drown the Eccho, with a
loud Volley of Oaths.   To remedy which Sin, the Prefident ordered every Man's Oaths to be numbered, and at
Night, for every Oath, to have a Can of Water poured
down his Sleeve; which fo wafhed and drenched the Offender, that in a fhort time, an Oath was not heard in a
Week.

IN the mean while, Mr. *Scrivener*, Captain *Waldo*, and
Captain *Wynne*, at the Fort, each, in their feveral Way,
carefully regarded their Charge.   But when the Prefident
returned, feeing the Time confumed, and no Provifions
got, and that the Ship lay idle at a great Charge,
and did nothing, he immediately embarked in the Difcovery Barge, taking with him eighteen Men and another
Boat, and leaving Orders with the Council, to fend
Lieutenant *Percy* after him, with the next Barge, that arrived at the Fort.   Going into *Chickahominy*, the *Indians*
were furly, and knowing his Wants, with much Scorn and
Infolence refufed to trade.   But the Prefident, perceiving,
it was *Powhatan's* Policy to ftarve the *Englifh*, told them,
that he came not fo much for Corn, as to revenge his own
Captivity and the Death of his two Men; which he pretended to attribute to them.   And fo, landing his Men,
and making ready to charge them, they immediately fled.
Soon after they fent Ambaffadors, with Corn, Fifh, Fowl,
and whatever elfe they had, to make their Peace.   Their
Corn being that Year but bad, they complained extremely
of their own Wants, yet freighted their Boats with an
hundred Bufhels, and in like manner Lieutenant *Percy's*,
that not long after arrived.   Returning to *James-Town*, the
Colony was much pleafed and revived by this feafonable
Supply.   Yet fuch was the Malice and Envy of fome, that
they had rather hazard a Starving, than that *Smith's* Endeavours fhould prove fo much more effectual, than theirs.
And *Newport* and *Ratcliffe* had projected, not only to de-
pofe

pofe him, but to keep him out of the Fort; under Pretence, that, being Prefident, he had left his Place and the Fort, without their Confent. But their Horns were too fhort, and they themfelves narrowly efcaped a greater Mifchief.

ALL this while, their old Tavern, the Ship, made as much of all them, that had either Money or Ware, as could be defired. By this time, they were become perfect on all Sides, the Sailers, the Soldiers, and the *Indians*; and much more Care was taken, to maintain their private and pernicious Trade, than to provide things neceffary for the Colony. *Newport* and his Mariners had fo many private Factors at the Fort, that in fix or feven Weeks, of two or three hundred Axes, Hoes, Pick-axes, and other Inftruments for the Ufe of the Colony, fcarce twenty could be found; and for Pike-heads, Powder, Shot, or any thing elfe they could fteal, they knew well, how to convey them fecretly, to trade with the *Indians* for Furs, Bafkets, young Beafts, and other fuch-like Commodities. So that, altho' *Virginia* afforded no Commodities for thofe, who were at the Expence of the Settlement, yet thefe Men found Means, by thefe indirect Methods, of driving on a very profitable Trade. And thus, by their falfe Excufes, Informations, and Advices in *England*, and by their unlawful Trade here, the Adventurers were coufened, and the Action almoft overthrown. Upon this Account therefore, as well as under Pretence, that his Orders were, not to return, without a Lump of Gold, a Certainty of the *South-Sea*, or one of Sir *Walter Ralegh*'s loft Company, the Prefident had once determined to fend away the Ship, and to oblige *Newport* to ftay one Year in the Country, to learn to fpeak of his own Experience. But upon his Submiffion and Acknowledgment, this Punifhment was remitted, and he was fuffered to return to *England* in the Ship; where, it is not to be doubted, but that he reprefented Matters in the worft Light.

IT is certain, that the Treafurer and Council in *England* were greatly difappointed in their Hopes. For they expected, upon their Difcoveries in *America*, to have fpeedy Returns, in Gold and Silver, and fuch other rich Commodities, as the *Spaniards* found at their firft Arrival. But *Virginia* is not a Country of Mines. It is formed by Nature for producing all the Neceffaries, or even Elegancies of Life, to as high a Degree, as perhaps any other Country whatfoever. It lies under the fame Clime, as fome Parts of *Spain*, *Italy*, and *Sicily*, and is a Country of Plenty and Abundance; and therefore, in the End, is more valuable,

1608.

John Smith
Prefident.

and even richer, than thofe Regions, which abound in Gold and Silver. The Truth of this is confirmed by Experience; and it is an undeniable Maxim in Politicks, that Commodities of the firft Neceffity, or fuch as are of abfolute Ufe for our Subfiftance and the Support of Life, have a much greater real and intrinfic Value, than thofe, which only receive an imaginary Worth, by Compact or Agreement, and are wholly defigned, as a Gage, or Meafure, of the real and intrinfic Value of other Commodities. The true Riches therefore, and Power of every Country, depend upon the plentiful Production of Corn, Stocks, Cloathing, and other fuch Commodities of the firft Neceffity; the Want of which can, by no means, be fupplied by ever fo great an Abundance of Gold and Silver. But the Want of them, on the contrary, may be, and often have been, fupplied, by ftamped Leather, Tallies, Shells, Paper, or other fuch arbitrary Reprefentations. But altho' thefe Neceffaries of Life are of this greater real Value, yet they are not to be had at once. Previous Preparations by Culture, Manufacturing, Stocks, and other Improvements, are neceffary; which often require a long Time, to bring them to any tolerable Degree of Perfection. And the *Englifh*, when they firft came to *Virginia*, happened upon a Land, juft as God had made it, little planted, manured or improved. The Inhabitants were an idle, improvident, vagabond People; knowing nothing of Gold and Silver, and other valuable Commodities; and carelefs of every thing, but juft from Hand to Mouth.

BUT however free they might be from Blame, the Council in *England* were certainly very much fretted with the Difappointment, and by this Ship, wrote the Prefident a very angry Letter. They complained of the vain Hopes, they had been fed with, and very fmall Proofs; and of their Factions and filly Projects about dividing the Country, concerning which the late Prefident and his Faction had written fome idle Story to the Earl of *Salifbury*, at that time chief Minifter of State. And they threatened, unlefs the Charge of this Voyage, amounting to about two thoufand Pounds, was defrayed by the Ship's Return, they fhould be deferted, and left to remain here, as banifhed Men. To this Letter Captain *Smith* gave a very plain and foldierly Anfwer by the Ship, which was at length difpatched, with the Trials of Pitch, Tar, Glafs, Frankincenfe, and Soap-Afhes, and with what Wainfcot and Clapboard could be provided. In it he endeavoured to lay open to them the Caufes, that kept them from laying fuch a Foundation, as might have given better Satisfaction; and

advifes

advifes them againſt expecting any profitable Returns at prefent. He declares his own Integrity and Sincerity towards them, and warns them againſt fome Perſons, who caufed them to believe much more, than was true. He tells them, that their Directions by *Newport* had been followed, altho' he himſelf was directly againſt them, as they were very prejudicial and to the imminent Hazard of the whole Colony, which was then, when it was too late, generally confeffed. He complains of *Newport*, expoſes the Vanity and ill Conſequences of his Projects, his Lingering in the Country, the good Cheer and Luxury of him and the Sailers, and their Embezzlement of the publick Stores. For of the two thouſand Pounds, which this Ship coſt them, he affures them, that the Colony had not Received the Value of an hundred Pounds. He blames *Ratcliffe*, *Archer*, and others, as the Authors of their Factions and Diſturbances; and tells them, that he had ſent *Ratcliffe*, a counterfeit Impoſtor, whoſe right Name was *Sicklemore*, home, leſt the Company ſhould cut his Throat. And he judiciouſly inſiſts upon their ſending uſeful Labourers and proper Tradeſmen for their preſent Condition; and upon providing, firſt of all, Food, Lodging, and ſuch other Neceſſaries, as were abſolutely requiſite for their Being and Subſiſtance, before they went on any other Projects of Gain or Curioſity, for which they were no ways fitted, in their preſent weak and infant Condition. At the fame time, he ſent them two Barrels of ſuch Stones, as he thought contained ſome Kind of Ore, with Notes, ſignifying in what Places he found them. And to ſhew, he could make as large a Diſcovery, as *Newport's* of the *Manakins*, for leſs Charge, than he ſpent them at every Meal, he ſent them a Map of the Bay and Rivers, with a Relation annexed, of the Countries, and of the Nations, that dwelt upon them. And this indeed was done with ſuch wonderful exactneſs, as ſhewed him to have travelled far, and ſeen much; and it has ever ſince been the Original, from which all later Maps and Deſcriptions of *Virginia* have been moſtly copied.

A N D now the Ship being gone, the grand Remora and Obſtacle to all neceſſary Buſineſs, the Colony began to look about them. The Proſpect was diſmal, and they were all in the utmoſt Conſternation, expecting nothing elſe but the moſt extreme Famine. However to make up, in ſome meaſure, their loſt Time, Mr. *Scrivener* had been ſent, before *Newport's* Departure, with the Bark and Barges to *Werowocomoco*. There he found the *Indians* more ready to fight, than to trade. But his Vigilancy prevented their Plots; and by the Means of *Namontack*, he got three or

1608.

John Smith
Preſident.

G 2   four

1608.

John Smith President.

four Hogfheads of Corn, and as much Pocones, a red Root, at that time efteemed an excellent Dye. Meeting *Newport* at *Point Comfort*, he returned to the Fort; and the Prefident, taking him and Captain *Wynne*, fet off immediately for *Nandfamond*. That Nation at firft denied him, not only the four hundred Bafkets of Corn, they had promifed, but any Trade at all. They excufed themfelves on Account of their Corn's being almoft fpent, and becaufe they were commanded by *Powhatan*, to keep what was left, and not to let the *Englifh* even enter their River. The Prefident finding, nothing was to be done in the Way of Peace, refolved to ufe Force. At the firft Onfet, the *Indians* all fled, without fhooting an Arrow. Then marching up to their Houfes, they fet Fire to the firft, they came to. When the *Indians* perceived that, they offered, if they would make no more Spoil, to give them half the Corn, they had. Accordingly, before Night, they loaded their three Boats; and for fparing them this Year, they promifed to plant Corn purpofely for them the next. With this they returned to *James-Town*, about the Time, that *John Laydon* was married to *Anne Burras*; which was the firft Chriftian Marriage, that ever was in *Virginia*. But the Prefident ftaid not long at the Fort. For he fitted himfelf and Captain *Waldo* out immediately with two Barges, and made a Voyage up the River. From *Wyanoake*, and all Parts there-abouts, he found the *Indians* fled; and therefore hafting up higher, he then firft difcovered the River and People of *Appamatox*. The little Corn, they had, was equally divided; and the Prefident gave them Copper for it, and fuch other Toys, as fully fatisfied them. At the fame time, Mr. *Scrivener* and Lieutenant *Percy* went abroad in Queft of Provifions, but could find nothing.

ABOUT this time, the Prefident was invited by *Powhatan* to come to him; and he promifed to load his Ship with Corn, provided he would fend fome Workmen to build him a Houfe, and would give him a Grind-ftone, fifty Swords, fome Mufkets, a Cock and a Hen, with much Copper and Beads. The Prefident was not ignorant of his Devices and Subtlety; yet was unwilling to negleét any Opportunity of getting Provifions, and refolved, fooner than fail, to take him and all his Store by Surprife. To this End, he took Order with Captain *Waldo*, whom he knew to be fure in Time of Danger, to fecond him, if Need required. But Captain *Wynne* and Mr. *Scrivener* did their utmoft to hinder their Projeét. For *Scrivener's* ftriét Friendfhip with Captain *Smith* was now much cooled; and he was thought to join with fome others, in a Plot to ruin him in *England*.

But

But the Prefident, whom no Eloquence could perfuade to ftarve, fent off two *Englifhmen* before by Land, and four *Germans*, to build the Houfe for *Powhatan* againft his Ar- rival. And then, having left Mr. *Scrivener* his Subftitute, he fet forward with the Bark and two Barges, manned only with fuch, as offered themfelves voluntarily to go upon the Service. In the Difcovery-Barge went himfelf, Mr. *Ralegh Chrofhaw*, *John Ruffel*, and feveral other Gentlemen and Soldiers; and Mr. *William Phittiplace*, as Captain, Lieute- nant *Percy*, Mr. *Francis Weft*, Mr. *Robert Ford*, Clerk of the Council, with many others, went on board the Bark.

THE 29th of *December* they left *James-Town*, being victualled only for three or four Days. That Night they lodged at *Warrafqueake*, where the Prefident got fufficient Provifion. The King of that Town did his utmoft to divert him from feeing *Powhatan*; but finding, he could not prevail, he told him, that *Powhatan* would ufe them kindly, although he had fent for them only to cut their Throats. He therefore advifed him, not to truft him, and to be fure to give him no Opportunity of feizing his Arms. The Prefident thanked him for his good Counfel; and having obtained Guides from him to the *Chowanocks*, a Nation dwelling in the Fork of *Chowan*, between *Notta- way* and *Meherrin* Rivers, he fent *Michael Sicklemore*, a very valiant, honeft, and painful Soldier, with Prefents to that King; but chiefly to look for Silkgrafs, and to en- quire after Sir *Walter Ralegh*'s loft Colony. The next Night they lodged at *Kicquotan*, and were detained there fix or feven Days by the extreme Wind, Rain, Froft, and Snow. This obliged them to keep their *Chriftmas* among the Savages; and they were never more merry in their Lives, lodged by better Fires, or fed with greater Plenty of good Bread, Oyfters, Fifh, Flefh, and Wildfowl. De- parting thence, they arrived on the 12th of *January*, thro' various Accidents, at *Werowocomoco*; where they found the River frozen near half a Mile from the Shore. But the Prefident, running his Barge up, as far as he could by breaking the Ice, was left by the Ebb upon the oozy Shoals. In this dangerous Situation, he plunged firft into the River himfelf; and by his Example, taught them to march, near Middle deep, a Flight-fhot, through the frozen Ooze. When the Barge fhould float, he appointed two or three to re- turn her aboard the Bark; where they, foon after, came into fuch Diftrefs for Want of Water, that the River being falt, they were obliged to make frefh Water, by melting the Ice.

THE Prefident and his Company quartered in the next Cabbins, they found, and fent to *Powhatan* for Provifions.

1609.

John Smith
Prefident.

He fent them Plenty of Bread, Turkey, and Venifon ; and the next Day, feafted them after his ufual Manner. But he pretended, he had not fent for them ; neither had he any Corn, and his People much lefs ; and foon began to be importunate with them to be gone. But the Prefident confronting him with the Perfons, who brought the Meffage, he endeavoured to put the Matter off with a Laugh, and afked for his Commodities. But he liked nothing, except Guns and Swords, and valued a Bafket of Corn higher than a Bafket of Copper ; faying, he could rate his Corn, but not the Copper. Captain *Smith*, feeing his Intent, told him ; that he had many Ways, to have got Provifions, but relying on his Promifes, he had negleƈed all to fatisfy his Defire, and had fent his Men to make his Buildings, whilft his own were undone : That he knew, he had engroffed his People's Corn, and forbid them to trade ; thinking, by confuming Time, to confume them : That as for Swords and Guns, he had none to fpare ; and that he muft know, thofe, he had, could keep him from ftarving : Yet he would neither rob nor wrong him, nor diffolve that Friendfhip, they had mutually promifed, unlefs conftrained to it by bad Ufage. The King liftened attentively to this Difcourfe ; and promifed, that both he and his People fhould fpare him, what they could, and that they fhould receive it within two Days. *But, fays he, I have fome Doubt about the Reafon of your coming hither. I am informed from many Hands, that you come, not to trade, but to invade my People, and to poffefs my Country. This makes me lefs ready to relieve you, and frightens my People from bringing in their Corn. And therefore to eafe them of that Fear, leave your Arms aboard, fince they are needlefs here, where we are all Friends, and for ever* Powhatans.

IN thefe, and many fuch infidious Difcourfes, that Day was fpent. But Captain *Smith* afterwards difcovered, that the *Germans*, whom he had fent to build *Powhatan's* Houfe, finding his Plenty and the Wants of the *Englifh*, and thinking it fcarce poffible, that they could efcape both him and Famine, had, to gain his Favour, revealed to him all, they knew, of the State and Defigns of the *Englifh*, and advifed him, how to counteraƈ and prevent them. And this Treachery was the more odious and unfufpeƈed, becaufe the Prefident had placed one of them, as a Spy upon *Powhatan*, being a Man of Judgment and Refolution, and therefore thought moft proper for that Employ. And as he was fure of his Wages for his Labour, and had ever been well ufed, both he and his Countrymen, there was at
that

that time little Doubt concerning his Honefty. But whilft
they expected the coming in of the Country, they wrangled
Powhatan out of eighty Bufhels of Corn for a Copper Ket-
tle; which the Prefident feeing him much affect, he told
him, it was of much greater Value, yet in Regard of his
Scarcity, he would accept that Quantity at prefent, pro-
vided he fhould have as much more the next Year, or the
Manakin Country. Both being fatisfied with the Condition,
Powhatan begun to expoftulate the Difference of Peace and
War, with Captain *Smith*, after this Manner.

HE told him, with a Vanity ufual to Perfons, who affect
to be thought very old, that he had feen the Death of all
his People thrice; and that not one of thofe three Genera-
tions was then living, except himfelf: That he knew the
Difference of Peace and War better, than any in his
Country: That he was now grown old, and muft die foon;
and that the Succeffion muft defcend, in Order, to his
Brothers, *Opitchapan*, *Opechancanough*, and *Catataugh*, and
then to his two Sifters, and their two Daughters. He wifhed
their Experience was equal to his; and that *Smith*'s Love
to them might be no lefs, than his to *Smith*. He afked
him; Why he would take that by Force, which he might
quickly have by Love? Why he would deftroy them, that
provided him Food? and, What he could get by War?
For they could hide their Provifions, and fly into the Woods;
and then he muft confequently famifh by wronging his
Friends. He defired to know the Reafon of his Jealoufy,
fince he faw them unarmed, and willing to fupply his Wants,
if he would come in a friendly Manner, and not with
Swords and Guns, as to invade an Enemy. And he told
him, that he was not fo fimple, as not to know, it was
better to eat good Meat, lie well, and fleep quietly with his
Women and Children; to laugh and be merry with the
Englifh, and being their Friend, to have Copper, Hatchets,
and whatever elfe he wanted; than to fly from all, to lie
cold in the Woods, feed upon Acorns, Roots, and fuch
Trafh, and to be fo hunted, that he could neither reft, eat,
or fleep. In that Circumftance, his tired Men muft watch,
and if a Twig did but break, all would be crying out,
Here comes Captain Smith; and fo, in this miferable Manner, to end his miferable Life; which might likewife foon
be Captain *Smith*'s Fate too, through his Rafhnefs and Un-
advifednefs. He therefore earneftly exhorted him to peaceable Counfels; and above all infifted, that the Guns and
Swords, the grand Caufe of their Jealoufy and Uneafinefs,
fhould be removed and fent away.

To

1609.

John Smith President.

To this crafty Difcourfe the Prefident replied: That it was the Fafhion of the *Englifh*, always to wear their Arms, like their Cloaths; and that they would, by no Means, part with them: That his People came frequently to *James-Town*, and were entertained with their Bows and Arrows, without any Exceptions: That if the *Englifh* had intended him any Hurt, they could long fince have effected it, as was evident to him, and all the World, efpecially confidering the Superiority of their Arms : That altho' Revenge was always in their Power, yet, out of an Inclination to Mercy and Friendfhip, they paffed over the daily Violations of the Peace by his Subjects: And as to hiding his Provifions, and flying into the Woods, he told him, they fhould not fo unadvifedly ftarve, as he imagined. For they had a Rule to find things hidden, beyond his Knowledge. After much more Difcourfe, they at laft began to trade. But the King, feeing that his Will would not be admitted as a Law, and that *Smith* was obftinate, not to difmifs his Guard, or difarm his Men, breathed out his Mind once more in this Manner, with a Sigh.

Captain Smith, *I never ufe any Werowance fo kindly as yourfelf; yet from you I receive the leaft Kindnefs of any. Captain* Newport *gave me Swords, Copper, Cloaths, or whatever elfe I defired, ever accepting what I offered him; and would fend away his Guns, when requefted. No one refufes to lie at my Feet, or do, what I demand, but you only. Of you I can have nothing, but what you value not, and yet you will have, whatfoever you pleafe. Captain* Newport *you call Father, and fo you call me; but I fee, in fpite of us both, you will do, what you will, and we muft both ftudy to humour and content you. But if you intend fo friendly, as you fay, fend away your Arms. For you fee, my undefigning Simplicity and Friendfhip caufe me, thus nakedly, to forget myfelf.*

Tʜᴇ Prefident, perceiving this Barbarian only trifled the Time to cut his Throat, refolved to treat him in his own Way. He therefore procured the *Indians* to break the Ice, that his Boat might come, to fetch him and his Corn; and at the fame Time, gave Order for more Men to come afhore, to furprife the King. In the mean while, to protract the Time, he endeavoured to entertain him with much fpecious and fallacious Difcourfe; promifing, the next Day to quit his Arms, and to fhew, by trufting to his Word, that he loved and confided in him, as a Father. But whilft the Ice was breaking, *Powhatan* conveyed himfelf away, with his Women, Children, and Luggage. Yet to avoid Sufpicion, he left two or three of his Women talking with the Prefident, whilft he fecretly ran off, and his Men as fecretly

fecretly befet the Houfe. Which being prefently difcovered, the Prefident iffued forth, with his Piftol, Sword, and
Target. At his firft Shot, thofe, next him, tumbled one
over another ; and the reft fled nimbly off, fome one Way,
fome another. And thus, without any Hurt, only accompanied with Mr. *John Ruffel*, he reached the main Body
of his Men. But when the *Indians* perceived him fo well
efcaped, they ufed their utmoft Art, to excufe and diffem-
ble the Matter. *Powhatan* fent him a great Bracelet and
Chain of Pearl by an ancient Orator, who told him, that
their Emperor was fled for Fear of his Guns: That knowing, when the Ice was open, there would come more Men
afhore, he had fent thofe Numbers, whom he had affaulted,
only to guard his Corn from being ftole, which might happen without the Prefident's Knowledge: That altho' fome
were hurt by his Miftake, yet *Powhatan* was ftill his Friend,
and for ever would continue fo. And he defired, fince the
Ice was open, that he would fend away his Corn ; and if
he expected his Company, that he would alfo fend away
his Guns, which fo frighted his People, that they were
afraid to bring in their Corn, as he had promifed they
fhould. And then Bafkets being provided for the *Englifh*,
to carry their Corn to the Boats, thofe *Indians* kindly offered their Service, to guard their Arms, left they fhould be
ftolen. There was a great Number of goodly, well-proportioned Fellows, painted and grimmed, like Devils. But
the very Sight of the *Englifh* cocking their Matches, and
being ready to charge, made them quit their Bows and Arrows, at Command, to the Guard, and carry down the
Corn upon their Backs. And there was no Occafion to
importune them, to make Difpatch.

B U T *Powhatan* and the *Germans* were ftill eager to have
the Head of Captain *Smith*. For if they could but kill him,
they thought, all would be their own. And therefore, the
Englifh being ftaid by the Ebb till late within Night, the
King fpent his Time in making ready his Forces, to furprife the Houfe and him at Supper. But *Pocahontas*, in a
very dark and difmal Night, came alone through the Woods,
and told the Prefident, that great Cheer would be fent them
foon ; but that *Powhatan*, with all the Power, he could
make, would come after to kill them all, if thofe, who
brought the Victuals, could not effect it with their own
Arms, while they were at Supper. And therefore, as they
tendered their Lives, fhe advifed them to be gone. The
Prefident would have given her fuch Things, as he knew,
fhe delighted in. But, with Tears running down her
Cheeks, fhe refufed them ; faying, fhe durft not be feen to
have

have any of them. For fhould her Father know it, it
would be certain and immediate Death to her. And fo fhe
ran away, by herfelf, as fhe came. Within lefs than an
Hour after, came eight or ten lufty Fellows, with large
Platters of Venifon and other Vi&uals; and they were very
importunate with the *Englifh*, to put out their Matches;
pretending, their Smoke made them fick. But the Prefident made them tafte of every Difh; and then fent fome of
them back to *Powhatan*, to bid him make Hafte; for he
was ready for his coming. Soon after came more Meffengers, to fee what News; and not long after them, others.
And thus was the Time fpent, with equal Vigilancy on both
Sides, but without any farther Hurt. At high Water, the
Englifh departed; but to oblige *Powhatan*, they left him,
at his Requeft, *Edward Brynton*, to kill him Fowl, and
the *Germans*, who were yet unfufpe&ed, to finifh his Houfe.

THEY had no fooner fet Sail, but *Powhatan* returned,
✓ and fent two of the *Germans* to *James-Town*. They pretended to Captain *Wynne*, that all things were well, and
that the Prefident had Occafion for their Arms; and therefore they defired new ones, with fome fpare Tools, and
fhift of Apparel; all which were readily granted them.
During their loitering there, by the Promife of *Powhatan*'s
Favour, and of an Exemption from the Miferies, which
would certainly happen to the Colony, they drew over to
their Confederacy fix or· feven more, fuch expert Thieves,
as prefently furnifhed them with fifty Swords, eight Mufkets, eight Pikes, and Powder and Shot; which were
fpeedily conveyed away, by *Indians* at Hand for that Purpofe. The other *German Powhatan* kept, as a Pledge;
whofe Diligence provided him with three hundred Toma-
hauks, or *Indian* Hatchets. In the mean time, *Edward
Brynton* and *Thomas Savage*, feeing the *Germans* fo diligent
to accommodate the *Indians* with Arms, attempted to make
their Efcape to *James-Town*. But they were apprehended
and brought back, and expe&ed, every Minute, to be put
to Death.

The Prefident and the reft, being arrived at *Pamunkey*,
were entertained fome Days by the King, with great Feafting and Mirth. The Day, appointed to begin their Trade,
he went afhore with Lieutenant *Percy*, Mr. *Weft*, Mr.
Ruffel, Mr. *Behethland*, Mr. *Crofhaw*, Mr. *Powel*, Mr.
Ford, and others to the Number of fifteen; and going up
to *Opechancanough*'s Houfe, a Quarter of a Mile from the
River, they found nothing but a lame Fellow and a Boy,
and all the Houfes round abandoned, and ftripped of every
thing. They ftaid not long, before the King came, and
after

after him feveral of his People, loaded with Bows and Arrows. But their Commodities were fo trifling, and thofe
held at fuch a Rate, that the Prefident began with the
King, and faid: That the Profeffions of his Tongue were
proved by his Actions to be mere Deceit: That laft Year
he kindly freighted his Veffel; but had how treacheroufly
invited him, with a View to famifh and deftroy him: That
as the King was not ignorant of his Wants, fo neither was
he of the King's Plenty; of which, by fome Means, he
muft have Part. And he told him, it was highly proper
and decent for Kings, above all others, to keep their Promife. And therefore, fhewing his Commodities, he offered
him his Choice, and the reft, he faid, he would proportion
in fit Bargains for his People. *Opechancanough* feemed kindly to accept his Offer; and the better to colour his Defigns,
fold them, what they had, at their own Price; promifing,
the next Day, more Company, better provided.

THE next Day, the Prefident, with the fame fifteen,
marched up to the King's Houfe, where they found four
or five Men, newly arrived, with each a great Bafket.
Soon after came the King; and putting on a ftrained Chear-
fulnefs, he entertained them in Difcourfe, about the great
Pains he had been taking, to keep his Promife; till Mr.
Ruffel brought in News, that at leaft feven hundred *In-*
dians, well armed, had invironed the Houfe, and befet the
Fields. The Prefident, feeing fome of the Company greatly difmaid at the Thought of fuch a Multitude, told them:
That he was lefs concerned at the Danger and Number of
the Enemy, than at the malicious Reprefentations, which
the Council, and their open mouthed Minions, would make
to *England*, of his breaking the Peace: That he, alone,
was once affaulted by three hundred; and had it not been
for an Accident, would have made his Way good among
them all: That they were now fixteen, and the Enemy
but feven hundred at the moft. And therefore he defired
them, to fight like Men, and not die like Sheep. For if
they dared to follow his Example, and to do, as he did,
he doubted not, by God's Affiftance, to extricate them out
of the prefent Difficulty and Danger. The Time not per-
mitting any Argument, they all chearfully vowed, to execute, whatever he attempted, or die. But that they might
not fight for nothing, or be even ruined and ftarved by
their Victory, the Prefident told *Opechancanough*: That he
faw his Plot to murder him, but he feared it not: That
their Men had done no Harm, but by their Directions:
That therefore, if each of his Men would bring a Bafket
of Corn, he would ftake againft it the Value in Copper,
and

and they two would go over into the Ifland, in the River,
againft that Place, and decide the Matter by fingle Combat :
John Smith That he fhould have his Choice, and all Advantage of Wea-
Prefident. pons : and, That the Conqueror fhould have all, and be
Lord and Mafter over all their Men.

BUT duelling in fair and open Field is not the Manner
of the *Indians.* Their chief Valour confifts in way-laying
and murdering the unfufpecting and unprovided, or perhaps
the weak and helplefs. Neither had *Opechancanough* fuch
Regard for the Lives of his Subjects, as to fave them from
Danger, at the Hazard of his own. He therefore kindly
endeavoured to appeafe the Prefident's Anger and Sufpicion,
by a Prefent at the Door, which he intreated him to accept. This was only to draw him out, where the Bait
was guarded with two hundred Men, befides thirty, which
lay behind a great Tree, fallen acrofs, with each his Arrow notched, ready to fhoot. But the Prefident, having
difcovered the Treachery, feifed the King, in the Midft of
his Men, by his long Lock of Hair, and prefented his Piftol, ready cocked, to his Breaft. Thus he led him, trem-
bling and half dead with Fear, among his People ; who
were eafily induced to throw down their Arms, and to deliver the King's Vambrace, Bow, and Arrows ; little
dreaming, that any one durft to ufe their King in that Manner. And now *Opechancanough,* to refcue himfelf, beftowed his Prefents in ferious Sadnefs ; and his Subjects, being
upbraided and threatened by the Prefident in a fmart and
angry Speech, mixed with fome Expreffions of Love and
Confidence, caft away their Bows and Arrows, and Men,
Women, and Children, brought in their Commodities.
For two or three Hours, they fo thronged and wearied him,
that he retired into the Houfe to reft, leaving others to
trade, and receive their Prefents. Whilft he was afleep,
fifty of their choice Men, with each an *Englifh* Sword or
Club in his Hand, and feconded by two or three hundred
more, preffed into the Houfe to murder him. But the Prefident, being waked from his Sleep, by the Noife of the
People and fhaking of the Houfe, betook himfelf to his
Arms, together with Mr. *Crofhaw* and fome others ; which
foon made them throng back, fafter than they came. But
Opechancanough and fome of his Ancients, who were kept
Prifoners with him, endeavoured, in a long Oration, to
excufe this Intrufion. The reft of the Day was fpent with
much Kindnefs, the *Indians* renewing their Prefents, and
feafting the *Englifh* with their beft Provifions.

WHILE thefe things were tranfacting, there happened
an unlucky Accident at the Fort. Mr. *Scrivener* had received

ceived Letters from *England*, which gave him towering
Thoughts, and made him decline entirely in his Affection and
Friendſhip to Captain *Smith*, who ſtill regarded and loved
him, as his Brother. This made him more headſtrong and
conceited, than was naturally conſiſtent with his Prudence
and Moderation. And having taken it into his Head to viſit
Hog-Iſlamd, he could not be turned from it, by the Advice
and repeated Entreaties of Captain *Waldo* and ſeveral others.
Therefore, taking with him Captain *Waldo*, who was not
to be abſent from the Fort, but to be ready to ſecond the
Preſident, if called for, and Mr. *Anthony Goſnold*, a very
worthy, honeſt, and induſtrious Gentleman, and Brother
to Captain *Bartholomew Goſnold*, with eight others, he
went into the Skiff. She was ſo overloaded, that ſhe ſcarce
could have lived in calm Weather; but, in that cold and
boiſterous Day, ſhe ſunk, none knowing how or where,
and all aboard were drowned. To advertiſe the Preſident
of this heavy News, none could be got, till Mr. *Richard
Wyffin* undertook it alone. He was encountered with many
Dangers and Difficulties, in all Places, as he paſſed. And
at *Werowocomoco*, not finding the Preſident, and perceiving
ſuch Preparations for War, he was certainly aſſured, that
ſome Miſchief was intended: But *Pocahontas* hid him for
a Time, and ſent thoſe, who purſued him, the quite contrary Way. At length, by her Means and extraordinary
Bribes and Trouble, in three Days Travel, he found the
Preſident at *Pamunkey*, in the Midſt of thoſe Broils and
Difficulties. The Preſident, having ſworn him to conceal
this unhappy News from the Company, and diſſembling
his Sorrow with the beſt Countenance, he could, went
ſafely aboard at Night, and left *Opechancanough* at Liberty,
according to his Promiſe, and likewiſe with a Deſign, the
better to entrap *Powhatan* in his Return. Soon after, he went
down the River, having ſearched the Countries of *Youghtanund* (now *Pamunkey* River) and *Mattapony*; where the
poor Creatures imparted the little Corn, they had, with
ſuch Complaints, and Tears from the Eyes of Women and
Children, as fully ſatisfied, and moved them with Compaſſion.

Powhatan had threatened Death to his Men, if they did
not, by ſome Means or other, kill Captain *Smith*. But
they hated fighting with him, almoſt as bad as hanging.
And the Preſident, on his Side, was as eager, to ſurpriſe
and take that ſubtle and perfidious Barbarian. Therefore,
in his Way down the River, there were many Feints and
Stratagems, on both Parts, but without any remarkabl Effect. Only the Preſident, with Mr. *Weſt* and ſome others,
would

would have been poifoned, had their Art been equal to
their Will. It only made them Sick, and fo worked itfelf

off. And thus, through many Dangers and Difficulties,
they returned to *James-Town*; where they delivered, near
200 *lbs.* of Deer's Suet, and 479 Bufhels of Corn, to the
Cape-Merchant.

AT *James-Town* they found nothing done, but their Provifions fpent, and a great Part of their Tools and Arms
conveyed to the *Indians*. But altho' what was left by the
Ship was fo rotten with the Rain, and fo mangled by the
Rats and Worms, that the Hogs would fcarcely eat it, yet
upon cafting up their Store, they found a fufficient Provifion for the Year. Wherefore, the Fear of ftarving being
laid afide, the Company was ranged into proper Divifions,
and fix Hours each Day fpent in Work, the reft in Paf-
time and merry Exercifes. And the Prefident, having called them together, told them: That their late Experience
and Mifery were fufficient to perfuade every one to a prefent Amendment: That they muft not think, that either
his Pains, or the Adventurers Purfes, would for ever maintain them in Sloth and Idlenefs: That he knew, many deferved more Honour, and a better Reward, than was yet
to be had; but that far the greateft Part of them muft be
more induftrious, or ftarve: That it was not reafonable,
that the Labours of thirty or forty honeft and induftrious
Men fhould be confumed, to maintain an hundred and fifty
Loiterers: and, That therefore every one, that would not
work, fhould not eat: That they had often been fcreened
and protected, in their Difobedience to his juft and neceffary
Commands, by the Authority of the Council: But that
now, all being either dead or gone, except Captain *Wynne*
and himfelf, that whole Power refted, in Effect, folely in
him. And therefore, he advifed them, not to feed themfelves up with the vain Prefumption, that his Authority was
but a Shadow, and that his Life muft anfwer for theirs.
For the Letters Patent, and other Powers, would prove
the contrary, and fhould, every Week, be read to them;
and every one, that offended, might affuredly expect his
due Punifhment. He alfo made a Table, as a publick Memorial of each Man's Deferts, to encourage the Good, and
to fpur on the reft by Shame. By this, many became very
induftrious; but more were driven to their Bufinefs, by
Punifhment, and the Prefident's extraordinary Vigor and
Diligence.

As they came down *Pamunkey* (fince called *York* River)
off of *Werowocomoco*, the Prefident had fent Mr. *Chrofbaw*
and Mr. *Ford* to *James-Town*, by Land. In their Way,
they

they met four or five of the *German*'s Confederates, going
to *Powhatan*; who to clear themfelves from thofe Gentle-
mens Sufpicion, that they were running to the *Indians*, returned with them to the Fort, and there continued. But
the *Germans*, to know the Reafon of their Stay, fent one
of their Company, a ftout young Fellow, difguifed like an
Indian, to the Glafs-houfe. This ftood in the Woods,
about a Mile from *James-Town*, and was the common
Place of Rendezvous for all their fecret Villany. The Prefident, hearing of this, immediately fent to apprehend this
German. But he being gone, he difpatched twenty good
Shot after, to intercept him in his Return to *Powhatan*.
They foon brought him back, and notwithftanding his fair
Tale and plaufible Excufes, he was thrown into Prifon.
However the Prefident fpared his Life, hoping thereby to
regain his Countrymen.

CAPTAIN *Smith*, having fent all his Men after the
German, returned from the Glafs-houfe alone, armed only
with a Faucheon. In his Way he met the King of *Pafpahey*, a Man of great Strength and gigantic Stature. At
firft, he endeavoured to draw the Prefident into his Ambufcade; but failing in that, he attempted to fhoot him.
But *Smith*, to prevent it, clofed in and grappled with him.
And the *Indian*, by mere Dint of Strength, bore him into
the River, with a Defign to drown him. Long they ftruggled in the Water, till the Prefident got fuch Hold of his
Throat, that he almoft ftrangled him. And then, having
difengaged himfelf, fo as to draw his Faucheon, the poor
Savage begged his Life, in fuch a pitiful Manner, that he
led him to *James-Town*, and put him into Chains, where
he continued for fome time, till by the Negligence of his
Keepers, he efcaped. Some Endeavours were ufed to re-
take him, but without Effect; only the Prefident took two
Indians Prifoners, *Kemps* and *Tuffore*, the two moft exquifite Villains in all the Country. Thefe Men would have
betrayed both King and Kindred for a Piece of Copper;
and had Captain *Wynne* and Lieutenant *Percy*, who were
fent upon the Bufinefs with fifty Men, followed their Directions, they would certainly have regained the King, and
been fully revenged for the Injury and Affault. However,
that this might not encourage them to farther Boldnefs,
they attacked and flew feveral of the Nation, burnt their
Houfes, took their Canoes and fifhing Weirs, and planted
fome of them at *James-Town*, and were refolved to profecute them with War, till they were fully humbled and
fubdued.

Not

1609.

John Smith Prefident.NOT long after, the Prefident, paffing by *Pafpahey* in his Way to *Chickahominy*, was affaulted by them. But as foon as they knew him, they all threw down their Arms, and fued for Peace. Their Spokefman was a lufty young Fellow, named *Okaning*, whofe Difcourfe well deferves to be remembered. He told the Prefident, that the King, his Mafter, was there prefent in the Company: That they took him for Captain *Wynne*, who purfued them in War, altho' they had never injured him: That if the King offended him in efcaping from Prifon, he ought to confider, that the Fifhes fwim, the Fowls fly, and the very Beafts ftrive to efcape the Snare and live: That therefore, his Mafter, who was a Man, ought not to be blamed, for following this neceffary Inftinct of Nature even in brute Animals. He reminded him of the Pains, his Mafter took, to fave his Life, when a Prifoner; and if he had fince injured him, he was compelled to it, and it had however been already fully revenged, to their too great Lofs. And he further told him, if he ftill perfifted in his Refolution to deftroy them, they muft abandon their Habitation, and fettle fomewhere beyond his Reach; which would only coft them more Labour, but would be of worfe Confequence to the *Englifh*, who could not well fubfift without their Corn and Fruits. And therefore he earneftly entreated him to grant them his Friendfhip, and to permit them to enjoy their Houfes, and plant their Fields, in Peace and Security. Concluding, that if he would promife them Peace, they would truft to his Word; but if he proceeded in his Revenge, they would quit the Country. Whereupon the Prefident promifed them Peace, if they would do no farther Injury, and would bring in Provifions to the Fort. To which they joyfully agreed, and parted good Friends, and fo continued, till *Smith* left the Country.

SOON after this, an *Indian*, who had been imprifoned at *James-Town* for Theft, had fo ftifled himfelf, by a Charcoal Fire in a clofe Room of the Prifon, that he feemed to be dead. But the Prefident, by the Application of Vinegar and *Aqua-vitæ*, brought him to himfelf, which was foon fpread abroad among the *Indians*, throughout the whole Country, as a Miracle; and it was generally believed, that Captain *Smith* could raife a dead Man to Life. And another at *Werowocomoco*, having got a large Bag of Powder, to fhew his extraordinary Skill among his Companions, dried it on the Back of an Armour, as he had feen the Soldiers at *James-Town* do. Many ftood peeping over, to fee his Skill; till at laft it took Fire, and blew him, with one or two more, to Death, and fo fcorched and mangled the reft,

that

that it raifed a vaft Dread and Aftonifhment in them, and
a great Admiration of the Power and Art of the *Englifh.*
Thefe, with fome other Accidents, fo frighted and amazed
Powhatan and his People, that they flocked from all Parts,
and with Prefents defired Peace ; returning many ftolen
Things, which had never been demanded, or thought of, by
the *Englifh.* And ever after, during the Remainder of Capt.
Smith's Adminiftration, both *Powhatan* and his People would
fend back to *James-Town* fuch, as had been taken ftealing, to
receive their Punifhment ; and the whole Country became
as abfolutely free and fafe to the *Englifh*, as to themfelves.

A N D now the Colony purfued their Bufinefs with Alacrity and Succefs. They made three or four Laft of Tar,
Pitch, and Soap-Afhes ; produced a Trial of Glafs ; funk
a Well in the Fort, of excellent Water, which till then
was wanting ; built about twenty Houfes ; new-covered
the Church ; provided Nets and Weirs for fifhing ; and to
ftop the Diforders of the Thieves and *Indians*, they built a
Block-houfe in the Neck of the Ifland, to receive the Trade
of the *Indians* ; and none, neither *Indian* nor Chriftian, was
fuffered to pafs or repafs, without the Prefident's Order.
Thirty or forty Acres of Ground were broke up and planted.
Of three Sows, in eighteen Months, increafed fixty odd
Pigs ; and near five hundred Chickens brought up them-
felves, without having any thing given them. But the
Hogs were tranfported to Hog-Ifland ; where alfo was built
a Block-houfe, with a Garrifon, to give Notice of any
Ships ; and for their Exercife at leifure Times, they made
Clapboard and Wainfcot. In this Time, died Captain
Wynne ; fo that the Government devolved wholly upon the
Prefident, as it had before in Effe&t done, by his having
two Voices in the Council.

B U T this Flow of Plenty and Profperity lafted not long.
For, upon Examination, they found half their Corn rotten,
and the reft confumed by Rats ; which, coming originally
from the Ships, had increafed to incredible Multitudes. So
that all Works were intermitted, and the People fufficiently
employed to get Provifions. But at firft, the *Indians*, to
exprefs their Love, brought in an hundred a Day, at leaft,
of Squirrels, Turkies, Deer, and other wild Beafts ; and
Powhatan fpared them near half his Stock of Corn. But
the Prefident was neverthelefs obliged to detach fixty or
eighty down the River, to live upon Oyfters. Twenty
were fent to the Falls with Mr. *Weft* ; and as many more
with Lieutenant *Percy* to *Point Comfort*, to try for a Fifhery.
But he being very fick, and forely burnt with Gun-powder,
they would not agree in fix Weeks, once to caft out their

Net. Many were billetted among the *Indians*, who knew, that they had fuch a commanding Power at *James-Town*, that they durft not wrong them in the leaft. And in all this Time of Diftrefs, they caught more Sturgeon than could be devoured by Man and Dog. This the induftrious, drying and pounding, would mingle with Caviare, Sorrel, and wholefome Herbs, and make Bread and good Meat. Others would gather as much Tuckahoe Root in a Day, as would make them Bread for a Week. So that, upon thefe wild Products, and what they caught, the deligent lived very well and plentifully.

YET fuch was the infufferable Sloth and unreafonable Perverfenefs of far the greater Number, that they would fooner have perifhed, than have been at the Pains to gather Food. And they were even importunate with the Prefident, to fell their Tools and Iron, nay, their Swords and Firelocks, and their very Houfes and Ordinance, to the *Indians* for this Trafh. And they took Occafion fronrhence, in a very turbulent and clamorous Manner, to infift on the Neceffity of leaving the Country. But the Prefident, having punifhed one of the worft and moft feditious among them, called the reft together, and reprefented to them the extreme Folly and Iniquity of their Proceedings. And he told them, that if any more were found attempting to run away to *Newfoundland* with the Bark, they might affuredly expect the Gallows, as their Fate: That he never had more from the Store than the worft of them; for they well knew and faw, that his extraordinary Allowance, as Prefident, was conftantly diftributed among the Sick: and, That fince he found, Neceffity had not Power to force them to gather the Fruits of the Earth, he was refolved, that they fhould gather, not only for themfelves, but alfo for the Sick; and that whofoever would not gather, every Day, as much, as he himfelf did, fhould, the next Day be fet beyond the River, and banifhed from the Fort, as a Drone. This Order raifed a great Clamour and Outcry; but it made moft of them beftir themfelves fo well, that they had Plenty of Food to eat, and continued very healthy and ftrong. Yet many of them, underftanding, how well they were ufed, that were billetted among the *Indians*, ran away to *Kemps* and *Tuffore*, their old Prifoners. But *Kemps* firft made himfelf Sport with them, fhewing his Countrymen, how he was ufed, when a Prifoner, and feeding them upon this Condition, that they, who would not work, fhould not eat; and then he carried them back, by Force, to the Prefident.

THIS deterred many others, who intended to follow; and made them content, rather to labour at home, than venture

among

For the Kings, and better Sort of that
People, were fo afraid, or fo friendly, that when the *En-*
glifh punifhed fome of their bafer Sort with great Severity,
they would hire them, not to tell it to their Kings or
Countrymen; left they fhould punifh them again, and fend
them to *James-Town,* to give full Satisfaction to the Prefident.

ABOUT this time, Mr. *Sicklemore* returned from *Cha-*
wonock; but without any Information of Sir *Walter Ralegh*'s
loft Company, or fatisfactory Account of the Silk-grafs.
And the Prefident, to purfue a Point, thought fo neceffary
by the Council in *England,* fent off Mr. *Nathaniel Powel*
and *Anas Todkill,* to the *Mangoags,* a Nation of *Indians,*
not fubject to *Powhatan,* dwelling on the upper Branches
of *Nottoway,* or fome fmall Streams of *Roanoke* River. He
obtained Guides from the King of the *Quiyoughquohanocks,*
a fmall Nation of *Indians,* feated on the *South* Side of *James*
River, about ten Miles above *James-Town.* This good
King did ever affect the *Englifh* above all others; and altho' he was very zealous to his falfe Gods, yet he confeffed, that the *Englifh* God as much exceeded his, as their
Guns did his Bow and Arrows; and in Time of Drought,
he would often fend Prefents to Captain *Smith,* to pray
to his God for Rain. His Guides conducted *Powel* and
Todkill, three Days Journey, into a high Country, towards
the *South-Weft*; where they faw, here and there, a Corn-
field, by fome little Spring or fmall Brook, but no large
River. The People were, in all Refpects, like the reft,
except their Language. They lived chiefly by hunting, and
on Fruits and Roots; and they trafficked their Skins with
thofe towards the Sea and fatter Countries, for dried Fifh
and Corn. But neither did they here, or ever after, hear
any thing of this Colony, left by Mr. *White,* in the Year
1587, on one of the Iflands of *Hatteras.*

ALL this while, they employed one *William Volday,* a
Zwitzer, by Promifes and Pardons to reclaim his Countrymen, the *Germans,* and one *Bentley,* another Fugitive. But
this vile Hypocrite, pretending highly to deteft their Villany, hereby got an Opportunity, to convey them every
thing, they wanted, to effect their Projects, and deftroy
the Colony. With much Devotion they looked for the
Spaniard, to whom they were willing and intended to do
good Service. And finding, the *Englifh* were obliged to
difperfe themfelves to gather Food, they importuned *Pow-*
hatan to lend them his Forces; and they undertook, not
only to deftroy the Hogs, fire the Town, and feize on the
Bark, but to bring moft of the Colony to his Service and
Subjection. This Scheme was communicated to many of
their Confederates at the Fort; but two, whofe Hearts re-
lented

lented at the Horror of the Act, revealed it to the Prefident. He ordered them to keep it ftill a Secret, and to
draw them into fuch Ambufcades, as he had prepared.
But the thing taking Air, and coming to the Ears of the
impatient Multitude, they were outrageous to go and deftroy them immediately. Lieutenant *Percy* and Mr. *John*
Codrington, two Gentlemen of high and refolute Spirits,
offered their Service, to go to *Werowocomoco*, and to cut
their Throats before the Face of *Powhatan*. But the Prefident cared not to hazard fuch Perfons, for whom he had
other Employment; and gave Way to Mr. *Wyffin* and Serjeant *Jeffery Abbot*, to undertake the Matter. But the
Germans fo blinded *Abbot*, with a fair Tale, that he relent-
ed; and *Wyffin*, tho' willing, cared not to attempt it alone.
When *Powhatan* underftood their Bufinefs, he fent immediately to the Prefident, to inform him, that he neither detained them, nor hindered his Men from executing his
Command. For he neither did, nor would, maintain them,
or any other, to his Difpleafure. But altho' thefe treacherous Foreigners did all, they could, to raife and incenfe
Powhatan and the *Indians* againft the *Englifh*, yet fuch exact Intelligence had Captain *Smith* of their Plots, that their
Machinations were his greateft Advantage and Security.
And if any Commotion had happened, he always had it in
his Power to take Revenge. For all the Country now ftood
more in Fear of him, than of *Powhatan*; and he had fuch
Parties among the bordering Nations, that, out of Love or
Fear, they would have done any thing, he commanded.
However, not long after, one of the *Germans* returned to
his Duty; but the other ftill remained with *Powhatan*.

WHILST thefe things were paffing, Captain *Samuel Ar-*
gall arrived, who was afterwards an active Perfon here,
and a noted Governor of the Country. He came to truck
with the Colony, and to fifh for Sturgeon, with a Ship
well furnifhed with Wine and other good Provifion. This
was, at that Time, a prohibited Trade; but he being a
Kinfman to Sir *Thomas Smith*, the Treafurer, it was con-
nived at and overlooked. The Neceffities of the Colony
obliged them to take his Provifions, by which his Voyage
was loft; but they revictualled him, when their next Supply arrived, and fent him to *England* with a full Account of
the State of their Affairs. By this Ship, they received Letters, which taxed the Prefident for his hard Ufage of the
Natives, and for not returning the Ships freighted. And
now alfo, they firft had an Account of the Alterations in
England, and of the great Preparations and large Supply,
to be fent by the Lord *Delawarr*, appointed Captain-General and Governor in Chief of *Virginia*.

THE

THE

HISTORY

OF

VIRGINIA.

BOOK III.

T HE Treafurer, Council, and Company in *England*, were ftill intent upon prefent Gain, and gaping after the Mines of *Mexico* and *Peru* from their Difcovery; and upon the laft Voyage, not finding that Profit and Return, they expeded, they were much difappointed and enraged. To this was added *Newport's* Account of things, which was certainly not very favourable to their Condud and Management in *Virginia*. The Company therefore made Intereft to his Majefty, to grant them a new Charter, which bears Date the 23d of *May* 1609, and contains larger Powers and more ample Privileges, than the former; as may be feen in the Original, printed at large in the Appendix. By this Charter the Power and Authority of the Prefident and Council in *Virginia* were exprefly abrogated; and they were ftreightly commanded, upon their Allegiance, to pay Obedience to fuch Governor or Governors, as fhould be appointed by the Council in *England*. In Confequence of which Power, the Council conftituted Sir *Thomas Weft*, Lord *Delawarr*, Captain-General of *Virginia*; Sir *Thomas Gates*, his Lieutenant-General; Sir *George Somers*, Admiral; Captain *Newport*, Vice-Admiral; Sir *Thomas Dale*, High-Marfhal; Sir *Ferdinando Wainman*, General of the Horfe; and fo, many other Offices, to feveral worthy Gentlemen, for their Lives.

H 3 THIS

THIS new Charter was granted to the Earls of *Salif-bury*, *Suffolk*, *Southampton*, *Pembroke*, and other Peers, to the Number of twenty one; to the Honourable *George Percy* and *Francis Weft*, Efqrs; to Sir *Humphrey Weld*, Lord Mayor of *London*, and ninety eight other Knights, ex-prefly named; and to Dr. *Matthew Sutcliffe*, with a great Multitude more, of Doctors, Efquires, Gentlemen, Officers, Merchants, and Citizens, together with many Corporations and Companies of *London*. So many Perfons of great Power, Intereft, and Fortune, engaging in the En-terprize, and the Lord *Delawarr*, with the other Gentle-men of Diftinction, appointed to the feveral Offices, foon drew in fuch large Sums of Money, that they difpatched away Sir *Thomas Gates*, Sir *George Somers*, and Captain *Newport*, with nine Ships, and five hundred People. Thefe three Gentlemen had, each of them, a Commiffion who firft arrived, to call in the old. But becaufe they could not agree for Place, it was concluded, that they fhould all go in one Ship, called the *Sea-Venture*. They failed from *England*, the latter End of *May* 1609; but the 25th of *July*, the Admiral-Ship was parted from the reft of the Fleet, by the Tail of a Hurricane, having on board the three Com-manders, an hundred and fifty Men, their new Commif-fion, and Bills of Lading, together with all Manner of In-ftructions and Directions, and the beft Part of their Provi-fions. She arrived not, but was foundered on *Bermudas*, as fhall be hereafter related. A fmall Catch likewife perifh-ed in the Hurricane; but the feven other Ships came fafe. In them, as Captains, came *Ratcliffe* (whofe right Name, as is faid, was *Sicklemore*) *Martin*, and *Archer*, with Cap-tain *Wood*, Captain *Webbe*, Captain *Moon*, Captain *King*, Captain *Davies*, Mr. *Ralph Hamer*, and divers other Gen tlemen, of good Fortune, and eminent Birth. The Prefi dent, being informed by his Scouts of the Arrival of th Fleet, little dreamed of fuch a Supply, but fuppofed then at firft, to be *Spaniards*. He therefore put himfelf into tl beft Pofture of Defence, he could; and being feconded the *Indians* (who, upon this Occafion, fhewed their Frien fhip, and prepared, with great Alacrity, to affift the *E glifh* with their utmoft Power) they thought themfelves well provided for the Reception of an Enemy, that tl little feared their Coming.

Ratcliffe, *Martin*, and *Archer*, had bred much Dif bance at Sea, and had paved the Way, for being even n troublefome afhore. For they had infufed fuch Jealo and Prejudices into the Company againft Captain *Sr* that they mortally hated him, before they had ever

him. But feveral of better Senfe and Experience among
them, from their firft landing, hearing the general good
Report of his old Soldiers, and feeing the Prudence and Uprightnefs of his Actions, were foon undeceived, and faw
into the Malice of *Ratcliffe* and his Faction. They therefore left their Society, and ever adhered to Captain *Smith*,
as his firm and faithful Friends. But a great Part of this
new Company confifted of unruly Sparks, packed off by
their Friends, to efcape worfe Deftinies at home. And the
reft were chiefly made up of poor Gentlemen, broken
Tradefmen, Rakes and Libertines, Footmen, and fuch
others, as were much fitter to fpoil or ruin a Commonwealth, than to help to raife or maintain one. This lewd
Company therefore were led by their feditious Captains,
into many Mifchiefs and Extravagancies. They affumed
to themfelves the Power of difpofing of the Government;
and conferred it fometimes on one, and fometimes on another. To-day, the old Commiffion muft rule; To-morrow,
the new; and next Day, neither. So that, all was Anar-
chy and Diftraction; neither were there any Hopes, from
the prefent Pofture of Affairs, but of the utmoft Mifery
and Confufion.

THE *German* alfo, that had returned to the *Englifh*,
feeing this diftracted State of things, and hoping for fome
Advantage from it, fled again, with one of his Conforts,
to *Powhatan*; to whom he promifed Wonders, at the Arrival of Lord *Delawarr*. But that fenfible Barbarian,
knowing the Wickednefs and Perfidy of their Nature, replied; That they, who would have betrayed Captain
Smith to him, would certainly betray him to this great
Lord, to make their Peace. And fo, he ordered his Men,
to beat out their Brains. But *Volday*, the *Zwitzer*, made
a fhift to get to *England*; where purfuading the Merchants,
what rich Mines he had found, and what Services he would
do them, he was well rewarded, and fent back with the
Lord *Delawarr*. But being found a mere Impoftor, he died
in a moft contemned and miferable Manner.

CAPTAIN *Smith*, all this Time of Turbulency and
Diftraction, was fadly troubled and perplexed, how to proceed. At firft, finding his Authority thus unexpectedly
cancelled and changed, he refolved to leave all, and return
for *England*. But afterwards, feeing, there was little Hope
of the Arrival of this new Commiffion, and that his own
was not legally fuperfeded, but by the actual Production of
another, he determined to bear up, and to act with Vigor
and Refolution. He therefore fet himfelf, with great Courage, and the perpetual Hazard of his Life, to oppofe this

Tor-

rent of Faction and Immorality; and at laft, fo far
ed it, that he caft *Ratcliffe*, *Archer*, and the other
into Prifon, till he had more Leifure, to bring the
fair and legal Trial. And the better to diffipate t
mours, and to break their Confederacies, he fent Mr
with an hundred and twenty, the beft, he could cl
make a Settlement at the Falls; and *Martin*, with r
fame Number, to *Nanfamond*; allowing each their d
portion of all the Provifions, according to their N
And now the Year of his Prefidency being near expi
made Captain *Martin*, who was become more tr:
Prefident in his Room. But *Martin*, knowing his o
fufficiency, and the People's Unrulinefs and little
for him, within three Hours, refigned it again to (
Smith. For as *Ratcliffe* had been removed from the
cil, and was not again reftored, *Martin* and *Smith* w
only two then in the Country, that could either elec
elected Prefident. And *Martin*, having thus wifel
gaged himfelf from an Office, which he was then n
able to execute or fupport, proceeded to make his
ment at *Nanfamond*. That Nation, having been red
Subjection and Contribution, ufed him kindly; y(
were his unreafonable Jealoufy and Fear, that he furpr
poor naked King, and his Monuments and Houfe
the Ifland, wherein he lived, and there fortified l
But the *Indians*, foon perceiving his Fear and Diftr
ventured to affault him; and they killed feveral of hi
releafed their King, and gathered and carried off a tl
Bufhels of Corn; whilft he, in the mean while, nev
offered to intercept them, but fent to the Prefider
at the Falls, for thirty Soldiers. Thefe were prefen
him, from *James-Town*. But he fo employed the
they did nothing, and foon returned, complaining
Tendernefs and Cowardice. And he likewife, leav
Company to their Fortunes, came away with tl
James-Town.

THE Prefident followed the other Company up
Falls, to fee them well feated. But he was furpri
his Way, to meet Captain *Weft*, fo foon returning to
Town; and he found the Settlement very inconfid
made, in a Place, not only liable to the River's Inun
but alfo fubject to many other intolerable Inconven
To remedy which, he immediately fent to *Powha*
purchafe the Place, called *Powhatan*. The Condit
their Agreement were thefe: That the *Englifh* fhot
fend him againft the *Manakins*: That he fhould re
them the Fort and the Houfes, with all that Country

Proportion of Copper: That all Thieves fhould be fent
thither, to receive their Punifhment: That every Houfe,
as a Cuftom, fhould pay the Prefident a Bufhel of Corn,
for an Inch fquare of Copper, and a certain Quantity of
Pocones to King *James*, for their Protection: and, That
they fhould barter, what elfe they could fpare, at their beft
Difcretion.   But Captain *Weft's* Company depended fo
much on the Lord General's new Commiffion, that they
regarded no Perfon or thing.   And fuppofing the *Manakins*' Country reached to the *South-Sea*, and was all Gold,
they pleafed themfelves with the vain Conceit, that it was
entirely under their Power and Command, and that none
fhould go thither, but whom they pleafed.   They therefore
rejected the Prefident with Infolence and Contempt.   However he ventured, with five Men, to land among them;
and committed the Heads of the Mutiny to Prifon, till, by
their Numbers, they obliged him to retire.   In making off,
he happily furprifed one of their Boats, with which he returned to the Ship; and had not the Mariners proved very
tractable and faithful to him, he had fmall Means and little
Probability of efcaping their Fury.

THE *Indians* alfo came to him; complaining, that he
had brought them, for Protectors, worfe Enemies, than
the *Manakins* themfelves; that they ftole their Corn, robbed their Gardens, broke open their Houfes, beat them,
and kept feveral in Prifon; and that, till then, they had
borne all this, out of Love to him, but defired Pardon, if
hereafter they defended themfelves.   They likewife offered
him their Affiftance, and to fight for him againft them, if
he would lead them on.   But having fpent nine Days, to
no Purpofe, in endeavouring to reclaim them, he departed
for *James-Town*.   The Ship was no fooner under Sail, but
twelve *Indians* affaulted thofe hundred and twenty in their
Fort.   And finding many ftraggling abroad in the Woods,
they killed fome, and fo frighted the reft, that their Countrymen in Prifon efcaped, and they went fafely off, with
the Swords and Cloaks of thofe, they had flain.   But before
the Ship had failed half a League, fhe grounded; which
gave the Prefident an Opportunity of fummoning them,
once more, to a Parley.   And now he found them fo
amazed with that filly Affault of the *Indians*, that they
furrendered themfelves, upon any Terms, to his Mercy.
He therefore laid fix or feven of the chief Offenders by the
Heels; and feated the reft at *Powhatan*, the ftrongeft and
moft pleafant Place, he had feen in the Country; and for
that Reafon, they called it *Nonfuch*.   Here they had dry
Houfes for Lodgings, near two hundred Acres of Land,

cleared

cleared and ready for planting, with a Savage Fort, ready built, and prettily fortified with Poles and Barks of Trees, and fufficient to have defended them againft all the *Indians* in the Country. He likewife appeafed the *Indians*, making Reftitution and Satisfaction, to each Party, for their former Loffes and Damages.

AND now, new Officers being appointed, and the Prefident ready to depart, juft at that Inftant arrived Captain *Weft*; whofe gentle Nature was fo wrought on and abufed, by Compaffion for the Prifoners, and the Perfuafions of the Mutineers, who alledged, they had only done this for his Honour, that all things were again thrown into Confufion and Mutiny. But the Prefident, having no Inclination to contend with Mr. *Weft*, and little Power to curb their Infolence, left them to their Fortunes, and returned to *James-Town*. And foon after they abandoned *Nonfuch*, and went back to their firft Settlement at *Weft's-Fort*.

BUT paffing down the River, as Captain *Smith* was afleep in the Boat, his Powder-bag, by fome Accident, was fired; which tore the Flefh from his Body and Thighs, nine or ten Inches fquare, in a moft dreadful Manner. To quench the Fire, which fryed and tormented him in his Cloaths, he leaped overboard, and was almoft drowned, before they could recover him. In this piteous State, he arrived at *James-Town*; where *Ratcliffe*, *Archer*, and the reft of their Confederates, were foon to come to the Trials. But their guilty Confciences mifgiving them, and feeing the Prefident unable to ftand, and almoft bereft his Senfes by reafon of his Torment, they entered into Confpiracy to Murder him in his Bed. But his Heart failed him, who was to have given Fire to the Piftol. And being difappointed in this Purpofe, they joined together, ufurp the Government, and thereby efcape their Punifhment. In the mean time, the Prefident's old Soldiers, being provoked, beyond all Patience, at their Malice and Sedition, flocked to him, and importuned him to give them but the Word, and they would fetch the Heads of the beft among them, that durft refift his Commands. Yet he would not fuffer them to bring the Matter to a civil Broil, but fent immediately for the Mafters of the Ships, and took Order with them for his Return to *England*. For there was neither Chirurgeon nor Chirurgery at the Fort, his Wounds were fo grievous, and Torments fo cruel, few expected, he could live. And he likewife highly refented, and was much chagrined, to fee his Authority oppreffed, he knew not why; himfelf and his Soldiers ill rewarded for their paft Labours and Dangers, he knew

how; and a new Commiſſion granted, to they knew not
whom.   And beſides, he found himſelf unable to follow his
Buſineſs, ſuppreſs thoſe Factions, and range the Country
for Proviſions, as he before intended.   And he well knew,
that his own Preſence and Activity were as requiſite in thoſe
Affairs, as his Advice and Directions.   For all which Reaſons, he reſolved upon leaving the Country, and went preſently on board one of the Ships.

CAPTAIN *Percy* had been, for ſome time, in a very
bad State of Health, and had taken his Paſſage in one of the
Ships, to go to *England*.   But now, upon *Smith*'s Departure, many came about him, and by Intreaties and Perſuaſions, prevailed with him to ſtay, and take upon him the
Government.   But there were many others up in Arms,
calling themſelves Preſidents and Counſellors; ſeveral of
which began now to fawn upon and ſollicite *Smith*, to give
up his Commiſſion to them.   And after much ado, and
many bitter Repulſes, that their Ruin and Confuſion might
not be attributed to him, for leaving the Country without
a Commiſſion, he permitted it to be ſtolen, but never could
be induced to reſign it into ſuch vile Hands.   In which he
ſeems to have been ſomething froward and peeviſh.   For
ſince the old Soldiers, and better Sort of new Comers, had
generally agreed upon Captain *Percy* for their Governor, a
Perſon every way fit for the Office, except in Point of
Health, it would have been but reaſonable in him, to have
endeavoured to confirm him in his Authority, and when
he departed, to have delivered up his Commiſſion to him.·

AND thus, about *Michaelmas* 1609, Captain *Smith* left
the Country, never again to ſee it.   He left behind him
three Ships and ſeven Boats; Commodities ready for Trade;
the Corn newly gathered; ten Weeks Proviſion in the
Store; four hundred ninety and odd Perſons; twenty four
Pieces of Ordinance; three hundred Muſkets, with other
Arms and Ammunition, more than ſufficient for the Men;
the *Indians*, their Language, and Habitations, well known
to an hundred trained and expert Soldiers; Nets for fiſhing;
Tools, of all Sorts, to work; Apparel, to ſupply their
Wants; ſix Mares and a Horſe; five or ſix hundred Hogs;
as many Hens and Chickens; with ſome Goats, and ſome
Sheep.   For whatever had been brought, or bred here, ſtill
remained.   But this ſeditious and diſtracted Rabble, regarding not any thing, but from Hand to Mouth, riotouſly
conſumed, what there was; and took Care for nothing,
but to colour and make out ſome Complaints againſt Captain *Smith*.   For this End, the Ships were ſtaid three
Weeks, at a great Charge, till they could produce and
bring

1609.
John Smith Preſident.

The Hon. *George Percy* Eſq; Governor.

1609.
The Hon.
George Percy
Efq; Gover-
nor.

. + +

bring them to bear. But, notwithstanding their perverse
Humours and unreasonable Clamours, Captain *Smith* was
undoubtedly a Person of a very great and generous Way of
thinking, and full of a high Idea of the publick Good and
his Country's Honour. To his Vigor, Industry, and undaunted Spirit and Resolution, the Establishment and firm
Settlement of this Colony was certainly owing; and therefore it may not be unacceptable to the Reader, to have
some farther Account of his Person and Actions. And this
we are enabled to do the more authenticly, as he hath himself, at the Request of Sir *Robert Cotton*, the famous Antiquarian, left a brief Relation of his principal Travels and
Adventures.

He was born a Gentleman, to a competent Fortune, at
Willoughby in *Lincolnshire*, in the Year 1579. From his
very Childhood, he had a roving and romantic Fancy, and
was strangely set upon performing some brave and adventurous Atchievement. Accordingly, being about thirteen
Years of Age at School, he sold his Satchel and Books, and
all, he had, to raise Money, in order to go secretly beyond
Sea. But his Father dying just at that Time, he was stopped for the present, and fell into the Hands of Guardians,
more intent on improving his Estate, than him. However,
at fifteen, in the Year 1594, he was bound to a Merchant
at *Lynne*, the most considerable Trader in those Parts.
But because he would not send him immediately to Sea, he
found Means, in the Train of Mr. *Peregrine Berty*, second
Son to the Lord *Willoughby*, to pass into *France*. Here
and in the Low-Countries, he first learnt the Rudiments c
War; to which Profession he was led, by a strong Proper
sity of Genius. He was afterwards carried into *Scotlan*
with delusive Hopes, from a *Scottish* Gentleman, of bei
effectually recommended to King *James*. But soon fin
ing himself baffled in his Expectations, he returned to *W*
loughby, his native Place; where meeting with no Comp
ny, agreeable to his Way of thinking, he retired into
Wood, at a good Distance from any Town, and th
built himself a Pavilion of Boughs, and was wholly e
ployed, in studying some Treatises of the Art of W
and in the Exercise of his Horse and Lance. But
Friends, being concerned at such a whimsical Turr
Mind, prevailed with an *Italian* Gentleman, Rider to
Earl of *Lincoln*, to insinuate himself into his Acquaintar
and as he was an expert Horseman, and his Talent and
dies lay the same Way with Mr. *Smith*'s, he drew him
his sylvan Retirement, to spend some time with hir
Tatterfall.

BUT *Smith*'s reftlefs Genius foon hurried him again into *Flanders*; where lamenting to fee fuch Effufion of Chriftian Blood, he refolved to try his Fortune againft the *Turks*. In order to this, he paffed through *France*, with Variety of Adventure and Misfortune, in which he always fhewed a high and martial Spirit. At *Marfeilles* he embarked for *Italy*. But the Ship meeting with much foul Weather, a Rabble of Pilgrims, on board, hourly curfed him for a Hugonot, railed at Queen *Elizabeth* and his whole Nation, and fwore, they fhould never have fair Weather, as long as he was in the Ship. At laft, the Paffions of thefe pious Chriftians rofe fo high, that they threw him overboard; trufting, we may fuppofe, in the Merit and Supererogation of that holy Pilgrimage, to expiate the trifling Offence and Peccadillo of Murder. However, *Smith*, by the Divine Affiftance, got fafe to a fmall uninhabited Ifland, againft *Nice* in *Savoy*. From thence he was, the next Day, taken off by a *French* Rover, who treated him very kindly, and with whom he therefore made the Tour of the whole *Mediterranean*, both on the *Mahometan* and the Chriftian Coafts. At length, after a defperate Battle, having taken a very rich *Venetian* Ship, the generous *Frenchman* fet him afhore, with his Share of the Prize; amounting to five hundred Sequeens in Specie, and a Box of rich Commodities, worth near as much more. And now out of Curiofity ranging all the Regions and Principalities of *Italy*, he at laft went to *Vienna*, and entered himfelf a Gentleman Volunteer, in Count *Meldritch*'s Regiment, againft the *Turk*.

HE had not been long in the Chriftian Army, before he was diftinguifhed for a Man of great perfonal Bravery; and in the Sieges of *Olumpagh* and *Alba-Regalis*, he was the Author of fome Stratagems, which fhewed a happy Talent for War, and did fignal Service to the Chriftian Caufe. He was thereupon immediately advanced to the Command of a Troop of Horfe; and was, foon after, made Serjeant Major of the Regiment, a Poft, at that Time, next to the Lieutenant Colonel. But Count *Meldritch*, a *Tranfilvanian* Nobleman by Birth, afterwards paffed with his Regiment, out of the Imperial Service, into that of his natural Prince, *Sigifmond Bathori*, Duke of *Tranfilvania*. And here, endeavouring to recover fome patrimonial Lordfhips, then in the Poffeffion of the *Turk*, he laid Siege to a ftrong Town, chiefly inhabited by Renegados and Banditti. Whilft their Works were advancing flowly, and with great Difficulty, a *Turkifh* Officer iffued forth of the Town, and challenged any Chriftian, of the Dignity of a Captain, to a fingle Combat. Many were eager of the Honour of humbling
this

this haughty Muffelman ; but it was at laft decided, by Lot,
in Favour of Captain *Smith*. Accordingly, the Ramparts
of the Town being filled with fair Dames and Men in Arms,
and the Chriftian Army drawn up. in Battalia, the Comba-
tants entered the Field, well mounted and richly armed, to
the Sound of Hautboys and Trumpets ; where, at the firft
Encounter, *Smith* bore the *Turk* dead to the Ground, and
went off triumphantly with his Head.   But the Infidel Garrifon being enraged at this, he afterwards engaged two o-
ther Officers ; and being a great Mafter of his Arms, and
the Management of his Horfe, he carried off their Heads,
in the fame Manner.   After which, being attended with a
Guard of fix thoufand Men, with the three *Turkifh* Horfes
led before him, and before each a *Turk*'s Head upon a
Spear, he was conducted to the General's Pavilion ; who
received him with open Arms, and prefented him with a
fine Horfe, richly caparifoned, and with a Scimitar and
Belt, worth three hundred Ducats.   Soon after, the Duke
himfelf, coming to view his Army, gave him his Picture,
fet in Gold ; fettled three hundred Ducats upon him, as a
Yearly Penfion ; and iffued his Letters patent of Nobleffe,
giving him three *Turks* Heads, in a Shield, for his Arms ;
which Coat he ever afterwards bore, and it was admitted
and recorded in the Herald's Office in *England*, by Sir *William Segar*, Garter, principal King at Arms.

B U T foon after, the Duke of *Tranfilvania* was deprive
of his Dominions by the Emperor ; and *Smith*, at the fat;
Battle of *Rottenton*, in the Year 1602, was left upon th
Field, among the dreadful Carnage of Chriftians, as dea
But the Pillagers, perceiving Life in him, and judging l
the Richnefs of his Habit and Armour, that his Ranfc
might be confiderable, took great Pains to recover hi
After that, he was publickly fold, among the other Pri
ners ; and was bought by a Bafhaw, who fent him to C
ftantinople, as a Prefent to his Miftrefs, *Charatza Tra
bigzanda*, a beautiful young *Tartarian* Lady.   *Smith*
then twenty three Years of Age, in the Bloom of l
and, as it feems, of a very handfome Perfon.   F o r
young Lady was fo moved with Compaffion, or ra
Love, for him, that fhe treated him with the utmoft ¯
dernefs and Regard.   And to prevent his being ill ufe
fold, by her Mother, fhe fent him into *Tartary*, tc
Brother, who was Timor Bafhaw of *Nalbrits*, on th
lus Mæotis.   Here, fhe intended, he fhould ftay, to
the Language, together with the Manners and Religi
the *Turks*, till Time fhould make her Miftrefs of herf

BUT the Bafhaw, fufpecting fomething of the Matter, from the affectionate Expreffions, with which fhe recommended and preffed his good Ufage, only treated *Smith* with the greater Cruelty and Inhumanity. *Smith*'s high Spirit, raifed alfo by a Confcioufnefs of *Tragabigzanda*'s Paffion, could but ill brook this harfh Treatment. At laft, being one Day threfhing alone, at a Grange above a League from the Houfe, the Timor came, and took Occafion, fo to kick, fpurn, and revile him, that forgetting all Reafon, *Smith* beat out his Brains, with his threfhing Bat. Then reflecting upon his defperate State, he hid the Body under the Straw, filled his Knapfack with Corn, put on the Timor's Cloaths, and mounting his Horfe, fled into the Deferts of *Circaffia*. After two or three Days fearful Wandering, he happened, providentially, on the Caftragan, or great Road, that leads into *Mufcovy*. Following this, for fixteen Days, with infinite Dread and Fatigue, he at laft arrived at a *Mufcovite* Garrifon, on the Frontiers. Here he was kindly entertained and prefented, as alfo at all the Places, through which he paffed. Having travelled through *Siberia*, *Mufcovy*, *Tranfilvania*, and the Midft of *Europe*, he at length found his old Friend and gracious Patron, the Duke of *Tranfilvania*, at *Leipfick*, together with Count *Meldritch*, his Colonel. Having fpent fome time with them, the Duke, at his Departure, gave him a Pafs, intimating the Services, he had done, and the Honours, he had received; prefenting him, at the fame Time, with fifteen hundred Ducats of Gold, to repair his Loffes. And altho' he was now intent on returning to his native Country, yet being furnifhed with this Money, he fpent fome time, in travelling through the principal Cities and Provinces of *Germany*, *France*, and *Spain*. From the laft, being led by the Rumour of Wars, he paffed over into *Africa*, and vifited the Court of *Morocco*. Having viewed many of the Places and Curiofities of *Barbary*, he at laft returned, through *France*, to *England*; and in his Paffage in a *French* Galley, they had a moft defperate Engagement, for two or three Days together, with two *Spanifh* Men of War. In *England*, all things were ftill, and in the moft profound Peace; fo that, there was no Room or Profpect for a Perfon of his active and warlike Genius. And therefore, having fpent fome time, in an idle and uneafy State, he willingly embarked himfelf with Captain *Gofnold*, in the Project of fettling Colonies in *America*, and came to *Virginia*.

HIS Conduct here hath been fufficiently related; and I fhall finifh his Character, with the Teftimonies of fome of his Soldiers and Fellow-Adventurers. They own him to
have

have made Juftice his firft Guide, and Experience his fecond : That he was ever fruitful in Expedients, to provide
for the People under his Command, whom he would never
fuffer to want any thing, he either had, or could procure:
That he rather chofe to lead, than fend his Soldiers into
Danger ; and upon all hazardous or fatiguing Expeditions,
always fhared every thing equally with his Company, and
never defired any of them, to do or undergo any thing, that
he was not ready, to do or undergo himfelf : That he hated
Bafenefs, Sloth, Pride, and Indignity, more than any Danger : That he would fuffer Want, rather than borrow;
and ftarve, fooner than not pay : That he loved Action,
more than Words ; and hated Falfhood and Covetoufnefs,
worfe than Death : and, That his Adventures gave Life and
Subfiftency to the Colony, and his Lofs was their Ruin and
Deftruction.   They confefs, that there were many Captains in that Age (as there are indeed in all Ages) who were
no Soldiers ; but that Captain *Smith* was a Soldier, of the
true old *Englifh* Stamp, who fought, not for Gain or
empty Praife, but for his Country's Honour and the publick Good : That his Wit, Courage, and Succefs here,
were worthy of eternal Memory : That by the mere Force
of his Virtue and Courage, he awed the *Indian* Kings, and
made them fubmit, and bring Prefents : That, notwithftanding fuch a ftern and invincible Refolution, there wa:
feldom feen a milder and more tender Heart, than his was
That he had nothing in him counterfeit or fly, but wa
open, honeft, and fincere : and, That they never knew
Soldier, before him, fo free from thofe military Vices, ‹
Wine, Tobacco, Debts, Dice, and Oaths.

FROM this Account of Captain *Smith*, extracted fro
his own Writings and the Teftimony of his Contempoi
ries and Acquaintance, it will be eafily feen, that he w
a Soldier of Fortune, who had run through great Vari‹
of Life and Adventure.   And indeed he was fo famous
this in his own Age, that he lived to fee himfelf brou
upon the Stage, and the chief Dangers, and moft inter
ing Paffages of his Life, racked, as he complains, and ı
reprefented in low Tragedies.   I cannot therefore for'
tranfiently obferving *Oldmixon*'s Miftake, who fays,
the Company took him into their Service, becaufe he
a noted Seaman, and famed for his Experience in mari
Affairs.   But to remark all the Errors of our Hiftoi
but moft efpecially of *Oldmixon*, the weakeft, moft
and erroneous of all others, would be an infinite V
and too often interrupt and break the Thread of my
ration.   I hope therefore, the courteous Reader will

tisfied with this ſhort Caution and Animadverſion, once for
all. For to ſpeak the Truth ingenuouſly, I had rather
find out and correct one Miſtake in my own, than expoſe
and ridicule twenty Blunders in the Hiſtories of others. But
to return to the Affairs of *Virginia*.

I T hath been before ſaid, that the Admiral-Ship, with
Sir *Thomas Gates*, Sir *George Somers*, and Captain *Newport*
on board, was ſeparated from the reſt of the Fleet in a Storm.
She was ſo racked and torn by the violent Working of the
Sea, and became ſo ſhattered and leaky, that the Water
roſe in the Hold above two Tire of Hogſheads; and they
were obliged to ſtand up to their Middles, with Kettles,
Buckets, and other Veſſels, to bail it out. And thus they
bailed and pumped, three Days and Nights, without Inter-
miſſion; and yet the Water ſeemed rather to gain upon
them, than decreaſe. At laſt, all being utterly ſpent with
Labour, and ſeeing no Hope, in Man's Apprehenſion, but
of preſently ſinking, they reſolved to ſhut up the Hatches,
and to commit themſelves to the Mercy of the Sea and
God's good Providence. In this dangerous and deſperate
State, ſome, who had good and comfortable Waters, fetched
them, and drank to one another, as taking their laſt Leaves,
till a more happy and joyful Meeting in the other World.
But it pleaſed God, in his moſt gracious Providence, ſo to
guide their Ship, to her beſt Advantage, that they were
all preſerved, and came ſafe to Shore.

F O R Sir *George Somers* had ſat, all this Time, upon the
Poop, ſcarce allowing himſelf Leiſure, either to eat or
ſleep, cunning the Ship, and keeping her upright, or ſhe
muſt, otherwiſe, long before this, have foundered. As
he there ſat, looking wiſhfully about, he moſt happily and
unexpectedly deſcried Land. This welcome News, as if
it had been a Voice from Heaven, hurried them all above
Hatches, to ſee, what they could ſcarce believe. But thereby, improvidently forſaking their Work, they gave ſuch an
Advantage to their greedy Enemy, the Sea, that they were
very nigh being ſwallowed up. But none were now to be
urged, to do his beſt. Altho' they knew it to be *Bermudas*, a Place then dreaded and ſhunned by all Men, yet
they ſpread all the Sail, and did every thing elſe, in their
Power, tô reach the Land. It was not long, before the
Ship ſtruck upon a Rock; but a Surge of the Sea caſt her
from thence, and ſo from one to another, till ſhe was moſt
luckily thrown up between two, as upright, as if ſhe had
been on the Stocks. And now the Danger was, leſt the
Billows, overtaking her, ſhould, in an Inſtant, have daſhed
and ſhivered her to Pieces. But all on a ſudden, the Wind

John Smith Preſident.

17   I   lay,

1609.   lay, and gave Place to a Calm; and the Sea became so
        peaceable and still, that, with the greatest Conveniency and
John Smith Ease, they unshipped all their Goods, Victuals, and Peo-
President. ple, and in their Boats, with extreme Joy, almost to A-
        mazement, arrived in Safety, without the Loss of a Man,
        altho' more than a League from the Shore.

        How these Islands came by the Name of *Bermudas*, is
not certainly agreed. Some say, that they were so named
after *John Bermudaz*, a *Spaniard*, who first discovered them,
about the Year 1522. Others report, that a *Spanish* Ship,
called the *Bermudas*, was cast away upon them, as she was
carrying Hogs to the *West-Indies*, which swam ashore, and
increased to incredible Numbers. But they had been, in
all Times before, infamous and terrible to Mariners, for
the Wreck of many *Spanish*, *Dutch*, and *French* Vessels.
They were therefore, with the usual Elegance of the Sea
Stile, by many called the *Isle of Devils*; and were esteemed
the Hell or Purgatory of Seamen, the most dangerous, unfortunate, and forlorn Place in the World.

        BUT the safe Arrival of this Company was not more
strange and providential, than their Feeding and Support
was beyond all their Hopes or Expectation. For they found
it the richest, pleasantest, and most healthful Place, they
had ever seen. Being safe on Shore, they disposed themselves, some to search the Islands for Food and Water, and
others to get ashore, what they could, from the Ship. Sir
George Somers had not ranged far, before he found such a
Fishery, that, in half an Hour, he took, with a Hook and
Line, as many, as sufficed the whole Company. In some
Places, they were so thick in the Coves, and so big, that
they were afraid to venture in amongst them; and Sir
George Somers caught one, that had before carried off two
of his Hooks, so large, that it would have pulled him into
the Sea, had not his Men got hold of him. Two of those
Rock-fish would have loaded a Man; neither could any
where be found, fatter, or more excellent Fish, than they
were. Besides, there were infinite Numbers of Mullets,
Pilchards, and other small Fry; and by making a Fire in
the Night, they would take vast Quantities of large Craw-
fish. As for Hogs, they found them in that Abundance,
that, at their first Hunting, they killed thirty two. And
there were likewise Multitudes of excellent Birds, in their Sea-
sons; and the greatest Facility, to make their Cabbins with
Palmeta Leaves. This caused them to live in such Plenty,
Ease, and Comfort, that many forgot all other Places, and
never desired to return from thence.

IN

IN the mean while, the Thoughts of the two Knights
were bufily employed, how to proceed, in this defperate
State of their Affairs. At laft, it was refolved, to deck
the Long-boat with the Ship's Hatches, and to fend Mr.
Raven, a ftout and able Mariner, with eight more in her,
to *Virginia*; to get Shipping from thence, to fetch them
away. But fhe was never more heard of; and fuch was
the Malice, Envy, and Ambition of fome, that, notwithftanding Sir *George Somers*'s eminent Services, there arofe
great Differences between the Commanders. So that, as
if, according to the Obfervation of a *Spanifh* Author, the
Air of *America* was infeﬅious, and inclined Mens Minds to
Wrangling and Contention, they lived afunder, in the
Height of this their Calamity, rather like mere Strangers,
than diftreffed Friends. But the feveral Parties, each refolved upon building a Veffel. In the mean while, two
Children were born. The Boy was called *Bermudas*, and
the Girl *Bermuda*; and in the Midft of all their Sorrows,
they had a merry *Englifh* Wedding. But the two Cedar
Ships being, at length, finifhed, and rigged with what they
faved from the *Sea-Venture*, they calked them, and paid
the Seams with Lime and Turtle's Oyl, inftead of Pitch
and Tar; which quickly became dry, and as hard as a
Stone. Sir *George Somers* had no Iron in his Bark, except
one Bolt in the Keel. And now, their Provifions being
laid in, and all Things in Readinefs, after about Nine
Months Abode there, they fet Sail, on the 10th of *May*,
1610. They left behind them two Men, *Chriftopher Carter* and *Edward Waters*; who, for their Offences, fled
into the Woods, and defired, rather there to end their
Days, than to ftand to the Event of Juftice. For one of
their Accomplices had been fhot to Death, and *Waters* was
aﬅually tied to a Tree to be executed; but he had, by
Chance, a Knife about him, with which he fecretly cut
the Rope, and ran into the Woods. There alfo came from
England with them two *Indians*, named *Namontack* and
Machumps. But, upon fome Difference, *Machumps* flew
Namontack; and having made a Hole to bury him, becaufe
it was too fhort, he cut off his Legs, and laid them by him.
Neither was the Murder ever difcovered, before he got to
Virginia.

WHILST thefe Things were paffing in *Bermudas*, the
Colony in *Virginia* was reduced to the utmoft Mifery and
Diftrefs. Captain *Percy*, their Governor, was fo fick and
weak the whole Time, that he could neither go nor ftand.
Wherefore he could not keep up his Authority with fuch a .
feditious Crew, nor aﬅ with that Vigor and Induftry, as

might juftly have been expected from him. Captain *Mar-*
tin from *Nanfamond,* and Captain *Weft* from the Falls,
having loft their Boats, and near half their Men, were returned to *James-Town.* For the *Indians* no fooner underftood, that *Smith* was gone, but they revolted, and fpoiled
and murdered all, they met. And now they had twenty
Prefidents, with all their Appurtenances of Parafites and
Profufion. They lavifhly fpent the Provifions, fent from
England in the laft Ships; which, however, were fo bad,
and fo infufficient in Proportion, that the poor famifhing
People, in the Bitternefs of their Heart, poured forth, the
whole Time, the moft dreadful Curfes and Execrations a-
gainft Sir *Thomas Smith,* the Treafurer. And they were
therefore foon obliged, to depend wholly, on what Captain
Smith left ; which he had provided, only to ferve his own
Company for fome Time, with Intention, afterwards to
lay in a much larger Stock. But before thefe Provifions
were quite confumed, Captain *Weft* and Captain *Ratcliffe,*
each with a fmall Ship, and thirty or forty Men well appointed, went abroad to trade. *Ratcliffe,* upon Confidence
of *Powhatan's* fair Profeffions, was flain, with thirty others,
as carelefs as himfelf. Only one Man of the Company
efcaped ; and *Pocahontas* faved a Boy, one *Henry Spilman,*
who lived for many Years, by her Means, among the *Pa-*
towmacks. But *Powhatan,* ftill as he found Opportunity,
cut off their Boats, and denied them Trade ; fo that Captain *Weft* failed off in his Ship to *England.*

A n d now, they were all deeply fenfible of the Lofs of
Captain *Smith.* Even his bittereft Enemies, and greateft
Maligners, would curfe their Deftiny for his Departure.
Inftead of Corn and Contribution from the *Indians,* which
his Induftry and Authority ftill wrefted from them, they
had nothing but Scoffs and mortal Wounds. And as for
their Hogs, Sheep, Goats, Hens, and other Animals, their
riotous Commanders, and the *Indians,* daily confumed and
deftroyed them. So that they traded away their Swords,
Firelocks, and any thing elfe, they had, with the *Indians;*
who were thereby enabled, the more eafily, often to em-
brue their cruel Hands in their Blood. Thofe, who had
Startch, made no little Ufe of it, in this Extremity ; and
the very Skins of their Horfes were prepared, by ftewing
and hafhing, into dainty and welcome Food. Nay, fo great
was the Famine, that the poorer Sort took up an *Indian,*
that had been flain and buried, and eat him ; and fo did feveral others, one another, that died, boiled and ftewed
with Roots and Herbs. And one, among the reft, killed
his Wife, powdered her up, and had eaten Part of her,
before

before it was difcovered; for which he was, afterwards, de-
fervedly executed. In fhort, fo extremewas the Famine and
Diftrefs of this Time, that it was, for many Years after, The Hon-
diftinguifhed and remembered, by the Name of the STAR- Efq; Gover-
VING TIME. And by thefe means, of near five hundred nor.
Perfons, left by Captain *Smith* at his Departure, within
fix Months, there remained not above fixty, Men, Wo-
men, and Children; and thofe moft poor and miferable
Creatures, preferved, for the moft part, by Roots, Herbs,
Acorns, Walnuts, Berries, and now and then a little Fifh.
Neither was it poffible for them, to have held out ten Days
longer, without being all utterly extinct and famifhed with
Hunger.

IN this calamitous State, did Sir *Thomas Gates* and Sir Sir *Thomas*
George Somers find the Colony, at their Arrival, on the *Gates*, Go-
24th of *May*. Thefe two noble Knights, being utter vernor.
Strangers to their Affairs, could underftand nothing of the
Caufe and Reafon of thefe Miferies, but by Conjecture from
their Clamours and Complaints, either accufing, or excufing one another. They therefore embarked them all, in
the beft manner, they could, and fet Sail for *England*. At
their Departure, many were importunate to burn the Houfes
and Fort at *James-Town*. But God, who did not intend,
that this excellent Country fhould be fo abandoned, put it
into the Heart of Sir *Thomas Gates*, to fave the Town and
Fortifications. For having fallen down to *Hog-Ifland*, and
thence to *Mulberry-Point*, they defcried the Long-boat of
the Lord *Delawarr*; who, being then Captain-General of
Virginia, a Title ever after given to our Governors in chief,
came up with three Ships, exceedingly well furnifhed with
all Neceffaries, and returned them back to *James-Town*.

HIS Lordfhip arrived the 9th of *June*, accompanied with Lord *Dela-*
Sir *Ferdinando Waynman*, General of the Horfe, (who foon *warr*, Go-
after died here) Captain *Holcroft*, and divers other Gentle- vernor.
men of Figure. The 10th he came up with his Fleet,
went afhore, heard a Sermon, read his Commiffion, and
entered into Confultation about the Affairs of the Colony.
Then he made a fhort Speech to the Company, juftly
blaming them for their Pride, Vanity, and Sloth, and earneftly entreating them to amend their Ways, left he fhould
be compelled to draw the Sword of Juftice, and cut off fuch
Delinquents; which, he profeffed, he had much rather
draw, to the fhedding his own vital Blood, in their Caufe
and Defence. He alfo conftituted proper Officers of all
Kinds, and allotted every Man his particular Place and Bufinefs. This Oration was received with a general Applaufe;
and you might foon fee the idle and refty Humours of a divided Multitude, by the Splendor, Unity, and Authority of
I 3   this

this Government, fubftantially healed. Captain *Martin*
was removed from the Council, for his weak, cruel, and
Lord *Dela-* diforderly Behaviour; and thofe, who knew not the Path
warr, Go- to Goodnefs before, would now chalk it out to their Fel-
vernor. lows, endeavouring to outftrip each other in Diligence and
Induftry. The *French* prepared to plant the Vines; the
Englifh laboured in the Woods and Grounds; and every
Man knew his particular Bufinefs and Vocation, which he
followed with Alacrity and Pleafure.

BUT altho' his Lordfhip's Stores were very plentiful for
his own Company, yet were they far from being enough to
fuffice the whole Colony. For it was computed, that all
the Provifion, landed from *England*, the whole firft three
Years, was not fufficient to have ferved the People, according to their Numbers, fix Months. Underftanding
therefore, what Plenty there was of Hogs and other good
Provifions in *Bermudas*, he determined to fend thither for a
fufficient Supply. Whereupon Sir *George Somers*, who, by
his Diligence in ranging thofe Iflands, was beft acquainted
with the Place, and whofe generous Mind ever regarded the
publick Good, more than his own private Ends, altho' of
above threefcore Years of Age, and of a Fortune in *England* fuitable to his Rank and Quality, yet offered his Service to perform this dangerous Voyage to thofe rocky and
unfortunate Iflands; and he promifed with God's Affiftance,
foon to return, with fix Months Provifion of Flefh. On
the 19th of *June*, he embarked, in his own Cedar Veffel,
of thirty Tons; and Captain *Samuel Argall* was alfo fent
with him, in another fmall Bark. But Captain *Argall* was
foon forced back, by Strefs of Weather; and was fent, by
the Lord Governor, to *Patowmack* River, to trade for Corn.
He there found the *Englifh* Boy, *Henry Spilman*, preferved
by *Pocahontas* and thofe *Indians*, from the Fury of *Powhatan.* He was a young Gentleman, well defcended; and,
by his Acquaintance and Help, Captain *Argall* received fuch
good Ufage from that kind People, that his Veffel was foon
freighted with Corn, with which he returned to *James-
Town.* But Sir *George Somers* ftruggled long with foul
Weather and contrary Winds; and was at laft forced to the
Northern Parts of the Continent, where he refrefhed himfelf and his Men on the unknown Coaft. But departing
thence again, he at length arrived fafe at *Bermudas.* Ufing
too much Diligence and Pains in difpatching his Bufinefs,
and the Strength of his Body not anfwering the ever memorable Vigor of his Mind, having lived long in honourable
Employments, much beloved, and highly efteemed, thro'
his whole Life, Nature at laft could no longer fupport the
Burthen,

Burthen, but funk under his too great Labour and Fatigue. Finding his Time but fhort, after having made a proper Difpofition of his Eftate, he called them together, and like a valiant Captain and worthy Patriot, exhorted them to be true and conftant to thofe Plantations, and with all Expedition and Diligence, to return to *Virginia*.

THUS died this virtuous and honourable Knight, in the very Place, where they afterwards built a Town, from him called *St. Georges*; and the Iflands themfelves have ever fince borne the Name of the *Somer-Iflands*, in Honour to his Memory. But Captain *Matthew Somers*, his Nephew, and all his Men, were in fuch Grief and Confternation at his Death, and were fo heedlefs and unconcernd for the Colony, that they utterly negle&ed his dying Inftru&ions, to return to *Virginia*. For having buried his Heart and Entrails, and ere&ed a Crofs over the Place; they embalmed his Body, and fet Sail with it, in his Cedar Ship, for *England*. Arriving fafe at *Whitchurch* in *Dorfetfhire*, he was there honourably enterred, with many Vollies of Shot, and the Rites of a Soldier. But the Crofs was accidentally found, nine Years after, in a Bye-place, overgrown with Bufhes, by Captain *Nathaniel Butler*, then Governor of thofe Iflands. Refolving to have a better Memorial of fo worthy a Soldier, and finding a large Marble Stone, brought from *England*, he caufed it to be handfomely wrought by Mafons, and laid over the Place; engraving an Epitaph, agreeable to the Tafte and Manner of the Times, and environing the whole with a fquare Wall of hewn Stone. But I underftand, that this Monument is now utterly obliterated, and the Place quite forgot and unknown in that Country.

UPON this Occafion, there alfo happened a very humourous Circumftance. *Carter* and *Waters* had been left here, when the reft went to *Virginia*, as hath been faid. And now, by *Carter*'s Perfuafions, *Waters* was ftill ftaid, and one *Edward Chard* joined himfelf to them. This Veffel once out of Sight, thefe three Lords and fole Inhabitants of all thofe Iflands, began to ere& their little Commonwealth, with equal Power and brotherly Regency, building a Houfe, preparing the Ground, planting their Corn, and fuch Seeds and Fruits, as they had, and providing other Neceffaries and Conveniences. Then making Search among the Crevices and Corners of thofe craggy Rocks, what the Ocean, from the World's Creation, had thrown up among them, befides divers fmaller Pieces, they happened upon the largeft Block of Ambergreafe, that had ever been feen or heard of, in one Lump. It weighed

four-

1610.   fourfcore Pounds; and is faid, itfelf alone, befides the others,
to have been then worth nine or ten thoufand Pounds. And
Lord *Dela-* now being rich, they grew fo refty and ambitious, that
warr, Go- thefe three forlorn Men, above three thoufand Miles from
vernor. their native Country, and with little Probability of ever
feeing it again, fell out for the Superiority and Rule. And
their Competition and Quarrel grew fo high, that *Chard*
and *Waters,* being of the greateft Spirit, had appointed to
decide the Matter in the Field. But *Carter* wifely ftole
their Arms; chufing rather, to bear with fuch troublefome
Rivals, than, by being rid of them, to live alone. So
doubtful a Good are Riches, and fo prepofterous a Thing
the Mind of Man!

IN the mean while, the Lord *Delawarr,* in *Virginia,*
built two Forts at *Kicquotan;* and called one, *Fort Hen-*
ry, the other, *Fort Charles.* They ftood on a pleafant
Plain, near a little River, which they named *Southampton*
River, in a wholefome Air, having plenty of Springs, and
commanding a large Circuit of Ground, which contained
Wood, Pafture, and Marfh, with fit places for Vines,
Corn, and Gardens. Here it was intended, that thofe,
who came from *England,* fhould be quartered at their firft
Landing, that the Wearifomenefs and Naufea of the Sea
might be refrefhed, in this pleafant Situation, and wholefome Air. Sir *Thomas Gates* he fent to *England;* and Captain *Percy,* with Mr. *Stacy* and fifty or threefcore good
Shot, was difpatched to revenge fome Injuries of the *Paf-*
pabeys. But thofe *Indians* flying, they burnt their Houfes,
and took the Queen and her Children Prifoners, whom not
long after they flew. So much was the Government already altered from the Clemency of *Smith's* Adminiftration,
who never did, nor would have been permitted, to fhed
the leaft Drop of *Indian* Blood, by Way of Punifhment;
but was obliged to fupply the Want of fufficient Vigor and
Power in his Authority, by his own Activity, Induftry,
Art, and Circumfpection.

SOME time after, as my Lord *Delawarr* was at the
Falls, the *Indians* affaulted his Troops, and killed three or
four of his Men. But his Lordfhip had now been long fick.
Immediately upon his Arrival, he was feized with an Ague,
which, being put by for the prefent, foon returned with
greater Violence than ever; and he began to be diftempered
with other grievous Sickneffes. He was firft affailed by the
Flux, then by the Cramp, and after that by the Gout;
all which reduced him to fo weak and low a State, that,
being unable to ftir, it brought upon him the Scurvy.
Therefore, by the Advice of his Friends, on the 28th of
March,

March, he fhipped himfelf, with Dr. *Bobun* and Captain *Argall,* for *Mevis,* in the *Weft-Indies,* an Ifland, at that time, famous for wholefome Baths. At his Departure, he committed the Colony to the Charge of Captain *Percy,* 'till the Arrival of Sir *Thomas Dale.* And he left behind about two hundred Perfons, moft of them in good Health, and well provided with Victuals, and the Natives, to all outward Appearance, tractable and friendly. But being croffed by *Southerly* Winds, they were obliged to fhape their Courfe to the *Weftern-Iflands;* where his Lordfhip met with much Relief from Oranges and Lemons, a fovereign Remedy for that Diforder. However he was advifed, not to hazard himfelf back to *Virginia* yet, but to return to *England,* for the perfect Recovery of his Health.

1611.

The Hon. *George Percy* Efq; Governor.

THE Council in *England* were, all this while, ftill eager after fome immediate Profit. Therefore, finding the Smalnefs of the Return by thofe Ships, which had carried the laft Supply, they entered into ferious Confultation, whether it were better, to come into a new Contribution, or in time to abandon the Country, and give over the Enterprife. Wherefore, upon the Arrival of Sir *Thomas Gates,* they adjured him to deal plainly with them; and he, with a folemn and facred Oath, gave them a full Account of the State and Profpect of Things. And he told them, that all Men knew, they lay at the Mercy of politic Princes and States; who, for their own proper Utility, devifed all Methods to grind their Merchants, and, on any Pretence, to confifcate their Goods, and draw from them all Manner of Gain; whereas *Virginia,* in a few Years, might furnifh all their Wants, with Honour and Security. But, by this time, fome of the Adventurers were become fufpicious of the Treafurer's Fairnefs in the Carriage and Management of the Bufinefs. To which the Lord *Delawarr's* Return added a farther Damp and Difcouragement, and bred fuch a Coldnefs and Irrefolution in many of them, that they endeavoured to withdraw their Payments. Being fued, fome pleaded in Chancery, upon their Oaths, that the Monies were not converted to the Ufe intended, but to private Mens Gains; and that no Accounts were kept, or at leaft legally audited and examined. But this was overruled, and no ways regarded or believed; and Sir *Thomas Smith's* Integrity was then thought fo unqueftionable, that they were obliged to pay their Sums fubfcribed. The Lord *Delawarr* alfo, being much pleafed with the Country, and cordial in the Affair, made a publick Oration in the Council; which he afterwards publifhed, to allay their Difcontents, and give Satisfaction to all. And his Lordfhip protefted himfelf willing,

1611.

Sir *Thomas*
Dale, Go-
vernor.

ling, to venture his whole Fortune upon the Succefs of the Enterprife; and rather than fo honourable an Action fhould fail, to return immediately in Perfon, if they would but fecond his Endeavours.

BUT before the Arrival of Lord *Delawarr* in *England*, the Council and Company had difpatched away Sir *Thomas Dale*, High Marfhal of *Virginia*, with three Ships, Men, and Cattle, and with all other Provifions, thought neceffary for a Year; which arrived fafe, the 10th of *May*, 1611. Sir *Thomas* found the People again falling into their former Eftate of Penury and Want.   For they were fo improvident, as not to put Corn into the Ground, but trufted wholly to the Store, then furnifhed with only three Months Provifions.   His firft Care, therefore, was to employ all Hands in planting Corn at the two Forts at *Kicquotan*; and the Seafon being then not fully paft, they had an indifferent Crop of good Corn.   And having taken Order for this Bufinefs, and committed the Care of it to his Under-Officers, he hafted back to *James-Town*; where he found moft of the Company, at their daily and ufual Work, bowling in the Streets.   But he foon employed them about things more neceffary; as felling Timber, and repairing their Houfes, ready to fall on their Heads.   He likewife fet many to providing Pales, Pofts, and Rails, to empale the new Town, he purpofed to build; but being yet unacquainted with the Country, he had not refolved, where to feat it.   He therefore fpent fome time, with an hundred Men, in viewing the River of *Nanfamond*, in Defpight of the *Indians*, at that time their Enemies.   And then he examined *James* River, up to the Falls; and at length pitched upon a Place for his new Town, on the Narrow of *Farrar*'s Ifland, in *Varina* Neck, upon a high Land, nearly invironed by the main River.

BUT he found it no eafy Matter, to reduce his turbulent and feditious People to good Order.   About this time, Sir *Thomas Smith* fent over a printed Book of Articles and Laws, chiefly tranflated from the martial Laws of the *Low Countries*.   Thefe were very bloody and fevere, and no ways agreeable to a free People and the *Britifh* Conftitution; neither had they any Sanction or Authority from the Council and Company in *England*.   However, Sir *Thomas Dale*, being fadly troubled and peftered with the mutinous Humours of the People, caufed them to be publifhed, and put into Execution with the utmoft Rigor.   And altho' the Manner was harfh and unufual to *Englifhman*, yet had not thefe military Laws been fo ftrictly executed at this time, there were little Hopes or Probability of preventing the utter

ter Subverfion of the Colony. For, this Summer, one
Webb and one *Price* entered into a Plot againft the Government; which was, foon after, followed by a more dan- Sir *Thomas*
gerous Confpiracy of *Jeffrey Abbot*. This *Abbot* had ferved *Dale*, Go-
vernor.
long as a Soldier, both in *Ireland* and the *Netherlands*, and
was here Serjeant of Captain *Smith*'s Company; who declares, that he never knew in *Virginia*, a more able Soldier,
lefs turbulent, of a better Wit, more hardy and induftrious, or more forward to cut off thofe, who endeavoured to
abandon the Country, or wrong the Colony. But from
what Caufe foever his Difcontents arofe, whether he refented his being neglected and unrewarded, and having others
put over his Head and preferred before him, or whether
there was any other Reafon of his Diffatisfaction, it is certain, that this Man, who never received any Reward for
his long Services and Deferts, now met with an immediate
Punifhment for this fudden and paffionate Deviation from
his Duty. One *Cole* alfo, and *Kitchens*, with three more,
plotted to run away to the *Spaniards*, whom they fuppofed,
from fome wrong Information, to be inhabiting, fome
where within five Days Journey of the Fort. And thefe
Commotions juftified Sir *Thomas Dale*'s neceffary Severities,
which might otherwife have been branded, as many were
then ready to do, with being too cruel and tyrannical.
But however falutary fuch fharp and fummary Proceedings
might be at that time, as I find them owned to have been,
and commended by all Parties; and however Sir *Thomas
Dale* might fafely be trufted with fo great a Power, a Man
of much Honour, Wifdom, and Experience; yet it is certain, that thefe Articles were utterly deftructive of the *Englifh* Freedom and Laws, and gave the Governor fuch a
commanding and defpotick Authority, as is, by no means,
to be lodged in any Hand, in a Country, that has the leaft
Thoughts or Pretenfions to Liberty.

IN the Beginning of *Auguft*, Sir *Thomas Gates* arrived Sir *Thomas*
in fix tall Ships, with three hundred Men, an hundred Cat- *Gates* Go-
vernor.
tle, two hundred Hogs, and with all Manner of other Mu-
nition and Provifion, that could be thought of, as needful
and proper. At his Arrival, Sir *Thomas Dale*'s Authority
determined, who, after mutual Salutations, acquainted him
with what he had done, and what he intended. And now,
being eafed of the Burthen of Government, and more at
Leifure, he fet himfelf heartily about building his Town;
and Sir *Thomas Gates*, highly approving the Defign, furnifhed him with three hundred and fifty Men, fuch as he
himfelf made Choice of. He fet Sail from *James-Town*,
the Beginning of *September*; and being arrived at the Place,
he

1611.

Sir *Thomas Gates*, Governor.

he environed it with a Palisade, and in Honour of Prince *Henry*, called it *Henrico*. And then he built a Church, and Storehouses; and at each Corner of the Town, high commanding Watch Towers. This being accomplished, he next provided proper and convenient Houses for himself and Men, which were finished with all possible Speed, to the great Comfort and Satisfaction of his Company and the whole Colony.

THE Ruins of this Town are still plainly to be traced and distinguished, upon the Land of the late Col. *William Randolph*, of *Tuckahoe*, just without the Entrance into *Farrar's* Island. It lay from River to River, upon a Plain of high Land, with very steep and inaccessible Banks, and the Neck without, being well empaled, gave it all the Security and Conveniency of an Island. It had three Streets of well-framed Houses, a handsome Church, and the Foundation of another laid, to be built of Brick, besides Store-houses, Watch-houses, and other publick Conveniences. Upon the Verge of the River Bank, stood five Houses, inhabited by the better Sort of People, who kept continual Sentinel for the Town's Security. About two Miles from the Town, into the Main, he run another Palisade, from River to River, near two Miles in Length, guarded with several Forts, with a large Quantity of Corn-ground empaled and sufficiently secured. Besides these Precautions, there may still be seen, upon the River Bank within the Island, the Ruins of a great Ditch, now over-grown with large and stately Trees; which, it may be supposed, was defended with a Palisade, to prevent a Surprise on that Side, by crossing the River. And for a still further Security to the Town, he intended, but never quite finished, a Palisade on the *South* Side of the River, as a Range for their Hogs; and he called it *Hope in Faith and Coxendale*. It was about two Miles and an half long, and was secured by five of their Manner of Forts, called *Charity Fort, Elisabeth Fort, Fort Patience*, and *Mount Malady*, with a Guest House for sick People, upon a high and dry Situation, and in a wholesome Air, in the Place, where *Jefferson's* Church now stands. On the same Side of the River also, Mr. *Whitaker*, their Preacher, chose to be seated; and he empaled a fair Parsonage, with an hundred Acres of Land, calling it *Rock-hall*.

ABOUT *Christmas*, Sir *Thomas Dale*, to revenge some Injuries of the *Appamattock Indians*, assaulted and took their Town, without the Loss of a Man. This Town stood at the Mouth of the River, and was accounted but five Miles, by Land, from *Henrico*. And Sir *Thomas*, considering how convenient it would be to the *English*, resolved to possess

and

and feat it, and, at the Inftant, called it *New Bermudas.*
And he annexed, to the belonging Freedom and Corporation for ever, many Miles of champion and wood-land
Ground, in feveral Hundreds, by the Names of the *Upper*
and *Nether Hundreds, Rochdale* (now called *Rockſdale*)
Hundred, Shirley Hundred, and *Digges's Hundred.* At
Bermudas, where was the moft Corn-ground, he firft be-
gan to plant; and with a Pale of two Miles, acroſs from
River to River, he encloſed and ſecured eight *Engliſh* Miles
in Compaſs. Upon this Circuit, there were ſoon built ma-
ny fair Houſes, to near the Number of fifty. *Rockſdale*
was alſo encloſed with a croſs Paliſade, near four Miles in
Length; and there were many Houſes, planted along the
Pale, within which their Hogs and Cattle had twenty Miles
Circuit to graze in ſecurely.

It will not be thought, I believe, foreign to the Hiftory
of *Virginia,* occaſionally to interſperſe ſome Account of
the Fortunes of Sir *Walter Ralegh,* our Founder, and the
firft Author, to the *Engliſh,* of ſettling Colonies in *America.*
Juft before the Death of Queen *Eliſabeth,* he received a
Challenge, upon ſome Quarrel, from Sir *Amias Preſton,*
one of *Eſſex's* Followers, and a Man of the Sword; which
howevǝr was made up, by the Mediation of a certain great
Nobleman, before it came to the laſt Deciſion. But on this
Occaſion, Sir *Walter,* like a prudent and affectionate Father of a Family, had conveyed all his landed Eſtate, which
conſiſted of about three thouſand Pounds a Year, to his
Wife and Son. This was fortunately a Bar to his Lands
falling abſolutely to the Crown, upon his Attainder. They
were only forfeited for his own Life; and the King, upon
ſome powerful Interceſſion, reſtored them to him again. So
that he lived, under his Confinement, with much Elegan-
cy, Neatneſs, and Affluence. For he was naturally a great
Lover of Propriety; and had been, in the Time of his
Proſperity, both in his Dreſs and Equipage, one of the moſt
ſumptuous and polite Perſons of the Age. And now, being
cut off from all the active Parts of Life, he indulged and
gave a Looſe to his noble Genius, and natural Thirſt of
Knowledge; and ſeemed (to uſe Prince *Henry's* Alluſion)
a ſinging Bird in a Cage; rather a Philoſopher, than a Cap-
tive; a Student in a Library, than a Priſoner in the Tower.
The Reſtraint of his Body was ſo far from damping and
confining his native Greatneſs of Mind and Sublimity of
Parts, that it only opened a new Field of Glory to him,
and rendered him as illuſtrious, in this ſtill and ſedentary
Scene of Life, as he had before been, in his moſt active and
proſperous Days. But at laſt, the Lawyers pretended to
find

1611.

Sir *Thomas*
Gates, Go-
vernor.

find fome Flaw in the Conveyance of his Lands; and an Information was exhibited againſt him, in the Court of Ex-
chequer. His chief Judge, we are told, was his greateſt
Enemy; which, I ſuppoſe, was Sir *Edward Coke*, then
Lord Chief Juſtice. For that famous Lawyer, notwith-
ſtanding his vaſt Abilities and Knowledge in the Common
Law, will be branded to all Futurity, for bawling and rail-
ing Sir *Walter Ralegh* out of his Life at his Trial. And
Wilſon, a contemporary Hiſtorian, tells us, that it was po-
pularly objeſted to him, as a Judge; That he made the
Law lean too much to his own Opinion, thereby becoming
a legal Tyrant, and ſtriking, whom he pleaſed, with that
Weapon, whoſe Edge he was able to turn any Way.
When the Cauſe came to Trial, it was determined againſt
Sir *Walter Ralegh*, only for the Want of one ſingle Word
in his Anſwer, ſetting forth that Conveyance; which was
neverthelefs an Overſight of the Clerk, and the Word was
in the original Inſtrument. And thus was he moſt iniqui-
touſly deprived of his Lands; and upon Lady *Ralegh*'s paf-
ſionate Application to the King, ſhe could obtain no other
Anſwer from him, but *I mun have the Land, I mun have
it for* Car. It was accordingly conferred upon that Favourite, juſt then in his Riſe; and Sir *Walter* wrote him a
Letter upon the Occaſion, which may be ſeen in his Life,
by Mr. *Oldys*; and which may be placed, perhaps, among
the moſt beautiful, wiſe, and pathetic Compoſitions, that
ever has appeared of that Kind. So invariable was this Monarch in his wrong Judgment of Men and Things, as to
aggrandize and enrich ſo inſignificant a Tool, and one ſo
infamouſly wicked, lewd, and inſufficient, as *Car*, with the
Spoils of a Perſon, ſo truly virtuous, great, and able, as
Sir *Walter Ralegh*. As if Fortune had conſpired to expoſe
his Weakneſs, and render his Injuſtice the more conſpicu-
ous and remarkable, by the Contraſt between the Man, he
oppreſſed, and the Man, he advanced. However, as ſome
Retaliation for the Injuſtice and Wrong, his Majeſty afterwards gave Lady *Ralegh* and her Son eight Thouſand
Pounds for the Eſtate.

1612.

CAPTAIN *Matthew Somers* and his Company, at their
Return to *England* with Sir *George*'s Body, had made very
advantageous Relations of *Bermudas*. But theſe were little
credited at firſt, and looked upon, as mere Traveller's
Tales; till ſome of the *Virginia* Company apprehended,
that a Settlement there might be very beneficial and helpful
to the Plantation in *Virginia*. But as by their former Letters-patent, they were only entitled to the Iſlands within an
hundred Miles of their Coaſt, and as *Bermudas* lay much
beyond

beyond that Diftance, they procured a new Charter from
his Majefty, bearing Date *March* 12, 1611-12. This
granted them all the Iflands in the Ocean Seas, within three
hundred Leagues of the Coaft, between the one and fortieth
and thirtieth Degrees of *Northerly* Latitude. It alfo gave
them a Power, to fet up Lotteries; to fue for the Monies
fubfcribed, requiring the Judges, to favour and further the
faid Suits, fo far forth, as Law and Equity would, in any
wife, further and permit; together with other ample Privi-
.leges and Authorities, as may be more fully feen in the
Charter at large, printed in the Appendix. But the *Virginia* Company fold thefe Iflands to about an hundred and
twenty of their own Members, who were erected into a
diftinct Society and Body Corporate, by the Name of the
Somer-Iflands Company.   Sir *Thomas Smith* was elected
their Treafurer, or Governor, in *England*; and fome time
this Year 1612, Mr. *Richard More* was fent Governor of
the Country, with fixty Men, to make a Settlement and
Plantation. They found the three Men, before fpoken of,
lufty and well. They were very comfortably feated, and
plentifully ftored with divers Sorts of excellent Provifions.
But under Colour, that they were fitted out, at the Charge,
and in the Service of the Company, thefe three poor Men
were profecuted, tormented, and threatned by the Governor, in the Company's Name, 'till they were entirely deprived of their great Treafure of Ambergreafe. However
a great Part was embezzled by Captain *Davies* and Mr.
Edwin Kendal, to whom they committed it, during the
Squabble and Contention. So that not above a Third came
into the Hands of the Company; for which, we are told,
they afterwards compounded with the Finders, and made
them a juft and reafonable Satisfaction.

I N the Beginning of the fame Year, two Ships arrived
in *Virginia*, with a Supply of Provifions and fourfcore Men.
But thefe Provifions, according to Cuftom, were very fcanty
and infufficient; and therefore Capt. *Argall*, who commanded one of the Ships, having recreated and refrefhed his
Company, was fent to *Patowmack* River, to trade for Corn.
For the *Indians* about *James-Town* were in a ticklifh State,
and little to be depended upon; being Friends or Foes, according as they found Advantage and Opportunity. Captain
Argall foon entered into a great Acquaintance and Friendfhip with *Japazaws*, King of *Patowmack*, an old Friend to
Captain *Smith*, and fo to the whole *Englifh* Nation, ever
fince the firft Difcovery of the Country. Hard by *Patowmack*, *Pocahontas* lay concealed, thinking herfelf fafe, and
unknown to all but trufty Friends. What was the Reafon
of

Margin notes:
1612.
Sir *Thomas*
Gates Go-
vernor.

of her abfconding from *Werowocomoco*, cannot eafily be
judged; except it was to withdraw herfelf from being a
Witnefs to the frequent Butcheries of the *Englifh*, whofe
Folly and Rafhnefs, after *Smith*'s Departure, put it out of
her Power to fave them. Captain *Argall*, having got Intelligence of this, engaged to give *Japazaws* a Copper Kettle, to bring her on board his Ship; promifing not to hurt
her, but to keep her fafe, 'till they could conclude a Peace
with her Father. This Savage would have done any thing
for the Copper Kettle; and therefore, having no Pretence
on Account of her own Curiofity, becaufe fhe had feen and
been in many Ships, he made his Wife pretend, how defirous fhe was to fee one, fo that he offered to beat her for
her Importunity, 'till fhe wept. But at laft he told her, if
Pocahontas would go with her, he was content. And
thus, taking Advantage of her Good-nature and obliging
Temper, they betrayed this innocent Creature aboard;
where they were all kindly received and entertained in the
Cabbin. The Captain, when he faw his Time, decoy'd
Pocahontas into the Gun Room; only to conceal from her,
that *Japazaws* was any way guilty of her Captivity. When
he had received his Reward, the Captain fent for her again;
and told her, fhe muft go with him, and be the Means and
Inftrument of Peace, between her Country and the *Englifh*.
At this, the old Traitor and his Wife began to howl and
cry, as much as *Pocahontas*; who, by the Captain's fair
Promifes and Perfuafions, pacified herfelf, by degrees. And
fo *Japazaws* and his Wife, with their Kettle and other
Baubles, went joyfully afhore, and fhe to *James-Town*;
where, altho' a frequent Vifitant before, and often a kind
Support and Preferver of the Colony, fhe had never been
'till now, fince Captain *Smith* left the Country.

A Meffenger was immediately difpatched to her Father;
that he muft ranfom his Daughter *Pocahontas*, whom he
loved fo dearly, with the Men, Guns, and Tools of the
Englifh, which he had treacheroufly ftolen and furprifed.
This unwelcome News much troubled *Powhatan*, becaufe
he loved both his Daughter and their Commodities well;
and it threw him into fuch Perplexity, that it was three
Months, before he returned any Anfwer. Then he fent
back feven of the *Englifh*, with each an unferviceable
Mufket; and fent Word, that when they fhould deliver his
Daughter, he would make full Satisfaction for all Injuries, and
give them five hundred Bufhels of Corn, and would be
their Friend for ever. But the *Englifh* anfwered; That
his Daughter fhould be well ufed; but that they could not
believe, the reft of their Arms were either loft, or ftolen
from

from him; and that therefore, they would keep his Daugh-   1612.
ter, till he had fent them all back.   But this Anfwer difpleafed him fo much, that they heard no more from him, Sir *Thomas*
for a long time after.   *Gates*, Go-
                                                                vernor.
   AT laft, in the Beginning of the next Year, Sir *Thomas*   1613.
Dale took *Pocahontas* with him, and went in Captain *Ar-*
gall's Ship, with fome other Veffels belonging to the Colony, up into his own River, to his chief Habitation at *We-*
rowocomoco, with a Party of an hundred and fifty Men,
well appointed.   *Powhatan* did not appear ; and although
the *Englifh* told them, their Bufinefs was to deliver up their
Emperor's Daughter, upon Reftitution of the reft of their
Men and Arms, yet were they received with many fcorn-
ful Bravades and Threats.   They told them, if they came
to fight, they were welcome; but advifed them, as they
loved their Lives, to retire; or elfe they would treat them,
as they had done Captain *Ratcliffe*.   But after fome fmall
Skirmifhes, and confiderable Damage done the *Indians*,
by burning their Houfes, and fpoiling all, they could find,
a Peace was patched up.   They immediately fent Meffengers to *Powhatan*; and they told the *Englifh*, that their
Men were run off, for fear they fhould hang them ; but
that *Powhatan*'s Men were run after, to bring them back;
and that their Swords and Mufkets fhould be brought, the
next Day.   But the *Englifh*, perceiving, that this was all
Collufion, only to delay the Time, till they could carry off
their Goods and Provifions, told them, that they fhould
have a Truce, till the next Day at Noon; but then, if
they had not a direct Anfwer to their Demands, or found
them inclinable to fight, they fhould know, when the *En-*
glifh would begin, by the Sound of their Drums and Trumpets.   Upon Confidence of this Truce, two of *Powhatan*'s
Sons came on board the Ship, to fee their Sifter; on whofe
Sight, finding her well, although they had heard the contrary, they greatly rejoiced ; and they promifed to perfuade
their Father, to redeem her, and for ever be Friends with
the *Englifh*.   Hereupon Mr. *John Rolfe* and Mr. *Sparks*
were fent to *Powhatan*, to acquaint him with the Bufinefs.
They were kindly received and entertained, but not admitted into the Prefence of the Emperor.   They only fpoke
with *Opechancanough*, who promifed to do his utmoft with
his Brother, to incline him to Peace and Friendfhip.   But
it now being *April*, and Time to prepare their Ground, and
fet their Corn, they returned to *James-Town*, without doing any thing more in the Affair.
   LONG before this, Mr. *John Rolfe*, a worthy young
Gentleman, and of good Behaviour, had been in Love with
 19   K   *Pocahontas*,

Pocahontas, and fhe with him. And at this time, he made the thing known to Sir *Thomas Dale*, through Mr. *Ralph Hamer*, and wrote him a Letter, entreating his Advice; and fhe likewife acquainted her Brother with it. Sir *Thomas Dale* highly approved of it; and the Report of this Marriage foon coming to the Knowledge of *Powhatan*, it was found a thing acceptable to him, by his fudden Confent. For within ten Days, he fent *Opachifco*, an old Uncle of hers, and two of his Sons, to fee the Manner of the Marriage, and to do in that Behalf, what they were required, for the Confirmation of it, as his Deputies. It was therefore folemnifed in the Beginning of *April* 1613; and ever after, they had friendly Trade and Commerce, as well with *Powhatan* himfelf, as with all his Subjects.

T H E *Chickahominies* were a ftout, daring, and free People. They had no Werowance, or fingle Ruler, but were governed, in a Republican Form, by their Elders. Thefe were their Priefts, and fome of the wifeft of their old Men, as Affiftants to them. In Confequence of thefe Principles of Government, they took all Opportunities of fhaking off *Powhatan*'s Yoke, whom they looked upon and hated, as a Tyrant. And therefore, they had taken Advantage of thefe late Times of Hoftility and Danger as well to the *Indians*, as to the *Englifh*, to affert their Liberty. But now, feeing *Powhatan* fo clofely linked with the *Englifh*, both in Affinity and Friendfhip, they were in great Concern and Dread, left he fhould bring them again to his Subjection. To prevent which, they fent Ambaffadors to Sir *Thomas Dale*; excufing all former Injuries, and promifing ever after to be King *James*'s faithful Subjects: That they would relinquifh the Name of *Chickahominies*, and be called *Taffauteffus*, or *Englifhmen*, and that Sir *Thomas Dale* fhould be their Governor, as the King's Deputy. Only they defired to be governed by their own Laws, under their eight Elders, as his Subftitutes. Sir *Thomas Dale*, hoping for fome Advantage from this, willingly accepted their Offer. At the Day appointed, with Captain *Argall* and fifty Men, he went to *Chickahominy*; where he found the People affembled, expecting his Coming. They treated him kindly; and the next Morning, having held a Council, the Peace was concluded on thefe Conditions:

I. T H A T they fhould for ever be called *Englifhmen*, and be true Subjects to King *James* and his Deputies:

II. T H A T they fhould neither kill, nor detain, any of the *Englifh*, or of their Cattle, but fhould bring them home:

III. T H A T

III. THAT they ſhould be always ready, to furniſh the 1613.
Engliſh with three hundred Men, againſt the *Spaniards*, or
any other Enemy :   : |Sir *Thomas*
    IV. THAT they ſhould not enter any of the *Engliſh*|*Gates,* Go-
Towns, before ſending in Word, that they were new *En-*|vernor.
gliſhmen :
    V. THAT every fighting Man, at gathering their Corn,
ſhould bring two Buſhels to the Store, as a Tribute ; for
which he ſhould receive as many Hatchets :
    VI. THAT the eight chief Men ſhould ſee all this per-
formed, or receive the Puniſhment themſelves ; and for
their Diligence, they ſhould have a red Coat, a Copper
Chain, and King *James's* Picture, and be accounted his
Nobleman.

THESE Articles were joyfully aſſented to and ratified,
by a great Shout and Acclamation ; and one of their Elders
began an Oration, addreſſing his Speech, firſt to the old
Men, then to the Young, and then to the Women and
Children, to make them underſtand, how ſtrictly they were
to obſerve theſe Conditions, and that then the *Engliſh* would
defend them from the Fury of *Powhatan,* or any other E-
nemy whatſoever.   And thus was their Liberty once more
ſecured ; which indeed had its uſual good Effects, even a-
mong theſe wild and ſavage Nations.   For altho' *Chickahominy* is far from being famous for good Land, yet we are
told, that they had the largeſt Fields, and moſt plentiful
Crops of Corn, and the greateſt Abundance of all other
Proviſions and Neceſſaries, of any People then in the Country.   Such a happy Influence had Liberty, and ſuch viſible
Incitement did firm Property give to the Induſtry of even
that lazy and improvident People.
    AND now the *Engliſh* began to find the Miſtake of for-
bidding and preventing private Property.   For whilſt they
all laboured jointly together, and were fed out of the common Store, happy was he, that could ſlip from his Labour,
or ſlubber over his Work in any Manner.   Neither had
they any Concern about the Increaſe ; preſuming, however
the Crop proſpered, that the publick Store muſt ſtill maintain them.   Even the moſt honeſt and induſtrious would
ſcarcely take ſo much true Pains in a Week, as they
would have done for themſelves in a Day.   The five Years
alſo, preſcribed in his Majeſty's Inſtructions under the Privy
Seal, for trading all together in common Stocks, and bringing the whole Fruit of their Labours into common Store-
houſes, were now expired.   Therefore, to prevent this Inconveniency and bad Conſequence, Sir *Thomas Dale* allotted

1613. each Man three Acres of cleared Ground, in the Nature
of Farms. They were to work eleven Months for the
Sir *Thomas* Store, and had two Bushels of Corn from thence; and only
Gates, Go- had one Month allowed them, to make the rest of their
vernor. Provisions. This was certainly very hard and pinching;
but his new and favourite Settlement at *Bermudas Hundred*
had better Conditions. For one Month's Labour, which
must neither be in Seed-time nor Harvest, they were exempted from all further Service; and for this Exemption
they only paid two Barrels and a half of Corn, as a Yearly
Tribute to the Store. However, the Prospect of these Farmers Labours gave the Colony much Content; and they
were no longer in Fear of wanting, either for themselves,
or to entertain their new Supplies.

S I R *Thomas Dale* had been very active and industrious
in ranging about and viewing the Country, and was vastly
delighted with its Pleasantness and Fertility. Being therefore much vexed and concerned, to find the Possession of
so noble a Territory set so light by at home, as even sometimes to be debated, whether it should be farther prosecuted, or entirely abandoned, he wrote a Letter to Sir *Thomas Smith*, the Treasurer; wherein he assures them all,
and prays them to remember it, that if they should give
over the Enterprise, and lose the Country, they would, in
their great Wisdom, commit an Error of such Prejudice
and Damage to *England*, as had never happened to it, since
the Loss of the Kingdom of *France*. He desires them not
to be gulled and deceived, by the clamorous Reports of
base People, but to believe *Caleb* and *Joshua*. And if the
Glory of God, and the Conversion of those poor Infidels,
had no Influence on the rich Mammons of the Earth; yet
he advises them to follow the Dictates of their own Avarice,
and only to consult their proper Interest and Advantage.
For he protests on the Faith of an honest Man, that the
more he ranged and saw of the Country, the more he admired it; and that having seen the best Parts of *Europe*,
yet he declares, with a solemn Asseveration, that put them
all together, he thought, this Country would be equivalent
to them, if it were once well cultivated, and seated with
good and industrious People.

1614. E A R L Y in the next Year, Sir *Thomas Gates* returned to
England, and left the Government again to Sir *Thomas*
Sir *Thomas* *Dale*. Understanding, that there was a Colony of *French*,
Dale, Go- in the *Northern* Part of *Virginia*, about the Latitude of
vernor. 45, he sent Captain *Argall* thither, to *Port Royal* and *St.
Croix*, two Towns, lying on each Side of the Bay of *Fun-
di*, in *Acadia*. Finding the *French* dispersed abroad in the
Woods,

Woods, he furprifed their Ship and Bark, lately arrived
from *France.*   In them was much good Apparel, with other
Furniture and Provifion, which he brought to *James-Town* ;
but the Men efcaped, and lived among the *Indians* of thofe
Countries.   The Pretence for this Depredation on the
French, was founded on their Right of firft Difcovery ;
and therefore the *Englifh,* in Imitation of the *Spaniards,*
laid Claim to the whole Continent, altho' they really poffeffed, and had feated fo fmall a Part of it.   But it is certain, that we were, at that time, in profound Peace, not
only with *France,* but the whole World.   In his Return,
Captain *Argall* likewife vifited the *Dutch* Settlement, on
Hudfon's River ; and he alledged, that Captain *Hudfon,* the
firft Difcoverer, under whofe Sale they claimed that Country, being an *Englifhman,* and licenfed to difcover thofe
Northern Parts, by the King of *England,* could not alienate
that, which was only a Part of *Virginia,* from the *Englifh*
Crown.   He therefore demanded the Poffeffion ; and the
Dutch Governor, being unable to refift, peaceably fubmitted both himfelf and his Colony, to the King of *England,*
and to the Governor of *Virginia* under him.   Soon after,
a new Governor arrived from *Amfterdam,* better provided.
Under Colour of their Right of Purchafe, and becaufe the
Country lay void and unoccupied, and confequently open
to the firft Poffeffor, he not only refufed to pay the Tribute
and Acknowledgment, which had been agreed upon, but
alfo began to fortify, and put himfelf into a Pofture of Defence.   And the Claim of the *Englifh,* being either wholly
waved for the prefent, or but faintly purfued, they, this
fame Year, made a firm Settlement, which foon became
very flourifhing and populous.   But Complaint being made,
fome Years after, to King *Charles* I. and by him reprefented to the States of *Holland,* they declared, by a publick
Inftrument, that they were no ways concerned in it, but
that it was a private Undertaking of the *Weft-India* Company of *Amfterdam* ; and fo referred it wholly to his Majefty's Pleafure.

M R. *Ralph Hamer,* who was afterwards one of our
Council, and to whofe Relation we are indebted for this
Part of the Hiftory of *Virginia,* having refided fome Years
here, ever fince the great Supply 1609, and being now a-
bout to return to *England,* was very defirous to vifit *Powhatan* and his Court, and to be able, when he went home,
to fpeak fomething of his own Knowledge.   Sir *Thomas
Dale* alfo thought it advifeable, to have fome further Pledge
of *Powhatan's* Friendfhip, befides *Pocahontas.*   It was therefore refolved, to fend this Gentleman, as his Ambaffador,

to demand his other Daughter. Wherefore, Mr. *Hamer*, taking *Thomas Savage* for his Interpreter, and two *Indians* Sir *Thomas* for his Guides, went off in the Morning from *Bermudas*, Dale, Go-vernor. (Sir *Thomas Dale's* favourite Seat, and chief Place of Re-fidence) and arrived the next Evening at *Matchot*. This was a Seat of the King's, where he then was, a few Miles higher up *York* River, than *Werowocomoco*. *Powhatan* knew the Boy, *Thomas Savage*, well, whom *Newport* had prefented to him, in the Year 1607; and he faid to him: *My Child, you were my Boy, and I gave you Leave, four Years ago, to go and fee your Friends; but I have never feen nor heard of you, nor my own Man* Namontack *fince, altho' many Ships have gone and returned.* Then turning to Mr. *Hamer*, he demanded the Chain of Pearl, which he fent to Sir *Thomas Dale*, when the Peace was concluded; and which was to be a Token between them, whenever Sir *Thomas* fent a Meffenger to him; otherwife, he was to bind him, and fend him back, as a Deferter. It was true, there was fuch an Agreement; and Sir *Thomas Dale* had ordered his Page to deliver the Chain to Mr. *Hamer*, but the Page either neglected or forgot it. Mr. *Hamer* there-fore replied, that he knew not of any fuch Order; and if there was fuch a Token, it was only intended, when Sir *Thomas*, upon the fudden, fhould fend an *Englifh* Meffen-ger, without an *Indian* Guide. But if his own People fhould conduct the Meffenger, which was the Cafe at pre-fent, that was a fufficient Teftimony and Credential. With this Anfwer *Powhdtan* was fatisfied, and conducted them to his Houfe, where a Guard of two hundred Bowmen atten-ded. Firft he offered Mr. *Hamer* a Pipe of Tobacco, and then afked after his Brother, Sir *Thomas Dale's* Health; and how his Daughter, and unknown Son, lived and liked. And being told, that his Brother was well; and that his Daughter was fo delighted with her Condition, that fhe would not, upon any Account, return and live again with him, he laughed heartily, and feemed much pleafed to hear it.

AFTER that, he demanded of Mr. *Hamer* his Bufinefs; who telling him, that it was private, he inftantly com-manded all out of the Houfe, except his two Queens, that always fat by him, and then bad him fpeak on. Mr. *Ha-mer* firft prefented him with feveral Toys, fent by Sir *Tho-mas Dale*; and then he told him, that his Brother *Dale*, having heard of the Fame of his youngeft Daughter, in-tended to marry her to fome worthy *Englifh* Gentleman, which would be highly pleafing and agreeable to her Sifter, who was very defirous to fee her, and to have her near her;

her; and that therefore, he defired, as a Teftimony of his
Love, that he would fend her to him. For fince they were
now become one People, and defigned to dwell together in
the fame Country, he conceived, there could be no firmer
Union, nor ftronger Affurance of Love and Friendfhip,
than fuch a natural Band of Intermarriage and Alliance.
Powhatan, who often interrupted him, and betrayed many
Signs of Uneafinefs, the whole Time, he was fpeaking,
immediately returned this Anfwer, with much Serioufnefs
and Gravity.

*I gladly accept my Brother's Salute of Love and Peace;
which, whilft I live, I will punctually and exactly keep. I
likewife receive his Prefents, as Pledges thereof, with no lefs
Thankfulnefs. But as to my Daughter, I fold her, a few
Days fince, to a great Werowance, for two Bufhels of Roanoke.*
Mr. *Hamer* told him, that the Roanoke was but a Trifle
to fo great a Prince; and by returning it, he might recall
her, and gratify his Brother. And he further affured him,
befides ftrengthening the ftrict Band of Peace and Friendfhip
between them, that he fhould have three times the Worth
of the Roanoke for her, in Beads, Copper, and other Commodities. This extorted the Truth from him; and he in-
genuoufly confeffed, that the Reafon of his Refufal, was
the Love, he bore his Daughter. Altho' he had many
Children, yet he delighted in none, he faid, fo much as
her; and he could not poffibly live without often feeing her;
which he could not do, if fhe lived among the *Englifh*.
For he had determined, upon no Terms, to put himfelf into their Hands, or come among them. He therefore defired him, to urge him no farther upon the Subject, but to
return his Brother this Anfwer: *That he held it not a brotherly Part, to endeavour to bereave him of his two darling
Children at once: That, for his Part, he defired no farther
Affurance of his Friendfhip, than the Promife, he had given:
and, That from him, Sir* Thomas *already had a Pledge, one
of his Daughters, which, as long as fhe lived, would be fufficient; but if fhe fhould happen to die, he promifed to give
another. And further, fays he, tell him, altho' he had no
Pledge at all, yet he need not diftruft any Injury from me or
my People. There hath been enough of Blood and War. Too
many have been flain already, on both Sides; and, by my Occafion, there fhall never be more. I, who have Power to perform it, have faid it. I am now grown old, and would gladly
end my Days in Peace and Quietnefs; and altho' I fhould have
juft Caufe of Refentment, yet my Country is large enough, and
I can go from you. And this Anfwer, I hope, will fatisfy
my Brother.*

WHILST

W H I L S T Mr. *Hamer* ſtaid here, by Chance there came an *Engliſhman*, who had been taken, three Years before, at *Fort Henry*, on the Mouth of *Hampton* River. He was grown ſo like an *Indian*, both in Complexion and Habit, that he could be diſtinguiſhed from them by nothing but his Language. He begged of Mr. *Hamer*, to procure his Liberty; which, with much Difficulty, he did. And now being about to return, *Powhatan* deſired him, to put his Brother *Dale* in Mind, to ſend him ſeveral Toys and Tools; which, leſt he ſhould forget, he made him write them down, in a Table-Book, that he had. However he got it, it was a very fair one; and Mr. *Hamer* deſired, he would give it to him. But he told him, he could not part with it: For it did him much Good, in ſhewing to Strangers. After which, having furniſhed them well with Proviſions, he diſmiſſed them; giving each a Buckſkin, extremely well dreſſed, and ſending two more, to his Son and Daughter.

A L L this while, Sir *Thomas Dale*, Mr. *Whitaker*, Miniſter of *Bermuda-Hundred*, and Mr. *Rolfe*, her Huſband, were very careful and aſſiduous, in inſtructing *Pocahontas* in the Chriſtian Religion; and ſhe, on her Part, expreſſed an eager Deſire, and ſhewed great Capacity in learning. After ſhe had been tutored for ſome time, ſhe openly renounced the Idolatry of her Country, confeſſed the Faith of Chriſt, and was baptized by the Name of *Rebecca*. But her real Name, it ſeems, was originally *Matoax*; which the *Indians* carefully concealed from the *Engliſh*, and changed it to *Pocahontas*, out of a ſuperſtitious Fear, leſt they, by the Knowledge of her true Name, ſhould be enabled to do her ſome Hurt. She was the firſt Chriſtian *Indian* in theſe Parts, and perhaps the ſincereſt and moſt worthy, that has ever been ſince. And now ſhe had no Manner of Deſire, to return to her Father; neither could ſhe well endure the brutiſh Manners, or Society, of her own Nation. Her Affection to her Huſband was extremely conſtant and true; and he, on the other Hand, underwent great Torment and Pain, out of his violent Paſſion, and tender Sollicitude for her.

W H I L S T theſe things were tranſacting in *Virginia*, Captain *Smith*'s reſtleſs and enterpriſing Genius could not brook a Life of Indolence and Inactivity at home. He therefore undertook a Voyage for ſome Merchants, to that Part of *Virginia*, which had been diſcovered by Captain *Goſnold*, in the Year 1602. Having made an advantageous Voyage for his Owners, and taken an exact Chart of the Coaſt, he then firſt called the Country *New-England*. This Name was afterwards confirmed and eſtabliſhed by Prince *Charles*, who likewiſe, at Captain *Smith*'s Deſire, gave
Names

Names to feveral Places and Rivers along the Coaft, from
Cape Cod as far as the Bay of *Fundi*. It was refolved, to
fettle the Country immediately, under the Conduct of Captain *Smith*; who was graced with the empty Title of Admiral of *New-England*. But he meeting with many crofs
Accidents the next Year, and being at laft taken by a *French*
Rover, the Project became abortive; and it was the Year
1620, before any Settlement was made there.

T H I S Year alfo, Sir *Walter Ralegh* firft publifhed his
Hiftory of the World; which was received with all due
Applaufe and Admiration by the Publick, but gave Umbrage, we are told, to the King. Some Authors have infinuated, that that Royal Pedant was piqued, as an Author,
and jealous of him in that Capacity. As if it would ever
come into any Man's Head, to put that admirable Work
in the Ballance with his old-wififh Garrulities; which are
now only to be found in the Collections of the Curious, as
a comic and ridiculous Entertainment, and a proper Subject for Laughter and Contempt. Others fay, that he was
fcandalized at the Freedom, which Sir *Walter Ralegh* had
taken with fome dead Princes, and particularly with *Henry*
VIII; thinking it perhaps an unpardonable Infolence, and a
Kind of Blafphemy, that any, below a Crowned Head,
fhould dare to cenfure their Actions. Whilft others tell us,
that, through the mifchievous Infinuations of fome Syco-
phants about him, he fufpected, that it contained an artful
Expofure of himfelf and Miniftry. And thus truly, as Mr.
Oldys obferves, the General Hiftory of the World was turned into a fecret Hiftory, or oblique Satire, upon his Court;
and *Scotch* Faces were to be feen in it, ftuck upon old *Jew-*
ifh, *Babylonian*, or *Affyrian* Shoulders. Altho', as it is re-
marked by another Author, he might eafily be led to fancy,
he faw in the Face of *Ninias*, the Son of *Semiramis*, his
own Features, as Succeffor to the *Britifh Semiramis*; and
that his particular Injuftice, to the Writer, was well reprefented and cenfured, in the Story of *Ahab*'s taking away
Naboth's Vineyard. But from whatever Caufe his Offence
arofe, I thought, it would not be unacceptable to the Reader, to make this fhort Digreffion, to the Honour of that
immortal Work. For next to the Praife and Approbation
of the Wife, it hath been ever efteemed a fecondary Honour to an Author, to be carped at, by the foolifh Cavils,
and vain Exceptions, of thofe of a contrary Character.

In *June*, Captain *Argall* fet Sail for *England*, and gave
an Account of the quiet and flourifhing State of the Colony;
which Report was ftrengthened by the Teftimony of Sir
Thomas Gates, who had returned from *Virginia*, the *March*
before.

1615.   before.   To back this Succefs with all Expedition, the
Council and Company refolved, that the great *Virginia*
Sir *Thomas* Lottery fhould be drawn, with all convenient Speed; which
Dale, Go-   was accordingly done, the following Year 1615.   The
vernor.   fame Year, a *Spanifh* Ship was feen to beat to and fro, off
Point Comfort; and at laft, fhe fent a Boat afhore, for a Pilot.
Captain *Davies*, the Governor of the Fort, readily granted
one, and fent Mr. *John Clarke*; who was no fooner on
board, but they fet Sail, and carried him off to *Spain*.   He
was there ftrongly follicited, to become their Inftrument
and Pilot, to betray the Colony.   But he bravely and honeftly refifted all their Temptations; and was, therefore,
obliged to undergo a long Captivity.   At laft, after four
Years Imprifonment, he was, with much Suit, returned to
England.   But the *Spanifh* Ship, by fome Accident, left
three of her own Men behind; who were immediately
feized, and ftrictly examined.   They faid, that having loft
their Admiral, they were forced into thefe Parts; and that
two of them were Captains, and in chief Authority in the
Fleet.   But fometime after, one was difcovered to be an
Englifhman; who had been a Pilot in the *Spanifh Armada*,
in the grand Expedition againft *England*, in the Year 1588.
And not content with this Perfidy and Bafenefs to his Country, he began here to plot, and perfuaded fome Malecon-
tents, to join with him, in running away with a fmall Bark.
But they were apprehended, and fome of them executed;
and he, now lying at Mercy, readily confeffed, that there
were two or three *Spanifh* Ships at Sea, fent purpofely to
difcover the State of the Colony.   But he faid, their Commiffion was not to be opened, 'till they arrived in the Bay;
fo that, of any thing further he was utterly ignorant.   One
of the *Spaniards* died here, and the other was fent to *England*.   But this Renegado was hanged at Sea, by Sir *Thomas Dale*, in his Voyage homeward.

1616.   FOR Sir *Thomas Dale* had now been five Years in the
Country; and he had been, for fome time paft, kept here,
George and fupported under a longing Defire to vifit his own Affairs
Yeardley, and Family, by a juft Senfe of his Duty to God and his
Governor. Country, and out of Compaffion to the poor Creatures committed to his Charge.   But now the Country being in perfect Peace, and having fettled all things in good Order,
and made Choice of Mr. *George Yeardley*, to be Deputy-
Governor in his Abfence, he embarked for *England*, with
Pocahontas and Mr. *Rolfe* her Hufband; and carrying with
them feveral young *Indians* of both Sexes, they all arrived
fafe at *Plimouth*, the 12th of *June*, 1616.   But at the time
of his Daughter's Departure, *Powhatan* had withdrawn
himfelf

himfelf to the King of *Moy-umps*, on *Patowmack* River ;
out of Fear, as it was fuppofed, of *Opechancanough*. For
he was then a Man very gracious and popular, both with
the *Indians* and the *Englifh*; and as *Opitchapan*, the fecond
Brother, was lame and decrepit, he was thought to look
upon *Powhatan*, a Perfon of equal Ambition and Capacity
for Government, as the only Obftacle to his afpiring Hop
and Defigns. And therefore, *Powhatan* fufpected at this
time, that he had entered into a Confpiracy with the *Englifh*, to betray him into their Hands; a Cafe, which he had
ever dreaded, and which, he had therefore turned the whole
Force of his Politicks, to prevent and avoid.

THIS worthy and honourable Knight, Sir *Thomas Dale*,
who may juftly be ranked among the firft and beft of our
Governors, had, by his fingular Vigor and Induftry, and
by his Judgment and Conduct of the Affairs of the Colony,
put things into fuch an eafy and profperous Condition, that,
from this Time, an Alteration was made, in the Right of
Adventure for Land. For before this, every one, that had
adventured his own Perfon, or had fent, or brought others
over, at his own Expence, was entitled to an hundred A-
cres of Land, perfonal Adventure, for each; which was
the utmoft that could be granted in any fingle Share, by
the King's Letters patent, and which are called, in the
Company's Journals, and other old Records, Great Shares,
or Shares of old Adventure. But now it was thought, all
Difficulties were fo far overcome, and the Country fettled
in fuch a Way of fubfifting and flourifhing, that, hence-
forward, fifty Acres only were allowed to thofe, who came,
or brought others over. This is the ancient, legal, and a
moft indubitable Method of granting Lands in *Virginia*, and
was intended for a great and ufeful End, the encouraging
People, to come themfelves, and to bring or fend others
over, to inhabit the Country ; and that they might, immediately upon their Arrival, have a Place, whereon to feat
themfelves and Families. And I likewife find, in the old
Records, that upon peopling and faving thefe hundred, or
fifty Acres (the Terms of which I can no where find) they
were entitled to the like Quantity more, to be held, and
feated at their Leifure. But befides this, there were two
other Methods of granting Lands. The one was upon Merit : When any Perfon had conferred a Benefit, or done
Service, to the Company or Colony, they would beftow
fuch a Proportion of Land upon him. However, to prevent Excefs in this Particular, they were reftrained, by his
Majefty's Letters patent, not to exceed twenty great Shares,
or two thoufand Acres, in any of thefe Grants. The other
                                                        was

1616. was called the Adventure of the Purſe; every Perſon, who paid twelve Pounds ten Shillings into the Company's Treaſury, having thereby a Title to an hundred Acres of Land, any where in *Virginia*, that had not been before granted to, or poſſeſſed by others.

Geo. Yeardley, Governor.

SIR *Thomas Dale*, among the many Praiſes, juſtly due to his Adminiſtration, had been particularly careful of the Supplies of Life; and had, accordingly, always cauſed ſo much Corn to be planted, that the Colony lived in great Plenty and Abundance. Nay, whereas they had formerly been conſtrained, to buy Corn of the *Indians* Yearly, which expoſed them to much Scorn and Difficulty, the Caſe was ſo much altered under his Management, that the *Indians* ſometimes applied to the *Engliſh*, and would ſell the very Skins from their Shoulders for Corn. And to ſome of their petty Kings, Sir *Thomas* lent four or five hundred Buſhels; for Repayment whereof the next Year, he took a Mortgage of their whole Countries. But as the Cultivation of Tobacco began to creep in, and to obſtruct their Crops of Corn, he made a Law, that no Tobacco ſhould be ſet, 'till ſuch a Proportion of Corn-Ground, for the Maſter and each Servant, had been firſt prepared and planted. And this was the firſt Beginning and Eſſay, towards making Tobacco here, which hath ever ſince continued the Staple-Commodity of our Country. But after his Departure, both his Law and his Example were utterly laid by and forgot; and the new Governor himſelf, together with all the People, being tempted with the View of preſent Gain, applied themſelves ſo eagerly to planting Tobacco, that they neglected the other neceſſary Article of Life. And beſides this Neglect of their Corn, the Supplies of People, ſent this Year, came, as uſual, ſo unprovided, that they ſoon eaſed them of the Plenty, left by Sir *Thomas Dale*, and reduced them to great Streights. Mr. *Yeardley* therefore, ſent to the *Chickahominies*, for the Tribute Corn. For there being about two hundred and fifty, or three hundred, fighting Men of the Nation, and each Man being obliged, by the Treaty, to bring two Buſhels of Corn to the Store, ſuch a Quantity would have been a great Relief to their Neceſſities. But receiving a ſlight and affrontive Anſwer, he drew together an hundred of his beſt Shot, and went to *Chickahominy*.

THE People there received him with much Scorn and Contempt. They told him, he was only Sir *Thomas Dale*'s Man; that they had indeed paid his Maſter, according to Agreement; but as for him, they had no Order, and leſs Inclination, either to obey, or give him any Corn. And being

being led by their Captain, *Kiffanacomen,* Governor of O-
zinies, they drew themfelves up, in martial Rank and Order, as they faw the *Englifh* do. But after many Remon-
ftrances, and much Bravade and Threatening on both Sides,
Mr. *Yeardley,* at laft, commanded his Men to fire upon
them. Twelve were flain, and as many taken Prifoners;
among whom, were two of their Senators, or Elders. For
their Ranfom, they had an hundred Bufhels; and the *Indians,* to buy their Peace, readily loaded their three Boats
with Corn; one of which, crowding on, to bring the firft
News to *James-Town,* was unhappily overfet, all her Corn
loft, and eleven Men drowned.

Opechancanough, a politick and haughty Prince, was much
vexed, that neither his Brother, nor he, could ever bring
this obftinate People, firmly to their Obedience. Being,
therefore, as attentive to enflave them, as they were watchful and tenacious of their Liberty, he took this Opportunity,
and agreed with Mr. *Yeardley,* to come to no Terms with
them, without his Advice and Confent. And as the *Englifh* paffed down the River with their Prifoners, he met
them at *Ozinies,* and pretended to the *Indians,* that he had,
with great Pains and Sollicitation, procured their Peace.
To requite which Service, they chearfully proclaimed him
King of their Nation, and flocked, from all Parts, with
Prefents of Beads, Copper, and fuch other Trifles, as were
in Value and Efteem among them. And he was glad to
be content with this precarious Acknowledgment, from a
free and refolute People. But this feafonable and vigorous
Chaftifement of the *Chickahominies,* and efpecially the ftrict
League and Friendfhip, with *Opechancanough,* and the whole
Imperial Family, kept the reft of the *Indians* in fuch Awe
and Dependance, that the *Englifh* followed their Labours,
with the utmoft Quietnefs and Security. Many alfo of
the Savages daily brought them fuch Provifions, as they
could get; and would be their Guides in hunting, and fometimes hunt for them themfelves. And thus, by fuch an Intercourfe and Familiarity, the *Englifh* and they lived together,
the reft of this Gentleman's Government, as if they had
been one People. And Captain *Smith* tells us, that Mr.
Yeardley had fome trained to their Pieces to kill him Fowl,
as had likewife feveral other Gentlemen in the Country;
and that thefe foon became as dextrous and expert, as any
of the *Englifh.* But the Captain's Authority is rendered
very fufpicious in this, by the Records of our General
Court. For long after, the Governor and Council received
fome Queries from *England,* the fourth whereof was:
What was the Caufe of the Maffacre, and who firft taught
the

the Indians *the Use of Fire Arms?* Whereupon, in a Court
held the 1ſt of *November*, 1624, *Robert Poole* and *Edward
Grindon*, Gentlemen, ancient Planters and Inhabitants of
the Country, appear, and declare, upon Oath, their Knowledge of the Matter. Their Depoſitions entirely clear Mr.
Yeardley, and ſhew him to have been very cautious and
careful in that Point; and they throw the whole Blame upon Captain *Smith* himſelf, Sir *Thomas Dale*, and ſome other
inferior Officers and private Perſons.

IN the mean while, *Pocahontas*, or the Lady *Rebecca*,
as they now affected to call her, was kindly received in *England*. She was, by this time, well inſtructed in Chriſtianity, ſpoke good and intelligible *Engliſh*, and was become
very civil and ceremonious, after the *Engliſh* Faſhion. She
was likewiſe delivered of a Son, of which ſhe was extremely
fond; and the Treaſurer and Company gave Order, for
the handſome Maintenance of both her and her Child.
Beſides which, her Company was courted, and ſhe kindly
treated, by many Perſons of higheſt Rank and Quality in
the Nation. There hath been indeed a conſtant Tradition,
that the King became jealous, and was highly offended at
Mr. *Rolfe*, for marrying a Princeſs. That anointed Pedant,
it ſeems, had ſo high an Idea of the *Jus divinum*, and in-
defeaſible Right, of *Powhatan*, that he held it a great Crime
and Miſdemeanor, for any private Gentleman to mingle
with his Imperial Blood. And he might perhaps likewiſe
think, conſiſtently with his own Principles, that the Right
to theſe Dominions would, thereby, be veſted in Mr. *Rolfe's*
Poſterity. However, it paſſed off, without any farther bad
Conſequence, than a little Diſpleaſure and Murmuring.

AT the time of *Pocahontas's* Arrival, Captain *Smith* was
preparing for a Voyage to *New-England*. He was much
concerned, that the Suddenneſs of his Departure put it out
of his Power, to do her that Service, which he deſired, and
ſhe well deſerved at his Hands. However, being well acquainted at Court, and particularly favoured and counte-
nanced by Prince *Charles*, he drew up, and preſented to the
Queen, before her Arrival in *London*, a Repreſentation of
her Caſe and Deſert. In this, he expreſſes a deep Senſe of
Gratitude to her; and ſets forth her great Affection, and
many Services, to himſelf, and the whole *Engliſh* Nation:
That by her, their Quarrels had oft been appeaſed, their
Wants ſupplied, and their Dangers averted: That ſhe, un-
der God, had been the chief Inſtrument, of preſerving the
Colony, and confirming the Settlement: That being taken
Priſoner, ſhe had become the Means of a firm Peace and
Alliance, with her Father: That ſhe was now married to
an

an *English* Gentleman; who, however, was not of Abi- 1616.
lity, to make her fit to attend her Majefty: That fhe was
the firft Chriftian, that ever was of that Nation; and the *Geo. Teard-*
firft *Virginian*, that ever fpoke, or became *English:* That *ley,* Gover-
being well received, and honoured by fo great a Queen,
beyond what her fimple Thought could imagine or conceive,
fhe might be the Means of adding another Kingdom, to his
Majefty's Dominions: But by bad Ufage, her prefent Love,
to the *English* and Chriftianity, might be turned to Scorn
and Fury; and all the Good, fhe had, or might do, diverted to the worft of Evil. And therefore, he humbly recommends her to her Majefty, as a proper Objeƈt of her Favour
and Regard, on Account of her Birth, Virtue, Simplicity,
and forlorn Condition in a ftrange Country.

Bᴜᴛ before Captain *Smith*'s Departure, *Pocahontas* came
up to *London*. Being offended by the Smoke of the Town,
fhe was immediately removed to *Brentford*; whither Smith,
with feveral of his Friends, went to vifit her. After a cold
and modeft Salutation, fhe turned from him in a paffionate
Manner, hid her Face, and could not be brought to fpeak
a Word for two or three Hours. But at laft, fhe began to
talk; and fhe reminded him, of the many Services, fhe
had done him, and of the ftriƈt Promife of Friendfhip, between him and her Father. *You,* fays fhe, *promifed him,
that what was yours, fhould be his; and that you and he
would be all one. Being a Stranger in our Country, you called*
Powhatan *Father; and I, for the fame Reafon, will now
call you fo.* But Captain *Smith*, knowing the jealous Humour of the Court, durft not allow of that Title, as fhe
was a King's Daughter; and therefore, he endeavoured to
excufe himfelf from it. But fhe, with a ftern and fteady
Countenance, faid: *You were not afraid to come into my Father's Country, and ftrike a Fear into every Body, but myfelf;
and are you here afraid, to let me call you Father? I tell you
then, I will call you Father, and you fhall call me Child; and
fo I will for ever be of your Kindred and Country. They
always told us, that you were dead; and I knew no otherwife,
'till I came to* Plimouth. *But* Powhatan *commanded* Tomocomo *to feek you out, and know the Truth; becaufe your Countrymen are much given to Lying.*

Tʜɪs *Tomocomo* (or *Uttamaccomack*, as *Smith* calls him)
had *Matachanna*, one of *Powhatan*'s Daughters, to Wife;
was one of the chief of his Council, and of their Priefts;
and was efteemed a very wife and underftanding Fellow a-
mong them. He was therefore fent upon this Voyage, by
Powhatan, to take the Number of the People in *England*,
and to bring him a full and exaƈt Account, of their Strength

and

1616.

Geo. Yeard-
ley, Gover-
nor.

and Condition. And accordingly, being arrived at *Plimouth*, he got a long Stick, intending to cut a Notch, for every one, he faw. But he was foon tired with fuch an endlefs Work, and threw away his Stick; and being afked, by the King, after his Return, how many People there were? it is faid, that he replied: *Count the Stars in the Sky, the Leaves on the Trees, and the Sand upon the Sea Shore; for fuch is the Number of the People in* England. But Sir *Thomas Dale* told Mr. *Purchas*, that he believed him to be fent by *Opechancanough*, their King and Governor in *Powhatan*'s Abfence and Retreat; and that he was fent, not fo much to number the People, as to take an Account of their Corn and Trees. For *Namontack*, and fuch others, as had been fent to *England* formerly, being ignorant and filly, and having feen little elfe befides *London*, had reported much of their Men and Houfes, but thought, they had fmall Store of Corn and Trees. And it was therefore a general Opinion among thefe Barbarians, that the *Englifh* came into their Country, to get a Supply of thefe; which might be ftrengthened and confirmed, by their fending large Quantities of Cedar, Clapboard, and Wainfcot, to *England*, and by their continual Want and Eagernefs after Corn. But *Tomocomo*, landing in the *Weft*, and travelling thence to *London*, was foon undeceived, and faw great Caufe, to admire the *Englifh* Plenty. However, he began to take an Account, untill his Arithmetick failed him. Meeting Captain *Smith* accidentally in *London*, they foon renewed their old Acquaintance. He told the Captain, that *Powhatan* had commanded him, to find him out, to fhew him the *Englifh* God, their King, Queen, and Prince; of which he had told them fo much. As to God, Captain *Smith* excufed and explained the Matter, the beft, he could; and as to the King, he told him, that he had already feen him, and fhould fee the reft, whenever he pleafed. But he denied, that he had feen the King, 'till, by Circumftances, he was convinced and fatisfied. And then, with a melancholly Countenance, he faid: *You gave* Powhatan *a white Dog, which he fed as himfelf; but your King has given me nothing, and yet I am better, than your white Dog.* Such an arch Senfe had this Barbarian, of the ftingy Treatment, with which he had been received at Court.

HOWEVER, *Pocahontas* was eagerly fought, and kindly entertained every where. Many Courtiers, and others of his Acquaintance, daily flocked to Captain *Smith*, to be introduced to her. They generally confeffed, that the Hand of God did vifibly appear, in her Converfion; and that they had feen many *Englifh* Ladies, worfe favoured, of lefs ex-

a

act

act Proportion, and genteel Carriage, than she was. She *1616.* was likewise carried to Court, by the Lady *Delawarr*, attended by the Lord, her Husband, and divers other Persons *Geo. Yeard-ley,* Gover-of Fashion and Distinction. The whole Court were charm-*nor.* ed and surprised, at the Decency and Grace of her Deportment; and the King himself, and Queen, were pleased, honourably to receive and esteem her. The Lady *Delawarr*, and those other Persons of Quality, also waited on her, to the Masks, Balls, Plays, and other publick Entertainments; with which she was wonderfully pleased and delighted. And she would, doubtless, have well deserved, and fully returned, all this Respect and Kindness, had she lived to arrive in *Virginia.*

THE Lord *Rich* was one of the Company in *England*; a great and powerful, but a most designing, interested, and factious Member. Not content with that lawful and regular Advantage, which might be justly expected, in a due Course of Time, from the Enterprise, but aiming at a sudden and extraordinary Profit, altho' it should be, by the Spoil of the Publick, and Oppression of the private Planters, and being likewise egged on and assisted, by some corrupt and avaritious Persons, he threw himself at the Head of a Faction in the Company, and drew over to his Party, as many Creatures and Dependents, as he possibly could. By their Means and Support, he hoped and endeavoured, to bear such a Sway, both in the *Virginia* and *Somer-Islands* Company, that the Management of all things at home, and the Placing all Governors abroad, should be entirely in his Power and Disposal. And altho' he met with a Check in his Designs, from many great and worthy Members, and a vast Majority of the whole Companies, yet he did, at this time, carry a very important Point. Captain *Samuel Argall*, a Friend and Relation of Sir *Thomas Smith*, the Treasurer, was one of Lord *Rich's* fastest Friends and Favourites. His Lordship therefore, having concerted Matters with him, and entered into a Partnership, procured him to be elected Deputy-Governor of *Virginia.* And altho' Martial Law was then the Common Law of the Country, yet the better to arm and strengthen him, with the Exercise of such a despotic Authority, and that no Man here might dare to open his Mouth against him, he obtained for him the Place of Admiral of the Country and Seas adjoining.

WITH these Views and Powers, was Captain *Argall* *1617.* fitted out, and sent to *Virginia*, in the Beginning of 1617. And the Treasurer and Council took Care, for the proper *Sam. Argall,* Accommodation of *Pocahontas* and her Husband, on board *Governor.*

21 L the

1617.

Sam. Argall, Governor.

the Admiral Ship. Mr. *Rolfe* was also made Secretary and Recorder-General of *Virginia*, which Place was now first instituted. But it pleased God, at *Gravesend*, to take *Pocahontas* to his Mercy, in about the two and twentieth Year of her Age. Her unexpected Death caused not more Sorrow and Concern in the Spectators, than her religious End gave them Joy and Surprise. For she died, agreeably to her Life, a most sincere and pious Christian. Her little Son, *Thomas Rolfe*, was left at *Plimouth* with Sir *Lewis Steukley*, who desired the Care and Education of him. This Gentleman was then Vice-Admiral of the County of *Devon*; but soon after, having seised Sir *Walter Ralegh*, and been guilty of a notable Piece of Treachery towards him, he drew upon himself the publick Scorn and Detestation. For however hard or unjust Kings and Statesmen may be to those Persons of their Age, who are of the most eminent Parts and Virtues, the Publick is generally more candid in it's Judgments, and apt to resent every Hardship or ill Usage to such Men. Sir *Lewis Steukley* therefore fell unpitied, when he was afterwards detected in corrupt Practices; for which he was obliged to purchase his Life at the Expence of his whole Fortune, and at last died, a poor, despised, and distracted Beggar. And as these Misfortunes happened soon after this Time, it is not to be supposed, that young Mr. *Rolfe* long enjoyed the Advantage of his Favour and kind Intentions. However he was carried up to *London*, and there educated by his Uncle Mr. *Henry Rolfe*, and afterwards became a Person of Fortune and Distinction in this Country. He left behind him an only Daughter, who was married to Col. *Robert Bolling*; by whom she left an only Son, the late Major *John Bolling*, who was Father to the present Col. *John Bolling*, and several Daughters, married to Col. *Richard Randolph*, Col. *John Fleming*, Dr. *William Gay*, Mr. *Thomas Eldridge*, and Mr. *James Murray*. So that this Remnant of the Imperial Family of *Virginia*, which long ran in a single Person, is now encreased and branched out into a very numerous Progeny.

BUT Governor *Argall*, with his Vice-Admiral Captain *Ralph Hamer*, pursued their Voyage to *Virginia*, where they arrived in *May*. He found all the publick Works and Buildings in *James-Town* fallen to Decay; not above five or six private Houses fit to be inhabited; the Market-place, Streets, and all other spare Places, planted with Tobacco; and the Colony dispersed all about, as every Man could find the properest Place, and best Conveniency, for Planting. But soon after his Arrival, he wrote to *England*, that the Colony was in great Peace and Plenty, and the People busily bufily employed, in preparing for their Crops of Corn and Tobacco. With him returned *Tomocomo*, who, in our old Records, is called by a third Name, *Tomakin*. Captain *Argall* sent him immediately to *Opechancanough*, who came to *James-Town*, and received a Present, with great Joy and Thankfulness. *Tomocomo* railed violently against *England*, and the *English*; and particularly, against his best Friend, Sir *Thomas Dale*. But all his Reports were so clearly disproved before *Opechancanough* and his Grandees, that much to the Satisfaction of the Grandees, he was rejected and disgraced. But *Powhatan*, all this while, leaving the Care and Charge of the Government chiefly to *Opechancanough*, went about from Place to Place, taking his Pleasure, and visiting the different Parts of his Dominions. However he still continued in good Friendship with the *English*. He greatly lamented the Death of his Daughter; but rejoiced, that her Child was living. He also, as well as *Opechancanough*, expressed much Desire to see him; but determined, that he ought not to come over, before he was stronger. And, this Year, one Mr. *Lambert* made a great Discovery, in the Trade of Planting. For the Method of curing Tobacco then was in Heaps. But this Gentleman found out, that it cured better upon Lines; and therefore the Governor wrote to the Company, to send over Line for that Purpose.

CAPTAIN *Argall* was a Man of Sense and Industry; and therefore, to secure a Plenty of Provisions, he sent out, the next Year, a Frigat and a small Bark to trade, which brought near six hundred Bushels of Corn, to the great Relief of the Colony. For the Company's Servants, that worked for the Store, were reduced to fifty four, Men, Women, and Children. But from the Farmers, who were at Captain *Argall's* Arrival eighty one, and from the Indians, as Tribute, they received annually above twelve hundred Bushels. But this Year, there was a great Drought, with a dreadful Storm, that poured down Hailstones, eight or nine Inches round, which did much Damage to both Corn and Tobacco. However, what Tobacco could be saved, was made up, the best at three Shillings a Pound, and the rest at eighteen Pence. The Governor also published several Edicts: That all Goods should be sold at twenty five *per Cent*, and Tobacco allowed for at three Shillings a Pound, and not under nor over, on the Penalty of three Years Slavery to the Colony: That there should be no private Trade or Familiarity with the Savages: That no *Indian* should be taught to shoot with Guns, on Pain of Death to Teacher and Learner: That no Person

should

fhould hunt Deer or Hogs, without the Governor's Leave : That all Hogs, found a fecond time in *James-Town*, fhould be forfeited to the Colony ; and thofe at *Bermuda*, ringed : That no Man fhould fhoot, except in his own neceffary Defence againft an Enemy, till a new Supply of Ammunition came in, on Pain of a Year's Slavery : That none fhould go on board the Ship, then at *James-Town*, without the Governor's Leave ; and that no Mafters of Ships fhould fuffer their Sailers to go afhore, or talk with the People at *Kicquotan* : That every Perfon fhould go to Church, *Sundays* and Holidays, or lye Neck and Heels that Night, and be a Slave to the Colony the following Week ; for the fecond Offence, he fhould be a Slave for a Month ; and for the third, a Year and a Day.

THE Lord *Delawarr*, who had withdrawn from the Government on Account of his Health, and whofe Commiffion, as Captain-General, was fupreme, and fuperfeded all others, being ardently wifhed for by the Colony, was now fent by the Council and Company, in a large Ship, with a Supply of two hundred People. But meeting with contrary Winds and much bad Weather, many fell fick, and thirty died. In this Number was the Right Honourable, the Lord Governor himfelf ; a Perfon of a moft noble and generous Difpofition, who had warmly embarked, and expended much Money, in this Bufinefs, for his Country's Good. *Cambden* tells us, that he had been feafted at the *Weftern-Iflands*, and that his Death was not without fufpicion of Poifon. And I think I have fomewhere feen, that he died about the Mouth of *Delawarr* Bay, which thence took it's Name from him. But being not able, now to recollect the Authority, I fhall leave it, as I found it, and not venture pofitively to affirm it. After his Death, they were forced on the Coaft of *New-England* ; where they got a Recruit of Wood and Water, and took fuch an Abundance of Fifh and Fowl, as plentifully ferved them to *Virginia*. They likewife here met a fmall *Frenchman*, rich in Bever and other Furrs, who feafted them with fo great a Variety of Fifh, Fowl, and Fruits, that they were all amazed ; little fufpecting, that wild Defert could afford fuch a wonderful Plenty of delicate and wholefome Food. This Ship bringing News, that Multitudes were preparing in *England* to be fent, Captain *Argall* called a Council, and wrote to the Treafurer and Council in *England* the State of the Colony ; and what Mifery muft neceffarily enfue, if they fent not Provifions, as well as People. And he likewife reprefented their Want of fkilful Hufbandmen, with Shares, Harnefs, and other Implements for Ploughing.

For

For their Land was exceeding good, and they had now about forty Bulls and Oxen, which were wholly idle and ufelefs, for want of fkilful Men to bring them to Labour. However, I find, in our old Records, that fome Ploughs, by this time, were fet to work.

ONE *Richard Killingbeck*, this Summer, attempting a fecret Trade with the *Indians*, was, together with his whole Company, flain by a Party of the *Chickahominies*; who fearing the Confequences, robbed the *Matchacomoco* Houfe of their Town, and fled. This was their Temple and religious Treafury; held, to the higheft Degree, facred and inviolable by the *Indians*. And the *Sunday* after, they flew two Boys and three young Children, within a Mile of *James-Town*, while their Parents were at Church. The Governor therefore fent to *Opechancanough*, who had the Title of their King, and the Power too, as far as Neceffity conftrained, or it fuited with their Humour or Intereft. But he excufed the Nation from the Guilt, and laid the whole Blame upon fome fugitive Robbers; of whofe Town he fent him a Bafket of Earth, as Poffeffion given; and promifed, to fend their Heads alfo for Satisfaction, as foon as they could poffibly catch them. But this he never performed; and confidering the Perfidy of his Nature, and the exterminating Hatred, he always bore to the *Englifh*, it is much to be queftioned, whether he was not privy to, or perhaps the chief Author and Contriver of the whole Matter. However, by thefe Acts of Hoftility and Barbarity, the whole Nation was rendered obnoxious to the *Englifh* Power and Refentment, and his Regal Authority thereby firmly riveted and eftablifhed among them. Altho' the Governor, being fatisfied with this Pretence and Excufe, never farther profecuted, or revenged, this perfidious Murder and Breach of the Peace.

CAPTAIN *Argall*, all this time, was not negligent or forgetful of the grand End of his coming to *Virginia*, but pufhed on his unrighteous Gains, by all imaginable Methods of Extortion and Oppreffion. For befides a Multitude of private Wrongs to particular Perfons, he converted in a manner wholly to his own Ufe and Poffeffion, whatfoever remained, at that time, belonging to the Publick, being the Fruits and Relicts of eighty thoufand Pounds Expence. So that he was loudly charged, with many Offences in Matter of State and Government, with Depredation and Wafte of the publick Eftate and Revenues of the Company, and with great Oppreffion of the Colony in general, as well as feveral private Men in particular. And the Cries of his Outrages and Rapine at laft became fo loud and numerous, and

and the Company in *England* was fo enraged at the Reports and Informations, they received, that they could fcarce be reftrained from flying to the King, for the Redrefs of fo many and fo great Mifchiefs. But Sir *Thomas Smith*, whether in Favour to Captain *Argall*, his Kinfman, or out of his real Judgment, alledged, that imploring his Majefty's Aid might prove prejudicial to the Company's Power, and of dangerous Confequence to their Liberties; and might alfo give Room to much publick Scandal and Reflection. And therefore he propofed a milder and lefs clamorous Way of Proceeding.

To this End, he himfelf, Alderman *Johnfon*, the Deputy-Treafurer, Sir *Lionel Cranfield*, and others of the Council, wrote Captain *Argall* a Letter, dated the 23d of *Auguft*, 1618; charging him, in very fharp and fevere Terms, with many Crimes and Mifdemeanors: That he was exceedingly chargeable to the Company, and converted the Fruits of their Expence to his own private Ufe: That he was grown fo proud and infolent, as to fcorn the Title of Deputy-Governor, declaring, that he would be no Man's Deputy: That he wronged the Magazine, by his Negligence and Connivency: That he had appropriated the *Indian* Trade to himfelf; ufing the Company's Frigat and other Veffels, together with their Men, to trade for his own Benefit, and prohibiting the Trade of Skins and Furs to all others: That he took the old Planters, who ought to be free, as well as the Company's Tenants and Servants, and fet them upon his own Employments: That he expended the publick Store-Corn, to feed his own Men: That he had, for fome private End and Purpofe of his own, informed the Company, that *Opechancanough* and the Natives intended to give their Country to Mr. *Rolfe*'s Child, and to referve it from all others, 'till he came of Age: That he neither looked into, nor regarded, their Inftructions; but had, under Pretence of their Commiffion, difpofed of all the Company's Cattle, againft their Exprefs Orders and Directions, and had converted the Profits thereof to his own Ufe: That he had, under Colour of his Right, as Admiral, feifed and detained fome Hides, unlawfully taken or purchafed, for which the Company had compounded, with the Lord High Admiral and the *Spanifh* Ambaffador, at the great Expence of four hundred Pounds: And in fhort, that all his Actions and Proceedings feemed to be, as if the Colony was wholly intended for his private Gain and Advantage, and as if he was fo great, and they fo mean and infenfible of Reafon, as to let things, of this publick and notorious Nature, pafs off without a ftrict and exact Account;

up-

upbraiding him alfo with thefe ungrateful Returns to their Favour and Friendfhip, in procuring him the Government.

AT the fame time, they wrote a Letter to my Lord *Delawarr*, whofe Death was yet unknown in *England*, containing the like Heads of Complaint and Accufation a-gainft Captain *Argall*; and informing him, that by the ftrange Infolence of his laft Letter, and by the Informations of fundry Witneffes, lately come from *Virginia*, there was more Difcontent raifed in the Adventurers, and more Dan-ger feared to the Colony, than had ever happened, by any other thing, fince the firft Beginning of the Enterprife. So that the Adventurers could hardly be reftrained from going to the King, altho' far off on a Progrefs, and procuring his Majefty's Command, to fetch him home as a Malefactor. But to avoid farther Scandal to their Management and Ad-miniftration, they befeech his Lordfhip, to fend him forth-with to *England*, to make his perfonal Appearance, and to give his Anfwers to fuch things, as fhould be laid to his Charge. And forafmuch as it was conceived, that there would be many things, for which he muft make Satisfaction to the Company, they defired his Lordfhip, to feife upon his Tobacco, Skins, Furs, and other Goods, to be fent to them as a Depofite, till all Matters fhould be fatisfied and adjufted; and that he would likewife return the Cattle, and other publick Goods, which he had embezzled, to their proper Places and Owners. And at the fame time, there was an Order of Court paffed in *England*, to fequefter all Captain *Argall's* Effects, which fhould be fent home, to make Reftitution to the Company for his Rapines and Ex-tortions.

THESE Letters, coming, by Lord *Delawarr's* Death, to Captain *Argall's* Hands, were fo far from diverting or repreffing his Exhorbitances, that they feemed, only to put him upon his Guard, and to render him the more ea-ger and ftudious to make the beft Ufe of his Time. For my Lady *Delawarr* complained, that he wrongfully took fome of her Goods from her late Hufband's Servants, with-out rendering any Account of them. And indeed he had, in general, affumed to himfelf a Power, of ordering and difpofing of his Lordfhip's Eftate, fetting his Tenants and Servants to his own Work, and thereby ruining and depo-pulating a very large and hopeful Plantation, begun by his Lordfhip. But one Captain *Edward Brewfter*, alledging Lord *Delawarr's* Order, for their being under his Manage-ment and Direction, endeavoured to withdraw them from the Governor's Work, and to employ them, for the Main-tenance of themfelves, and for the Benefit of his Lordfhip's

Heirs,

Heirs and Fellow-Adventurers. But one of them refufed

to obey him, which drew from him fome threatening Expreffions againft the Fellow.   This he immediately ran with
to the Governor; who being drunk with Power, and impatient of Oppofition, (a Diftemper, very incident to our
American Viceroys) and being alfo vexed perhaps, to find
any one dare to withftand his arbitrary Schemes of Gain,
he caufed Captain *Brewfter* to be feifed, tried by a Court
Martial, and condemned to Death.

T H E Legality of this Proceeding was founded on an Article of the Martial Laws of the Low Countries, introduced among thofe Articles, fent over by Sir *Thomas Smith.*
This decreed, " That no Man fhould offer any Violence,
" or contemptuoufly refift or difobey his Commander, or
" do any Act, or fpeak any Words, which might tend to
" breed Diforder or Mutiny, in the Town or Field, or
" difobey any principal Officer's Directions, upon Pain of
" Death."   But altho' it was evident from his Majefty's
Charter, that the Governor had Power to execute Martial
Law only in Times of Mutiny and Rebellion, in like Manner as Lords Lieutenants in *England* had, and that in all
other Cafes, as well civil as criminal, their Proceedings
were to be as agreeable, as conveniently might be, to the
Laws, Statutes, Government, and Policy of the Realm of
England; and altho' it was as evident, that there was at
that time no Pretence of Rebellion or Mutiny, but the Colony enjoyed an univerfal Peace and Tranquility; yet was
this innocent Gentleman's Condemnation moft unmercifully
driven on, and his Life fubjected to the Pleafure of a furious and enraged Enemy.   And this, not in an Affair of
publick Concern, but in a Dispute of private Right; and
when it did not appear, that he had uttered any thing a-
gainft the Governor, but only fome threatening Language againft a Servant, that difobeyed his lawful Commands.   And the whole was carried on and tranfacted, under Colour and Pretence of a Law, which could have no
legal Force or Validity in the *Britifh* Dominions.   Altho'
it muft be confeffed, that Martial Law was then the reigning Law of *Virginia*, to the great Difcouragement of the
Colony, and to the manifeft Infringement of the Rights and
Liberties of the People, as *Britifh* Subjects.   And this
Courfe, at times introduced and ufed from the firft, as being in a State of War and Danger, was firmly riveted and
confirmed by thofe bloody Articles, fent in by Sir *Thomas
Smith*, which were unfortunately, at their firft coming, applied to a good Purpofe and Effect by Sir *Thomas Dale*, in
quelling the diforderly and mutinous Humours of the People.

ple. And thus, by this Example and Authority, and by 1618.
eafy Acquiefcence and Ignorance in the People of their native Rights and Privileges, it was made the ftanding Rule *Sam. Argall*
of Proceeding, and became the Common Law and Cuftom Governor.
of the Country.

BUT fome of the Court, reflecting on the extreme Severity of thefe Martial Laws, and being alfo moved perhaps by the particular Hardfhip and Unrighteoufnefs of the
prefent Cafe, prevailed on the reft, to go in a Body, and
intercede for Captain *Brewfter's* Life. And being alfo joined
by fuch of the Clergy, as were at Hand, they did, with
much Intreaty, and after many Repulfes and Allegations of
Captain *Argall*, at laft prevail to fave his Life. But it
was upon this exprefs Condition, that he fhould take a folemn Oath, neither directly nor indirectly, in *England* or
elfewhere, to utter any contemptuous Words, or do any
thing elfe, that fhould turn to the Difhonour or Difparagement of Captain *Argall*; and that he fhould never return
more to *Virginia*, by any direct or indirect Means. All
which was this poor Gentleman, a Perfon of fome Figure
and Confideration, obliged to fubmit to, to refpite and put
off an immediate Execution. But after his Return to
England, being deeply fenfible of this oppreffive and injurious Treatment, as alfo to clear his Reputation, and to
wipe off the Stain of being a condemned Man, he appealed
from the Sentence of the Court Martial in *Virginia*, to the
Treafurer and Company in *England*. And the Profecution
of this Appeal did greatly contribute, to fhew and expofe
the extreme Rapicioufnefs and tyrannical Adminiftration of
Captain *Argall*.

A Ship, called the *Treafurer*, was alfo, this Year, fent
from *England* by the Lord *Rich*, who was now become
Earl of *Warwick*, a Perfon of great Note afterwards in the
Civil Wars, and commander of the Fleet againft the King.
He had afpired to the Title of Earl of *Clare*; but that
being then efteemed the fame with *Clarence*, and a Royal
Title, it was judged too high an Honour for a Family in a
Manner new and upftart, and that of *Warwick* conferred
upon him. This Ship was here new victualled, and manned
with the ftouteft and ableft Recruits, that could be picked
out of the whole Colony. And then, under Colour of an
old Commiffion of Hoftility from the Duke of *Savoy*, againft
the *Spaniards*, which they had by fome Means procured,
fhe was fent to rove on the *Spanifh* Dominions in the *Weft-
Indies*; where fhe committed much Ravage, and gained
fome Booty. But they had the Confcience even to defraud
the Mariners, who afterwards made Complaint to the

Company, that they had cheated them of their Share of the Negroes taken ; all which were placed on the Earl of *Sam. Argall Governor.* *Warwick*'s Lands in *Bermudas*, and there kept and detained to his Lordſhip's Uſe. And this Proceeding was eſteemed, not only a manifeſt Act of Piracy, but alſo a thing of great Danger to the Colony, conſidering our weak Condition at that time, and the great Strength of the *Spaniards* in the *Weſt-Indies*. Mr. *Beverley* alſo gives a particular Account of an Expedition, made this Year by Captain *Argall* in Perſon, to diſlodge the *French* at *St. Croix* and *Port-Royal* in *Acadia*. But as I cannot find the leaſt Mention of it, in any contemporary Writer, or in any of the old Records, that I have peruſed and examined, I am apt to think, he is miſtaken in the Time, and confounds this with the Expedition, he made under Sir *Thomas Dale*, in the Year 1614.

But the Company in *England*, receiving Advice of Lord *Delawarr*'s Death, and finding, that Sir *Thomas Smith*'s Project had thereby failed of Succeſs, came to a Reſolution of ſending over a new Governor, with Power to examine all Complaints and Accuſations againſt Captain *Argall* upon the Spot. And therefore Captain *Yeardley*, who was upon this Occaſion knighted, was choſen Governor and Captain-General, and ſent upon this Buſineſs. But Captain *Argall*, in the mean while, was fully appriſed, by the Earl of *Warwick* and others, his Aſſociates in *England*, of every thing, that had paſſed in their Courts concerning himſelf. Wherefore, to prevent the Seiſure of his Goods, he conſigned all his Effects, under other Men's Names, and into the Hands of great and powerful Perſons. And as to thoſe Goods, which were ſent home, before he knew of the Order to ſequeſter them, the Earl of *Warwick*, by his Intriguing and Intereſt, got them all into his own Hands, under Pretence of taking out the Share, which belonged to him by his Right of Partnerſhip, and upon expreſs Promiſe, to return the reſt into the Company's Hands. But this Promiſe he could never be brought to perform ; ſo that the Company were deprived of the Means to right themſelves, and defrauded of that juſt Reſtitution, which they had great Reaſon to expect and demand.

This Year 1618 is likewiſe memorable, for the Death of two Perſons of principal Figure in the *Virginian* Hiſtory. The firſt of theſe was *Powhatan*, Emperor of the *Indians*, a Prince of excellent Senſe and Parts, and a great Maſter of all the Savage Arts of Government and Policy. He was penetrating, crafty, inſidious, and cruel; and as hard to be deceived by others, as to be avoided in his own Strategems and Snares. But as to the great and moral Arts of

Policy,

Policy, fuch as Truth, Faith, Uprightnefs, and Magnanimity, they feem to have been but little heeded or regarded
by him.   He was fucceeded in his Dominions, according to
the regular Order of Succeffion, by his fecond Brother,
Opitchapan; who is fometimes called *Itopatin*, and *Oeatan*.
And now upon his Acceffion to the fupreme Power, he
again changed his Name to *Safawpen*, as *Opechancanough*
did his to *Mangopeeomen*.   Upon what Reafon of Cuftom,
or Dignity, or Humour, thefe Changes were made in their
Names, I cannot fay; but to avoid Confufion, I fhall take
no Notice of fuch nominal Differences, but fhall always
fpeak of the fame Perfon by the fame Name.   *Opitchapan*,
being an eafy, decrepit, and unactive Prince, was foon
obfcured by the fuperior Parts and Ambition of his younger
Brother, *Opechancanough*; whofe Figure and Activity firft
drew the Attention, and at laft, by degrees, engroffed the
whole Power of the Government; altho' for fome time,
he was content with, and feemed chiefly to affect, the Title
of *King of Chickahominy*.   However they both renewed
and confirmed the League with the *Englifh*; under the Protection of which, every Man peaceably followed his Building and Planting, without any remarkable Accidents or Interruption.

THE other Perfon was Sir *Walter Ralegh*, the Father
and firft Mover of thefe *American* Colonies; to whom we
owe our Name, as we do our Settlement alfo to the Profecution of his Defign.   In *October* this Year, he ended a
Life of much Glory and Adverfity, on the Scaffold, to the
everlafting Infamy and Reproach of King *James*.   For he
was a Perfon of very great Worth, and of a vaft and moft
extenfive Genius; being equally fitted, to fhine in every
Part of Life, or Branch of Art, to which he applied himfelf.   And he was accordingly alike famed, as a Seaman,
a Soldier, a Statefman, and a Scholar.   He was therefore
univerfally pitied and lamented, and even interceded for by
feveral Princes; by the Queen, Prince *Henry*, the King of
Denmark, and King of *France*, whofe Agent in *England*,
even at the laft, endeavoured to contrive his Efcape.   But
King *James*, perverfely bent on the Wrong, could, by no
means, be prevailed upon, to fpare the greateft and wifeft
Head in his Dominions; but fhamefully made him a Sacrifice to his darling Dotage, the *Spanifh* Match, à Meafure
weak in itfelf, but profecuted and carried on, with ftill
greater Weaknefs and Indifcretion.   But his Death hath
been fo often deplored and condemned, that I fhall not add
to the general Complaint any farther, than by making fome
brief Extracts out of a Letter, preferved by Mr. *Rufhworth*

in

in his Collections, to shew the shameful Cruelty and Injustice of the Act.

THIS Letter is written, by a great Minister of State in
England, to Mr. *Cottington*, afterwards Lord *Cottington*,
the *British* Resident at the Court of *Spain*. In it he complains, as by Order from the King, of the Insincerity and
Chicanry of the *Spanish* Court in that Affair, and sets forth
the upright and sincere Intentions of his Majesty. And he
says, that he is particularly commanded by his Majesty, to
advertise him of the Execution of Sir *Walter Ralegh*, who
was lately put to Death, chiefly for their Satisfaction, and
concerning whom he promises speedily to send a Declaration: That, to please them, his Majesty of late had, in
many things, strained upon the Affections of his People;
and most especially, in this last of Sir *Walter Ralegh*, who
died with great Courage and Constancy, and had raised
much Remorse and Compassion in the People, who all attributed his Death, to the *Spanish* Machinations, and his
Majesty's Desire to do them a Pleasure: And further, he
orders him, strongly to insist upon and represent, how able
a Man Sir *Walter Ralegh* was to have served his Majesty, if
he had been pleased to have employed him: And that yet,
to give them Content, he had not spared him, altho' he
might, by saving his Life, have given infinite Satisfaction
to his People, and have had at Command, upon all Occasions, as useful a Man, as served any Prince in Christen-
dom.

THUS fell one of the last-surviving, and the brightest
of all the Commanders, bred under Queen *Elisabeth*, and
by her fleshed in *Spanish* Blood and Spoil. And what is the
most reproachful Part of it, he fell a Victim to his own
great Merit and Abilities, the Memory and Danger of
which, to the *Spanish* Nation, had been revived, by his late
Expedition to *Guiana*; as also, out of the old Grudge, for
his many eminent Services, under his former Royal and
illustrious Mistress, Queen *Elisabeth*, and to place him beyond a Possibility of ever rendering the like Services, to
King *James* or his Son. As the King's whole Conduct towards him was a strange Medley of Injustice and Incon-
sistency, so was it smartly observed by his Son, *Carew Ralegh*; That his poor Father was first condemned, for being
a Friend to the *Spaniards*, and afterwards lost his Life, by
the same Sentence, for being their Enemy. He died, as he
had lived, with great Lustre and Honour; with the Charity, Serenity, and Resignation of a Christian, joined to
the Magnanimity and intrepid Courage of an old *Roman*.

IN

In the Beginning of the Year 1619, Sir *George Yeardley* was
difpatched and fent Governor, with divers Commiffions and
Inftru&ions for proceeding againft Captain *Argall* in *Virgi-*
nia, were the Fa&s were committed, and where the Proofs,
on both Sides, might readily be had. The Earl of *War-*
wick and his Fa&ion had violently oppofed this, but not being able to prevail, he was obliged to betake himfelf to
other Meafures. Mr. *Rolfe's* Commiffion was either now
expired; or elfe, as I rather believe, he had given Offence
to the Company, and was turned out of his Place of Secretary. And this, I find fome Reafon to fufpe&, proceeded from his too great Submiffion and Subferviency to
Captain *Argall's* male Pra&ices. But however that was,
the Earl of *Warwick* obtained that Place from Sir *Thomas*
Smith, for Mr. *John Pory*, who now went over with the
Governor. For the Nomination to that Office was a Com-
pliment, made by the Company to their Treafurer; till afterwards the Earl of *Southampton*, in the Time of his Treafurerfhip, returned it back to the Company, and referred it
wholly to their Choice. By the Means of .this *Pory*, as it
was vehemently fufpe&ed, the Earl of *Warwick* got the
Ship fo long ftopped and retarded on the Coaft of *England*,
that he difpatched a fmall Bark, before from *Plimouth*, to
fetch away Captain *Argall*, with all his Goods and Booty.
This Bark arriving the Beginning of *April*, Captain *Argall*
took immediate Order for his Affairs, and within four or
five Days, embarked in her for *England*. He left Captain
Nathaniel Powel Deputy-Governor; a worthy Gentleman,
who had come in at the firft with Captain *Smith*, and ever
fince continued, an honeft and ufeful Inhabitant. But his
Government was of very fhort Duration. For in ten or
twelve Days after Captain *Argall's* Departure, Sir *George*
Yeardley arrived; and was received with the greater Joy and
Welcome, as he brought with him feveral Charters from
the Company, of Grants and Liberties to the Colony. For
the honefter Part and Majority of the Company, being
alarmed at thefe late Proceedings, refolved to be more attentive to the Affair, and to prevent all fuch Exorbitancies for
the future. One of thefe Charters only have I feen, containing Dire&ions to the Governor and Council of State, to
lay off Lands for feveral publick Ufes; and likewife confirming Titles, and afcertaining the Methods of obtaining
Lands in *Virginia*, and for preventing fraudulent and fur-
reptitious Grants; two of which, of a very extraordinary
and inconvenient Nature, had been obtained by Captain
Martin and Captain *Argall*. But Sir *George Yeardley*, having thus narrowly miffed of the Quarry, applied himfelf to
the

1619. the Affairs of Government. And firſt he added the following Gentlemen to the Council; Captain *Francis Weſt*,
Captain *Nathaniel Powel*, Mr. *John Pory*, Mr. *John Rolfe*,
Mr. *William Wickham*, and Mr. *Samuel Macock*. For although Captain *Powel* had been appointed Deputy-Governor, yet was he not of the Council. For, till this time,
the Governors, in Caſe of their Abſence, always aſſumed
to themſelves the Power of naming their Deputies. Soon
after Sir *George* publiſhed his Intention, of holding a General Aſſembly in a ſhort time; which, I ſuppoſe, was one
of the chief Privileges and Powers, granted and ſent over
with him. And I likewiſe find, by an Inſtrument of Writing to one *Richard Kingſmil*, that he had a Power to grant,
and accordingly did grant, to all the ancient Planters, who
had been here before Sir *Thomas Dale*'s Departure, a full
Releaſe and Diſcharge from all further Service to the Colony, excepting only ſuch Services, as they ſhould willing-
undertake, or were bound in Duty to perform by the Laws
of all Nations; together with a Confirmation of all their
Eſtates real and perſonal, in as full and ample Manner, as
the Subjects of *England* held and enjoyed them. And this
Precaution was undoubtedly occaſioned by Captain *Argall*'s
Rapines, and many perſonal Impoſitions on the ancient Planters and Freemen of the Colony.

THE Earl of *Warwick* was highly incenſed at theſe late
Proceedings againſt Captain *Argall*; and finding Sir *Thomas
Smith* not ſtanch, and fit for his Purpoſe, he purſued, with
great Vehemence, the Removal of him and Alderman *Johnſon*, the Deputy, from the Government of the Company.
Thoſe two Gentlemen had alſo given much Offence, to
the greater and better Part of the Adventurers; and lay under a ſtrong Suſpicion, as well of Negligence in their Office,
as of Colluſion and unfair Dealing. Sir *Thomas Smith* too
himſelf, being far advanced in Years, of tender Health,
and very rich, was willing to ſurrender a Place, of ſo great
Trouble and Fatigue, and ſo little fair Profit. And therefore, being already Governor of the *Eaſt-India* Company,
and lately appointed a Commiſſioner of his Majeſty's Navy,
he declared, at a Quarter Court, held the 28th of *April*,
that he was unable to give that Attendance, which he deſired, and which the Affairs of the Company demanded;
and for that reaſon, requeſted the Favour of them, to be
diſcharged from his Office. And altho' he was afterwards
named by ſome to be a Candidate, yet he was fixed in his
Reſolution, and abſolutely refuſed to ſtand in Election. In
his Room, Sir *Edwin Sandys*, Sir *John Wolſtenholme*, and
Alderman *Johnſon*, were propoſed; and the Choice fell on
Sir

Sir *Edwin Sandys*, he having fifty nine Voices, Sir *John*
Wolftenholme twenty three, and Alderman *Johnfon* eighteen.
Sir *Edwin* was a Gentleman of *Kent*, and a Member of
Parliament ; a Perfon of excellent Underftanding and Judgment ; of great Induftry, Vigor, and Refolution ; and in-
defatigable in his Application to the Bufinefs of the Company and Colony. He had, before this, on Account of his
Iduftry and Knowledge of their Affairs, been often joined,
by the Courts, with Sir *Thomas Smith*, in the Management
of feveral weighty things, relating to the Colony. So that
fcarce any thing, whilft he was in Town, paffed without
him. But he afterwards complained, that what was done,
during his Abode in Town, was commonly undone, when
he was abfent in the Country. Mr. *John Farrar*, an eminent Merchant of *London*, with a like Majority, was chofen
Deputy-Treafurer ; a worthy Second to Sir *Edwin Sandys*,
and every way fit for the Poft, conferred upon him.

BUT not to caft off an old Servant with Difregard, who
had, in the Time of greateft Trouble and Difficulty, continued above twelve Years in the principal Office of the
Company, at the Motion of Sir *Edwin Sandys*, twenty
great Shares, or two thoufand Acres of Land, were beftowed, as a Gratuity, upon Sir *Thomas Smith*. But there
was not the leaft Notice taken, or Reward given, to Alderman *Johnfon*. And thefe Alterations in the Government of the Company gave not only much Satisfaction in
England, but were alfo received with great Joy in *Virginia* ;
where the old Officers had been long and bitterly exclaimed
againft, by the general Voice of the Colony. But the
Earl of *Warwick* was fo far from gaining by the Change,
that he had now a Perfon of much greater Honour and Integrity, and a Gentleman of principal Figure and Intereft
in the Nation, to oppofe his Schemes and Defigns. For
altho' Sir *Edwin Sandys* was much wronged in the Execution of his Office, and even fought to be deterred by Threats
of Blood, yet they could no way turn him, from a vigorous
Profecution and Enquiry into the late Diforders in *Virginia*.
At the Expiration of Sir *Thomas Smith*'s Government, after fourfcore thoufand Pounds Expence and twelve Years
Labour, the Colony confifted of about fix hundred Perfons,
Men, Women, and Children. And they had about three
hundred Head of Cattle, fome Goats, and infinite Numbers of Hogs, both wild and tame. But all the Company's Lands and Plantations were utterly ruined and depo-
pulated by Captain *Argall*, there being only three Tenants
left thereon, and fix Men of what he called his Guard.
And notwithftanding Sir *Thomas Smith*'s Boaft, that he had

left

1619. left four thousand Pounds, for the new Treasurer to proceed
upon, yet it was found, upon Examination, that the Com-
Sir George pany was above that Sum in Debt. However Sir *Edwin*
Yeardley, *Sandys*, and all the founder and more publick-spirited Part
Governor. of the Company, applied themselves, with a laudable Dili-
gence and Industry, to reform the Abuses, and by all the
Methods, they could devise, to set forward and advance the
Plantation.

S I R *George Yeardley*, upon his Arrival in *Virginia*, finding a great Scarcity of Corn, made it his first Care to supply that Defect. And therefore he wrote to the Treasurer
and Company in *England*, to excuse him, if he made not
such Returns in Tobacco, this Year, as might be expected.
For he was determined, by the Blessing of God, to raise
such a plentiful Crop of Corn, that the Colony should not,
in haste, be in any further Danger of Want. And about
the latter End of *June*, he called the first General Assembly, that was ever held in *Virginia*. Counties were not yet
laid off, but they elected their Representatives by Town-
ships. So that the Burroughs of *James-Town*, *Henrico*,
Bermuda Hundred, and the rest, each sent their Members to
the Assembly. And hence it is, that our Lower House of
Assembly was first called the House of Burgesses, a Name
proper to the Representatives of Burroughs or Towns ;
and it hath, by Custom, ever since retained that Appella-
tion, altho' the Burgesses, or Members for Towns and Corporations, are very few and inconsiderable at present, in
Comparison of the Representatives for Counties. Mr. *Beverley* says, they sate in the same House with the Governor and Council, after the Manner of the *Scotch* Parliament ; and we are told by *Smith*, that they debated all
Matters, thought expedient for the Good of the Colony.
The Acts of this General Assembly were remitted to *England*, and presented to the Company, to be read in their
Court, the 20th of *March* following. For the Company
then had the regal Power of confirming, or disanulling our
Acts of Assembly. I can no where find, among the Records now extant, any Account of the Particulars, that
passed. Only Sir *Edwin Sandys*, upon Perusal of them,
assures the Company, that they were very well and judiciously formed ; but they were very intricate, and difficult
to be reduced into distinct and proper Heads.

H O W E V E R we may be certain of this happy Effect, that
by the Introduction of the *British* Form of Government,
by Way of Parliament or Assembly, the People were again
restored to their Birthright, the Enjoyment of *British* Liberty ; and that most grievous and oppressive Custom of
Trial

Trial by Martial Law was thereby, if not at once, yet by Degrees, entirely banifhed and abolifhed. It is true indeed, that before, both by the Royal Charters, and by all other Law and Reafon, the *Englifh*, tranfplanted hither, had a Right to all the Liberties and Privileges of *Englifh* Subjects. And certainly no Perfon, in his Senfes, would have left the Liberty of *England*, to come hither (in order to improve the Commerce, and increafe the Riches of the Nation) to a State of Slavery; when without that, it was natural to fuppofe, that they muft undergo much Hardfhip and Labour. Yet by the Neceffity of the Times, by the Ignorance of the People, and by the Oppreffion and Tyranny of Governors, they had, thus far, been deprived of that their native Right. But with the *Englifh* Form of Government, the *Englifh* Liberty again revived and flourifhed; and together with the Nation, they now tranfplanted and diffufed into *America* their moft happy Conftitution. From this Time therefore, we may moft properly date the Original of our prefent Conftitution, by Governor, Council, and Burgeffes; which altho' defective perhaps in fome material Points, yet comes fo near to the excellent Model of the *Englifh* Government, that it muft be the hearty Prayer and Defire of all true Lovers of their Country, that it may long flourifh among us and improve. For this happy Change, we are chiefly indebted to the Change of the Officers and Governors of the Company in *England*, and to the Activity and Attention of Sir *Edwin Sandys*, and many other worthy Members of the Company, to the Affairs of the Colony.

THIS Summer, they laid off four new Corporations; which encreafed the Number of their Burroughs, that had Right to fend Members to the Affembly, to eleven in all. And *Japazaws*, the King of *Patowmack*, came to *James-Town*, and invited the *Englifh* into his River to trade; for a more plentiful Year of Corn had not been known, in a long time. But Captain *Ward*, being fent thither, was treacheroufly dealt with by the Natives; and the thing coming to open Hoftility, he took from them eight hundred Bufhels by Force, and fo returned to *James-Town*. One Captain *Stallings*, this Year, had the Misfortune, firft to have his Ship caft away, and not long after to be flain, in a private Quarrel, by *William Eppes*. And the whole Colony laboured under fo great a Mortality, that no lefs than three hundred of the Inhabitants died within the Year. But in Mitigation of this, they had the moft plentiful Crop of Grain, that had ever yet been raifed, fince the firft Plantation of the Country. And indeed the Company received fuch an Account of it, as will not eafily gain Credit; which

I there-

I therefore leave entirely to the Reader's good Pleasure, to believe or disbelieve, as he thinks fit ; neither should I have related it, had I not found it authentically recorded, in the Company's Journals. For by Letters from *Virginia,* they were informed, that they had had two Harvests of Wheat, the first being shaken by the Wind, and producing a second ; and their Ground was so extraordinary fat and good, that they planted *Indian* Corn upon the Stubble, and had an ex- · cellent Crop of that. But it must be remembered, that rare-ripe Corn was the Corn of those Times, and that they usually had two Crops of it in a Year.

W h i l s t things were in this State in *Virginia,* Sir *Edwin Sandys* was, by no means, idle or negligent of his Charge in *England.* For turning the whole Bent of his Thoughts, towards the Improvement and Furtherance of this noble Enterprise, he got a Committee appointed, consisting of Sir *Dudley Digges,* Sir *Edward Harwood,* and divers other Knights, Gentlemen, Merchants, and Citizens, as well for compiling and reducing the standing Rules and Orders, for the Government of their own Company, into one entire Body, as more especially for constituting Laws, and settling a Form of Government for *Virginia,* appointing Magistrates and Officers, and declaring their several Functions and Duties. And this was one of the chief Powers and Injunctions of his Majesty's Letters patent and Instructions to the Company. As to the former Part, concerning the Government of themselves, it was easily brought to a tolerable Head. But the latter being a vast Design, of very great Weight and Difficulty, and comprehending no less, than a Project for rearing, constituting, and forming a compleat Commonwealth, in all its Parts, it never could, notwithstanding Sir *Edwin Sandys's* great Pains and Diligence, be brought to any satisfactory Conclusion. So that *Virginia* was left to the best Means of forming its Government ; that is to say, to work after the *English* Plan, with the Assistance of Time and Experience, and the united Sense and Endeavours of its Representatives and Officers of State.

T h e King had formerly issued his Letters to the several Bishops of the Kingdom, for collecting Money, to erect and build a College in *Virginia,* for the training up and educating Infidel Children in the true Knowledge of God. And accordingly, there had been already paid near fifteen hundred Pounds towards it, and more was expected to come in. For besides other Particulars, Sir *Edwin Sandys,* upon some Conference with the Bishop of *Litchfield,* found, that he had never heard of any Collection in his Diocese ; but he promised, as soon as he should have a Warrant, to further

ther

ther fo good a Defign, with the utmoft Diligence. Sir
Edwin therefore recommended it to the Company, as a
thing moft worthy of their Confideration, both for the Glory of God, and their own Honour. And he told them,
that it was an Affair of that Weight and Dignity, that they
muft expect to render an Accout of their Proceedings to the
State; and that Negligence therein could never efcape publick Notice and Cenfure, efpecially of thofe, who had generoufly contributed towards it. He therefore had Sir *Dudley Digges*, Sir *Nathaniel Rich*, Sir *John Wolftenholme*, Mr.
Deputy *Farrar*, Dr. *Anthony*, and Dr. *Gulftone*, appointed
a Committee, to meet, as he fhould order and direct, and
to confult thereupon. And he likewife moved and obtained,
that ten thoufand Acres of Land fhould be laid off for the
Univerfity at *Henrico*, a Place formerly refolved on for that
Purpofe. This was intended, as well for the College for the
Education of *Indians*, as alfo to lay the Foundation of a Se-
minary of Learning for the *Englifh*. In Confequence of
thefe Refolves, Sir *Edwin* procured fifty Men to be fent this
Summer, and fifty more the Beginning of the next Year,
to be feated on thefe College Lands, as Tenants at Halves.
They were to have half the Profit of their Labour to themfelves, and the other half was to go, towards forwarding
the Building, and the Maintenance of the Tutors and Scholars. And as a Man's Labour was then computed at ten
Pounds *Sterling* a Year, it was intended, hereby to eftablifh
an annual Revenue of five hundred Pounds, for this good
and pious Work. Mr. *George Thorpe* alfo, a Kinfman of
Sir *Thomas Dale's*, being a Gentleman of his Majefty's Privy Chamber, and one of the Council in *England* for *Virginia*, accepted of the Place, and was fent over the next Spring,
as the Company's Deputy and Superintendent for the College. And for his Entertainment and Support, they granted
three hundred Acres of Land, to be for ever annexed and
belonging to that Place, with ten Tenants thereon.

IN a great and general Quarter Court of the Company,
held in *November* this Year, Sir *Edwin Sandys* told them,
that his Duty and Inclination running equally for the Advancement of this good Action, he had many things to lay
before them. And accordingly, he reminded them, that
the Maintenance of the Publick, in all States, was of no
lefs Importance, even for the Benefit of private Men, than
the Root and Body of a Tree are to the particular Branches.
And he recalled to their Remembrance, how by the admirable Care and Diligence of two worthy Knights, Sir *Thomas Gates* and Sir *Thomas Dale*, the publick Eftate and Revenue of the Company had been fet forward, in a Way to
great Perfection: That the former, Sir *Thomas Gates*, had

the

the Honour to all Posterity, to be the first named, in his
Majesty's Patent and Grant of *Virginia*, and was also the
first, that by his Wisdom, Industry, and Valour, accompanied with exceeding Pains and Patience, in the Midst of
many Difficulties, had laid the Foundation of the present
prosperous State of the Colony: And the latter, Sir *Thomas
Dale*, building upon those Foundations, with great and
constant Severity, had reclaimed, almost miraculously, those
idle and dissolute Persons, and reduced them to Labour and
an honest Fashion of Life: That proceeding with great
Zeal for the good of the Company, he had laid off publick
Lands, to yield them a standing Revenue, placed Servants
thereon, as also upon other publick Works, for the Company's Use; established an annual Rent of Corn from the
Farmers, and of Tribute from the Barbarians; together
with a great Stock of Cattle, Goats, and other Animals:
That this had since been the Occasion of drawing so many
private Plantations, to seat in *Virginia*; upon Hope and
Promise of Plenty of Corn and Cattle, to be lent them by
the Publick, for their Ease and Benefit, at their first Arrival: But that since their Times, all this publick Provision
had been utterly laid waste and destroyed: And that besides,
for about an hundred Persons, which appeared to have been
sent, at the Company's Charge, within the two or three
last Years, Sir *George Teardley* wrote Word, that, at his
Arrival, only three could be found, remaining to the Publick:

THAT as to the Means and Causes of these Dilapida-
tions, he doubted not, but that hereafter, in due time, they
would be made fully manifest; but that he forbore, at present to touch upon them, left he should, by Glance of
Speech, give Offence to any Person present (for Captain
Argall, the known Author thereof, was then in Court)
But as to the Remedies of these Mischiefs, he related to
them, what Methods had been already taken. For whereas, not much above three Years before, there had been remitted from *Virginia* twelve several Commodities, sold
openly in Court, to the great Honour of the Action, and
Encouragement of the Adventurers; yet since that time,
there had been little returned, worth speaking of, except
Tobacco and Saffafras; to which the People there applied
themselves so entirely, that they would have been reduced
to the Necessity of starving, the last Year, had not the Magazine supplied them with Corn and Cattle from *England:*
That this had been the Occasion of stopping and discouraging many Hundreds of People, who were providing to remove themselves thither: That frequent Letters had therefore been sent, from the Council there to the Governor in
Virginia, to restrain that immoderate planting of Tobacco,

and

and to caufe the People to apply themfelves to other and
better Commodities: And that he had alfo, by the Advice
and Confent of the Council, and according to an Order now
to be propofed, caufed to be drawn a new Covenant, to be
inferted in all future Grants of Land, that the Patentees
fhould not apply themfelves, wholly, or chiefly, to Tobacco, but to other Commodities, therein fpecified; an
Example whereof they would now fee, in a Patent, lying
before them for their Approbation.

B u t altho' they had been, by no means, negligent in
thefe Affairs, yet he faid, that his principal Care and Study
had been employed, to fet up again and reftore the publick
Stock and Revenue, to as great, or a greater Degree of
Perfection, than they had heretofore been at. And to that
End, he recounted, how three thoufand Acres of Land
had been laid off, for the Governor; twelve thoufand for
the Company; and ten thoufand, for the Univerfity at *Henrico.* And that feventy two Perfons had already been placed
on the Company's Land, fifty three on the Governor's, and
fifty on the College's; an hundred and feventy five in all.
But not content with this, he told them, that he had ftill
fome farther Propofitions to make to them.

A n d firft, he propofed to them, that thefe Tenants for
the publick might, the next Spring, be encreafed to the
Number of three hundred; an hundred for the Company's
Land, an hundred for the College, and an hundred for the
Governor, who fhould be obliged, at the Expiration of his
Office, to leave the fame Number to his Succeffor; which
would thereby raife a ftanding Revenue of a thoufand Pounds
a Year, and eafe the Company of all further Expence for
his Provifion and Entertainment. And whereas Care had
been, and ftill fhould be taken, during his Office, to fend
over to thefe Lands, divers ftaid and difcreet Perfons, he
propofed, in the fecond Place, that an hundred Boys and
Girls, of about twelve or thirteen Years of Age, might be
fent to be their Servants and Apprentices; in the Charge
whereof, he hoped, that the honourable City of *London*
would partake with the Company, as they had formerly
done. And becaufe he underftood, that the People in *Virginia*, tho' feated there in their Perfons for fome few Years,
yet were not fettled in their Minds, nor intended to make
it their Place of Reft and Continuance, but propofed, after
having got fome Wealth, to return again to *England*, which
tended to the utter Overthrow and Diffolution of the Plantation; he therefore advifed, and made it his third Propofition, that there fhould be fent over one hundred Maids,
young and uncorrupt, to make Wifes for the Inhabitants;

that

that Wives, Children, and Families, might render them lefs moveable, and fix and fettle them, together with their Pofterity, in that Soil: And that fuch of thefe Maids, as were married to the publick Farmers, fhould be tranfported at the Company's Expence; but if any were married to others, that then thofe, who took them to .Wife, fhould repay the Company their Charges of Tranfportation. And in Confequence of this ʼPropofition, ninety Maids were accordingly fent the following Spring. As to the Manner of tranfporting thefe Perfons, to make up five hundred in all for the Publick, he propofed, in the fourth Place, that they fhould not hire Shipping, as heretofore, fince each Ship, at its Return, in bare Freight and Wages, emptied the publick Cafh of eight hundred, and fometimes a thoufand Pounds; but that they fhould, as he had already done this prefent Year, take the Advantage of the Ships trading to *Newfoundland,* and fo tranfport them, at fix Pounds a Perfon, without any after Reckonings. Fifthly, he propofed, the fending twenty Heifers, for every hundred Tenants, threefcore in the whole; which, with their Breed, might foon raife them a tolerable Stock; and which he had Hopes of having tranfported, taking the Opportunity of Shipping in the *Weftern* Parts, at ten Pounds a Head, to be delivered in *Virginia.*

LASTLY, as to the Charges, he obferved to them, that there never could be a more proper Time, for fuch large Tranfportations, than the prefent; Corn being fo exceedingly cheap and plentiful at home, and there being, by their Advices from *Virginia,* fo great Promifes of an excellent Crop there. And he alfo fhewed, how much the Company was bound to give Thanks to Almighty God, for all his Bleffings, who continually raifed Means, to fupport and carry on this great Work; and he particularly mentioned one unknown Gentleman alone, who promifed five hundred Pounds, on Demand, for the Converfion and Education of threefcore *Indian* Children; and that he had likewife, upon his Letters, received Affurance from fundry Parts, and fome of them very remote, that if they proceeded with the Undertaking, they fhould not want for Money. But not to rely upon fuch precarious Funds and Hopes, he related to them, particularly, the feveral Ways and Means, by which the Money would arife. And he eftimated the whole Charge, at four thoufand Pounds, to be done fparingly; and bountifully, at five thoufand. He alfo promifed, not to leave the Company one Penny in Debt, for any Act or Thing, to be performed within his Year; and that he would moreover difcharge three thoufand Pounds of former

Debts,

Debts, according to the Stock, left at the time of his coming to his Place. And thefe things done, he hoped, the
Publick would again be fully reftored, a Foundation laid
for a future great State, the Adventurers and Planters well
comforted and encouraged, and all Matter of Scandal and
Reproach to them and the Enterprife removed. And fo
he concluded, by recommending thefe Points to their moft
ferious Confideration, and the whole Enterprife to the Bleffing of Almighty God. Thefe Propofitions, which had
been before made in two feveral Courts, and were now repeated at the particular Defire of fome noble Lords prefent,
were received with that Applaufe, they well deferved; and
they paffed, upon the Queftion, with an unanimous Approbation, altho' Sir *John Wolftenholme*, in a former Court,
had made fome vain Exceptions againft them. And Sir *Edwin Sandys*, with an extreme Care and Diligence, faw them
all afterwards put effectually into Execution.

BUT befides thefe reputable People, to be tranfported at
the Company's Charge, the Treafurer and Council received
a Letter from his Majefty, commanding them, forthwith
to fend away to *Virginia* an hundred diffolute Perfons, which
Sir *Edward Zouch*, the Knight Marſhal, would deliver to
them. In Obedience to his Majefty's Command, it was
refolved, to fend them over with all Conveniency, to be
Servants, which Mr. Treafurer underftood, would be very
acceptable to the Colony. But as it was *November*, and
Shipping, at that Seafon, not eafily procured, it was thought
they could not be fent off before *January* at fooneft. But
to fatisfy his Majefty, the Company agreed to be at the Expence of their Maintenance, in the mean while. The
Treafurer was therefore defired, to deliver this their Anfwer to his Majefty, by Secretary *Calvert*. But he was
told, that the King's Command was urgent, and admitted
no Delay; and that fifty, at leaft, muft with all Speed be
ſhipped off. And notwithftanding his juft Reprefentations,
how great Inconveniency and Expence would thence accrue to
the Company; that they could not well go in lefs than four
Ships, left, being fo many together, they ſhould mutiny,
and run away with the Veffel; that thofe four Ships, to be
got thus fuddenly, without taking Advantage of the Veffels
trading to *America*, would not ftand the Company in lefs
than four thoufand Pounds; and that, notwithftanding all,
Ships were not to be procured fo fpeedily, at that Time of
the Year. Yet nothing, he could alledge, giving Satisfaction,
the Company were obliged to appoint a Committee of the
Deputy and other feleēt Merchants, to employ all their Endeavours, for compaffing Shipping, with all poffible Speed.

1619.
Sir *George*
Teardley,
Govern.*r.*

And by good Fortune, for the additional Premium of an hundred Pounds, they procured a large Ship, to carry them off; but which neverthelefs could not fail before *February.*

THOSE, who are acquainted with Hiftory, and know, with how high and magifterial a Hand, this King fometimes carried it, even with his Parliaments, will not be furprifed, to find him thus unmercifully infult a private Company, and load them, againft all Law, with the Maintenance and extraordinary Expence of tranfporting fuch Perfons, as he thought proper to banifh; and that perhaps, without any colourable Pretext, or fufficient Warrant of Law at that time. And I cannot but remark, how early that Cuftom arofe, of tranfporting loofe and diffolute Perfons to *Virginia*, as a Place of Punifhment and Difgrace; which altho' originally defign'd for the Advancement and Increafe of the Colony, yet has certainly proved a great Prejudice and Hindrance to it's Growth. For it hath laid one of the fineft Countries in *Britifh America*, under the unjuft Scandal of being a mere Hell upon Earth, another *Siberia*, and only fit for the Reception of Malefactors and the vileft of the People. So that few People, at leaft few large Bodies of People, have been induced, willingly to tranfport themfelves to fuch a Place; and our younger Sifters, the Northern Colonies, have accordingly profited thereby. For this is one Caufe, that they have outftripped us fo much, in the Number of their Inhabitants, and in the Goodnefs and Frequency of their Cities and Towns.

HIS Majefty had, by his Letters patent, bearing Date the 23d of *May* 1609, granted the Company a " Freedom " from all Cuftom and Subfidy, for twenty one Years, ex-" cepting only five *per Cent.* upon all fuch Goods and " Merchandifes, as fhould be imported into *England*, or " any other of his Majefty s Dominions, according to the " ancient Trade of Merchants." Notwithftanding this, which was intended for the Eafe and Encouragement of the Infant Colony, the Farmers of the Cuftoms, upon a general Rate made of Tobacco, both *Spanifh* and *Virginia*, at ten Shillings the Pound, demanded fix Pence a Pound, equally upon all; altho' *Spanifh* Tobacco was ufually fold at eighteen Shillings a Pound, and fometimes more, and *Virginia* would feldom bear above three or four Shillings. Mr. *Jacob* alfo, Farmer of the Impoft upon Tobacco, did moft oppreffively impofe another fix Pence a Pound, contrary to the clear and indubitable Tenor of his Majefty's Grant. And the Company, in *June* this Year, importing twenty thoufand Weight, the whole Crop of the former
Year,

Year, had delivered it all into the Cuſtom-Houſe, as they   1619.
were required, that the Tobacco might be weighed, and
the Cuſtom anſwered.   But Mr. *Jacob*, of his own Au-   Sir *George*
thority, ſtopped and ſeiſed the Tobacco, till that Impoſt of   *Yeardley*,
ſix Pence a Pound ſhould be diſcharged.   And this alſo will   Governor.
ſoon be perceived by thoſe, who are any thing verſed in the
Hiſtory of thoſe Times, to be entirely conſonant to the
Behaviour of the Cuſtomers then; whoſe Inſolence and
arbitrary Proceedings, ſupported by the Royal Authority,
and even encreaſed and carried to a greater Height in the
next Reign, was one of the chief and moſt viſible Cauſes
of the general Diſcontent of the Nation, and of the unhappy
Civil War, which enſued.

THE Company, being thus wronged and abuſed, applied themſelves to the Lords of his Majeſty's Privy Council, and obtained their Letter to Mr. *Jacob*, to deliver the
Tobacco, upon their entering into Bond to pay him, whatſoever ſhould appear to be his due, upon Certificate from
his Majeſty's learned Council, within a Month.   But *Jacob*
rejecting this, and all other Conditions offered by the Company, and likewiſe exacting twelve Pence a Pound at *Plimouth*, upon the *Somer-Iſlands* Tobacco, it was reſolved to
try the Strength of their Charter, and to enter an Action
againſt him for the Damage, which was already computed
at two thouſand five hundred Pounds *Sterling*.   But afterwards, conſidering, that their Commodity was very periſh-
able, and that their Suit could not be determined that
Michaelmas Term, they altered their Method of Proceeding, and by the Advice of a great Lord of the Privy Council to Sir *Edwin Sandys*, they brought the Matter before
the Council Board; where, upon the Attorney-General's
delivering his Opinion clearly, that the Company, by their
Letters patent, were free from all Impoſition, and after
ſome Delay and Chicanry of Mr. *Jacob*, it was ordered,
upon a full Hearing of the Allegations on both Sides, that
he ſhould deliver the Tobacco to the Company, paying all
lawful Duties appertaining thereto.   And thus, at length,
they regained their Goods out of the Hands of this Harpy;
but were obliged to ſit ſilently by the great Loſs and Damage, occaſioned partly, by impairing it's Worth through
Drying and other Corruption, and partly by the Fall of the
Price, upon the Sale of *Engliſh* Tobacco, made ſince it's
Importation.   To which was added the daily Expectation
of more, both from *Virginia* and the *Somer-Iſlands*, which
rendered the Market ſo mean and dead, that they were ſadly
puzzled and perplexed, how to diſpoſe of it.   And at laſt,
after many Schemes and Efforts to raiſe the Price, they were

obliged to fell it very low, and were confiderable Lofers by it.

IT was one peculiar Mark and Property of this Family of our Kings, that they were always craving, and for ever poor and in Want, notwithftanding the frequent Contributions of the People, to fome of them efpecially ; the Reafons of which, it lies not within my Province at prefent, to open and explain. And accordingly King *James*, notwith-ftanding his natural Antipathy to Tobacco, began now to tafte the Sweets of the Revenue, arifing from it ; and was therefore very ill fatisfied, with this Determination of the Privy Council. For in the very Beginning of the next Year, within a Month after, under Colour, that fome *Spanifh* Tobacco had fold at twenty Shillings a Pound, he demanded of the Company twelve pence a Pound, Cuftom and Impoft, for theirs. But it was unanimoufly agreed, to ftand refolutely upon the Privilege of their Charter, which they could not give up or betray, without the greateft Breach of their Truft and Duty. And therefore, as *Virginia* Tobacco had never been actually fold for more, than five Shillings a Pound, but generally much lower, they fubmitted to pay three Pence a Pound Cuftom, which was full five *per Cent.* on their higheft Price, But however, to avoid all Conteft with the King, as his Majefty had given Order for prohibiting, by Proclamation, the planting *Englifh* Tobacco, for five Years enfuing, they agreed, in Return to that his Majefty's Favour, during the faid Term of five Years, if the Proclamation took Effect, and continued fo long, to add nine Pence a Pound more, and thereby to make it up twelve Pence; which was the Full of his Majefty's Demand, tho' not in the fame Form. But it was conceived, unlefs this Offer, and the true Meaning thereof, fhould be entered, as an Act, in the Lords Commiffioners of the Treafury's Books, it would be very difficult, at the Expiration of the five Years, to withdraw the Payment, but continuing fo long, it might be demanded for ever, as due from the Company to the King. They therefore appointed a Committee, to repair to the Clerk of the Council, and to take Care, that this Bargain be exactly recorded, and alfo to procure a Copy of the faid Record, to be entered in the Company's Journals. But as to the Farm of the Impoft on Tobacco, the Refufal whereof the King, at the fame time, offered them, they held it inconvenient at prefent to be undertaken ; but not entirely to reject his Majefty's Offer, they permitted fome of their Society, to join for a Part, in the Company's Name, but in reality, for their own proper Ufe and Behoof.

THE

THE Trade of *Virginia* had been thus far reftrained,
and kept in the Adventurers Hands, except a few Inter-
lopers, that ftraggled in by Chance; and the Method of
carrying on this Trade was thus. Every Adventurer, that
pleafed, fubfcribed, what he thought proper, to a Roll;
which Money, together with a certain Sum perhaps, contributed out of the publick Cafh of the Company, made
their Capital or Stock. With this they bought Goods, and
fent them to the Cape-Merchant in *Virginia*, who had,
long before this, loft his original Office of being Keeper of
the publick Storehoufes, and was become the Company's
chief Factor. The Cape-Merchant, having fold thefe
Goods to the Inhabitants, for Tobacco or other Commodities, remitted the Effects to *England*. This Society for
Trade, called the Magazine, was a diftinct Body from the
publick Company; but always under its Controle, as it received its Being and Authority from the Company, and as
the Joint-Stock of the Company was always the greateft
and principal Adventurer in it. Alderman *Johnfon* had
ever been at the Head of this Magazine, under the Title of
Director; and fince the Removal of himfelf and Sir *Thomas
Smith* from their Offices, it had been the Subject of much
Faction and Difcord. For they had made many Difficulties,
in fubmitting to the Orders of the Company, concerning
the Place of their Meetings; had neglected to bring their
Accounts to an Audit, tho' very clear and fairly kept; and
had delayed and kept off the making any Dividend; which
things had caufed much Difturbance and Diffenfion. To
remove therefore fuch a Block of Offence, it was now a-
greed to diffolve this Magazine, and to leave the Trade free
and open to all; only with this Provifo, that the Goods of
the Magazine, then upon hand in *Virginia*, fhould be firft
fold off, before any of the fame Kinds fhould be vended.

BUT the Diligence, Vigor, and Fidelity of Sir *Edwin
Sandys*, and of others of the Company, had now raifed the
Reputation of the Action very high. And accordingly there
had been prefented, by an unknown Perfon, the former
Year, a Communion Cup, with a Cover and Cafe, a
Trencher Plate for the Bread, a Carpet of Crimfon Velvet,
and a Damafk Table-Cloth, for the Ufe of the College;
and another had given a fair Set of Plate, with other rich
Ornaments, to Mrs. *Mary Robinfon's* Church, who had,
the Year before, bequeathed two hundred Pounds, towards
the Building of it. And now, in the Beginning of this
Year, another unknown Perfon fent five hundred Pounds,
directed; *To Sir* Edwin Sandys, *the faithful Treafurer of*
Virginia. This was for the Maintenance of a convenient
Number

1620.

Sir *George Yeardley,* Governour

Number of young *Indians,* from seven or under, to twelve Years of Age, to be instructed in Reading and the Principles of the Christian Religion; and then to be trained and brought up in some lawful Trade, with all Gentleness and Humanity, till they attained the Age of twenty one; and after that, to have and enjoy the like Liberties and Privileges, with the native *English* in *Virginia.* And he likewise sent fifty Pounds, to be given into the Hands of two religious and worthy Persons, who should, every Quarter, examine and certify, to the Treasurer in *England,* the due Execution of this Design, together with the Names of the Children, and of their Tutors and Overseers. This Charity, the Company thought not proper, to entrust to private Hands, but committed the Management of it to *Smith's* Hundred chiefly. This lay in the Parts above *Hampton,* up into *Warwick,* and was so called, in Honour to Sir *Thomas Smith.* But after this, Sir *Thomas,* with the Earl of *Warwick,* and the rest of that Faction, sold out their Shares in this, and other private Plantations, and only reserved their Part in the Company's publick Stock, in order to be present, and to have a Vote at their Courts. Wherefore, this was afterwards changed to the Name of *Southampton* Hundred; either in Honour to the Earl of *Southampton,* their next Treasurer, or rather, as that Nobleman became the chief Adventurer in the Plantation. And further, for the better procuring and retaining the *Indian* Children, the Company ordered a Treaty and Agreement to be made with *Opechancanough,* and authorised Sir *George Yeardley,* to make him such Presents, out of the Magazine, as would be most grateful to him, and best promote the Design. Mr. *Nicholas Farrar,* the Elder (Father, as I take it, to the present and succeeding Deputy-Treasurer of the Company) also bequeathed three hundred Pounds, for converting Infidel Children in *Virginia.* He ordered this to be paid into the Hands of Sir *Edwin Sandys* and Mr. *John Farrar,* at such time, as it should appear by Certificate, that ten *Indian* Children were placed in the College; and then, by them to be disposed of, according to his true Intent and Meaning. And in the mean time, he obliged his Executors to pay eight *per Cent.* for the Money, to be given to three several honest Men in *Virginia,* of good Life and Fame, and such as Sir *Edwin Sandys* and Mr. *John Farrar* should approve of, each to bring up one of the said Children, in the Grounds and Principles of the Christian Religion.

THERE was, at this time, a great Scarcity of Clergy in *Virginia;* there being but five Ministers and eleven Burroughs, each of which, being some very distant from each other,

other, was erected into a diſtinct Pariſh. The Company
indeed had before, in their Charter by Sir *George Yeardley*,
taken Care of a handſome Proviſion for the Clergy. For
they had ordered an hundred Acres of Land, in each of the
Burroughs, to be laid off for a Glebe; and that there
ſhould, for their further Maintenance, be raiſed a ſtanding
and certain Revenue, out of the Profits of each Pariſh, ſo
as to make every Living, at leaſt two hundred Pounds *Sterling* a Year. And this Stipend I find, two Years after, ſettled in the following Manner: That the Miniſter ſhould receive Yearly fifteen hundred Weight of Tobacco, and ſixteen Barrels of Corn, which was then eſtimated at two
hundred Pounds *Sterling*: That this ſhould be raiſed by ten
Pounds of Tobacco and a Buſhel of Corn a Head, for every
labouring Man or Boy, above ſixteen Years of Age; provided, it did not exceed fifteen hundred Weight of Tobacco and ſixteen Barrels of Corn: But if any Plantation
was not able, to make up that Quantity, by ten Pounds of
Tobacco and a Buſhel of Corn a Head, that, in ſuch Caſe,
the Miniſter ſhould be contented with leſs, according to
the Number of Tithables. And now, for a farther Encouragement, that pious, learned, and painful Miniſters
might be invited to go over, the Company ordered ſix Tenants to be placed on each of thoſe Glebes, at the publick
Expence; and they applied to the Biſhop of *London*, for his
Help and Aſſiſtance in procuring proper Miniſters, which
his Lordſhip readily promiſed, and undoubtedly performed.
For he had ever been a great Favourer and Promoter of the
Plantation, and had himſelf alone collected and paid in a
thouſand Pounds towards the College; which he would not
permit the Company to diminiſh, by a Preſent to his Re-
giſter, who had been very active and uſeful in the Collection.
And for this, and other his Deſerts towards them, he was
made free of the Company, and choſen one of his Majeſty's
Council for *Virginia*.

As the Country was very defenceleſs and unfortified,
and as the Intereſts and Improvements of the Inhabitants
were now much encreaſed, and become conſiderable, they
began to grow uneaſy in that Particular; and they wrote
to the Treaſurer and Company in *England*, to procure them
ſkilful Engineers, to raiſe Fortifications; promiſing, themſelves to bear the Charge of it. Wherefore, to give them
preſent Satisfaction, and as regular Fortifications, to endure
Aſſault and Battery, were not ſo needful, as the chuſing
and improving ſome Places of natural Strength and Advantage, Sir *Thomas Gates* was entreated by the Company, as
well in Regard of his military Skill, as of his Knowledge of
the

the Country, to write them his private Letters of Advice and Direction. And he was alfo defired, together with Sir *Nathaniel Rich*, to confer with General *Cecil* about it, another eminent and military Member of their Society, and youngeft Son to the famous Lord Treafurer *Burleigh*, who likewife promifed, if other Methods failed, to write them fuch particular Directions and Inftructions, that they might eafily themfelves proceed. To them was afterwards added Sir *Horatio Vere*, who was efteemed the Perfon of the greateft military Skill and Reputation of any in that unwarlike Age. He was therefore, this Summer, fent Commander of the fingle Regiment, which King *James*, in his great Wifdom, thought fit to furnifh out, for the Relief and Support of his diftreffed Son in Law, the *Palatine* of the *Rhine*. For altho' General *Cecil* had been firft defigned for that Service, yet he was afterwards laid afide, and this Gentleman appointed in his Room.

THE Governor and Council, in *Virginia*, had fettled and allowed certain Fees to the Secretary, which were, this Year, fent to *England* for Confirmation. But the Treafurer and Company were become, from the late Exactions, very jealous and cautious in that Point; and did moreover judge thofe Fees to be very oppreffive and intolerable. And therefore, for the Eafe of the Colony, they declared, that the Secretary fhould receive no Fees at all; but in Recompence of all Services, they allotted five hundred Acres of Land, for him and his Succeffors, with twenty Tenants thereon. This was laid off on the *Eaftern* Shore, and the Grant was afterwards enlarged. But whereas Captain *Argall*, in the time of his Sufpenfion from the Place of Admiral, had deputed *Abraham Peirfey*, the Cape-Merchant, to be his Vice-Admiral, the Company declared that Deputation, to be utterly void and unlawful, and committed the Execution of that Office, to the Governor and Council of State, and to fuch under them, as they fhould authorife and appoint.

THERE had been many fcandalous Reports fpread (as was intimated in a private Letter to Mr. *Bland*, a very confiderable Merchant of the Company) of the Barrennefs and Infertility of the Soil in *Virginia*. And it alfo had been one efpecial Piece of Captain *Argall's* Policy, in order to difhearten and difgrace the Company, to vilify the Country, both by himfelf and his Engines, and to reprefent it as lefs fertile, than the moft barren arable Lands in *England*. And altho' thefe Afperfions were fufficiently contradicted by his own former Letters and Reports, yet, for a fuller Anfwer to them, a Commiffion was fent to *Virginia*, and a Return made

made upon Oath, of the Strength and Goodnefs of the Soil. 1620. But as Malice is more induftrious than Truth, thefe unjuft Scandals prevailed but too much, and difcouraged many Adventurers from making their Tranfportations. To obviate therefore all fuch ill Confequences, it was refolved upon the Motion, and committed to the Care, of Sir *Edwin Sandys* and Dr. *Winftone*, to prepare and publifh a fmall Book, containing a Refutation of all· fuch flanderous Reports; and to adjoin, at the End, an alphabetical Index of the Adventurers Names. This laft had a double Ufe. For, in the firft Place, it did great Honour to the Enterprife, by fhewing, that many of the chief Perfons in the Nation, for Wifdom, Fortune, and Dignity, were deeply concerned in, and great Encouragers of it. And next, as this Index was drawn from Sir *Thomas Smith*'s Books, which were very carelefly kept and incorrect, it gave the Alarm to all fuch, as had paid in their Monies to him, and found themfelves omitted in this Lift. And it accordingly made them bring in his Receipts, or Bills of Adventure; whereby many Sums of Money appeared to have been received by him, which could otherwife never have been made out by his Books, or proved by any other Method.

Sir George Yeardley, Governor.

THE

THE
HISTORY
OF
VIRGINIA.

BOOK IV.

1620.

Sir *George Yeardley,* Governor.

T HE Time of Sir *Edwin Sandys*'s Office being expired, there was held a great and general Quarter Court of Election, at Mr. Deputy *Farrar*'s House, in St. *Sithe*'s Lane, on the 17th of *May*, confisting of three Earls, one Vifcount, four Lords, thirty Knights, feveral Doctors and Efquires, and largely above an hundred other Gentlemen, Merchants, and Citizens. To this fplendid Meeting, Sir *Edwin Sandys* made a long and very handfome Speech, laying before them the State of their Affairs, at the time of his Acceffion to the Office of Treafurer, and then. In this he was naturally led to fet forth, as well the Negligence and bad Government at home, as particularly the vaft Lofs and Damage, which the Company had fuftained, in the Time of their Deputy Governor, Captain *Argall*. And he informed them, that there had, within his Year, been fet out eight Ships at the Company's Expence, and four others by private Adventurers; and that thefe Ships had tranfported twelve hundred and fixty one Perfons, whereof fix hundred and fifty were for the publick Ufe, and the other fix hundred and eleven for private Plantations. He alfo gave them an Account of the feveral Gifts, which had been made, this Year, for pious Ufes; and of the many Patents, that had paffed to various private Adventurers and their Affociates, who had
under-

undertaken, to tranfport to *Virginia* great Multitudes of People, with much Cattle. And he recounted to them the feveral Methods, which had been taken, to draw the People off from their greedy and immoderate Purfuit of To- bacco, and to turn them to other more ufeful and neceffary Commodities: That for this Purpofe, an hundred and fifty Perfons had been fent, to fet up three Iron Works: That Directions had been given for making Cordage, as well of Hemp and Flax, as more efpecially of Silk-grafs, which grew there naturally in great Abundance, and was found, upon Experience, to make the beft Cordage and Line in the World; and that therefore each Family had been or- dered and obliged, to fet an hundred Plants of it, and the Governor himfelf five thoufand: That, befides, it had been recommended to them, to make Pitch and Tar, together with Pot and Soap-Afhes, and to provide Timber of all Sorts, for Shipping, and other Ufes; to which End, fuffi- cient Men and Materials had been fent over, for erecting fundry Sawing-Mills: That the Country abounding in Mul- berry Trees of the beft Sort, whereon fome Silkworms had been found naturally, producing excellent Silk, they had therefore preffed upon them the Culture and Improvement of that Manufacture; and that his Majefty, now the fecond time, after the Mifcarriage of the former, had beftowed upon the Company Plenty of Silkworm Seed, of the beft Sort, out of his own Store: That moreover, as the Coun- try yielded naturally a wonderful Variety of excellent Grapes, there had been fent divers fkilful Vignerons, together with Store of Vine Slips, of the beft *European* Kinds: And laft- ly, that the Salt-Works, which had been fuffered to run to Decay, were again reftored and fet up; and that there were now Hopes of fuch Plenty, as not only to ferve the Colony for the prefent, but alfo fhortly to fupply the great Fifhery on thofe *American* Coafts.

HE then exhibited to the Court the Book of his Accounts, examined and approved by five of the feven publick Auditors of the Company, the other two being abfent. And he fur- ther declared, that for any Bufinefs, done within his Year, he had not left the Company, to his Knowledge, one Pen- ny in Debt, except perhaps the Remain of fome Charges, which had not been delivered in, or were not yet become due; and that he had alfo left in Stock twelve hundred Pounds more, than had been left to him the former Year. And next, he proceeded to inform the Company of the De- puty's Accounts, who himfelf prefented them, exactly kept, after the Manner of Merchants, in three Books, fubfcribed and approved, as well by the Company's Committees, as

1620.

Sir George Yeardley, Governor.

N

all

all the Auditors. And then Sir *Edwin Sandys* went on, and told the Court, that he could not but greatly commend Mr. Deputy-Treasurer's Fidelity, Care, and Industry; who, to the Neglect of his own private Affairs, had bestowed his whole Time, together with the great Help and Assistance of his Brothers, on the Business of his Office, which he had discharged, with wonderful Exactness, and an incredible Diligence and Labour. And lastly, he concluded, with his respective Thanks to the several Orders of the Company: First, to the Company in general, for their good Opinion and Affection, in chusing him their Treasurer: Then, particularly to the Lords, for their frequent Presence, to the great Grace and Honour of the Court, and Furtherance of the Enterprise: Next, to the Officers, for their Fidelity and Diligence, in joining with him to support the great Burthen of the Company's Business: And lastly, to the Court, for their Goodness and Patience, in bearing with his involuntary Errors and other Infirmities. After which, delivering up his Office, together with the Seals, he desired them to proceed to their Election, according to the Message, lately received from his Majesty; and thereupon withdrew himself out of Court.

For at the Beginning of this Court, before they had entered upon any Business, a Gentleman from the King presented himself to the Board, and signified; that it was his Majesty's Pleasure, out of his especial Care and Affection for the Colony, that the Company should elect one of the four, which he should name to them, and no other, to be their Treasurer. These were Sir *Thomas Smith*, Sir *Thomas Roe*, Mr. Alderman *Johnson*, and Mr. *Maurice Abbot*. Sir *Thomas Smith* and Alderman *Johnson* had before been in their chief Offices, and the Company conceived themselves to have little Reason, to be satisfied with their Conduct and Proceedings. But in *Virginia* more especially, where the Effects of their Management had been more sensibly felt, they were notoriously infamous, and utterly detested and cursed by the whole Colony. So that this may be looked upon, as an additional Instance of the unhappy Turn of that Monarch, in his Choice of publick Officers. Sir *Thomas Roe* was indeed an eminent Person, a Man of Letters, and a very great Traveller, and is well known to the Learned, by the Intimacy and Dearness, that was between him and Dr. *Donne*, Dean of St. *Paul*'s; who was himself afterwards one of the Company, and of his Majesty's Council for *Virginia*. But Sir *Thomas Roe* is most noted, for his Embassy from King *James* to the Court of the Great *Mogul*, and for his Journal of that Embassy, a most judicious and exquisite

Book

Book of Travels. But fince his Return from the Great *Mogul*'s Court, he had been concerned in the Cuftoms, and was likewife well known, to have had a long and intimate Friendfhip with Sir *Thomas Smith*; both which, being fuf-picious Circumftances to the *Virginia* Company, would but little contribute towards recommending him to their Choice. As to Mr. *Abbot*, little is known of him; only that he was a Merchant, and may feem, from fome obfcure Circum-ftances, to have been of Kin to his Grace, Dr. *George Ab-**bot*, then Archbifhop of *Canterbury*.

BUT the greateft Obftacle, to the Election of either of thefe Gentlemen, was, that the Company had, almoft una-nimoufly, caft their Eye upon the Earl of *Southampton* for their future Treafurer, a Nobleman of eminent Quality, Grandfon to the Lord Chanceller *Wriothefly* (one of King *Henry* VIII's Executors, and of the Regents during the Minority of *Edward* VI.) and Father to the great and vir-tuous Earl and Duke of *Southampton*, in the Reigns of *Charles* the Firft and Second. He is alfo famed in Hiftory, for his Friendfhip to the unfortunate Earl of *Effex*, by whofe Rafhnefs and Impetuofity, he was betrayed into fome un-warrantable Actions; and was therefore, at the fame time with that Nobleman, condemned to Death, but pardoned by Queen *Elifabeth*, and kept in Prifon, during her Life. He was, in Truth, an early, conftant, and great Encou-rager of this Settlement of *Virginia*, as well as of all other noble Works and Enterprifes; and is particularly memora-ble, for his generous Patronage, and fingular Munificence, to *Shakefpear*, the Glory and Prodigy of the *Englifh* Stage. For he is faid, to have given him, at one time, a thoufand Pounds, to enable him to go through with a Purchafe, which he underftood, he had an Inclination to make. But altho' he had been a ftrenuous Friend of *Effex*'s, to all whom King *James* declared a particular Regard and Obli-gation, as that Lord was thought to have acted for his In-terefts, and altho' he was admitted of the Privy Council, yet was he but little affected or liked at Court. For his Friendfhip to the former Earl of *Effex* was continued down to his Son; whofe hard Ufage, in fome Meafure from the Court, in the Cafe of his Wife, could not but have been much difapproved and difgufted by him. And befides, a-bout this Time, the Encroachments of the Prerogative, and the avowed Principles of arbitrary Power, began to raife a Spirit of Liberty in the Nation; and the Earl of *Southampton*, together with the Earls of *Effex* and *Oxford*, were foon diftinguifhed, as the undoubted Heads of the patriot Party in the Houfe of Lords; whilft Sir *Dudley*

N 2 *Digges,*

Digges, Sir *Nathaniel Rich*, Mr. *Selden*, and others of
the *Virginia* Company, as well as divers Members not of
that Company, appeared with equal Vigor and Refolution,
in the Houfe of Commons.

BUT however the Affections of the Company might
ftand, they were much troubled and perplexed, by this
Meffage from the King. For fhould they proceed according to that Nomination, they would certainly admit a very
great and evident Breach, in their Privilege of free Election.
And fhould they reject it, they might incur the Sufpicion
of Defect in Point of Duty and Obedience; an Imputation,
ever hateful and eafy of Accefs to the jealous Minds of weak
and pufillanimous Princes, and which many of their own
difaffected Members would be too ready to improve, to the
Difadvantage of the Company. Having therefore confulted
the Letters patent, it was at length agreed to adjourn to
Election to the next Quarter Court; and after much and
earneft Refufal, they prevailed on Sir *Edwin Sandys*, to
continue in his Office, till that time. In the mean while,
as it evidently appeared, that the King had been much a-
bufed and mifinformed, concerning the Management of
their Affairs, they appointed the Earl of *Southampton*, the
Vifcount *Doncafter*, Lord *Cavendifh*, Lord *Sheffield*, Sir
John Davers, Sir *Nicholas Tufton*, Sir *Lawrence Hyde*, with
others, Gentlemen and Merchants, to deliver in, to his
Majefty, a full and true Account, as well of the former, as
of the laft Year's Adminiftration of their Affairs; and to
befeech his Majefty, not to take from them the Privilege of
their Charters, but to leave it to their own Choice, to have
a free Election. To which Requeft, his Majefty readily
condefcended; and farther fignified, that it would be highly
pleafing and agreeable to him, if they made Choice of fuch
a Perfon, as might, at all times, and on all Occafions, have
free Accefs to his Royal Prefence. And he likewife declared, that the Meffenger, in excluding them from the Liberty of chufing any other, but one of the four nominated,
had miftaken his Intention; which was indeed, to recommend thofe Gentlemen to their Choice, but not fo, as to
bar the Company from the Election of any other.

THIS Anfwer being received by the Company with great
Thankfulnefs, Mr. *Herbert* obferved to them, that their
Bufinefs had, of late, fuffered much, as well in Reputation,
as otherways, by Reafon of fome unhappy Diffenfions a-
mong them: That they ought, therefore, ferioufly to think,
of applying a prefent and effectual Remedy to this Evil:
That the late Treafurer was a Gentleman of fuch acknowledged Sufficiency, and of fo great Integrity and Induftry,

, that

that of his Rank, there could not certainly be any found to surpaſs him : That therefore, there ſeemed to him no Hope left, except ſome of thoſe honourable Perſonages, then preſent, would vouchſafe to accept of the Place of Treaſurer ; who, by the Addition of Nobility, and by the Luſtre and Influence of their high Station, might effect that, which, they had found by Experience, could not be effected, by mere Dint of Ability and Induſtry. Hereupon, the whole Court, beſeeching his Lordſhip to redeem this noble Enterpriſe from imminent Danger and Deſtruction, did, with univerſal Joy and Applauſe, nominate the Earl of *Southampton* ; and to teſtify their Thankfulneſs and Reſpect, they elected him Treaſurer, without the Ballot, by a general Acclamation and Erection of Hands. And his Lordſhip, after a ſhort Pauſe, declared his Acceptance ; and exhorted them all, to put on the ſame Mind, with which he accepted that Place, and laying aſide all private Feuds and Animoſities, to labour chearfully and unanimouſly, for the Promotion of the publick Good, and the Advancement of the Colony. But as his Lordſhip's Attendance in Parliament, and other weighty Affairs, might not always permit him, to be ſo conſtant at their Courts, as might otherwiſe be wiſhed, they voluntarily, and without his Motion, diſpenſed with him, in that Particular. And they alſo re-elected Mr. *John Farrar*, to the Place of Deputy-Treaſurer ; whoſe Experience, and known Integrity and Diligence, might well ſupply the occaſional Abſence of their Treaſurer. Sir *Edwin Sandys* likewiſe, who was in a cloſe and intimate Friendſhip with the Earl of *Southampton*, was afterwards authoriſed, at his Lordſhip's Deſire, to ſet his Hand, upon Occaſion, to Receipts of Money, for the Company's Uſe ; and did otherwiſe, by his private Diligence and Activity, give him great Eaſe and Aſſiſtance, in the Execution of the Office.

CAPTAIN *Brewſter*'s Appeal from the Sentence of the Court-Martial, in *Virginia*, had, all this while, hung in Suſpence ; and it had even been declared, by a Meeting of the Council at the Earl of *Warwick*'s Houſe, the former Year, that Trial by Martial Law was the nobleſt kind of Trial, being judged by Soldiers and Men of Honour. But now, proper Certificates and atteſted Copies of the Proceedings being returned from *Virginia*, the Cauſe came to a final Hearing and Determination, in an extraordinary Court, held for that Purpoſe, and compoſed of ſeveral Lords and others of eminent Quality and Diſtinction. But here there ſeems to have reigned a quite different Spirit from that, which appeared at the Earl of *Warwick*'s. For they were

no

no way inclined, to give up the many Rights and Advantages of Juries and the Laws of *England*, for the extraordinary Privilege of being fummarily tried by Martial Law,
and dying honourably by the Verdict of Gentlemen of
the Sword. And therefore, being fhocked at the Cruelty
and Terror of the Proceedings againft Captain *Brewfter*,
they declared them to be unjuft and unlawful, and not war-
rantable, either in Matter or Form, by the Laws of *England*, or by any Power or Authority, derived from his Majefty's Charters: That Captain *Brewfter* had committed
nothing, any way worthy of the fevere Penalty of Death:
That the Manner of Trial by Martial Law, in time of
Peace, and when there was no Mutiny or Rebellion, was
utterly unlawful and of no Validity: And confequently,
that Captain *Brewfter* was to be held a legal Man, and not
lawfully condemned. And all this then paffed and was ratified by the univerfal Affent of the Court; altho' Sir *Thomas
Wroth*, who had married the Earl of *Warwick*'s Sifter, did,
in a fubfequent Court, declare his Diffent, on fome falfe
and frivolous Pretences. Captain *Brewfter* had alfo, upon
his Requeft, a Copy of this Act of Court granted him, ex-
emplified under the legal Seal of the Company; of which
he fent a Duplicate to *Virginia*.

IN *May* this Year, there was held another General Af-
fembly, which has, through Miftake, and the Indolence and
Negligence of our Hiftorians, in fearching fuch ancient Re-
cords, as are ftill extant in the Country, been commonly
reputed the firft General Affembly of *Virginia*. But that
Privilege was granted fooner, immediately upon the Difguft
taken, by the worthier Part of the Company, at Sir *Thomas
Smith*'s ill Government, and the infufferable Tyranny and
Iniquity of Captain *Argall*'s Proceedings. And upon Sir
George Yeardley's Reprefentation of the Want of more
Counfellors, the Company appointed the following Gentlemen to be of the Council; Mr. *George Thorpe*, Deputy for
the College; Mr. *Thomas Newce*, who had alfo been fent
over Deputy for the Company's Lands, with the Allowance of twelve hundred Acres, and forty Tenants; Mr.
Tracy; Mr. *Pountis*; Mr. *Middleton*; Mr. *Bluet*; and
Mr. *Harwood*, the Chief of *Martin*'s Hundred. And we
are likewife told by Mr. *Beverley*, that a *Dutch* Ship, putting in this Year, fold twenty Negroes to the Colony,
which were the firft of that Generation, that were ever
brought to *Virginia*.

TOBACCO, a ftinking, naufeous, and unpalatable Weed,
is certainly an odd Commodity, to make the Staple and
Riches of a Country. It is neither of Neceffity nor Ornament

ment to human Life; but the Ufe of it depends upon Humour and Cuftom, and may be looked upon, as one of the moft fingular and extraordinary Pieces of Luxury, that the Wantonnefs of Man hath yet invented or given into. It is not therefore to be wondered, that the Colony's Eagernefs and Application, almoft folely, to Tobacco, was much diftafted and oppofed by the Company; efpecially in thofe early Times, before it had yet obtained fuch a general Reception and Dominion in the World. To which may be added, that the King himfelf, to whom the Age in general, and the Company in particular, did, on many Occafions, pay great Deference, had a Sort of natural Antipathy to it, and was perpetually haranguing, railing, and even writing againft it. For that *Solomon* of *England* thought it not below his Royal Wifdom and Dignity, to write a Treatife, entitled; *A Counter-Blaft to Tobacco.* The Company therefore entered into and admitted various Projects, for raifing other things of more immediate Neceffity and Benefit to Mankind; fuch as the feveral Commodities, mentioned and recommended by Sir *Edwin Sandys,* in his late Speech, at the delivering up of his Office, with many others. For this Purpofe, they procured plenty of Silkworm Seed out of *France, Italy,* and *Spain*; and fent over a Perfon, who had been brought up, many Years, in tending the King's Silkworms at *Oatlands,* and was thereby become very fkilful, in breeding the Worms, and winding the Silk, and undertook to inftruct others therein. And they alfo laid out for, and had Hopes of procuring, many more fuch fkilful Artifts from *France.* And as the Inhabitants were very eager, to have the Servants and Apprentices, fent over by the Company, they made an Order, for the greater Encouragement of thefe Commodities, that fuch Planters, as had excelled, in building fit Rooms for Silkworms, and in planting Mulberry Trees and Vines, fhould have the firft Choice of fuch Apprentices and Servants; and that the Company would be paid for them, not a Whit in Smoke and Tobacco, but in Corn, Silkgrafs, Silk, and other fuch ufeful Commodities. At Sir *Edwin Sandys's* Motion, there was likewife tranflated, by fome of the Company, a *French* Treatife (recommended, as excellent in that Kind) concerning the Management of Mulberry Trees and Silk; which was printed at the Company's Expence, and fent over in fufficient Numbers, and diftributed among the People. And they alfo appointed a felect Committee of Merchants, to rate all thofe feveral Commodities at fuch a juft Price, that the Company and Merchants might be no Lofers thereby, and yet that the Planter might have good Encouragement to raife them.   N 4   BE-

1620.

BESIDES thefe, they entered into Projeds and Con-
trads, for raifing various other Commodities. And Sir
Edwin Sandys in particular, who was ever ftudious and in-
defatigable in the Company's Bufinefs, prefented a long and
judicious Writing, containing many ufeful Inftrudions and
Projeds, for the Peace and better Government of the Company at home, and for the Advancement of the Colony
abroad ; all which, in its feveral Parts and Branches, was
entrufted to proper Committees, to ripen and bring into
Execution. Sir *William Monfon* alfo, a Perfon of great E-
minence and Note (being Admiral in the Reigns of Queen
Elifabeth, *James* I. and *Charles* I. and Author of the Naval
Trads) together with his Affociates, offered to the Company, if they would, for feven Years, grant them the fole
Benefit and Importation, from *Virginia,* of two fuch new
Commodities, as had not yet been difcovered or planted by
any other, to pay them an hundred Pounds *per Annum,* to
plant twenty five Men, every Year during the faid Term,
and then to refign the Whole up into the Company's Hands.
A Patent was therefore accordingly granted, with proper
Reftridions ; but what thefe Commodities were, or what
was the Succefs or Confequence of this Undertaking, I do
not find.

THIS Year 1620, Count *Gondomar,* the *Spanifh* Ambaffador, who had a great Afcendant at Court, and governed
the King, as he pleafed, prevailed with him, to fit out a
Squadron, of fix Ships of War and twelve ftout Merchant-
men, in order to humble the *Algerines,* who then infefted
the *Spanifh* Coafts and Trade, but were not any way particularly troublefome to our Nation. And thus was this weak
and timorous Prince, who could not be drawn to make any
Steps, towards the Vindication of his own Honour, or to
fupport the Rights of his Family, or the Interefts of his
Subjeds, ftrangely engaged in a warlike Expedition, in Defence of a treacherous and delufive Ally. This Squadron
was put under the Command of Sir *Robert Manfel,* as Admiral ; together with whom, Sir *Richard Hawkins,* Vice-
Admiral, Sir *Thomas Button,* Rear-Admiral, Sir *Henry
Palmer, Arthur Manwaring,* and *Thomas Love,* Efqrs.
Captains of the other Men of War, and *Samuel Argall,* Efq;
who commanded one of the ftouteft Privateers, were appointed a Council of War. But this Enterprife was very
weakly managed; and to ufe Sir *William Monfon's* Remark,
altho' it was defigned to find out and deftroy the Pirates of
Algiers, yet the Fleet did not fpend twenty Days at Sea, the
whole time, they continued in the *Mediterranean* ; but retired into Harbour, where the Pirates might find them, but

not

not they the Pirates. So that, this ill-conducted Action afforded fufficient Subject of Scorn and Laughter to all Nations; efpecially confidering the great Reputation, the *Engliſh* had juftly gained, in their former Expeditions at Sea. 1620.
Sir *George*
Yeardley,
Governor. But *Cambden* tells us, that, in Revenge for this Injury and Affault, the *Algerines* took, by the 9th of *October* following, thirty five Sail of *Engliſh* and *Scotch* Ships.

ABOUT this time, there arofe a warm Difpute between the two Colonies, concerning the *Virginia* Company's Right to fifh at *Cape Cod*, within the Limits of the *Northern* Colony; and upon Reference to the Letters-patent, it was found clearly, that their Pretenfions were juftly grounded. But Sir *Ferdinando Gorges*, with others principally concerned in the *Northern* Grant, endeavoured privately to obtain a new Patent, whereby the *Southern* Colony fhould be utterly excluded from fifhing upon that Coaft, without their Leave and Licence firft obtained. This gave a juft Alarm to the *Virginia* Company. For befides fix thoufand Pounds, which they had already expended upon that Fifhery, it was at prefent of main Confequence to them, as well for the Support and Suftenance of the Plantation, as for defraying the vaft Charge of Shipping and Tranfportation of People, by Returns made from thence in Fifh. They therefore applied to his Majefty, and got this Patent of Sir *Ferdinando Gorges* ftopped and fequeftered, in the Lord Chancellor's Hands. And finding, how precarious their Privileges were, upon his Majefty's foleGrant, and how liable to be perpetually violated and impeded, it was refolved, upon the Motion of Mr. *Smith*, a fenfible, worthy, and ufeful Member of the Company, to obtain a new Grant, with all fuch further Immunities, and larger Privileges, as were fitting and requifite, and to have it ftrengthened and confirmed in the Parliament, which was to meet foon after; and upon the Earl of *Southampton*'s Application to his Majefty, he readily gave his Confent to it. But notwithftanding the Earl of *Southampton*'s Intereft and Endeavours, and Sir *Edwin Sandys*'s great Pains and Induftry therein, it was never brought to any final Iffue or Conclufion.

BUT the Remedy, propofed by Mr. *Herbert*, for curing the Factions and Difcords of the Company, by fetting a Nobleman of eminent Diftinction and Authority at the Head of their Affairs, was far from having the intended Effect. For their Animofities and Diffenfions grew higher, towards the latter End of this Year, and never ended, but with the Diffolution of the Company. As therefore they were the chief Occafion and Pretence of that Diffolution, it will not be improper here, to give a fuller and more diftinct Account of them. BE-

BESIDES the Affairs of the Magazine, which, notwi
ftanding its Diffolution, ftill afforded Matter of Contentic
there were two other principal Subjects of Difpute and Ci
fufion in the Company; the fettling Sir *Thomas Smith*'s /
counts, and the Profecution of Captain *Argall*, for his mi
Outrages and exorbitant Proceedings in *Virginia*. Sir 7
mas *Smith* had been Treafurer, from the firft Conftitut
of the Company in the Year 1606, till *April* 28, 161
and in that time, there had paffed through his Hands ab
eighty thoufand Pounds. He had, in thofe Days, a v
great Intereft and Sway in the Company; and to put
beft Conftruction upon the Matter, he never expected
be called to a ftrict and rigorous Account, and his Serva
had been very carelefs and remifs, in keeping his Boo
But feveral of the Company fufpected, that he had emb
zled and converted much of the publick Money, to
own private Ufe; and were therefore very eager, to br
him to an Account. Sir *Thomas*, on his Side, was very
in his Profeffions, and preffed, with much Warmth,
full Settlement and finifhing the Affair; offering to pay,
only what fhould appear due from himfelf, but whate
Wrong or Damage fhould have happened to the Compa
from his Under-Officers or Servants. But then his Rece
were fo very faulty and deficient, and his Difburfements
void of all Warrant and proper Vouchers, that the Cc
pany's Auditors, although they took much Pains, cc
bring nothing tp a Head; and the whole only ferved
adminifter frefh Fuel to Animofities and Quarrels, with
any Profpect of coming to a fatisfactory Conclufion.

As to Captain *Argall*, altho' he was under Profecut
from the Company, yet by his Craft and Management,
the Power and Influence of his Friends, by his fhifting
turning, and by going on the Expedition againft the *A*
rines, he fo fhuffled and perplexed the Company, that
at laft efcaped, without any Punifhment or Reftitution at
And altho' Sir *Thomas Smith*, overpowered with the Juf
and Neceffity of the thing, had firft commenced the Pr
cution againft him, yet being now Fellow-Sufferers,
equally aggrieved at the prefent upright and vigorous /
miniftration of the Company's Affairs, they joined Fori
and did every thing in their Power, to difgrace, and vil
and retard the Succefs of the Enterprife. The princ
Perfons of their Faction were, the Earl of *Warwick*;
Nathaniel Rich, the Earl's Brother; Sir *Thomas Wroth*, \
was nearly allied to them by Marriage; Sir *John Wolf*
holme, a wealthy Merchant and a Farmer of the Cuftoi
with Alderman *Johnfon*, Mr. *Canning*, and Mr. *Effing*
tl

three factious Citizens, and others of lefs Note, to the
Number of twenty fix in the whole, when their Faction
was ftrongeft ; a very inconfiderable Party, had they not
gained the Ear and Support of a weak King, who had a
wonderful Inftinct and Propenfity to the wrong Side of every
Queftion, and with much Formality of Wifdom and Learning, for ever miftook the true Intereft of himfelf and his
Subjects. On the other Side appeared the Earl of *Southampton*, the Earl of *Dorfet*, the Earl of *Devonfhire*, the Vifcount *Doncafter*, Lord *Cavendifh*, Lord *Sheffield*, Lord
Paget, Sir *Edward Sackvil*, Sir *Dudley Digges*, Sir *Edwin
Sandys*, Sir *John Davers*, Sir *Samuel Sandys*, with a long
Roll of others, and in fhort, the whole Body of Adventu-
rers in general, which confifted of near fifty Noblemen, fome
hundreds of Knights, and many hundreds of Gentlemen,
eminent Merchants, and Citizens, to the full Amount of
a thoufand Perfons in all. But none acted in the Support of
Truth and Juftice, with greater Spirit and Vigor, than the
Lord *Cavendifh*, afterwards Earl of *Devonfhire*, and Sir
Edward Sackvil. The former was a young Nobleman of
much Generofity, Spirit, and Eloquence ; and he fucceeded
Sir *Thomas Smith*, in the Place of Governor to the *Somer-
Iflands* Company. The latter, who afterwards became
Earl of *Dorfet*, was the Perfon of the greateft Fame in that
Age, for a facetious Vivacity, fparkling Wit, and undaunt-
ed Courage, joined to a found and comprehenfive Under-
ftanding, and an excellent Turn for Bufinefs. He was one
of the firft, that raifed the Reputation of the *Dorfet* Family,
for Wit and Exactnefs of Tafte and Difcernment; but is
beft known to common Readers, for his Duel with Lord
Bruce, which is related in my Lord *Clarendon* and the Guar-
dian, Books defervedly popular and in the Hands of every
Body. And as he appeared thus early in the Caufe of the
Colony (for fuch is it owned to be by our Affemblies of thofe
times) fo did he continue, to the laft, a conftant Friend and
Favourer of *Virginia*.

As Sir *George Yeardley* had expreffed his Defire to leave
the Government, at the Expiration of his Commiffion,
which would be in the *November* following, the Earl of
Southampton recommended to the Company the Confideration of a proper Perfon, to fucceed him. His Lordfhip propofed to their Choice Sir *Francis Wyat*, a young Gentleman,
thought every way fufficient and equal to the Place, and
highly efteemed, as he faid, on Account of his Birth, Education, Integrity of Life, and fair Fortune. However, he
earneftly preffed on the Company the Nomination of fuch
other Perfon or Perfons, as they fhould think proper, to
ftand

1621.　ftand in Election with him. But no other being fo m
as named, Sir *Francis Wyat* was chofen Governor, to t
Sir *George*
Yeardley,
Governor.
his Place at the Expiration of Sir *George Yeardley*'s C
miffion, and not before. And to do him the greater G
and Honour, as well as the better to enable and encou
him in the Execution of his Office, they elected him
of his Majefty's Council in *England* for *Virginia*. T
alfo allowed him two hundred Pounds, for all necef
Provifions for his Voyage, with the free tranfport of I
felf-and Attendants, provided they did not exceed the N
ber of twenty Perfons.

　　DR. *Lawrence Bohun*, who had left *Virginia* in the Y
1611, with the Lord *Delawarr*, had now obtained a 1
Grant of Land, for the Tranfportation of three hun
Perfons. He was alfo appointed the Company's Phyfic
General to the Colony, with the Allowance of five hun
Acres of Land and twenty Tenants; under Covenani
maintain and make them good, from time to time, an
his Deceafe, or other Removal, to leave the like Nun
of Men and Stock of Cattle, as was allowed by the Cor
ny, and by them annexed to the Place. He accordingl
fail, in the Beginning of *February*, with eighty Paffeng
in a Ship of an hundred and fixty Tons and eight Iron (
and a Falcon, commanded by Captain *Anthony Che*
But about the Middle of *March*, they were attacked,
Nevis in the *Weft-Indies*, by two *Spanifh* Men of Wa
three hundred Tons and fixteen or twenty Brafs Car
apeice. The Fight was fharp and defperate; but the
glifh fo beftowed their Shot, and managed the Engager
with fuch Dexterity and Bravery, that the *Spaniards*
glad to ftand aloof, and after following them a Day or
without any other remarkable Annoyance, at laft fell af
and left them. There was made a very great Slaught
the *Spaniards*, fo that their Scuppled ran with Blood;
the Captain of the Admiral-Ship, who acted the Part
brave Commander, was flain. On the *Englifh* Side,
were killed; among whom was Dr. *Bohun*, whofe L
was greatly lamented. He had ftudied long among
learned Phyficians of the *Low-Countries*, and behaved
felf in this Battle, like a worthy and valiant Gentlei
In his Room, Mr. *John Pot* was elected, by the Comp
Phyfician-General to the Colony. He was recomme
by Dr. *Gulftone*, an eminent Member of their Societ
a Mafter of Arts, well practiced in Chirurgery and Ph
and expert in Chymical Proceffes and other ingenious I
of his Profeffion; whofe Service, he therefore conce
would be of great Ufe to the Colony. He was accord

fent, upon the fame Foot, as Dr. *Bohun*; and was allowed his own, his Wife's, and two Servants Paffages. Dr. *Gul-*
ftone was likewife defired, to buy a Cheft of Phyfic of twen-
ty Pounds Value, and ten Pounds of Books, proper for the
Profeffion, which fhould always belong to the Place.

CAPTAIN *William Newce* offered, to tranfport and fettle a thoufand Perfons in *Virginia*, by Midfummer, 1625;
and defired to be appointed their General, and to have a
Patent, with that Proportion of Land, and fuch other Privileges, as were ufually granted on the like Occafion. A
Patent was readily granted, in the largeft and moft ample
Manner. But as to the Title and Command of General,
they refufed to grant it him; becaufe it was a Power, properly belonging to the Governor only. Befides, it gave
fuch an Independency, as was deftructive of all Order and
good Government; and had therefore been loudly cried out
againft, in Captain *Martin*'s extravagant Patent, and in a
Grant furreptitioufly and illegally obtained by Captain *Argall*, and therefore exprefly ftopped, by the Company's Orders to the Governor in *Virginia*. But Captain *Newce* farther requefted, in order to enable him the better to go
through the Charge of fo great an Undertaking, to be appointed Marfhal of *Virginia*; for which Poft he was eminently qualified, having ever been exercifed in military Affairs and Arms, and of noted Experience and Skill in Martial
Difcipline; as appeared by his many Services in *Ireland*, and
by the Teftimony of divers honourable Perfons, upon their
own Knowledge. He was therefore conftituted Marfhal of
Virginia; to take into his Charge, as well the Fortifications, Arms, and Forces of the Colony, as to caufe the
People, to be duly trained up in Military Difcipline, and to
the Ufe and Exercife of Arms. And they annexed fifteen
hundred Acres of Land and fifty Tenants to the Place, to
be tranfported and furnifhed by himfelf, at eight Pounds
Charge to the Company a Man. And the King alfo, being
highly pleafed at the Nomination of this Gentleman, conferred the Honour of Knighthood upon him; calling him
his Knight-Marfhal of *Virginia*, and expreffing great Hopes
from the Management of a Perfon of his acknowledged Capacity and Skill. However, he did not long furvive his Arrival in *Virginia*; but died, two Days after the reading his
Patent and Commiffion.

THERE was, at this time, above a thoufand Pounds,
due in *Virginia* to the Company, for Rents and Duties;
and they were likewife greatly fcandalifed and offended, to
find their frequent and preffing Orders, for raifing good and
ftaple Commodities, entirely flighted and neglected. It was
therefore

therefore thought neceffary, to appoint a particular Office
by the Name of Treafurer; who fhould have the Charg
not only of their Rents and Duties, but fhould alfo tal
into his more efpecial Regard and Care, to fee all Orde
and Directions, fent from *England*, duly and faithfully ex
cuted, from time to time; or otherwife to render a fuffic
ent Reafon to the contrary. To this Office Mr. *Geor*
Sandys, the noted Poet and Traveller was unanimouf
elected, as a Perfon every way fit, on Account of his Ab
lity and Integrity. And they likewife allotted fifteen hu:
dred Acres of Land, perpetually to belong to the faid Pla
of Treafurer, with fifty Tenants thereon; and allow
Mr. *Sandys* an hundred and fifty Pounds, to furnifh himf
for the Voyage, with the free Paffage of his Family, n
exceeding the Number of ten Perfons. And it was thoug
proper, that two fuch eminent Officers as Marfhal a
Treafurer, to which Places fuch worthy Gentlemen h
been preferred, fhould be admitted of his Majefty's Cou
cil in *England*, and appointed of the Council of State
Virginia.

SOON after, Mr. *Richard Norwood*, a Man famous,
thofe Days, as a Mathematician, who had laid off t
Tribes and Lands, and made an exact Plot of the Iflan
of *Bermudas*, was recommended to the Company for St
veyor of *Virginia*, and was accordingly elected to the Pla
But I know not, how the Change came to be made, ye
find, very foon after, Mr. *William Clayborne* appointed a
fent Surveyor. The Company allowed him thirty Poun
a Year and a convenient Houfe, for his publick Service
laying off their Lands; with twenty Pounds paid in Ha
to furnifh himfelf with Inftruments and Books, which
was obliged to leave to his Succeffors. They likewife
lowed him the Tranfport of three Perfons, and gave h
two hundred Acres of Land in Fee-fimple; and in cafe
was employed in any private Survey, he was to receive
Shillings a Day, and to be found in Diet and Lodging.

MR. *Pory*'s Commiffion of Secretary was to determine
the fame Time, as Sir *George Yeardley*'s. He had given
Company little Satisfaction in that Office, but had b
plainly detected, although a fworn Officer, of betray
the Proceedings, and fecretly conveying the Proofs, aga
Captain *Argall*, to the Earl of *Warwick*. And as he
befides known, to be a profeffed Tool and Inftrument
that Faction, the Company was at no Lofs or Hefitati
about renewing his Commiffion. But four Gentlemen
ing ftrongly recommended to them, as fully qualified
that Poft, in Point of Learning, Honefty, and Experier

t

they made Choice of Mr. *Chriſtopher Daviſon*, and admitted him a free Brother of the Company, and one of the
Council of State in *Virginia*. And as the Company's
Ships were often delayed in the Country, through Negligence and Miſmanagement, it was reſolved, to appoint
an Officer, by the Title of Vice-Admiral, who ſhould
take into his Charge the Care and Diſpatch of them.
Mr. *John Pountis* therefore, one of the Council, who
had deſerved well of both the Company and Colony,
was, this Summer, appointed to that Place proviſionally,
and afterwards confirmed by the Quarter Court in *November*, with the Allowance of three hundred Acres of Land
and twelve Tenants.

THE late large Tranſportations of People, the furniſh-
ing and fitting out the new Governor and theſe other Officers, with the vaſt Charge of providing them with Tenants
and Servants, and other needful and well-deſigned Expences,
did ſo entirely exhauſt the publick Treaſury of the Company, that it never afterwards recovered itſelf to any tolerable
Degree of Affluence or Wealth. And beſides, the Lotteries were now at an End, which were the only Means of
raiſing a Fund again, and which alone had brought twenty
nine thouſand Pounds *Sterling* into the Company's Stock.
Wherefore Mr. *Smith* obſerved to them, that the Lotteries,
which had thus far ſupplied the real and ſubſtantial Food,
by which *Virginia* had been nouriſhed, did now no longer
ſubſiſt. To the End therefore, that ſhe might ſtill be preſerved, by divulging Fame and good Report, he propoſed,
in the Name of himſelf and many others of the Society,
to have a fair and perſpicuous Hiſtory compiled of the Country, from the firſt Diſcovery to that Time ; wherein the
Memory and Deſerts of many of her worthy Undertakers,
as Sir *Walter Ralegh*, Sir *George Somers*, the Lord *Delawarr*, Sir *Thomas Dale*, and Sir *Thomas Gates* (for both
thoſe Knights, after their Return from *Virginia*, had gone
to the *Eaſt-Indies*, and there died) together with divers
others then living, might be commended to eternal Thankfulneſs. He regretted their preſent Inability, in having no
other Coin, wherewith to recompence the great Pains and
Merit of the well-deſerving. But he affirmed, that the beſt
planted Parts of *America*, under the *Spaniſh* Government,
at the like Age, afforded not better Matter of Relation,
than *Virginia* then did. And he ſaid, that the Effect, which
ſuch a general Hiſtory, deduced to the Life, would have,
throughout the Kingdom, on the popular Opinion of the
common Subject, might be gathered, from the Succeſs of
the little Pamphlets or Declarations, lately publiſhed. And
he

he further urged the immediate Performance thereof, becaufe a few Years would confume the Lives of many,
whofe Memories retained much, and might alfo devour
thofe Letters and Intelligences, which yet remained in loofe
and neglected Papers.

T H I S Speech was received by the whole Court, with
very great Applaufe, as fpoken freely, and to an excellent
Purpofe ; and it was refolved, to have it confidered, and
put in Practice, in due Time. Mr. *Smith* was alfo exceedingly commended, as well for this, as for always preferring
Motions of efpecial Confequence. And it was from this
Motion, I fuppofe, that Captain *Smith* was requefted, in
the Company's Name, to write his Hiftory of *Virginia* ;
as he himfelf tells us, *p.* 168. However the Captain's Deferts feem not, about this Time, to have been fully underftood or regarded. For I find him, foon after, preferring
a Petition to the Company, fetting forth ; That he had
not only adventured Money, but had alfo twice built *James-
Town*, and four other Plantations ; and had difcovered the
Country, and relieved the Colony, three Years together,
with fuch Provifions, as he got from the Savages, with great
Peril and Hazard of his Life ; and therefore he defired, in
Confideration thereof, that the Company would be pleafed
to reward him, either out of their Treafury at home, or
their Profits in *Virginia*. And certainly, confidering his
many great and extraordinary Services, he was highly worthy their Regard. But the Court referred him to the Committee, appointed for rewarding Men upon Merit ; and from
whatever Caufe it happened, I find nothing farther done
in the Matter. . So that he, with a Fate very ufual to publick Spirits, had Reafon to complain, that every Shilling,
which he had gained by thefe Enterprizes, had coft him a
Pound ; and that what he had got, in fome fuccefsful Cam-
paigns at War, had been chearfully fpent on *Virginia* and
New-England, for the publick Good. Yet he begrudges
it not, but fhould think himfelf happy, to fee their Profperity and Advancement.

A T the Court of Election, the Earl of *Southampton* was
again chofen Treafurer for the enfuing Year, with an unanimous Voice. His Lordfhip was then abfent, having been
long detained, that Day, in Parliament. But at his coming
to Court, he was pleafed to accept the Place, in a very noble Manner ; and he had the hearty Thanks of the whole
Court returned him, for his honourable Care and Pains,
ever fince his Entrance into that Place of Government, to
uphold and advance the Plantation. And at his Lordfhip's
Requeft, Mr. *John Farrar*, of whofe Fidelity and Sufficiency

ciency they already had fo much Experience, was moft willingly continued in his Office of Deputy.

THE Earl of *Warwick* was highly offended at Sir *George Yeardley*, for intercepting a Pacquet of Letters, and difcovering the Correfpondence between Secretary *Pory* and himfelf. He therefore loudly declared his Difpleafure, and took all poffible Methods to daunt and difcourage him, from proceeding vigoroufly in *Argall's* Profecution. To this End, he caufed it to be rumoured over all *Virginia*, even to *Opechancanough*, and had it confirmed by Letters from *England*, that he himfelf was coming over fhortly, in Perfon, to be their Governor, with Captain *Argall* for his Pilot; and that then he would call Sir *George Yeardly* feverely into Queftion, for his own Government, and would take a fharp and full Revenge. Thefe Reports much weakened the Strength and Authority of the Government; and they likewife fo affeted Sir *George Yeardley*, a Man of a meek and gentle Nature, and threw him into fuch a Dejetion of Spirit, that he fell into a long and languifhing Sicknefs, to the general Hurt and Negle of the publick Bufinefs, as well as Captain *Argall's* Affair in particular.

THE Company alfo, this Year, entertained fome Projets for producing ufeful Commodities; and as three of the Mafter Workmen of their Iron Works were dead, they fent over Mr. *John Berkeley*, and *Maurice*, his Son, who were commended, as very fkilful in that Way, with twenty other experienced Workmen. They likewife ordered a Bill to be prepared for the Parliament, for fending over the Poor, which were now become very numerous and burthenfome to the feveral Parifhes, to be fet to work, and ufefully employed, in *Virginia*. Sir *George Yeardley* complained, that the Council of State lived very diftant and difperfed; and having no Allowance for their Attendance, could fcarce be got together. Whereupon the Company ordered, that the Council fhould meet, four times a Year, and fhould hold Quarter Seffions, a whole Week together; to affift the Governor, from time to time, as well in Matter of Counfel and of State, as in all Caufes of Importance, and for Redrefs of general and particular Grievances. And that their Number might make their Meetings the more eafy, befides the feven, laft Year appointed, and the new Officers of State, now going over, they alfo added, in the Room of Dr. *Bohun* and two others, that were dead, Mr. *Pot*, the Rev. Mr. *Robert Pawlet*, Captain *Roger Smith*, and Mr. *Leech*. This laft Gentleman was going over, to view the Country, and to pitch upon a proper Place of Settlement, for the famous and munificent *William* Earl of *Pembroke*; who had

under-

1621.   undertaken, with his Affociates, to plant thirty thoufand
Acres of Land, and confequently to tranfport fix hundred
Sir *George*   Perfons.
Yeardley,
Governor.   THE latter End of *July*, or Beginning of *Auguft*, Sir
Francis Wyat fet out for his Government, with the Treafurer, Secretary, Phyfician-General, and Surveyor, in Com-
pany with nine Sail of Ships; all which arrived fafe in *Vir-
ginia*, about *October*, without the Lofs of one fingle Paf-
fenger.   With him, was fent a Body of Inftructions to the
Governor, for the time being, and the Council of State in
Virginia; confifting of forty feven Articles, and figned by
the Earl of *Southampton*, Sir *Edwin Sandys*, Sir *John Davers*, and others of the Council.   In thefe, it was firft recommended to them, to take into their efpecial Regard the
Service of Almighty God, and the Obfervance of his divine
Laws; and that the People fhould be trained up, in true
Religion and Virtue.   And fince their Endeavours, for the
Eftablifhment of the Honour and Rights of the Church and
Miniftry, had not yet taken due Effect, they were required,
to employ their utmoft Care, to advance all things appertaining to the Order and Adminiftration of Divine Service,
according to the Form and Difcipline of the Church of
England; carefully to avoid all factious and needlefs Novelties, which only tended to the Difturbance of Peace and
Unity; and to caufe, that the Minifters fhould be duly re-
fpected and maintained, and the Churches, or Places appointed for Divine Service, decently accommodated, according to former Orders in that Behalf.   They were, in
the next Place, commanded, to keep the People in due
Obedience to the King; to provide, that Juftice might be
equally adminiftered to all, as near as could be, according
to the Forms and Conftitution of *England*; to prevent all
Corruption, tending to the Perverfion or Delay of Juftice;
to protect the Natives, from Injury and Oppreffion; and to
cultivate Peace and Friendfhip with them, as far as it fhould
be confiftent with the Honour of the Nation and Safety of
the People.   They were likewife required, to make the
People apply themfelves to an induftrious Way of Life;
and to fupprefs all Gaming, Drunkennefs, and Excefs in
Apparel.   To this End it was ordained, that no Perfon,
except the Council, or the Heads of Hundreds and Plantations, with their Wives and Children, fhould wear Gold
on their Cloaths, or any Apparel of Silk, except fuch as
had been raifed by their own Induftry.   But the Governor
and Council anfwered to this, that they knew of no Excefs
in Apparel, except in the Price of it; and had it not come
from them, they fhould have thought it a Flout upon the
Colony, for their Poverty and Nakednefs.   THEY

1621.

Sir *George
Yeardley,*
Governor.

THEY were also enjoined, to use great Care, that no
juſt Cauſe of Offence be given to any other Prince, State, or
People; to permit no Captain, or other Perſon, under Pretence of Trade, to ſail to the *Weſt-Indies*, to rob and ſpoil;
not to give Harbour or Refuge, on the Coaſts or in the
Country, to any Pirates or Banditti, but ſeverely to proſe-
cute and puniſh them; and to take better Care, for proper
and effeĉtual Fortifications. They further preſſed upon
them, in a particular Manner, the uſing all probable Means
of bringing over the Natives, to a Love of Civility, and to
the Knowledge of God, and his true Religion. To which
Purpoſe, they obſerved to them, that the Example, given
by the *Engliſh* in their own Perſons and Families, would be
of ſingular and chief Moment: That it would be proper,
to draw the beſt diſpoſed among the *Indians*, to converſe
and labour with our People, for a·convenient Reward; that
thereby, being reconciled to a civil Way of Life, and
brought to a Senſe of God and Religion, they might afterwards become Inſtruments in the general Converſion of their
Countrymen, ſo much deſired: That each Town, Bur-
rough, and Hundred, ought to procure, by juſt Means, a
certain Number of their Children, to be brought up in the
firſt Elements of Litterature: That the moſt towardly of
theſe ſhould be fitted for the College; in building of which,
they purpoſed to proceed, as ſoon as any Profit aroſe from
the Eſtate, appropriated to that Uſe; and they earneſtly
required their utmoſt Help and Furtherance, in that pious
and important Work; not doubting the particular Bleſſing
of God upon the Colony, and being aſſured of the Love of
all good Men, upon that Account.

THEY next proceeded to give Inſtruĉtions, for the
Reception and Accommodation of the new Governor,
and of the other Officers and People, then ſent. And
they preſſed upon them the raiſing ſeveral uſeful Commodities; as well Corn, Wine, Silk, and others heretofore frequently mentioned, as alſo the making Oil of
Walnuts, employing their Apothecaries in Diſtillation, and
ſearching the Country for Minerals, Dyes, Gums, Drugs,
and the like. And they ordered them particularly, by the
King's Advice and Deſire, to draw the People off of their
exceſſive planting of Tobacco. To that End, they were
commanded to permit them, to make only an hundred
Pounds of Tobacco a Head; and to take all poſſible Care,
to improve that Proportion in Goodneſs, as much as might
be, which would bring their Commodity into Requeſt, and
cauſe a more certain Benefit to the Planter. They likewiſe
added many other Advices and Inſtruĉtions, for the Admini-

ſtration

1621.   ſtration of Juſtice, the good Government, and happy Ad-
          vancement of the Colony.

Sir *George*   IN Caſe of the Death, Removal, or Suſpenſion of the
Yeardley,   Governor, the Council, or major Part of them, then reſi-
Governor.   dent in *Virginia*, were ordered, immediately to aſſemble
          themſelves, within fourteen Days, or ſooner, and out of
          their own Body, to elect a Perſon, to ſupply the Place, for
          the Time. But if the Voices ſhould happen to be equal,
          then Election was to be made of the Lieutenant-Governor;
          and in his Abſence, or neceſſary Cauſe of declining it, the
          Marſhal ſhould ſucceed; next, the Treaſurer; and then
          one of the two Deputies, for the College and Company's
          Lands; till the Government ſhould be ſettled in one of thoſe
          chief Officers. And the Governor was authoriſed, to de-
          termine and puniſh, at his Diſcretion, any ſudden and emer-
          gent Buſineſs, and all Neglect or Contempt of Authority,
          in any Kind or Perſon whatſoever; except only the Coun-
          cil in their own Perſons, who were, in ſuch Caſes, to be
          ſummoned to appear, at the next Quarter Seſſion of the
          Council, and there to abide their Cenſure. But if the Go-
          vernor thought, it concerned the Peace and Welfare of the
          Colony, to proceed more ſpeedily with ſuch Offender, that
          then it ſhould be lawful for him, to ſummon an extraordi-
          nary Council, at which ſix of the Council, at leaſt, ſhould
          be preſent with the Governor; and by Majority of Voices,
          any Counſellor might be committed, or obliged to give Bail
          for his Appearance.

              SIR *Francis Wyat* alſo brought over with him an Ordi-
          nance or Charter, from the Treaſurer, Council, and Com-
          pany in *England*, for ſettling the Conſtitution and Govern-
          ment of *Virginia*, in the Governor, the Council of State,
          as his Aſſiſtants, and the General Aſſembly. This Aſſem-
          bly was to conſiſt of the Governor, Council of State, and
          two Burgeſſes, choſen by every Town, Hundred, or par-
          ticular Plantation. All Matters were to be decided, deter-
          mined, and ordered in it, by the Majority of Voices, then
          preſent; reſerving to the Governor a Negative upon the
          Whole. And they were empowered, to treat, conſult, and
          conclude, as well concerning all emergent Occaſions, re-
          lating to the publick Weal of the ſaid Colony, and every
          Part thereof, as alſo to make, ordain, and enact ſuch gene-
          ral Laws and Orders, as ſhould, from time to time, appear
          neceſſary : Provided neverthelefs, that no Law, or Ordi-
          nance, made in the ſaid General Aſſembly, ſhould be of
          Force or Validity, unleſs the ſame ſhould be ſolemnly con-
          firmed and ratified, in a General Quarter Court of the
          Company in *England*, and returned under their Seal : As
                                                              alſo,

alfo, when this Form of Government fhould be once well
framed and fettled, that no Orders, of the Court in *England*,
fhould bind the Colony, before they were ratified and confirmed, in like Manner, by the General Affembly in *Virgi-*
nia. But in all other things, they were commanded, to
follow the Policy, Form of Government, Laws, Cuftoms,
Manner of Trial, and other Adminiftration of Juftice, ufed
in *England*.

THE Company's Treafury was fo reduced, that it could
not now fuffice for feveral things of the utmoft Neceffity and
Advantage. Wherefore, to fupply this Deficiency, they
entered into a Method of preparing Rolls, and offering them
to the voluntary Subfcription of the Adventurers. Whatever was fent to *Virginia* upon thefe Rolls, was there fold,
by the Cape-Merchant or fome other Factor, at fuch a moderate Price, as fhould indemnify the Subfcribers for their
Money advanced, and for all Charges incident thereupon.
At this time, four Rolls were prepared and brought into
Court, for the Company's Subfcription. The firft was for
Apparel, and other neceffary Provifions and Utenfils, for
the Colony. The fecond, for fending an hundred more
Maids, to make Wives; and fixty were accordingly fent,
young, handfome, and well recommended to the Company,
for their virtuous Education and Demeanor. With them
was fent over the feveral Recommendations and Teftimonials of their Behaviour, that the Purchafers might thence
be enabled to judge, how to chufe. The Price of thefe
Wives was ftated at an hundred and twenty Pounds of Tobacco, and afterwards advanced to an hundred and fifty, and
proportionably more, if any of them fhould happen to die ;
fo that the Adventurers might be refunded their original
Charge. And it was alfo ordered, that this Debt for Wives
fhould have the Precedency of all others, and be firft re-
coverable. And it was ftrictly enjoined, that they fhould
be well ufed, and not married to Servants, but to fuch Freemen and Tenants, as could handfomely fupport them ; that,
by their good Fortune, Multitudes of others might be allured to come over, on the Profpect of advantageous Matches. And the Company likewife declared their Intention,
that, for the Encouragement of fettled Families, and fecuring a Pofterity, they would prefer and make Confignments
to married Men, before fingle Perfons ; and that as many
Boys fhould be fent, as there were Maids, to be 'Prentices
to thofe who married them. They alfo granted the Adventurers, who fubfcribed to this Roll, a ratable Proportion
of Land, according to the Number of the Maids fent, to be
laid off together and formed into a Town, by the Name of

O 3   *Maidftown*.

1621.
Sir *George*
Yeardley,
Governor.

Maidftown. The third Roll was for a Glafs Furnace, to make Beads, which was the current Coin in the *Indian* Trade; and one Captain *Norton*, with fome *Italian* Workmen, was fent over for that Purpofe. The fourth was for fetting out a trading Voyage with the *Indians*, for Skins and Furs. For, the Company was informed from feveral Hands, that the *French* and *Dutch* carried on a very profitable Trade of that fort, in *Delawarr* and *Hudfon*'s Rivers, which were within the Limits of their Grant, and then efteemed Parts of *Virginia*. They therefore refolved, to vindicate their Right, and not to permit Foreigners to run away with fo lucrative a Branch of their Trade. One Captain *Jones* was accordingly fent upon the Voyage; but by the Wickednefs of him and his Mariners, the Adventure was loft, and the whole Project overthrown. To thefe Rolls, the Earl of *Southampton* and Sir *Edwin Sandys*, each fubfcribed two hundred Pounds; and fuch was the Zeal and Refolution of the Adventurers to advance the Colony, that they were foon compleated, and put into Execution. At the fame time, the Company, in their Letters to the Governor and Council, recommends to them the Prevention of Fraud and Deceit in Tobacco; and that fome Provifion fhould be made, for burning all bafe and rotten Trafh, and none fuffered to go home, but what was very good; whereby, they faid, there would certainly be more advanced in the Price, than loft in the Quantity.

B U T Tobacco was, at this time, a very finking Commodity. For altho' the Planters magifterially forced it on the Company and others, at the current Price of three Shillings a Pound, yet it would not turn out at home, after Shrinkage and Wafte, and the Difcharge of the Duty and Freight, (which laft alone was three Pence, and fometimes four Pence, a Pound) at above two Shillings for the beft, and the inferior Sort at fcarce eighteen Pence a Pound. And befides, the Trade was ftrangely hampered and perplexed, by the weak and unfteady Counfels of the puny Monarch, then on the Throne. For altho', in the Beginning of the former Year, the Company had yielded to his unreafonable Demand of twelve Pence a Pound, yet foon after, in the fame Summer, he iffued a Proclamation, prohibiting a general Importation of Tobacco, and reftraining the Quantity from *Virginia* and the *Somer-Iflands*, to fifty five thoufand Weight. At the fame time, taking Advantage of an Offer of Sir *Thomas Smith* and Alderman *Johnfon*, in the Name of the Company, but without their Knowledge or Authority, and fo utterly difclaimed by them, he granted a Monopoly of Tobacco; the fole Importation whereof was

granted,

granted by Letters patent, firſt to Sir *Thomas Roe* and his 1621.
Aſſociates (at whoſe Deſire and Inſtigation the Proclamation,
above mentioned, was iſſued) and the Year after, to Mr. Sir George
Jacob and certain other Patentees.　They proceeded moſt Governor.
injuriouſly againſt both Companies, not only ſtinting them
to too ſcant a Proportion, but alſo reſtraining them from
ſelling their Tobacco, without their Seal and Allowance
firſt had ; for which, under the Pretence and Title of Garbling, they were obliged to pay four Pence a Pound.　This
Garbling was an ancient Cuſtom of the City of *London* ; and
an Officer was appointed, who had Power to enter into any
Shop or Warehouſe, to view and ſearch Drugs and Spices,
and to garble the ſame ; that is, to make them clean from
all Garbles or Traſh.　And it was now put into Execution,
and arbitrarily applied to Tobacco (a new Commodity in
England, and therefore not legally ſubject to Garbling,
without an expreſs Law) in order the more effectually to
oppreſs the Companies and Plantations, and to ſqueeze the
greater Gain out of them.

　THUS injured and diſtreſſed, the Company preſented
their Petition and Repreſentation to his Majeſty, to which
they received a gracious Anſwer, with large Profeſſions of
his Love to the Colonies, and that it never was his Intention
to grant any thing to their Prejudice; but without any Redreſs of their Grievance.　It was therefore at laſt reſolved,
to prefer a Petition to the Houſe of Commons, and therein
to complain of theſe Oppreſſions, which tended to the utter
Deſtruction and Overthrow of the Colonies; and as that
Houſe had called into Queſtion, and intended to ſuppreſs,
other Monopolies (a great and crying Grievance of thoſe
Times) they doubted not, to receive from them a full and
ample Redreſs.　They likewiſe, at the Motion of Sir *Edwin Sandys*, preſented Mr. *Edward Bennet*, a Citizen of
London, with the Freedom of their Company ; becauſe he
had written a Treatiſe, ſetting forth, in a clear and lively
Manner, the great Inconvenience and Damage to the Nation, by the Importation of *Spaniſh* Tobacco ; and becauſe
he had frequently attended the Committees of the Houſe of
Commons, who were well inclined, to afford their utmoſt·
Aſſiſtance, for the Prohibition of foreign Tobacco.　This
Mr. *Bennet* immediately became the moſt deeply engaged,
and was far the largeſt and moſt conſiderable Adventurer
of any, then known, in the Affair of *Virginia* ; whoſe
Foundations, in that early time, have continued down to
the preſent.　For his Nephew, *Richard Bennet*, Eſq; was
the firſt Governor of *Virginia*, by the Election of the Colony, in the time of *Cromwell's* Uſurpation ; and the Re-

main of the Family, now feated in *Maryland*, is ftill t
richeft and moft wealthy, in all Kinds of Fortune and
Sir *George* ftate, of any in this Part of *America*.   However, fince t
Yeardley, *Somer-Iflands* could not well fubfift without the Profits
Governor. *Somer-Iflands* could not well fubfift without the Profits
their Tobacco, and as the Territory of *Virginia* was larg
their Soil good, and great Hopes conceived, that many oth
valuable Commodities would foon be produced and returne
from thence, it was agreed, that the whole 55,000 Weigł
fhould be imported from thofe Iflands; and the *Virgini*
Company procured Storehoufes, and appointed Factors, a
Middleburg and *Flufhing*, and compounded with the State
of thofe Cities, for a Half Penny a Pound Cuftom, for th
Import, and ·the fame Rate for the Export, of their Tobacco.   So that no *Virginia* Tobacco was imported into
England, this Year, but all was carried and difpofed of in
Holland.

THE News of this State of their Affairs coming to *Virginia*, the Colony was greatly alarmed, and drew up an
humble Petition to the King, fetting forth : That his Ma-
iefty, out of his religious Defire to fpeed the Gofpel of
Chrift, and princely Ambition to enlarge his Dominions,
had given Encouragement to fuch, as would go to *Virginia*, and granted them many goodly Privileges and Liberties,
under the great Seal of *England*, than which they thought
no earthly Affurance more firm and inviolable : That in
Confidence hereof, they, his Majefty's poor Subjects, had
adventured their Lives and Fortunes thither ; and in the
Profecution of the Enterprife, had undergone fuch incredible Difficulties and Sufferings, as would be fhocking, in the
Relation, to his Majefty's facred Ears : That they had now,
by the Divine Affiftance, in fome Meafure, overcome thofe
Difficulties, and brought themfelves to an Ability of fubfifting, without any other Help from *England*, than the ufual
Courfe of Commerce ; but that they had, of late, been
brought into Danger, of returning into their former, or even
worfe Circumftances, by the finifter Practices of fome Members of the Company at home ; who, pretending his Majefty's Profit, but really aiming at their own exorbitant
Gain, had obtained a Proclamation, to prohibit the Importation of Tobacco into *England* : That other things, of
greater real Value, required more time, than their preffing
Neceffities would allow, and more Help, to bring them to
Perfection, than they had, till of late, been furnifhed withal ; and that, therefore, Tobacco was the only Commodity,
they had yet been able to raife, in order to fupply themfelves
and Families with Apparel, and other needful Supplements
of Life : That, if it fhould be thus fuppreffed and prohibited,

bited, they muſt all, of Neceſſity, perish, for Want of
Cloathing, and ſuch Neceſſaries, as both their Nature and
Education required: That his Majeſty would, thereby, not
only loſe ſo many good and loyal Subjects, as had adventured their Lives and Subſtance to *Virginia*, for the Promotion of thoſe great Ends, the Glory of God, and his Majeſty's Service, but muſt likewiſe be deprived of the Hope
and Profpect, of acquiring a Territory, as large, and capable of becoming as opulent, as any of thoſe Kingdoms, he
at preſent poſſeſſed: Since therefore they were aſſured, that
his Majeſty tendered the Lives and Welfare of his Subjects,
above Thouſands of Gold and Silver, and ſince his Royal
Word was engaged, and even ratified under the great Seal
of *England*, they beſought him, out of his princely Compaſſion, either to revoke that Proclamation, and to reſtore
them to their ancient Liberty, or elſe to ſend for them
home, and not ſuffer the Heathen to triumph over them.

THIS Petition was tranſmitted to the Treaſurer and Company, and was ſeconded by a Letter, from Sir *George Teardley* and the Council, to the Company; deſiring, that it
might be preſented to his Majeſty, in as humble and effectual a Manner, as poſſible; becauſe, as they conceived, the
very Life of the Colony depended upon the Succeſs of it.
But before it came to hand, the King was become ſenſible
of the Damage, that hence accrued to himſelf, by the Di-
minution of his Cuſtoms. The Deputy therefore, and ſome
others of the Company, were ſent for, in *October* this Year,
and received an angry Rebuke from the Lords of the Privy
Council; importing, that Complaint had been made to that
Board, that the Company had ſet up a Trade in *Holland*,
and carried all their Commodities thither; and requiring an
Anſwer, whether they would bring all their Commodities
into *England*, or continue their Trade in the *Low-Countries*.
To the former Part of this, the Anſwer was ready and obvious; that they had indeed carried their Tobacco to *Middleburg*, not out of Choice, but being conſtrained thereto
by his Majeſty's Proclamation, and an Order of their own
Board. And as to the latter Part, concerning bringing all
their Commodities into *England*, as it was a new and unexpected Propoſition, and a Point of great Weight and future Conſequence, they took ſome time to conſider of it,
and then returned a long and very reſpectful Anſwer:

THAT it was a Liberty and Privilege, generally taken
and enjoyed, by all his Majeſty's Subjects, to carry their
Commodities to the beſt Markets: That many Commodities were now ſet on Foot, and expected ſoon to be returned
from *Virginia*, which, altho' in ſome Demand in other
Countries,

Countries, yet would not be vendible in *England*, nor pay
the Expence of Freight and Cuftom : That neither the
Mufcovy Company, nor any other ancient Corporation, was
under fuch a Reftraint, to whofe greateft Privileges and Immunities, they were entitled, by the exprefs Words of his
Majefty's Charter : That the Company had granted feveral
Patents, with the fame Privileges, as they themfelves enjoyed, to divers Perfons of noble and worthy Families, who
had thereupon expended great Sums of Money, and fome
their whole Eftates in the Plantation; and that it was not
in their Power, nor would it be confonant to Law or Equity, now to revoke or reftrain them : That they conceived
themfelves to have no Right or Authority, to difpofe of the
Goods of the private Planters in *Virginia*, who are declared,
by his Majefty's Charter, to be as free, as any other his Subjects, and who had merited, by their long and hard Services,
all Manner of Immunity and Encouragement : That they
could not forbid or reftrain them, from trading and barter-
ing their Commodities freely, with fuch Ships, as carried
Paffengers, moft of which proceeded on trading Voyages,
and returned not directly to *England* : That a Trade had
lately begun between *Ireland* and *Virginia*, for Cattle and
other Neceffaries, for which Contracts were made in Tobacco ; and that this Trade would hereby be nipped in the
Bud, to the exceeding great Prejudice, and the Hazard of
the utter Ruin of the Colony : And laftly, That it was not
in the Power of the few Members of the Company, then in
Town in the time of Vacation, to conclude any thing pofi-
tive, in an Affair of that vaft Importance ; wherein above a
thoufand Adventurers in *England*, and near four thoufand
Inhabitants of *Virginia*, were deeply interefted and concerned.   After which they concluded, with affuring their Lordfhips, that they affected no foreign Trade, but in Cafes of
mere Neceffity, and for the better Support and Advancement of the Colony ; that they fhould always endeavour at
fuch a mutual Commerce between *England* and *Virginia*,
as fhould be confiftent with the Honour and Benefit of both ;
and that, next to God's Glory, they chiefly aimed at the
Good of their Country, his Majefty's Honour, and the Advancement of his Profit and Revenue ; for which Ends,
they had, out of their own private Eftates, befides their
Labour and Time, expended above an hundred thoufand
Pounds, without any Return, not only of Profit, but even
of the leaft Part of the Principal itfelf, to any one of the Adventurers, that they knew of.

T H I S Anfwer gave no Satisfaction to their Lordfhips;
but they were referred to Mr. *Jacob*, their old Antagonift
and

and Oppreffor; and were likewife ordered, to give in their peremptory Anfwer, whether they would import, not all their Commodities, but all their Tobacco only, into En-gland. With Mr. *Jacob*, they could come to no fatisfactory Accommodation; and as to importing all their Tobacco into *England*, they befought their Lordfhips, to be left at Liberty, either to import, or not import it into *England*, as they fhould find it moft beneficial to the Colony. But if they muft be obliged to import all or none, they declared, it was their Choice, to import none into *England*, the enfuing Year. But their Lordfhips termed this an undutiful Anfwer, and commanded them, at their Peril, to bring all their Tobacco into *England*. And the Deputy and Committee, appointed to attend their Lordfhips, offering fome Reafons, they were told, that they were not to difpute at that Board, but to obey; and fo were difmiffed, with high Marks of their Difpleafure and Indignation.

THESE Proceedings, being reported to the Company, caufed great Grief and Dejection among them. For the Importation of *Spanifh*, and all other Tobaccoes, was then free; and altho' the Houfe of Commons, in their laft Seffion, had entered into fome Confideration about it, yet I cannot find, that any thing material was done in the Matter. And as to the King, out of his doating Fondnefs for the *Spanifh* Match, and his eager Defire, to give all poffible Pleafure and Advantage to his good Friend and Brother, the King of *Spain*, he was even active and diligent, to protect and advance the Importation of *Spanifh* Tobacco. However the Deputy exhorted the Company, not to be difcouraged at thefe Difafters. For he hoped, that God would ftill exert himfelf in the Protection of *Virginia*, who had turned for the beft, divers former Projects, which threatned the Ruin and Deftruction of the Colony. And he defired, that having put their Hands to the Plough, they would not now look back, or be weary of well-doing. For the Action was univerfally confeffed, to be moft chriftian, honourable, and glorious, and of extreme Confequence to the Commonwealth and Realm of *England*; and altho' they might feem to have caft their Bread upon the Waters, yet after many Days, he doubted not, but they fhould find it again, to their great Comfort and Advantage. And he farther told them, that altho' their exhaufted Treafury had been able to do little, that Year, for fending People to *Virginia*, yet it had pleafed God, to ftir up fo many worthy Minds, for the Advancement of the Colony, that no lefs than twenty Ships were already gone, or ready to go, in which would be tranfported above a thoufand Perfons. But

by

1621.   by Captain *Smith*'s Account, there were twenty one Sail
of Ships sent this Year, with thirteen hundred, Men, Wo-
Sir *George*   men, and Children; which might likewise be true, as it
Yeardley,   was only *October*, and the Year not concluded, when Mr.
Governor.   Deputy *Farrar* made this Report to the Company.

    MR. *Copeland*, Chaplain to the *Royal James*, an *Eaſt-
India* Ship juſt returned to *England*, by his Example and
Perſuaſions, prevailed on the Ship's Company, to contribute
ſeventy Pounds, towards building a Church or a Free-ſchool
in *Virginia*; and an unknown Perſon gave thirty Pounds
more, to make the Benefaction an hundred; to which twenty five Pounds were afterwards added, by another unknown
Perſon. It was therefore determined, to build a School at
Charles-City (which was judged the moſt commodious Place,
and moſt convenient to all Parts of the Colony) by the Name
of the *Eaſt-India* School; and the Company allotted, for
the Maintenance of the Maſter and Uſher, a thouſand A-
cres of Land, with five Servants and an Overſeer. This
School was to be collegiate, and to have Dependence upon
the College at *Henrico*; into which, as ſoon as the College
was ſufficiently endowed, and capable to receive them, the
Scholars were to be admitted and advanced, according to
their Deſerts and Proficiency in Learning. Mr. *Copeland*
was alſo preſented with the Freedom of the Company, and
with three hundred Acres of Land in *Virginia*. And Carpenters were accordingly ſent over for this Purpoſe, early
the next Year.

Sir *Francis*   ON the 18th of *November*, Sir *Francis Wyat* entered
Wyat, Go-   upon his Government; but inſtead of his hundred Tenants,
vernor.   he received only forty ſix from Sir *George Yeardley*, who
refuſed to make the Number good, as he was under no
ſuch Contract with the Company, when he came Governor, and as he had even offered to ſurrender them all back
again, into the Company's Hands. Sir *Francis* ſent Mr.
Thorpe immediately, to *Opitchapan* and *Opechancanough*, to
confirm all former Leagues, between the *Engliſh* and them.
They both expreſſed great Satisfaction at the Arrival of this
new Governor, and were content, that the *Engliſh* ſhould
inhabit the Country; and Mr. *Thorpe* thought, that he perceived more Motions of Religion in *Opechancanough*, than
could eaſily be imagined, in ſo great Ignorance and Blind-
neſs. He acknowledged his own Religion, not to be the
right Way; and deſired, to be inſtructed in the *Chriſtian*
Faith. He confeſſed, that God loved the *Engliſh* better
than them; and he thought, the Cauſe of God's Anger
againſt them was their Cuſtom of conjuring their Children,
and making them black Boys. He had alſo ſome Knowledge

ledge of the Heavens ; had obferved the North Star and the Courfe of the Conftellation about it ; and called the Great Bear, *Manguahaian*, which, in their Language, fig- nified the fame. He gave Mr. *Thorpe* Hopes of their en- tertaining fome *Englifh* Families among them, and their fending fome of theirs to cohabit with the *Englifh* ; and confirmed a former Promife, of fending a Guide with the *Englifh* to fome Mines beyond the Falls. But all thefe fair Profeffions and Promifes feem to have been only Diffimula- tion and Policy. For that favage Prince certainly never had any real Friendfhip or Love for the *Englifh* ; but watched all proper Opportunities and Pretences, to do them Mifchief, or even utterly deftroy them. It was likewife ordered, upon the Acceffion of this new Governor, that the Colony fhould only tend a thoufand Plants, for every Head, with nine Leaves on each Plant ; which, by their Compu- tation, would amount to about an hundred Weight, ac- cording to the Company's exprefs Inftructions, in Confe- quence of his Majefty's Defire and Advice. Mr. *Gookin* too, who was under Contract with the Company for Cat- tle, arrived with them out of *Ireland*, on the 22d of *No- vember* ; and he brought with him fifty Men of his own, and thirty Paffengers, exceedingly well furnifhed with all Kinds of Provifion, and feated himfelf at *Newport's-News*. The Inhabitants alfo made a Contribution of fifteen hundred Pounds, to build a Gueft-Houfe, for the Reception and Entertainment of New-Comers ; which was accordingly undertaken, and in a Way of being well executed, by Lieutenant *Jabez Whitaker*, to his own great Commenda- tion, and to the general Satisfaction of the People here, and the Company in *London*.

BEFORE I finifh this Year, it will not be improper, briefly to remark, what•then paffed in the Parliament of *England*. There were two Seffions of Parliament, this Year. The firft began in *January*, and paffed off peace- ably. They granted the King Money, to fupport the *Pa- latine* of the *Rhine*, againft the Houfe of *Auftria* ; and were content to fupprefs fome Monopolies, without touch- ing on their Author, the Marquifs of *Buckingham*, altho' he was generally known, and even plainly accufed of it, by Sir *Henry Yelverton*, the late Attorney General. However I do not find, that the Monopoly of Tobacco came under their Reftraint. Only the eminent Lawyers of the Houfe of Commons declared the Patent for Garbling utterly ille- gal, and a great Grievance in the Erection, but much more fo, if it fhould be brought into Execution. And this Seffion had alfo another good Effect : For at their very firft Meet- ing,

ing, the Reſtraint on Tobacco was taken off, and Liberty
given, at leaſt by Connivance, freely to import it into *En-*
gland ; which indeed, I ſuppoſe, was the Reaſon, that neither the Company's Petition was delivered, nor any thing
elſe done in the Houſe of Commons, with Relation to that
unlawful, unjuſt, and oppreſſive Monopoly.

T H E ſecond Seſſion began the 20th of *November*, and
was hot and angry. The Diſpute between the King and
the Houſe of Commons, concerning the Extent of the
Royal Prerogative, and the Rights, Franchiſes, and Privileges of Parliament, roſe ſo high, that the King firſt ad-
journed, and then diſſolved them, in a Paſſion. However,
before that could be done, the Commons entered upon
their Journals a Proteſtation, aſſerting their Parliamentary
Rights and Privileges. But the King, eleven Days after
the Adjournment, called for the Clerk of the Houſe of
Commons ; and demanding the Journals, he declared, in
full Council, and in the Preſence of all the Judges then in
Town, that it was invalid, annulled, void, and of no Effeƈt ; and did moreover, with his own Hand, take the ſaid
Proteſtation, out of the Journal-Book of the Houſe of
Commons. And not content with theſe Marks of his Diſpleaſure, he proceeded farther againſt ſome of the warmeſt
of the Houſe of Commons ; whom he ſtiled fiery, popular, and ill-tempered Spirits. Sir *Edwin Sandys* was impriſoned; during the Seſſion, which cauſed a great Tumult
in the Houſe. And altho' the King, upon the Houſe's
ſending a Meſſage to Sir *Edwin*; to know the Reaſon of his
Confinement, declared, in a Letter to the Speaker, that it
was not for any Miſdemeanor in Parliament, yet I ſuſpeƈt,
his Impriſonment was deſigned, to prevent him from aƈt-
ing with Vigor, in the Caſe of the Monopoly, and other
illegal Oppreſſions on Tobacco ; and this the more eſpecially, as I can no where find, that any Reaſon or Pretence
was given for his Commitment. However the King's
Opinion, concerning his Power over the Members, was
plainly expreſſed in that Letter. For he orders the Speaker, to tell the Houſe, in his Name, that he conceived
himſelf, to have both Right and Ability, to puniſh any
Man's Miſdemeanors in Parliament, as well during their
ſitting, as after ; which Power he meant not hereafter to
ſpare, as Occaſion ſhould be adminiſtered, by the inſolent
Behaviour of any of their Members. And agreeably to
this Declaration, Sir *Edward Coke*, the great Lawyer, Sir
Robert Philips, Mr. *John Selden*, another Prodigy of Law
and all Kinds of Knowledge, Mr. *Pym*, and Mr. *Mallery*,
were impriſoned, after the Receſs, profeſſedly for their Behaviour

haviour in Parliament. And Sir *Dudley Digges*, Sir *Thomas*
Crew, Sir *Nathaniel Rich*, and Sir *James Perrot*, were fent
into *Ireland*, under Pretence of enquiring into fundry Matters, relating to his Majefty's Service in that Kingdom, but,
in reality, by Way of Banifhment. The Earls of *Oxford*
and *Southampton* were likewife fent to the Tower, soon after the Diffolution, on fome far-fetched, Pretences. But the
true Reafon was eafily and publickly perceived, and that
their real Crime was, having fpoke too freely in Parliament,
concerning the King's Conduct.

I have made this Relation, not fo much as it is a remarkable Æra in the *Englifh* Hiftory, which gave Rife to two
profeffed Parties, the one for the King's Prerogative, and
the other for the Rights of Parliament and the Liberty of
the Subject; nor as it was alfo the firft open breach, between the King and the People, which, by fubfequent Pro-
vocations and Heart-burnings, at laft broke out, into a moft
unhappy and virulent Civil War. But I have mentioned
thefe things chiefly, as they relate to my Subject, and will
contribute to let the Reader more fully, into the Springs
and Motives of fome future Tranfactions. For it will be
readily perceived, that many of the moft eminent and active
Oppofers in Parliament, of the King's arbitrary Views,
were alfo principal and leading Members of the *Virginia*
Company; and it is well known, with what an Eye of
Jealoufy and Difpleafure, that Prince ever looked upon fuch,
as dared to ftand up for the Liberty of their Country, or
were fo far infected, with the mortal Taint of a publick
(or as he thought it) a republican Spirit, as to oppofe his
Claim to an unlimited and defpotic Power. It will not
therefore be furprifing, to find him hereafter, notwithftanding his many affected and anile Profeffions of Love and Affection to the Colonies, not only much difgufted at the
Company, and little inclined to do them any Favour, but
even, in their Diffolution, making a Stretch of that Prerogative, which many of them had the Boldnefs, to queftion
and withftand.

BUT the Colony being now much enlarged and encreafed, it was found very troublefome, to bring all Caufes
to *James-Town*. Inferior Courts were therefore, in the
Beginning of the Year 1622, appointed in convenient Places,
to relieve the Governor and Council from this vaft Burthen
of Bufinefs, and to render Juftice the more cheap and ac-
ceffible. This was the Original and Foundation of our
County Courts; altho' the Country was not yet laid off in
Counties, but ftill continued in Townfhips and particular
Plantations, as they called thofe Settlements, which were
not

1622. not confiderable enough, to have the Title and Privileges of Burroughs.

Sir *Francis. Wyat,* Go- vernor. B u t this Year is rendered moſt memorable in our Annals, by a cruel and bloody Maſſacre, concerted by *Opechancanough* and the *Indians,* and executed on the *Engliſh* Colony, upon the 22d of *March,* on the following Occaſion and Manner. There was a noted *Indian,* called *Nemattanaw,* who was wont, out of Bravery and Parade, to dreſs himſelf up, in a ſtrange antic and barbaric Faſhion, with Feathers ; which therefore obtained him, among the *Engliſh,* the Name of *Jack of the Feather.* This *Indian* was highly renowned among his Countrymen, for Courage and Policy ; and was univerſally eſteemed by them the greateſt War-Captain of thoſe Times. He had been in many Skirmiſhes and Engagements with the *Engliſh,* and bravely expoſed his Perſon ; yet by his Activity, Conduct, and good Fortune, he had always eſcaped without a Wound. This, aided by his Craft and Ambition, eaſily wrought, in the Minds of thoſe ignorant and ſuperſtitious Barbarians a fond Conceit, that he was invulnerable and immortal. This Captain came to the Houſe of one *Morgan,* who had many ſuch Commodities, as ſuited the rude Taſte of the *Indians.* Being ſmit with the Deſire of ſome of thoſe Baubles, he perſuaded *Morgan* to go with him to *Pamunkey,* upon the Promiſe and Aſſurance of a certain and advantageous Traffick. But, upon the Way, he murdered the poor credulous *Engliſhman* ; and within two or three Days, returned again to his Houſe. There were only two ſturdy Lads there, the late *Morgan's* Servants ; who ſeeing him wear their Maſter's Cap, aſked for their Maſter, and *Jack* frankly told them, he was dead. Being confirmed in their Suſpicion, they ſeiſed him, and endeavoured to carry him before Mr. *Thorpe,* who then lived at *Berkeley.* But *Jack* ſo provoked them, by his Reſiſtance and Inſolence, that at laſt they ſhot him down, and put him into a Boat, in order to carry him before the Governor, who was then within ſeven or eight Miles of the Place. On the Way, our fainting Immortal felt the Pangs of Death very ſtrong upon him, and earneſtly entreated the Boys, to grant him two things ; firſt, never to make it known, that he was ſlain by a Bullet ; and ſecondly, to bury him among the *Engliſh,* that the certain Knowledge, and Monument of his Mortality, might be ſtill concealed, and kept from the Sight of his Countrymen. Such was the Vanity of this poor Barbarian, and ſo ſtrong his Deſire of falſe Glory in the Opinion of others, againſt the Experience and plain Conviction of his own Senſe.

Opechancanough

Opechancanough was a haughty, politic, and bloody Man, ever intent on the Deftruction of the *Englifh*, and ready to catch at every Pretence, for effecting his Purpofe. He had been difcovered, the Year before, tampering with a King on the *Eaftern Shore*, to furnifh him with a Poifon, either real or fuppofed, in order to Poifon the *Englifh* Colony.   He had alfo been accufed to the Governor, of a Defign, to draw together a very great Force, under Colour of celebrating fome funeral Rites to *Powhatan*, but really with Intent to cut off all the *Englifh*.   But Sir *George Yeardley*, by this Information, was rendered very watchful of his Motions; fo that he was either difappointed in his Scheme, or elfe, as Sir *George* thought, had never really formed any fuch Defign.   As to this Warrior, he was fo far from being in his Favour, that he had fent Word to. Sir *George Yeardley*, fome time before, that he fhould be content, if his Throat were cut.   Yet he being a popular Man, and much lamented by the *Indians*, *Opechancanough* pretended, the better to enflame and exafperate them, to be much grieved at his Death, and was very loud, at firft, in his Threats of Revenge.   But the Reafon and Juftice of the thing being evinced, and receiving alfo fome ftern and refolute Anfwers from the *Englifh*, he cunningly diffembled his Intent for the prefent, and treated a Meffenger, fent to him about the Middle of *March*, with extreme Civility and Kindnefs; affuring him, that he held the Peace fo firm, that the Sky fhould fall fooner, than it fhould be violated on his Part. And fuch was the Treachery and Diffimulation of the reft of the *Indians*, that, but two Days before, they kindly conducted the *Englifh* through the Woods, and fent home one that lived among them, to learn their Language.   Nay, on the very Morning of that fatal Day, as alfo the Evening before, they came, as at other times, unarmed into the Houfes of the *Englifh*, with Deer, Turkies, Fifh, Fruits, and other things to fell; and in fome Places fat down to Breakfaft with them.   Yet fo general was the Combination, and their Plot fo well laid, to cut off the whole Colony, in one Day, and at the fame Inftant, that they had all Warning, one from another, through all their Habitations, though far diftant from each other, and every Party and Nation had their Stations appointed, and Parts affigned, at the Plantations of the *Englifh*, fome being directed to one Place, and fome to another.

THE *Englifh*, on the other hand, were by this Behaviour, as well as on other Accounts, lulled into a fatal Security.   They thought the Peace fure and inviolable, not fo much becaufe of their folemn Promifes and Engagements,

ments, as becaufe it was highly ufeful and neceffary to the *Indians* themfelves. For thofe poor, weak and naked Barbarians were, every way, advantaged by the *Englifh*. By the Peace, they were fafely fheltered and defended from all other Enemies; they were fupplied with feveral neceffary Tools and Utenfils, and other Commodities of Pleafure and Entertainment; they were fomething acquainted with, and got a Tafte of Civil Life; and were befides no ways in a Condition to withftand an *Englifh* War, becaufe of the Superiority of their Arms, the Advantage of their Difcipline and native Courage, and their greater Skill in all military Arts and Stratagems. The *Englifh* had likewife ever treated them, with the utmoft Humanity and Kindnefs, out of the Hope and Defire, of thereby alluring and bringing them over, to the Knowledge of God and his true Religion. For nothing was more earneftly recommended from *England*, or more heartily defired and endeavoured by many good and pious Perfons of the Colony, than their Converfion; which, agreeably to the Spirit of the Gofpel, and of the Proteftant Religion, and greatly to the Honour of our Nation, was always purfued, by the Ways of Gentlenefs and Perfuafion, and never by thofe unchriftian Arguments of Fire and Sword. On all thefe Accounts, the *Englifh* were fo confident and fecure, that there could feldom be met with, in their Houfes, a Sword or a Firelock, and moft of their Plantations were feated in a fcattered and ftraggling Manner, as a convenient Situation, or a choice Vein of rich Land invited them; and indeed it was generally thought, the further from Neighbours the better. All *Indians* were kindly received into their Houfes, fed at their Tables, and even lodged in their Bedchambers; fo that they feemed, entirely to have coalefced, and to live together, as one People. And the *Englifh* were fo far infatuated, by an Opinion of their Simplicity, and of their Inclination, and even Intereft, to maintain the Peace, that they lent them their Boats, as they paffed backwards and forwards, to concert their Meafures, and to confult upon the execrable Defign of murdering and utterly extirpating the whole Nation.

THE Hour appointed being come, and the *Indians*, by reafon of their Familiarity, knowing exactly, in what Places and Quarters every *Englifhman* was to be found, rofe upon them at once, fparing neither Sex nor Age, Man, Woman, nor Child; and they were fo quick and fudden in their Execution, that few perceived the Weapon or Blow, that brought them to their End. Some entered their Houfes, under Colour of Trade; others drew them abroad, upon fpecious Pretences; whilft the reft fell fuddenly on
thofe,

thofe, that were at their feveral Works and Labours. And
thus, in one Hour, and almoft at the fame Inftant, fell
three hundred and forty feven, Men, Women, and Children; moft of them, by their own Tools and Weapons,
and all, by the Hands of a perfidious, naked, and daftardly
People, who durft not ftand the prefenting of a Staff, in
Manner of a Firelock, nor an uncharged Piece, in the
Hands of a Woman. Neither were they content with their
Lives only; but they fell again upon their dead Bodies, de-
facing, dragging, and mangling them into many Pieces, and
carrying fome Parts away, with a bafe and brutifh Triumph.

In this Havock, fix of the Council were flain. For
thofe Blood-hounds, with equal Spight and Barbarity, murdered all before them, without any Remorfe or Pity, and
without having any Regard to Dignity, or even to thofe
Perfons who were beft known to them, or from whom
they had daily received many Benefits. Among thefe was
that pious, worthy, and religious Gentleman, Mr. *George
Thorpe*, Deputy to the College Lands, and both in Command and Defert, one of the Principal in *Virginia*. He
had been of the King's Bed-Chamber, and was a Perfon of
confiderable Figure in *England*. Yet fo truly and earneftly
did he affect their Converfion, that he left all at home, and
came over chief Manager to the College, a Foundation
defigned for their Education and Converfion. And here he
feverely punifhed, whofoever, under him, did them the
leaft Difpleafure. He thought, nothing too dear or precious
for them, nor ever denied them any thing. Infomuch that,
being frightened at the *Englifh* Maftives, he caufed fome of
them to be killed in their Prefence, to the great Grief of
their Owners, and would fain have had all the reft gelt,
to make them mild and peaceable. He alfo built the King
a handfome Houfe, after the *Englifh* Fafhion; in which he
took fuch Pleafure, efpecially in the Lock and Key, that he
would lock and unlock his Door, an hundred Times a Day,
and was fo taken with the Device, that he thought nothing
in the World comparable to it. And thus infinuating himfelf into that Barbarian's Favour, he would often confer
with him about Religion; and that treacherous Infidel
would feem much pleafed with his Difcourfe and Company, and very defirous to requite all his Courtefy and Kindnefs. Yet did this ungrateful and viperous Brood, not only
murder this good Gentleman, but with fuch Spight and
Scorn abufe his dead Corps, as is unfit to be heard, or related. At the very Minute of the Execution, his Man,
perceiving fome Treachery, warned him to look to himfelf;

and

and withal ran off, and so saved his own Life. But his
Master, out of his good Meaning, was so void of Suspicion,
and full of Confidence, that they had slain him before he
could, or would believe, they intended any Harm. Captain
Nathaniel Powel, another of the Council, who had some
time been Governor of the Country, was also killed. He
was one of the first Planters, a brave Soldier, had deserved
well in all Ways, was universally valued and esteemed by
all Parties and Factions, and none in the Country better
known among the *Indians*. Yet they slew both him and
his Family; and afterwards haggled their Bodies, and cut
off his Head, to express their utmost Height of Scorn and
Cruelty.

THIS Slaughter was a deep and grievous Wound to the
yet weak and Infant Colony; but it would have been much
more general, and almost universal, if God had not put it
into the Heart of a converted *Indian*, to make a Discovery.
This Convert, whose Name was *Chanco*, lived with one
Richard Pace, who treated him, as his own Son. The
Night before the Massacre, another *Indian*, his Brother,
lay with him; and telling him the King's Command, and
that the Execution would be performed the next Day, he
urged him to rise and kill *Pace*, as he intended to do by
Perry, his Friend. As soon as his Brother was gone, the
Christian Indian rose, and went and revealed the whole
Matter to *Pace*; who immediately gave Notice thereof to
Captain *William Powel*, and having secured his own House,
rowed off before Day to *James-Town*, and informed the
Governor of it. By this Means, their Design was prevented at *James-Town*, and all such Plantations, as could
possibly get Intelligence in time. For where-ever they saw
the *English* upon their Guard, or a single Musket presented,
they ran off, and abandoned their Attempt.

SUCH also, at other Places, as had sufficient Warning
to make Resistance, saved their Lives. *Nathaniel Causie*,
one of Captain *Smith*'s old Soldiers, being cruelly wounded,
did, with an Ax, cleave down one of their Sculls; and
tho' they were all about him, yet they fled away, and he
escaped. At another Place, two Men only, having Notice
of their Design, defended a House against sixty or more,
that assaulted it. At *Warrasqueake*, one Mr. *Baldwin*,
when his Wife was so wounded, that she lay for dead, yet
by often discharging his Piece, drove them off, and saved
both her and his House, together with himself and divers
others. At Mr. *Harrison*'s, about half a Mile from *Baldwin*'s, was Mr. *Thomas Hamer*, with six Men, and eighteen or nineteen Women and Children. To him the *Indians,*

dians came, with many Prefents and fair Profeffions. They
pretended, they wanted Captain *Ralph Hamer*, to go to
their King, then hunting In the Woods. Mr. *Hamer* fent
immediately for his Brother, who was at a new Houfe, he
was then building. But he not coming according to their
Wifh, they fet Fire to a Tobacco Houfe, and came and
told them in the Dwelling Houfe of it. The Men ran towards it; and the *Indians* following, firft fhot them full of
Arrows, and afterwards beat out their Brains. Mr. *Hamer*,
having finifhed a Letter he was writing, ran out to fee
what was the Matter. But he foon received an Arrow in
his Back, which obliged him to retire into the Houfe, and
barricade the Doors. Hereupon the *Indians* fet Fire to the
Houfe; but *Harrifon*'s Boy, juft at that Inftant, finding
his Mafter's Gun loaded, fhot at Random. At the bare
Report, the *Indians* all fled; and thereby left the Way
open, to Mr. *Hamer* and twenty two more, to get to *Baldwin*'s Houfe. Captain *Ralph Hamer*, all this while, was
wholly ignorant of what was paffing; but coming to his
Brother, who had fent for him, he met the *Indians*, cha-
fing fome of the *Englifh*. Whereupon he retired to his
new Houfe, and with only Spades, Axes, and Brickbats,
defended himfelf and his Company, till the Savages departed. Soon after, the Mafter of a Ship, lying near, and perceiving the Confufion, fent him fix Mufketeers; with whom
he recovered their Merchant's Store-houfe, and armed ten
more; and fo, with thirty other unarmed Workmen, he
found out his Brother and the reft, at *Baldwin*'s. But in
the Midft of this miferable Slaughter and Uproar, a little
Houfe and fmall Family, not far from *Martin*'s Hundred,
at which Place alone feventy three were flain, not only
efcaped, but never heard any thing of it, till two Days after.

AT this time alfo, Captain *Ralegh Crofhaw* was in *Patowmack* River, trading in a fmall Bark, commanded by
Captain *Spilman*. There an *Indian* ftole aboard, and told
them of the Maffacre; and that *Opechancanough* had been
practifing with his King and Country, to betray them, which
they refufed to do; but that the *Indians* of *Wighcocomoco* had
undertaken it. Hereupon Captain *Spilman* went thither.
But they, feeing his Men fo vigilant and well armed, fufpected themfelves to be difcovered; and therefore, the better to colour their Guilt, and delude him, they gave him
fuch Satisfaction in his Trade, that his Veffel was foon near
loaded. After this, Captain *Crofhaw* went up to *Patowmack*. He had been long acquainted with that King; who
now very earneftly entreated him, to ftay with him, and to
be his Friend, his Director, and Captain, againft feveral

neigh-

1622.

Sir *Francis
Wyat*, Go-
vernor.

neighbouring Nations, his mortal Enemies. *Croſhaw* very
readily embraced his Offer; as well to promote ſome private Views of his own in Trade, as to keep him firm to the
Engliſh Intereſt, and make him an uſeful Opponent and Inſtrument againſt *Opechancanough*. Therefore, relying on
the Faith of this Barbarian, he ventured, with one Man
only, to ſtay behind at *Patowmack*.

IN the Beginning of this Year, before the Contrivance
and Perpetration of this bloody Conſpiracy in *Virginia*, the
unknown Gentleman in *England*, who had given five hundred and fifty Pounds, towards the Converſion and Education of *Indian* Children, having waited two Years, and received no ſatisfactory Account of the effectual Proſecution
of his Deſign, wrote a Letter to the Company. Herein
he complains, that what was done in that Affair, did by no
means anſwer his Expectation or Intent. And he requires,
of the whole Body of the Company, towards which he expreſſes much Reſpect, and an entire Confidence in their
Uprightneſs and Integrity, that, as he had entruſted the Diſ-
poſal of that Money, a great and painfully gotten Part of his
Eſtate, to their Care and Management, ſo they would ſee
the ſame, ſpeedily and faithfully applied, to the Uſe intended.
And he further propoſed to them, the procuring ſome of the
male Children of the *Indians* to be brought over into *England* (where they might be immediately under the Company's Eye and Inſpection) there to be educated and taught,
and to wear a Habit, as the Children of *Chriſt-Church* Hoſ-
pital do. In that Caſe, he deſires, that the five hundred
and fifty Pounds might be converted to that Uſe; and he
faithfully promiſes, to add four hundred and fifty Pounds
more, to make the former Sum a thouſand, as ſoon as
eight or ten *Indian* Children ſhould be placed in *London*,
either in *Chriſt's-Hoſpital*, or in the *Virginia* School or Hoſ-
pital, as it might be called; which, he doubted not, would
be Yearly augmented, by the Legacies and Gifts of good
Men. But if they liked not this Propoſition, then it was
his humble Suit and Motion, that the former Gift, of five
hundred and fifty Pounds, ſhould be immediately applied,
and wholly beſtowed, upon a Free-ſchool in *Southampton*
Hundred, or ſuch other Place, as he or his Friends ſhould
approve: That in this School, properly endowed with ſuch
Privileges, as they, in their Wiſdom, ſhould think fit, both
Engliſh and *Indians* ſhould be promiſcuouſly taught and
brought up together; and that great Care ſhould be taken,
to ſend over ſuch a Maſter, as ſhould bring a ſound Teſti-
monial, of his Sufficiency in Learning, and Sincerity of Life.
And ſo praying, that the Lord would give them wiſe and
under-

underftanding Hearts, that his Work herein might not be negligentl erroi ed, he concludes, and fubfcribes himfelf *Duft and Afhes*; a Name which he had ever, from the firft, affumed and made Ufe of, in this Affair.

THIS important Letter being read in Court, Sir *Edwin Sandys* gave the Company a particular Account of that whole Bufinefs: That the Money had been brought, in the Time of his being Treafurer: That, upon mature Deliberation, it was refolved by the Company, to divide it between *Smith*'s, since called *Southampton* Hundred, and *Martin*'s Hundred; each to undertake for a certain Number of *Infidel* Children: That *Martin*'s Hundred, being then in a very weak and confufed Condition, was afterwards, at the Entreaty of the Adventurers, eafed from that Burthen and Charge, and the Whole laid on *Southampton* Hundred: That that Society, confidering the Weight and Difficulty, as well as the Hazard of fucceeding, were alfo very unwilling to meddle with it, and offered an hundred Pounds, to be added to the former five hundred and fifty, if they might be excufed from it; but being earneftly preffed, they did at laft yield to accept and undertake it: That after much and careful Confultation, it was agreed by that Society, to employ the faid Money, together with a far greater Sum out of the Society's Purfe, to furnifh out Captain *Bluet*, with eighty able and fufficient Workmen, for fetting up an Iron-Work in *Virginia*; whereof the Profits accruing, were intended and ordered, in a ratable Proportion, to be faithfully employed, in educating thirty *Indian* Children, according to the Directions and Intent of the Donor: That Letters were likewife fent to Sir *George Yeardley*, then Governor of *Virginia*, and Captain alfo of *Southampton* Plantation; not only giving him large Advice and Direction therein, but alfo commending the Excellency and Piety of the Defign, and adjuring him to employ his utmoft Care and Induftry in it, as a Work, whereon the Eyes of God and Men were fixed: That in Anfwer hereto, Sir *George* informed them, how difficult it was to obtain any of the Children, with the Confent and good Liking of their Parents; as well on Account of their Tendernefs and Fondnefs of them, as out of their Fear of hard Ufage from the *Englifh*: That he therefore recommended a Treaty with *Opechancanough*; which was accordingly ordered, and Sir *Gaorge* promifed, to ufe his utmoft Endeavours therein: That this Backwardnefs and Jealoufly of the *Indians* was not the only Hindrance to that pious Work; for Captain *Bluet* dying foon after his Arrival, it occafioned another great Stop: That, however, Care had fince been taken, to reftore that

Iron-

Iron-Work, by a fresh Supply ; so that he hoped, the Gentleman would soon receive good Satisfaction, concerning the Disposal and Effect of his Charity, as he was sure, they would, at all times, be both ready and willing to give a faithful Account of the Employment of the said Money.

SIR *Edwin Sandys* further said, that as he could not but highly commend the Gentleman, for this his worthy and most christian Action, so he had observed great Inconveniency to arise from his Modesty, by shunning Ostentation and vain Glory, and concealing his Name. For they were thereby deprived of that mutual Help and Advice, which they might otherwise have, by Conference with him. Neither could he receive such clear Satisfaction, or fully know, with what Integrity and Care, the Affair had been managed ; the success whereof must be submitted to the Will and Pleasure of Almighty God, as it had been already commended to his Blessing. But as to the two Methods, now proposed in his Letter, he doubted greatly for his Part, whether either of them would attain the desired Effect. For, to send for them to *England*, would be far from answering the End, if he might judge from the Experience of those, brought over by Sir *Thomas Dale*. And to build a Free-school for them in *Virginia*, he feared, considering, in their present Dotage on Tobacco, that no proper Workmen could be had, but at excessive Rates, it would rather tend to exhaust this sacred Treasure in some small Edifice, than to accomplish such a Foundation, as might satisfy Mens Expectations and Desires. He therefore again wished, that a Meeting might be had, between the Gentleman, or his Friends, and the Society of *Southampton* Hundred. That so, all things being fully debated, and judiciously weighed, some Course might be entered upon and pursued, for advancing and bringing to Effect so pious and excellent a Work ; for which he prayed the Blessing of Almighty God to be upon the Author : And all the Company answered, and said, *Amen.*

BUT this charitable Gentleman, however studious he was to conceal himself, was afterwards (if any Credit may be given to Captain *Martin*'s Report) found to be Mr. *Gabriel Barber*, the chief Manager and Book-keeper of their Lotteries, and a very worthy, honest, and useful Member of the Company. He was himself then present, and heard this Account, with which he seems to have been satisfied. For he made no farther Demand or Stir in the Matter ; but continued afterwards, in the time of their subsequent Quarrels and Dissensions, a very hearty and strenuous Friend to the Company. Mr. *George Ruggles* also, Fellow of *Clare-Hall*, in *Cambridge*, and a Brother of the Company, did,

the

the latter End of this Year, notwithstanding the News of the Massacre, bequeath an hundred Pounds, for the Education of *Indians*. He is represented as a Gentleman, who was esteemed, in that University, second to none in Knowledge and Learning, of very great Wisdom and Understanding, of singular Honesty and Integrity of Life, and very sincere and zealous in Religion. And he had, for the three last Years of his Life, almost wholly exercised and employed his Time and Abilities, in the Service of the Colony. For, besides the Counsels and Assistances of himself and his Brethren, in their several Places, he wrote divers Treatises, for the Benefit of the Plantation; particularly one concerning the Government of *Virginia*, which is often mentioned, in the Company's Records, with Commendation, especially by Sir *Edwin Sandys*.

BUT there succeeding, immediately upon this violent and injurious Assault, a continual and exterminating War between the *English* and the *Indians*, all the Difficulties of their Conversion were greatly encreased; and I do not find, what farther was done, with Relation to these Benefactions. The College People also received a great and deadly Slaughter in the Massacre; which, together with the Death of Mr. *Thorpe*, their grand Principle of Life and Action, caused them to abandon the College Lands, and to retire lower down the River, to such Places as were more defensible against the sudden Assaults and Inroads of the *Indians*, because of the greater Numbers of People, and the nearer Situation, and more ready Assistance, of other Plantations. Thus did that brutish and unhappy People tear up, as it were, with their own Hands, the Foundations, which had been laid, for their Conversion to Christianity and Civility of Life. For altho' the Company, in *London*, did afterwards frequently enter upon serious Consultation, about restoring again and setting forward this charitable Work, yet by reason of their own Troubles, and of the Factions and Discords among themselves, nothing therein was ever brought to Effect. So that, from this time, there was no publick Attempt, nor any School or Institution, purposely designed for their Education and Conversion, before the Benefaction of the late Honourable *Robert Boyle*, Esq; which shall be fully related, in its proper Time nd Place.

BUT whilst the Colony in *Virg. ia* lay under the Pressure and Calamity of this bloody Massacre, the Company in *England* were greatly rejoiced and encouraged, by the favourable Account of things, which they received, about that time, from the Governor and Council. For they were informed, by their Letters, that all the Ships were safely arrived,

without

1622. without the Lofs of one Perfon, by Sea or Land ; that Mr.
John Berkeley had put the Iron Works in fo good a For-
Sir *Francis* wardnefs, that he doubted not to begin to make Iron, by
Wyat, Go- *Whitfuntide* ; that the Cotton Trees profpered exceedingly
vernor. well ; that the *Frenchmen* declared the Mulberry Trees of
Virginia to be of the very beft Kind ; and daily, by their
Example, encouraged the People to plant them in Abundance, fo that they were in high Expectation, of fhortly
fucceeding in, and bringing to Perfection, that rich Commodity of Silk ; that the *French* Vignerons had conceived
great Hopes, of fpeedily making Plenty of good Wine,
whereof they had already made an Experiment, and fent
home a Tafte by that Ship; and in fhort, that they now
had a fairer Profpect, and more certain Hope, than ever yet,
of foon becoming a rich and flourifhing Country. For
which joyful News, and happy Succefs, the Company voted
and refolved, that a Sermon fhould be preached, to teftify
and exprefs their Thankfulnefs to God, for his Blefling on
their Labours and Undertaking. And Mr. *Copeland*, a Brother of the Society, who, by his hearty Zeal for the Enterprife, was well acquainted with the Succefs of their Affairs, for the laft Year, was requefted to undertake the
Performance of this holy Exercife ; which he accordingly
did, at *Bow* Church, the 17th Day of *April*.

M R. *Copeland* was alfo himfelf, foon after, publickly entreated by the Company, to go over in Perfon to *Virginia*,
and to apply himfelf to the Miniftry there. And in Confideration of his good Services and worthy Endeavours,
which had redounded much to the Honour and Benefit of
the Colony, as alfo in Refpect of his known Sufficiency and
Worth, they conftituted him one of the Council of State,
and appointed him Rector of the College for the Converfion
of *Indians*, to receive, as a Salary, the tenth Part of the
Profits arifing from their Lands and the Labours of their
Tenants ; and alfo to have the Paftoral Charge of the College
Tenants about him, which were to be erected into a Par-
fonage, according to the Company's general Order in that
Behalf. But this Defign, together with all their fanguine
Hopes and Ideas of an immediately rich and profperous
Country, was dafhed to Pieces, and cut off, by the Maffacre. The Iron-Work on *Falling* Creek, in particular,
was entirely ruined and demolifhed, and Mr. *John Berkeley*
flain, with all his Workmen and People, except one Boy
only and a Girl, who found Means to hide themfelves, and
efcape. Their Preparations likewife, for other Commodities and Manufactures, were quite deftroyed and deferted ;
the People, all this Summer, being in fuch a State of Terror

ror and Flight, that they did not even make Corn for their Support and Subfiftence.

To this fad Pofture of Affairs in the Colony, was added the continual Increafe of the Company's Diffenfions and Animofities at home, which became daily more furious and irreconcileable. Captain *Argall* and that Faction, omitted no imaginable Methods of Vexation and Trouble; and the more to difparage and perplex the Company's Proceedings, they were perpetually raifing new Authors and frefh Subjects of Complaint, as well to the Publick, as moft efpecially to the King, and to the great Lords and powerful Perfons of his Court. It hath been already faid, that Captain *John Martin* came over, one of the Council of State, in the firft Adventure; and there hath been frequent Occafion fince, to mention his weak Conduct and Behaviour here. This Gentleman was well born, and nearly related to Sir *Julius Cæfar*, then Mafter of the Rolls. In the Time of Sir *Thomas Smith*'s Treafurerfhip, he had furreptitioufly obtained a Grant, to be Mafter of the Ordinance in *Virginia*; as alfo a moft extravant and illegal Patent for Land, at the Place, which he himfelf named *Martin*'s Brandon. For, by the exprefs Words of his Majefty's Charter, the Company was reftrained to their four great and general Quarter Courts, one to be held each Term, for tranfacting any Bufinefs of great Importance, and particularly for granting Lands in *Virginia*. But both thefe Grants, to Captain *Martin*, had been paffed in a private Court, called purpofely for that Jobb, and could never after receive the Affent and Confirmation of a Quarter Court. For the Company, being apprifed of the Matter, ftrongly oppofed their Execution, and endeavoured to keep them from taking Effect. Captain *Argall* in particular, when Governor of *Virginia*, had fent home grievous Complaints, againft the Exorbitancies of *Martin*'s Patent and Behaviour; and both Sir *Thomas Smith* and Alderman *Johnfon*, at that time Treafurer and Deputy of the Company, had been willing and affifting, to ftop and prevent thefe Grants from being further confirmed, and receiving the legal Sanction of a Quarter Court.

BUT now, the Company's witholding Captain *Martin* from the Fruition of thofe Privileges and Immunities, which appeared to have been granted under their Seal, being, at firft Sight, a fpecious Pretence of Clamour and Complaint, which might be turned to difgrace and vilify the Juftice and Honour of their Proceedings, thefe very Gentlemen inftigated and affifted him, to get a Certificate under the Hands of feveral noble Lords, and others, and to have it delivered in to the Company, by one Captain *Hafwell*. The Purport

port of this Writing was : That whereas *John Martin* Efq;
having been a long and faithful Servant to the Colony of
Virginia, defired a Teftimonial of his Carriage and Demeanor in all things, according to their Knowledge and
the Truth, they did thereby certify : That, by the general
Confent of his Majefty's Council in *England*, for *Virginia*,
the faid Captain *John Martin* was, in the Face of the publick and open Court, elected, chofen, and fworn, one of
his Majefty's firft Council of *Virginia* : That afterwards,
in the faid honourable and open Court, he was, with the
free and full Confent thereof, appointed, chofen, and
fworn, Mafter of the Ordinance in the faid Colony : That,
befides his firft Adventure, which was very laudable and
good, he had, ever fince, conftantly and very worthily endured all the Miferies and Calamities ◆f fore-paft Times,
with the Lofs of his Blood, the Death of his only Son (the
fole Hope and Comfort of his Age) together with Sicknefs,
Famine, and many other inexpreffibly hard and miferable
Sufferings : That he had alfo providently and very carefully endeavoured all the Good and Benefit to the Plantation,
that was in his Power ; in all things, upholding and labouring to maintain, with equal Juftice and Clemency, all his
Majefty's Laws, Prerogatives, and Rights whatfoever :
That for thefe honeft and worthy Services, They, the Company and Council for his Majefty, refident in *England*, had
formerly granted him fundry Privileges, by Charter under
their Great Seal, for fettling a private Plantation upon his
own Allotment of Land in *Virginia* ; wherein he had fince
proceeded with much Charge and Expence, and for which
they neither faw nor knew any Reafon, why he fhould not
be permitted to enjoy the fame, according to the true Intent
and Meaning of his faid Grant.

THIS Certificate was figned by the Earls of *Pembroke*,
Warwick, *Leicefter*, and *Montgomery*, by Lord *Sheffield*,
Sir *Robert Manfel*, Sir *Thomas Smith*, Alderman *Johnfon*,
Captain *Argall*, and a few others, to the Number of twelve
in all. Being prefented to the Company, they conceived
themfelves much wronged and affronted, that a few Members of their Body fhould, in this Paper, affume to themfelves the Name and Authority of the whole Company ;
ftiling themfelves, *We, the Company and Council for his*
Majefty, here refident in England. And they found themfelves under a Neceffity of doing fomething, to avoid the
foul Afperfion, contained therein, as if they now went a-
bout to difavow their own Act and Deed ; as alfo to prevent the evil Confequences, that might follow, and the ill
Conftructions, that might be made thereon. Being therefore

fore fully apprifed, that fome of the Lords, and others, had
been miflead and betrayed into it, by the falfe Reprefentations and malicious Practices of the reft, they drew up an
Anfwer, and ordered their Secretary to make divers Copies
thereof, which they entreated Sir *John Davers* and Mr.
Tomlins, to deliver, as well to fuch Lords as had figned
the Certificate, as alfo to his Majefty's Mafters of Requeft.
For, by reprefenting Captain *Martin*, as labouring to maintain the King's Laws, Prerogatives, and Rights (a Stile
exactly fuited to the Tafte and Views of the Court) it was
eafy to perceive, which Way it was chiefly intended and
addreffed. But as to the other Subfcribers, the Secretary
was commanded, to deliver each of them a Copy himfelf.

IN this Anfwer they fet forth : That the Company are
limited and directed, by his Majefty's Charters, to their
Quarter Courts only, for paffing of all Matters of greateft
Weight, and particularly for difpofing of Lands in *Virginia* :
That, contrary to this fundamental Law, notoriously known
to all the Company, and frequently publifhed and declared
to the Planters, as an Ordinance from his Majefty to be in-
violably obferved, Captain *Martin's* two Grants were prefented to an inferior private Court, ready engroffed, the
Company not being before acquainted with the Matter :
That by this Court, called extraordinarily, and as it feems,
for this Bufinefs only, the faid Patents were unlawfully and
unduly paffed, notwithftanding the Diffent and Oppofition
of divers then prefent ; and that they never could afterwards have the Confirmation of a Quarter Court : That
the faid Patent for Land contained fundry tranfcendent Liberties and exorbitant Privileges, apparently repugnant to
Juftice and the good Government of the Colony, and
which the Company, by his Majefty's Charters, had no
Power to grant : That therein was given an Exemption of
all the People within the Limits of his Patent, from the
Command and Government of the Governor and Council,
and from all other Charges and Services of the Colony
whatfoever, except in Cafe of War only ; as likewife a
Grant of an unlimited Fifhing, of the fifth Part of all rich
Mines, with many other general and indefinite Liberties :
That, under Colour of thefe extraordinary Privileges, many great Inconveniences had arifen, to both the Company
and Colony : That Captain *Martin* refufed to fubmit himfelf to the Laws and Orders of Government there : That
his Plantation was made a Receptacle and Harbour for all
diffolute Perfons, who fly thither from ordinary Juftice :
That all thefe, and many other Mifchiefs, had been often
complained of by the Colony, in their particular and general

Wyat, Go-
vernor.

ral Affemblies; as alfo by the Governors there, and moft
efpecially by Captain *Argall,* notwithftanding his Subfcription to this Certificate : That, upon his Letter to the Company, an Order was made, in a Great and General Quarter
Court, held in *May* 1618, and a Committee appointed, to
examine and reform the faid Patent : That Sir *Thomas
Smith* and Alderman *Johnfon* then prefided, as Treafurer
and Deputy to the Company ; fo that it feemed ftrange to
them, to find their Hands alfo to that Certificate, contra-
dicting the Act of that Great Court, wherein themfelves
were the principal Managers and Directors : That the faid
Inconveniencies had moreover been lately teftified, by feveral
Perfons, before the Company, in open Court : But that the
Company had neverthelefs frequently offered, and was always
ready to grant Captain *Martin* (whofe Merits they fhould
be glad to hear of, and to cherifh) upon the Surrender of
his former, a new Patent, with as large and ample Privileges, as any other had, or could enjoy.

NOTWITHSTANDING the Truth, Juftice, and Rea-
fonablenefs of this Anfwer, Captain *Martin* preferred a
Petition to the King, containing many fcandalous Suggestions, as well againft the whole Body of the Company, as
againft fome fpecial Members in particular. And he obtained an Order from his Majefty, to have his Caufe heard
and determined, at Sir *Thomas Smith*'s Houfe, before fuch
Referees, as he himfelf named ; among which were thofe,
who chiefly inftigated and fet him on. In Anfwer to this,
the Company made two Addreffes ; one to the Referees, in
like Manner as they had done in the Cafe of the Certificate ; and the other to the King, as well to clear the Company and fuch particular Perfons, as ftood accufed and defamed in *Martin*'s Petition, as alfo to inform his Majefty,
that fome of thofe, unto whom the Reference was procured, were violently fufpected, to be Captain *Martin*'s chief
Abettors and Supporters in this Affair. They therefore
defired, that the Matter might be referred, together with
thofe Lords in *Martin*'s Reference, to certain other Lords
of the Privy Council, whom they named. But upon Lord
Cavendifh's prefenting this, his Majefty faid, that he was
much furprifed at this new Cuftom, lately fprung up, that
Petitioners fhould chufe their own Referees. To which his
Lordfhip anfwered ; that, in that Point, Captain *Martin*
had been their Example, who in his Petition, which his
Lordfhip then produced and fhewed his Majefty, had named
his own Referees, which his Majefty had approved and appointed accordingly.

BUT

BUT not content to give the Company this Trouble and Diſturbance, Captain *Martin*, together with one Captain *Robert Haſwell*, preſented another Petition to his Majeſty, ſetting forth: That in the Time of Sir *Thomas Dale's* Government, there was a large Quantity of Woodland, Marſh, and other Ground, being in Circumference by Eſtimation about fourſcore Miles, for which Sir *Thomas Dale* compounded with *Powhatan*, the *Indian* King, and bounded the ſame by Trees, and other Marks of perpetual Knowledge and Remembrance, with a ſolemn Proceſſion of many of his Majeſty's Subjects, then and there living, commanding Notice to be taken thereof, to be, and always ſo called and entitled, *The King's Foreſt*: That within the ſaid Foreſt, there was of Deer and wild Hogs a very great Number; which being preſerved, with Care and Judgment, from the Spoil and Havock, which continually was, and would be made, both of them and their Brood, the Colony might therein have a conſtant Stock and Support, and Shipping might, at all times, be plentifully victualled and ſupplied: And that there were beſides, within thoſe Limits, many other profitable Commodities, already known. They therefore humbly beſought his moſt ſacred Majeſty, to take the ſaid Foreſt into his own Royal Hands, and to appoint ſome honourable Perſon, to be Commander thereof, authoriſing him, to give Order for converting the Plantations thereon to his Majeſty's beſt Uſe and Behoof, and for appointing a Juſtice of Oyer, and Rangers, with ſuch other Officers, as ſhould be thought moſt proper and convenient for the ſaid Foreſt and Plantation.

To ſuch a Height of Falſhood, Fraud, and Impoſture, did the Paſſions of theſe unhappy Men carry them, as thus to give the King at once, as far as it was in their Power, all the Lands and Poſſeſſions of a very great and principal Part of the Colony; who had, by their Labours and Sufferings, ſtruck out new Branches of Trade and Profit to the King and Nation, and well deſerved all Manner of Indulgence, and the utmoſt Security and Stability in their Properties. But King *James* was not of a Temper, to forego any Views of Profit and Advantage. He therefore referred the Examination of the Matter to Sir *Chriſtopher Perkins*, one of the Maſters of Requeſts; who ſummoning the Company, received for Anſwer:

THAT they held not their Lands from King *Powhatan*, nor acknowledged any King of *Virginia*, but King *James*: That it was true, for a perpetual Memorial and permanent Honour to his Majeſty and his Royal Iſſue, they had named their chief Towns, and other moſt remarkable Places, after

the

the King and his Children: That they however fuppofed, this did no way alter the Property of Inheritance in thofe Places, which his Majefty, by Letters-patent under the Great Seal of *England*, had granted to the faid Company, for and throughout all *Virginia* : That as to the King's Foreft, it was a Name happily known to Captain *Martin* and his Affociates, but never before heard of by the Company : That within the Circuit, which they had been pleafed to appropriate for the Foreft, were placed *James-City*, their chief Town, and Place of Refidence for the Governor and Council, and divers other principal Seats and Plantations : That as for the Deer, it was true, the whole Country did generally abound in them; but the Swine were no other, but the Breed of fuch as had been tranfported thither by the Company : That Captain *Martin* was a Perfon, who had ruined his own Eftate, (if ever he had any) as alfo the Eftates of others, who had put him in Truft : That he made his Territory in *Virginia* a Receptacle of Vagabonds and Bankrupts; and was famous for nothing, but all Kinds of bafe Conditions and Actions, as had been publifhed in Print, above ten Years before : That he had been therefore difplaced from the Council, by Lord *Delawarr*, as a moft unworthy Perfon, who had prefumed, of his own Authority, no ways derived from his Majefty, to pafs unjuft Sentence of Death upon divers of his Majefty's Subjects, and to fee the fame put into cruel Execution : That it was therefore a Matter of great Surprife to them, to find fuch a Man dare to offer himfelf to his Majefty, as an Agent, either for Matter of good Hufbandry, or good Government : That as to Captain *Hafwell*, he was neither Adventurer in the Company, nor Planter in the Colony, but a mere Stranger to both; nor otherwife known to them, than as Interpreter to a *Polonian* Lord, of his own creating : That however, if the King was pleafed, to have a Royal Domain laid off for him in *Virginia*, nothing could be more joyful and agreeable to the faid Council and Company, nor wherein they would more willingly employ their Endeavours.

AT the fame time, Mr. *Pierce*, who had been Cape-Merchant in *Virginia*, underftanding, that Captain *Martin* denied, that he ever protected any within his Territories, averred, that he had delivered feveral Warrants, to be ferved upon Perfons, that lived loofely within Captain *Martin*'s Plantation, and that the Provoft Marfhal made Return, that the faid Captain *Martin* refifted the Officer, and drew Arms upon him, and would not fuffer him to execute the faid Warrants. Others alfo affirmed, that it

was

was generally reported in *Virginia*, that Captain *Martin*'s Plantation was a Place of Refuge for all Debtors; and that, if he had been of Power, there would have been no living in *Virginia*. To which Mr. *Jefferson* added; that, to his Knowledge, Captain *Martin*, being fummoned, had refufed to obey the General Affemblies. All which, they all declared themfelves to be ready and willing, whenever required, to confirm and juftify upon Oath. Wherefore, in a Cafe of this clear Evidence and Truth, Captain *Martin* was not able to carry his Point againft the Company. He was afterwards induced to deliver up his illegal Patent in open Court, to be cancelled; and Orders were given for drawing a new one, with as large and ample Privileges, as the Earl of *Southampton*, or any other Adventurer had. But when this was drawn, Captain *Martin* complained, that he was therein abridged of a great Quantity of Land, granted in his former Patent. For, in that, ten Shares were given him, in Reward of his Services; and he pretended, that each of thofe Shares ought to be five hundred Acres of Land; and he therefore claimed five thoufand Acres. For this, he defired that Spot of Land, as he called it, at *Martin*'s *Brandon*, where he had formerly feated, containing about fix thoufand Acres, with all Marfhes and funken Grounds thrown in, as an Overplus. But the Court, having never heard of any Shares of five hundred Acres, and finding it exprefly directed by their Charters, that no Share fhould exceed an hundred Acres, abfolutely refufed to grant his Demand. However, to give him Satisfaction, if poffible, they gave him to a certain Day, to produce any Inftance or Evidence, that there had ever been Shares of five hundred Acres, and promifed, to fhew him all lawful Favour. But he afterwards perverfely demanded the Re-delivery of his old Patent; and the Court, being quite wearied out with his Obftinacy and Impertinence, gave him for their laft and refolute Anfwer; That, if he would accept fuch a Patent, as they could lawfully grant, he might have it; but as for his old Patent, they could not deliver it to him again, being void, not fo much by his Refignation, as by the Extravagance and Illegality of the Grant itfelf. Whereupon he went away, and never fpared, upon all Occafions, to load many very worthy and deferving Members of the Company, with all poffible Scandal and Reproach. But at laft he accepted the new Patent, and pretended to be fully reconciled to the Company; and came to *Virginia*, with a Recommendation from the Privy Council, and by their Means and Interpofition, even from the Company themfelves; which Favour he

1622.

Sir *Francis* Wyat, Governor.

accordingly requited, by propagating and spreading through the Country all the Falshoods and Calumnies against them, that he could invent or utter.

BUT besides Captain *Martin*, some others were raised up and suborned, to give in Complaints to the King, against the Company. One *Adam Dixon*, in his Petition, pretended to have been hired, for the Service of the Company and Colony, as Master-Calker of their Ships and Vessels in *Virginia*, at thirty six Shillings a Month, and that having served them many Years, he only had received three Pounds thirteen Shillings; so that there was now due to him an hundred and fifty Pounds, or there-abouts: That Captain *Argall* also, in the time of his Government, had given him and one *John Berry* a Piece of uncleared Ground, on which they had expended an hundred Pounds in a House; but that, contrary to all Justice and Equity, they had been turned out of their said House and Ground, the former Year, by Sir *George Yeardley*, to their great Discomfort and utter Undoing. To this the Company answered: That the Matters of the said Petition were to them utterly unknown; that there was not, in their Books, the least mention of any such Officer or Contract; neither had they any Inducements, to believe it to be true: That if any such thing had passed, it must have been in Sir *Thomas Smith*'s Time, to whom they referred him, for Answer and Satisfaction: That as to the Outrage and Wrong, pretended to have been done by Sir *George Yeardley*, the Petitioner had never yet complained thereof to them; but they would take a Course for speedy Justice therein, by commending the Matter to the Care and Examination of the Governor and Council in *Virginia*. And the Affair was accordingly examined and tried in our General Court, the 21st of *January* 1623-4. It then appeared, by the Oath of *Thomas Gates* and the said *Adam Dixon*, that they, together with *John Berry* and *Thomas Dingley*, were hired by Sir *Thomas Smith*, upon Wages, for a certain Term; that their Wages were not only never paid, but they themselves were detained, many Years longer, in very hard Servitude; and that at last, to free themselves, they were obliged to give Captain *Argall* an Acquittance, under their Hands, for their Wages; without which, he threatened, they should never be set free. And they further swore, that Captain *Argall* kept them a Year after, in his own proper Service, without any Allowance of either Wages or Cloaths. But I cannot find, in our Records, that they prosecuted or made any Complaint here, against Sir *George Yeardley*, about their House and Land.

ONE

ONE *William Kemp* alfo prefented a Complaint to his *1622.* Majefty, of the Grievances of certain Inhabitants of *Kic-* *quotan* in *Virginia*; that *William Julian*, *John Bufh*, and *Sir Francis Wyat, Governor.* fome others, ancient Planters, and deferving Inhabitants of the beft mechanical Trades, had been turned out of their lawful Poffeffions, by Sir *George Yeardley*, with many Circumftances of Oppreffion and Cruelty. To which the Company anfwered: That the Parties, pretended to be wronged, had never made any Complaint to them: That *Kemp* had been in *England* above a Year, and had never laid the Matter before the Council and Company, where Juftice might have been done: That he did not even pretend to have Authority from the Parties grieved, to exhibit this Complaint to his Majefty: That they therefore faw no Caufe, to believe his Allegations to be true; but fufpected him, rather to be fet on by the Malice of others, than moved by his own Zeal for Right and Juftice: That however, according to their Cuftom in Caufes of the like Nature, they would, by the firft Opportunity, tranfmit this Complaint to the Governor and Council in *Virginia*; that, if there appeared any Truth in any Part thereof, they might proceed, as well to the due Redrefs of the faid Grievances, as to the condign Punifhment of the Authors and Delinquents. And this Complaint appears, from our Records, to have had this Foundation in Truth and Matter of Fact; that fome Perfons had fet down, at *Kicquotan*, upon the publick Land of the Company, and were obliged, by the Governor and Council, to go off. But they however had, either by this time or afterwards, (I cannot exactly fay which) Satisfaction made them for their Clearing and Improvements.

CAPTAIN *Matthew Somers*, who had returned to *England* with his Uncle's Body, in the Year 1610, had, long before this, been a Prifoner in the King's Bench. From thence he often pelted and tiezed the Company, with an extravagant Demand for his Uncle's Adventure; and altho' fomething confiderable in Adventure appeared, by their Books, to be due to Sir *George Somers*, yet they refufed to pafs it over to him, becaufe he had an elder Brother in the Country, who was Heir at Law to Sir *George*, and he could not make fufficient Proof, that either his Uncle had bequeathed it by Will, or that his Brother had made over all his Right and Intereft therein to him. In this time therefore of prefenting Petitions to the King, Captain *Somers* alfo preferred his; informing his Majefty: That Sir *George Somers* was forced, by Strefs of Weather, to fave himfelf and Company, on the Iflands of *Bermudas*, where he loft his

Q 2 Ship,

Ship, and soon after, his Life: That he, the Petitioner, being his immediate Heir, and then present, built a small Bark, to convey his Company to *England*; and left three Men, to continue the Possession of those Islands, in his Majesty's Name: That the *Virginia* Company, hearing of this Discovery, challenged those Islands, as their Right, altho' they were above an hundred Leagues without the Limits of their Grant; and they sent a Governor, with Men, to take the Possession from his Majesty: That finding the Petitioner's Men had, by their Industry, found a Cake of Ambergrease of an hundred and sixty Pounds Weight, the said Governor took it violently from them, for the Use of the Company, who sold it for twelve thousand Pounds, and likewise threatened Violence to the poor Men, to make them confess more: That the said Company, shortly after, sold the said Islands to a particular Company, for two thousand Pounds; and the poor Petitioner could never yet obtain any thing, either for his Adventure or otherwise, altho' he had long and often solicited it, to his great Charge and utter Undoing: That these, and no other Comforts, could they, the ancient Adventurers, receive from the Company; and therefore he humbly besought his Majesty, to take into Consideration his own Royal Rights therein, and to give Order for the Relief of him, the poor Petitioner.

To this false and exaggerated Account of that Affair, the *Somer-Islands* Company gave in, for Answer, much the same in Substance and Purport, as I have before related concerning it. And as for Captain *Somers*, they deny him to have any just Pretence, to stile himself, either an ancient Adventurer, or Planter. For he made a very short Abode there; and contrary to his Duty and Trust, returned suddenly to *England*, where he had ever since continued, without performing the least Service to either Plantation. They confess, that a Block of Ambergrease of very great Value was found, of which they got about a third Part; but were not able to deliver in an exact Account of its Worth, because Sir *Thomas Smith*, at that time Governor and Treasurer of their Company, had hitherto refused to give in any Account of their Treasury. And they further say, that they conceived the Right to that Ambergrease to be in the *Virginia* Company, at whose Charge, and in whose Service, those three Men had been set out and employed; but that they had nevertheless, since compounded with the Finders, so that none of them had any just Cause of Complaint, and least of all Captain *Somers*, who could have no Title or Pretence of Interest therein.

As

As Captain *Argall* had been long and actively employed in *Virginia*, and was confequently well acquainted with moft Perfons and Paffages there, he was ftrongly fufpected to be at the Bottom of thefe Complaints and Petitions againft the Company. They therefore, on their Part, refolved to purfue their Profecution againft him with greater Vigor; and they appointed a felect Committee, to warn him peremptorily to exhibit his Accounts, and to make a full and fubftantial Anfwer to fuch things, as the Company fhould charge him withal. But he, being a Man of good Senfe and Capacity, and of great Induftry and Refolution, ftill foiled and perplexed their Proceedings, and gave them much Trouble and Annoyance, without their being able to bring him to any Account or Punifhment, for all his unrighteous Gains and Extortions in *Virginia*.

CAPTAIN *Samuel Each* was fent, this Summer, in a large Ship of three or four hundred Tons, to build a Blockhoufe or Fort, on thofe Banks which lie out in *James* River, near *Blunt Point*. This was defigned, to command the Paffage up the River; and it was judged, by divers of the Inhabitants, to be that, which ought firft to be attempted, and would be moft eafily effected. Captain *Each* alfo, who was efteemed a very honeft and fkilful Man, having viewed the Place, when in *Virginia*, thought the thing very feafible. But this Undertaking, like many others, ended with great Charge to the Company, and without any real Effect or Advantage. However, in this Ship went over the Lady *Wyat*, and Mr. *Barret*, a Mafter-Shipwright, (whom Captain *Smith* calls Captain *Barwick*) with twenty five Men, to build Ships and Boats, together with many Houfe-carpenters for the *Eaft-India* School, and other Ufes. All thefe Perfons, for publick Services, were fent in the common Method, ufed ever fince the Company's Fund was exhaufted, by the voluntary Subfcription of the Adventurers to a Roll. And I likewife find, that one Mr. *Howe*, who ftiles himfelf a Chronicler, made a Demand upon the Company, about this time, for twelve Pounds of Tobacco; which, he faid, had been promifed him annually, in Confideration of his Pains and Willingnefs to ferve the Company, and to relate, in his Book, the feveral Paffages concerning *Virginia*. They granted him his Penfion for that Year, which he moft thankfully accepted. But he either never performed the Service, or is at leaft a Writer of that Obfcurity and Infignificancy, that I neither know, nor can find any thing of him.

BEFORE the Election of Officers came on this Year, the Company, in a previous Court, expreffed their great

Satif-

Satisfaction in the Earl of *Southampton*'s Administration; and they made it their humble Desire and Entreaty to his Lordship, which was entered upon their Records, that he would vouchsafe, to hold the Place of Treasurer, for one Year more. But the Earl of *Southampton* was very obnoxious to the Court, on Account of his Principles of Liberty, and his bold and resolute Opposition to an excessive Prerogative. The King therefore endeavoured once more, to put him out of the Government of the Company. For, at the time of Election, Alderman *Hamersley* and Mr. *Bell* delivered a Message, in his Majesty's Name, signifying: That altho' it was not his Design or Desire, to infringe their Freedom of Election, yet it would be highly pleasing to his Majesty, if they would make Choice, for Treasurer and Deputy, of any of those Gentlemen, whose Names were written in a Paper, then presented to the Court. In this, Sir *John Wolstenholme*, Sir *William Russel*, Mr. *Clitheroe*, Mr. *Maurice Abbot*, and Mr. *Handford*, were proposed to their Choice for Treasurer; and for Deputy, Mr. *Leat*, Mr. *Robert Offley*, Mr. *Stiles*, Mr. *Abdy*, and Mr. *Bateman*. The Company expressed great Joy and Satisfaction, for this Testimony of his Majesty's Notice and good Wishes to the Colony, and of his gracious Intention, not to infringe their Privilege of free Election. But because, by their Rules and Orders, three only at a time could stand for either of those Places, they first put it to the Vote, which two, of the five recommended by the King for Treasurer, should be put in Election, with one, whom the Company should name. Mr. *Clitheroe* and Mr. *Handford* were chosen to stand in Election, and the Company named the Earl of *Southampton*; who was, upon the Ballot, chosen by a vast Majority, he having an hundred and seventeen Balls, Mr. *Clitheroe* thirteen, and Mr. *Handford* seven. In like Manner, they chose Mr. *Leat* and Mr. *Bateman*, to stand for the Place of Deputy Treasurer, to whom the Company added Mr. *Nicholas Farrar*, who was also elected, by having an hundred and three Balls, Mr. *Bateman* ten, and Mr. *Leat* eight.

THE Earl of *Southampton* was then absent; and indeed seems, purposely to have abstained from their Courts at such times, to shew, that these things were carried, not by any Art or Ambition of his own, but merely by the free Choice, and unbiassed Affection of the Company. But Mr. *Nicholas Farrar*, being present, took his Place, as Deputy Treasurer, and returned Thanks to the Company, for this honourable Testimony of their Love and Esteem, wherein he should, all his Life, exceedingly glory and rejoice. And he farther declared his Sense of the Weight and Difficulty of the

Office,

Office, and of his own Inability. But not to trouble them
with any felf-denying Intreaties, he promifed, to the Utmoft
of his Power, to perform the Charge they had laid upon
him; and befought the Honourable the Lords, and the other
worthy Gentlemen and Officers, with their Counfels to direct, and the whole Court, with their Prefence to affift him,
in the Execution of his Office. And, in particular, he defired them, to requeft his Brother, Mr. *John Farrar* (in
Confidence of whofe Affiftance and Direction, he well knew,
they had chofen him) to continue the fame Care and Pains,
he had formerly done. Whereupon Mr. *John Farrar* promifed, not to flack any thing of his former Zeal and Diligence, in the Bufinefs; and the Company, in thankful Ac-
knowledgement and Approbation of his great and faithful
Services, in the Place of Deputy-Treafurer, for the three
laft Years, beftowed upon him twenty Shares of Land, old
Adventure. And they further ordered, that together with
the Gift, it fhould be entered on their Records, that the
Court conceived his Services and Merits to be fo great, that
had not their Liberality been bounded, within the Compafs
of twenty great Shares, they would, for him, have exceeded it with a much larger Proportion. And the fame Quantity had alfo been beftowed upon Sir *Edwin Sandys,* in his
Abfence, the former Year, with a like honourable Teftimony and Acknowledgment of his Services and Deferts.

THE Company alfo requefted the Lords *Cavendifh, Paget,* and *Houghton,* to prefent their moft humble Thanks to
his Majefty, for his Remembrance and good Wifhes to
their Affairs; and to inform him, with what Reverence
and Refpect, his Meffage was received; but that the Election had fallen upon the Earl of *Southampton,* with an almoft unanimous Confent, the Company having found, that
the Plantation had profpered, each of the three laft Years,
more than in ten before; and that more had been done
with ten thoufand Pounds, than formerly with fourfcore
thoufand. And they further conceived, that as their Staple
Commodities were then in eftablifhing and perfecting, and
as the Government of the Country was to be fettled and
confirmed, equal Sufficiency, in their Governors and Directors, would not fo much advance the Plantation, as the
Variablenefs of Inftructions and Methods, in the Change of
Officers, proceeding from different Conceptions and Ways
of thinking, would prejudice and retard the Bufinefs. But
his Majefty was not well pleafed to find, that out of fo large
a Number, as were recommended by him, not one had
been chofen; and he faid, he conceived Merchants to be
fitteft, for the Management of fuch Undertakings, becaufe

of

1622.

Sir *Francis*
Wyat, Go-
vernor.

of their Experience and Skill in Staple Commodities. In
Confirmation of which, he inſtanced Sir *Thomas Smith's*
Government, in whoſe time many Staple Commodities had
been ſet up, which were now laid down, and only Tobacco
raiſed or attempted. To which Lord *Cavendiſh* replied,
that in this, as well as many other Particulars, relating to
the Company and their Proceedings, his Majeſty had been
very groſly miſinformed ; that the following Tobacco only,
and neglecting all other Staple Commodities, had been the
Fruits of Sir *Thomas Smith's* and Alderman *Johnſon's* Government ; but that ſince, they had laboured, with all Induſtry, Care, and Diligence, to erect Iron-Works, plant
Vineyards, make Silk, and raiſe other ſuch valuable Commodities, of ſome whereof, they hoped, ſhortly to give his
Majeſty a Proof ; and he ſaid, that ſince Sir *Thomas Smith's*
Time, the Colony had grown to almoſt as many thouſands
of People, as he left hundreds, beſides a very great Increaſe
of their Cattle. And his Lordſhip further aſſured his Majeſty, that ſome of the Perſons recommended, being in
Court, did then, and moſt of them have otherwiſe ſince,
publickly acknowledged and declared, that they would never have accepted thoſe Places ; profeſſing themſelves, thro'
Want of Experience, and a Multitude of other Buſineſs, ſo
very unfit and unequal to the Charge, that they ſhould certainly have brought back the Buſineſs more, in one Year,
than it had gone forward and proſpered, in the laſt three.

SOON after this, the News of the Maſſacre in *Virginia*
arrived. This Event, ſo unexpected, and ſo contrary to
all their Hopes and Proſpects, was received, by the Company, with inexpreſſible Grief ; which was not a little ag-
gravated, that ſo many had fallen, by the Hands of Men ſo
contemptible, and after ſuch plain Warnings, as *Opechan-*
canough's Attempt to poiſon the whole Colony, and eſpecially the Death of *Nemattanow* had given. And they were
therefore very loud in their Complaints againſt the Conduct
of the Governor and Colony ; never conſidering, how eaſy
and natural it would be, to retort upon them (as the Governor and Council actually did) their own conſtant and
preſſing Inſtructions, to win the *Indians* over by Courteſy
and Kindneſs, to give them familiar Entertainment in their
Houſes, and if it were poſſible, to draw them to live together and cohabit with the *Engliſh.* However, all good and
ſenſible Men thought not the worſe of the Enterpriſe, for
theſe Diſaſters ; but many publick-ſpirited Adventurers undertook ſeveral new Plantations, and divers Ships were diſ-
patched away, with ſuch Supplies and Aſſiſtance, as were
thought ſufficient. The King alſo was ſo far ſenſible of the
Loſs

Lofs of fo many of his Subjects, and of the miferable State **1622.**
of the Colony, that he made them a Gift of Arms out of the
Tower; fuch indeed, as were unferviceable in *Europe* a- *Sir Francis*
gainft equal Enemies, yet might, with a little Trimming *Wyat, Go-*
and Repair, be made very ufeful againft the *Indians.* And *vernor.*
for immediate Difpatch, his Majefty lent twenty Barrels of
Powder, upon the Security of the Company's Seal, afterwards to repay it. He likewife promifed, to levy four hundred young Men, out of the feveral Shires, to be fent to
Virginia, in Supply of thofe, that had perifhed in the Maffacre; but he never could be brought, tho' often follicited
by the Company, to make that Promife good. The Lord
St. John of *Bafing*, alfo gave fixty Coats of Mail, for the Defence of the Colony.; and the City of *London*, with many
private Perfons, were much concerned at, and very forward
to contribute towards the Repair of this Lofs.

CAPTAIN *Smith*, with Mr. *Stockham* and Mr. *Whita-*
ker, two Clergymen of Note in the Colony, had ever been
of Opinion, that the Ways of Gentlenefs and Kindnefs would
never be fufficient to bring the *Indians* over; and had therefore recommended, that *Mars* and *Minerva* fhould go Hand
in Hand, as well in their Converfion, as in all other Tranfactions and Intercourfe with them. But they were too fan-
guinary in their Notions of the Matter. For Mr. *Stockam*
plainly declares, that, until the Throats of their Priefts and
Elders were cut, there could be no Hopes of their Converfion; and Captain *Smith* frequently mentions, and infinuates
to Imitation, the deteftable Example of the *Spaniards*, in
their Conqueft of the *Weft-Indies.* They were indeed fomething excufable, if, their Patience being worn out by a long
Experience of the Perfidioufnefs, Bafenefs, and almoft invincible Brutality of that People, they at laft gave too much
Way to the Dictates of Anger and Violence. Captain *Smith*,
in particular, thought, that there had long fince been given
juft Occafion, to profecute them with War, and entirely to
conquer and fubdue them; and he now looked upon the
Maffacre, as rather an 'Advantage than Detriment, as it
would open the Eyes of the *Englifh*, and fet them upon their
Guard, and would give them juft Grounds for a War, even
to their utter Extirpation, and thereby contribute to the future Security and fpeedy Advancement of the Colony. And
this indeed feems to have been the general Opinion of the
Times. For the Company themfelves, in a Letter this
Year to the Governor and Council, declare, that they faw
fuch a Difpofition in Mens Minds, as made them think,
that this Addition of Price had endeared the Purchafe, and
that the Blood of thefe People would be the Seed of the

Planta-

1622.

Sir *Francis Wyat,* Governor.

Plantation. And, for their own Parts, they thought it a Sin againſt their dead Brethren, who had loſt their Lives in it, to abandon or give over the Enterpriſe, till they had fully ſettled and got Poſſeſſion of the Country.

✗ CAPTAIN *Smith* likewiſe, upon this Occaſion, offered his Service to the Company. He propoſed, that they ſhould tranſport him, with an hundred Soldiers and thirty Sailors, and all proper Proviſions and Ammunition; and ſhould give him a Bark of an hundred Tons, with Means and Materials, to build ſix or ſeven Shallops, to tranſport his Men from Place to Place, as Occaſion required; and then he undertook, to form a flying Camp, and to range about and torment the *Indians,* till he either obliged them to quit the Country, or brought them into ſuch Fear and Subjection, that every Man ſhould follow his Buſineſs in Peace and Security. And as to the Support and Subſiſtence of this Party, he thought, if his Majeſty were truly informed of the Neceſſity and Benefit of the thing, he would give the Cuſtoms of *Virginia* for a time. For, without ſome ſuch Method, it was much to be doubted, whether there would come, in a few Years, either Cuſtom, or any thing elſe, from thence to *England.* And he doubted not, but that the Planters would, according to their ſeveral Abilities, contribute towards ſo uſeful and neceſſary a Deſign. But he inſiſted, that the Governors ſhould not be permitted, by Virtue of their Authority, to take his Men away, or any thing elſe, to employ them, as they thought proper. And he farther promiſed, to make the beſt Uſe of his Experience, as well within the Limits of *Virginia,* as *New-England,* to bring them both into one Map, with all the Countries, that lay between them. As to the Reward of his own Pains and Danger, he aſked not any thing, but what he could raiſe, from the proper Labour of the Savages themſelves.

THIS Propoſal was well approved by moſt, that heard it; but ſuch were their Diviſions and Confuſion at that time, that he could obtain no other Anſwer, but that the Expence would be too great, and their Stock was exhauſted; and they thought, the Planters ſhould do ſomething of that Nature themſelves, if they could find ſufficient Means to effect it. However, he was given to underſtand, as he tells us, that if he would undertake the thing upon his own private Account, he might have the Company's Leave; provided, they might have half the Pillage. But he rejected this Intimation with Scorn; thinking, that all the Pillage of thoſe poor and naked Barbarians, except a little Corn, to be had at ſome times of the Year, would not, in twenty Years, amount to twenty Pounds. But I ſuſpect, that all
this

this only paffed in Converfation, or was at moft privately
talked at their Courts, without ever being brought regularly before the Company. For I have the Company's Records of that time, now in my Poffeffion, in which there
is not the leaft Mention of any fuch Propofition, altho'
things of a trivial and much more minute Nature are moft
exactly entered. Neither does it feem confiftent with the
Character of the Company and its Leaders, who gave a
fair Courfe and Debate to all Propofitions offered, and were
rather profufe in their Expences for the good of the Colony,
than lying upon the Catch for little Advantages and mean
Gains. However, the Captain's open Nature, and Simplicity of Honefty, might be blinded by crafty and defigning
Men, and eafily made believe, that that came from the
Company, which had really never come under their Cog-
nifance, or been laid before them.

In the mean time, the Colony in *Virginia*, being much
frightened at this lamentable and unexpected Difafter, refolved to abandon all the petty Plantations, and to draw the
People together, to make good five or fix of the beft and
moft defenfible Places. Nay, fo great was the Terror and
Alarm, that many Perfons were urgent, to abandon *James*
River, and to retire to the *Eaftern Shore*, where they might
eafily fortify and defend themfelves againft the Indians. And
for quieting thofe, who were many, the Governor was
obliged to hold fome Councils, under Colour of confidering
their Propofal, but yet with a full Refolution, never to take
fo unadvifed and deftructive a Step. However, many Plantations were quitted by Authority; and all the People were
drawn together to *Shirley Hundred*, *Flower-de-Hundred*,
James-Town, with *Pafpahey* and the Plantations right oppofite, *Kicquotan*, and *Southampton Hundred*; to which
were added, by the Obftinacy and Refolution of their Owners, Mr. *Samuel Jordan*'s Plantation, now called *Jordan*'s
Point, and *Newport's-News*. For Want of Boats and other
Conveniencies, it was impoffible, on fuch a fudden, to fecure and bring off all their Cattle and other Goods, which
were, for the moft part, after their Departure, burnt, ruined, and deftroyed by the *Indians*. But Mr. *Gookin*, at
Newport's-News, refufed to obey the Order of Government,
and draw off his People; and having got together thirty
five of all Sorts, he fecured his Plantation, and defended
himfelf and Company againft all their Affaults and Incur-
fions. The like was alfo done by Mr. *Samuel Jordan*; and
by Mrs. *Proctor*, a proper, civil, and modeft Gentlewo-
man, who, with an heroic Spirit, defended her Eftate for
a Month, till fhe, with all with her, were obliged, by the
Englifh

1622.

Sir Francis
Wyat, Go-
vernor.

Englifh Officers, to go with them, and to leave their Subftance to the Havock and Spoil of the Enemy.   Mr. *Edward Hill* alfo, at *Elifabeth-City*, altho' much Mifchief
was done to his Cattle, yet did himfelf alone defend his
Houfe, whilft all his Men were fick and unable to give him
any Affiftance.

CAPTAIN *Thomas Newce*, Deputy and Superintendant
of the Company's Lands, forefeeing the Difficulties and
Famine, that muft neceffarily enfue, caufed as much Corn
as poffible, to be planted at *Elifabeth-City*, where he commanded; whilft others deftroyed even that, which had
been before planted, fearing, it might be of Service to the
Indians, and trufted wholly to Relief by Trade or from
England, which had ever been one of the principal Caufes
of their Miferies.   For, Supplies from *England* were very
precarious, and liable to many Accidents and Difappointments, and had been, formerly at leaft, very ftingily afforded :   And the Trade for Corn; with the Natives, was
ufually carried on by Men of Subftance, to their own Gain
and Advantage, and as it was complained, efpecially by
the Company's Enemies, to the great Oppreffion of the
poor and fuffering Inhabitants.   But Captain *Newce* called
all his next adjoining Neighbours to his Houfe, and omitted
nothing, to relieve their Wants and Neceffities.   He likewife, with all Speed, entrenched himfelf; mounted three
Pieces of Ordinance; funk a Well of frefh Water; and
foon put himfelf into a Pofture of Defence, above the Fear
of any Danger or Affault from the Enemy.   In all thefe
Works, he acted the Part of a Sawyer, a Carpenter, or a
Labourer; till he brought upon himfelf many Sickneffes,
and at laft a Dropfy, to the very great Grief of his Family, and of all under his Government.   The latter End of
June, Sir *George Yeardley*, in his Way to *Accomack*, ftaid
three or four Days with Captain *Newce*, being accompanied by the Council, and many other gay Gentlemen.   The
Captain, being oppreffed with fo large a Company, complained, to one of the chief among them, of the Want of
Provifions.   Whereupon he gave the Word to the reft,
and they entered the Fields of Corn near the Fort, which
were the beft guarded and preferved from the Ravage of
the Enemy, and altho' the Ears were fcarce half grown,
they devoured and made a miferable Wafte among it.   But
it muft be obferved, that this Particular relies wholly on
the Authority of Captain *Smith*, who was himfelf abfent,
and whofe Relations of thefe times were chiefly taken from
Perfons of the opponent Faction.   They are therefore always
to be fomewhat fufpected ; and efpecially in this Story, as it
- clafhes

clafhes fo much with Sir *George Yeardley*'s general Character, and the univerfal Love and Efteem, which he obtained
from the Colony. However Captain *Newce* was certainly a
Man of great Goodnefs and Merit. As long as he had any
thing, his Company fhared it equally with him ; and when
all was fpent, being obliged to live on Crabs and Oyfters,
they fell into a very weak and feeble Condition. Yet
Captain *Newce* diftributed among them, as he faw Occafion, a little Milk and Rice, which he ftill had left ; and
behaved himfelf, in all things, with fuch a fatherly Tendernefs and Care, that he obtained the Reputation, of being the Commander, throughout the whole Country, that
took the moft continual Pains for the Publick, and did the
leaft Good for himfelf, of all others. On the 9th of *September*, his Men were attacked at their Labours, by the
Indians, which was the firft Affault, they had made fince
the Maffacre, and four were flain. The Captain, altho'
extremely fick, fallied forth to engage them ; but they,
hiding themfelves in the Corn and other lurking Places,
efcaped his Vengeance. Soon after, this worthy Gentleman died ; and the Company, in Confideration of his, as
well as her own Merit, granted his Widow a Moiety of
the Labours of the Tenants, due to his Place, till another
Perfon fhould be appointed to fucceed him. And afterwards, in a Letter to the Governor and Council, they ordered her the whole Profits of their Labour for the following Year, with no fmall Commendation of, her Virtue and
Defert.

CAPTAIN *Ralegh Chrofhaw* was, all this while, at *Patowmack*, with one Man. He had not been long there,
before *Opechancanough* fent two Bafkets of Beads to *Japazaus*, the King, to kill them ; affuring him of the Slaughter he had made, and that before the End of two Moons,
there fhould not be an *Englifhman* left in all their Countries. *Japazaus* difclofed this to Captain *Chrofhaw*, who
expreffed great Scorn and Contempt for *Opechancanough*,
whofe Treachery and Cowardife he had feen fufficiently
tried by Captain *Smith*, when he took him Prifoner, at the
Head of feven hundred Men. After two Days Deliberation, *Japazaus* made Anfwer, that the *Englifh* were his
Friends, and *Opitchapan*, the *Indian* Emperor, his Brother ;
and that therefore, there fhould be no Blood fhed between
them, by his Means. He alfo returned the Prefent of
Beads, advifing the *Pamunkeys* to come no more into his
Country, left the *Englifh*, though againft his Will, fhould
do them a Mifchief. But the *Englifh* Colony concluded
Chrofhaw undoubtedly dead, till Captain *Hamer* came to *Patowmack*,

1622.

towmack, in *June*, to trade for Corn; where he found him safe, and was kindly entertained by both him and the King. By the King's Direction and Affiftance, he affaulted and took a Town, where was fome Corn; and at his Departure, he left Captain *Chrofhaw* four Men more. *Chrofhaw* receiving continual Alarms, retired with thefe to a Place of Advantage, where, with the Affiftance of the *Patowmacks*, he foon fortified himfelf, fufficiently againft all fuch wild Affailants. Soon after, he was vifited by Captain *Newce*; from whom underftanding the miferable State of the Colony, he offered, if they would fend him a bold Shallop, with Provifion to trade, and proper Arms and Men, to provide them Corn fufficient, after the getting in their Corn; but as yet, it being but the latter End of *June*, he told him, there was little or none in all the Country.

Newce communicating this to the Governor and others, Captain *Ifaac Maddifon* was fent, with thirty odd Men, in a Ship and fmall Bark. His Commiffion from the Governor, exprefly charges and requires him, to affift and defend their Friends and Confederates, the *Patowmacks*, againft the common Enemy; to protect them and their Corn, to his utmoft Power; and in his Carriage, as well towards them as the Enemy, to difcharge, faithfully and circumfpectly, the great Truft, repofed in him, as he would anfwer the fame, at his Peril. But juft at that time, Captain *Chrofhaw* had received a Letter from Mrs. *Boyce*, a Woman of Figure, who was Prifoner, with nineteen more, at *Pamunkey*. Having fome Profpect of recovering their Liberty, he went to *James-Town*, with two Chiefs of the *Patowmacks*, to follicit the Governor, and to enter into Meafures for their Releafe. But before this, *Opechancanough* had returned an infolent Anfwer to the Governor's Meffage, concerning reftoring the *Englifh* Captives, and had treated the King's Picture with great Difhonour and Contumely. The *Englifh* alfo diffembled their Intents, and pretending Peace and Friendfhip, invited the *Indians* back, to plant their Corn at their ufual Habitations; which being now grown up, fo as to make the Lofs irreparable by a new Crop, the Governor was preparing, with five hundred Men, to make a fharp and vigorous War upon them, efpecially upon *Opechancanough* and his bloody Adherents; and hoped, by deftroying their Corn, and other Means, to drive them quite out of the Country. As to the lawful Emperor, *Opitchapan*, who by this time indeed was only an Emperor in Name, he feems very greatly to have difapproved of the Maffacre. For I find him, early the next Year, fending *Chanco*, *Pace*'s *Chriftian* Convert, who difcovered the *In-*

dian

1622.

Sir *Francis*
Wyat, Go-
vernor.

dian Conspiracy, to assure Sir *Francis Wyat*, that if he would send ten or twelve Men, he would give up the rest of the *English* Prisoners, that were in his Possession; and would also deliver his Brother *Opechancanough*, the Author of the Massacre, into the Hands of the *English*, either alive or dead. Captain *Tucker* was accordingly sent upon this Service, but without the desired Success. However *Opitchapan* sent back Mrs. *Boyce*, naked and unapparaled, in Manner and Fashion, like one of their *Indian* Queens.

For these Reasons, the Governor was unwilling, at that Juncture, to hear of any Treaty with *Opechancanough*; and Captain *Chroshaw's* Journey to *James-Town* was in vain; but his Absence from *Patowmack* had a very unhappy Consequence, on another Account. For, *Maddison* was a Man of a jealous and timorous Nature; and not liking to live among the *Savages*, as *Chroshaw* did, he built himself a strong House, within *Chroshaw's* Fort, and there soon rose great Coldness and Reserve between him and the *Patowmacks*. There was also then at *Patowmack* an exile King, who was inwardly exasperated at *Japazaus*, because he would not assist him in the Recovery of his Kingdom. This subtle and malicious Barbarian did therefore, in Revenge, forge a Plot, as if *Japazaus* and the *Patowmacks* were in Treaty with *Opechancanough*, how to cut off and destroy the *English* there. And to give his Lye the greater Credit and Air of Probability, he wrested and applied several Circumstances, that had lately happened, to this Design. *Maddison*, naturally fearful and suspicious, was alarmed at this, and made his Men stand punctually to their Arms. Some time after, under Pretence of Business, he sent for the King to his strong House; where having locked him, his Son, and four others up, and set a Guard of five *Englishmen* upon the House, he fell on the Town, with the rest of his Company, and slew thirty or forty, Men, Women, and Children. The poor King, being surprised at such an unexpected Assault, called out, and begged him to cease from so undeserved a Cruelty. But he gave not over the Execution, till he had slain, or put to Flight, all in the Town. Then he returned, and taxed the King of Treachery, who denied it bitterly, and told him, it was some Contrivance of those, who wished his Destruction, for being a Friend to the *English*. After that, *Maddison* led him, his Son, and two others to his Ship, promising to set them at Liberty, as soon as his Men were all safely shipped; and the King, very readily and effectually, ordered his Subjects, not to shoot at, or annoy the *English*, whilst they were going on board. But notwithstanding this,

Mad-

Maddifon, contrary to all good Faith, carried them Prifoners to *James-Town* ; where they lay, till the *October*
following, when they were carried home by Captain *Hamer*, who took a Quantity of Corn for their Ranfom.
However, this perfidious Dealing did not pafs off, entirely
without Notice or Animadverfion. For, Mr. *John Pountis*,
as a Cafe properly belonging to his Office of Vice-Admiral,
afterwards lodged a Complaint againft fome Perfons, who
going out to trade with the *Indians*, under Pretence of
Friendfhip, and in the Governor's Name, had feifed their
Perfons, and fometimes taken their Lives, and fometimes
their Goods, for nothing, or at their own Rates, contrary
to all Laws human and divine, and to the Difhonour of
God's Name, of the King, and the whole *Englifh* Nation.
Altho' this was conceived in general Terms, fo as to reach
all other Perfons, guilty of the fame Crime, yet we are
told, in the Aƈt of Court itfelf, that it was chiefly levelled
againft *Maddifon* and *Hamer*. And fome Examinations a-
gainft them were accordingly taken ; but by Reafon of *Hamer*'s Sicknefs, and *Maddifon*'s Abfence, who foon after
returned to *England*, the Suit dropped, and never proceeded to full Trial.

THIS rafh and unadvifed Aƈtion of *Maddifon* (not to
call it by any worfe Name) was of very ill Confequence to
the Colony. For they were thereby cut off from all Hopes
and Pretenfions, to trade for Corn on that River ; which
was then their only Refuge and Dependance, as the *Indians*, in all the other Parts of the Country, were in an
open and declared War with them, and as they themfelves
had not attempted any thing of a Crop, left the Corn,
when grown up, fhould give Means and Opportunity for
Affaults and Ambufcades. Captain *Chrofhaw*'s Defign was
alfo quite defeated ; who intended to make *Japazaus* a proper Inftrument and Ally againft *Opechancanough*. For he
had at his Command above two hundred fighting Men, in
the Town of *Patowmack* ; and was, befides, a Perfon of
great Intereft and Authority, throughout the whole River,
being a Kind of petty Emperor there, and unwilling to
own Subjeƈtion to the other Emperors, whom he always
affeƈted to treat, rather as Brethren than Superiors. It was
therefore probably thought, that *Chrofhaw* would have
fucceeded in his Scheme, and might eafily have made him
rife againft a Power, which he was before jealous of, and
always looked upon, as ufurped and oppreffive.

HOWEVER Captain *Henry Spilman*, who had been preferved by the Means of *Pocahontas*, and had lived feveral
Years at *Patowmack*, relying on his Intereft and Acquaintance

tance with them, ventured to go thither, in a Bark, with
twenty fix Men, to trade for Corn. But himfelf, with
twenty one more, were furprifed and flain by the *Pafcoti-*
cons, the greateft People in thofe Parts. They immediately boarded the Veffel in their Canoes, and entered fo faft,
that the five Men, left to guard her, were in the utmoft
Amazement, till a Sailor gave fire to a Piece of Ordinance
at Random; the bare Report whereof fo frightened the
poor Savages, that they leaped overboard, and forgetting
their Canoes, fwarm afhore. Soon after, they heard a great
Noife among them, and faw a Man's Head thrown down
the Bank; whereupon they weighed Anchor, and returned.
And thus died this unfortunate Gentleman, who was of a
good Family in *England*. He had, three Years before,
been tried and found guilty, of depreciating and under-
mining the Governor's Authority, by telling *Opechancanough*,
that a Great Man (meaning the Earl of *Warwick*) would
foon come, and take his Place. For which Crime, they
thought it a Mercy to fpare his Life; but they however
degraded him from his Captainfhip, and condemned him,
to be a Servant to the Colony for feven Years, in Quality
of Interpreter; for which Office he was peculiarly fitted,
by having long lived, and been very converfant, among the
Indians.

Edward Waters, one of the three, that ftaid in the Iflands
of *Bermudas*, and found the great Block of Ambergreafe,
dwelling in *Virginia*, at the time of the Maffacre, was
himfelf, together with his Wife, taken and kept Prifoners
by the *Nandfamonds*. But this Fall, fome *Englifh*, near
Newport's-News, were furprifed in fo great a Storm, that
altho' the Men faved their Lives, the Boat was loft; which
was caft, by the Winds and Waves, upon the Shore of
Nandfamond. The *Indians*, finding it, were fo bufied,
with Songs, and Dances, and Invocations, according to
their Manner of Triumph, that *Waters* and his Wife found
Means, to get fecretly into one of their Canoes, and croffed
the River, nine or ten Miles over, to *Kicquotan*; where
they were received with no lefs Joy and Wonder by the
Englifh, than their Efcape gave Anger and Vexation to the
Indians.

SHORTLY after, Sir *George Yeardley* and Captain *Powel*,
each with a Company of Gentlemen Volunteers, went to
feek the Enemy. But all being fled, except three, which
Captain *Powel* met by Chance and flew, they burnt their
Houfes, deftroyed every thing, they could find, and fo returned. Three hundred Soldiers, the beft, they could
chufe, were, not long after, raifed and embarked in con-

venient

venient Veffels, under the Condu&t of Sir *George Yeardley*, with all things neceffary for the Expedition. They went firft to *Nandfamond*; where the *Indians* fet fire to their own Houfes, fpoiled all they could, and then fled away, with what they could carry off. So that the *Englifh* had no Opportunity to make any Slaughter of them. But their Corn being newly gathered, they feized all, they could find; burnt the Houfes, which the Inhabitants had in their Hurry left unburnt; and fo departed. From thence they went to *Pamunkey*, the chief Seat of *Opechancanough*. He did not appear himfelf; but the *Indians* there feemed exceedingly aftonifhed, and promifed to bring them all the *Englifh*, yet living, and to reftore their Arms, and what-ever elfe they had; pretending, much to defire Peace, and to give them any Satisfaction in their Power. But this was only a Device, to procraftinate the Time, till they could convey away their Corn from all other Places, except where the *Englifh* were quartered. At length, the *Englifh*, perceiving their Defign, feifed on the Corn in their Power, burnt their Houfes, and purfued them into the Woods. But they fled before them, and eafily efcaped, not without Contempt and Infult. For fome lurked about in Ambufh, and difcharged fome Shot out of *Englifh* Pieces, which hurt and wounded feveral diforderly Stragglers. After this, Sir *George* returned, with a thoufand Bufhels of Corn, and each of the Soldiers had three Bufhels a piece. Captain *Smith* tells us, that they were however obliged to pay ten Shillings a Bufhel, before they received it, for Freight and other Charges of the Expedition. But the Governor and Council's Letters to the Company, an Authority not to be contefted, exprefly fay, that Sir *George Yeardley* freely em-ployed his own Shipping, Shallops, Mariners, and Servants, without any Recompence or Freight at all. But this is not the only Inftance, in which that Gentleman's A&tions are mifreprefented in *Smith*'s Hiftory. For, he immediately pre-ceeding and coming after Captain *Argall*'s Government, and having a Commiffion to examine and punifh his Of-fences, became a peculiar Mark of Hatred and Calumny to that Fa&tion. The fame Letters inform us, that three thoufand Bufhels of Corn more were taken from the Ene-my, by Force or Trade, and brought in, by different Par-ties of Men. By thefe, and other fuch fmall Inroads and Depredations, the *Indians* were reduced to great Want and Neceffity that Winter, and endured no fmall Mifery and Famine. So that many of the *Englifh*, in Confidence of their Weaknefs, and Inability to hurt them, returned to their former Habitations. For, befides plundering and ruin-

ing

ing their Corn, and other Ways of diftreffing and deftroying them, the Governor and Council, in the aforefaid Letter, affure the Company, that more *Indians* were flain that Autumn and Winter, than had ever fallen by the Hands of the *Englifh*, put them all together, from the firft Beginning and Settlement of the Colony.

THE Earl of *Warwick,* not fatisfied with the Spoils of *Virginia,* had alfo, by his Intereft and Intrigues, procured his Follower and Dependent, Captain *Nathaniel Butler,* to be fent Governor of *Bermudas* for three Years; where he exercifed the fame bare-faced Oppreffion and Extortion, that Captain *Argall* had done here. But from the petty Offence of plundering the Colony, he proceeded to a higher Crime and Mifdemeanor, and committed fome Pillage upon a *Spanifh* Wreck. This incenfed *Gondomar,* and the Lords of the Privy Council fent a fharp Order to the Company, to make an immediate and ftrict Enquiry into the Matter. The Time of his Government being therefore now expired, a Commiffion was given to Mr. *Bernard,* who was going over to fucceed him, to enquire into the Affair of the *Spanifh* Wreck, as well as the Truth of many other Complaints and Allegations, fent over againft him to *England.* But, as had been done in Captain *Argall's* Cafe, a Bark was difpatched from *Barnftaple,* in which he efcaped, juft before the Arrival of the new Governor, and came to *Virginia.* He left thofe Iflands in a moft miferable Plight, being reduced to Beggary and Ruin, by his Rapines and Extortions; and coming hither in the Extremity of Winter, he found the Colony labouring under the Diftreffes and unhappy Confequences of the Maffacre. Sir *Francis Wyat* received and entertained him, with great Hofpitality and Good-manners; but his Behaviour here was infamoufly lewd and riotous. Among other things, he demanded to be admitted of the Council, and grievoufly refented his being refufed, altho' he could fhew no Colour of Right or Title to it. After about three Month's Stay, and having gone up as high as *Chickahominy,* where, like a common Robber or free Booter, he fell upon, and made Spoil of Lady *Dale's* Cattle, he fet Sail, and returned for *England.*

BUT before this, in the Beginning of the Summer, there had been fet afoot a moft unhappy Affair for the Company; which gave it, as it were, a fettling Blow, and not without fome Face of Reafon, was the Occafion of greater Clamours and Animofities than ever. It hath been frequently related, how the King took all Opportunities of grinding the Company and infant Colony, by laying op-

preffive

preffive and illegal Impofitions on Tobacco. This he
did, partly out of his natural Abhorrence and Averfion to
that Weed, but chiefly out of a Defire of Gain. For,
with a Conjunction not unufual to be found in Men's Characters, Profufion, and a voracious Appetite after Money,
had met together in that Prince's Nature. In all thefe
Exactions, Sir *Lionel Cranfield* had been his principal Inftrument. He had been at firft a Merchant of *London*, and
then an Officer in the Cuftoms, from whence he was introduced to Court, as a Projector; which, in the Language of thofe Times, fignified a Perfon, who could furnifh Expedients to the Minifters, to raife Money, in the
Vacancy, and without the Affiftance, of Parliament. He
was a very wife and dextrous Officer; and in this Execrable
Function, had been fo ufeful and fuccefsful, that, together
with the Advantage of having married one of *Buckingham*'s
Relations (an extraordinary Merit then, and an infallible
Road to the higheft Preferments) he had rifen, before this
time, to the Dignity of Earl of *Middlefex*, and Lord High
Treafurer of *England*. He was himfelf an ancient Ad-
venturer in the Affair of *Virginia*; and well knew, how
uneafy they were, under the Preffure of the Monopolies,
Garbling, and other illegal Patents. He therefore refolved
to try, whether he could not make the Company confent
to their own Oppreffion, and fqueeze out of them a greater
Profit and Revenue to his Majefty, by making a particular
Contract with themfelves.

To this End, he firft broached the Matter privately to
Sir *Edwin Sandys*; offering a Grant, to the two Companies
of *Virginia* and the *Somer-Iflands*, for the fole Importation
of Tobacco into the Realms of *England* and *Ireland*, referving to his Majefty a certain valuable Rent. This he
did, with large Profeffions of his Love and Affection to the
Colony of *Virginia*, whereof he was an ancient Counfellor;
and declared, that, befides the perfonal Duty of his Place,
as Lord High Treafurer, his principal Motive herein was
the Profit and Advancement of the Colonies. Sir *Edwin*
profeffed his Ignorance, in Affairs of that Nature; but
after fome Thought, he confulted with Sir *Arthur Ingram*,
another Member of the *Virginia* Company, then prefent,
but a faft Creature and Retainer to the Lord Treafurer.
At length, confidering, that Tobacco was a deceiveable
Weed, and the Ufe of it wholly founded on a Humour,
which, might foon vanifh into Smoke, and come to nothing, he told his Lordfhip, that to fettle any great Rent
in Money, upon fuch an uncertain Commodity, might
foon bankrupt the Companies, and utterly ruin the Plantations.

tions. Wherefore, he conceived it much the fafer Way for the Companies, to yield his Majefty a certain Proportion, in Specie, out of the Tobacco itfelf; whereof, he thought, they might be induced to give a fourth Part, provided they might be difcharged from all other Burthens upon it. But his Lordfhip, falling into a Calculation, told him, that without the Grant of a Third, there could not be that Revenue raifed to his Majefty, as was expected; and for the old Cuftom, of fix Pence a Pound upon Roll, and four Pence upon Leaf Tobacco, it was already granted to his Majefty's Farmers, and could not be reverfed.

AFTER this, Sir *Edwin Sandys*, by his Lordfhip's Command, communicated this Propofal to the Lords *Southampton* and *Cavendifh*, and the two Deputies; who having imparted it to their Councils, brought it before the Companies. Such a Contract, if it could be concluded on any reafonable Terms, was certainly of very great and vifible Advantage to the Companies and Colonies. For it would enable them, by having the whole Commodity in their own Hands, to exclude all foreign Tobacco, and to raife, or at leaft keep up, the Price of their own; and would as well eafe them from the Extortions and Infults of other monopolifing Patents, as fecure them from any farther Impofitions. For the Court, as the Colonies advanced in Strength, was ftill loading them with new Impofitions, and kept them always ftaggering, and fcarce able to go forward, under the Burthen of Taxes and Impofts. And this was then done, folely by the King's Authority, without granting Parliaments their undoubted Right, of giving Money, and laying new Duties on the Subject. And what was a notorious, and (if the facred Character of Kings and Minifters would allow the Expreffion) an impudent Breach of Faith, it was done againft the plaineft and moft exprefs Words and Tenor of former Grants; which was, beyond Doubt, the prefent Cafe of the *Virginia* Company, as hath been before obferved and recited.

HOWEVER, the Companies, fitting down peaceably under thefe Oppreffions, readily embraced this Overture, and appointed each a Committee, to treat with the Lord Treafurer about it. But in the Progrefs of the Bufinefs, his Lordfhip was ftill fqueezing in new Hardfhips upon them; and particularly furprifed and fhocked them with a Propofal, that for each of the two Years, then next enfuing, the Companies fhould be obliged, to bring in fixty thoufand Weight of *Spanifh* Tobacco, or otherwife permit forty thoufand Weight to be imported by fome other. This Propofition feemed very grievous to the Committees, and croffed

one

one of their chief Purpofes. They therefore replied : That no fuch Obligation was laid on the former Patentees for the fole Importation of Tobacco : That the Example of obliging Men to bring in any foreign Commodity, whereof there was fufficient of the Growth of the King's own Dominions, would feem very ftrange and accountable ; and fuch a thing, as they thought, had not been heard of, in any Part of the World : That to prohibit the planting Tobacco in *England*, and yet to command the importing fo large a Quantity from a foreign Country (efpecially when it was confeffedly a great Drain of the Cafh of the Nation) would be very grievous to the *Englifh* Subject ; and was fo odious a thing, that they were afhamed to be concerned in it : That the Quantity of fixty thoufand Weight of *Spanifh* Tobacco was very exceffive, and more than had been imported, in divers Years, when there was no Reftraint at all : That fo large a Proportion (the whole Import of Tobacco into *England*, upon an Average for the laft feven Years, being only an hundred forty two thoufand and eighty five Pounds Weight a Year) muft utterly abafe the Price of the Plantation Tobacco, as manifeftly appeared from that Year's Experience ; fo that the Colonies would part with a third of their Tobacco to the King, without any Retribution in the Price of the reft, as was at firft propofed : And that, in excluding all *Spanifh* Tobacco, there could be no Room for Fraud or Error ; whereas, under the Colour of fo large an Importation, it would be impoffible to prevent the running and ftealing in a much greater Quantity.

THESE Objections were certainly very fharp and home, and did not a little expofe the partial and moft unpatriot Meafures of the Court. But it was the Misfortune of that Time, that the Company dealt much in Reafon, and the Courtiers in Command. They were therefore peremptorily told, that this was a Point of fuch Importance, that it could not be difpenfed with, without diffolving the whole Contract. For we muft remember, that the *Spanifh* Match was ftill on Foot ; and therefore his Majefty would facrifice fo large an Intereft of his own Subjects to that Nation, to gratify and oblige his good Friend and Ally, the King of *Spain* ; who had been now, for many Years, bubbling and abufing him, to the open Scorn and Mockery of all *Europe*. Befides which, it is not to be fuppofed, that *Gondomar*, who, about this time, bore a very great Sway in the Affairs of *England*, would let flip fuch an Opportunity, of acquiring fo great a Profit to his Country. And indeed we are told by Mr. *Oldys*, that the Obftruction of thefe Plantations, was a main Branch of the Aims and Endeavours of that *Spanifh*
Buffoon ;

Buffoon ; and that he oppofed all Voyages to the *Weft-Indies*,
and particularly croffed thefe Undertakings of *Virginia* and
Bermudas, left from them there fhould afterwards arife ano-
ther *England* in *America*, of equal Dread and Annoyance to
New Spain, as that in *Europe* was to the Old. But the
Company, having had fome Gleams of Hope, and dreading
nothing fo much, as falling into their former Calamities and
Oppreffions, did at laft, after much Difpute and Contefta-
tion, confent to this Article ; and the whole Contract was
concluded and agreed upon, chiefly on thefe Conditions.
For I fhall in this, as I have done in other Cafes, take the
Liberty, for Brevity's Sake, only to give the main Subftance
of Matters, and to leave out fuch Points, as are immaterial, and of little or no Confequence to be known.

I. THAT the fole Importation of Tobacco, into the
Realms of *England* and *Ireland*, fhould be granted to the
Virginia and *Somer-Iflands* Companies, by Patent under the
Great Seal of *England* ; which Grant fhould be drawn and
conftrued, in the moft beneficial Manner for the Companies Behoof, and the Advancement of the Colonies ; his Majefty's Profit, hereafter recited, only referved.

II. THAT his Majefty fhould, by Proclamation, prohibit all others from importing, as alfo from planting Tobacco in *England* and *Ireland*, during the faid Contract, under grievous Penalties ; and that what was already planted,
fhould, by Virtue of the former Proclamation, be confif-
cated.

III. THAT his Majefty, and the Lord High Treafurer,
fhould take all proper Methods, for preventing and confif-
cating all Tobacco, unduly imported ; and fhould endeavour, in all Points, to keep up effectually to the true Intent
and Meaning of this Contract ; and particularly, that his
Majefty fhould grant no Licences to Retailers of Tobacco,
that the Market might ftill remain free and open, as it had
hitherto done.

IV. THAT in Confideration hereof, as alfo for that the
Companies fhould be difcharged from all other Payments on
Tobacco (excepting only the ancient Cuftom, in the Book
of Rates, of fix Pence a Pound on Roll Tobacco, and four
Pence upon Leaf) the faid Companies fhould pay to his Ma-
jefty the clear Proceed of a full third Part of all Tobacco,
Yearly imported and landed by them in the faid two Realms :
Provided neverthelefs, that they fhould not be obliged to
import more Tobacco of the Growth of the two Colonies,
than they themfelves thought proper.

V. THAT

V. THAT the Lord High Treafurer fhould caufe the
Cuftom to be reduced to a Medium for feven Years laft
paft, ending at *Michaelmas,* 1621 ; wherein fhould be fpecified, how much was Roll Tobacco, and how much
Leaf, becaufe of the different Cuftom ; and that the Whole
fhould be reduced to a certain Sum of Money, whereof one
Third to be paid by the King, for his Part, and two Thirds
by the Companies, and the Cuftomers to make no farther
Demand on any Tobacco, either imported or exported.

VI. THAT his Majefty fhould be difcharged from Payment of Freight, and all other previous Charges; but that
immediately upon the Arrival of the faid Tobacco (at which
time his Majefty's Intereft therein would commence) he
fhould bear the third Part of all Charges, for landing, houfing, keeping, and tranfporting by Land, Sea, or frefh Water, into divers Parts; as alfo his third Part of all Law-fuits,
of the Salaries of all Officers, Agents, Factors, and Servants; and in general, of all Matters and Bufineffes whatfoever, incident to the faid Tobacco, or Contract.

VII. THAT all the Tobacco imported, fhould be configned into fuch Hands, as fhould be appointed by the faid
Companies ; who fhould, in their General Courts, have the
fole Nomination of all Officers, Agents, Factors, Minifters,
and Servants, and the entire Management of the faid Tobacco : Yielding to his Majefty, a true and perfect Account
thereof, and paying the clear Profits, which fhould become
due to his Majefty for his Third, and come into their Hands :
In which Account the third of all Charges fhould be allowed
and defalcated, as aforefaid.

VIII. THAT the Companies fhould be obliged to import, not above fixty thoufand, nor under forty thoufand
Weight of *Spanifh* Tobacco, for each of the firft two Years
of this Contract, and no longer : Upon Condition neverthelefs, that the King and State of *Spain* did not purpofely
(upon Knowledge of their being obliged to import fo large a
Quantity) raife the Cuftom, or impofe new Burthens and
Charges upon their Tobacco ; and on Condition likewife,
that the Price of Tobacco, at which it was then fold in *Spain,*
be not purpofely enhanced, and that the Markets be, in all
refpects, as free and open, as formerly they have been:
Provided alfo, if any of the faid Quantity of *Spanifh* Tobacco do, in any wife, mifcarry by Cafualties at Sea, that
in that Cafe, the faid Companies fhould not be bound, to
reftore and make good the Proportion fo loft, by any new
Provifion and Importation.

IX. THAT this Contract fhould commence at *Michaelmas,* 1622, and continue for the Space of feven Years, then
next enfuing.   THIS

THIS Contract was certainly very well and cautiously worded, by Sir *Edwin Sandys*, who drew it, and was indeed their conftant Draughtfman upon all fuch Occafions. But it was at laft efteemed a very hard and pinching Bargain upon the Trade; and as a certain noble Perfon expreffed it, was not to be looked upon as a pleafant Difh, well fauced and feafoned, but as a bitter Potion, which muft, of neceffity, be fwallowed down, for avoiding greater Evils. The Earl of *Southampton* therefore, earneftly defired the Company, duly to confider each Article, and not to fpare to give their beft Counfel and Advice, in fo weighty a Bufinefs, which fo nearly concerned themfelves and the Colonies, it being not only free, but demanded, as a Duty, from every Man, to fpeak his Mind boldly, as his own Reafon fhould fuggeft. But after a long Paufe, it appearing, that nothing more could be faid, than had formerly been delivered, his Lordfhip, at the Company's Requeft, put it to the Queftion, and it was ratified and confirmed, by an almoft unanimous Confent, one Hand only being held up againft it. After which, it was, by the Lord *Cavendifh*, their Governor, propofed to, and confirmed by the *Somer-Iflands* Company, with the like Unanimity. For the Adventurers in that Plantation, being about an hundred and twenty fix in Number, were all likewife Members of the *Virginia* Company.

BUT before the Bargain was throughly concluded and ratified by the Lord High Treafurer, he preffed in upon them an Obligation, to import the forty thoufand Weight of *Spanifh* Tobacco, in the beft *Varinas*, with a Promife (which however he did not keep) not to trouble them any farther, if that was granted. The Company therefore yielded to it; on Condition, that fuch a Quantity of beft *Varinas* could be procured. For there had been fome Years, when the whole Importation of that Kind of Tobacco into *Spain* did not amount to forty thoufand Weight. But if *Varinas* could not be had, they undertook (to give his Majefty and the Lord Treafurer Satisfaction) to import the reft of their Quantity, in the beft and moft coftly Sorts of *Spanifh* Tobacco. It will doubtlefs be very furprifing to every thinking Reader, to find a King thus load and opprefs his Subjects, with the Importation of a foreign Commodity, of no Ufe or Neceffity, but of mere Luxury and Wantonnefs, and that too, in the deareft and moft grievous Manner; efpecially when that Commodity might be fupplied by our own Colonies, and muft, in *Spain*, be paid for in hard Cafh, as the Cafe then was. But to account for fo unconfcionable a Proceeding, it muft ftill be obferved, that herein were anfwered the two grand Ends, which at that time lay neareft

1622.

Sir *Francis Wyat*, Governor.

to that Prince's Heart; fince by taking off their deareft Tobaccoes, he did the more oblige the *Spanifh* King and Nation, and threw more Money into their Pockets, out of his
Subjects Purfes (which was, in Truth, fo much clear Lofs
to the *Englifh* Nation) and did alfo, at the fame time, advance his own Profit and Revenue. For as the King was,
by the Contract, to have the clear Proceed of one Third
of all Tobacco imported, it was more to his Gain and Advantage, to have the beft *Spanifh* Tobaccoes, which would
then fell for eighteen or twenty Shillings a Pound, and fometimes more, than the Plantation Tobacco, which would
fcarcely fetch two and fix Pence a Pound.

T H E Affair of the Contract, being thus fettled and concluded, the next thing that fell under their Confideration,
was appointing proper Officers, with their Salaries; and the
refolving on a fteady Courfe, for the Management of the
Bufinefs. For this Purpofe, a Committee was appointed
out of both the Companies, confifting of the Earl of *Southampton*, the Lords *Cavendifh*, *Paget*, and *Houghton*, Sir
John Brooke, Sir *Edwin Sandys*, Sir *John Davers*, Meffirs.
Nicholas and *John Farrars*, the Deputies of the two Companies, Mr. *Samuel Wrote*, and others, Gentlemen and
Merchants, to the Number of twenty one in all. After a
whole Day's Confultation and Debate, they at laft agreed
upon all Matters; and the Lords *Southampton* and *Cavendifh*,
Treafurer and Governor of the Companies, reported the
Refult of their Deliberations, to their refpective Courts.
But firft, the Earl of *Southampton*, with much Candor and
Earneftnefs, entreated the *Virginia* Company, to deliver
their Opinions freely, either for, or againft, what he fhould
then propound; which (he faid) himfelf, the Council, and
Committee, had confulted upon, not with Intent to conclude or determine any thing, nor to prejudice the Courts
in their Judgment, but only the better to prepare the Bufinefs for their Confideration; looking upon themfelves, as
his Lordfhip expreffed it, only as Servants to the Court.

A F T E R which Declaration, he proceeded and told them,
that, as it was propofed, and in fome Meafure concluded,
in the Preparative Court, they judged it neceffary, that there
fhould be one principal Officer, by the Name of Director,
on whofe Sufficiency, Care, and Integrity, the whole Succefs of the Bufinefs did chiefly depend; and that they conceived the faid Director would well deferve, for his Salary of
that Year, five hundred Pounds. Next to him, was a Deputy: For without fuch an Affiftant, it would be impoffible
for the Director, to undergo all the Burthen of Bufinefs,
that would lie upon him. And to this Office they conceived
requifite

requisite an extraordinary Deal of Pains and Industry, and no small Sufficiency. The Third Officer was a Treasurer, to keep the Cash. But altho' the Offices of Deputy and Treasurer were distinct in themselves, and would require two Persons, yet the better to husband the Expences for that Year, they thought it best (according to the Resolution of the Preparative Court) to join them both in one Person, for the present. And to this Officer, they allotted a Salary of four hundred Pounds, for the current Year. Next they conceived it necessary, to have a Committee of, at least, eight able and judicious Persons, chosen out of the two Companies, for selling and disposing of their Tobaccoes, and for assisting the Director, with their Counsels, and Help, in the several Parts of his Office ; which would be very many and exceedingly weighty and important. And to these, they appointed a Salary of fifty Pounds, a Man. And besides these principal Officers, he told them, there would be necessary, two Cashiers, the one to be constantly resident in the Treasury, the other to receive and gather in the Monies ; a Book-keeper ; two Clerks ; a Sollicitor ; a Husband, to whom the Custody of the Warehouses should be committed ; and a Beadle ; with a House, for the Meetings of the Officers ; and Warehouses, for the Reception of the Tobacco. And the whole Amount of all these Salaries and Expences, was computed at two thousand Pounds a Year, which must be raised upon the Tobacco. But as the *Spanish* vastly exceeded the Plantation Tobacco in Price, it was agreed, that it should bear a double Proportion in the Rate of the Charges.

His Lordship farther told them, that they conceived it necessary, that there should be five hundred Pounds more set apart, for such contingent Expences, as should occasionally arise ; which Money, if it were not, by the Consent and Order of the Courts, expended for the Advantage and Improvement of the Price of Tobacco, was to be again repaid, to each Adventurer proportionably. And altho' this Sum, of twenty five hundred Pounds a Year, might to many seem very great and extraordinary ; yet, he said, considering, that five hundred Pounds was not to be expended, except for the evident Advantage of the Commodity ; and that, of the two thousand Pounds remaining, his Majesty was to bear one third Part, and the *Spanish* Tobacco a Proportion double to the rest, he conceived, it would be found no great Burthen upon the Plantations (whose Benefit was the grand Point in View) but such, as it was hoped, would be manifoldly repaid, by the Advancement of the Price. And as to the Officers Salaries, he declared it to be his Opinion, that they were far below the Pains, Care, and Charge, that they must, of necessity, be at.   THE

THE Earl of *Southampton* having thus finished his Report, there followed, for some time, a general Silence among the Adventurers. Whereupon his Lordship entreated them, freely to speak their Minds concerning all these things, and to declare, what and how they would have them done. And he repeated it again, that they esteemed themselves only as their Ministers or Servants, to prepare Business for the Court, in whom alone, was Power and Authority to determine and conclude Matters. He therefore earnestly entreated them, without Respect to himself, or any others, from whom those Propositions came, to declare their Opinions freely, especially concerning the Salaries, which, he perceived, was the grand Rock of Offence.

HEREUPON, Mr. *Robert Smith*, the Under-Chamberlain, said; that he thought, many able Gentlemen might be found, who, for Conscience Sake, would do the Business for far less Salaries. To which Sir *Edward Sackvil* replied ; that for his Part, he thought Men bound in Conscience, to give those whom they employed, some reasonable Satisfaction for their Labour and Pains ; and that he had found by Experience, that some Men, who had, for Conscience Sake, served the Company, had also, for Conscience Sake, undone it. But the Earl of *Southampton*, to soften the Quickness of Sir *Edward Sackvil's* Reply, and to encourage a Freedom of Debate, declared, that Mr. *Robert Smith* was a very worthy and honest Man ; and he thanked him, for speaking his Mind freely, desiring all others to do the same. After which, there ensued a short Debate ; and it was often observed, in the Progress of the Affair, that this was properly a Point of Merchandise, and not of settling Colonies ; and that it was not just or reasonable, to expect, that Men, fit to be trusted with, and capable to perform, so important a Business, should expend their whole Time and Labour, for the Advancement of other Mens Estates, without any Reward or Retribution at all. Mr. *Barker* also now said ; that, having been, many Years, a Member of that Court, he had never heard of such great Salaries, as four and five hundred Pounds a Year ; but that he had however heard of five hundred, and a thousand Pounds, deficient in the Accounts of some Officers, who did their Business for nothing. Soon after, the Earl of *Southampton* was called upon, to put the several Propositions to the Vote. But his Lordship said, he would once more read them over to them ; which having done, and no Man making any Objection, after a good Pause, he put the several things, concerning the Officers and Salaries, above related, distinctly to the Question, and they were all approved and confirmed.

THEY

THEY then proceeded to the Election of their Officers. Sir *Edwin Sandys* had been nominated, in a former Court, to the Place of Director; but he earneftly refufed it, as be- ing unexperienced in Matter of Trade and Merchandife, in which that Officer ought to have an exact Knowledge; and as he could not conftantly refide in Town, having a great Family in the Country. Befides which, he faid, he began, as he now grew old, to wax weak; and therefore purpofed, rather to withdraw from all Bufinefs of the World, than to engage himfelf farther in it. But the Court, efpe- cially the Earl of *Southampton* and the other Lords, being not fatisfied with this Excufe, earneftly preffed him, not to refufe a Place, wherein he might do fuch fingular Ser- vice to the Colonies; the whole Welfare of which did, al- moft entirely depend, upon the wife and upright Manage- ment of this Contract. No other Perfon therefore being fo much as named againft him, and himfelf rather not op- pofing, than confenting to accept the Place, he was, upon the Ballot, chofen Director, by having fixty five Balls for, and only five againft him. Mr. *John Farrar* had alfo, at the fame Court, been named to the joint Place of Deputy and Treafurer; but he likewife refufed, alledging, that the Company had laid fuch a Burthen of Bufinefs upon him, for now almoft four Years together, that he had been obli- ged to neglect his own private Affairs, which required his immediate and diligent Infpection. All which the Court acknowledged to be true; yet declared, they held him fo fit a Man for that Place, that they would not propofe any other to ftand in Election with him; and fo he was chofen, by having fixty eight Balls for, and only two againft him. They then made Choice of their Committee, and inferior Officers; and alfo added a Committee extraordinary, to be chofen out of the Council, without Salaries. They were not obliged to a conftant Attendance; but were only to give their Ad- vice and Affiftance to the Director and other acting Com- mittee, in Cafes of a high and extraordinary Nature. And this Committee confifted of the Lords *Paget* and *Maynard*, Sir *Edward Sackvil*, Sir *John Brooke*, Sir *John Davers*, Sir *Henry Mildmay*, Mr. *Thomas Gibbs*, Mr. *Samuel Wrote*, Mr. *John Smith*, and Mr. *Robert Smith*.

THE

THE

H I S T O R Y

O F

V I R G I N I A.

BOOK V.

1622.

Sir *Francis Wyat,* Governor.

I HAVE, in the former Book, been the more full and exact, in relating the Affair of the Officers and Salaries, as it afterwards became the Subject of much Wrangling and Contention. There was one Mr. *Samuel Wrote,* a Gentleman of Fortune and Diftinction in the Company, who had, ever till now, behaved himfelf with great Moderation, Judgment, and Induftry, and had therefore been elected of his Majefty's Council for *Virginia.* This Gentleman did fuddenly, in a fubfequent Court, held on the 4th of *December* this Year, break forth into much Violence, Indecency, and Opprobrioufnefs of Language; and endeavoured, to call into queftion and cancel, in an inferior and ordinary Court, what had been fettled and determined, by the Authority of a Great and General Quarter Court. He faid, that this Affair, which was of efpecial Confequence to the Company, had been propofed and paffed, without that due Preparation, which the Laws and Orders of the Company required in the like Cafes; that the lawful and regular Courfe had not been taken for preparing Matters, but they had been haftily fhuffled over; that the Bufinefs of the Salaries, in particular, was not duly committed, but

carried

carried fouly, and diforderly, and with much Art, furreptitioufly, and to private Ends; and that divers of the Company did, both then and fince, as well publickly as privately, in his Hearing, complain much againft thofe Proceedings, but that they durft not fpeak their Minds freely, becaufe they were overawed. He called the Laws of the Company Sir *Edwin Sandys's* Laws, becaufe that Gentleman had been very active and induftrious, in contriving and framing many of them; and being reprimanded by Lord *Cavendifh*, for an Infinuation fo unjuft and opprobrious to the Company, and for fo unfuitable a Return to Sir *Edwin Sandys* for doing publick Service, his Lordfhip added, that he had done more Harm by that Day's Work, than Captain *Martin*, Captain *Argall*, or Captain *Bailie*; the laft of which was Captain *Somers's* Sollicitor, and had given their Courts much Trouble and Abufe. To this Mr. *Wrote* replied; that, in terming their Laws Sir *Edwin Sandys's* Laws, he called them no otherwife, than a great Lord did; and fince his Lordfhip was fo difpleafed with him, he declared, he would never more trouble that Court, where his Lordfhip prefided, but would, at their next Meeting, deliver up his Share in the *Somer-Iflands* Company.

HE farther objected, that the Committee, in which thefe things paffed, was very diforderly, fome Men talking privately by the Fire fide; which he imputed to Mr. Deputy's Fault and Negligence, who ought to have moderated and kept Order in their Meetings. And he faid, that neither the Council, nor the Committee, had any Authority to treat of the Matter of Salaries; and that there were things reported to the Court, as the Judgment of the Committee, concerning Points, referred to them by the Company, which neverthelefs were not the Committee's Acts and Doing. And laftly, he charged and challenged the Deputy, with wrong entering the Proceedings of a Court, the 7th of *October* before. And to this Violence of Accufation, and Acerbity of Speech, he joined an equally rude and infolent Behaviour. All which was the more inexcufable in him, as he was himfelf one of the Committee, who prepared and brought this Matter before the Court, and had, when prefent, concurred with them in their Proceedings, but through Abfence and Negligence in attending that Committee, had now fpoke moft of thofe bitter and reproachful things, merely upon Hearfay and Conjecture.

So many, and fuch various Accufations and Abufes, which affected divers of the greateft Lords and principal Members of the Company, did naturally produce a long

and

and various Debate; in which Mr. *Wrote's* Arguments and Allegations were fully anfwered and difproved, by feveral of the Company; particularly by the Deputy, Lord *Cavendifh*, Sir *Edwin Sandys*, and Mr. *John Farrar*. Many alfo expreffed much Grief and Concern, for this unhappy Altercation; as well out of their private Regard for Mr. *Wrote*, who had thus far been much beloved and efteemed, as out of Fear, left it fhould give a Handle to the Malicious, and be the Occafion of much Reproach and Scandal to the Company. But Mr. *Wrote*, with great Violence and Obftinacy, ftill perfifted to have feveral Propofitions, which he made, relating to the Contract, put to the Vote; and being refufed, he declared, that fince he could not have things put to the Queftion, and for divers other juft Caufes of Offence, he appealed to the Quarter Court. Neither could he be filenced or repreffed, till the Deputy, at the Court's Requeft, put it twice to the Vote, and it was, by a general Confent (Mr. *Wrote* himfelf, and one other only diffenting) a fecond time ordered and refolved; That fince the Points, now moved, had paffed the Judgment of a Great and General Quarter Court, they fhould no more be called into queftion or difputed, before the next Quarter Court, at which time, if any Perfon had any thing to oppofe againft them, they might come prepared, and do it.

THE whole Court, and particularly the Lord *Cavendifh*, were much fcandalifed at this turbulent and offenfive Behaviour of Mr. *Wrote*; which was fufpected to proceed, not fo much from any evil Mind in himfelf, as from the malicious Infufions of fome others, in order to caufe Variance and Diftraction in the Company. For Alderman *Johnfon*, and others of the Faction, were now prefent; who had of late been generally obferved, never to appear at their Courts, but againft fome Storm and Confufion. Lord *Cavendifh* therefore, without naming the Perfon, immediately wrote a full and particular Account of it to the Earl of *Southampton*, who was then in the Country. Whereupon the Earl, being willing to fupprefs, in the Beginning, an Affair of fuch dangerous Confequence, haftened up to Town, and called a Meeting of his Majefty's Council for *Virginia*, on the 11th of the fame Month of *December*. But Mr. *Wrote* protefted againft their Power and Jurifdiction, as he had appealed to the Quarter Court; to which, he declared, he would only fubmit himfelf. He then renewed his Accufation againft the Deputy, for wrong entering a Court, the 7th of *October* laft paffed, and thereby bringing the Company three thoufand Pounds in Debt. And he did, from his firft coming into the Room, behave himfelf in a moft violent

violent and contemptuous Manner, towards the Earl of 1622.
Southampton, Lord *Cavendish,* and the whole Council.

MR. Deputy said, that the Accusation against himself Sir *Francis* *Wyat,* Go-
was of a very high Nature, and deeply concerned the Com- vernor.
pany. For the Entries of their Courts being the Company's Records, to charge them with Falsity, was to call into
question all the Records and Proceedings of the Company.
He therefore declared the Manner of entering their Courts:
First, the Secretary drew them up, and brought them to
him, which Draught he, according to the Company's Order, perused and corrected; that then it was read in the
next Court, distinctly, Article by Article, and after a sufficient Pause and Examination, either confirmed, or amended; after which, it was admitted to Record. And he said,
that the very Court, now spoken of by Mr. *Wrote,* had
accordingly gone through this Course; and that no Exceptions had been taken to it, not even by Mr. *Wrote,* who
was then present, and ought to have objected, if there had
been any thing wrong. For he would otherwise himself
become privy and consenting to the Falsification, which he
now laid to his Charge. But he averred, that there was
nothing in it, to his Knowledge, wrong entered or amiss;
but the whole was truly and faithfully set down, by the Secretary and himself, according to the Meaning of the Court,
as they conceived; which he would, by the Persons, that
were present at it, sufficiently prove. And as to bringing
the Company three thousand Pounds in Debt, there was,
and could be, no Manner of Colour or Pretence for any
such thing. He therefore solemnly protested his Innocency; and as, if he should be found guilty of this grievous
Charge, he would deserve the greatest of Punishments, so
he humbly insisted, for his own Justification, that the Matter might be strictly looked into and examined.

THE Earl of *Southampton* also told Mr. *Wrote,* that he
seemed to take himself to be so great a Man, that they
were all, as Pigmies, in his Sight; but as he did not know
him to be any Prince of the Blood, so he desired, he
would carry himself with more Calmness and Decency.
And as to his affrontive Behaviour to Lord *Cavendish,* the
Earl said; that altho' they were all there equal, as Coun-
sellors of the *Virginia* Company, yet there was a very
great Difference between the Persons of divers of them;
and particularly between him and the Lord *Cavendish,* to
whom he owed a more respectful Language and Behaviour.
And some time after, pressing him upon his Rashness and Indiscretion, and on his Failure in his Duty, as a *Virginia* Counsellor, Mr. *Wrote* went out abruptly and departed; saying,

S that

1622. that he came not thither, to hear ill Words. Whereupon

Sir *Francis* the Earl appealed to the Judgment of the Council, then
present, what juft Occafion of Offence had been given to

Wyat, Go-
vernor. Mr. *Wrote*, that he fhould go off in that rude and unre-
fpectful Manner. They therefore ordered and agreed, that
a Collection fhould be made of thofe Matters, which
fhould be objected againft Mr. *Wrote* at the next Quarter
Court, to which he had appealed. And in the mean while,
in Regard to the great Contempt, he had that Day fhewed, they fufpended him from the Council, till he fhould
clear himfelf of the Matters laid to his Charge, and fhould
come to a better Temper and Deportment.

BEFORE the next Meeting of the Company, Sir *John*
Brooke, accompanied with Mr. *John Farrar*, went to the
Lord *Cavendifh*, and told him ; that he found Mr. *Wrote*
forry, for what he had done ; and had the Earl of *Sou-*
thampton been in Town, he would have gone to his Lordfhip, and given him Satisfaction. He therefore defired
Lord *Cavendifh*, on Mr. *Wrote*'s Behalf, that the Court,
which was the next Day to fit, might be put off. For if
the Proceedings of the former Court, of the 4th of *De-*
cember, fhould be openly read, Mr. *Wrote* would be put
upon his Defence and Juftification ; which would tend to
widen the Breach, and to render the thing irreconcileable,
which there were now Hopes of having compromifed and
fettled upon amicable Terms. And the Lord *Cavendifh*,
out of this Hope, and in Compliance with Sir *John Brooke*'s
Requeft, did accordingly caufe the Court to be put off and
deferred. But Mr. *Wrote* was fo far from anfwering Sir

1623. *John Brooke*'s Expectation, that at the next Meeting of the
Company, which was not before the 29th of *January*, he
made this very thing a Subject of Complaint ; as if that
long Intermiffion of Courts had been purpofely contrived
to his Prejudice. But being fully anfwered and filenced
on this Head, by the joint Teftimony of Lord *Cavendifh*
and Sir *John Brooke*, he infifted, that the Salary Men, as
being interefted Perfons, and the Deputy, whom he moft
unjuftly called his Accufer (for both he and his Brother
were ftill faft Friends to Mr. *Wrote*, and endeavoured to
palliate and make up the Affair) fhould not be prefent,
when his Bufinefs was difcuffed. He alfo excepted, in the
grofs, againft the Entry of that Court ; faying, he fpoke
not thofe Words, neither in Manner nor Form, as they
were there fet down. Whereupon a long Debate enfued ;
Whether it was agreeable to the Cuftom of Courts, and
would not be productive of great Inconveniency and Diforder, and raife much Queftion and infinite Trouble to
the

the Company by the Precedent and Example, if they
should suffer that, which had been entered by sworn Officers, to be recommitted, and called afresh in question,
whenever it should please any Man, to make Exceptions
against it. But for Mr. *Wrote*'s Satisfaction, and to take
away all Pretence of Cavil and Complaint, an extraordinary
Court was appointed, to examine by Parts, and to rectify
the said Court of the 4th of *December*; to which they
only, who were that Day present, were warned or admitted, as being the only proper Witnesses and competent
Judges of the Matter.

AT that Court, Mr. *Wrote* still behaved, in the same
unaccountable and distempered Manner. He said, he suf-
fered for the Service of his Majesty, and for doing his Duty. He repeated his Appeal to the Quarter Court; and
thanked the Gentlemen, then present, for prejudging him
to that Court. He also declared, if the Quarter Court
righted him not, he would appeal to the King, the Foun-
tain of Justice and Mercy; often repeating the same
Words, with great Passion and Vehemence. Mr. *John
Farrar* having said, that something was untrue, he ran to
him, and whispered in his Ear, that he durst not have said
Untrue to him in another Place. For which rude Swag-
gering, he was justly and sharply reproved, by the Earl of
Southampton. He alledged, that Mr. *Withers*, an eminent
Lawyer of the Company, had somewhere said, that the
Earl of *Southampton*, as a Privy Counsellor, might commit
him; and protested, that under that Fear, he durst not
speak freely. He likewise, in a very rude and affrontive
Manner, charged the Earl of *Southampton* with saying;
that he blundered out his Indiscretion; and for giving him
the Lye in the third Person, his Lordship having said; That
whoever should say, that Men were in any thing overawed,
and durst not speak their Minds, it was put into his Mouth
by the Father of Lies; for a fouler Lye himself never
told. The Earl owned, that he had spoke those Words;
and he said, he would justify and maintain them; and if Mr.
Wrote applied them to himself, he could not help it. But as
to committing him, he desired him to be under no such Fear.
For whatever Honours and Respects were due to him, he
laid them all aside, when he came to that Place, and only
appeared there, as their Treasurer. But he declared, that
had Mr. *Wrote* behaved himself towards him so, in any
other Place but that, he would not have endured it so patiently; and he therefore willed him, to be more mannerly
and discreet. As to the Court of the 4th of *December*,
which they then met to examine and rectify, it was found

to

1623.

Sir *Francis*
Wyat, Go-
vernor.

to be rightly entered, in the main Points and moft material Paffages; and it was accordingly, after a few flight Additions and Alterations, fo voted and determined, by an almoft unanimous Voice, one Perfon only diffenting. And to put the Matter ftill further out of Difpute, the Earl of *Southampton* fummoned another Court, confifting of the fame Perfons, to meet three Days after, and to fee, that the faid Court was rightly entered, according to thofe Reformations and Amendments.

Soon after, Mr. *Wrote* prefented a Project, for the better and more thrifty Management of the Contract; wherein he propofed, to have the whole Bufinefs performed for twelve hundred Pounds a Year, and thereby to fave thirteen hundred Pounds annually to his Majefty and the Companies. And to give the thing the fairer Courfe and Hearing, the Earl of *Southampton* fummoned another Court extraordinary, to meet and examine his Propofal. They went through the Whole, Article by Article; and after a full Deliberation and Debate, which lafted a whole Day, till late at Night, each Point was difapproved and rejected, generally unanimoufly, and never with above three or four diffentient from the reft of the Company.

THE 5th of *February* being the Quarter Court Day, to which Mr. *Wrote* had appealed, and his Affair having made a great Noife, and been the Subject of much Scandal and Defamation to the Company, there was a very numerous and fplendid Meeting, confifting of fix Lords, thirty Knights, Dr. *Donne*, Dean of St. *Paul's*, and a vaft Concourfe of others, Doctors, Efquires, Gentlemen, Merchants, and Citizens. And the Lord *Cavendifh* alfo, to the fame Time and Place, fummoned a Court of the *Somer-Iflands* Company, as they were equally concerned and engaged in the Bufinefs of the Contract. But Mr. *Wrote*, having appeared in Court, foon withdrew; declaring to Sir *Samuel Sandys* (who met, and afked him, whither he was going) that he was ill at Eafe, and could not ftay. However Mr. *Brooke*, and other Gentlemen, learned in the Law, delivered their Opinions clearly; that notwitftanding his Departure, and his pretended Appeal to his Majefty, as there was no Evidence, that he had really made fuch Appeal, or that his Majefty had accepted it, they were no way debarred from proceeding againft him, in a due and legal Manner. Whereupon Sir *Edwin Sandys* obferved, that Mr. *Wrote* was not accufed, or profecuted, to that Court, but was himfelf the Profecutor and Accufer. If therefore his Accufation was well and juftly grounded, why did he forfake it then, when that Day and that Court were come, to

which

which he himſelf had appealed; and when the Perſons, by him accuſed, ſtood there, in the Face of the Court, ready to ſubmit themſelves to the Trial, by him called for and demanded? But, he ſaid, Truth and Innocency are bold and ſettled, whereas Calumny and Falſhood are fugitive, fearful. Wherefore, as it was apparent, that the King's Ears had been poſſeſſed, and all Parts of the Town and Country filled, with cauſeleſs Clamours, by Mr. *Wrote* and his Friends; and whereas his Wrongs to the Council, Committee, and whole Company, were ſo great, ſo groundleſs, and ſo pernicious, he concluded, that unleſs ſome Courſe was taken, to puniſh and repreſs him, he could not ſee, but that the whole Government. of the Company, muſt utterly diſſolve, and fall into the moſt extreme Confuſion and Contempt.

HEREUPON, at Sir *John Davers*'s Motion, it was firſt unanimouſly voted and agreed, that all Mr. *Wrote*'s Exceptions, Charges, and Imputations, at the late Courts, were utterly falſe and ſlanderous. And then proceeding to his Sentence, after a long Debate, in which ſome propoſed ſevere, and others more gentle Methods, it was at laſt concluded and reſolved; that he ſhould be diſplaced, and for ever excluded from being of his Majeſty's Council for *Virginia*; and that he ſhould not be entirely diſenfranchiſed from the Company, but ſhould only be ſuſpended and excluded from their Courts, for one whole Year abſolutely, in which his Submiſſion ſhould not be accepted, altho' he ſhould offer it. But if, at the Expiration of that Year, he ſhould make his Submiſſion to the next Quarter Court, that then it ſhould be left to the Pleaſure of that Court, whether they would re-admit him or not. But without a full Submiſſion, and due Acknowledgment of his Fault, it was ordered, that he ſhould never be received at all. And it was further reſolved, upon Sir *John Davers*'s Motion, that, if Mr. *Wrote* ſtill perſiſted in his wilful Courſes and unjuſt Aſperſions, or ſhould any way wrong or moleſt the Company, then, for his Conviction and Diſgrace, and for the Company's Juſtification, his Sentence, together with an authentic Copy of his whole Proceedings, ſhould be put into Print.

IT was the Company's great Unhappineſs, that whatever Conteſts or Diſſenſions happened among them, the thing was always carried to his Majeſty in the worſt Light; who was but too ready and willing, to receive Impreſſions to their Prejudice. And ſo it happened in this Caſe of Mr. *Wrote*. For Sir *Henry Mildmay*, profeſſing himſelf, to be neither of the Faction, nor the Factious, and that he came

1623.   not to ftir up Storms, but to allay them, informed the
Company, that upon fome late Difcourfe with the King,
Sir *Francis* his Majefty took Notice of thefe Differences, which were
Wyat, Go- a great Hindrance to the main Bufinefs, and to things of
vernor. efpecial Confequence to the Colony; to which he alfo attributed the great Difcouragement of divers Adventurers,
and their Willingnefs to give up their Shares. And his
Majefty farther fignified his Will, that the Liberty of the
Company, in every kind, fhould be preferved and kept
entire; and particularly, that no Man fhould be abridged
of the Liberty to fpeak his Mind freely, fo he did it with
due Refpect and Decorum. But this, he faid, he fpoke,
not as from the King, but as his private Advice and Admo-
nition. And afterwards at this Quarter Court, when Mr.
Wrote's Bufinefs came on, he informed the Company, that
what he had before intimated to them, as from himfelf, he
had now Warrant from his Majefty to tell them; who, by
Way of Advice and Council, but no way to command
them, wifhed, that they would leave verbal Differences,
and go on with the Bufinefs of the Plantation.

UPON Occafion of this Information of Sir *Henry Mild-*
may, Sir *Edwin Sandys* obferved, that of all Mr. *Wrote*'s
Calumnies and Accufations, none was more unjuft, nor
more apparently falfe and groundlefs, than that, wherein
he charged the Earl of *Southampton* (though not by Name,
yet by neceffary Inference) of overawing the Company,
and depriving them of the Liberty of Speech. And the
Earl told Sir *Henry Mildmay*, if it was his Majefty's Pleafure, that they fhould not meddle with any evil Words,
or feditious Behaviour, they would all obey and defift from
the prefent Bufinefs. But Sir *Henry* declaring, that he had
no fuch Command, but only Warrant, to fpeak by Way
of Advice, what he had now delivered, the Court proceeded to the Cenfure of Mr. *Wrote*. And the Earl of
Southampton farther faid, that this thing feemed very ftrange
and unaccountable to him, but he muft attribute it wholly
to Mifinformation; and he wondered, that any Man fhould
be found, fo fhamelefs and void of all Truth and Confcience, as thus to abufe the Ears, and mifinform the Mind
of a King. Whereupon he appealed to the Court, to bear
Witnefs in that Point; and they all, with an univerfal
Confent and unanimous Voice, declared, that it was a falfe
and unjuft Imputation; and that they were not overawed,
but enjoyed fuch Freedom and Liberty of Speech, as was
in no other Company permitted. And this Declaration they
often afterwards repeated, with the fame Unanimity; the
opponent Faction themfelves, altho' they infinuated and
kept

kept up the Lye at a Diſtance, not being ſo abandoned to
all Senſe of Shame, as to ſay any ſuch thing, in the Face
of the Court, where there were ſo many Witneſſes to diſ-
prove and confound them.   Divers of the Company alſo farther ſaid, that if Men ſhould uſe half the Liberty of Speech
in ſome Companies of the City, or demean themſelves with
ſo much Rudeneſs and Diſorder, as ſeveral Members did
in that Court, it would not be ſuffered or endured, but they
would be either puniſhed in the Purſe, or ſent to the Coun-
ters.   And in Truth, the grand Fault of the Earl of *Southampton* and this Court was, not a tyrannical Government,
or imperious Reſtraint of the Freedom of Speech and Debate, but rather, out of a Principle of Candor and Fairneſs,
the giving too much Way to Impertinence and Licentiouſ-
neſs of Tongue ; which had it been properly reſtrained,
and duly puniſhed, it would, in all Probability, have preſerved the Being and Privileges of the Company, and prevented that Diſſolution, which followed.

F R O M the very Beginning of this Commotion, Sir *Edwin Sandys* deſired Mr. *Wrote,* not to be diſturbed at his
Office and Salary.   For as he had accepted them with much
Reluctancy, and in ſole Obedience to the Company's Requeſt, as they all knew and could teſtify, ſo he would reſign
both the one and the other, with a much better Will, than
he had ever received them.   And he accordingly often made
and declared his Reſignation, and very ſeriouſly proteſted,
that he would never again accept the Place ; and that, in
Reſentment of the late Courſes taken to defame the Officers
and Salaries, he would not, for any Reward whatſoever,
any longer put up with, and endure ſuch Affronts and A-
buſes.   He therefore deſired the Company, to make Choice
of ſome other to the Place of Director, that the Buſineſs,
for the Want of that Officer, might not ſtand ſtill, or receive any Prejudice.

B U T as Mr. *Wrote* had thus moved a freſh the Affair of
the Officers and Salaries, Sir *Henry Mildmay* confeſſed, that,
altho' he was not directly of Mr. *Wrote's* Opinion, and the
Salaries had formerly paſſed with his Vote, yet upon ſecond
Thoughts, he had ſince changed that Opinion, and now
conceived, that ſuch large Salaries was the ready Way to
ruin and overthrow the whole Buſineſs ; which, in his Judgment, might have been better huſbanded.   And he particularly inſiſted, that as the Salaries were to be raiſed upon the
Tobacco, it would be a great Burthen and Oppreſſion on
the poor Planter ; which had alſo been a popular and conſtant Theme of Declamation with Mr. *Wrote.*   In this O-
pinion, Sir *Henry Mildmay* was ſeconded by Sir *Thomas*
Wroth,

Wroth, Mr. *Edward Johnson,* and some others. This
Point therefore of the Officers and Salaries was again called
wholly into Queſtion and reconſidered, at a Court, held for
that Purpoſe, on the 12th of *February.* At that time, the
Oppoſers of the Salaries deſired, for various Reaſons and
Allegations, that the Conſideration might be referred to a
farther Day. But Mr. Deputy ſaid, it ſeemed wonderful
to him, that Men, who had raiſed ſuch Storms and Clamours about the Salaries, not only to the Diſparagement of
the Company's Proceedings, but alſo much to the Hindrance
of the Plantation, and to the Diſgrace and Defamation of
ſome very worthy Perſons, for accepting thoſe Places, ſhould
now, after all this Scandal raiſed, and Miſchief done, be yet
unprepared with plain and evident Reaſons, to overthrow
them. And he ſaid, he marvelled the more at this, as he
then ſaw, before his Eyes, ſome Perſons, who declared, at
the Council of the 11th of *December,* when the Conſideration of the Salaries was referred to that preſent Day, that
they would, againſt this Time, arm and fortify themſelves,
to cut the Throat of the Salaries. Wherefore he earneſtly
beſought them, not to interpoſe any farther Delays, but
now at length produce thoſe Reaſons, for which they had
ſo much traduced and defamed both the Salaries and the Officers. For they had certainly had ſufficient Time, to conſider and ripen the Matter ; and nothing would be Reaſon
in any future Day, which was not then ſo. Hereupon
there aroſe a very long Debate ; till the Company, being
little ſatisfied with the Reaſons given, and much wearied
with the many Diverſions, made from the main Queſtion,
eſpecially by Alderman *Johnson,* called upon the Earl of
Southampton to put it to the Vote ; and it was again voted
and agreed, with an unanimous Voice (the Gentlemen in
the Oppoſition either retiring, or elſe finding, how inconſi-
derable their Number was, giving no Vote at all) that the
Officers and Salaries ſhould ſtand, as they had been formerly ordered and appointed.

T H I S was indeed a very great Concurrence and Unanimity of the Company, in the only Affair, for which the
opponent Faction ever ſeemed to have had the leaſt Colour
or Shadow of Reaſon. But altho' the Sum of five and twenty hundred Pounds a Year, for the Management of this Buſineſs, may, at a ſlight View, be thought very great and
extraordinary, yet if it be conſidered, that thoſe Officers (as
it was then calculated and agreed) would have an hundred
thouſand Pounds *per Annum,* running through their Hands,
it will not be found ſo exorbitant and exceſſive. For it only
amounts to two and a half *per Cent.* whereof five hundred
Pounds

Pounds a Year, or the half *per Cent.* was not to be expended,
except it could be evidently applied for raifing the Price of
Tobacco. And the two great Salaries, arifing to nine hundred Pounds a Year, againft which their Exceptions chiefly
lay, did not amount quite to one *per Cent.* whereas the
whole Strefs and Burthen of the Bufinefs would lie upon
thofe two Officers, and its Succefs entirely depend upon their
Induftry, Care, and Dexterity, in the Management of it.

AT this Court, the Lord *Cavendifh* alfo moved, that fince
Sir *Edwin Sandys* would, by no means, hold the Place of
Director any longer, they would propofe fome other Perfon
for that Office. Whereupon fome named Sir *Nathaniel
Rich*; but he excufed himfelf, as uncapable of difcharging
fuch an Office, and would not therefore undertake it, for
ten thoufand Pounds a Year. But he declared, if he thought
himfelf fit for the Bufinefs, he would willingly do it for nothing. Then Sir *Thomas Wroth*, and Mr. *Edward Johnfon*,
an eminent Lawyer, and very worthy Member of the Society, were propofed; but they both refufed, as no way
fkilled in fuch Bufinefs, or able to execute the Place. Afterwards it was put to the Queftion; Whether the Company would accept of Sir *Edwin Sandys*'s Refignation, and it
was, by a general Erection of Hands, denied. He was
therefore very preffingly entreated, not to leave the Place,
upon any Difcouragement whatfoever; the Company pro-
feffing, that, without his Affiftance, they much doubted of
the good Management and Succefs of fo difficult a Bufinefs.
Even fome of the moft violent in the Oppofition did, at
other times, exprefs great Satisfaction in the Choice of Sir
Edwin Sandys; and declared, that he, or no Body, was
able to go through with fo thorny and troublefome an Employment: Whilft others feemed difinclined and backward,
to be any way engaged in it, except it was under his Management and Direction. And thus the Office of Director
was, a fecond Time forced upon Sir *Edwin Sandys*, with a
very general and honourable Teftimony of the Company;
and he accordingly, with the Committee, entered into Confultation, about a proper Courfe and Regulation of the Bufinefs; which, being brought before the Company, was
generally approved and confirmed.

BUT the Gentlemen in the Oppofition, finding all Attempts with the Company vain, took another and more
effectual Way to deftroy the Contract. For, twelve Days
after the Thing had been thus examined a frefh, and again
fettled and determined, the Earl of *Southampton* and Lord
Cavendifh, the Treafurer and Governor of the two Companies, with the two *Farrars*, the Deputies, Sir *John Da-*

1623.
Sir *Francis Wyat*, Governor.

vers, Sir *Edwin Sandys*, and some others, were called before the Lord Treasurer; where appeared, on the other Part, the Earl of *Warwick*, Sir *Nathaniel Rich*, Alderman *Johnson*, Mr. *Wrote*, Mr. *Bing*, and others of that Faction, who were seconded and assisted by Sir *John Wolstenholme* and the Customers. There passed much Dispute and Contradiction between the two Parties, which the Lord Treasurer heard with great Patience, and without the least Interruption to either Side. And it was here confidently averred, especially by Mr. *Wrote* and Mr. *Bing*, that the Companies, in carrying the Contract, had been overawed by the Earl of *Southampton*; and threatened, unless the Contract proceeded, the Colonies would be taken from them. At length, one of the Customers proposed to the Lord Treasurer, that since the Contract had been the Subject of so much Contention and Discord, it might be immediately dissolved; and that the Companies should be obliged, to bring all their Tobacco into *England*, and pay the old twelve Pence a Pound, Custom and Impost; which, he said, would be more satisfactory to the Planters, and more beneficial to the King. And he then proceeded to calculate and shew, that a Revenue, of twenty thousand Pounds a Year upon Tobacco, would be thence raised for his Majesty; which was the utmost, that had been aimed at or expected. The Lord Treasurer also reminded the Companies of the great Grace and Favour, his Majesty had shewed them, by granting them Lotteries, and other Means, for the Advancement of the Colonies. And this, by the bye, was always insisted on, as a vast and infinite Obligation, which the Companies could never return; and it was therefore for ever urged as an Argument, for their granting his Majesty, whatever he demanded. And his Lordship concluded, that it was a very unfit and ungrateful thing, whether there was a Contract, or no Contract, not to bring all their Tobacco into *England*, to pay Duty, that his Majesty's Revenue might be thereby advanced.

THESE Expressions of the Lord Treasurer were received with great Applause and Approbation, by the *Warwickian* Faction; who declared, that it had ever been their Desire, that all the Tobacco should be brought into *England*. And Mr. *Wrote* farther said, that the Colony in *Virginia* had sent a Petition, to be exhibited to his Majesty, to that Purpose; which was however never presented to the King, but had been concealed and suppressed by the Deputy. By this he meant the Petition, already recited (*p.* 200) which was sent, when no Tobacco from *Virginia* was imported into *England*; but coming after the Prohibition was taken off, it was therefore

fore never prefented. The Earl of *Southampton* therefore replied, that the Colony meant nothing lefs by that Petition, than what he now pretended. For the Scope of it was, to obtain Liberty to bring Tobacco into *England*, at a time, when they were utterly debarred from importing any. At laft they were difmiffed; and the Lord High Treafurer told them, they might ftill proceed with the Bufinefs of the Contract, notwithftanding thefe Diffenfions and Oppofitions.

BUT foon after, they were again fummoned, to meet before the Lords of the Privy Council, on the 4th of *March*; Sir *Edwin Sandys* (the Earl of *Southampton* being then out of Town) and the two *Farrars*, with fuch, as they fhould bring with them, for the *Virginia* Company, and for the other Side, Sir *Thomas Smith* and Alderman *Johnfon*, with fuch Advocates and Affiftants, as they fhould chufe; for the *Somer-Iflands* Company, the Lord *Cavendifh*, and fuch, as he would bring with him, and of the oppofite Party, the Earl of *Warwick*, or Sir *Nathaniel Rich*, with fuch others, as they thought proper. On that Day, they appeared accordingly, being attended by the Lord *St. John*, Lord *Paget*, Sir *Edward Sackvil*, Sir *John Brooke*, Sir *John Davers*, Sir *Robert Killigrew*, and divers other eminent Members of the Company; and they were told by the Lord High Treafurer, that this Meeting had been appointed to examine fundry Complaints, that had been exhibited againft the Contract, by fome particular Members of their Companies. Whereupon the Lord *Cavendifh* made Proteftation, that, as the Contract had often been, moft fairly and regularly, voted and concluded, in feveral Quarter Courts, neither himfelf, nor the reft of the Company, which then attended, came to give any Satisfaction to thofe Members, which now oppofed it. For they were not only, as the leffer Part, involved in the general Agreement of the Majority, but had, moft of them, actually given their Votes and Confent to the Contract; and it would be to the Prejudice and Deftruction of all good Government, to be perpetually tampering and treating with them about it. But he faid, if their Lordfhips, upon any finifter Surmifes or Informations, had conceived any Doubts about the Matter, himfelf, and the reft, were both ready and willing, to give their Lordfhips an Account of their whole Proceedings, and fuch an Account, as they trufted and were affured, would, in every Particular, give all reafonable Satisfaction.

HEREUPON, the Lords of the Council requiring fome of the Complainants to make known their Grievances, Mr. *Bing* ftepped forth, and made a long and very bitter Invective againft the Contract, and the Manner of paffing it. In this,

this, he ufed great Sharpnefs and Freedom of Speech againft the Earl of *Southampton*; and endeavoured, by ridiculous Sir *Francis* and mimick Geftures, to mock, and turn him into Con-*Wyat*, Go- tempt. But Mr. *Bing* was not now in the *Virginia* Court; vernor. where he and his Party had long indulged themfelves, in a moft immoderate Licentioufnefs of Speech, and Indecency of Behaviour. And therefore, altho' the Earl of *Southampton* was no ways gracious at Court, nor confequently to the Lords of the Privy Council, his Majefty's immediate Creatures, yet they fharply checked and rebuked him. But the Lord *Cavendifh* appealed to their Lordfhips for Juftice a-gainft him, for having fo wronged and abufed the Earl of *Southampton*, a Peer of the Realm, and a Member of that Board, as well now in their Lordfhips Prefence, as at other Times and Places, as he was ready, abundantly to prove. Wherefore Mr. *Bing* was afterwards committed to the Mar-fhelfea, by an Order of the Privy Council; from whence he was not to be releafed, until he had made due Submiffion to the Earl of *Southampton*, and given him all fitting Satif-faction.

BUT as to the main Subject of Complaint in Mr. *Bing's* Speech, the Lord Treafurer propofed to the Companies Three Points, to be confidered : Firft, whether the Companies had been overawed ? Secondly, whether the Contract was for the Good of the Colonies ? And Laftly, if it was not for the Good of the Colonies, how it might be made fo ? The debating and clearing up thefe Points took the whole Day, both Forenoon and Afternoon. At length, after a long Hearing and Deliberation, the Lord *Cavendifh*, Sir *Edwin Sandys*, and Mr. *Nicholas Farrar*, Deputy of the *Virginia* Company, were called in, and told by the Lord Prefident of the Council; that they had given a good Account, both of the Reafons, which induced them to conclude the Con-tract, and of their fair and upright Proceeding in paffing it. And he promifed, that a Report fhould be made to his Ma-jefty, by that Board, accordingly; and he doubted not, but that the Contract would be confirmed to them, or elfe fome other Bargain granted, as much to their Content and Advantage. The Lord Treafurer likewife gave them a moft honourable Teftimony, of their upright Proceedings, and wife Adminiftration of the Affairs of the Colonies, for the four laft Years; in which, he faid, they had thriven won-derfully, and profpered beyond Belief. And his Lordfhip further added, that in the former Years, when Alderman *Johnfon* was Deputy, and the Bufinefs was in other Hands, it was carried fouly and diforderly; fo that, if the Perfons, then in the Government of the Companies, fhould be called

to

to an Account for their Proceedings, he queſtioned, whether their Eſtates would anſwer it.

A N D thus did this Affair go off, in all Appearance, greatly to the Honour of the Companies, and to the utter Diſgrace and Confuſion of the oppoſite Faƈtion.   But whilſt
the Companies were engaged in debating the Matter before
the Council, the Earl of *Warwick* and Mr. *Wrote* were with
the King; and what Effeƈt their Calumnies and Inſinua-
tions might have on the Mind of that weak Prince, may be
eaſily judged by the Event.   For the *Virginia* Company,
being incouraged by the Third Point, propoſed by the Lord
Treaſurer, to be conſidered, *viz.* If the Contraƈt was not
for the Good of the Colonies, how it might be made ſo?
reconſidered the Whole, in each Article and Particular, and
propoſed ſuch Alleviations in the hardeſt Parts, as they conceived reaſonable, or thought there were any Hopes of obtaining.   And to this End, the Gentlemen in the Oppoſition
were expreſly invited and deſired, to join with them ; that,
laying aſide all Study of Party and Contradiƈtion, they might
unanimouſly, and with the Calmneſs of Reaſon, examine
and find out, what was moſt neceſſary and beneficial for the
Colonies.   But the Principal of thoſe Gentlemen not vouch-
ſafing their Preſence, they proceeded, and drew up a long
and particular Repreſentation of the whole Matter to the
Lords of the Privy Council ; that they might aſſiſt their
Suit, and be Interceſſors to his Majeſty for them.   But
whilſt theſe things were in Agitation, the whole Contraƈt
was ſuddenly declared by his Majeſty, to be void and of none
Effeƈt.   But I cannot diſcover the exaƈt Day, when this
was done ; nor what were the Reaſons or Pretences for it.

A N D this was the End of the Company's Contraƈt with
his Majeſty, for the ſole Importation of Tobacco ; an Affair, which raiſed vaſt Heats and Animoſities, and gave a
Handle, eſpecially on Account of the two great Salaries,
to much Clamour and Reproach.   And by this Means, the
Warwickian Faƈtion were ſtrengthened by the Acceſſion of
Mr. *Wrote,* Mr. *Gibbs,* Mr. *Bing,* and other Perſons of Conſideration and Figure ; and it was now encreaſed to twenty ſix
in the whole, whereas it had before been even leſs numerous and potent.   As to the Contraƈt itſelf, it was acknowledged, by thoſe, who were moſt vigorous in upholding it,
not to be abſolutely and in itſelf advantageous, but only
comparatively good, with Reſpeƈt to their former State of
Slavery and Oppreſſion under the Cuſtomers and Farmers
of his Majeſty's Revenues, and as it would ſhield them from
their farther illegal and arbitrary Impoſitions.   And the
Breach of it was, at this time, the more apprehended, as it
was

1623.

Sir *Francis Wyat,* Governor.

was likely, that a fole Importation would be granted to fome other Perfons, who made Offer of fo exceeding and large a Revenue to his Majefty, as could not poffibly be raifed, but with the extreme Oppreffion of the Colonies, and greatly to the Prejudice, if not to the utter Deftruction, of their growing Trade and Staple of Tobacco.

BUT the Faction, that oppofed the Companies, did not only, by the Diffolution of the Contract, endanger the Trade, and render it again fubject to the Rapacioufnefs and Extortions of the Farmers and Cuftomers, but their Contentioufnefs and Malice had another unhappy Confequence. It hath been already related, that, in *October* 1621, the Lords of the Privy Council commanded all the Tobacco and other Commodities, to be brought from *Virginia* into *England*; but upon Reafons given, and a Reprefentation made by the Company, the Matter refted, and had been no farther infifted on. But now, chiefly at the Inftigation, and by the Offers and Motions of the opponent Faction, their Lordfhips renewed that Order, in very ftrong and peremptory Terms. For, on the 4th of *March*, when the Companies were before the Council, the Lord *Cavendifh*, Sir *Edwin Sandys*, and Mr. Deputy *Farrar*, of the *Virginia* Company, were very. fharply reprimanded and threatened, becaufe fome Ships had lately gone from the Colonies to *Holland*; and they were ordered, to fignify and declare to their Companies, that it was the Pleafure and exprefs Command of that Board, that all the Tobacco and other Commodities of the Plantations, fhould be brought directly to *England*.

WHEN this Affair came before the Company, Sir *Edwin Sandys* faid, that he fhould always be the Son of Obedience, and yield a ready Submiffion to the Commands of the higher Powers; as he well knew, it was the Intent and Inclination of the Company to do. Yet, in Cafes of evident Impoffibility or publick Detriment, he thought it the Part of well-ordered Duty, to make a juft and true Reprefentation of the Matter, and modeftly propofe their Reafons againft it. He therefore obferved, that the Commodities of *Virginia* had three feveral Sorts of Owners: Firft, the Company; fecondly, particular Hundreds and Plantations, belonging to private Adventurers in *England*, as *Southampton* Hundred, *Martin's* Hundred, and the like; and thirdly, Planters inhabiting and refiding in *Virginia*, whofe Part he conceived to be far the largeft and moft confiderable. As to the firft, the Company's Commodities, they certainly had them in their own Power, and could always import them into *England*. But over the two latter Sorts, he conceived

the

the Company to have no Power, by Law, to command or controle them. For the Inhabitants of *Virginia* were, by his Majefty's original Charters and Grants, declared to be as free, as the reft of his Majefty's Subjects, which inhabited the Realm of *England*, or any other of his Dominions. And befides, the particular Societies, and divers of the private Brothers in *England*, and of the Inhabitants in *Virginia*, had Ships of their own ; and it was not in the Power of the Company, to prevent or reftrain them, from carrying their Goods to the beft and moft promifing Markets.

HE farther obferved, that *Virginia* had, or would probably foon have, many Commodities, as Salt, Fifh, Pipeftaves, Caviary, and the like, which in other Countries might be vendible at an indifferent Price, but not in *England*. Confidering therefore, that within a few Years, when the Term granted in their Letters-patent was expired, the King was to have Cuftom of all Merchandife in *Virginia* itfelf, if thefe Goods fhould pay a fecond Cuftom in *England*, and afterwards a third Cuftom in foreign Parts, where they were vended, there could be no Doubt, but that thefe three Cuftoms, together with the Freight of fuch cheap and bulky Kinds of Merchandife, and the other contingent Charges, would fo feed upon the Commodity, as to leave little or nothing, for the Suftenance and Profit of the Adventurer and Planter.

HOWEVER, he faid, as the *Virginians* had been driven, by the Rigor of former Contractors with the Crown, to feek foreign Markets for their Commodities, fo he doubted not, but by gentle Ufage and good Treatment, they would be eafily induced to return back to *England*, their beft and moft natural Market. But as for what had been alledged by a very honourable Perfon, that the *Spanifh* Colonies brought all their Merchandifes into *Spain*, and to no other Place, he faid, there was a very evident and important Difference between the Cafe of the *Spanifh* Colonies and the *Englifh*. For the State of *Spain* fuffered no other Commodities of the fame Kind, to be brought into that Kingdom, which was an exceeding great Encouragement and Benefit to their *American* Plantations ; whereas in *England*, the Commodity, which could be eafily and abundantly fupplied from our own Colonies, was not only permitted, but even ftrictly enjoined, and fternly commanded, to be imported from a foreign Country. But if his Majefty would afford them the fame Privilege and Favour, that the King of *Spain* did to his Colonies, and would prohibit the Importation of all Commodities from foreign Parts, that could be furnifhed by our own Plantations, there would doubtlefs be all ready and

joyful

joyful Obedience yielded to this Command, of bringing all
their Commodities into *England*. But without fuch a Qua-
lification and Privilege, he declared it to be his Opinion,
that this was a Propofition extremely oppreffive and hurtful
to the Colonies, and muft foon bring them to utter Ruin
and Deftruction.

THIS clear and pathetic Account of the Cafe was received with the general Applaufe and Approbation of the
Company; and Mr. *Rider* added, that there feemed to
him to be another material Difference, between the *Spanifh* and *Englifh* Plantations. For the *Spanifh* Colonies
were founded by the Kings of *Spain*, out of their own
Treafury and Revenues, and they maintained the Garrifons
there, together with a large Navy, for their Ufe and Defence; whereas the *Englifh* Plantations had been at firft fettled, and fince fupported, at the Charge of private Adventurers; unlefs it might be excepted, that his Majefty, out
of his great Grace and Favour, had granted them fome
Lotteries and Collections, the Produce of which had neverthelefs been expended, merely for the publick Service. To
which it might have been juftly added, that thofe vaft Obli-
gations of Lotteries and Collections were very cheap to his
Majefty, he never having contributed one Farthing himfelf
in them, altho' he was a very great, and in a manner the
only Gainer yet, by thefe Settlements. At length, in order to lofe no Time, Sir *Edwin Sandys* and Mr. *Chriftopher
Brooke* were defired, to take both the Reafons, which had
been formerly prefented to their Lordfhips by the Company, together with fuch new ones, as had been now alledged, and to draw up a brief Anfwer to this Order of the
Privy Council. And whereas the Matter was already fo
well prepared and digefted to their Hands, it was thought,
they might eafily do it, during the fitting of the Court.
Whereupon they withdrew, and foon returned with an
Anfwer, containing much the fame in Purport with that,
prefented to their Lordfhips, about a Year and a Half before,
by Mr. *John Farrar*, then Deputy-Treafurer of the *Virginia* Company. This Draught, being deliberately read in
the Court, was ratified and approved by the Company;
and Lord *Cavendifh*, Lord *Paget*, and Sir *Edward Sackvil*
were entreated, to deliver it to the Lords of the Privy
Council, in the Company's Name.

BUT this Stifnefs and Refolution of the Company did,
by no means, turn their Lordfhips from their Purpofe.
For I find, by another Order of the Privy Council, dated
the 28th of *April* this Year, that they ftill ftrenuoufly infifted on, and ftrictly enjoined them, to import all their
Com-

Commodities into *England*. But as some Alleviation and Encouragement, the King, in the same Order of Council, declares ; that, instead of the twelve Pence, formerly answered to his Majesty, he would, for the future, be content with nine Pence a Pound on Tobacco (the Customers having abated three Pence a Pound Custom) and that all Tobacco, then lately imported into *England*, should be delivered to the Proprietors, on paying that nine Pence only. And for the Information of the People in *Virginia*, that they might know, how to comport themselves herein, this Order was transmitted hither, and is still extant among the Records of our Council. At the same time, the Lords of the Privy Council wrote a Letter to the Governor and Council here ; informing them, of his Majesty's gracious Intentions, towards the Colony ; and commanding them, not to be discouraged by any loose Advertisements, proceeding from Faction, Malice, or private Ends. But they streightly charged and required them, in his Majesty's Name, to live together, in that Concord, Unity, and joint Care of the common Good of the Plantation, as became the Undertakers of such an Action, the Subjects of such a King, and the Professors of such a Religion. They told them also, that they were informed by some, who had lately been Eye-witnesses, that their Fortifications, Houses of Habitation, and Provision of Victual, were not cared for in such sort, as they ought to be ; which was highly displeasing to his Majesty. And therefore they required them, to be more careful hereafter, as well for themselves, as for the publick Weal and Subsistence of the Colony.

B u t the Contract being dissolved, and the Benefit of sole Importation taken from the Company, the *Warwickian* Faction themselves were soon alarmed, at the Apprehension of a general and unlimited Importation of Tobacco. Wherefore Sir *Nathaniel Rich* proposed to the Company, their entering into a new Treaty with his Majesty, for the sole Importation, and for farming the forty thousand Weight of *Spanish* Tobacco ; which he gave them to understand, from some Speech, he had lately had with the Lord Treasurer, there were great Hopes of obtaining. But his Proposition was slighted and rejected, as a Scheme, which had lately been rendered abortive, by himself and his Faction ; and as it would be necessarily productive of those Salaries and Expences, which they had so loudly exclaimed against. But soon after, the same Gentleman informed the Company, that there was like to be a free Importation of all Sorts of foreign Tobacco, without Stint or Limitation ; and that there was a Proclamation shortly to come forth,

87   T   to

1623.   to that Purpofe. This was a thing before not fufpected or
━━━━━   imagined ; and it was unanimoufly judged, to be utterly
Sir *Francis* deftrudive of the Colonies. For as the meaneft Tobaccoes
Wyat, Go- might be bought in *Spain*, for fix Pence a Pound, the Price
vernor.   of the Plantation Tobacco, after the Difcharge of Freight,
.   Cuftom, Impoft, and other Charges, would be reduced to
little or nothing. The Company therefore unanimoufly
entered upon feveral Schemes and Meafures, to prevent fo
unfortunate an Event ; all which at laft ended, in a bare
Promife from the Lord Treafurer (and the Court Promifes
of that Time were not greatly to be depended upon) that
forty thoufand Weight of *Spanifh* Tobacco only, fhould be
imported into *England*.

SIR *Thomas Smith*'s Accounts remained ftill unfettled,
and Sir *Edward Sackvil* was among the freeft in his Cen-
fures and Complaints of this Matter. About this time,
Sir *Thomas Smith*, cafually meeting him, complained and
expreffed much Concern, that he fhould publickly, and in
divers Places, fay, that Sir *Thomas* was indebted to the
Company. Sir *Edward Sackvil* was a young Nobleman of
a frank and generous Nature. He fpoke freely, whatever
he thought, and was not at all of a Turn to deny, what
he had once faid. He therefore confeffed it to be true, and
gave his Reafons for it. Whereupon Sir *Thomas Smith* folemnly protefted his Clearnefs and Integrity, and as a Proof
of it, afked Sir *Edward Sackvil* ; If he was fo much in the
Company's Debt, why they did not, efpecially in this their
Time of Want and Neceffity, fue and recover it ? For he
was undoubted folvent, and able to make them full Satif-
fadion. But, he faid, it was fo far from this, that he had
been now, for the Space of three Years, in vain impor-
tuning and folliciting an Audit of his Accounts, and had,
for that End, delivered in all his Books to the Company.
This was alfo confirmed by Sir *Humphrey Handford*, then
Sherif of *London*, and one Mr. *Abdy*, a rich Merchant ;
who told Sir *Edward Sackvil* further, that they had formerly, by the Company's Appointment, examined Sir
Thomas Smith's Accounts, and found the Ballance five hundred and odd Pounds in his Favour, which they had accordingly witneffed under their Hands, and delivered in to
the Court. As to this Affertion of thefe two Gentlemen,
I find, at a Court held *May* 12, 1619, on the Motion of
Sir *Thomas Smith*, Mr. *Maurice Abbot*, Mr. *Humphrey
Handford*, and Mr. *Anthony Abdy* were admitted to be
prefent at the auditing the Account, to fee, that Sir *Thomas Smith* received no Wrong. But it was alfo ordered,
that three of the old Auditors, *viz.* Sir *Edwin Sandys*, then
Trea-

Treafurer, Sir *John Davers*, and Mr. *John Wroth* fhould
be of the *Quorum*, and that nothing fhould be concluded,
without the Confent of two of them at· the leaft. And
foon after, at a Quarter Court, Mr. *Abbot* and thofe two
Gentlemen, together with Mr. *Thomas Keightly* for the
Company, were admitted extraordinarily into the Number
of legal Auditors. But that the Accounts had ever been
fully audited and paffed by them, is plainly falfe, by the
whole Courfe and Tenor of the Company's Records. And
if thefe Gentlemen, who were only Auditors *ex parte*, on
Sir *Thomas Smith*'s Behalf, did give in any Paper to the
Court, relating to the full Settlement and Ballance of thofe
Accounts, it could never furely, either in Law or Reafon,
be received as authentic and definitive. But Sir *Edward
Sackvil* being unacquainted with the Proceedings of thofe
Times, Sir *Thomas Smith* befought him, that his Accounts
might be paffed ; and that he might be no farther molefted
upon that Head, but permitted to go in Peace to his Grave,
being already far ftricken in Years, and fufficiently afflicted
with the many Infirmities, incident to old Age. But he
declared, that none of thofe Pains and Afflictions were
comparable to the Grief and Anguifh of Mind, which he
received from thefe injurious Attacks on his Good-name
and Reputation ; efpecially as they proceeded from Perfons,
from whom he had hoped, by his many Years Services, a
far different Ufage and Return.

Sir *Edward Sackvil's* generous Nature was affected
with this Difcourfe ; and he very earneftly and warmly
moved the Company, to appoint fome Perfons, to put an
immediate and effectual End to this Bufinefs. For, as Sir
Thomas Smith had thus fairly put himfelf upon his Trial, he
thought, that to delay it, would hardly be juft, and to deny it quite, would be an evident and downright Injuftice.
Whereupon Sir *Edwin Sandys* faid, that the Office of Auditors, as he conceived, was not to make, but to examine
and fettle an Account ; that the Accounts, exhibited by Sir
Thomas Smith, had been found by the Auditors, after great
Labour and Pains fpent upon them, to be fo diforderly,
intricate, and defective, that they fcarce merited the Name
of Accounts ; that he fpoke not this, to lay any Afperfion
on Sir *Thomas Smith*, further than of Neglect (for it was
well known, that he neither made, nor kept thofe Accounts himfelf) but to clear the Auditors and the Company, from all Imputation and Blame. For they had often
declared their Exceptions and the Difficulties of thofe Accounts, as well to Sir *Thomas Smith*, as to the Company ;
and he then had a Writing, which contained many weighty

Ex-

Exceptions againſt them. However, altho' they ſeemed to
him to be altogether bottomleſs and unexaminable, yet he
promiſed, that the Auditors ſhould proceed in them, with
all poſſible Expedition.

ALDERMAN *Johnſon* and Mr. *Effington* were now
likewiſe found, to be clearly indebted eight hundred Pounds
to the Company, beſides the old Magazine Accounts,
which they kept ſo dark and intricate, that the Auditors
had not yet been able, fully to explicate and unravel them.
And Sir *Samuel Argall* (for, about this time, he received
the Honour of Knighthood) was ſtill under Proſecution
from the Company, for his Rapines and extortionate Adminiſtration in *Virginia*. So that it was evident, that theſe
Gentlemen could never be ſafe or ſecure, as long as the
Company continued in Being; and it is greatly to be ſuf-
pected, that they, by the Part they acted in the late Commotions, aimed not ſo much at the Diſſolution of the Contract, as the Diſſolution of the Company. But now the
Contract being annulled, and the Diſturbances ſomewhat
allayed, they reſolved to keep the Company ſtill in Employment, and not permit them to enjoy any long Leiſure
or Tranquility. For ſoon after the Diſſolution of the Contract, Alderman *Johnſon* preſented, in a private and concealed Manner, a Writing to his Majeſty, entitled; *The*
humble Petition of ſundry Adventurers and Planters in the
Virginia and Somer-Iſlands Plantations. The Subſtance of
this was:

THAT among the many memorable Works of his Majeſty's gracious Reign, the Plantations of *Virginia* and the
Somer-Iſlands were not the leaſt conſiderable: That theſe
were the firſt *American* Colonies, attempted and brought to
Effect, by the *Engliſh* Nation: That the Beginning of the
Enterpriſe was attended with ſo great an Expence, without
any preſent Hope of Retribution, as was ſufficient, at the
firſt View and Computation, to have diſcouraged the moſt
forward and reſolute Adventurers: That however, by the
Divine Aſſiſtance and his Majeſty's gracious Encouragement, together with that mild and diſcreet Government,
at firſt ſettled and appointed by his Majeſty, all ſorts of
Men were, in ſuch kind and friendly Manner, invited and
induced to engage themſelves in it, that notwithſtanding
thoſe many Difficulties, that great Action, which muſt
otherwiſe have periſhed in the Birth, not only took Life
and Being, but alſo proceeded, for many Years, in a moſt
hopeful and comfortable Courſe: That there was then
Unity and Love among themſelves at home, and Peace and
Quiet with the Savages abroad; by which means, ſundry
of

of thofe Infidels, and fome of eminent Rank, were converted to the *Chriftian* Religion, and many Staple Commodities began to be raifed and imported into *England*: Sir *Francis*
That fuch were the Bleffings, in thofe Times, upon their *Wyat*, Go-
juft and peaceable Proceedings; whereas it had come to vernor.
pafs, they knew not how, that notwithstanding his Majefty's Subjects had been, in great Multitudes, tranfported to
the Plantations, yet the aforefaid Commodities, and the
other Fruits of the Enterprife, had not appeared of late,
as in former Times; their Unity at home was turned into
civil Difcord and Diffenfion; and their Peace abroad, into
Maffacre and Hoftility between the Natives and the Colony;
and that many of the ancient Adventurers and Planters
conceived themfelves, to be many ways injured, abufed,
and oppreffed:

T HAT fearing, upon thefe Accounts, without the Help
of a fupreme Hand, the utter Ruin and Deftruction of thofe
great and noble Undertakings, and not holding it fit, to
trouble his Majefty's facred Ears with all particular Complaints and Allegations, they humbly befought him, to nominate and appoint fome worthy Perfons, by Commiffion
under the great Seal of *England*, who by Oath, or otherwife, by all lawful Ways and Means, fhould enquire and
examine; What was the true State of the Colonies, at
the Time, when Sir *Thomas Smith* left the Government of
the Companies; what Monies had fince been collected for
the Plantations; by whom received, and how the fame had
been procured· and expended; and what, after fo vaft an
Expence, was the prefent State and Condition of the Colonies: That the faid Commiffioners fhould alfo enquire into
all Grievances and Abufes; what Wrongs had been done
to any of the Adventurers or Planters, together with the
Grounds and Caufes thereof; and fhould propofe, how the
fame might in time to come, be reformed and prevented;
and how the Bufinefs of the Colonies might be better managed and carried on. So that, all Contentions being reconciled, the Authors thereof condignly punifhed, Peace
and Unity reftored, and the Government of Affairs better
eftablifhed, thofe noble Works might go on and profper
with a Bleffing from Heaven, to his Majefty's great Honour and Profit, and to the religious and publick Ends, for
which they were at firft undertaken.

A BOUT the fame time, Captain *Nathaniel Butler*, a
Creature of the Earl of *Warwick*'s, who had been fent to
pillage *Bermudas*, and had fled thence to *Virginia*, as hath
been already mentioned, was introduced to the King, and
obliged, as it was pretended, to give his Majefty an Account

1623. count of the State of the Colony in *Virginia*. This he
presented, under the starched and affected Title of, *The*
Sir *Francis* *unmasked Face of our Colony in Virginia, as it was in the*
Wyat, Go- *Winter* 1622. This contained the following Particulars
vernor. and Allegations.

1. THAT he found the *English* Plantations generally
seated upon mere Marshes, full of infectious Bogs and mud-
dy Creeks and Lakes; and thereby subject to all those Inconveniencies and Diseases, which are commonly found in
the most unhealthy Parts of *England*, whereof every Country and Climate hath some.

2. THAT he found the Shores and Sides of those Parts
of the main River, where the Plantations were settled,
every where so shallow, that no Boat could approach them.
So that, besides the Difficulty, Danger, and Spoil of Goods
in landing, the poor People were forced to a continual
Wetting and Wading, and that in the Midst of Winter,
when the Ships commonly arrived; and that they thereby
got such violent Surfeits of Cold upon Cold, as never left
them, till they were brought to their Graves.

3. THAT the People, sent over, arriving, for the most
part, very unseasonably in Winter, found neither Guest-
house, Inn, nor any such Place, to shelter themselves from
the Weather; no, not so much as a Stroke given, towards
any such charitable and necessary Work. So that many,
for want hereof, were not only seen dying under Hedges,
and in the Woods, but being dead, lay some of them many
Days, unregarded and unburied.

4. THAT the Colony, that Winter, was in great Di-
stress for Provisions, so that *English* Meal was sold for thirty, and their own native Corn, called Maize, for ten and
fifteen Shillings a Bushel. But that, however heavy this
might lay upon the poor People, there were Reasons to
suspect, it was not unaffected by the Chief Men. For they
only having the Means, in these Extremities, to trade with
the Natives, did hereby engross all into their Hands, and
sell it out at their own Prices. To which he added, that
he himself had heard from the Mouth of a prime one
among them, that he would never wish their own Corn
cheaper, than eight Shillings a Bushel.

5. THAT their Houses were generally the worst, that
he had ever seen; the meanest Cottages in *England* being
every way equal, if not superior, to the best Houses in
Virginia. And that besides, they were seated, so improvidently, and scatteringly one from another, as partly by
their Distance, but especially by the Interposition of Creeks
and

1623.

Sir *Francis Wyat,* Go-
vernor

and Swamps, they offered all Advantages to the favage Enemy, and were utterly deprived of the Means of fudden Re-
collection, upon any emergent Occafion.

6. THAT he found not the leaft Piece of Fortification :
That three Pieces of Ordinance only were mounted at *James-
City*, and one at *Flower-de-hundred*, but not one of them
ferviceable. So that it was certain, that a fmall Bark of
an hundred Tons might take it's Time, to pafs up the
River, and coming to an Anchor before *James-Town*, might
beat all their Houfes about their Ears, and fo forcing them
to retreat into the Woods, land under the Favour of their
Ordinance, and rifle the Town at Pleafure.

7. THAT expecting, according to their printed Accounts, to find fundry Commodities in great Forwardnefs,
he found not any one of them fo much as in any Toward-
nefs of Being. For the Iron-works were utterly wafted,
and the People dead ; the Glafs Furnaces at a Stand, and
in fmall Hopes of proceeding ; and as for the reft, they
were had in general Derifion, even among themfelves ; and
the Pamphlets concerning them, being fent thither by hundreds, were laughed to Scorn, and every bafe Fellow gave
them the Lye in divers Particulars. So that Tobacco was
their only Bufinefs, and for ought he could obferve, every
Man madded upon that, and little thought of, or looked
after, any thing elfe.

8. THAT he found the ancient Plantations of *Henrico*
and *Charles-City* quite deferted, and abandoned to the Spoil
of the *Indians* ; who not only burnt the Houfes (faid to be
once the beft in the Country) but fell upon their Stocks of
all Kinds, and killed and deftroyed them, to the great
Grief, as well as utter Ruin of the old Inhabitants ; who
ftuck not to affirm, that thefe were not only the beft and
moft healthy Parts of the Country, but might alfo, by
their natural Strength of Situation, have been the moft eafily preferved of all others.

9. THAT whereas, according to his Majefty's gracious
Letters-patent, his People in *Virginia* were to be governed,
as near as poffibly could be, according to the excellent
Laws and Cuftoms of *England*, he found, not only ignorant and forced Errors in divers Particulars, but alfo wilful
and defigned Deviations from Law. Infomuch that fome
Perfons, who urged due Conformity to his Majefty's gracious Intentions, were termed, in Contempt, *Men of the
Law*, and were even excluded from thofe Rights, which
they were elected and fworn unto in *England*.

10. THAT there having been, as it was thought, ten
thoufand Souls tranfported to *Virginia*, there were not, at

T 4   that

1623. that prefent, through the aforefaid Abufes and Neglects,
above two Thoufand of them to be found, and many of
Sir *Francis* thofe alfo, in a moft fickly and defperate State.   So that it
Wyat, Go-
vernor. might be undoubtedly expected, unlefs the Confufions and
private Ends of fome of the Company in *England*, and the
bad Execution of their Agents in *Virginia*, were fpeedily
redreffed, by a divine and fupreme Hand, inftead of a Plantation, it would fhortly get the Name of a Slaughter-houfe,
and fo juftly become odious to themfelves, and contemptible to all the World.

THE End and Defign of thefe Reprefentations, together
with their Falfhood and Unjuftnefs in the main, will be
eafily feen from the foregoing Narration.   But however
flily and covertly they were prefented to the King, the
Knowledge of them could not be long kept from the Company.   For the Lord *Cavendifh* and Sir *Edward Sackvil*
were foon advertifed, by their Friends at Court, of Alderman *Johnfon*'s Petition; and they had an extraordinary
Court of the Company immediately warned, in order to
enter upon fome prefent Courfe, to prevent it's making any
finifter Impreffions upon his Majefty's Breaft.   This Court
fent fome of their Body to defire Alderman *Johnfon*, either
to bring, or fend them, a Copy of the Petition, he had
lately prefented to his Majefty.   But he faid, he had neither himfelf a Copy, nor knew of any Perfon that kept
a Copy of it.   However he affured them, that the Petition
was no ways againft the Company.   This was likewife affirmed by fome, then prefent in Court, who had been at
the Delivery of the Petition.   They alfo profeffed themfelves, to be as ftudious of the Good of the Plantation and
of the Company, as any other whatfoever; and therefore
defired the Company, not to intermeddle or engage themfelves in the Matter, before they had feen the Petition.
But this not fatisfying the Court, they were defired to declare, what was the Subject of their Complaint, and againft
what Perfons.   For Lord *Cavendifh* faid, if they did not
find themfelves aggrieved with the Company, they ought
not to have complained to his Majefty at all, 'till they had
firft made known their Grievances to the Court, and feen,
what Remedy would have been by them applied.   At
length, Sir *Edward Sackvil* faid, that altho' Alderman
Johnfon and his Accomplices would give them no Light
into the Affair, yet himfelf, and fome others in Court,
could fully and certainly inform the Company, what was
the Subftance of that Petition.   Whereupon he gave them
a fhort and exact Account of it's Purport and Aim, and
declared

declared it to be true, upon his own certain Knowledge ; 1623. which was likewife confirmed by the Lord *Cavendifh*. The Court was in no Doubt or Hefitation about the Matter, but clearly judged it, to be directly againft the Company ; and accordingly refolved, to juftify their Conduct. But as to the Iffue of the Alderman's Petition, they readily joined in it, and ordered a Petition to be prefented in the Company's Name, to befeech his Majefty, that the Examination of thefe things might be referred to the Lords of the Privy Council ; that fo their Innocency, or their Guiltinefs, might be either cleared, or punifhed. And in the mean time, to prevent all Prepoffeffion againft them, they ordered a Declaration of the prefent State of *Virginia*, comparatively with it's former State under Sir *Thomas Smith*, which had, by the Earl of *Southampton*'s Order, been drawn up by a Committee of the Council, about the *Chriftmas* before, to be now read in the Court, and being, with fome fmall Alterations, confirmed, to be delivered to his Majefty, as the Company's Act. This Declaration fet forth :

Sir *Francis Wyat*, Governor.

THAT in *December*, 1618, being the twelfth Year from the firft Settlement of the Colony, after fourfcore thoufand Pounds Expence, and upwards, of the publick Stock, befides other Sums of private Planters and Adventurers, there were remaining in *Virginia* about fix hundred Perfons, Men, Women, and Children, and of Cattle about three hundred at the moft ; and that the Company was then left in Debt near five thoufand Pounds : But that then (*Chriftmas* 1622) through the Divine Bleffing, notwithftanding the late Mortalities in all thofe Parts of *America*, and notwithftanding the Maffacre, and the great Mortality, confequent thereon, by the People's being driven from their Habitations and Provifions, there were ftill remaining (as was computed) above five and twenty hundred Perfons, fent over at the Expence only of thirty thoufand Pounds of the publick Stock, befides the Charges of particular Societies and Planters ; that the Cattle were alfo encreafed to above a thoufand Head, befides Goats, and infinite Numbers of Swine ; and that the old Debt, left on the Company by Sir *Thomas Smith*, was wholly difcharged :

THAT at the faid Time, *December*, 1618, the only Commodities of Value, returned from *Virginia*, were Tobacco and Saffafras ; whereas, during the four laft Years, great Sums had been expended, and infinite Care and Diligence beftowed, by the Officers and Company, for fetting forward various Commodities and Manufactures ; as Iron-Works, Wine, Silk, Sawing-Mills, Salt-Pans, and other things of the like Nature ; And that they had been particu-

larly

larly careful, according to his Majesty's Advice and Directions, to restrain the Colony from their too eager Pur-
suit of Tobacco, as did abundantly appear, from their frequent Letters, Instructions, and Charters to that Effect,
with sundry printed Books and Pamphlets, made purposely
and published for their Use and Direction:

THAT as to the Government, it had been, within the
four last Years, reformed according to his Majesty's original
Directions, in the Letters-patent; and the People were no
longer discontented and mutinous, but now lived in great
Peace and Tranquility: And to the End, that Persons of
Worth might be allured to the Places of Power and Profit,
and all Occasion of Rapine and Extortion removed, they
had raised a competent annual Provision and Revenue, for
the Governor, and all other Officers and Magistrates, and
particularly for the Clergy, according to the Degree and
Quality of each Place:

THAT these their Cares were, by no means, lost or in-
effectual; but as they had settled the Colony in perfect Quiet
and Content, so they had raised at home so great a Fame of
Virginia, that Men now, not only out of Necessity, as at
first, but many Persons of good Quality and Fortune had,
out of Choice, removed themselves thither, and were daily
providing to remove:

THAT there had been granted, in the last four Years,
forty four Patents for Land, for each of which the Patentees
had undertaken to transport one hundred Men at the least;
whereas, in the former twelve Years, there had not been
granted above six:

THAT, in the said time, there had been employed forty
two Ships, most of great Burthen (whereof seventeen Sail
were, about *Christmas* last, in *James* River at once) whereas, in four Years before, there were not above twelve employed:

THAT, in the said four last Years, there had come in
ten times the Number of Adventurers, as had done in twice
the time before: So that, whereas before the legal Number
of twenty could scarce be got together, to make a Quarter
Court, it seldom now consisted of less than two hundred,
and sometimes of many more:

THAT they could not omit the extraordinary Blessing
of God, in exciting the Hearts of many zealous and devout
Persons, to extend their Aid towards this glorious Work,
who had contributed, within the four last Years, to the
Value of fifteen hundred Pounds, for pious and religious U-
ses; a Fruit, whereof the preceeding Years were altogether
barren:

THAT

THAT however it could not be denied, but that the
Encreafe and Profperity of the Colony had lately received
a fatal Blow and Interruption, by the *Indian* Maffacre; and
their Peace and Unity at home had been much broken and
difturbed, by divers troublefome Oppofitions. But the one,
they hoped, would foon be fharply punifhed and revenged;
and the other muft, with Patience be borne, and overcome
with Conftancy.

AND laftly, they concluded with befeeching his Majefty
(as being the firft Founder, and gracious Supporter of this
great Enterprife, which would continue to all Pofterity a
conftant Monument of his glorious Name) to grant them the
four hundred young Men, long fince promifed to be levied
on the feveral Counties, in order to be fent to *Virginia*, to
root out the barbarous Enemy, and to fupply the Colony,
in Parts yet defective and unfettled; and they doubted not,
in a fhort time to be able, to yield him fo good and fo real
an Account of the Fruit of their Cares and Labours, as
might, in fome fort, be anfwerable to their Duty, and to
his Majefty's princely Expectation.

BESIDES this Declaration, the Lord *Cavendifh* produced
another Writing, containing a Vindication of the late Conduct of the *Virginia* and *Somer-Iflands* Companies. His
Lordfhip had drawn this up himfelf, for the Satisfaction of
fome very noble Perfons, who had, from finifter Informations, conceived a hard Opinion of the Companies Proceedings; and as, he faid, thofe Noblemen, upon reading that
Difcourfe, were fully fatisfied of the Juftice and Fairnefs of
their Actions, fo he hoped, it might work the like Effect
upon his Majefty's Mind. Whereupon that Writing was
deliberately read, and every Article and Branch thereof,
being duly weighed and confidered, was feverally put to the
Queftion, and it was ordered to be delivered to his Majefty,
as the Company's Act and Anfwer; there being not above
three Voices againft any Part thereof, and moft of them being confirmed and approved, by an unanimous Confent.
This long Difcourfe contained three different Heads: Firft,
Anfwers to the feveral Objections againft the Company's
Proceedings: Secondly, the true Caufes of the late Difagreement and Difturbances: And thirdly, it propofed Remedies, for preventing the like Inconveniencies and Factions
for the future.

I am fenfible, that the long Detail of Declarations and
Anfwers, is a moft tedious and unpleafant Part of Hiftory
to the common Reader; and I have obferved, that fuch
Pieces, even in the Hands of our beft Writers, and however neceffary to clear up Points of Hiftory, have neverthelefs

1623.

Sir *Francis*
Wyat, Go-
vernor.

lefs been much diftafted by feveral Perfons. But as thefe
publick Papers contain the moft authentic Reafon and Account of things, and as they are the fureft and moft indubitable Materials, for an Hiftorian to proceed upon, I fhall
not be turned from my Courfe, by the accidental Diflike of
fome Readers. For the Diffolution of the Company now
draws on, and I intend to give a full View of the Motives
and Proceedings in that Affair; which can be from nothing
drawn fo well, as from the publick Acts and Writings of
both Parties, and their outward Pretences at leaft, and different Allegations. However, I efteem it my Part and Duty, to fave the Reader from all unneceffary Forms and Re-
petitions; and to give him the Subftance of thofe original
Acts and Records, in the fhorteft Manner I poffibly can,
without injuring or obfcuring their main Senfe and material
Points. As for this Difcourfe therefore, now prefented by
Lord *Cavendifh*, and adopted by the Company, it fet forth:
That it was manifeft, his Majefty's Ears had been abufed
by divers Mifinformations, to which they held it their Duty
to give a true and juftifiable Anfwer.

I. I T was objected, that fome few of the Company led
and overfwayed the reft; and that, in the particular Bufinefs of the Contract, thefe Perfons, aiming at their own
private Advantage, efpecially in the Point of Salaries, had
therefore perfuaded and mifled the Court.

To this it was anfwered; that it was true, fome particular Perfons, with great Labour and Pains, and without
any Hope or Profpect of Reward, had employed much of
their Time and Endeavours, in ftudying, what might tend
to the Good and Benefit of the Colonies; and this only with
the View, to propofe and communicate to the Courts their
faithful and impartial Advice; which was the Duty, and
in the Power, of every Member of thofe Societies, to do.
But that this honeft Diligence, and thefe clear and difinterefted Views, fhould be interpreted an enflaving or mif-
leading the Courts, was, in their Opinion, a moft unjuft
Cenfure, and a hard Requital to thofe Perfons, who, for
the publick Good, had beftowed fo much of their Time,
and neglected many Opportunities of private Gain.

A N D as to the Suppofition, that thefe Men, in Refpect
of the Salaries, had mifguided the Courts in the Cafe of the
Contract, they made his Majefty a clear and faithful Nar-
rative of their Proceedings in that Bufinefs; much the fame
in Effect as I have already related it. And they declared,
that the Gentlemen, elected to the two great Salaries, a-
gainft which the opponent Faction chiefly exclaimed, did,
at fundry times, both in publick and private, ufe all poffible

ble Endeavour and Induſtry, to keep themſelves from being choſen: But that the Company's Experience of their Faith-fulneſs and Ability, had cauſed them to be elected, and in a manner forced to thoſe Employments, againſt their Wills: And that they had ſince, in ſeveral Courts, as much as in them lay, ſurrendered their Offices; but their Reſignation would never be received or admitted by the Company.

2. It was objected, that the Courts were overawed, eſpe-cially in the Buſineſs of the Contract.

To which it was replied, that it was a ſtrange Boldneſs in any, eſpecially in any of the Company, who knew their Proceedings therein, to affirm a thing ſo manifeſtly falſe and groundleſs; which the Company were ſo perfectly con-vinced of, that this was one of the principal Cauſes, why Mr. *Wrote,* who firſt broached that Slander, was cenſured and ſuſpended. And they told his Majeſty, that this Point had been put to the Vote, often and in different Courts, when different Perſons were preſent, and it had always been unanimouſly adjudged a falſe and ſcandalous Imputation.

3. It was alledged, that theſe Perſons, when they could not carry Matters by Plurality of Voices, ſpun out the Courts 'till eleven o'Clock at Night; by which Means, thoſe, who would have oppoſed their Schemes, being over-wearied with ſo long ſitting, departed.

They owned, that the Day, here meant, the Courts ſat 'till about ten o'Clock. But they gave his Majeſty the Reaſons of it: That many long Courts were to be read and examined; that Mr. *Wrote's* Affair took up much Time; and that they were afterwards obliged, to enter upon ſeve-ral Points relating to the Contract, which muſt be then de-termined, or elſe deferred for above three Months, till the next Quarter Court; and that this would have been much to the Prejudice of that Buſineſs, as they daily expected the Arrival of a great Quantity of Tobacco. But as to what was chiefly inſinuated by this Objection, they declared it to be utterly falſe. For altho' ſome perhaps departed before the Riſing of the Court, yet not one of the opponent Party went away; and at the very laſt, when the Queſtion was put, there were, beſides divers Noblemen and Knights, a-bout an hundred Perſons in the Court.

4. It was alledged, that whilſt the Contract was in Agi-tation, the Courts were purpoſely put off, for ſeven Weeks together; that ſome Planters who were ſhortly to go away, might not have Opportunity to complain againſt it.

This Objection they averred to be manifeſtly falſe and impoſſible. For the Contract, which could only be ratified in a Quarter Court, was concluded upon at their laſt Mid-
ſummer

1623. ſummer Quarter Court, when all the old Planters, being about thirty in Number, were, or might have been in the Court ; for none went away, till about eight Weeks after. Neither could it then be diſcovered, that any of them were diſcontented with it ; but on the contrary, ſome argued very earneſtly for it.   And beſides, it was untrue, that the Courts were at all put off ſo long.   For altho', by the Orders of the Companies, there might be a Ceſſation of their Meetings, in the long Summer Vacation, when the Noblemen and Gentlemen of principal Figure and Conſequence were in the Country, unleſs there ſhould occur ſome extraordinary and preſſing Occaſion, yet the Courts met more frequently that Summer, than had been uſual at ſuch Times, by reaſon of ſending out ſeveral Ships, and with them the Company's Orders and Directions to the Colonies.

Sir *Francis Wyat,* Governor.

5. It was confidently affirmed, that the *Virginia* Planters had petitioned his Majeſty, to bring all their Tobacco into *England* ; and that this Petition was, by the Officers of the Company, ſuppreſſed.

In Confutation of this, they referred to the original Petition itſelf, then in the Hands of the Lord High Treaſurer ; and they ſaid, that no Man, that had ever ſeen that Petition, and had not a Mind wilfully to put Wrongs upon the Company, could ever ſcrew ſuch a Senſe out of it.   They likewiſe gave his Majeſty an Account of the Occaſion of the Petition, and the Reaſon why it was not preſented ; the ſame, that has been already given, in the foregoing Parts of this History.

6. It was objected, that no Buſineſs could be done in their Courts, by reaſon of Faction and Wrangling.

To this they anſwered, that it was an odd thing, for Men to complain of that, wherein themſelves were principally faulty.   Yet they denied this to be true, in ſo general and extenſive a Senſe ; altho' it muſt be confeſſed, that ſome diſcontented Perſons, who had lately joined together to oppoſe the Contract, had long waited for all Occaſions, to raiſe Troubles and Contentions in the Companies ; whoſe Faces, for ſeveral Years paſt, had never been ſeen in the Courts, except when they came to raiſe a Tempeſt and Diſturbance.   However, they aſſured his Majeſty, that this Faction, when they had muſtered all their Forces, and ſent for their whole Strength out of the Country, amounted to but twenty ſix Perſons ; whereas the *Virginia* Company, in particular, conſiſted of about a ʼthouſand Adventurers, and oftentimes two hundred, or more, were aſſembled at once.   So that this Objection of Faction and Wrangling muſt neceſſarily return back and reflect on themſelves ; as

in

in all well-governed Societies, the major Part was ever understood to involve the Consent of the minor, which, by making Opposition and Clamour, did undoubtedly thereby render themselves the factious Party.

7. IT was objected, that the Government of the Companies, as it then stood, was democratical and tumultuous, and ought therefore to be altered, and reduced into the Hands of a Few——And this was properly *argumentum ad hominem*, and very weighty in the Eyes of that Prince; who had a noted Aversion to all republican Forms of Government, and was, in Truth, for a Monarchy, in the strictest and highest Sense of the Word.

HOWEVER, the Company replied, that as to the Tumultuousness objected, it was already answered in the former Article of Faction, and plainly appeared to proceed only from themselves. And as to the Democracy, they said, that the Government of the Companies was no other, than what was prescribed in his Majesty's Letters-patent; and it was a bold Censure, thus to tax a Government, ordained and constituted by such an Authority. But yet they denied this Allegation to be just, or that their Government was properly democratical. For the Companies had not supreme Authority over the People of the Plantations, but governed them by an Authority derived from the King, according to his Laws, and were accountable to his Majesty for their Conduct; and therefore that Government could not properly be termed democratical, where the King was supreme, and where the People swore Allegiance only to him. And they added farther, that the Companies were so far from having supreme Power over the People of the Colonies, that when any Man had committed Offences, of what high Nature so ever (as lately appeared by two notorious Instances) if they could escape Punishment in the Plantations, where the Companies had Power, by his Majesty's Letters-patent, to call them to Trial and Account, they might, there in *England*, outface the Companies (as those two did) and they could have no Means of Redress, but by appealing to higher Justice.

HOWEVER, they owned, that, according to his Majesty's Institution, their Government had some Shew of a democratical Form; which was nevertheless, in that Case, the most just and profitable, and most conducive to the Ends and Effect aimed at thereby. For those Plantations, tho' much furthered by his Majesty's Grace, were yet chiefly founded by the Purses of private Men; who would never have adventured their Fortunes in such an Enterprise, if, in the Regulation and Government of the Business, their own

Votes

Votes and Opinions had not been admitted.   Befides which,
fuch infant Undertakings often called for large and fpeedy
Supplies, which could not be fent, but by the Purfes of
many Men ; who, had their Voices been excluded, and
the Management committed to a Few, would not perhaps
have been over-forward and hafty in contributing towards
their Relief.

L AST LY, they obferved, that the opponent Faction
cried out loudly againft Democracy, and yet called for O-
ligarchy ; which would, as they conceived, make the Government neither of better Form, nor more monarchial.
But they however hereby difcovered their Aim and Defire,
which was to draw all things into their own Hands and
Power, as had been fufficiently manifefted before, by fome
of their late Steps and Actions.

H AVING thus given Anfwers to the moft material Scandals againft the Companies, they next proceeded, to inform
his Majefty of the true Caufes, tho' difguifed, why thefe
twenty fix, by their fecret Whifperings and Infinuations,
and by their continual under-hand Practices, fo much laboured, to difgrace the Government of the Companies, and
in Effect, to bring the Plantations to utter Ruin.   And they
affured his Majefty, that, whatever Imputations they might
lay on the Companies behind their Backs, they never yet
had the Confidence, openly to avow and maintain them in
their Courts, but always qualified them with fuch Diftinc-
tions and Equivocations, as amounted to a flat Denial of
what they had faid.   And

1. T HE firft Caufe of thefe Mens Malice was the ill
Affection of the old Officers ; out of whofe Hands (the Colonies having not profpered under them) the Government
was neceffarily taken ; and their Profperity fince, implying
the evident Benefit of that Removal, and a manifeft Proof
of their ill Government, it had fo offended them, that they
endeavoured, the better to cover that Fault, by publick
Difturbances, and private Practice and Confederation, to
interrupt the prefent Profperity of the Colonies, and to ble-
mifh the Reputation, and difturb the Peace of the Companies : And that, to this End, they had not forborn to fet to
their Hands in Atteftation of moft falfe and fcandalous Petitions ; frequently to lay Imputations themfelves on the
Courts ; fometimes to procure Complaints from others a-
gainft them ; and at all times to yield a public Encouragement and Protection to fuch Perfons, as had done Wrong,
or were declared Enemies, to the Companies.

2. T HE fecond Caufe was, that the principal of thofe
Citizens, and fome others, who had wove themfelves into
the

the Oppofition, were for the moft Part fuch, as had for- merly borne Office, either in the Companies, or the Plan- tations; who having not cleared their many Accounts (fome of which were very fufpicious) and being preffed by the Companies, ufed all the Art, that Malice could invent, to do Prejudice, and give Difturbance, to the prefent Govern- ment; hoping, by that means to fhroud themfelves from a due Examination, and fo, in the Storm and Confufion, to go off, unconvicted and unpunifhed.

3. SOME others of thefe Opponents, of a different Rank and Quality, had either been concerned in fpoiling and fleec- ing the Plantations, and in fetting forth a piratical Ship, called the *Treafurer*; or elfe had abetted and protected thofe, who had done it, with fuch Violence, as was greatly to the Offence, Scandal, and Wrong of the Company. But their Ends not fully anfwering their Expectations, they had there- fore abandoned the *Virginia* Courts, except when they came to raife Troubles and Diffentions, in order, by that means, to keep the Company from calling thofe Offences into Queftion.

4. MOST of the twenty fix were involved in fome, or all thefe Caufes of Diffenfion; and the few that remained, were either Servants to, or had neceffary Dependency upon, fome of the reft.

LASTLY, they went on to propofe fome Remedies, to prevent the like Inconveniences and Difturbances for the fu- ture. Since therefore thefe Colonies were chiefly fettled, for the Honour of his Majefty's Times, in propagating the *Chriftian* Religion in thofe barbarous Parts; for the Enlarge- ment of his Dominions; for the Encreafe of his Revenue; for the enriching his People; and for the future Strength and Ornament of the Kingdom of *England*; they befought his Majefty, to give Countenance and Encouragement to their Labours; to believe well of the Companies, and not give too ready a Credit to the malicious and pre-concerted Informations of fome of their Members; and to grant them fome fuch prefent Teftimony of his good Opinion, and gra- cious Acceptance of their Endeavours, by Letter or other- wife, as might do Honour to the Company, and ftrengthen their Authority. And this they were the rather induced to hope, as the late great Breach in the Companies had been occafioned, by their Forwardnefs and Defire, to advance his Majefty's Profit and Revenue by the Contract. And they farther befought his Majefty, to be gracioufly pleafed to declare his Intention, that, in all Bufinefs of the Courts for the future, they fhould be left freely to govern them- felves, by their Charters and Laws; and withal, to give

prefent Order to the Lords of the Privy Council, that, if
there fhould be any fuch private Confpiracy, Confederation,
or Oppofition, as the Companies themfelves could neither
remedy nor punifh, to afford them their Help and Affiftance,
in the Remedy and Punifhment of the fame. And laftly
they prayed, that for fuch, as had been accufed of henious
Crimes, committed in the Plantations, and had thence efcaped, and then braved the Companies in *England*, his Majefty would be gracioufly pleafed, to extend his Power, and
fend them back to the Plantations, there to receive their juft
and legal Trials. And by thefe Affiftances, the Companies
would be enabled, chearfully to proceed, and in fhort time
fo to advance thofe great and noble Undertakings, as would
give his Majefty full Content, and juft Caufe to believe,
that thefe his Favours had been well beftowed, and rightly
ufed.

THE Earl of *Southampton* was not prefent, when thefe
things paffed ; and as he was obnoxious at Court, and had
received fome ill Ufage from it, it may be furmifed, that he
kept out of the Way purpofely, to avoid being farther em-
broiled. But it is, I think, much more agreeable to the
Character of that worthy and patriot Nobleman, to fuppofe, that he did not defert his Station in fuch a Manner,
but was abfent on other juft and neceffary Occafions. In
his Abfence therefore, thefe two Papers (together with a
Petition to his Majefty, to refer the Hearing of the Complaints of Alderman *Johnfon* and his Affociates, to the Body
of his moft Honourable Privy Council) were committed to
Lord *Cavendifh*, Lord *Delawarr*, Sir *Edward Sackvil*, Sir
John Brooke, and Colonel *Ogle*, to take the firft proper Opportunity to prefent them to his Majefty, and to make
Choice of fuch others of the Company, as they thought
fit, to atend them.

THIS Court alfo, at Mr. Deputy *Farrar's* Motion,
conferred the Freedom of the Company on *Carew Ralegh*
Efq; the only furviving Son of Sir *Walter*. He had gone,
after his Father's Death, a Gentleman Commoner, to *Wad-
ham* College, in *Oxford*; where he continued his Studies,
about five Years. About this time, being yet fcarce twenty
Years of Age, he came up to *London*, and went to Court ;
hoping by the Favour of *William*, Earl of *Pembroke*, his
noble Kinfman, to obtain fome Redrefs, in the Hardfhips
and Wrongs done him. But the King did not like his
Countenance there ; and faid, that he appeared in his Court,
like his Father's Ghoft. Wherefore, by the Earl's Advice,
he removed himfelf from his Majefty's Sight, and went
upon his Travels, till a more favourable Conjuncture fhould
offer.

offer. But however fixed this Monarch might be in his
Antipathy, and however fteady and conftant in doing an
eternal Difhonour to his own Judgment and Fame, by dif-
gracing and depreffing every thing that had Relation to
this Great Man, the *Virginia* Company feems to have had
a quite different Notion of things. For they willingly embraced the Pretence, of Sir *Walter Raleigh*'s being the firft
Difcoverer of *Virginia*, to teftify their Refpeét to his Memory and Merit, by conferring extraordinarily, upon his
Son, the Freedom of the Company, and a Voice in their
Courts. And he accordingly appears at their Courts, commonly ranked with the Knights, till *June* the next Year,
at which time, it may be fuppofed, he went on his Travels.

Soon after this, authentic Copies of Alderman *Johnfon*'s Petition and Captain *Butler*'s Information were, by
fome Perfon, fent to the Company; which being publickly
and diftinétly read, the Court was informed by Perfons of
Worth, that this Report, in particular, of the Unhealthi-
nefs of the Country, and of the Colony's being feated
among Bogs and Marfhes, having been induftrioufly fpread
by Captain *Butler* and his Affociates, not only over all
Parts of the City, but likewife into divers Parts of the
Country, was likely to ftop many hundreds of People, who
were preparing to tranfport themfelves thither; and that it
was therefore abfolutely neceffary, to make an immediate
Enquiry about that Matter. Whereupon fome, then prefent, who had been long and often in *Virginia*, affirmed
upon their certain Knowledge, that, at all the Plantations
on the main River, they might land, with Boats drawing
three Foot Water, from half Flood to half Ebb, fafe and
dry, without wetting their Foot; and that they had found,
by their own Experience, the Air to be as wholefome, and
the Soil for the moft Part, as fertile, as in any Part of *England*, or of any other Country, where they had been.
But the better to obviate the ill Confequences and Calumnies of Captain *Butler*'s Information, an Anfwer was drawn
up in Writing againft the next Meeting of the Company,
and fubfcribed by the Rev. Mr. *William Meafe*, a Minifter,
who had lived ten Years in *Virginia*; by one Mr. *John
Proéter*, a Man of good Sort, who had lived there fourteen
Years; and by fourteen others, Mafters of Ships, Mariners, and Inhabitants, who had been and lived, fome more
and fome lefs, in the Country, and were perfeétly acquainted with the River, and all Parts of the Colony.
This Anfwer, which they declared themfelves ready to
juftify upon Oath, contained a flat Denial and Difproof of

1623.   the feven firft Articles of *Butler's* Information. As to the
three laft, they left them to be anfwered by the Governor
Sir *Francis* and Company, as relating immediately to themfelves, and
Wyat, Go- containing things, either above their Determination, or out
vernor.   of their Knowledge. And as this Writing contained the
Teftimony of Eye-witnefles to Matters of Fact, it agreed
fo exactly in Subftance with an Anfwer, afterwards returned from *Virginia* by the Governor and General Affembly,
that I fhall not detain the Reader, at prefent, with an Ab-
ftract of it, but fhall refer to that more authentic Teftimony of the whole Body of the Colony, which will be hereafter recited, in it's proper Time and Place.

BUT befides this Difproof of Captain *Butler's* Information, the farther to detect and expofe his malicious Defigns and unfair Proceedings, two Papers were produced in
Court, and admitted to Record, under the Hands of *John*
Severne, Mafters-Mate, and *John Lowe,* Boatfwain, of the
James. In thefe they affirmed, that coming, one Morning, to Captain *Nathaniel Butler,* about fome Bufinefs, the
faid Captain brought a Writing in his Hand, and began to
read fome Part of it; telling them, he had been with the
King, and protefting, the Writing was for the Good of the
Country. Whereupon they, being in great Hafte, having
heard a few Lines only read, and not attending much to
the Matter, and befides conceiving Captain *Butler* to be a
very honeft Man, did readily fet their Hands to the faid
Writing. But having fince underftood, that it was in Difgrace and Difparagement of the Country, they, the faid
John Severne and *John Lowe,* did thereby difavow the faid
Writing, as falfe and unjuft; and farther protefted, that,
upon their Oaths, they muft declare the contrary. And all
thefe Proofs of his wilful Malice and Injuftice did Captain
Butler fit in the Court and hear, and calmly demanded a
Copy of the Anfwer to his Information.

BUT as his Majefty intended, in Compliance with the
Petitions of both Alderman *Jahnfon* and the Company, to
appoint Commiffioners to enquire into all thefe Matters and
Allegations, the Court thought it proper, to prepare be-
times to make their Defence. To this End, as the Company confifted of many Members of both Houfes of Parliament, they were naturally led to the Parliamentary Methods of proceeding, and refolved themfelves into a grand
Committee of the whole Company, which had Power, to
fubftitute and ordain other Sub-Committees, for expediting
Matters; that fo the Bufinefs, being parted among many
Hands, might be the more fpeedily and better accomplifhed.
And now having Copies of Alderman *Johnfon's* and Cap-
                                                        tain

tain *Butler*'s Complaints, they foon after drew up direct and particular Anfwers to them both.

IN Anfwer to Alderman *Johnfon*'s Petition, they obferved, that it was founded upon three main Allegations : Firft, that the former Government, under Sir *Thomas Smith*, as Treafurer, and Mr. *Canning* and himfelf, as Deputy-Treafurers, was mild and difcreet ; whereby all Sorts of Perfons were induced to engage themfelves in that great and difficult Action, which thence proceeded in a moft hopeful Way, and with Peace and Concord ; whereas it had of late come to pafs, that their Love and Unity at home were turned into civil Difcord and Diffenfion ; and that divers of the ancient Adventurers and Planters conceived themfelves, to be many ways injured, abufed and oppreffed.

To this they replied : That as to the Government at home in thofe times, all his Majefty's particular Inftructions therein were clean fuppreffed and extinguifhed, and the Originals no longer extant ; and that there were no Orders made for the Government of the Company, except now and then one, upon prefent Occafion. And as to the Government abroad in the Colony, it was, for the moft part, left abfolutely to the Governor's Will and Pleafure ; only inftead of a Body of moderate Laws, agreeable to the Conftitution and Government of *England*, there was printed at home, and with great Honour dedicated to Sir *Thomas Smith*, and afterwards by him fent to *Virginia*, by his own Authority, and without the Company's Order or Confent, a Book of moft truculent Laws, written in Blood ; which, altho' they might ferve for Martial Government in time of War, being tranflated moft of them from the Martial Laws of the United Provinces, yet were abfolutely deftructive of all the native Rights and Liberties of *Englifh* Subjects, and very far from deferving the Name of a mild Government, here given it by the Petitioners : And that, for this Caufe, People in *England* were deterred from going over in Perfon, to live there under fuch bloody and tyrannical Laws, and many of his Majefty's Subjects in *Virginia* were put to moft unjuft and undeferved Deaths. But moft efpecially, fuch a Weapon was hereby put into the Hands of one of the Governors, a Kinfman of Sir *Thomas Smith*, that he, in a manner, fpoiled and deftroyed the whole Colony, as was ftill extant and to be feen, in the Letters of Sir *Thomas Smith* himfelf and Alderman *Johnfon*.

THAT the Confequence of this Mifgovernment was, that the Colony was wafted to a few hundreds of People, who had neverthelefs no Intent to proceed in the Plan-

·tation,

tation, but being deftitute of Food, both fpiritual and temporal, cried out loudly againft the Company, for Injuftice
and Cruelty; being fome times, in Defpair, all fhipped to
return, and at other times, in Revenge, adopting to themfelves new Patrons and Defenders againft their bad Government. And that Adventurers at home did indeed, at firft,
come plentifully in, as to a new Thing; but that, at laft,
they abandoned the Courts, and refufed to pay their Monies fubfcribed; for which being fued, they pleaded in
Chancery, upon their Oaths, that the Monies were not
converted to the Ufe intended, but to particular Men's
Gains; and that no Accounts were kept, or were at leaft
to be feen. But on the contrary, they faid, what Reformations had been made, and what Meafures taken, in Point
of Government, for the four laft Years, might be apparent to all Men; and that their Labours herein had given
fuch Satisfaction to the Plantations, that the Colony of *Virginia* had, in particular, by a publick Act in their General
Affembly, returned Thanks to the Company, for their
great Love, Juftice, and Care.

As for Difcord and Diffenfion, they acknowledged,
within the Compafs of the four laft Years, there had been
fome great Rents made in the Council and Company; but
that thefe proceeded wholly from the Alderman and his
Party, the greateft Number of whom were feldom feen in
their Courts, but when they came to raife, or to nourifh,
this very Difcord and Faction, they here complained of.
And as to the Wrongs and Oppreffion of the ancient Adventurers and Planters, they challenged him to fhew, that
the Juftice, which it was in the Company's Power to give,
had ever been denied to any Man whatfoever; much lefs
had the Goods of fome particular Perfons in the Colonies,
by private Directions and underhand Letters, been taken
violently from them, contrary to all Juftice and due Courfe
of Law, and configned into the Hands of their potent Ad-
verfaries in *England*; as was notorioufly done, in the Cafe
of Captain *Miles Kendal,* formerly Governor of *Bermudas,*
who was fpoiled by Captain *Butler,* his Succeffor, of fourteen Negroes, granted him by a *Dutch* Captain, under a
falfe and groundlefs Pretence, that they belonged to their
piratical Ship, the *Treafurer.*

THE fecond Allegation of Alderman *Johnfon*'s Petition
was: That, under the former Government, they had
Peace with the *Indians,* by which means fundry of thofe
Infidels, and fome of eminent Rank, were converted to the
Chriftian Religion; whereas, of late, there had been a
Maffacre and Hoftility between the Natives and the Colony
of *Virginia*.   IN

IN Anfwer to this, they denied, that except *Pocahontas* (whom they here call *Matoax*) there had happened any thing of Note in the Converfion of thofe Infidels, under Sir *Thomas Smith*'s Adminiftration.   And they farther affirmed, that, during his time, the *Englifh* were almoft in a continual War and Hoftility with the *Indians*; and that, in particular, Captain *Argall* came away, in the laft Part of that time, and left unpunifhed the Murder of ten of the *Englifh*, by a Party of the *Chickahominies*.   But on the contrary, how great, and what chargeable Attempts, had been made, within the laft four Years, for the Converfion and Education of thofe Infidels, was fufficiently evident, from the Plantation for the College; on which, notwithftanding the late Maffacre, they conceived, there were yet remaining fixty Tenants, or thereabouts.   And the Company had indeed, in their firft Letter after the Knowledge of the Maffacre, propofed Methods, and given ftrict Orders, to the Governor and Council, for the Renewal of the College, and Refettlement of it's Lands; but Means being wanting, the Governor and Council could do nothing in it to Effect.   However they promifed, that that pious Work fhould, by the Divine Affiftance, again proceed, in due time.   And as to the Hoftility with the *Indians*, they declared, there had been none, within the four laft Years, before the late treacherous and bloody Maffacre; which had it not happened, thefe Maligners muft have been mute, and would have had nothing to alledge to the Difgrace of the Company and Plantation.

THE third Allegation of the Alderman's Petition was: That, in the firft twelve Years, divers Staple-Commodities began to be raifed and imported into *England*; whereas, of late Years, the aforefaid Commodities did not appear.

THEY replied, that this Objection reflected ftrongly on the Objector himfelf.   They owned, that fome Samples of thofe Commodities had been, by the Induftry of Sir *Thomas Dale*, fent home, in the ninth and tenth Years of the firft twelve; but that none had appeared, in the two laft, under the Government of Captain *Argall*.   The Reafon of which was, that the Magazine being then on foot, whereof the Alderman was Director, it pleafed him, to fet no Price upon any other Commodity, except Tobacco and Saffafras, being Commodities of his own Trade, and for the greateft Part whereof he himfelf became the Company's Chapman; and that, by this means, all Endeavours for thofe other Commodities were abandoned, and the Colony poffeffed with that doating Affection for Tobacco, which the Company had not fince, with all their Care, been able to extinguifh.

1623.

Sir *Francis Wyat,* Governor.

tinguifh.   And they then proceeded, to recount their late Endeavours for raifing divers Commodities; which had indeed lately received a fore Interruption from the Maffacre, but it was their Intent and Refolution, fhortly again to reftore and fet them up.

As for that Pretence, that the Petition aimed at no other End, but that after the Work of fome neceffary Reformation, the Work of the Plantations might be again renewed and profper; they faid, they were obliged, therein to detect the Alderman's unclear Proceedings.   For it fhould be juftified againft him, by undeniable Proof: That he had laboured of late, by ftrange and falfe Allegations, to difcourage fome Perfons of Eminence and Fortune, from favouring or proceeding in the Enterprife: That he had brow-beaten and found Fault with fuch, as had commended the Country, fo much extolled formerly by himfelf, in fundry printed Treatifes; and had declared, that the World had been cheated and deluded by *Virginia :* That he had faid, there were too many of the *Englifh* Nation there already; that the Staple-Commodities, fpoken of, would come to nothing; that the Iron was bafe, and not worth the Freight; the Grapes four, and the Climate improper for Wine; that the Mulberry Trees had a Prickle in them, which deftroyed the Silk-worms, when they came to any Bignefs; and that the Converfion of the Infidels was a vain and impoffible Attempt, they being defcended of the curfed Race of *Ham.*   And now, whether a Perfon of this Malice and Virulency of Difpofition was a proper Inftrument to work out the Good of the Colonies, they left to the Judgment of all clear and impartial Minds.

LASTLY, touching the Iffue of the Petition, that all Abufes might be examined and reformed, the Company declared, they willingly concurred with the Petitioners therein, but could not forbear remarking their too evident Partiality.   For they defired only, that the Accounts fince Sir *Thomas Smith*'s Time might be examined, which had always been fairly kept, and legally audited, according to the Orders of the Court, (except by one only of the Petitioner's Society) and yet they paffed the Accounts of the former Years over in Silence, which were neverthelefs three times as large, and thrice three times more queftionable.

In their Anfwer to Captain *Butler*'s Information, they recited, that the feven firft Articles had been anfwered by fixteen Eye-witneffes of the Matters alledged, Men of unqueftionable Character and Veracity, who were ready, at any time, to juftify the fame upon their Oaths.   They therefore referred to that, as being the higheft and moft
unex-

unexceptionable Evidence, that could be had in such a Case; and they proceeded themselves, to give Answers to the three last Articles. But as the Answer, afterwards returned from *Virginia* by the Governor and General Assembly, was much the same in Purport with this, I shall still, to avoid all tedious and needless Repetition, refer to that, hereafter to be given. But as to *Butler*'s last Clause, of the Confusions and private Ends of some of the Company in *England*, and of the bad Execution of their Agents in *Virginia*, they besought his Majesty, that he might not be permitted to wander in such general and indeterminate Accusations, which only tended to Slander and Defamation, but might be obliged to make an express and particular Discovery of those Persons and Measures before the Commissioners, that were soon to be appointed. And in the mean while, they protested against it, as calumnious and unjust, and of the self-same Truth with the rest of his Informations.

MR. *Berblock* also desired, that a short Passage, out of one of Sir *Thomas Dale*'s Letters to Sir *Thomas Smith*, might be read; which he had accidentally happened upon, in perusing the Company's Books, by Order of the Court. This was dated in *June* 1613, and has been already mentioned and extracted. In it, he desires them not to be gulled by the clamorous Reports of base People, but to believe *Caleb* and *Joshua*, and gives a very great and lavish Commendation of the Country; which Mr. *John Smith* declared to agree exactly, with what he, and divers other Persons of Worth, had heard from his own Mouth in *England*; and Mr. *Copeland* affirmed, that Sir *Thomas Dale* had told him the same in Effect, at *Japan* in the *East-Indies*. There was also read Part of a Letter from Sir *Samuel Argall* to the Company, dated in *July* 1617, highly commending the Healthiness and Conveniency of *James-Town*. To these was added, at the Lord *Cavendish*'s Motion, a long Declaration, by his Majesty's Council for *Virginia*, and the principal Assistants for the *Somer-Islands*; in which, they plainly, and without Disguise or Palliation, laid open the whole Scene of the Earl of *Warwick*'s Proceedings, with the iniquitous Practices of himself and his Faction, but most especially of his too grand Instruments of Rapine, Sir *Samuel Argall* and Captain *Butler*. This long and particular Relation has been of singular Service, and given great Light, in the fuller Detection of their fraudulent Arts and Management; but as it contains nothing materially different from the foregoing Relation of their Proceedings, I shall ease both myself and the Reader from the Trouble of an Abstract.

ALL

298
288

1623.

Sir Francis Wyat, Go-vernor.

ALL thefe Publick Acts, Declarations, and Teftimonials were laid before his Majefty, the Lords of the Privy Council, and the Commiffioners. For, two Days after this, on the 9th of *May*, a Commiffion iffued, under the Great Seal of *England*, to Sir *William Jones*, Knight, one of his Majefty's Juftices of the Court of Common Pleas, Sir *Nicholas Fortefcue*, Sir *Francis Gofton*, Sir *Richard Sutton*, Sir *William Pit*, Sir *Henry Bourchier*, and Sir *Henry Spilman*, Knights, or any four of them, to examine and enquire into all Matters and Bufineffes, any ways relating or appertaining to the Plantations of *Virginia* and the *Somer-Iflands*. Altho' the Points, to be enquired into, ran very much, in this Commiffion, according to the general Heads, and even the very Words, of the latter Part of Alderman *Johnfon's* Petition, yet the Lords of the Privy Council had the Alderman's Partiality reformed, and their Enquiry was not confined to the four laft Years, but extended to all Acts and Things, from the firft Incorporation of the Companies, and Settlement of the Colonies. Who thefe Commiffioners were, and what were their real Characters and Conduct through Life, I cannot fay. I only find, that *Cambden*, in his Annals for the Year 1619, briefly mentions *Fortefcue*, *Gofton*, *Sutton*, and *Pit*, late Commiffioners for the Navy, and for Domeftick Affairs, to be then knighted.

FROM this time, all Letters from the Colonies, both publick and private, were intercepted by his Majefty's Command; in order to furprife, and find out, any fecret Combinations and underhand Practices of the Companies, or their Officers. All their Books and Records were likewife fequeftered, by an Order of the Privy Council; and both the Mr. *Farrars*, the Deputy-Treafurers to the two Companies, were laid under Arreft, and confined. I cannot difcover, by what Colour or Pretence this was done; but it was a great Interruption, in preparing the Company's Bufinefs, which was to be laid before the Commiffioners. For their Defence depended entirely on their Books and Records, from which, they doubted not, to make their Innocency abundantly appear. And they were fo fenfible of the Prejudice, that would arife to the Companies, by their Deputies Reftraint, who were their greateft Accomptants, and by reafon of their Places, the moft converfant of all others in the Bufinefs of late Years, that they petitioned the Privy Council, fo far at leaft to fet them at Liberty, that they might be able to go forward with the Company's Bufinefs, and attend the Commiffioners. And their Books were accordingly foon after reftored, and the Deputies releafed.

BUT

299
289

Sir *Francis* *Wyat,* Governor.

BUT from thefe, and other difcouraging Circumftances, it was an eafy Matter to conjecture, what was aimed at, and how things were going.   And therefore the great Officers of the Company, the Earl of *Southampton,* Sir *Edwin Sandys,* and the two *Farrars,* through whofe Hands all the Company's Bufinefs and Money had of late Years paffed, fued out their general Acquittances in the Court.   And as their Accounts had undergone the Examination of the Company's Auditors, and had laid, all their legal time, and fome much longer, open in the Courts, for any Perfon to examine, and make Exceptions againft them, their Difcharges were granted, under the legal Seal, by a chearful and unanimous Concurrence of the whole Company. The Proportions of Land, formerly granted, were alfo confirmed to them in the ftrongeft Manner, and Mr. *John Farrar* had the beft Security they could give him, for three hundred and twenty Pounds, which he had taken up at Intereft, for the Ufe, and by the Order of the Company ; all their Effects from *Virginia* being ordered, to be configned into his and his Brother *Nicholas Farrar's* Hands (who was likewife foon after found to be about eighty Pounds in Advance for the Company) till their Ballances, with all other Damages incident thereto, were difcharged.

IN Confideration of the ill Confequences, of having continued Sir *Thomas Smith* fo many Years in the Place of Treafurer, the Company had made it a ftanding Rule and Order, that no Perfon, after that, fhould hold the Place of Treafurer or Deputy, above three Years together.   The Earl of *Southampton's* three Years being therefore now expired, Lord *Cavendifh* and Lord *Paget* were named, to ftand in Election to fucceed him.   The King had always been endeavouring, to get fuch a Perfon chofen into that Place of chief Government, as fhould be perfectly fubmiffive to his Pleafure and Command.   And now, on the Day of Election, the Court received a Letter from his Majefty, fignifying ; That he had appointed Commiffioners, to examine into the prefent State of the Colony of *Virginia* ; and as he expected to receive, within a few Days, fome Account of their Labours therein, it was his Will and Pleafure, that all Officers fhould continue, as they were ; and that they fhould not proceed to any new Election, before the Morrow fortnight after, at the fooneft.   This unexpected Order, and myfterious Reafon, caufed a long and general Silence in the Court.   But at length, confidering, that they were reftrained, by their Charters, to Quarter Courts only for the Election of Officers ; and that, all Offices expiring that Day, their Government would become

void,

1623.

Sir *Francis*
Wyat, Go-
vernor.

void, and their Patents forfeited, unlefs fomething was done
therein, they continued all Officers in their Places, not a
Fortnight longer, but 'till the next Quarter Court, when
only Election could legally be made.   And thus, the King
never after having expreffed his Pleafure herein, and the
Company, to avoid Mifconftruction, forbearing to do any
thing, 'till his Majefty's Pleafure was farther known, the
Earl of *Southampton* and Mr. *Nicholas Farrar* were, from
time to time, continued in their Places, 'till the Suppreffion
of the Courts and Diffolution of the Company.

IN fome of the intercepted letters from *Virginia*, the
Lords of the Privy Council found great Complaints of the
Scarcity of Provifions.   This had been occafioned by the
Maffacre, and the confequent War with the *Indians*; by
which much of their Corn and Stocks had been deftroyed,
and a general Interruption given to the Culture of their
Lands.   Their Lordfhips therefore called the Deputy, and
a few more of the Company, before them; and acquaint-
ing them therewith, commanded them, to fend an immediate Relief to the Colony.   And they propofed, that the
whole Company fhould be obliged to contribute their Parts
towards it, according to the Number of each Man's Shares,
by rating them at twenty, or at leaft ten Shillings, a Share;
and that they fhould be compelled to pay the fame, by an
Order of that Board.   But Mr. *Farrar* and his Affociates
feem, not to have been perfectly convinced of the Legality
of fuch a Proceeding; and conceived themfelves to have no
Power by Law, to lay fuch a general Affefment on the Company, without their Confent.   Wherefore, after much Debate, they prevailed on their Lordfhips, to permit them to
proceed, in their ufual Method of voluntary Subfcriptions.
And as the opponent Faction had been loud before the Lords
of the Council, and preffed much the fending a fpeedy Supply, thereby endeavouring to infinuate and reflect on the
Negligence and finifter Views of the Company, a Roll of
Subfcription was prepared purpofely, and prefented to them,
to fubfcribe by themfelves; and Sir *Edward Sackvil* earneftly entreated them, to be liberal and exemplary in their
Contributions, fince they had expreffed, before the Council,
fo tender a Senfe of the diftreffed State of the Colony.   But
they had the Confidence to withftand fo ftrong a Snare; and
the Colony was obliged to the other Side for the Supply, as
I find intimated, in a Letter from Mr. Deputy *Farrar*, fent
at the fame time, in the Name of the Council and Company.   However, it was not of that vaft Ufe and Relief, as
was imagined or pretended.   For, as the Deputy and Company had judged, the Colony had gathered in their Corn,
before it could poffibly arrive.   BUT

BUT notwithstanding these lowering Prospects, and this 1623. unpromising Aspect of their Affairs, the Company proceeded chearfully and boldly in their Defence. And therefore, as soon as the Commissioners were known, they deputed Sir *Edward Sackvil*, Sir *Robert Killigrew*, and Sir *John Davers*, to wait upon them, in the Company's Name; and to declare their Joy and Satisfaction, in the Commission's being issued. And they very earnestly and unanimously besought them, to take into their immediate Consideration Captain *Butler*'s Information to his Majesty, entitled; *The unmasked Face of the Colony in* Virginia; which had given a deadly Wound to the happy Progress and Prosperity of that Plantation. So that until, by their Wisdom and Integrity, the Truth should be discovered, and the World again possessed with their former Hopes and good Opinion of that Colony, it must undoubtedly languish, if not shortly perish, for Want of those daily Supplies, which its Reputation alone had before raised, in great Abundance. But I do not find, that the Commissioners took the least Notice, or did any thing in Consequence, of this just and reasonable Request; altho' the Company urged it often, as a Point of great Importance, which required an immediate Examination and Dispatch. But soon after, they issued their Warrant to Mr. *Collingwood*, the Secretary, and to all other the Clerks and Officers of the *Virginia* Company, to bring before them, to the Quest-House, adjoining to St. *Andrew*'s Church in *Holborn*, all and singular Letters-patent, Proclamations, Commissions, Warrants, Records, Orders, Books, Accounts, Entries, and all other Notes and Writings whatsoever, in their Custody. Hereupon the Company appointed a Committee, consisting of Sir *Robert Killigrew*, Sir *John Davers*, Mr. *Herbert*, Mr. *Tomlyns*, Mr. *White*, Mr. *Withers*, Mr. *Bland*, Mr. *Barber*, and Mr. *Berblock*, who should all, or any three of them, with the Secretary, attend the Commissioners, from time to time, with the Letters-patent, Books of Accompt, and other Writings. But they charged them, at every Rising of the Commissioners, to bring back the original Letters-patent, and to leave with them only a Copy; which, they hoped and conceived, would be sufficient. The Commissioners were likewise desired, in the Company's Name, to respite the Delivery of their Books of Account, 'till their Accomptant had taken Copies of them; when they were, together with all other Writings and Records, delivered into their Hands, and never afterwards returned to the Company.

WHILST the Company urged to the Commissioners an immediate Enquiry into the Truth of Captain *Butler*'s Allegations,

1623.

Sir *Francis* Wyat, Governor.

legations, they, at the fame time, recommended to their View and Perufal, as a thing relative to that Affair, the Declaration of the Council for *Virginia* and of the principal Affiftants of the *Somer-Iflands* Company, which hath been before mentioned, and which charged, in a home and open Manner, the Earl of *Warwick* and his Faction, but particularly Sir *Samuel Argall* and Captain *Butler*, with many illegal and oppreffive Practices. This, I prefume, gave Occafion to a Letter, which the Company foon after received from the King; wherein he utterly forbids, that any Complaints fhould be brought before the Commiffioners againft any Man, in the Name of the Council or Company, becaufe that Courfe only tended to Defamation, and to raife more Contention; and becaufe to bring Matters, determined by the Council or Company, before the Commiffioners, was to preoccupate the Commiffioners Judgments, or elfe to oppofe the Act and Opinion of the Council and Company, to the Act and Opinion of the Commiffioners. It was therefore his exprefs Pleafure and Command, that whofoever would exhibit Complaints againft any Man, either for publick Wrong to the Company, or for private Injuries to himfelf, he fhould bring the fame in Writing, fubfcribed with his Name, to the Commiffioners, who fhould receive the Anfwer thereto in Writing, and thereupon proceed, as they fhould fee Caufe.

WHAT was the End or Defign of fuch an Order is not eafily conceived, I think; unlefs it was to prevent the Company from acting with that Unanimity and Agreement, which it plainly appeared, they would, and which, in the Eyes of all impartial Men, would give the greater ·Weight and Authority to their Proceedings. And where the Juftice was, or Legality, of forbidding the Company to profecute *for publick Wrong to themfelves*, as a Body corporate, and to leave it only to private Men, who could not legally do it, without being firft authorifed and impowered by the Company (and then it became their Act and Deed). is to me equally myfterious and inconceiveable. I am unwilling to make hard and uncharitable Interpretations; but this whole Affair of the Commiffioners appears to have very little of the Face of Juftice, but feems to have been fet on Foot for quite different Ends and Purpofes.

BUT befides this, that Letter contained another exprefs Command; That no Man, of what Degree or Quality foever, fhould be admitted to their Courts or Committees, who, befides his Freedom and Land, had not fome Men then, or lately before, planted upon his Shares; or that was not, at that time, actually engaged in, and accordingly ly purfued, the fending of Men or Supplies over. And he farther ordered, if any other prefumed to be prefent at their Meetings, that they fhould be proceeded againft, as factious and feditious Perfons. This was likewife a manifeft Infringement of their Charters, which had fpecified the different Ways, by which Men fhould become free, and act as Members of the Company. Being therefore much ftaggered and furprifed at both thefe Points, they refolved to hold no more Courts, 'till the King's Pleafure was farther underftood. To this End, they prefented a Petition to his Majefty; in Anfwer to which, he, in effect, took off and reverfed thofe two Prohibitions and Commands. After which, the Company again proceeded, as a Body corporate, in their Bufinefs before the Commiffioners; and they laid before them their Reafons and Exceptions againft Sir *Thomas Smith's* Accounts, together with all the other Declarations, Anfwers, and Writings, which had been drawn up, and fo unanimoufly agreed to, by the Committee of the whole Company. And they ftill particularly infifted upon, and ftrenuoufly preffed, the expediting Captain *Butler's* Affair, as that Bufinefs was the moft urgent, and moft immediately hurtful and pernicious to the Colony.

BUT what the Commiffioners did, what Enquiries they entered upon, and what Reports they made to his Majefty, was a dead Secret to the Company; who, in a Letter to the Colony, acknowledge themfelves to be entirely in the Dark, as to what was paffing, or what was intended. At length, after long waiting for the Iffue of their Enquiries and Determinations, Mr. Deputy *Farrar*, with fome few more of the Company, were called, on the 8th of *October*, before the Lords of the Privy Council, who made fome Propofals to the Deputy. But thefe being of a very weighty and important Nature, and Mr. *Farrar* conceiving himfelf to have no Power to give an Anfwer to them, they were, at his Requeft, drawn up into an Order of that Board; that fo he might, under that Form, prefent them to the Company. This Order of Council fet forth:

THAT his Majefty had taken into his princely Confideration the diftreffed State of the Colony of *Virginia*, occafioned, as it feemed, by the ill Government of the Company: That this could not well be remedied, but by reducing the Government into fewer Hands, near the Number of thofe, that were, in the firft Patent, appointed: That therein efpecial Provifion fhould be made, for continuing and preferving the Interefts of all Adventurers and private Perfons whatfoever: That his Majefty had therefore refolved, by a new Charter, to appoint a Governor and twelve Affiftants,

1623.

Sir *Francis Wyat*, Governor.

Affiftants, to be refident in *England*, to whom fhould be committed the Government of the Company and Colony : That the faid Governor and Affiftants fhould be nominated and chofen, for the firft time, by his Majefty ; and that their Election afterwards fhould be in the following Manner, *viz.* the Affiftants fhould prefent the Names of three to his Majefty, of whom he fhould nominate one, to be Governor ; and the Affiftants themfelves fhould be chofen, by the major Part of their own Body for the time being, the Names of thofe to be chofen being firft prefented to the King, or the Council Board, to be allowed of, or difallowed, by his Majefty ; and that the Governor, and fix of the Affiftants, fhould be changed, once in two Years :. That there fhould alfo be refident in *Virginia*, a Governor and twelve Affiftants, to be nominated by the Governor and Affiftants in *England*, they firft prefenting their Names to his Majefty, or the Council Board, for their Allowance or Difallowance of the fame : And that, as the Governor and Affiftants, refident in *Virginia*, fhould have Relation and Dependence on the Governor and Affiftants in *England*, fo the Governor and Affiftants in *England*, fhould have Relation and Dependence upon the Council Board, that fo all Matters of Importance might thereby be under his Majefty's immediate Direction at that Board : And that his Majefty further purpofed, to make the like Grants, as well of Lands, as of other Franchifes and Benefits, as had been granted in the former Charters ; with Declaration, that for fettling and eftablifhing all private Interefts, this new Company fhould confirm, or grant anew to all Perfons, the like Interefts, as they enjoyed by the Grant, Order, or Allowance of the former Company. And therefore, the Deputy and the reft were, by their Lordfhips, required, to affemble a Court forthwith, to refolve, whether the Company would fubmit, and furrender their former Charters, and be content to accept a new one, with the aforefaid Alterations ; and they were commanded to return their Anfwer with all Expedition, his Majefty being determined, in Default of fuch Submiffion, to proceed for recalling their former Charters, in fuch Sort, as to him fhould feem juft and meet.

THIS Order of Council fo ftruck and amazed the Company, that, as if they diftrufted their own Ears, they caufed it to be read over three feveral times ; and after that, no Man, for a long while, fpoke a Word to it. However, eight of the Faction of Twenty-fix, being prefent with Sir *Samuel Argall* at their Head, moved the Company, in Conformity to their Lordfhips Order, to make an immediate Surrender of their Charters ; but far the major Part of the

Court,

Court, to the Number of an hundred and twelve Perfons, declared refolutely againft it. They faid, it was a Matter of fuch Weight and Confequence, that they thought themfelves to have no Power to give an Anfwer to it, in that ordinary Court. For fuch Courts were, by their Charters, only permitted, to treat of cafual and particular Occurrences of lefs Confequence ; but all weighty Affairs, and particularly all things relating to Government, were reftrained, by the precife Words of their Letters-patent, to Quarter Courts only. Wherefore, whilft their prefent Patents were in Force, that ordinary Court had no Authority, to determine fuch a Matter as this, being of the higheft and moft important Nature, that had ever been propounded to them. To which it was added, that, in Obedience to their Charters, they had never taken to themfelves the Liberty, to difpofe of fo much as a fingle Share of Land, but in their Quarter Court ; and they conceived themfelves much more, even in Confcience, bound, not to betray their Truft, and fo fuddenly pafs away all the Rights of themfelves and the reft of their ¡numerous Society, and of all the Planters in *Virginia* alfo, who were equally interefted with them in their Letters-patent. They therefore befought their Lordfhips, that their Anfwer might, upon thefe juft Grounds, be refpited till the Quarter Court ; which, being the 19th of *November*, was not far off ; and againft then, they fhould have Leifure to confider well of fo weighty a Propofition. And to this End, they ordered a very large and particular Summons to be given to all the Adventurers, againft that Day ; and that their Officers fhould give them efpecial Notice of the Bufinefs, then to be treated ; and defire them, in the Company's Name, not to fail to be prefent ; which if they did, they would be without Excufe, and would have no Manner of Pretence, to complain afterwards.

THIS Anfwer, however confonant to both Law and Reafon, gave no Satisfaction to the Lords of the Privy Council ; who, by another Act of their Board, dated the 17th of the fame Month of *October*, declared it to be merely delatory. Wherefore, as his Majefty expected a fpeedy Account of their Proceedings in that Bufinefs, and as it did likewife, in itfelf, require all Expedition, in Regard of the Importance and Confequence thereof (which, by the bye, was an odd Reafon for being hafty) they ordered, and exprefly charged, the Deputy and the reft, to affemble themfelves again immediately, and on the *Monday* following, being the 20th of the faid Month, to deliver a clear, direct, and final Anfwer to that, which had been before propounded, and was that Day reiterated unto them : *viz.* Whether the

1623.

Sir *Francis Wyat*, Governor.

the Company would be content, to submit and surrender their former Charters, and to accept a new one, with the Alterations, mentioned in the aforesaid Act of Council. And the Deputy was likewise commanded, to propound the Question to the Company, in those clear and precise Terms, in which it was then delivered.

IN Obedience to this Order of the Privy Council, Mr. *Farrar* called an extraordinary Court; at which, by reason of the Shortness of the Warning, there were only seventy Persons present. And having proposed the Question to them, in the express Terms, prescribed in the Act of Council, nine Voices only were for submitting, Sir *Thomas Wroth* being added to the former eight. But all the rest being strenuously against the Surrendry of their Charters, an Answer was accordingly returned to their Lordships.

THESE Proceedings, which struck plainly at the Root and Foundation of all the Rights and Franchises of both the Company and Colony, made a great Noise, and naturally gave the Alarm to all such, as were any way deeply, or immediately, engaged in the Action. Some Ships therefore, which were preparing to sail, were stopped, till the Issue and Intent of these Acts of Power were farther seen into and understood. But the Lords of the Council, being apprised of this ill Consequence, made another Order of their Board, on the 20th of *October*, importing: That their Lordships were that Day informed, there was so great a Discouragement among many of the *Virginia* Adventurers, on Account of the intended Reformation and Change of the Government, as rendered them fearful to prosecute their Adventures; so that it would probably occasion some Stop to those Ships, which were then ready freighted, and bound to that Country. That, altho' their Lordships much marvelled, that any Man should so far mistake their Meaning, considering the Declarations, that had been made at that Board, *viva voce*, as also by an Act of Council, and otherwise, yet for the better satisfying of those, who, through their own Error, or the false Suggestions of others, had conceived any such Fear or Discouragement, they thereby again declared, that there was no other Intention, than merely and only the Reformation and Change of the present Government; whereof his Majesty had seen so many bad Effects, as would endanger the whole Plantation, if it was not corrected and amended: That nevertheless, for so much as concerned the private Interest of every Man, his Majesty's Royal Care was such, that no Man should receive any Prejudice in his Property, but should have his Estate fully and wholly conserved to him, and if any thing was
found

found defective, better secured ; so that none needed to ap- 1623.
prehend any such Fears or Inconveniencies, but contrariwise
chearfully proceed.   It was therefore ordered by their Lord- *Sir Francis*
ships, and thought fit to be published to the Company, that *Wyat, Go-*
it was his Majesty's absolute Command, that the Ships, then *vernor.*
intended for *Virginia*, and in some Readiness to go, should
be forthwith dispatched away, for the Relief of the Colony
and Good of the Plantation, without any farther Hindrance
or Stop.

W H A T were the Proceedings of the Commissioners all
this while, I cannot tell ; nor whether his Majesty found
sufficient Matter, as he thought, from their Reports, to
suppress the Company, and revoke their Charters.   But the
better to fortify this Design, and to raise Matter of Complaint and Accusation, the Lords of the Privy Council, on
the 24th of *October*, appointed *John Harvey*, Esq; (afterwards well known, as Governor of *Virginia*, by the Title
of Sir *John Harvey*) *John Pory*, (formerly Secretary, and a
noted Tool of the Earl of *Warwick*'s) *Abraham Piersey*,
Samuel Matthews, and *John Jefferson*, Gentlemen, to be
their Commissioners, to make particular and diligent Enquiry, touching divers Matters, which concerned the State
of the Colony of *Virginia*.   And that they might the better
perform the Orders they had received, and discharge the
Trust committed to them, their Lordships strictly willed
and required the Governor and Council here, to yield them
their best Aid and Assistance, upon all Occasions, and in
all Matters, wherein they should find Cause to make Use
of the same.   The three Acts of Council also, just before
recited, were committed to Mr. *Pory*, and particularly the
last, to be published in such Places in *Virginia*, as he should
judge fit, for the Quieting and Satisfaction of the Inhabitants here.   Captain *Harvey* indeed and Mr. *Pory* seem, to
have been the most active, and most depended upon, in
this Business ; and therefore Captain *Smith*, who had probably never seen their Commission, and knew nothing of
the others, only mentions two, as sent upon this Errand.
As for Mr. *Jefferson*, he never appeared in it, but seems
all along a hearty Friend to the Company, and their present
Constitution and Government.   Besides, he was present
at their Courts in *England*, at such times, as were incon-
sistent with his prosecuting that Commission in *Virginia*.
And Captain *Matthews* expresly joins with the General Assembly, in their Opposite Representations to his Majesty,
as will be hereafter related.

T H I N G S being laid in this Train, soon after, on the
10th of *November*, Mr. Deputy-Treasurer *Farrar*, and di-
X 2   vers

1623.   vers others of the Company, were ferved with a Procefs of
Sir Francis *Quo Warranto* out of the King's Bench ; to fhew, by what
Wyat, Go- Authority, they claimed to be a Body corporate, and to
vernor. have and enjoy thofe Liberties and Privileges, which they
did.   The Company chearfully acknowledged this to be a
fair and legal Manner of proceeding ; and they defired the
Defendants, to take efpecial Care of the Bufinefs, as being
the Company's Caufe, altho' profecuted in particular Names ;
and as their Charter was called in Queftion by it, which,
they conceived, was therefore to be pleaded.   As for the
Charge of this Suit (which, it was judged, would be very
great) it was agreed, that it fhould be borne by the Company's general Stock.   Wherefore it was unanimoufly ordered, that whatever Difburfements fhould be made by the
Defendants, or others, in the Procefs of the Suit (provided, it were for the Company's Caufe and Defence, and
not for Matters, that in the Iffue would fall upon particular Perfons, or their Actions) they fhould all be duly repaid, and made good by the Company.   But the entertain-
ing Counfel and Attornies was wholly left and entrufted to
the Choice and Care of the Defendants.

B U T for this Caufe, fince another Courfe had been taken
to bring the Bufinefs to a legal Trial, by the Attorney General's profecuting a *Quo Warranto* againft the Company,
they refufed, at their Quarter Court on the 19th of *November*, to enter into any Confideration about the Matter.   But
that Court, with a general Unanimity, (feven only diffenting) folemnly ratified and confirmed all the Proceedings of
the former Courts, which had refufed to furrender up their
Charters.   And for the better Management of fo weighty an
Affair, which would require often and ferious Confultation,
a Grand Committee was appointed, to direct all Matters
appertaining thereto ; and the Deputy had Authority given
him, at all times to call them together, or fuch a Part of
them, as he fhould think proper.   And that the Company
might be the better enabled to prepare their Proofs, and
make good their Defence, a Petition was ordered to be delivered to the Lords of the Privy Council, for reftoring their
Books and Writings ; which had now, for fome time, been
in theirs and the Commiffioners Hands.   But Mr. *Bing*
faid, let them make as many Petitions as they pleafe, they
fhould as foon have an Halter, as have their Writings;
which gave fuch univerfal and juft Offence, that Complaint
was made thereof to the Lords of the Council.   But I do
not find, that any Right was done them, for fo atrocious
an Infult and Affront on the Court, or that they ever afterwards recovered their Records.

B U T

B u t soon after, on the 8th of *December*, the more to perplex and difcourage the Company, and to opprefs thofe private Members, who were Defendants in this Suit, Alderman *Johnfon*, with others of his Faction, prefented a Petition to the Lords of the Privy Council, fignifying; That they had always been, and ftill were ready, according to his Majefty's exprefs Will and Pleafure, to render up their Charters to his Majefty's Difpofal : But forafmuch as Mr. *Nicholas Farrar*, and fome others, withftood the Surrendry, and the better to free themfelves from the Charge of the Suit, and to enable them to oppofe his Majefty, they had lately made an Order of their Court, that the Expence of defending that Caufe fhould be borne by the Company's publick Stock; they therefore humbly prayed, that it might be ordered by their Lordfhips, that the Charge of thofe Suits fhould be borne by the Defendants themfelves, and no Part by the Company's publick Stock, nor by the Goods of any of the Adventurers or Planters, that fhewed themfelves conformable to his Majefty's Pleafure. And they further befought their Lordfhips, to order, for better Affurance in this Point, that all fuch Goods, as fhould thereafter be imported for the General Company, fhould be fequeftered in the Cuftom Houfe, till their Lordfhips farther Order, for difpofing thereof to the Ufe and Benefit of the Plantation.

T h i s laft Claufe was purpofely aimed and defigned, to deprive the Deputy and his Brother, with fome others, (to whom the Company had made over all fuch Goods, as Security for confiderable Sums of Money, now due to them) of ever having it in their Power, to get their faid Debts. Their Lordfhips therefore, being apprifed of this, would not concur with the Alderman in a Defign, fo plainly fraudulent and iniquitous. However, they made an Order of their Board, that all they, who were queftioned by the *Quo Warranto*, fhould make their Defence, at their own private Charge, without any Help or Expence from the publick Stock; and that fuch, as were willing to furrender their Charters, fhould be difcharged from all Contribution towards the Expence of the faid Suit, both in their Perfons and Eftates. And this perhaps will be thought fufficiently hard and oppreffive. But however, confidering the noble Fortunes and generous Difpofitions of the Earl of *Southampton* and many others of the Company, who entirely agreed to, and abetted the Proceedings of the Courts and Deputy, the Expence was, in all Probability, made very eafy, and did not fall upon the Defendants fo heavily, as was hereby defigned. And I cannot here forbear re-

X 3

marking

marking the Generofity and publick Spirit of the Deputy, and other Merchants and Citizens. For the Noblemen, and other Gentlemen of capital Fortune and Figure, were not returned out of the Country, when the *Quo War-ranto* was iffued; fo that it was ferved entirely upon Merchants and Citizens, who neverthelefs bravely undertook the Defence of the Company, at the Rifk of their own Fortunes. And this was the more meritorious then, as the Rights of the Crown, and the Liberties of the Subject, were not fo well limited and underftood at that time, as they now are; but the little Finger of Regal Power was fuppofed two heavy, for the Loins of any private Man to bear. To which may be added, that Acts of Power, at that Juncture, ran very high, and were plainly attempted to be carried ftill higher; and the Deputy and Company had no Reafon to expect any Favour, but had found from manifold Experience, that all Advantages, even beyond what was ftrictly fair and legal, would be taken againft them.

IT will alfo doubtlefs feem ftrange to many Perfons, that the Privy Council fhould affume to themfelves fuch a Judicature, as thus arbitrarily to difpofe of Men's Fortunes, and load a few private Perfons with the Expence of defending the publick Caufe of the Company, even againft the Company's Will and Defire. But to clear this Point, it muft be known, that the Privy Council of that time affumed a moft extraordinary Power and Jurifdiction, and were plainly drawing into their Hands all the Parts of Government; or perhaps to fpeak more properly, the King, through them, was endeavouring to draw them into his own Hands. And this, as I take it, was the Occafion of a great and very dangerous Error in the Conftitution of this Colony. For as our Council was fettled and conftituted at the Time, that the Privy Council's Authority was ftrained to fuch a Height, there was perhaps too great a Power affigned to them. I fpeak freely, and I hope, without Offence; for what I mean, is fimply this. Our Council act in a double Capacity: Firft, as his Majefty's Council of State, from which all Acts of Power and Government iffue; and fecondly, as the fupreme Judicature of the Colony, and the laft Interpreters of Law. Now, if the Council fhould exert any Act of Power againft a Man, and he fhould appeal from it, the Caufe muft be brought before the fame Perfons again in the General Court, who would be naturally led to fupport their own Act. But in *England*, the Cafe is quite different. For fhould the Privy Council exercife any Act of Power upon the Subject there, he may appeal from them, to the Courts in *Weftminfter-Hall*; where

where the Caufe muft be determined by the Law, which is
always impartial and unbiaffed. So that all Acts of Power
there, are expofed to an immediate and fevere Check from
the Law. And indeed this is the great Beauty and Strength
of all free Conftitutions of Government, to have all their
Parts, but moft efpecially the higheft and moft dangerous
to Liberty, continually under the Check and Coercion of
the Law. But if we confider the many Infirmities of human Nature and Contingencies of human Governments,
the Charms and Allurements of Ambition and the ftrange
grafping and infatiable Nature of Power, the natural Pride
and Peremptorinefs of Men in Authority, their falfe Shame
of owning themfelves in the Wrong, and Pronenefs to defend and perfift in their Errors, together with the natural
and perpetual Conteft between Liberty and Power, this
muft, I think, be acknowledged, to be a very great and
material Defect in our Conftitution. It is true, there are
not perhaps any great Inconveniences felt from this at prefent, at leaft that I know of; which I fpeak not, with Intent to flatter our prefent Government or Governors: For
I flatter no Man. But however, altho' the Sword did not
actually fall upon the *Sicilian* Sycophant, yet no Perfon, I
believe, would chufe to be in his Situation, and have a
Sword perpetually hanging over his Head by a Hair. Whoever therefore fhould contrive and effect an Alteration in
this dangerous Point, he fhould have my Suffrage for a Sta-
tue, or any other, the moft honourable, or moft beneficial
Reward, for fo fignal a Service to the Country. But to
return from this Digreffion.

BESIDES the Petition, formerly recited, Alderman
Johnfon, being much galled by the Company's home Anfwers and Expofure of his and Sir *Thomas Smith*'s Conduct, drew up another Writing, under the Title of; *A
Declaration of the profperous Eftate of the Colony, during
Sir Thomas Smith's Time of Government*. In this, fubfcribed
by himfelf, Sir *Samuel Argall*, and Mr. *Wrote*, he faid:
That notwithftanding the many difaftrous Accidents, to
which Enterprifes of that Nature, efpecially in their In-
fancy, are fubject, yet it pleafed God, fo to blefs their Labours and Endeavours, who were then employed, that in
the firft twelve Years, during all which Time Sir *Thomas
Smith* was Treafurer and Governor of the Company, with
the Expence of feventy thoufand Pounds, or thereabouts,
brought in for the moft part by voluntary Adventurers, being a great many of them Sir *Thomas*'s near Friends and
Relations, and for his Sake joining in the Bufinefs, and
with the Help and Ufe of a very few of his Majefty's Sub-

jects,

312

1623. jects, and thofe moftly People of the meaneft Rank, a large
and very fpacious Part of the Country was fully difcover-

ed; the Coafts, Havens, Ports, Creeks, and Rivers thereof
perfectly known; the moft commodious Places of Strength,
and for Conveniency of Habitation, felected and made
Choice of; thofe Places partly recovered, or procured from
the Savages, and partly with infinite Labour, being generally overfpread with Wood, cleared, enclofed, and cultivated; many Houfes, Barns, and Forts built; Churches,
Bridges, and Storehoufes, with all other publick and neceffary Works, erected; not lefs, as he judges, than a
thoufand *Englifh*, when Sir *Thomas Smith* left the Government, being there inhabiting, with Plenty of Corn, Cattle,
Swine, Poultry, and other good Provifions, to feed and
nourifh them: That there was a competent Number of
able and fufficient Minifters, to inftruct them; worthy and
expert Commanders, Captains, and Officers, to direct and
govern them; and Store of Arms and Ammunition, to defend them: That divers Staple Commodities, befides Tobacco, were found out, at the prefent to encourage, and
in procefs of time to enrich them; Barks, Pinnaces, Shallops, Barges, and Boats, built in the Country, the better
to accommodate and fecure them: That the Natives were
in fo awful a League and Amity with them, that many of
thofe Heathens voluntarily yielded themfelves Subjects and
Servants to our moft gracious Sovereign; and priding themfelves in that Title, paid, together with moft of the reft, a
Yearly Contribution of Corn, for Suftentation of the Colony; and they were kept in fuch good Refpect and Corre-
fpondency, that they became mutually helpful and profitable, each to other: That to this Growth of Perfection
was that Plantation advanced, even in the firft twelve
Years; the Affairs thereof being, with great Unanimity,
Moderation, Integrity, and Judgment, chiefly directed by
Sir *Thomas Smith*; and the Accompts of Monies, received
and difburfed, being audited upon Oath, by Men of Credit
and Reputation, without all Exception.

THE Commiffioners were ftill fitting; and the Company, being wearied with long waiting for the Iffue of
their Labours, appointed their Grand Committee, to prefs
them to make fome Report to the Lords of the Council,
what they had done in the feveral Affairs, brought before
them by the Company and their Opponents. For they
faid, they greatly depended, that the Fairnefs and Uprightnefs of their Proceedings would be thence manifefted to
all the World. And they were likewife entreated, to require Sir *Thomas Smith*, either to fhew fufficient Caufe,

why

why he fhould not pay the eight hundred Pounds, found
againft him on the firft two Heads of Exception againft his
Accounts; or elfe, that he might be compelled to pay the
fame, as the Company was now in great Want of Money.
But I cannot difcover, that the Commiffioners, who were,
properly fpeaking, a Committee of Secrecy, ever did any
thing in either of thefe Points.

WHILST Things were in this Pofture in *England*, the
Colony in *Virginia* had recovered a tolerably eafy and comfortable State of their Affairs. Their Health, which had
been much affected by the Famine, and by the Hardfhips
and Inconveniences, they underwent by being driven from
their Habitations, was now well reftored; and the Famine
itfelf entirely relieved by a plentiful Crop of Corn. Having
likewife, by pretending Peace and Friendfhip, come to the
Knowledge of the *Indians* principal Places of Refidence, they
had cut up and deftroyed their Corn, when it was too late
for them to have another Crop; and by a fuccefsful Attack,
they had flain a great Number of them, among whom were
fome of their Kings, and feveral of their greateft War-
Captains and Commanders; of which *Opechancanough* was
hoped to be one. For the Stratagem was chiefly aimed at
him, and things, as they thought, fo well laid, that he
could fcarce poffibly efcape the Snare. The Governor
alfo went himfelf, this Year, in Perfon into *Patowmack*
River, and took a full Revenge upon the *Pafcoticons*, who
had flain Captain *Spilman*; putting many to the Sword,
and burning their Houfes, with a prodigious Quantity of
Corn, which they had conveyed into the Woods, and the
Englifh were not able to bring to their Boats. And he
iffued Commiffions to Captain *William Pierce*, Captain of
his Guard and Lieutenant-Governor of *James-City*, to go
againft the *Chickahominies*; to Captain *Nathaniel Weft*, to
go againft the *Appamatocks* and the *Taux-Wyanokes*; to
Captain *Samuel Matthews*, againft the *Taux-Powhatans*;
and to Captain *William Tucker*, Commander of *Kicquotan* and
thofe lower Parts of the Country, to go againft the *Nandfamonds* and *Warrafqueakes*; all which Parties fell upon
them the very fame Day, the 23d of *July*, with vaft Spoil
to their Corn and Habitations, and no fmall Slaughter.
And a Week after, Captain *Maddifon* marched againft the
great *Wyanokes*, and Captain *Tucker* made a fecond Expedition to *Nandfamond*.

BUT in the Midft of thefe Tumults and Alarms, the
Mufes were not filent. For at this time, Mr. *George Sandys*, the Company's Treafurer of *Virginia*, made his Tranflation of *Ovid's Metamorphofes*, a very laudable Performance

1623. for the Times. In his Dedication of that Piece to King
—⌣— *Charles* I. he tells him, that it was limned by that imper-
Sir *Francis* fect Light, which was fnatched from the Hours of Night
Wyat, Go- and Repofe. For the Day was not his own, but dedicated
vernor. to the Service of his Father and himfelf; and had that Service proved as fortunate, as it was faithful, in him, as well
as others more worthy, they had hoped, before the Revo-
lution of many Years, to have prefented his Majefty with
a rich and well-peopled Kingdom. But as things had turned, he had only been able to bring from thence himfelf
and that Compofition, which needed more than a fingle
Denization. For it was doubly a Stranger, being fprung
from an ancient *Roman* Stock, and bred up in the new
World, of the Rudenefs whereof it could not but partici-
pate; efpecially as it was produced among Wars and Tumults; inftead of under the kindly and peaceful Influences
of the Mufes.

1624.   THE Beginning of the next Year 1624, Captain *Harvey* and Mr. *Pory* arrived, as Commiffioners from the Privy
Council; and the 26th of *January*, Warrants were iffued
for fummoning a General Affembly. However this Affembly was not called, at the Commiffioners Motion or Requeft. For they kept their Commiffion fecret from the
Colony, and did every thing, they could, to conceal their
Powers and Defigns. The King alfo and the Privy Council
had, the laft Year, given very ftrict and menacing Orders
to the Company, and to all private Adventurers, to write
nothing to *Virginia*, concerning the Differences, then fubfifting among them; becaufe, as they faid, it would give
great Difcouragement to the Planters, and bring Prejudice
to the Colony. To this End, the Privy Council had often
perufed, and angrily returned, the Company's general Letters, before they could be formed entirely to their Liking;
and they had taken all Methods, to intercept and prevent
any Accounts going from private Hands. But notwithftanding thefe Precautions, the Colony was, by this time,
well informed, of what had paffed in *England*; and Copies
of the feveral Writings had been fent over to them efpecially of Alderman *Johnfon's* Declaration of the profperous
Eftate of the Colony, during Sir *Thomas Smith's* Government, and of Captain *Butler's* Information to his Majefty.
For thofe Papers related more particularly to them, as being upon the Spot, and therefore the beft Judges of the
Truth or Falfhood of the feveral Matters, therein alledged.
Wherefore, when the General Affembly met, which was
the 14th of *February*, the firft thing, they entered upon,
was the Confideration of thofe two Pieces; and by the 20th
of

of the fame Month, they had drawn up Anfwers to them.
Their Anfwer to the Alderman's Declaration fet forth:

THAT holding it a Sin againft God and their own Suf- *Sir Francis Wyat, Governor.*
ferings, to permit the World to be abufed with falfe Reports,
and to give to Vice the Reward of Virtue, They, in the
Name of the whole Colony of *Virginia*, in their General
Affembly met, many of them having been Eye-witneffes
and Sufferers in thofe Times, had framed, out of their
Duty to the Country, and Love to Truth, the following
Anfwer to the Praifes given to Sir *Thomas Smith*'s Government, in the faid Declaration.

THEY averred, that, in thofe twelve Years of Sir *Thomas Smith*'s Government, the Colony for the moft part,
remained in great Want and Mifery, under moft fevere
and cruel Laws, which were fent over in Print, and were
contrary to the exprefs Letter of the King's moft gracious
Charters, and as mercilefly executed here, oftentimes without Trial or Judgment: That the Allowance for a Man,
in thofe Times, was only eight Ounces of Meal and half a
Pint of Peafe a Day, both the one and the other being
moldy, rotten, full of Cobwebbs and Maggots, loathfome
to Man, and not fit for Beafts; which forced many to fly
to the Savage Enemy for Relief, who, being again taken,
were put to fundry Kinds of Death, by hanging, fhooting,
breaking upon the Wheel, and the like: That others were
forced, by Famine, to filch for their Bellies; of whom one,
for ftealing two or three Pints of Oatmeal, had a Bodkin
thruft through his Tongue, and was chained to a Tree,
till he ftarved: That if a Man, through Sicknefs, had not
been able to work, he had no Allowance at all, and fo confequently perifhed: That many through thefe Extremities, dug Holes in the Earth, and there hid themfelves, till
they famifhed: That they could not, for thofe their Miferies, blame their Commanders here; for their Suftenance
was to come from *England*, and had they given them better Allowance, they muft have perifhed in general: That
their Scarcity fometimes was fo lamentable, that they were
conftrained to eat Dogs, Cats, Rats, Snakes, Toadftools,
Horfe-hides, and what not? That one Man, out of the
Mifery he endured, killed his Wife, and powdered her up
to eat; for which he was burnt: That many others fed
on the Corpfes of dead Men; and that one, who, through
Cuftom, had got an infatiable Appetite to that Food, could
not be reftrained, till he was executed for it: And that,
indeed, fo miferable was their State, that the happieft
Day, many ever hoped to fee, was, when the *Indians*
had killed a Mare; the People wifhing, as fhe was boil-
ing,

1624. ing, that Sir *Thomas Smith* was upon her Back in the Kettle.

Sir *Francis Wyat,* Governor.   AND whereas it was affirmed, that very few of his Majesty's Subjects were lost in those Days, and those Persons of the meanest Rank, they replied ; that for one, that then died, five had perished in Sir *Thomas Smith*'s Times, many being of ancient Houses, and born to Estates of a thousand Pounds a Year, some more, some less, who likewise perished by Famine : That those, who survived, and had in Ventures both their Estates and Persons, were constrained to serve the Colony seven or eight Years for their Freedom, and underwent as hard and as servile Labour, as the basest Fellow, that was brought out of *Newgate :* As for Discovery, they owned, that much had been discovered in those twelve Years, but in the four or five last Years, much more than formerly : That the Houses and Churches, then built, were so mean and poor by reason of these Calamities, that they could not stand above one or two Years ; the People going to work indeed, but out of the Bitterness of their Spirits, breathing execrable Curses upon Sir *Thomas Smith* ; neither could a Blessing from God be hoped for in those Buildings, which were founded upon the Blood of so many *Christians :* That the Towns were only *James-City, Henrico, Charles Hundred, West* and *Shirley Hundred,* and *Kicquotan* ; all which were ruined in those Times, except ten or twelve Houses in *James-Town :* That at that Present, there were four for every one then, and forty times exceeding them in Goodness : That Fortifications there were none against a foreign Enemy, and those against the domestick Foe very few and contemptible : That there was only one Bridge, which also decayed in that time : That if, through the aforesaid Calamities, many had not perished, there would doubtless have been largely above a thousand People in the Country, when Sir *Thomas Smith* left the Government ; but they conceived, when Sir *George Yeardley* arrived Governor, he found not above four hundred, most of them in Want of Corn, and utterly destitute of Cattle, Swine, Poultry, and other necessary Provisions to nourish them : That there were some Ministers to instruct the People, whose Ability they would not tax, but divers of them had no Orders : That they were never over furnished with Arms, Powder and Ammunition ; yet that in Quality almost entirely useless : They acknowledge, that in those times a Trial was made of divers Staple Commodities, which they had not Means to proceed in ; but they hoped, in time a better Progress would be made therein, and had it not been for the Massacre, many by that

time

time would have been brought to Perfection: That for
Boats, there was only one serviceable one left in the Colony, at the End of that Government; for which one, besides four or five Ships and Barks, there were not then so
few as forty: That the Barks and Barges, then built, were
in Number so few, and so unwillingly and weakly by the
People effected, that in the same time they perished: That
they never knew, that the Natives did voluntarily yield
themselves Subjects to the King, took any Pride in that
Title, or paid any Contribution of Corn towards the Support of the Colony; neither could they, at any time, keep
them in such good Correspondency, as to become mutually
helpful to each other; but contrariwise, whatever was done,
proceeded from Fear, and not Love, and their Corn was
got by Trade or the Sword.

AND now, to what a Growth of Perfection the Colony
could arrive at the End of those twelve Years, they left to
be judged, by what had been said; and they besought his
Majesty, rather than be reduced to live under the like Government again, that he would send Commissioners over to
hang them. As to Alderman *Johnson*, one of the Authors
of that Declaration, they said, he had great Reason to commend Sir *Thomas Smith*, to whose Offences and Infamy he
was so inseparably linked. And all this they affirmed to be
true by the general Report of the Country, which they
never heard contradicted; many of them also having been
Eye-Witnesses, or else resident in the Country, when every
Particular here reported, happened.

THIS Declaration was signed by Sir *Francis Wyat*, the
Governor; by *George Sandys*, *John Pot*, *John Pountis*, *Roger Smith*, and *Ralph Hamer*, Esqrs. of the Council; and
by *William Tucker*, *William Pierce*, *Ralegh Croshaw*, *Samuel Matthews*, *Jabez Whitaker*, and others, to the Number of twenty four, of the House of Burgesses. And this,
I judge (or the Number of twenty five, which subscribed
the Answer to Captain *Butler*'s Information) was nearly
about the full Number of the House of Burgesses at that
time. For there were, three Years before, eleven Boroughs
which had Right to send Members to the Assembly; and
there might be, and undoubtedly were, a few others since
added to them. Their Answer to Captain *Butler*'s Information, ran in the following Manner.

Most gracious Sovereign,

WHEREAS a *Copy of an Information, presented
to Your Majesty by Captain* Nathaniel Butler, *entitled,* The Unmasking *of* Virginia, *is come to our Hands;*
and

1624.   *and whereas the same is full of notorious Slanders and Falshoods,*

proceeding from the Malice of his corrupt Heart, and abetted
Sir Francis *by private Enmity and publick Division, which aim at the Sa-*
Wyat, Go- *tisfaction of their particular Spleen, altho' it be to the Subver-*
vernor.   *sion of this whole Colony; Wee, the Governor, Council, and
Colony of* Virginia, *in our General Assembly, out of Zeal and
Respect to Your Majesty and this our Country, not to suffer
Your sacred Ears to be prophaned with false Suggestions, nor
Your Royal Thoughts to be diverted from so hopeful a Plan-
tation, which may add in time a principal Flower to Your
Diadem, do, in all Humbleness, submit this our Answer to
Your Princely Survey, annexed to the several Untruths of the
said Informer.*

1. I found the Plantations generally feated, &c. *

THE Plantations, for the moft Part, are high and pleafantly feated; and the reft not low, nor infefted with Marfhes, which, we wifh, were more frequent. The Creeks
are rather ufeful, than noifome; and no Bogs have been
feen here by any, that have lived twice as many Years, as
he did Weeks, in the Country; the Places which he fo
mifcalls, being the richeft Parts of the Earth, if we had a
fufficient Force to clear their Woods, and to give the frefh
Springs, which run through them, a free Paffage. The
Soil is generally rich, and reftores our Truft with Abundance; the Air is fweet, and the Clime healthful, all Circumftances confidered, to Men of found Bodies and good
Government.

2. I found the Shores, &c.

IN this he traduceth one of the goodlieft Rivers in the
habitable World, which runs for many Miles together within
upright Banks, till at length, enlarged with the Receipt of
others, it beats on a fandy Shore, and imitates the Sea in
Greatnefs and Majefty. It is approachable on both Sides,
from half Flood to half Ebb, for Boats of good Burthen;
neither is there any River in the World of this Vaftnefs,
without Cranes or Wharfs, more commodious for landing.
And it is equally contrary to Truth, that by wading we
get violent Surfeits of Cold, which never leave us, till we
are brought to our Graves.

3. THE new People, fent over, arriving for the moft
Part, &c.

WE affirm, that the Winter is the only proper time for
the Arrival of new Comers; whereof the Governor and
Council have often, by their Letters, informed the Com-

---

* *Vide* Captain *Butler's* Information, *p.* 268.

pany; and the like Advice has been given to their Corref-
pondents, from time to time, by private Planters, for their
Supply of Servants. As to Houfes of Entertainment, there
was a general Subfcription, amounting to an unexpected
Sum, and Workmen actually employed, to build a fair Inn
in *James* City, and every principal Plantation had refolved
on the like, for the Entertainment of their new Supplies;
when it pleafed God, to punifh our Crimes by the bloody
Hands of the *Indians*, which obliged us to divert that Care
to the Houfing ourfelves, many of us having been unfur-
nifhed by that Difafter. But Buildings of late have every
where encreafed exceedingly; neither have new Comers any
Reafon to complain, when every Man's Houfe is, without
Recompence, open to the Stranger, even to the difaccom-
modating ourfelves. So that we may with Modefty boaft,
that no People in the World do exercife the like Hofpitality. As for dying under Hedges (whereof there are none
in *Virginia*) or lying unburied in the Woods, by reafon of
this Defect, it is utterly falfe. However, if fuch things
fhould fometimes be feen accidentally here, the like may,
and often doth happen, in the moft flourifhing Countries of
Europe.

4. T h e Colony was, this Winter, in great Diftrefs, *&c.*

T h e Colony, that Winter, was in no Diftrefs of Victual, as the Accufer well knoweth. For he bought Corn
himfelf for eight Shillings a Bufhel, cheaper, as we hear,
than it was then fold in *England*. It is true, a fucceeding
Scarcity was feared. But what lefs could be expected, after
fuch a Maffacre; when near half the Colony were driven
from their Habitations in time of planting, others ftreigh-
tened in their Ground by receiving them, and all interrupted
in their Bufinefs by fupporting a fudden War? *Englifh*
Meal fold, as he affirmeth, at thirty Shillings the Bufhel,
was only fold for ten Pounds of Tobacco; for which, in
truck, we ordinarily receive under twelve Pence a Pound,
real Value. And it is not to be fuppofed, that any of the
Great fhould affect Scarcity, in order to enrich themfelves
by Trade. For Trade hath ever been free for us all; neither have they, who have brought in moft Corn, fold it
out at unconfcionable Rates, but have often freely imparted
it to the Neceffity of others, without any other Advantage
than Repayment. We agree with that Prime-one, who
wifhed, that Corn might never be under eight Shillings a
Bufhel; meaning in Tobacco at three Shillings a Pound.
For fo there would be fome Proportion between the Profit
of making the one and the other, and Corn would thereby
be planted in greater Abundance.

5. T h e i r

1624.

Sir *Francis Wyat,* Governor.

5. THEIR Houses are generally the worst, &c.

OUR Houses, for the most Part, are rather built for Use than Ornament; yet not a few for both, and fit to give Entertainment to Men of good Quality. If we may give Credit to those, who are accounted the most faithful Relaters of the *West-Indies*, many Cities of great Rumour there, after threescore Years Progress, are not to be compared in their Buildings to ours. And so far are they from the meanest Cottages in *England*, that many Towns there have hardly one House in them, which exceedeth ours in Conveniency or Structure. The greatest Disparagement, that some of them received, proceeded from his Riots and lascivious Filthiness with lewd Women, purchased with Rials of Eight and Wedges of Gold, the Spoils of the distressed *Spaniards* in *Bermudas*; which, as we are informed by a Gentleman of good Credit, who casually surveyed his Inventory, did, with other Treasure, amount to divers Thousands. As for the Interposition of Creeks, which Men are most desirous to seat upon, where we cannot go by Land, we have Boats and Canoes, for our sudden Transport on any Occasion.

6. I found not the least Piece of Fortification, &c.

WE have, as yet, no Fortifications against a foreign Enemy, altho' it hath been endeavoured by the Company, with a Success unanswerable to their Care and Expence; as also lately ,by ourselves. But the Work, being interrupted by the Scarcity of last Summer, shall proceed again, God willing, with all convenient Expedition; and almost all our Houses are sufficiently fortified against the *Indians*, with strong Palisadoes. His Envy would not let him number truly the Ordinance at *James* City; four Demi-Culverins being there mounted, and all serviceable. At *Flower-de-Hundred*, he makes but one of six; neither was he ever there, but, according to his Custom, reporteth the unseen as seen. The same Envy would not let him see the three Pieces at *Newport's-News*, and those two at *Elisabeth-City*. Two great Pieces there are at *Charles Hundred*, and seven at *Henrico*. Besides which, several private Planters have since furnished themselves with Ordinance. So that it were a desperate Enterprise, and unlikely to be attempted by a Man of his Spirit, to beat down our Houses about our Ears, with a Bark of that Burthen.

7. EXPECTING, according to their printed Books, &c.

THE time that this Informer came over, was in the Winter, after the Massacre; when those Wounds were green, and the Earth deprived of her Beauty. His Ears were open to nothing but Detraction, and he only enquired

after

after the Factious, of which there were none among us,
and how he might gather Accusations against those in the
Government, being, as it should seem, sent over for that
Purpose. Otherwise he could not but hear of our Proclamations for the Advancement of Staple Commodities, and
with what Alacrity and Success they proceeded; Vines and
Mulberry Trees being planted throughout the whole Country, the Iron-Works in great Forwardness and shortly to
receive Perfection, and the Glass-Works laboured after with
all possible Care, till the Slaughter by the *Indians,* and the
succeeding Mortality, gave a Ruin to some, and Interruption to all. So that he hath nothing but our Misfortunes
to accuse and upbraid us with; which have obliged us, still
to follow that contemptible Weed, as well to sustain the
War, as to enable us again to erect those Works. As for
deriding the Books, that were sent over by the Company,
it was done by himself, and no other, that we know of.

8. I found the ancient Plantations of *Henrico, &c.*

STILL he abuseth your Majesty with these Words, *I
found,* in Places, where he never was by some Score of
Miles; having never been higher up the River, than the
Territories of *James City. Henrico* was quitted in Sir *Thomas Smith's* Time, only the Church and one House remaining. *Charles City,* so much spoken of, never had but six
Houses. The Soil of both is barren, worn out, and not
fit for Culture. The Loss of our Stocks the Informer
hath less Reason to urge. For he joined with the *Indians*
in killing our Cattle, and carried the Beef aboard his Ship;
which would have cost him his Life, if he had had his De-
serts.

9. WHEREAS according to his Majesty's gracious, *&c.*

THE Governor and Council, whom it only concerned,
replied to this; that they had followed the Laws and Cus-
toms of *England* to their utmost Skill; neither could he,
or any other, produce any Particular, wherein they had
failed. As to their Ignorance, they held him to be no
competent Judge of those, who so far transcended him in
Point of Learning and Ability. For he had never been
bred to the Law (as was not unknown to some of them)
nor yet in any other of the liberal Sciences. But his principal Spleen in this Article, appeared to proceed from his
not being admitted of the Council, which they could by
no means, consistently with their Instructions, do.

10. THERE having been, as it is thought, ten thousand, *&c.*

HIS Computation of ten thousand Souls falleth short of
four thousand; and those were, in great part, wasted by

1624.

Sir *Francis*
Wyat, Go-
vernor.

the more than *Egyptian* Slavery and *Scythian* Cruelty, which
was exercifed on us, your poor and miferable Subjeæts, by
Laws written in Blood, and executed with all Sorts of Tyranny, in the Time of Sir *Thomas Smith*'s Government;
whereof we fend your Majefty the true and tragical Relation, from which it will plainly appear, that the pretended
Confufions and private Ends will ftrongly refleæt upon him
and his Inftruæors. And how unfit fuch Men are, to reftore that Plantation, which fuffered fo much under their
Government, we humbly refer to your princely Confideration; invoking, with him, that divine and fupreme Hand,
to proteæt us from fuch Governors and their Minifters,
who have poured out our Blood on the Earth like Water,
and have fatted themfelves with our Famine. And we befeech your Majefty, to fupport us in this juft and gentle
Authority, which has cherifhed us of late by more worthy
Magiftrates; and We, our Wives, and poor Children, as
is our Duty, fhall ever pray to God, to give you in this
World all Increafe of Happinefs, and to crown you in the
World to come, with immortal Glory.

T H I S Anfwer was fubfcribed by the fame Perfons as
the former; only with the Addition of the Honourable
Francis Weft, Brother to the late, and Uncle to the then
Lord *Delawarr*, and Sir *George Yeardley*, of the Council,
and of one more Member of the Houfe of Burgeffes. Mr.
John Pountis alfo, one of the Council of State, was appointed to go to *England*, to follicite the general Caufe of the
Colony (for fo they call it); and four Pounds of Tobacco
was levied upon every Male Tithable, that had been a Year
in the Country, to fupport his Expences. But this Gentleman, in his Voyage home, died upon the Coaft of *England*; and was therefore able to do nothing in the Affair.
But to thefe, the General Affembly added two other Writings; the one a Petition to the King, and the other a Letter to the Lords of the Privy Council.

I N their Petition to the King, they declared their great
Joy and Satisfaæion, that his Majefty, notwithftanding the
late unjuft Difparagement of this Plantation, had taken it
into his nearer and more efpecial Care. And that his Royal
Intentions might have their due Effeæ, they humbly befought him, being urged thereto by their Duty and Experience, to give no Credit to the late Declarations of the
happy, as it was called, but in Truth, miferable Eftate of
the Colony, during the firft twelve Years, nor to the malicious Imputations, which had been laid on the Government of late; but that he would be pleafed to behold, in
                                            Miniature.

Miniature, the true Eftate of both Times by their Relations, which they then prefented by the Hands of Mr. *John Pountis,* a worthy Member of their Body; and which contained nothing but the Truth, without Difaffection or Partiality. From thefe they doubted not, but that his Majefty would clearly underftand the true Condition of both Times; and would be pleafed, according to their earneft Defire, to continue, and even farther confirm, the Government, under which they then lived. But if it fhould pleafe him otherwife to determine, they befought him, by all the Ties of Compaffion and Humanity, not to fuffer them, his poor Subjects, to fall again into the Hands of Sir *Thomas Smith,* or his Confidents; but that he would gracioufly protect them from thofe Storms of Faction, which threatened the Ruin of fome Perfons (whofe Endeavours had deferved a better Reward) and in general the Subverfion of the whole Colony. And if the Government muft be altered, they defired, fince the Action was of fuch Honour and Confequence, that they might ftill depend upon fuch great and noble Perfons, as they lately had done. And farther, in Confideration of the late Maffacre and fubfequent Calamities, they befought his Majefty, to grant them and the *Somer-Iflands* the fole Importation of Tobacco; affuring him, that they affected not that contemptible Weed, as a thing good and defirable in itfelf, but as a prefent Means of Support. And if it fhould pleafe his Majefty, to fend over that Aid of Soldiers, whereof they had been put in Hopes, or any other Affiftance, they humbly defired, that the Governor and General Affembly might have a Voice in their Difpofal; fince none at that Diftance, by reafon of Accidents and emergent Occafions, could direct fuch an Affair fo advantageoufly, as they were enabled to do, by their Prefence and Experience in the Country. IN their Letter to the Privy Council, they acknowledged the Receipt of feveral of theirs, and returned their Thanks to his Majefty for his princely Care of the Colony; particularly for remitting three Pence a Pound in the Cuftom of Tobacco, and for his gracious Intention to grant them a fole Importation, than which nothing could give greater Life, or a more fpeedy Advancement, to the Colony. For little or nothing could be expected from Poverty, to which the mean Prices of Tobacco, and great Expence of the War againft the *Indians,* had reduced them. Neither had they, in their prefent State, the Means to fortify themfelves, or to fet up Staple Commodities, which would require a long Expectation of Profit; the Fruit of their Labours at prefent amounting to no more, if fo much, as

would

would barely feed and cloath them. They therefore humbly entreated their Lordſhips, to be a Means to his Majeſty to confirm his gracious Intention; and to take into
their Conſideration the heavy Burthen, of paying for Cuſtom above a Third of their Labour; which, they deſired,
might be reduced to five *per Cent.* according to the expreſs
Tenor of their original Charters.

THEY further told their Lordſhips, that they underſtood
by their Letters, that they had been accuſed by one, who
went from hence, of Neglect in Fortifications, in building
Houſes, and in providing themſelves Suſtenance; but they
proteſted againſt his Relation, which was, as in other things,
ſo in this, moſt falſe and ſlanderous. They had, in due
Submiſſion, publiſhed their Orders, ſent over by Mr. *Pory*;
by which they underſtood his Majeſty's Intention, to change
the Government. They profeſſed themſelves ignorant of
the Dangers and Ruin, that threatened them from the Government, as it then ſtood; and declared, they had nothing to accuſe thoſe Gentlemen of, who had ſwayed their
Affairs, ſince the Expiration of Sir *Thomas Smith*'s Authority; their Slavery having ſince been converted into Freedom, and the Colony cheriſhed under a juſt and moderate
Government. Neither would they have been ſubject to
Cenſure, had not the bitter Effects of the Maſſacre clouded
the Company's Zeal and their Endeavours.

BUT however it might pleaſe his Majeſty to diſpoſe of
them, it was their humble Deſire, that the Governors,
ſent over, might not have abſolute Authority, but might
be reſtrained to the Conſent of the Council; which Title,
they deſired, might ſtill be retained to the Honour of the
Colony, and not converted to the Name of Aſſiſtants, as
was propoſed in an Order of their Board. They ſaid, they
had found ſome Inconveniencies, by the ſtrict Limitations
of the Governor and Council, to proceed according to their
Inſtructions out of *England.* For in ſo far a Diſtance, and
imperfect Knowledge of the Country, thoſe things might
ſeem good in Advice, which might happen to prove very
inconvenient in Execution; neither was it fit, that any main
Project ſhould be ſet on Foot, which had not firſt Approbation from hence. They conceived, the preſent ſhort
Continuance of Governors to be very diſadvantageous to the
Colony. The firſt Year, they were raw and unexperienced in the Country, and for the moſt part in ill Diſpoſition
of Health, through the Change of Climate; the ſecond,
they began to underſtand ſomething of the Affairs of the
Colony; and the third, they were providing to return. But
above all, they made it their moſt humble Requeſt to their
Lordſhips,

Lordships, that they might still retain the Liberty of their General Assemblies; than which nothing could more conduce, to the publick Satisfaction, and publick Utility.

THESE two were signed by almost the same Persons as the former; and I cannot but observe, to the immortal Honour of Sir *Francis Wyat*, that he was so far from desiring the Tyranny of an absolute Authority, that he was most strenuous and active, and joined very cordially in all these Petitions and Representations, for restraining the exorbitant Power of Governors. All these things were carried, in the Assembly, with the utmost Unanimity and Dispatch; and they were kept secret from the Commissioners, whom they found to be in other Interests, and to have quite different Views from themselves. For, having at first promised to communicate all their Representations and Papers to the Governor and Assembly, expecting the like Favour from them, they afterwards stood off, and indeed absolutely refused to let them know any thing they were doing; under Pretence, that the Lords of the Privy Council ought to have the first View of what they intended to present. Whereupon the Governor and Assembly, suspecting some sinister Designs, endeavoured to conceal from the Commissioners what was passing among them. But Mr. *Pory*, a Tool of Power, and versed in Corruption, by the Promise of a Reward, obtained Copies of all these Writings from *Edward Sharples*, Clerk of the Council; and altho' Captain *Harvey* had no Hand in corrupting him, he afterwards promised him fifty Pounds of Tobacco, in Reward of his Treachery. This *Sharples* had been entertained, by the late Mr. Secretary *Davidson*, as a Writer in his Office; and after the Secretary's Death, which happened towards the last of the former Year, he was admitted, far above his Condition and Desert, Clerk of the Council, and took an Oath (a Copy whereof is still extant in our Records) to deliver no Copies of any Papers or Writings, without the Governor's Leave. Wherefore I find, at a Court held the 10th of *May* following, as it appeared by sufficient Evidence, and by his own Confession, that he, being sworn Clerk of the Council of State, had betrayed their Councils to the Commissioners, he was sentenced to stand in the Pillory, and there to have his Ears nailed to it, and cut off. However, he was only just set on the Pillory, and lost a Piece of one of his Ears. A Letter was also sent by the Governor and Council to the Company, to inform them of his Crime and his Punishment; and to complain of Mr. *Pory*'s Subornation of him, that they, understanding his double Dealing, might thence be upon their Guard, and prevent his corrupt Practices. But

it

1624. it was now too late for the Company to do any thing in it. For such a mean and proftitute Inftrument of their Aims **Sir Francis Wyat, Governor.** and Defigns, as *Pory*, had long before this more Power and Intereft at Court, and was likely to be more regarded, than all the noble, great, and worthy Members of the Company.

BUT the Commiffioners, finding, that things were going in the Affembly quite contrary to their Hopes and Defires, refolved to lay fome of their Powers before them, which might probably intimidate and influence them, and reftrain them from proceeding with fo much Sharpnefs and Vigor. They therefore opened fome Part of their Commiffion to the Affembly, on the 24th of *February*. A Week after, they wrote them a Letter, importing : That they fuppofed, in a Week's Time, fince their publifhing the Orders of the Lords of the Privy Council, the Affembly could not but have maturely confidered the fame : That therefore, for the fpeedier Advancement of the Colony in general, and for the fecuring every Man's Intereft in particular ; and that they might all, by Submiffion and Thankfulnefs, as by Obedience and Sacrifice both together, ingratiate themfelves and their common Caufe to his Majefty's renowned Clemency, They, as Remembrancers, thought it no lefs than their Duty, to propofe to their Confideration the Form enclofed ; which, they hoped, they would apprehend very fit to be fubfcribed by the whole Affembly, it being no other, than what they themfelves would, moft readily, and moft humbly, fet their Hands unto. The Form propofed was, as follows.

WHEREAS we underftand by three Acts of Council in England, lately publifhed in this General Affembly, that his Majefty hath fignified his gracious Pleafure, for the univerfal Good of this Plantation, which by reafon of our late Calamities is in an unfettled State, to inftitute another Form of Government, whereby the Colony may be upheld, and profper the better in time to come, and to that End hath required a Surrendry of the prefent Patents, declaring his Royal Intention, to fecure to the particular Members of the Company fuch Lands and Privileges in the faid Country, as, according to the Proportion of each Man's Adventure and private Intereft, fhall be found due unto him ; We of this General Affembly do, by Subfcription of our Names, not only profefs and teftify our Thanfulnefs, for that his Majefty's moft gracious and tender Care over us, but do moreover, for our Parts, in all Humility and Willingnefs, fubmit ourfelves to his princely Pleafure, of revoking our old Charters, and of vouchfafing his
new

THUS to draw the General Aſſembly to ſurrender and petition for a Revocation of their Charters, which the Courts in *England* would by no means ſubmit to, was certainly a very crafty and effectual Way, to difgrace the Company, and to make the Colony ſeem difaffected to them, and willing to throw off their Yoke; and would alfo have given ſome Colour to their violent Suppreſſion afterwards. But the Aſſembly ſeems fully to have underſtood their Aim, and even to ſuſpect, that this was Part of their Errand and Inſtructions from *England*. For in their Anſwer, they endeavoured to draw from them, by what Authority they made ſuch a Propoſal, and ſaid; As they could not ſee, how this Propoſition had any Ground in the Inſtructions, they had yet ſeen, they defired, before the Aſſembly returned an Anſwer, that the Commiſſioners would ſhew them the Depth of their Authority; or otherwiſe ſet it down under their Hands, that they had no further Commiſſions or Inſtructions, which might concern them.

BUT this Anſwer gave the Commiſſioners great Offence, and drew from them a very fierce and menacing Reply: That they had acknowledged, in delivering their Papers, that they had neither Commiſſion nor Inſtruction, to move them to ſubſcribe the Form propoſed; neither could the leaſt Shadow of any ſuch thing be collected from their Letter: That what they had propoſed, was out of their Diſcretion, as wholeſome Counſel for the Good of the Colony; neither was it precipitate or ſudden, but proper to the Time, Occaſion, and Perſons: That the Mark, aimed at, was no leſs than his Majeſty's Favour upon their Perſons and common Cauſe, to be obtained by Obedience and Thankfulneſs: That as there needed neither Commiſſion nor Inſtruction, for them to propound the Practice of ſo eminent a Duty, ſo it was lawful for them, as being Freemen and Planters, to offer to the General Aſſembly any reaſonable Motion, tho' of far leſs Conſequence; and had they not vouchſafed to return an Anſwer, they might juſtly have ſeemed diſcontented, or at leaſt diſcourteous: That they had no Reaſon, upon this Occaſion, to ſearch into the Depth of their Authority (ſince their Motion depended not, nor needed to depend, on their particular Commiſſion) much leſs, to urge them to ſet down any thing under their Hands: That they could not profeſs, that they had no farther Commiſſions, which might concern them, beſides that already put in Execution; for their Commiſſions, yet unperformed, con-

Y 4

cerned

1624. cerned them in their Houfes, Perfons, Servants, Corn,
Cattle, Arms, &c. That however they need not fufpect,
Sir *Francis* that they would attempt any thing to any Man's Wrong,
Wyat, Go- or which they could not very well anfwer.
vernor.
To this the Affembly calmly replied: That they had
already prefented their humbleft Thanks to his Majefty,
for his gracious Care of them; and had returned their Anfwer to the Lords of the Privy Council: That when their
Affent to the Surrendry of their Charters fhould be required
by Authority, it would then be the moft proper Time to
make a Reply: But in the mean while, they conceived,
his Majefty's Intention to change the Government had proceeded from wrong Information; which, they hoped,
would be altered upon their more faithful Declarations.
But the better to enable them to take a View of the Plantations, and to render an exact Account of the State of the
Colony, the Affembly ordered, upon the Commiffioners
Application for their Affiftance, that the feveral Plantations
fhould tranfport them from Plantation to Plantation, as
they fhould defire; and fhould accommodate them in the
beft Manner, their Houfes and Rooms would afford. The
Commiffioners alfo made the Affembly four Propofitions;
concerning the beft Places of Fortification and Defence;
the State of the Colony, with Refpect to the Savages; the
Hopes, that might be really and truly conceived of the
Plantation; and the propereft Means, to attain thofe
Hopes: To all which the Affembly gave full and particular Anfwers. And I cannot but remark, that Captain
Matthews, who had joined with the General Affembly in
their publick Acts and Reprefentations againft the former
Government, did likewife join with the Commiffioners in
all thefe Proceedings: Whether he was brought over by the
almighty Force and irrefiftable Allurement of private Advantage; or whether he thought himfelf obliged to do
fomething in Conjunction with them, as he was included
in the fame Commiffion.
THE Laws of this Affembly confifted of thirty five
Articles. For that Manner (taken, I prefume, from the
Articles, fent over by Sir *Thomas Smith*) was at this time,
and continued long after, the ufual Way of drawing up
and enacting their Laws; which indeed had this Good in
it, that all tedious Forms were thereby cut off, and the
main Senfe and Subftance of their Acts appeared at once,
in clear and precife Terms. As thefe Laws are the oldeft,
that I can now find upon our Records, and as they contain
fome things of efpecial Note, I fhall here prefent them to
the Reader.

THE

THE firſt ſeven related to the Church and Miniſtry, and
enacted: That in every Plantation, where the People were
wont to meet for the Worſhip of God, there ſhould be a
Houſe, or Room, ſet apart for that Purpoſe, and not converted to any temporal Uſe whatſoever; and that a Place
ſhould be empaled and ſequeſtered, only for the Burial of
the Dead: That whoſoever ſhould abſent himſelf from Divine Service any *Sunday*, without an allowable Excuſe,
ſhould forfeit a Pound of Tobacco, and that he, who ab-
ſented himſelf a Month, ſhould forfeit fifty Pounds of Tobacco: That there ſhould be an Uniformity in the Church,
as near as might be, both in Subſtance and Circumſtance,
to the Canons of the Church of *England*; and that all
Perſons ſhould yield a ready Obedience to them, upon Pain
of Cenſure: That the 22d of *March* (the Day of the
Maſſacre) ſhould be ſolemniſed and kept holy; and that all
other Holidays ſhould be obſerved, except when two fell together in the Summer Seaſon (the Time of their Working and
Crop) when the firſt only was to be obſerved, by reaſon of their
Neceſſities and Employment: That no Miniſter ſhould be
abſent from his Cure, above two Months in the whole
Year, upon Penalty of forfeiting half his Salary; and whoſoever was abſent above four Months, ſhould forfeit his
whole Salary and his Cure: That whoſoever ſhould diſ-
parage a Miniſter, without ſufficient Proof to juſtify his
Reports, whereby the Minds of his Pariſhioners might be
alienated from him, and his Miniſtry prove the leſs effectual, ſhould not only pay five hundred Pounds of Tobacco,
but ſhould alſo aſk the Miniſter Forgiveneſs, publickly in
the Congregation: That no Man ſhould diſpoſe of any of
his Tobacco, before the Miniſter was ſatisfied, upon For-
feiture of double his Part towards the Salary; and that one
Man of every Plantation ſhould be appointed, to collect the
Miniſter's Salary, out of the firſt and beſt Tobacco and Corn.

THE eighth and ninth Articles related to the Governor's Power: That he ſhould not lay any Taxes or Impoſitions upon the Colony, their Lands, or Commodities,
otherwiſe than by the Authority of the General Aſſembly;
to be levied and employed, as the ſaid Aſſembly ſhould appoint: That he ſhould not withdraw the Inhabitants from
their private Labours to any Service of his own, under any
Colour whatſoever; and if the publick Service ſhould require the Employment of many Hands, before another
General Aſſembly met to give Order for the ſame, in that
Caſe, the levying Men ſhould be done, by the Order of the
Governor and whole Body of the Council; and that in
ſuch Sort, as to be leaſt burthenſome to the People, and

1624. moſt free from Partiality. Thus early was the Aſſembly,
out of the Memory of their paſt Miſeries and Oppreſſions,
Sir Francis ſtudious and careful to eſtabliſh our Liberties ; and we had
Wyat, Go- here, by the ready Concurrence and Co-operation of this
vernor. excellent Governor, a *Petition of Right* paſſed, above four
Years, before that Matter was indubitably ſettled and explained in *England.* For theſe two Articles contain the
ſame in Effect, as that famous explanatory and fundamental
Law of the *Engliſh* Conſtitution ; *viz.* The firm Property
of the Subjects Goods and Eſtates, and the Liberty of
their Perſons.

THE other Articles enacted : That all the old Planters,
who were here before, or came in at the laſt Arrival of
Sir *Thomas Gates* (in *Auguſt* 1611.) ſhould both themſelves
and their Poſterity, except ſuch as were employed to command in Chief, be exempted from their perſonal Service in
the Wars, and from all other publick Charges (Church
Duties only excepted) but without the like Exemption of
their Servants and Families : That no Burgeſs of the General Aſſembly ſhould be arreſted, during the ſitting of the
Aſſembly, and a Week before and Week after ; upon Pain
of the Creditor's forfeiting his Debt, and ſuch Puniſhment
upon the Officer, as the Court ſhould award : That there
ſhould be Courts kept once a Month, in the Corporations
of *Charles-City* and *Eliſabeth-City,* for deciding Suits and
Controverſies, not exceeding the Value of one hundred
Pounds of Tobacco, and for puniſhing petty Offences ;
and that the Commanders of the Places, with ſuch others,
as the Governor and Council ſhould appoint by Commiſſion,
ſhould be Judges, the Commanders to be of the *Quorum,*
and Sentence given by Majority of Voices ; with Reſerva-
tion neverthelefs of Appeal, after Sentence, to the Governor and Council ; and that whoſoever appealed and was caſt
upon ſuch Appeal, ſhould pay double Damages : That
every private Planter's Dividend of Land ſhould be ſurveyed
and laid off ſeparately, and the Bounds recorded by the Surveyor, who ſhould have ten Pounds of Tobacco for every
hundred Acres ſurveyed ; and that all petty Differences, between Neighbours about their Bounds, ſhould be decided
by the Surveyor, but if of Importance, referred to the
Governor and Council : That, for the People's Encouragement to plant Store of Corn, the Price ſhould be left
free, and every Man might ſell it, as dear as he could :
(For the Governor and Council did then, and long afterwards, ſet a Rate Yearly upon all Commodities, with Penalties upon thoſe, who exceeded it) That there ſhould be
a publick Granery in each Pariſh, to which every Planter,
above

above eighteen Years of Age, who had been in the Country a Year, and was alive at the Crop, ſhould contribute a Barrel of Corn, to be diſpoſed of, for the publick Uſes of the Pariſh, by the major Part of the Freemen; the Remainder to be taken out by the Owners, Yearly on St. *Thomas*'s Day, and the new brought and put in it's Room: That three capable Men, of every Pariſh, ſhould be ſworn, to ſee, that every Man planted and tended Corn ſufficient for his Family; and that thoſe, who neglected ſo to do, ſhould be preſented by the ſaid three Men, to the Cenſure of the Governor and Council: That all Trade with the *Indians* for Corn, as well publick as private, ſhould be prohibited, after the *June* following: That every Freeman ſhould fence in a Quarter of an Acre of Ground, before the *Whitſuntide* next enſuing, for planting Vines, Herbs, Roots, and the like, under the Penalty of ten Pounds of Tobacco a Man; but that no Man, for his own Family, ſhould be obliged to fence above an Acre; and that whoſoever had fenced a Garden, and was outed of the Land, ſhould be paid for it by the Owner of the Soil; and that they ſhould alſo plant Mulberry Trees: That the Proclamations againſt Swearing and Drunkenneſs, ſet forth by the Governor and Council, were ratified by this Aſſembly; and it was farther ordered, that the Churchwardens ſhould be ſworn, to preſent all Offenders, to the Commanders of their reſpective Plantations; and that they ſhould collect the Forfeitures for publick Uſes: That a Proclamation ſhould be read aboard every Ship, and afterwards fixed to the Maſt, prohibiting them, without ſpecial Order from the Governor and Council, to break Bulk, or make private Sale of any Commodities, till they came up to *James-City:* That the ancient Rates of Commodities ſhould be ſtill in Force; and that Men ſhould be ſworn, in every Plantation, to cenſure the Tobacco: (So old are the firſt Rudiments of our Tobacco-Law; which nevertheleſs, after ſuch long Experience, raiſed much Oppoſition and Diſturbance:) That there ſhould be no Weights or Meaſures uſed, but ſuch as were ſealed, by Officers appointed for that Purpoſe: That every Dwelling-houſe ſhould be Paliſadoed in, for Defence againſt the *Indians:* That no Man ſhould go, or ſend abroad, without a ſufficient Party, well armed: That Men ſhould not go to Work, without their Arms and a Sentinel ſet: That the Inhabitants of the Plantations ſhould not go on board Ships, or upon any other Occaſion, in ſuch Numbers, as thereby to weaken and endanger the Plantation: That the Commander of every Plantation ſhould take Care, that there be ſufficient of Powder and Ammunition within his Plantation; and that their

Pieces

1624. Pieces be fixed, and Arms compleat : That there be fufficient Watch kept, every Night : That no Commander of
Sir *Francis* any Plantation fhould either fpend himfelf, or fuffer others
Wyat, Go-
vernor. to fpend Powder unneceffarily, in Drinking, Entertainments, and the like : That fuch Perfons of Condition, as
were found delinquent in their Duty, and were not fit to
undergo corporal Punifhment, might notwithftanding be
imprifoned at the Difcretion of the Commander, and for
greater Offences be fubje&t to a Fine, inflicted by the Month-
ly Court ; fo that it did not exceed the Value abovefaid :
That every Perfon who had not found a Man at the Caftle
(then building at *Warrafqueake*) fhould pay, for himfelf and
Servants, five Pounds of Tobacco a Head, towards defraying the Charge of thofe, who had their Servants there :
That, at the Beginning of *July* following, every Corporation fhould fall upon their adjoining *Indians* ; and that thofe
who fhould be hurt upon the Service, fhould be cured at
the publick Expence ; and if any were lamed, they fhould
be maintained by the Country, according to their Perfon
and Quality : That for difcharging fuch publick Debts, as
their Troubles had brought upon them, there fhould be levied ten Pounds of Tobacco upon every Male, above fixteen
Years of Age, then living ; but not including fuch, as had
arrived fince the Beginning of *July* laft : That no Perfon,
within this Colony, fhould prefume, upon the Rumour of
any fuppofed Change and Alteration in *England*, to be dif-
obedient to the prefent Government, nor Servants to their
private Mafters, Officers, or Overfeers, at their utmoft
Peril. And the laft Article related to fending Mr. *Pountis*
to *England*, and levying four Pounds of Tobacco a Head,
to fupport his Expences. Moft of thefe Laws were taken
from preceeding Proclamations and Orders of the Governor
and Council ; and I find, that the Governor was obliged,
foon after, to iffue a Proclamation, forbidding Women to
contra&t themfelves to two feveral Men at one time. For
Women being yet fcarce and much in requeft, this Offence
was become very common ; whereby great Difquiet arofe
between Parties, and no fmall Trouble to the Government.
It was therefore ordered ; That every Minifter fhould give
Notice in his Church, that what Man or Woman foever
fhould ufe any Word or Speech, tending to a Contra&t of
Marriage, to two feveral Perfons at one time, altho' not
precife and legal, yet fo as might entangle or breed Scruple
in their Confciences, fhould, for fuch their Offence, either
undergo corporal Corre&tion, or be punifhed by Fine, or
otherwife, according to the Quality of the Perfon fo offending.

BUT

BUT whilft the Commiffioners were pufhing the Court
Defigns in *Virginia*, the opponent Faction in *England* were
not lefs diligent and induftrious to blacken and defame the
Company. To this end, they engaged, according to their
ufual Method, fome Planters, lately returned from *Virginia*, to petition and complain to his Majefty. Neither was
it a difficult thing, among fo many weak, indigent, or
wicked Perfons, as were concerned in the Plantations, to
procure fome to fecond and abet any Complaint, however
falfe and unjuft. Among other Matters of Grievance, they
complained of the many Impofitions and Levies, laid upon
the Planters towards the Support of the Company, from
whom they were wont formerly to receive Relief; and
therefore they befought his Majefty, to take them into his
Royal Mercy and Protection, and to free them for the future
from the grievous Impofitions of the faid Company. But
Mr. Deputy *Farrar* defired them, to fet down in Writing
the particular Grievances and Oppreffions, which they thus
complained of in general; that the Company might thereby
be enabled to return a full and particular Anfwer. This
they promifed to do, but afterwards, upon better Advice,
refufed; till at length, being farther preffed, they brought
nine Articles, which however they could not be induced to
fubfcribe, being reftrained by thofe behind the Scene. Thefe
Articles contained criminal Charges of a very high Nature,
and fome of them Capital, againft the Governor and Council in *Virginia*; fo that the Lawyers of the Company declared, that the Perfons who prefented them, except they
could maintain and make them good, had incurred the Penalty of Libellers. But at laft, after much Shuffling and
Abfurdity of Complaint and Accufation, the Complainants
in general, and one *Perry* in particular, confeffed, that altho' they pretended to have Authority and Commiffion from
the Planters in *Virginia* to make thefe Complaints, yet the
Whole, both the Petition and Grievances, were entirely
framed in *England*. Wherefore the Company, perceiving,
they had been abufed and drawn into it by the Malice of
others, thought fit to pafs it over, in Favour and Compaffion to their Ignorance and Credulity.

UPON Occafion of thefe grievous Accufations againft the
Governor and Council, Sir *Francis Wyat's* Character and
Conduct were called much into Queftion and canvaffed.
But he was fufficiently cleared by the reft of the Planters
then in *England*; who gave ample Teftimony to the Worthinefs and Uprightnefs of his Proceedings, and declared
upon their Confciences, that they efteemed him to be a moft
juft and fincere Gentleman, and free from all Manner of
Cor-

Corruption and private Ends. As therefore he had, by a
Letter to the Company, declared his Defire to leave the
Government at the Expiration of his Commiffion, which
would be fhortly, they took the . Matter into their ferious
Confideration. But finding, that he had given very great
Satisfaction to the Colony, as appeared by the Report of
the Planters; and confidering alfo, how much the Company was in his Debt, by not furnifhing him with his legal
Number of Tenants, and that they had no Means left to
make good their Promife to him, much lefs were they able
to fet out a new Governor, it was thought beft and moft
advifeable, to continue him ftill in his Office. But fome of
the opponent Faction moving, that Sir *Samuel Argall*, in
Regard of his Worth, and of his Defire for the Place, might
ftand in Election with him, they were both ballotted; and
Sir *Francis Wyat* was chofen by having fixty nine Balls, and
Sir *Samuel Argall* only eight. And as the Company was
then unable to fend over more Men to him, it was ordered,
that he fhould be fupplied with his full Complement, out
of the Company's Tenants in *Virginia*; and the Confideration of fome Recompence, for his former Lofs and Difappointment, was referred to the next Quarter Court.

THE laft Parliament, out of their Love and Efteem for
Virginia, but more efpecially out of Regard to the Advancement of the Trade of *England*, had taken into their Confideration the Cafe of the Plantation Tobacco, and had entered into a very good Courfe about it; but by Reafon of their
fudden Adjournment and Breach with the King, they were
obliged to leave it unfinifhed. The Company therefore,
being encouraged by this, and quite wearied out by the
equivocal and fufpicious Conduct of the King and his Minifters, prefented a Petition to the Houfe of Commons, fetting forth:

THAT after divers Difcoveries had confirmed the Opinion, that *Virginia* was fituate in a temperate and wholfome
Climate, that the Soil was rich and fertile, the Country
well watered with fruitful and navigable Rivers, and that
their Ships, through a fair Sea, might have a comfortable
falling in on a fafe Coaft, it pleafed God fo to affect the
Minds of divers worthily difpofed Noblemen, Gentlemen,
and others, as to think it a Matter of great Religion and
Honour, to endeavour the Propagation of Chriftianity among
thofe barbarous People, and to gain fuch a hopeful Addition
of Territory to his Majefty's Dominions: That his Majefty alfo, being informed thereof, and apprehending, that
great Honour and Commodity would thence arife to this
Kingdom, was pleafed, by his moft gracious Letters-patent
of

355

of Incorporation, from time to time renewed and enlarged, 1624.
to confer as ample Privileges and Immunities, both for their
Affiftance, who fhould become Directors of the Bufinefs at Sir Francis
home, and for their Comfort and Encouragement, that Wyat, Governor.
would fettle and inhabit the Country, as could be then fore-
feen or defired : That this gave fo general an Encouragement, that Noblemen, Knights, Gentlemen, Citizens, and
others, in great Numbers, became Adventurers ; who, befides their Money, afforded many other Helps by their Induftry, towards the Advancement and Perfection of this
noble Work : And that, notwithftanding a Multitude of
Accidents and Difafters, incident to fuch Undertakings in
a remote and favage Country, yet it pleafed God, often to
enliven their Hopes and Endeavours, by fuch an undoubted
Probability of obtaining, at leaft for the Publick and Pofterity, fo beneficial a Retribution for all their Pains and Expence, as would, in the End, crown their Labours with
as much Glory, Honour, and Profit to the Realm of *England*, as could be well wifhed or expected.

THEY then proceeded to recount the feveral Emoluments and Advantages to *England*, which they had in their
View and Expectation. 1. The Converfion of the Savages
to *Chriftianity*, and eftablifhing the firft Colony of the Reformed Religion. 2. The difcharging the Overplus of
neceffitous People, which adminiftered Fewel to dangerous
Infurrections, and the leaving greater Plenty for thofe, who
remained. 3. The gaining a large Territory, already
known to be great, and which might prove much greater ;
whofe Fertility of Soil, and Temperature of Clime, agreed
well with the *Englifh*, and produced by Nature and Induftry, whatever ufeful Commodities were found in any
known Country. 4. The beneficial Fifheries difcovered ;
which, together with the continual Intercourfe and Commerce between People of the fame Nation, would contribute exceedingly to the Increafe of the *Englifh* Trade and
Navigation. 5. The vaft Quantity of Timber and Materials, for building and fetting forth Ships ; whereof there
was a great Scarcity throughout all *Europe*. 6. The Affurance, that many rich Trades might be found out there,
and driven on to the incredible Benefit of the Nation ; befides the no fmall Hopes of an eafy and fhort Paffage to
the *South* Sea, either by Sea or Land. 7. The ineftimable
Advantage, that would be gained, in Cafe of War, both
for the eafy affaulting the *Spanifh Weft-Indies*, and for the
relieving and fuccouring all Ships and Men of War ; the
Want whereof had in former times, difappointed and overthrown fo many Voyages. But hereby the Benefit to the
Englifh

English would be certain, and the Enemy's Lofs and Annoyance inevitable. After which, they went on in the following Manner:

But fo it is, that now, when the natural Difficulties,
incident to all new Plantations, are by Diligence and Tract
of Time, but moft efpecially by the Blefling of Almighty
God, in a great Meafure overcome; yet there have rifen
other unnatural Impediments, proceeding from Faction and
Difcord, from the cunning Courfes and Practifes of fome
Perfons, who tended wholly to their own Profit, from Mif-
employment of the publick Stock, falfe Accounts, and the
like Corruptions and Diverfions from the main Bufinefs; and
that thefe were fo encreafed of late, and fupported by ftrong
Hand, as threatened fpeedy Ruin and Deftruction to that
excellent Work, if Remedies were not timely applied : That
they, the Council and Company of *Virginia*, differed not
a little from other Companies ; as well in their Compofition,
confifting of principal Noblemen, Gentlemen, Merchants
and others ; as in the Ends, for which they were eftablifhed, being not fimply for Matter of Trade, but for things
of a higher and more publick Nature : That neverthelefs,
finding themfelves, in their Body, as it was then diftempered,
unable to be their own Phyficians without higher Affiftance,
they thought it their Duty, as well to clear their own Reputation, as in Difcharge of their Confcience, and of the
Truft repofed in them, to reprefent to the Parliament this
Child of the Nation, expofed, as in the Wildernefs, to extreme Danger, and then fainting, as it were, and labouring
for Life.

They therefore humbly entreated that honourable
Houfe, to take into their Commiferation, the diftreffed Colony and oppreffed Company; and to receive an Account
from fuch of his Majefty's Council for *Virginia*, as, being
Members of their Houfe, had been appointed by the Company, to give them a full and exact Relation of all their
Grievances and Oppreffions : Which, tho' of fundry Kinds,
yet had received (as they doubted not to make evident) either their Original or Strength from the Lord High Treafurer, out of his private and unjuft Defigns; not only to
almoft the Overthrow of the Colony, but alfo to the Decep-
tion of his Majefty in his Profit and Revenue, to the great
Prejudice of the whole Kingdom in Matter of Trade, and
even to Points of dangerous Confequence to the Liberty of
the Subject.

This Proceeding was certainly no ways grateful to the
King, who conceived himfelf much injured and affronted,
if the Parliament entered upon any Confideration, which
was

was not recommended to them by himfelf. For he looked upon them, not as the grand Council of the Nation, but of the King; and expected, that they fhould proceed with the abject Adulation and Submiffion of his Privy Council, and never touch upon any difagreeable Subjects. But above all, Matters of Grievance were the Points, on which he was moft tender and touchy, and would often winch grievoufly; and altho' the thing was difguifed, and even Praifes were given him in fome Parts of this Petition, yet it was evidently levelled, in the main, againft him and his Minifters. However, as his Majefty had called this Parliament with quite different Views, and treated it in a quite different Manner from the laft, he took no Notice of it, but permitted it to take its Courfe in the Houfe. Its Reception was alfo fecured by the Complaints, in the latter Part, againft the Lord High Treafurer; whom *Buckingham* and the Prince were, at this time, pulling down and tearing, as it were, with great Violence from the King's Side, not without very great Pain and Grief to his Majefty.

THIS Petition was committed to the Deputy, and fuch others of the Council, as were alfo Members of the Houfe of Commons; to prefent it to their Houfe, in the Name of the Council and Company of *Virginia*. It was received by the Commons very acceptably, notwithftanding fome Oppofition at firft; and a Committee was appointed to hear and examine their Grievances and Oppreffions, to which all of the Company, that were Members of the Houfe, were admitted, to come and to hear, but not to have any Voice. But conceiving, that Counfel at Law could not be fo fully informed of all Paffages, as was requifite, and would not perhaps be fo cordially concerned, or favourably heard, they divided their Grievances into four feveral Heads, and committed them to the following Gentlemen, to deliver and fpeak to them. 1. The Cafe of their Tobacco, with all the Oppreffions and Impofitions upon it, was committed to Mr. Deputy-Treafurer, *Nicholas Farrar*: 2. The Bufinefs of the Contract, to Sir *Edwin Sandys*: 3. The Proceedings of the Commiffioners, to the Lord *Cavendifh*: 4. All Paffages and Meafures fince, to Sir *John Davers*. And all thefe Gentlemen, but efpecially the Lord *Cavendifh*, did very nobly and chearfully undertake, to perform and make good their feveral Parts.

IT was the Misfortune of thefe Affairs, to be brought into Parliament very late in the Seffions; and they were befides of a very tender and delicate Nature. For, in their Procefs and Iffue, they muft have turned to a plain Arraignment of the Weaknefs and Unfairnefs, or even of the

downright Injuſtice and Oppreſſiveneſs of the King's Conduct towards the Company and Colony. The main Buſineſs therefore of their Oppreſſions and Grievances did not
proceed in Parliament, but was waved and ſlurred over in
Silence. But the particular Caſe of Tobacco, by the exceeding Care and Wiſdom of Sir *Edwin Sandys*, aſſiſted by
the Lord *Cavendiſh*, and the other Gentlemen of the Company, who had Seats in Parliament, was brought to a happy Iſſue. For the Importation of foreign Tobacco was put,
as one of the nine Grievances of the Realm in Point of Trade,
which this Seſſion preſented to his Majeſty, and deſired Relief in. And altho' this was done profeſſedly for the Good
of *England*, without any Mention or Relation to *Virginia*,
yet the Deputy told the Company, that he doubted not,
but the whole Houſe had, in their Hearts, an eſpecial Regard to the Advancement of the Colonies. And as this
Courſe was as effectual for Excluſion of *Spaniſh* Tobacco,
as if it had been done by Bill, ſo was it much better, than
if it had been done by the Bill, which was drawn the laſt
Parliament. For ſince that Time, the State and Price of
Tobacco was ſo much altered, that it could then no ways
bear the twelve Pence a Pound Duty, which that Bill laid
upon it, but muſt thereby have been as certainly ruined and
overthrown, as by any other Courſe. But this ſecond Way
brought with it all the Good of the Bill, and left out all its
Evil. Wherefore, he ſaid, it could not be too much commended, nor Sir *Edwin Sandys*, to whom they were be-
holden for it, ſufficiently thanked. And it may be here farther obſerved, that the King's Meaſures by this time were
entirely reverſed. For the *Spaniſh* Match was now broke
off, and even War was declared againſt the King of *Spain*,
and the whole Houſe of *Auſtria*. So that the Intereſt of
England would no longer be obliged to ſtoop to the Intereſt
of *Spain*; and a Prohibition of their Tobacco would be eaſily granted, as it agreed with the preſent Paſſions and Meaſures of the Court.

THIS was the laſt Service that Sir *Edwin Sandys*, or the
Company, were able to do the Colony and Trade. For
ſoon after, Captain *Harvey* and Mr. *Pory*, the Privy Council's Commiſſioners, returned from *Virginia*. What their
Report was of the State of the Colony, I cannot diſcover;
but we may eaſily judge, by the Principles and Diſpoſitions
of the Men, that it was not much to the Honour or Advantage of the preſent Government. Upon their Return therefore, his Majeſty was pleaſed, by a Proclamation bearing
Date the 15th of *July*, 1624, to ſuppreſs the Courſe of their
Courts at Deputy *Farrar's*. And for the preſent Ordering
of

of the Affairs of the Colony, 'till a fuller and more perfect
Settlement of them could be made, the Lord President of
his Majefty's Privy Council, with other Privy Counfellors,
and feveral Knights and Gentlemen, were appointed to
meet, every *Thurfday* in the Afternoon, at Sir *Thomas Smith*'s
Houfe, in *Philpot-Lane*; whither all Perfons, whom it
might concern, were ordered to repair.   And thus Sir *Thomas Smith* triumphed over the Companies and the Colonies;
and notwithstanding the authentic Reprefentations of the
Company in *England*, and our General Affembly here a-
gainft him, and the plain Detection of his Cruelties and Oppreffions, to all Men of common Senfe and common Juftice,
yet he did at laft recover his Power again, and was the Perfon chiefly depended upon, by the *Solomon* of that Age, in
all Matters relating to them.   For the *Somer-Iflands* Courts
had been fuppreffed fome Months before, by a fimple Letter from the King; and Meetings appointed, at Sir *Thomas
Smith*'s, for the Management of their Affairs.   But thefe
Meetings were without the Mixture of any Privy Counfellors, and wholly confifted of himfelf and his Creatures.
And by this time, in the Abfence of Sir *Edward Sackvil*,
now Earl of *Dorfet*, their Governor, who had, the Year
before, fucceeded the Lord *Cavendifh*, now alfo Earl of *Devonfhire*, and under Colour of fome Complaints and Diffentions, the Lords of the Privy Council appointed Sir *Thomas
Smith* again Governor of that Company; affuming to themfelves a boundlefs Power of placing and difplacing legal Officers, as they pleafed.   This Appointment, Captain *Smith*
tells us, was afterwards confirmed, and Sir *Thomas Smith*
elected by the Court.   But this Court was only his Faction,
who affumed to themfelves that Name and Character.   For
I find, that many of the Company, and as it appears, a vaft
Majority, complained of them, and declared againft their
Meetings, as Ufurpations upon the Government of the Company, and no ways legal or valid.

T H I S was the End of the *Virginia* Company; one of
the nobleft, moft illuftrious, and publick-fpirited Societies,
that ever yet perhaps engaged in fuch an Undertaking.   It
was an Event certainly of Benefit and Advantage to the
Country, as we in *America* find by Experience, that it is
better to be under a Royal Government, than in the Hands
of Proprietors, in what Shape or Manner foever.   But yet
it muft be at laft confeffed, that it was brought about with
all imaginable Inftances of Unrighteoufnefs and Oppreffion;
and that not even the Decency of Forms of Law were kept
up or regarded in it.   For altho' a Writ of *Quo Warranto*
(an oppreffive Writ in itfelf, and for the moft part turned

to very bafe and illegal Purpofes) was iffued againft the Company, yet I cannot underftand, altho' I have taken no fmall Pains to find it out, that it ever came to an Iffue or Determination. And to diffolve them by the arbitrary Authority of a Proclamation, whilft a legal Procefs was depending, feems but a more bare-faced Injuftice and Oppreffion. Far the greater Part of the Company did, by no means, deferve fuch Treatment. They appear, from all the Papers and Records that I have perufed, to have been Gentlemen of very noble, clear, and difinterefted Defigns; who, as they were above the Neceffity of any Accefs to their own Fortunes, were willing and intent to fpend much of their Time and Money, in advancing an Undertaking which they juftly conceived to be of very great Confequence to their Country. And even Captain *Smith*, who was certainly no Friend to the Company, and whofe Hiftory feems much in Honour and Vindication of Sir *Thomas Smith* and his Government, yet owns, that fcarce any of the Nobility and Gentry expected or aimed at any thing elfe, but the Profperity of the Action: And he was confidently perfuaded, that fome Merchants, and others, took more Care and Pains, even at their own continual great Charge, than they could be hired to, for the Love of Money; fo honeftly regarding the general Good of the Enterprife, that they would hold it worfe than Sacrilege, to wrong it but a Shilling, or to extort a Penny upon the common People.

IT may indeed be thought fomething ftrange, how fo many Gentlemen, of the nobleft Fortunes and moft publick Spirits in the Nation, could fo patiently fubmit to fuch evident Injury and Wrong, without bringing the Matter to a legal Trial. But they had been much harraffed and fatigued of late, by the Difcords and Factions in the Company; which, they plainly faw, were fupported and abetted by the King, for fome unjuft and partial Views of his own, being much charmed with the unexpectedly large and rifing Revenue from Tobacco, and therefore defirous to get the Plantations wholly into his own Hands. They had alfo expended largely above an hundred thoufand Pounds, out of their own private Fortunes, without any probable Profpect of prefent Retribution or Gain to themfelves; and they could not but fee, that proceeding in the Enterprife would ftill engage them in farther Expences, for which they would only be expofed to the Abufes and Affronts of the opponent Faction, and to Injuries and Oppreffions from the King and his Council. They might alfo confider perhaps the State of the Courts of Law at that time, which could give them but flender Hopes of obtaining any Redrefs there. For the
Judges

Judges and Oracles of Law are greatly wronged and abufed, if they were not then, like the lying Oracle of old, much addicted to *philippizing*, and willing to raife the Royal Prerogative above all Reftraints of Law, or of any other earthly Power. Their original Records, on which their Proofs muft chiefly depend, had likewife been taken from them by the Privy Council. And the Earl of *Southampton*, who had all their Eyes and Hearts fixed upon him, after languifhing fome time, and having firft loft his eldeft Son, the Lord *Wriothfley*, died this following Winter 1624. To which may be added, that the Succefs of the Colonies was ftill doubtful, without the King's Favour and Protection; or at leaft againft his Will, and the perpetual Stretch of his Power thwarting and oppreffing them. They therefore filently acquiefced and fubmitted to this illegal Diffolution; and quietly withdrew from an Affair, which had coft them fo much Money and Pains, and had given them fuch continual Trouble and Vexation.

F I N I S.

An

A N

APPENDIX

TO THE

Firſt Part of the

HISTORY

OF

VIRGINIA:

CONTAINING

A Collection of ſuch ancient Charters or Letters Patent, as relate to that Period of Time, and are ſtill extant in our publick Offices in the *Capitol*, or in other authentic Papers and Records.

WILLIAMSBURG: Printed by W. PARKS, M,DCC,XLVII.

THE
PREFACE.

O F the two *firft* of the following *Charters*, I have *feen four Copies*; one among the *oldeft Records* in the *Secretary's Office*, much mangled and defaced; another in the *Council Office*, tolerably legible; a third, in a very fair *Book of Records*, which belongs, as I take it, to the *Houfe of Burgeffes Office*; and the *fourth and moft correct*, I found among Sir John Randolph's *Papers, tranfcribed by his Clerk*, and collated, as I *fuppofe*, from different *Copies*. However, I can venture to *affure* the *Reader*, that the *Edition*, which I here give by the *Help* of the two *laft* mentioned *Copies*, is *ftill fuller* and more *correct* than any of them. Of the third *Charter* I have never met with but one *Copy*, likewife in Sir John Randolph's *Collection of publick Papers*. It is pretty *correctly tranfcribed*; and I hope, it will be found, with the *neceffary Emendations*, I have made in it, very complete and *exact*. *Thefe* are all the *King's Charters* to the *Company*, that I have been able to find; although they certainly are not all, he *granted*. For many things are mentioned in the *Company's Records*, as drawn from their *Charters*, which, are *neverthelefs* not to be found in *thefe*. But to *thefe Royal Charters* I have added a fourth, The *Company's Charter* and *Conftitution* of a Council of State and a General *Affembly*; which I found in the above-mentioned *Book*, belonging to the *Clerk's Office* of the *Houfe* of *Burgeffes*. As their *Authority* for granting it was *unqueftionable*, and as it is of an important *Nature*, and the *firft Draught* and *Foundation* of the *Conftitution* of this *Colony*, *I* thought, an *Edition* of it would not be unacceptable to the learned and curious *Reader*.

I once intended (as *Bifhop* Burnet has done, in a very *ufeful* and *fatisfactory Manner*, in his *Hiftory of the Reformation*) to have added feveral other very curious *Papers* and original *Pieces of Record*. But I perceive, to my no *fmall*

Sur-

Surprife and Mortification, that fome of my Countrymen (and thofe too, Perfons of high Fortune and Diftinction) feemed to be much alarmed, and to grudge, that a complete Hiftory of their own Country would run to more than one Volume, and coft them above half a Piftole. I was therefore obliged to reftrain my Hand, and only to infert thefe few moft neceffary Inftruments, for fear of enhancing the Price, to the immenfe Charge and irreparable Damage of fuch generous and publick-fpirited Gentlemen.

I thought the Publication of thefe Charters the more proper, as I conceive, that they have never been legally revoked, and as they contain things of very great Confequence and Concern. For if the Inhabitants and Natives of these Colonies are en-titled to all Liberties, Franchifes, and Immunities of free Denizens and natural Subjects, to all Intents and Purpofes, as if they had been abiding and born within the Realm of *England,* or any other of his Majefty's Dominions (*as is exprefly declared in. Sect.* xv. *of the firft, and Sect.* xxii. *of the fecond Charter*) *what Room can there be for that flavifh Doctrine, which was broached by a Judge of* New-York, *in a criminal Trial,* (*the Cafe of Col.* Bayard, *publifhed in the printed Collection of State Trials*) *that altho'* petitioning the King was no Crime, yet it might be fo, to petition the Houfe of Commons in the Plantations, where the King governs by his PREROGATIVE ; *a Word always doubtful, equivocal, and fufpicious, but to be fure fruitful of Tyranny and of all arbitrary and illegal Oppreffion, when unfixed and unreftrained by the Law. And what Law in the Plantations can curb the Royal Prerogative, which is faid to be as ancient as the Crown of* England *itfelf, and to be always inherent and infeperable from it ? But it is not to be fuppofed, that that Dragoon of the Long-Robe, and legal Pander to Slavery, had any Thought or Defire, to ftop with the Laws the Breach, which he endeavoured to make in the Liberties of the Colonies ; or to ftay, with old moldering Parchments, the lawlefs and overwhelming Waves of Prero-gative.*

BUT *farther : If we have a Right to* all the Liberties, Franchifes, and Immunities *of* Englifhmen, *in vain was the Chicanery of K.* Charles *II, and at laft his abfolute Refufal, in the Charter which he granted the Colony,* to ratify and con-firm the Power and Authority of the Grand Affembly, confifting of the Governor, Council, and Bugeffes ; *as alfo to grant and declare,* that no Manner of Impofitions or Taxes fhould be laid on the Colony, but by the common Confent of the Governor, Council, and Burgeffes, as had been theretofore ufed. *For what* Liberty, Franchife, or

Im-

Immunity *is dearer or more essential to* Englishmen, *than to be subject to such Laws, as are enacted, and to be liable to no Taxes, but what are laid upon them, by their own Consent, in a Parliamentary Way? And besides, it was then too late to abridge the Liberties of our General Assemblies, and to keep them in a precarious and dependent State, as that Prince (never a Friend to the Liberties of his People or Mankind, but about that time particularly plunged in arbitrary Schemes and Designs) endeavoured to do. For above fifty Years before that, the Company had expresly established the General Assembly, by the fourth Charter in this Collection, and by a Power immediately derived from the King. And supposing their own Charters were afterwards legally revoked, yet that (which they granted by his Majesty's express Authority and Direction, and whilst their own Powers were in full Force and Validity) will not, I presume, consequently fall and be annulled with them.*

THESE, and the like Conclusions, will naturally arise from the following Charters. And I therefore hope, I shall need no other Reason or Apology, for thus giving them to the Publick.

No. I.

N°. I.

K. James *I.'s Letters Patent to Sir* Thomas Gates, *Sir* George Somers, *and others, for two several Colonies and Plantations, to be made in* Virginia, *and other Parts and Territories of* America. *Dated* April 10, 1606.

I. JAMES, by the Grace of God, King of *England, Scotland, France,* and *Ireland,* Defender of the Faith, *&c.* WHEREAS our loving and well-difpofed Subjects, Sir *Thomas Gates,* and Sir *George Somers,* Knights, *Richard Hackluit,* Clerk, Prebendary of *Weftminfter,* and *Edward-Maria Wingfield, Thomas Hanham,* and *Ralegh Gilbert,* Efqrs. *William Parker,* and *George Popham,* Gentlemen, and divers others of our loving Subjects, have been humble Suitors unto us, that We would vouchfafe unto them our Licence, to make Habitation, Plantation, and to deduce a Colony of fundry of our People into that Part of *America,* commonly called VIRGINIA, and other Parts and Territories in *America,* either appertaining unto us, or which are not now actually poffeffed by any *Chriftian* Prince or People, fituate, lying, and being all along the Sea Coafts, between four and thirty Degrees of *Northerly* Latitude from the Equinoctial Line, and five and forty Degrees of the fame Latitude, and in the main Land between the fame four and thirty and five and forty Degrees, and the Iflands thereunto adjacent, or within one hundred Miles of the Coafts thereof;

II. AND to that End, and for the more fpeedy Accomplifhment of their faid intended Plantation and Habitation there, are defirous to divide themfelves into two feveral Colonies and Companies; The one confifting of certain Knights, Gentlemen, Merchants, and other Adventurers, of our City of *London* and elfewhere, which are, and from time to time fhall be, joined unto them, which do defire to begin their Plantation and Habitation in fome fit and convenient Place, between four and thirty and one and forty Degrees of the faid Latitude, alongft the Coafts of *Virginia* and Coafts of *America* aforefaid; And the other confifting of fundry Knights, Gentlemen, Merchants, and other Adventurers, of our Cities of *Briftol* and *Exeter,* and of our Town of *Plimouth,* and of other Places, which do join themfelves unto that Colony, which do defire to begin their Plantation and Habitation in fome fit and convenient Place, between eight and thirty Degrees and five and forty Degrees of the faid Latitude, all alongft the faid Coaft of *Virginia* and *America,* as that Coaft lyeth:

III. WE, greatly commending, and gracioufly accepting of, their Defires for the Furtherance of fo noble a Work, which may, by the Providence of Almighty God, hereafter tend to the Glory of his Divine Majefty, in propagating of *Chriftian* Religion to
fuch

ſuch People, as yet live in Darkneſs and miſerable Ignorance of the true Knowledge and Worſhip of God, and may in time bring the Infidels and Savages, living in thoſe Parts, to human Civility, and to a ſettled and quiet Government; D O, by theſe our Letters Patents, gracioufly accept of, and agree to, their humble and well intended Defires;

IV. A N D do therefore, for Us, our Heirs, and Succeſſors, G R A N T and agree, that the ſaid Sir *Thomas Gates*, Sir *George Somers*, *Richard Hackluit*, and *Edward-Maria Wingfield*, Adventurers of and for our City of *London*, and all ſuch others, as are, or ſhall be, joined unto them of that Colony, ſhall be called the *firſt Colony*; And they ſhall and may begin their ſaid firſt Plantation and Habitation, at any Place upon the ſaid Coaſt of *Virginia* or *America*, where they ſhall think fit and convenient, between the ſaid four and thirty and one and forty Degrees of the ſaid Latitude; And that they ſhall have all the Lands, Woods, Soil, Grounds, Havens, Ports, Rivers, Mines, Minerals, Marſhes, Waters, Fiſhings, Commodities, and Hereditaments, whatſoever, from the ſaid firſt Seat of their Plantation and Habitation by the Space of fifty Miles of *Engliſh* Statute Meaſure, all along the ſaid Coaſt of *Virginia* and *America*, towards the *Weſt* and *Southweſt*, as the Coaſt lyeth, with all the Iflands within one hundred Miles directly over againſt the ſame Sea Coaſt; And alſo all the Lands, Soil, Grounds, Havens, Ports, Rivers, Mines, Minerals, Woods, Waters, Marſhes, Fiſhings, Commodities, and Hereditaments, whatſoever, from the ſaid Place of their firſt Plantation and Habitation for the Space of fifty like *Engliſh* Miles, all alongſt the ſaid Coaſt of *Virginia* and *America*, towards the *Eaſt* and *Northeaſt*, or towards the *North*, as the Coaſt lyeth, together with all the Iflands within one hundred Miles, directly over againſt the ſaid Sea Coaſt; And alſo all the Lands, Woods, Soil, Grounds, Havens, Ports, Rivers, Mines, Minerals, Marſhes, Waters, Fiſhings, Commodities, and Hereditaments, whatſoever, from the ſame fifty Miles every way on the Sea Coaſt, directly into the main Land by the Space of one hundred like *Engliſh* Miles; And ſhall and may inhabit and remain there; and ſhall and may alſo build and fortify within any the ſame, for their better Safeguard and Defence, according to their beſt Diſcretion, and the Diſcretion of the Council of that Colony; And that no other of our Subjects ſhall be permitted, or ſuffered, to plant or inhabit behind, or on the Backſide of them, towards the main Land, without the Expreſs Licence or Conſent of the Council of that Colony, thereunto in Writing firſt had and obtained.

V. A N D we do likewiſe, for Us, our Heirs, and Succeſſors, by theſe Preſents, G R A N T and agree, that the ſaid *Thomas Hanham*, and *Ralegh Gilbert*, *William Parker*, and *George Popham*, and all others of the Town of *Plimouth* in the County of *Devon*, or elſewhere, which are, or ſhall be, joined unto them of that Colony, ſhall be called the *ſecond Colony*; And that they ſhall and may begin their ſaid Plantation and Seat of their firſt Abode and Habitation, at any Place upon the ſaid Coaſt of *Virginia* and *America*, where they ſhall think fit and convenient, between eight
and

and thirty Degrees of the ſaid Latitude, and five and forty Degrees of the ſame Latitude; And that they ſhall have all the
Lands, Soils, Grounds, Havens, Ports, Rivers, Mines, Minerals,
Woods, Marſhes, Waters, Fiſhings, Commodities, and Hereditaments, whatſoever, from the firſt Seat of their Plantation and Habitation by the Space of fifty like *Engliſh* Miles, as is aforeſaid,
all alongſt the ſaid Coaſt of *Virginia* and *America*, towards the
Weſt and *Southweſt*, or towards the *South*, as the Coaſt lyeth,
and all the Iſlands within one hundred Miles, directly over againſt
the ſaid Sea Coaſt; And alſo all the Lands, Soils, Grounds, Havens, Ports, Rivers, Mines, Minerals, Woods, Marſhes, Waters,
Fiſhings, Commodities, and Hereditaments, whatſoever, from the
ſaid Place of their firſt Plantation and Habitation for the Space of
fifty like Miles, all alongſt the ſaid Coaſt of *Virginia* and *America*, towards the *Eaſt* and *Northeaſt*, or towards the *North*, as
the Coaſt lyeth, and all the Iſlands alſo within one hundred Miles
directly over againſt the ſame Sea Coaſt; And alſo all the Lands,
Soils, Grounds, Havens, Ports, Rivers, Woods, Mines, Minerals,
Marſhes, Waters, Fiſhings, Commodities, and Hereditaments,
whatſoever, from the ſame fifty Miles every way on the Sea
Coaſt, directly into the main Land, by the Space of one hundred
like *Engliſh* Miles; And ſhall and may inhabit and remain there;
and ſhall and may alſo build and fortify within any the ſame for
their better Safeguard, according to their beſt Diſcretion, and the
Diſcretion of the Council of that Colony; And that none of our
Subjects ſhall be permitted, or ſuffered, to plant or inhabit behind, or on the Back of them, towards the main Land, without
the expreſs Licence of the Council of that Colony, in Writing
thereunto firſt had and obtained.

VI. P r o v i d e d always, and our Will and Pleaſure herein
is, that the Plantation and Habitation of ſuch of the ſaid Colonies, as ſhall laſt plant themſelves, as aforeſaid, ſhall not be made
within one hundred like *Engliſh* Miles of the other of them, that
firſt began to make their Plantation, as aforeſaid.

VII. A n d we do alſo ordain, eſtabliſh, and agree, for Us,
our Heirs, and Succeſſors, that each of the ſaid Colonies ſhall
have a Council, which ſhall govern and order all Matters and
Cauſes, which ſhall ariſe, grow, or happen, to or within the ſame
ſeveral Colonies, according to ſuch Laws, Ordinances, and Inſtructions, as ſhall be, in that behalf, given and ſigned with Our
Hand or Sign Manual, and paſs under the Privy Seal of our
Realm of *England*; Each of which Councils ſhall conſiſt of thirteen Perſons, to be ordained, made, and removed, from time
to time, according as ſhall be directed and compriſed in the ſame
Inſtructions; And ſhall have a ſeveral Seal, for all Matters that
ſhall paſs or concern the ſame ſeveral Councils; Each of which
Seals ſhall have the King's Arms engraven on the one Side thereof, and his Portraiture on the other; And that the Seal for the
Council of the ſaid firſt Colony ſhall have engraven round about,
on the one Side, theſe Words; *Sigillum Regis Magnæ Britanniæ,
Franciæ, & Hiberniæ*; on the other Side this Inſcription, round
about; *Pro Concilio primæ Coloniæ Virginiæ.* And the Seal for
the

the Council of the ſaid ſecond Colony ſhall alſo have engraven, round about the one Side thereof, the aforeſaid Words; *Sigillum Regis Magnæ, Britanniæ, Franciæ, & Hiberniæ*; and on the other Side; *Pro Concilio ſecundæ Coloniæ Virginiæ:*

⫸VIII. A n d that alſo there ſhall be a Council eſtabliſhed here in *England*, which ſhall, in like Manner, conſiſt of thirteen Perſons, to be, for that Purpoſe, appointed by Us, our Heirs and Succeſſors, which ſhall be called our *Council of Virginia*; And ſhall, from time to time, have the ſuperior Managing and Direction, only of and for all Matters, that ſhall or may concern the Government, as well of the ſaid ſeveral Colonies, as of and for any other Part or Place, within the aforeſaid Precinĉts of four and thirty and five and forty Degrees, abovementioned; Which Council ſhall, in like manner, have a Seal, for Matters concerning the Council or Colonies, with the like Arms and Portraiture, as aforeſaid, with this Inſcription, engraven round about on the one Side; *Sigillum Regis Magnæ Britanniæ, Franciæ, & Hiberniæ*; and round about the other Side, *Pro Concilio ſuo Virginiæ.*

IX. A n d moreover, we do G r a n t and agree, for Us, our Heirs and Succeſſors, that the ſaid ſeveral Councils, of and for the ſaid ſeveral Colonies, ſhall and lawfully may, by Virtue hereof, from time to time, without any Interruption of Us, our Heirs or Succeſſors, give and take Order, to dig, mine, and ſearch for all Manner of Mines of Gold, Silver, and Copper, as well within any Part of their ſaid ſeveral Colonies, as of the ſaid main Lands on the Backſide of the ſame Colonies; And to H a v e and enjoy the Gold, Silver, and Copper, to be gotten thereof, to the Uſe and Behoof of the ſame Colonies, and the Plantations thereof; Y i e l d i n g therefore, to Us, our Heirs and Succeſſors, the fifth Part only of all the ſame Gold and Silver, and the fifteenth Part of all the ſame Copper, ſo to be gotten or had, as is aforeſaid, without any other Manner of Profit or Account, to be given or yielded to Us, our Heirs, or Succeſſors, for or in Reſpeĉt of the ſame:

X. A n d that they ſhall, or lawfully may, eſtabliſh and cauſe to be made a Coin, to paſs current there between the People of thoſe ſeveral Colonies, for the more Eaſe of Traffick and Bargaining between and amongſt them and the Natives there, of ſuch Metal, and in ſuch Manner and Form, as the ſaid ſeveral Councils there ſhall limit and appoint.

XI. A n d we do likewiſe, for Us, our Heirs, and Succeſſors, by theſe Preſents, give full Power and Authority to the ſaid Sir *Thomas Gates*, Sir *George Somers, Richard Hackluit, Edward-Maria Wingfield, Thomas Hanham, Ralegh Gilbert, William Parker*, and *George Popham*, and to every of them, and to the ſaid ſeveral Companies, Plantations, and Colonies, that they, and every of them, ſhall and may, at all and every time and times hereafter, have, take, and lead in the ſaid Voyage, and for and towards the ſaid ſeveral Plantations and Colonies, and to travel thitherward, and to abide and inhabit there, in every the ſaid Colonies and Plantations, ſuch and ſo many of our Subjeĉts, as ſhall willingly accompany them, or any of them, in the ſaid Voyages and Plantations,

tations; With fufficient Shipping, and Furniture of Armour, Weapons, Ordinance, Powder, Victual, and all other things, neceſſary for the ſaid Plantations, and for their Uſe and Defence there: PROVIDED always, that none of the ſaid Perſons be fuch, as ſhall hereafter be ſpecially reſtrained by Us, our Heirs, or Succeſſors.

XII. MOREOVER, we do, by theſe Preſents, for Us, our Heirs, and Succeſſors, GIVE AND GRANT Licence unto the ſaid Sir *Thomas Gates,* Sir *George Somers, Richard Hackluit, Edward-Maria Wingfield, Thomas Hanham, Ralegh Gilbert, William Parker,* and *George Popham,* and to every of the ſaid Colonies, that they, and every of them, ſhall and may, from time to time, and at all times for ever hereafter, for their ſeveral Defences, encounter, expulfe, repel, and refift, as well by Sea as by Land, by all Ways and Means whatſoever, all and every fuch Perſon and Perſons, as without the efpecial Licence of the ſaid ſeveral Colonies and Plantations, ſhall attempt to inhabit within the ſaid ſeveral Precincts and Limits of the ſaid ſeveral Colonies and Plantations, or any of them, or that ſhall enterpriſe or attempt, at any time hereafter, the Hurt, Detriment, or Annoyance, of the ſaid ſeveral Colonies or Plantations:

XIII. GIVING AND GRANTING, by theſe Preſents, unto the ſaid Sir *Thomas Gates,* Sir *George Somers, Richard Hackluit, Edward-Maria Wingfield,* and their Aſſociates of the ſaid firſt Colony, and unto the ſaid *Thomas Hanham, Ralegh Gilbert, William Parker,* and *George Popham,* and their Aſſociates of the ſaid ſecond Colony, and to every of them, from time to time, and at all times forever hereafter, Power and Authority to take and furprife, by all Ways and Means whatſoever, all and every Perſon and Perſons, with their Ships, Veſſels, Goods, and other Furniture, which ſhall be found trafficking, into any Harbour or Harbours, Creek or Creeks, or Place, within the Limits or Precincts of the ſaid ſeveral Colonies and Plantations, not being of the ſame Colony, until fuch time, as they, being of any Realms or Dominions under our Obedience, ſhall pay, or agree to pay, to the Hands of the Treaſurer of that Colony, within whoſe Limits and Precincts they ſhall ſo traffick, two and a half upon every Hundred, of any thing, ſo by them trafficked, bought, or ſold; And being Strangers, and not Subjects under our Obeyfance, until they ſhal! pay five upon every Hundred, of fuch Wares and Merchandifes, as they ſhall traffick, buy, or ſell, within the Precincts of the ſaid ſeveral Colonies, wherein they ſhall ſo traffick, buy, or ſell, as aforeſaid; WHICH Sums of Money, or Benefit, as aforeſaid, for and during the Space of one and twenty Years, next enfuing the Date hereof, ſhall be wholly emploied to the Uſe, Benefit, and Behoof of the ſaid ſeveral Plantations, where fuch Traffick ſhall be made; And after the ſaid one and twenty Years ended, the ſame ſhall be taken to the Uſe of Us, our Heirs, and Succeſſors, by fuch Officers and Miniſters, as by Us, our Heirs, and Succeſſors, ſhall be thereunto aſſigned or appointed.

XIV. AND we do further, by theſe Preſents, for Us, our Heirs, and Succeſſors, GIVE AND GRANT unto the ſaid Sir *Thomas Gates*, Sir *George Somers, Richard Hackluit*, and *Edward-Maria Wingfield*, and to their Aſſociates of the ſaid firſt Colony and Plantation, and to the ſaid *Thomas Hanham, Ralegh Gilbert, William Parker*, and *George Popham*, and their Aſſociates of the ſaid ſecond Colony and Plantation, that they, and every of them, by their Deputies, Miniſters, and Factors, may tranſport the Goods, Chattles, Armour, Munition, and Furniture, needful to be uſed by them, for their ſaid Apparel, Food, Defence, or otherwiſe in Reſpect of the ſaid Plantations, out of our Realms of *England* and *Ireland*, and all other our Dominions, from time to time, for and during the Time of ſeven Years, next enſuing the Date hereof, for the better Relief of the ſaid ſeveral Colonies and Plantations, without any Cuſtom, Subſidy, or other Duty, unto Us, our Heirs, or Succeſſors, to be yielded or paid for the ſame.

XV. ALSO we do, for Us, our Heirs, and Succeſſors, DECLARE, by theſe Preſents, that all and every the Perſons, being our Subjects, which ſhall dwell and inhabit within every or any of the ſaid ſeveral Colonies and Plantations, and every of their Children, which ſhall happen to be born within any of the Limits and Precincts of the ſaid ſeveral Colonies and Plantations, ſhall HAVE and enjoy all Liberties, Franchiſes, and Immunities, within any of our other Dominions, to all Intents and Purpoſes, as if they had been abiding and born, within this our Realm of *England*, or any other of our ſaid Dominions.

XVI. MOREOVER, our gracious Will and Pleaſure is, and we do, by theſe Preſents, for Us, our Heirs, and Succeſſors, declare and ſet forth, that if any Perſon or Perſons, which ſhall be of any of the ſaid Colonies and Plantations, or any other, which ſhall traffick to the ſaid Colonies and Plantations, or any of them, ſhall, at any time or times hereafter, tranſport any Wares, Merchandiſes, or Commodities, out of any our Dominions, with a Pretence to land, ſell, or otherwiſe diſpoſe of the ſame, within any the Limits and Precincts of any the ſaid Colonies and Plantations, and yet neverthelefs, being at Sea, or after he hath landed the ſame within any of the ſaid Colonies and Plantations, ſhall carry the ſame into any other foreign Country, with a Purpoſe there to ſell or diſpoſe of the ſame, without the Licence of Us, our Heirs, and Succeſſors, in that Behalf firſt had and obtained; That then, all the Goods and Chattels of ſuch Perſon or Perſons, ſo offending and tranſporting, together with the ſaid Ship or Veſſel, wherein ſuch Tranſportation was made, ſhall be forfeited to Us, our Heirs, and Succeſſors.

XVII. PROVIDED always, and our Will and Pleaſure is, and we do hereby declare to all *Chriſtian* Kings, Princes, and States, that if any Perſon or Perſons, which ſhall hereafter be of any of the ſaid ſeveral Colonies and Plantations, or any other, by his, their or any of their Licence and Appointment, ſhall, at any time or times hereafter, rob or ſpoil, by Sea or by Land, or do

any

any Act of unjuft and unlawful Hoftility, to any the Subjects of Us, our Heirs, or Succeffors, or any the Subjects of any King, Prince, Ruler, Governor, or State, being then in League or Amity with Us, our Heirs, or Succeffors, and that upon fuch Injury, or upon juft Complaint of fuch Prince, Ruler, Governor, or State, or their Subjects, We, our Heirs, or Succeffors, fhall make open Proclamation, within any of the Ports of our Realm of *England,* commodious for that Purpofe, That the faid Perfon or Perfons, having committed any fuch Robbery or Spoil, fhall, within the Term to be limited by fuch Proclamations, make full Reftitution or Satisfaction of all fuch Injuries done, fo as the faid Princes, or others, fo complaining, may hold themfelves fully fatisfied and contented; And that, if the faid Perfon or Perfons, having committed fuch Robbery or Spoil, fhall not make, or caufe to be made, Satisfaction accordingly, within fuch Time fo to be limited, That then it fhall be lawful to Us, · our Heirs, and Succeffors, to put the faid Perfon or Perfons, having committed fuch Robbery or Spoil, and their Procurers, Abetters, or Comforters, out of our Allegiance and Protection; And that it fhall be lawful and free, for all Princes and others, to purfue with Hoftility the faid Offenders, and every of them, and their and every of their Procurers, Aiders, Abetters, and Comforters, in that Behalf.

XVIII. A n d finally, we do, for Us, our Heirs, and Succeffors, G r a n t and agree, to and with the faid Sir *Thomas Gates,* Sir *George Somers, Richard Hackluit,* and *Edward-Maria Wingfield,* and all others of the faid firft Colony, that We, our Heirs, and Succeffors, upon Petition in that Behalf to be made, fhall, by Letters-patent under the Great Seal of *England,* G i v e and G r a n t unto fuch Perfons, their Heirs, and Affigns, as the Council of that Colony, or the moft Part of them, fhall, for that Purpofe nominate and affign, all the Lands, Tenements, and Hereditaments, which fhall be within the Precincts limited for that Colony, as is aforefaid, T o b e h o l d e n of Us, our Heirs, and Succeffors, as of our Manor of *Eaft-Greenwich* in the County of *Kent,* in free and common Soccage only, and not in Capite:

XIX. A n d do, in like Manner, G r a n t and agree, for Us, our Heirs, and Succeffors, to and with the faid *Thomas Hanham, Ralegh Gilbert, William Parker,* and *George Popham,* and all others of the faid fecond Colony, that We, our Heirs, and Succeffors, upon Petition in that Behalf to be made, fhall, by Letters-patent under the Great Seal of *England,* G i v e and G r a n t unto fuch Perfons, their Heirs, and Affigns, as the Council of that Colony, or the moft Part of them, fhall, for that Purpofe, nominate and affign, all the Lands, Tenements, and Hereditaments, which fhall be within the Precincts limited for that Colony, as is aforefaid, T o b e h o l d e n of Us, our Heirs, and Succeffors, as of our Manour of *Eaft-Greenwich* in the County of *Kent,* in free and common Soccage only, and not in Capite.

XX. A l l which Lands, Tenements, and Hereditaments, fo to be paffed by the faid feveral Letters-patent, fhall be fufficient

Affurance from the faid Patentees, fo diftributed and divided amongft the Undertakers for the Plantation of the faid feveral Colonies, and fuch as fhall make their Plantations in either of the faid feveral Colonies, in fuch Manner and Form, and for fuch Eftates, as fhall be ordered and fet down by the Council of the faid Colony, or the moft Part of them, refpectively, within which the fame Lands, Tenements, and Hereditaments fhall lye or be; Although exprefs Mention of the true yearly Value or Certainty of the Premifes, or any of them, or of any other Gifts or Grants, by Us or any of our Progenitors or Predeceffors, to the aforefaid Sir *Thomas Gates*, Knt. Sir *George Somers*, Knt. *Richard Hackluit, Edward-Maria Wingfield, Thomas Hanham, Raleigh Gilbert, William Parker,* and *George Popham,* or any of them, heretofore made, in thefe Prefents, is not made; Or any Statute, Act, Ordinance, or Provifion, Proclamation, or Reftraint, to the contrary hereof had, made, ordained, or any other Thing, Caufe, or Matter whatfoever, in any wife notwithftanding. I N W I T N E S S whereof, we have caufed thefe our Letters to be made Patents; Witnefs Ourfelf at *Weftminfter,* the tenth Day of *April,* in the fourth Year of our Reign of *England, France,* and *Ireland,* and of *Scotland* the nine and thirtieth.

Lukin

Per breve de privato Sigillo.

N°. II.

King James *the* I.*'s fecond Charter to the Treafurer and Company for* Virginia, *erecting them into a Corporation and Body Politick, and for the further Enlargement and Explanation of the Privileges of the faid Company and firft Colony of* Virginia. *Dated* May 23, 1609.

I. *J A M E S,* by the Grace of God, King of *England, Scotland, France,* and *Ireland,* Defender of the Faith *&c.* To all, to whom thefe Prefents fhall come, Greeting. W H E R E A S, at the humble Suit and Requeft of fundry our loving and well difpofed Subjects, intending to deduce a Colony, and to make Habitation and Plantation of fundry our People, in that Part of *America,* commonly called V I R G I N I A, and other Parts and Territories in *America,* either appertaining unto Us, or which are not actually poffeffed of any *Chriftian* Prince or People, within certain Bounds and Regions, We have formerly by our Letters-patents, bearing Date the tenth Day of *April,* in the fourth Year of our Reign of *England, France,* and *Ireland,* and of *Scotland* the nine and thirtieth, G R A N T E D to Sir *Thomas Gates,* Sir *George Somers,* and others, for the more fpeedy Accomplifhment of the faid Plantation and Habitation, that they fhould divide themfelves into two Colonies (the one confifting of divers Knights, Gentlemen, Merchants, and others, of our City of *London,* called the F I R S T
Co-

Colony; And ·the other confifting of divers Knights, Gentlemen, and others, of our Cities of *Briftol, Exeter,* and Town of *Plimouth,* and other Places, called the second Colony) And have yielded and granted many and fundry Privileges and Liberties to each Colony, for their quiet Settling and good Government therein, as by the faid Letters-patents more at large appeareth:

II. Now, forafmuch as divers and fundry of our loving Subjects, as well Adventurers, as Planters, of the faid firft Colony, which have already engaged themfelves in furthering the Bufinefs of the faid Colony and Plantation, and do further intend, by the Affiftance of Almighty God, to profecute the fame to a happy End, have of late been humble Suitors unto us, that (in Refpect of their great Charges and the Adventure of many of their Lives, which they have hazarded in the faid Difcovery and Plantation of the faid Country) We would be pleafed to grant them a further Enlargement and Explanation of the faid Grant, Privileges, and Liberties, and that fuch Counfellors, and other Officers, may be appointed amongft them, to manage and direct their Affairs, as are willing and ready to adventure with them, as alfo whofe Dwellings are not fo far remote from the City of *London,* but that they may, at convenient Times, be ready at hand, to give their Advice and Affiftance, upon all Occafions requifite.

III. We, greatly affecting the effectual Profecution and happy Succefs of the faid Plantation, and commending their good Defires therein, for their further Encouragement in accomplifhing fo excellent a Work, much pleafing to God, and profitable to our Kingdom, Do, of our fpecial Grace, and certain Knowledge, and mere Motion, for Us, our Heirs, and Succeffors, Give, Grant, and Confirm, to our trufty and well beloved Subjects, *Robert,* Earl of *Salifbury, Thomas,* Earl of *Suffolk, Henry,* Earl of *Southampton, William,* Earl of *Pembroke, Henry,* Earl of *Lincoln,* Earl of *Dorfet, Thomas,* Earl of *Exeter, Philip,* Earl of *Montgomery, Robert,* Lord Vifcount *Lifle, Theophilus,* Lord *Howard* of *Walden, James Montague,* Lord Bifhop of *Bath* and *Wells, Edward,* Lord *Zouche, Thomas,* Lord *Lawarr, William,* Lord *Mounteagle, Ralph,* Lord *Ewre, Edmond,* Lord *Sheffield, Grey,* Lord *Chandois,* Lord *Compton, John,* Lord *Petre, John,* Lord *Stanhope, George,* Lord *Carew,* Sir *Humphrey Weld,* Lord Mayor of *London, George Percie,* Efq; Sir *Edward Cecil,* Knt. Sir *George Wharton,* Knt. *Francis Weft,* Efq; Sir *William Wade,* Knt. Sir *Henry Nevil,* Knt. Sir *Thomas Smith,* Knt. Sir *Oliver Cromwell,* Knt. Sir *Peter Manwood,* Knt. Sir *Drue Drury,* Knt. Sir *John Scot,* Knt. Sir *Thomas Challoner,* Knt. Sir *Robert Drury,* Knt. Sir *Anthony Cope,* Knt. Sir *Horatio Vere,* Knt. Sir *Edward Conway,* Knt. Sir *William Brown,* Knt. Sir *Maurice Berkeley,* Knt. Sir *Robert Manfel,* Knt. Sir *Amias Prefton,* Knt. Sir *Thomas Gates,* Knt. Sir *Anthony Afhly,* Knt. Sir *Michael Sandys,* Knt. Sir *Henry Carey,* Knt. Sir *Stephen Soame,* Knt. Sir *Califthenes Brooke,* Knt. Sir *Edward Michelborn,* Knt. Sir *John Ratcliffe,* Knt. Sir *Charles Wilmot,* Knt. Sir *George Moor,* Knt.

Sir *Hugh Wirral*, Knt. Sir *Thomas Dennis*, Knt. Sir *John Holles*, Knt. Sir *William Godolphin*, Knt. Sir *Thomas Monfon*, Knt. Sir *Thomas Ridgwine*, Knt. Sir *John Brooke*, Knt. Sir *Robert Killigrew*, Knt. Sir *Henry Peyton*, Knt. Sir *Richard Williamfon*, Knt. Sir *Ferdinando Weynman*, Knt. Sir *William St. John*, Knt. Sir *Thomas Holcroft*, Knt. Sir *John Mallory*, Knt. Sir *Roger Afhton*, Knt. Sir *Walter Cope*, Knt. Sir *Richard Wigmore*, Knight, Sir *William Coke*, Knight, Sir *Herbert Crofte*, Knt. Sir *Henry Fanfhaw*, Knt. Sir *John Smith*, Knt. Sir *Francis Wolley*, Knt. Sir *Edward Waterhoufe*, Knt. Sir *Henry Seekford*, Knt. * Sir *Edwin Sandys*, Knt. Sir *Thomas Waynam*, Knt. Sir *John Trevor*, Knt. Sir *Warwick Heele*, Knt. Sir *Robert Wroth*, Knt. Sir *John Townfend*, Knt. Sir *Chriftopeer Perkins*, Knt. Sir *Daniel Dun*, Knt. Sir *Henry Hobart*, Knt. Sir *Francis Bacon*, Knt. Sir *Henry Montague*, Knt. Sir *George Coppin*, Knt. Sir *Samuel Sandys*, Knt. Sir *Thomas Roe*, Knt. Sir *George Somers*, Knt. Sir *Thomas Freake*, Knt. Sir *Thomas Harwell*, Knt. Sir *Charles Kelke*, Knt. Sir *Baptift Hicks*, Knt. Sir *John Watts*, Knt. Sir *Robert Carey*, Knt. Sir *William Romney*, Knt. Sir *Thomas Middleton*, Knt. Sir *Hatton Cheeke*, Knt. Sir *John Ogle*, Knt. Sir *Cavallero Meycot*, Knt. Sir *Stephen Riddlefdon*, Knt. Sir *Thomas Bludder*, Knt. Sir *Anthony Aucher*, Knt. Sir *Robert Johnfon*, Knt. Sir *Thomas Panton*, Knt. Sir *Charles Morgan*, Knt. Sir *Stephen Pole*, Knt. Sir *John Burlacie*, Knt. Sir *Chriftopher Cleave*, Knt. Sir *George Hayward*, Knt. Sir *Thomas Davis*, Knt. Sir *Thomas Sutton*, Knt. Sir *Anthony Foreft*, Knt. Sir *Robert Payne*, Knt. Sir *John Digby*, Knt. Sir *Dudley Digges*, Knt. Sir *Rowland Cotton*, Knt. Dr. *Matthew Sutcliffe*, Dr. *Meadows*, Dr. *Turner*, Dr. *Poe*, Capt. *Pagnam*, Capt. *Jeffrey Holcrofte*, Captain *Romney*, Captain *Henry Spry*, Captain *Shelton*, Captain *Sparks*, Captain *Thomas Wyat*, Captain *Brinfly*, Captain *William Courtney*, Captain *Herbert*, Captain *Clarke*, Captain *Dewhurft*, Captain *John Blundell*, Captain *Fryer*, Captain *Lewis Orwell*, Captain *Edward Loyd*, Captain *Slingefby*, Captain *Hawley*, Captain *Orme*, Captain *Woodhoufe*, Captain *Mafon*, Captain *Thomas Holcroft*, Captain *John Coke*, Captain *Holles*, Captain *William Proude*, Captain *Henry Woodhoufe*, Captain *Richard Lindefey*, Captain *Dexter*, Captain *William Winter*, Captain *Pearfe*, Captain *John Bingham*, Captain *Burray*, Captain *Thomas Conway*, Captain *Rookwood*, Captain *William Lovelace*, Captain *John Afhley*, Captain *Thomas Wynne*, Captain *Thomas Mewtis*, Captain *Edward Harwood*, Captain *Michael Everard*, Captain *Comock*, Captain *Mills*, Captain *Pigot*, Captain *Edward-Maria Wingfield*, Captain

---

* The Adventurers Names are vaftly confufed and different in the different M. S. Copies of this Charter. I chofe the two faireft and moft correct Copies, that I had met with, to tranfcribe this from; and altho' they both agree in writing this Name, Sir *Edward Sands*, or *Sandis*, yet they are both certainly wrong, as might be eafily proved, were it worth while, and would not be too tedious. I was alfo much puzzled to adjuft and fet right others of the Names; and altho' I was at no fmall Pains in collating the Copies, and in confulting and referring to other ancient Letters Patents and Papers, yet I will not affirm that I am not often miftaken. But however erroneous and perplexed the Names of the Adventurers may be, yet I found the main Body, and material Parts, of the Charter, very clear, full, and correct.

Chriftopher

Chriftopher Newport, Captain *John Sicklemore,* alias *Ratcliffe,*
Captain *John Smith,* Captain *John Martin,* Captain *Peter Wynne,*
Captain *Waldoe,* Captain *Thomas Wood,* Captain *Thomas Button,*
George Bolls, Efq; Sheriff of *London, William Crafhaw,* Clerk,
Batchelor of Divinity, *William Seabright,* Efq; *ChriftopherBrooke,*
Efq; *John Bingley,* Efq; *Thomas Watfon,* Efq; *Richard Percival,*
Efq; *John Moore,* Efq; *Hugh Brooker,* Efq; *David Woodhoufe,*
Efq; *Anthony Aucher,* Efq; *Robert Bowyer,* Efq; *Ralph Ewens,*
Efq; *Zachary Jones,* Efq; *George Calvert,* Efq; *William Dobfon,*
Efq; *Henry Reynolds,* Efq; *Thomas Walker,* Efq; *Anthony Barnars,*
Efq; *Thomas Sandys,* Efq; *Henry Sandys,* Efq; *Richard Sandys,*
Efq; Son of Sir *Edwin Sandys, William Oxenbridge,* Efq; *John*
Moore, Efq; *ThomasWilfon,* Efq; *John Bullock,* Efq; *JohnWaller,*
Efq; *Thomas Webb, Jehu Robinfon, William Brewfter, Robert E-*
velyn, Henry Danby, Richard Hackluit, Minifter, *John Eldred,*
Merchant, *William Ruffel,* Merchant, *John Merrick,* Merchant,
Richard Banifter, Merchant, *Charles Anthony,* Goldfmith, *John*
Banks, William Evans, Richard Humble, Richard Chamberlayne,
Merchant, *Thomas Barber,* Merchant, *Richard Pomet,* Merchant,
John Fletcher, Merchant, *Thomas Nicholls,* Merchant, *John Stoke,*
Merchant, *Gabriel Archer, Francis Covel, William Bonham, Ed-*
ward Harrifon, JohnWolftenholme, Nicholas Salter, HughEvans,
William Barnes, Otho Mawdet, Richard Staper, Merchant, *John*
Elkin, Merchant, *William Coyfe, Thomas Perkin,* Cooper, *Hum-*
ohry James, Cooper, *Henry Jackfon, Robert Singleton, Chriftopher*
Nicholls, John Harper, Abraham Chamberlayne,Thomas Shipton,
Thomas Carpenter, Anthony Crew, George Holman, Robert Hill,
Cleophas Smith, Ralph Harrifon, John Farmer, James Brearley,
William Crofby, Richard Cox, John Gearing, Richard Strongarm,
Ironmongers, *Thomas Langton, Griffith Hinton, Richard Ironfide,*
Richard Dean, Richard Turner, William Lawfon, Mercer, *James*
Chatfield, Edward Allen Tedder, Robert Hildebrand Sprinfon, Ar-
thur Moufe, John Gardiner, James Ruffel, Richard Cafwell, Rich-
ard Evans, John Hawkins, Richard Kerril, Richard Brooke, Mat-
thew Scrivener, Gentleman, *William Stallenge,* Gentleman, *Ar-*
thur Venn, Gentleman, *Sandys Webbe,* Gentleman, *Michael Phet-*
tiplace, Gentleman, *William Phettiplace,* Gentleman, *Ambrofe*
Prufey, Gentleman, *John Taverner,* Gentleman, *George Pretty,*
Gentleman, *Peter Latham,* Gentleman, *Thomas Montford,* Gentleman, *William Cantrel,* Gentleman, *Richard Wiffin,* Gentleman,
Ralph Moreton, Gentleman, *John Cornelius, Martin Freeman,*
Ralph Freeman, Andrew Moore, Thomas White, Edward Perkin,
Robert Offley, Thomas Whitley, George Pit, Robert Parkhurft, Tho-
mas Morris, Peter Harloe, Jeffry Duppa, John Gilbert, William
Hancock, Matthew Brown, Francis Tyrrel, Randal Carter, Otho-
well Smith, Thomas Hamond, Martin Bond, Haberdafher, *John*
Moulfoe, Robert Johnfon, William Young, John Woodal,William
Felgate, Humfrey Weftwood, Rcihard Champion, Henry Robinfon,
Francis Mapes,William Sambach,Ralegh Crafhaw, Daniel Tucker,
Thomas Grave, Hugh Willefton, Thomas Culpepper, of *Wigfel,* Efq;
John Culpepper, Gentleman, *Henry Lee, Jofias Kirton,* Gentleman,
John Pory, Gentleman, *Henry Collins, George Burton, William*
Atkinfon,

Atkinson, Thomas Foreft, John Ruffel, John Holt, Harman Har-
rifon, Gabriel Beedel, John Beedel, Henry Dawkes, George Scot,
Edward Fleetwood, Gentleman, *Richard Rogers,* Gentleman, *Ar-*
thur Robinfon, Robert Robinfon, John Huntley, John Gray, Wil-
liam Payne, William Field, William Wattey, William Webfler,
John Dingley, Thomas Draper, Richard Glanvil, Arnold Hulls,
Henry Roe, William More, Nicholas Gryce, James Monger, Ni-
cholas Andrews, Jeremy Haydon, Ironmonger, *Philip Durette,*
John Quarles, John Weft, Matthew Springham, John Johnfon,
Chriftopher Hore, Thomas Snead, George Berkeley, Arthur Pet,
Thomas Careles, William Berkeley, Thomas Johnfon, Alexander
Bents, Captain *William King, George Sandys,* Gentleman, *James*
White, Gentleman, *Edmond Wynne, Charles Towler, Richard Rey-*
nold, Edward Webb, Richard Maplefden, Thomas Lever, David
Bourne, Thomas Wood, Ralph Hamer, Edward Barnes, Mercer,
John Wright, Mercer, *Robert Middleton, Edward Littlefield, Ka-*
tharine Weft, Thomas Web, Ralph King, Robert Coppin, James Af-
kew, Chriftopher Holt, William Bardwell, Alexander Chiles, Lewis
Tate, Edward Ditchfield, James Swifte, Richard Widdowes, Gold-
fmith, *Edmond Brudenell, Edward Burwell, John Hansford, Edward*
Wooller, William Palmer, Haberdafher, *John Badger, John Hodg-*
fon, Peter Mounfel, John Carril, John Bufhridge, Wm. Dun, Tho-
mas Johnfon, Nicholas Benfon, Thomas Shipton, Nathaniel Wade,
Randal Wetwood, Matthew Dequefter, Charles Hawkins, Hugh
Hamerfley, Abraham Cartwright, George Bennet, William Cater,
Richard Goddart, Henry Cromwell, Phineas Pet, Robert Cooper,
John Cooper, Henry Newce, Edward Wilkes, Robert Bateman, Ni-
cholas Farrar, John Newhoufe, John Cafon, Thomas Harris, Gentleman, *George Etheridge,* Gentleman, *Thomas Mayle,* Gentleman,
Richard Stafford, Thomas   , Richard Cooper, John Wef-
trow, Edward Welch, Thomas Britain, Thomas Knowles, Octa-
vian Thorne, Edmond Smith, John March, Edward Carew, Tho-
mas Pleydall, Richard Let, Miles Palmer, Henry Price, John Jo-
fhua, Gentleman, *William Clauday, Jeremy earfye, John Bree,*
Gentleman, *William Hampfon, Chriftopher Pickford, Thomas Hunt,*
Thomas Trufton, Chriftopher Salmon, John Howard, Clerk, *Rich-*
ard Partridge, Allen Caffen, Felix Wilfon, Thomas Bathurft, George
Wilmer, Andrew Wilmer, Maurice Lewellin, Thomas Godwin,
Peter Burgoyne, Thomas Burgoyne, Robert Burgoyne, Robert Smith,
Merchant-taylor, *Edward Cage,* Grocer, *Thomas Cannon,* Gen-
tleman, *William Welby,* Stationer, *Clement Wilmer,* Gentleman,
John Clapham, Gentleman, *Giles Francis,* Gentleman, *George*
Walker, Sadler, *John Swinhow,* Stationer, *Edward Bifhop,* Sta-
tioner, *Leonard White,* Gentleman, *Chriftopher Baron, Peter Ben-*
fon, Richard Smith, George Proctor, Minifter, *Millicent Ramfden,*
Widow, *Jofeph Soane, Thomas Hinfhaw, John Baker, Robert*
Thornton, John Davis, Edward Facet, George Newce, Gentleman,
John Robinfon, Captain *Thomas Wood, William Brown,* Shoema-
ker, *Robert Barker,* Shoemaker, *Robert Pennington, Francis Bur-*
ley, Minifter, *William Quick,* Grocer, *Edward Lewis,* Grocer,
Laurence Campe, Draper, *Aden Perkins,* Grocer, *Richard Shepherd,*
Preacher, *William Sherley,* Haberdafher, *William Taylor,* Haber-
dafher,

dafher, *Edwin Lukin,* Gentleman, *John Franklyn,* Haberdafher,
John Southwick, Peter Peate, George Johan, Ironmonger, *George
Yeardley,* Gentleman, *Henry Shelley, John Prat, Thomas Church,*
Draper, *William Powel,* Gentleman, *Richard Frith,* Gentleman,
Thomas Wheeler, Draper, *Francis Hafelrig,* Gentleman, *Hugh
Shipley,* Gentleman, *John Andrews* the Elder, Doctor of *Cam-
bridge, Francis Whiftler,* Gentleman, *John Vaffal,* Gentleman,
Richard Howle, Edward Berkeley, Gentleman, *Richard Keneridg-
burg,* Gentleman, *Nicholas Exton,* Draper, *William Bennet,* Fifh-
monger, *James Haywood,* Merchant, *Nicholas Ifaac,* Merchant,
William Gibbs, Merchant,　　*Bifhop, Bernard Mitchel, Ifaac
Mitchel, John Streate, Edward Gall, John Martin,* Gentleman,
Thomas Fox, Luke Lodge, John Woodliffe, Gentleman, *Richard
Webb, Vincent Low, Samuel Burnham, Edmund Pears,* Haber-
dafher, *John Googe, John St. John, Edward Vaughan, William
Dunn, Thomas Alcocke, John Andrews* the Younger, of *Cam-
bridge, Samuel Smith, Thomas Gerrard, Thomas Whittingham,
William Canning, Paul Canning, George Chandler, Henry Vincent,
Thomas Ketley, James Skelton, James Mountaine, George Webb,*
Gentleman, *Jofeph Newbridge,* Smith, *Jofiah Mand,* Cap-
tain *Ralph Hamer,* the Younger, *Edward Brewfter,* the Son of
William Brewfter, Leonard Harwood, Mercer, *Philip Druerdent,
William Carpenter, Triftian Hill, Robert Cock,* Grocer, *Laurence
Green,* Grocer, *Samuel Winch,* Grocer, *Humphrey Stile,* Grocer,
Averie Dransfield, Grocer, *Edward Hodges,* Grocer, *Edward
Beale,* Grocer, *Thomas Culler,* Grocer, *Ralph Bufby,* Grocer,
John Whittingham, Grocer, *John Hide,* Grocer, *Matthew
Shepherd,* Grocer, *Thomas Allen,* Grocer, *Richard Hooker,* Gro-
cer, *Lawrence Munks,* Grocer, *John Tanner,* Grocer, *Peter
Gate,* Grocer, *John Blunt,* Grocer, *Robert Phips,* Grocer, *Ro-
bert Berrisford,* Grocer, *Thomas Wells,* Grocer, *John Ellis,*
Grocer, *Henry Colthurft,* Grocer, *John Cavady,* Grocer, *Thomas
Jennings,* Grocer, *Edmond Pafhall,* Grocer, *Timothy Bathurft,*
Grocer, *Giles Parflow,* Grocer, *Robert Milmay,* Grocer, *Richard
Johnfon,* Grocer, *William Johnfon,* Vintner, *Ezekiel Smith,
Richard Martin, William Sharpe, Robert Rich, William Stan-
nard,* Innholder, *John Stocken, William Strachey,* Gentleman,
George Farmer, Gentleman, *Thomas Gypes,* Clothworker, *Abra-
ham Davies,* Gentleman, *Thomas Brocket,* Gentleman, *George
Bache,* Fifhmonger, *John Dike,* Fifhmonger, *Henry Spranger,
Richard Farrington, Chriftopher Vertue,* Vintner, *Thomas Bayley,*
Vintner, *George Robins,* Vintner, *Tobias Hinfon,* Grocer, *Vrian
Spencer, Clement Chicheley, John Scarpe,* Gentleman, *James
Campbell,* Ironmonger, *Chriftopher Clitheroe,* Ironmonger, *Philip
Jacobfon, Peter Jacobfon,* of *Antwerp, William Berkeley, Miles
Banks,* Cutler, *Peter Higgons,* Grocer, *Henry John,* Gentleman,
John Stokeley, Merchant-taylor, The Company of Mercers, the
Company of Grocers, the Company of Drapers, the Company
Fifhmongers, the Company of Goldfmiths, the Company of
Skinners, the Company of Merchant-taylers, the Company of
Haberdafhers, the Company of Salters, the Company of Iron-
mongers, the Company of Vintners, the Company Clothworkers,

the Company of Dyers, the Company of Brewers, the Company
of Leatherfellers, the Company of Pewterers, the Company of
Cutlers, the Company of Whitebakers, the Company of Wax-
Chandlers, the Company of Tallow-Chandlers, the Company of
Armorers, the Company of Girdlers, the Company of Butchers,
the Company of Sadlers, the Company of Carpenters, the Company of Cordwayners, the Company of Barber-Chirurgeons, the
Company of Paintftainers, the Company of Curriers, the Com-
pany of Mafons, the Company of Plumbers, the Company In-
holders, the Company of Founders, the Company of Poulterers,
the Company of Cooks, the Company of Coopers, the Company
of Tylers and Bricklayers, the Company of Bowyers, the Company of Fletchers, the Company of Blackfmiths, the Company
of Joiners, the Company of Weavers, the Company of Wool-
men, the Company of Woodmongers, the Company of Scrive-
ners, the Company of Fruiterers, the Company of Plaifters, the
Company of Brownbakers, the Company of Stationers, the
Company of Imbroiderers, the Company of Upholfters, the
Company of Muficians, the Company of Turners, the Company of Gardiners, the Company of Bafketmakers, the Company of Glaziers, *John Levet*, Merchant, *Thomas Nornicot*, Clothworker, *Richard Venn*, Haberdafher, *Thomas Scot*, Gentleman,
Thomas Juxon, Merchant-taylor, *George Hankinfon*, *Thomas Seyer*,
Gentleman, *Matthew Cooper*, *George Butler*, Gentleman, *Thomas
Lawfon*, Gentleman, *Edward Smith*, Haberdafher, *Stephen Spar-
row*, *John Jones*, Merchant,   *Reynolds*, Brewer, *Thomas
Plummer*, Merchant, *James Duppa*, Brewer, *Rowland Coitmore*,
William Southerne, *George Whitmore*, Haberdafher, *Anthony Gofnold*, the Younger, *John Allen*, Fifhmonger, *Simon Yeomans*,
Fifhmonger, *Lancelot Davis*, Gentlemen, *John Hopkins*, Alderman of *Briftol*, *John Kettleby*, Gentleman, *Richard Clene*, Goldfmith, *George Hooker*, Gentleman, *Robert Chening*, Yeoman;
AND to fuch, and fo many, as they do, or fhall hereafter, admit to be joined with them, in Form hereafter in thefe Prefents
exprefled, whether they go in their Perfons, to be Planters there
in the faid Plantation, or whether they go not, but adventure
their Monies, Goods, or Chattels; THAT they fhall be one
Body or Commonalty perpetual, and fhall have perpetual Succeffion, and one Common Seal, to ferve for the faid Body or
Commonalty; And that they, and their Succeffors, fhall be
KNOWN, CALLED, and INCORPORATED by the Name of, *The
Treafurer and Company of Adventurers and Planters of the City of
London for the firft Colony in Virginia:*

IV. AND that they, and their Succeffors, fhall be, from henceforth, for ever enabled to TAKE, ACQUIRE, and PURCHASE,
by the Name aforefaid (Licence for the fame, from Us, our
Heirs or Succeffors, firft had and obtained) any Manner of Lands,
Tenements, and Hereditaments, Goods, and Chattels, within
our Realm of *England*, and Dominion of *Wales:*

V. AND that they, and their Succeffors, fhall likewife be enabled, by the Name aforefaid, to PLEAD, and BE IMPLEADED,
before any of our Judges or Juftices, in any of our Courts, and
in any Actions or Suits whatfoever.   VI.

VI. AND we do alfo, of our fpecial Grace, certain Knowledge, and mere Motion, GIVE, GRANT, and CONFIRM, unto the faid Treafurer and Company, and their Succeffors, under the Refervations, Limitations, and Declarations, hereafter expreffed, all thofe Lands, Countries, and Territories, fituate, lying, and being, in that Part of *America* called VIRGINIA, from the Point of Land, called *Cape* or *Point Comfort*, all along the Sea Coaft, to the *Northward* two hundred Miles, and from the faid Point of *Cape Comfort*, all along the Sea Coaft, to the *Southward* two hundred Miles, and all that Space and Circuit of Land, lying from the Sea Coaft of the Precinct aforefaid, up into the Land, throughout from Sea to Sea, *Weft*, and *Northweft*; And alfo all the Iflands, lying within one hundred Miles, along the Coaft of both Seas of the Precinct aforefaid; Together with all the Soils, Grounds, Havens, and Ports, Mines, as well Royal Mines of Gold and Silver, as other Minerals, Pearls, and precious Stones, Quarries, Woods, Rivers, Waters, Fifhings, Commodities, Jurifdictions, Royalties, Privileges, Franchifes, and Preheminences, within the faid Territories, and the Precincts thereof, whatfoever, and thereto and thereabouts, both by Sea and Land, being, or in any fort belonging or appertaining, and which We, by our Letters Patents, may or can grant, in as ample Manner and Sort, as We, or any our noble Progenitors, have heretofore granted to any Company, Body politick or corporate, or to any Adventurer, or Adventurers, Undertaker or Undertakers, of any Difcoveries, Plantations, or Traffick, of in or into any foreign Parts whatfoever, and in as large and ample Manner, as if the fame were herein particularly mentioned and expreffed; TO HAVE AND TO HOLD, poffefs and enjoy, all and fingular the faid Lands, Countries, and Territories, with all and fingular other the Premifes, heretofore by thefe Prefents granted, or mentioned to be granted, to them, the faid Treafurer and Company, their Succeffors and Affigns for ever; To the fole and proper Ufe of them, the faid Treafurer and Company, their Succeffors and Affigns for ever; To BE HOLDEN of Us, our Heirs, and Succeffors, as of our Manour of *Eaft-Greenwich*, in free and common Soccage, and not in Capite; YIELDING and PAYING, therefore, to Us, our Heirs, and Succeffors, the fifth Part only of all Ore of Gold and Silver, that, from time to time, and at all times hereafter, fhall be there gotten, had, or obtained, for all Manner of Services.

VII. AND neverthelefs, our Will and Pleafure is, and we do, by thefe Prefents, charge, command, warrant, and authorife, that the faid Treafurer and Company, or their Succeffors, or the major Part of them, which fhall be prefent and affembled for that Purpofe, fhall, from time to time, under their Common Seal, DISTRIBUTE, convey, affign, and fet over, fuch particular Portions of Lands, Tenements, and Hereditaments, by thefe Prefents, formerly granted, unto fuch our loving Subjects, naturally born, or Denizens, or others, as well Adventurers as Planters, as by the faid Company (upon a Commiffion of Survey and Diftribution, executed and returned for that Purpofe) fhall be nominated, appointed, and allowed; Wherein our Will and Pleafure is, that

Refpect

Refpeȼt be had, as well of the Proportion of the Adventurer, as to the fpecial Service, Hazard, Exploit, or Merit of any Perfon, fo to be recompenced, advanced, or rewarded.

VIII. A N D forafmuch, as the good and profperous Succefs of the faid Plantation cannot but chiefly depend, next under the Bleffing of God, and the Support of our Royal Authority, upon the provident and good Direȼtion of the whole Enterprize, by a careful and underftanding Council, and that it is not convenient, that all the Adventurers fhall be fo often drawn to meet and affemble, as fhall be requifite for them to have Meetings and Conference about the Affairs thereof; Therefore we do O R D A I N, eftablifh, and confirm, that there fhall be perpetually one C O U N- C I L here refident, according to the Tenour of our former Letters-patents; Which Council fhall have a Seal, for the better Government and Adminiftration of the faid Plantation, befides the legal Seal of the Company or Corporation, as in our former Letters-patents is alfo expreffed.

IX. A N D further, we E S T A B L I S H and O R D A I N, that *Henry*, Earl of *Southampton*, *William*, Earl of *Pembroke*, *Henry*, Earl of *Lincoln*, *Thomas*, Earl of *Exeter*, *Robert*, Lord Vifcount *Lifle*, Lord *Theophilus Howard*, *James*, Lord Bifhop of *Bath* and *Wells*, *Edward*, Lord *Zouche*, *Thomas*, Lord *Lawarr*, *William*, Lord *Monteagle*, *Edmond*, Lord *Sheffield*, *Grey*, Lord *Chandois*, *John*, Lord *Stanhope*, *George*, Lord *Carew*, Sir *Humfrey*, *Weld*, Lord Mayor of *London*, Sir *Edward Cecil*, Sir *William Wade*, Sir *Henry Nevil*, Sir *Thomas Smith*, Sir *Oliver Cromwell*, Sir *Peter Manwood*, Sir *Thomas Challoner*, Sir *Henry Hobart*, Sir *Francis Bacon*, Sir *George Coppin*, Sir *John Scot*, Sir *Henry Carey*, Sir *Robert Drury*, Sir *Horatio Vere*, Sir *Edward Conway*, Sir *Maurice Berkeley*, Sir *Thomas Gates*, Sir *Michael Sandys* Sir *Robert Manfel*, Sir *John Trevor*, Sir *Amias Prefton*, Sir *William Godolphin*, Sir *Walter Cope*, Sir *Robert Killigrew*, Sir *Henry Fanfhaw*, Sir *Edwin Sandys*, Sir *John Watts*, Sir *Henry Montague*, Sir *William Romney*, Sir *Thomas Roe*, Sir *Baptift Hicks*, Sir *Richard Williamfon*, Sir *Stephen Poole*, Sir *Dudley Digges*, *Chriftopher Brooke*, Efq; *John Eldred*, and *John Wolftenholme*, fhall be our Council for the faid Company of Adventurers and Planters in *Virginia*.

X. A N D the faid Sir *Thomas Smith* we do O R D A I N to be Treafurer of the faid Company; which Treafurer fhall have Authority to give Order, for the Warning of the Council, and fummoning the Company, to their Courts and Meetings.

XI. A N D the faid Council and Treafurer, or any of them, fhall be from henceforth, nominated, chofen, continued, difplaced, changed, altered, and fupplied, as Death, or other feveral Occafions, fhall require, out of the Company of the faid Adventurers, by the Voice of the greater Part of the faid Company and Adventurers, in their Affembly for that Purpofe: P R O V I D E D always, that every Counfellor, fo newly eleȼted, fhall be prefented to the Lord Chancellor of *England*, or to the Lord High Treafurer of *England*, or to the Lord Chamberlain of the Houfehold of Us, our Heirs, and Succeffors, for the time being,

to

to take his Oath of a Counsellor to Us, our Heirs, and Successors, for the said Company of Adventurers and Colony in *Virginia.*

XII. A N D we do, by these Presents, of our special Grace, certain Knowledge, and mere Motion, for Us, our Heirs and Successors, G R A N T unto the said Treasurer and Company, and their Successors, that if it happen, at any time or times, the Treasurer for the time being to be sick, or to have any such Cause of Absence from the City of *London,* as shall be allowed by the said Council, or the greater Part of them, assembled, so as he cannot attend the Affairs of that Company, in every such Case, it shall and may be lawful for such Treasurer for the time being, to assign, constitute and appoint, one of the Council or Company, to be likewise allowed by the Council, or the greater Part of them, assembled, to be the Deputy Treasurer of the said Company; Which Deputy shall have Power, to do and execute all things, which belong to the said Treasurer, during such time, as such Treasurer shall be either sick, or otherwise absent upon Cause allowed of by the said Council, or the major Part of them, as aforesaid, so fully and wholly, and in as large and ample Manner and Form, to all Intents and Purposes, as the said Treasurer, if he were present, himself might or could do and execute the same.

XIII. A N D further, of our special Grace, certain Knowledge, and mere Motion, for Us, our Heirs, and Successors, we do, by these Presents, G I V E and G R A N T full Power and Authority to our said Council, here resident, as well at this present Time, as hereafter from time to time, to nominate, make, constitute, ordain, and confirm, by such Name or Names, Stile or Stiles, as to them shall seem good, And likewise to revoke, discharge, change, and alter, as well all and singular Governors, Officers, and Ministers, which already have been made, as also which hereafter shall be by them thought fit and needful to be made or used, for the Government of the said Colony and Plantation:

XIV. A N D also to make, ordain, and establish all Manner of Orders, Laws, Directions, Instructions, Forms, and Ceremonies of Government and Magistracy, fit and necessary, for and concerning the Government of the said Colony and Plantation; And the same, at all times hereafter, to abrogate, revoke, or change, not only within the Precincts of the said Colony, but also upon the Seas in going and coming, to and from the said Colony, as they, in their good Discretion, shall think to be fittest for the Good of the Adventurers and Inhabitants there.

XV. A N D we do also declare, that, for divers Reasons and Considerations us thereunto especially moving, our Will and Pleasure is, and we do hereby O R D A I N, that immediately from and after such time, as any such Governor or principal Officer, so to be nominated and appointed, by our said Council, for the Government of the said Colony, as aforesaid, shall arrive in *Virginia,* and give Notice unto the Colony there resident of our Pleasure in this Behalf, the Government, Power, and Authority of the President and Council, heretofore by our former Letters Patents there established, and all Laws and Constitutions, by them formerly
merly

merly made, (hall utterly ceafe and be determined, And all Officers, Governors, and Minifters, formerly conftituted or appointed,
fhall be difcharged, any thing, in our faid former Letters Patents
concerning the faid Plantation contained, in any wife to the contrary notwithftanding; Straightly charging and commanding the
Prefident and Council, now refident in the faid Colony, upon
their Allegiance, after Knowledge given unto them of our Will
and Pleafure, by thefe Prefents fignified and declared, that they
forthwith be obedient to fuch Governor or Governors, as by our
faid Council, here refident, fhall be named and appointed, as a-
forefaid, and to all Directions, Orders, and Commandments,
which they fhall receive from them, as well in the prefent Refign-
ing and Giving up of their Authority, Offices, Charge, and Places,
as in all other Attendance, as fhall be by them, from time to
time, required.

XVI. AND we do further, by thefe Prefents, ORDAIN and
eftablifh, that the faid Treafurer and Council here refident,
and their Succeffors, or any four of them, being affembled (the
Treafurer being one) fhall, from time to time, have full Power
and Authority, to admit and receive any other Perfon into their
Company, Corporation, and Freedom; And further, in a General Affembly of the Adventurers, with the Confent of the greater
Part, upon good Caufe, to disfranchife and put out any Perfon
or Perfons, out of the faid Freedom and Company.

XVII. AND we do alfo GRANT and confirm, for Us, our
Heirs and Succeffors, that it fhall be lawful for the faid Treafurer and Company, and their Succeffors, by Direction of the Go-
vernors there, to dig and to fearch for all Manner of Mines or
Gold, Silver, Copper, Iron, Lead, Tin, and all Sorts of Mine-
rals, as well within the Precinct aforefaid, as within any Part of
the main Land, not formerly granted to any other; And TO
HAVE and ENJOY the Gold, Silver, Copper, Iron, Lead, and
Tin, and all other Minerals, to be gotten thereby, to the Ufe
and Behoof of the faid Company of Planters and Adventurers;
YIELDING thereof, and paying Yearly, unto Us, our Heirs and
Succeffors, as aforefaid.

XVIII. AND we do further, of our fpecial Grace, certain
Knowledge, and mere Motion, for Us, our Heirs, and Succeffors, GRANT, by thefe Prefents, to and with the faid Treafurer
and Company, and their Succeffors, that it fhall be lawful and
free for them, and their Affigns, at all and every time and times
hereafter, out of our Realm of *England*, and out of all other our
Dominions, to take and lead into the faid Voyages, and for and
towards the faid Plantation, and to travel thitherwards, and to
abide and inhabit there in the faid Colony and Plantation, all
fuch and fo many of our loving Subjects, or any other Strangers,
that will become our loving Subjects and live under our Obedience, as fhall willingly accompany them in the faid Voyage and
Plantation; With fufficient Shipping, Armour, Weapons, Ordinance, Munition, Powder, Shot, Victuals, and fuch Merchandifes or Wares, as are efteemed by the wild People in thofe
Parts, Cloathing, Implements, Furniture, Cattle, Horfes, and
                                                           Mares,

Mares, and all other things, neceffary for the faid Plantation, and for their Ufe, and Defence, and Trade with the People there; and in paffing and returning to and fro; Without yielding or paying Subfidy, Cuftom, Impofition, or any other Tax or Duty, to Us, our Heirs or Succeffors, for the Space of feven Years from the Date of thefe Prefents: PROVIDED, that none of the faid Perfons be fuch, as fhall be hereafter, by efpecial Name, reftrained by Us, our Heirs, and Succeffors.

XIX. AND for their further Encouragement, of our fpecial Grace and Favour, we do, by thefe Prefents, for Us, our Heirs, and Succeffors, YIELD and GRANT, to and with the faid Treafurer and Company, and their Succeffors, and every of them, their Factors, and Affigns, that they, and every of them, fhall be free of all Subfidies and Cuftoms in *Virginia*, for the Space of one and twenty Years, and from all Taxes and Impofitions, for ever, upon any Goods or Merchandifes, at any time or times hereafter, either upon Importation thither, or Exportation from thence, into our Realm of *England*, or into any other of our Realms or Dominions, by the faid Treafurer and Company, and their Succeffors, their Deputies, Factors, or Affigns, or any of them: EXCEPT only the five Pounds *per Cent.* due for Cuftom, upon all fuch Goods and Merchandifes, as fhall be brought or imported into our Realm of *England*, or any other of thefe our Dominions, according to the ancient Trade of Merchants; WHICH FIVE POUNDS *per Cent.* ONLY being paid, it fhall be thenceforth lawful and free for the faid Adventurers, the fame Goods and Merchandifes to export, and carry out of our faid Dominions, into foreign Parts, without any Cuftom, Tax, or other Duty, to be paid to us, our Heirs, or Succeffors, or to any other our Officers or Deputies: PROVIDED, that the faid Goods and Merchandifes be fhipped out, within thirteen Months, after their firft Landing within any Part of thofe Dominions.

XX. AND we do alfo GRANT and confirm to the faid Treafurer and Company, and their Succeffors, as alfo to all and every fuch Governor, or other Officers and Minifters, as by our faid Council fhall be appointed to have Power and Authority of Government and Command, in or over the faid Colony and Plantation; That they, and every of them, fhall and lawfully may, from time to time, and at all times for ever hereafter, for their feveral Defence and Safety, encounter, expulfe, repel, and refift, by Force and Arms, as well by Sea as by Land, and all Ways and Means whatfoever, all and every fuch Perfon and Perfons whatfoever, as (without the fpecial Licence of the faid Treafurer and Company, and their Succeffors) fhall attempt to inhabit, within the faid feveral Precincts and Limits of the faid Colony and Plantation; And alfo, all and every fuch Perfon and Perfons whatfoever, as fhall enterprife or attempt, at any time hereafter, Deftruction, Invafion, Hurt, Detriment, or Annoyance, to the faid Colony and Plantation, as is likewife fpecified in the faid former Grant:

XXI. AND that it fhall be lawful for the faid Treafurer and Company, and their Succeffors, and every of them, from time to

time,

time, and at all times for ever hereafter, and they shall have
full Power and Authority, to take and surprise, by all Ways and
Means whatsoever, all and every Person and Persons whatsoever,
with their Ships, Goods, and other Furniture, trafficking in any
Harbour, Creek, or Place, within the Limits or Precincts of the
said Colony and Plantation, * not being allowed by the said
Company to be Adventurers or Planters of the said Colony, until
such time, as they, being of any Realms and Dominions under
our Obedience, shall pay, or agree to pay, to the Hands of the
Treasurer or of some other Officer, deputed by the said Governor of *Virginia* (over and above such Subsidy and Custom, as the
said Company is, or hereafter shall be, to pay) five Pounds *per
Cent.* upon all Goods and Merchandises so brought in thither,
and also five *per Cent.* upon all Goods by them shipped out from
thence; And being Strangers, and not under our Obedience,
until they have paid (over and above such Subsidy and Custom, as
the said Treasurer and Company, or their Successors, is, or hereafter shall be, to pay) ten Pounds *per Cent.* upon all such Goods,
likewise carried in and out, any thing, in the said former Letters Patents, to the contrary notwithstanding; And the same
S u m s of M o n e y and Benefit, as aforesaid, for and during the
Space of one and twenty Years, shall be wholly employed to the
Benefit, Use, and Behoof of the said Colony and Plantation;
And after the said one and twenty Years ended, the same shall
be taken to the Use of Us, our Heirs, and Successors, by such
Officers and Ministers, as by Us, our Heirs, or Successors, shall
be thereunto assigned and appointed, as is specified in the said
former Letters Patents.

XXII. A l s o, we do, for Us, our Heirs, and Successors, d e -
c l a r e, by these Presents, that all and every the Persons, being
our Subjects, which shall go and inhabit within the said Colony
and Plantation, and every of their Children and Posterity, which
shall happen to be born within any the Limits thereof, shall
h a v e a n d e n j o y all Liberties, Franchises, and Immunities of
free Denizens and natural Subjects, within any of our other Dominions, to all Intents and Purposes, as if they had been abiding
and born, within this our Realm of *England,* or in any other of
our Dominions.

XXIII. A n d forasmuch, as it shall be necessary for all such
our loving Subjects, as shall inhabit within the said Precincts of
Virginia, aforesaid, to determine to live together, in the Fear
and true Worship of Almighty God, Christian Peace, and civil
Quietness, each with other, whereby every one may, with more
Safety, Pleasure, and Profit, enjoy that, whereunto they shall
attain with great Pain and Peril; We, for Us, our Heirs and
Successors, are likewise pleased and contented, and by these Presents, do g i v e and g r a n t unto the said Treasurer and Com-
pany, and their Successors, and to such Governors, Officers, and
Mi-

---

* It is *and being* in the Original; but the Sense carried me so clearly to it,
that I ventured to make this Correction, letting the Reader at the same
time know it.

Miniſters, as ſhall be, by our ſaid Council, conſtituted and appointed, according to the Natures and Limits of their Offices
and Places reſpectively, that they ſhall and may, from time to
time for ever hereafter, within the ſaid Precincts of *Virginia*, or
in the Way by ‡ Sea thither and from thence, have full and abſolute Power and Authority, to correct, puniſh, pardon, govern,
and rule, all ſuch the Subjects of Us, our Heirs, and Succeſſors,
as ſhall, from time to time, adventure themſelves in any Voyage
thither, or that ſhall, at any time hereafter, inhabit in the Precincts and Territories of the ſaid Colony, as aforeſaid, according
to ſuch Orders, Ordinances, Conſtitutions, Directions, and Inſtructions, as by our ſaid Council, as aforeſaid, ſhall be eſtabliſhed; And in Defect thereof, in caſe of Neceſſity, according to
the good † Diſcretions of the ſaid Governor and Officers, reſpectively, as well in Caſes capital and criminal as civil, both
marine and other; So always, as the ſaid Statutes, Ordinances,
and Proceedings, as near as conveniently may be, be agreeable
to the Laws, Statutes, Government, and Policy of this our
Realm of *England.*

XXIV. AND we do further, of our ſpecial Grace, certain
Knowledge, and mere Motion, GRANT, DECLARE, and OR-
DAIN, that ſuch principal Governor, as, from time to time,
ſhall duly and lawfully be authoriſed and appointed, in Manner
and ' Form in theſe Preſents heretofore expreſſed, ſhall have full
Power and Authority, to uſe and exerciſe Martial Law, in Caſes
of Rebellion or Mutiny, in as large and ample Manner, as our
Lieutenants in our * Counties, within this our Realm of *En-
gland,* have, or ought to have, by Force of their Commiſſions of
Lieutenancy.

XXV. AND furthermore, if any Perſon or Perſons, Adventurers or Planters of the ſaid Colony, or any other, at any time
or times hereafter, ſhall tranſport any Monies, Goods, or Mér-
chandiſes, out of any of our Kingdoms, with a Pretence or
Purpoſe, to land, ſell, or otherwiſe diſpoſe of the ſame, within
the Limits or Bounds of the ſaid Colony, and yet neverthelesſ,
being at Sea, or after he hath landed within any Part of the ſaid
Colony, ſhall carry the ſame into any other foreign Country,
with a Purpoſe there to ſell and diſpoſe thereof; That then, all
the Goods and Chattels of the ſaid Perſon, or Perſons, ſo offending and tranſported, together with the Ship or Veſſel, wherein ſuch Tranſportation was made, ſhall be forfeited to Us, our
Heirs and Succeſſors.

XXVI. AND further, our Will and Pleaſure is, that in all
Queſtions and Doubts, that ſhall ariſe, upon any Difficulty of
Conſtruction or Interpretation of any thing, contained either in
this or in our ſaid former Letters Patents, the ſame ſhall be taken
and interpreted, in moſt ample and beneficial Manner for the ſaid
Treafurer and Company, and their Succeſſors, and every Member thereof.

---

‡ M. S. *Seas.*   † M. S. *Directions.*   * M. S. *Countrys.*

XXVII. And further, we do, by thefe Prefents, RATIFY and CONFIRM unto the faid Treafurer and Company, and their Succeffors, all the Privileges, Franchifes, Liberties, and Immunities, granted in our faid former Letters Patents, and not in thefe our Letters Patents revoked, altered, changed, or abridged. ,

XXVIII. And finally, our Will and Pleafure is, and we do further, hereby, for Us, our Heirs, and Succeffors, GRANT and agree, to and with the faid Treafurer and Company, and their Succeffors, that all and fingular Perfon and Perfons, which fhall, at any time or times hereafter, adventure any Sum or Sums of Money, in and towards the faid Plantation of the faid Colony in *Virginia*, and fhall be admitted, by the faid Council and Company, as Adventurers of the faid Colony, in Form aforefaid, and fhall be enrolled in the Book or Records of the Adventurers of the faid Company, fhall and may be accounted, accepted, taken, held, and reputed, Adventurers of the faid Colony, and fhall and may enjoy all and fingular Grants, Privileges, Liberties, Benefits, Profits, Commodities, and Immunities, Advantages, and Emoluments, whatfoever, as fully, largely, amply, and abfolutely, as if they, and every of them, had been precifely, plainly fingularly, and diftinctly, named and inferted in thefe our Letters Patents.

XXIX. And laftly, becaufe the principal Effect, which we can defire or expect of this Action, is the Converfion and Reduction of the People in thofe Parts unto the true Worfhip of God and Chriftian Religion, in which Refpect we fhould be loath, that any Perfon fhould be permitted to pafs, that we fufpected to effect the fuperftitions of the Church of *Rome*; We do hereby DECLARE, that it is our Will and Pleafure, that none be permitted to pafs in any Voyage, from time to time to be made into the faid Country, but fuch, as firft fhall have taken the Oath of Supremacy; For which Purpofe, we do, by thefe Prefents, give full Power and Authority, to the Treafurer for the time being, and any three of the Council, to tender and exhibit the faid Oath, to all fuch Perfons, as fhall, at any time, be fent and employed in the faid Voyage. Although exprefs Mention of the true Yearly Value or Certainty of the Premifes, or any of them, or of any other Gifts or Grants, by Us or any of our Progenitors or Predeceffors, to the aforefaid Treafurer and Company heretofore made, in thefe Prefents is not made; Or any Act, Statute, Ordinance, Provifion, Proclamation, or Reftraint, to the contrary hereof had, made, ordained, or provided, or any other Thing, Caufe, or Matter, whatfoever, in any wife notwithftanding. In WITNESS whereof, We have caufed thefe our Letters to be made Patent. Witnefs ourfelf at *Weftminfter*, the 23d Day of *May*, in the feventh Year of our Reign of *England, France,* and *Ireland*, and of *Scotland* the ****

Per ipfum Regem

Lukin.

N°. III.

Nᵒ. III.

A third Charter of K. James *I. to the Treasurer and Company for* Virginia. *Dated* March 12, 1611-2.

I. *JAMES,* by the Grace of God, King of *England, Scotland, France,* and *Ireland,* Defender of the Faith; To all, to whom thefe Prefents fhall come, Greeting. W H E R E A S, at the humble Suit of divers and fundry our loving Subjeƈts, as well Adventurers as Planters of the firƈt Colony in *Virginia,* and for the Propagation of *Chriƈtian* Religion, and reclaiming of People barbarous to Civility and Humanity, We have, by our Letters Patents, bearing Date, at *Weƈtminƈter,* the three and twentieth Day of *May,* in the feventh Year of our Reign of *England, France,* and *Ireland,* and the two and fortieth of *Scotland,* G I V E N and G R A N T E D unto them, that they, and all fuch and fo many of our loving Subjeƈts, as fhould, from time to time for ever after, be joined with them, as Planters or Adventurers in the faid Plantation, and their Succeffors, for ever, fhould be one Body politick, incorporated by the Name of, *The Treafurer and Company of Adventurers and Planters of the City of London for the firƈt Colony in Virginia;*

II. A N D whereas alfo, for the greater Good and Benefit of the faid Company, and for the better Furtherance, Strengthening, and Eƈtablifhing of the faid Plantation, we did further G I V E, G R A N T, and C O N F I R M, by our faid Letters Patents, unto the faid Treafurer and Company, and their Succeffors, for ever, all thofe Lands, Countries, or Territories, fituate, lying, and being, in that Part of *America* called V I R G I N I A, from the Point of Land, called *Cape* or *Point Comfort,* all along the Sea Coaƈts, to the *Northward,* two hundred Miles, and from the faid Point of *Cape Comfort,* all along the Sea Coaƈt, to the *Southward,* two hundred Miles, and all that Space and Circuit of Land, lying from the Sea Coaƈt of the Precinƈt aforefaid, up or into the Land, throughout from Sea to Sea, *Weƈt* and *Northweƈt,* and alfo all the Iƈlands, lying within one hundred Miles, along the Coaƈt of both the Seas of the Precinƈt aforefaid, with divers other Grants, Liberties, Franchifes, and Preheminences, Previleges, Profits, Benefits, and Commodities, granted, in and by our faid Letters Patents, to the faid Treafurer and Company, and their Succeffors, for ever:

III. N o w, forafmuch as we are given to underƈtand, that in thofe Seas, adjoining to the faid Coaƈts of *Virginia,* and without the Compafs of thofe two hundred Miles, by Us fo granted unto the faid Treafurer and Company, as aforefaid, and yet not far diƈtant from the faid Colony in *Virginia,* there are, or may be, divers Iƈlands, lying defolate and uninhabited, fome of which are already made known and difcovered, by the Induƈtry, Travel, and Expences of the said Company, and others also are supposed to be and remain, as yet, unknown and undiscovered, all and every of which it may import the said Colony, both in Safety and Policy of Trade, to populate and plant, in Regard whereof, as well for the preventing of Peril, as for the better Commodity and Prosperity of the said Colony, they have been humble Suitors unto us, that we would be pleased to grant unto them † an Enlargement of our said former Letters Patents, as well for a more ample Extent of their Limits and Territories into the Seas, adjoining to and upon the Coast of *Virginia*, as also for some other Matters and Articles, concerning the better Government of the said Company and Colony, in which Point our said former Letters Patents do not extend so far, as Time and Experience hath found to be needful and convenient:

IV. W E therefore, tendering the good and happy Success of the said Plantation, both in Regard of the general ‡ Weal of human Society, as in Respect of the Good of our own Estate and Kingdoms, and being willing to give Furtherance unto all good Means, that may advance the Benefit of the said * Company, and which may secure the Safety of our loving Subjects, planted in our said Colony under the Favour and Protection of God Almighty, and of our Royal Power and Authority, have therefore, of our especial Grace, certain Knowledge, and mere Motion, given, granted, and confirmed, and for Us, our Heirs and Successors, we do, by these Presents, G I V E, G R A N T, and C O N F I R M, to the said Treasurer and Company of Adventurers and Planters of the City of *London* for the first Colony in *Virginia*, and to their Heirs and Successors, for ever, all and singular those Islands whatsoever, situate and being in any Part of the Ocean Seas bordering upon the Coast of our said first Colony in *Virginia*, and being within three hundred Leagues of any the Parts heretofore granted to the said Treasurer and Company, in our said former Letters Patents, as aforesaid, and being within or between the one and fortieth and thirtieth Degrees of *Northerly* Latitude, Together with all and singular Soils, Lands, Grounds, Havens, Ports, Rivers, Waters, Fishings, Mines, and Minerals, as well Royal Mines of Gold and Silver, as other Mines and Minerals, Pearls, Precious Stones, Quarries, and all and singular other Commodities, Jurisdictions, Royalties, Privileges, Franchises, and Preheminences, both within the said Tract of Land upon the Main, and also within the said Islands and Seas adjoining, whatsoever, and thereunto or thereabouts, both by Sea and Land, being or situate ; And which, by our Letters Patents, we may or can grant, and in as ample Manner and Sort, as We, or any our noble Progenitors, have heretofore granted to any Person or Persons, or to any Company, Body politick or corporate, or to any Adventurer or Adventurers, Undertaker or Undertakers, of any Discoveries, Plantations, or Traffick, of in or into any foreign Parts, whatsoever, and in as large and ample Manner, as if the

---

† *and*, M. S.   ‡ M. S. *Wheel.*   * M. S. *Companies.*

same

fame were herein particularly named, mentioned, and expreffed : Provided always, that the faid Iflands, or any the Premifes herein mentioned, or by thefe Prefents intended or ‡ meant to be granted, be not actually poffeffed or inhabited by any other *Chriftian* Prince or Eftate, nor be within the Bounds, Limits, or Territories of the *Northern* Colony, heretofore by Us granted to be planted by divers of our loving Subjects, in the *North* Parts of *Virginia.* To HAVE AND TO HOLD, poffefs and enjoy, † all and fingular the faid Iflands, in the faid Ocean Seas fo lying, and bordering upon the Coaft and Coafts of the Territories of the faid firft Colony in *Virginia,* as aforefaid ; With all and fingular the faid Soils, Lands, and Grounds, and all and fingular other the Premifes, heretofore by thefe Prefents granted, or mentioned to be granted, to them, the faid * Treafurer and Company of Adventurers and Planters of the City of *London* for the firft Colony in *Virginia,* and to their Heirs, Succeffors, and Affigns, for ever, to the fole and proper Ufe and Behoof of them, the faid Treafurer and Company, and their Heirs, and Succeffors, and Affigns, for ever ; TO BE HOLDEN of us, our Heirs, and Succeffors, as of our Manor of *Eaft-Greenwich,* in free and common Soccage, and not in Capite ; YIELDING AND PAYING therefore to Us, our Heirs, and Succeffors, the ‖ fifth Part of the Ore of all Gold and Silver, which fhall be there gotten, had, or obtained, for all Manner of Services whatfoever.

V. AND further, our Will and Pleafure is, and we do, by thefe Prefents, GRANT AND CONFIRM, for the Good and Welfare of the faid Plantation, and that Pofterity may hereafter know, who have adventured and not been fparing of their Purfes in fuch a noble and generous Action for the general Good of their Country, and at the Requeft, and with the Confent, of the Company aforefaid, that our trufty and well-beloved § Subjects, *George,* Lord Archbifhop of *Canterbury, Henry,* Earl of *Huntington, Edward,* Earl of *Bedford, Richard,* Earl of *Clanrickard, &c.* who fince our faid laft Letters Patents are become Adventurers, and have joined themfelves with the former Adventurers and Planters of the faid Company and Society, fhall, from henceforth, be reputed, deemed, and taken to be, and fhall be Brethren and free Members of the Company, and fhall and may, refpectively, and according to the Proportion and Value of their feveral Adventures, HAVE, HOLD, and ENJOY all fuch Intereft, Right, Title, Privileges, Preheminences, Liberties, Franchifes, Immunities, Profits, and Commodities, whatfoever, in as large, and ample, and beneficial Manner, to all Intents, Conftructions, and Purpofes, as any other Adventurers, nominated and expreffed in any our former Letters Patents, or any of them, have or may have, by Force and Virtue of thefe Prefents, or any our former Letters Patents whatfoever.

---

‡ M. S. *mean.*   † M. S. *and and fingular.*   * M. S. *Treafurers.*
‖ M. S. *firft.*   § M. S. *Subject.*

VI. AND

VI. And we are further pleaſed, and we do, by theſe Preſents, Grant and confirm, that *Philip,* Earl of *Montgomery, William* Lord *Paget,* Sir *John Starrington,* Knt. *&c.* whom the ſaid Treaſurer and Company have, ſince the ſaid laſt Letters Patents, nominated and ſet down, as worthy and diſcreet Perſons, fit to ſerve us as Counſellors, to be of our Council for the ſaid Plantation, ſhall be reputed, deemed, and taken, as Perſons of our ſaid Council for the ſaid firſt Colony, in ſuch Manner and Sort, to all Intents and Purpoſes, as thoſe, who have been formerly elected and nominated, as our Counſellors for that Colony, and whoſe Names have been or are inſerted and expreſſed, in our ſaid former Letters Patents.

VII. And We do hereby Ordain and Grant, by theſe Preſents, that the ſaid Treaſurer and Company of Adventurers and Planters aforeſaid, ſhall and may, once every Week, or oftener, at their Pleaſure, hold and keep a Court and Aſſembly, for the better Order and Government of the ſaid Plantation, and ſuch things, as ſhall concern the ſame ; And that any five Perſons of our Council for the ſaid firſt Colony in *Virginia,* for the time being, of which Company the Treaſurer, or his Deputy, to be always one, and the Number of fifteen others, at the leaſt, of the Generality of the ſaid Company, aſſembled together in ſuch Manner, as is and hath been heretofore uſed and accuſtomed, ſhall be ſaid, taken, held, and reputed to be, and ſhall be a *ſufficient Court* of the ſaid Company, for the handling, and ordering, and diſpathcing of all ſuch caſual and particular Occurrences, and accidental Matters, of leſs Conſequence and Weight, as ſhall, from time to time, happen, touching and concerning the ſaid Plantation :

VIII. And that nevertheleſs, for the handling, ordering, and diſpoſing of Matters and Affairs of greater Weight and Importance, and ſuch, as ſhall or may, in any Sort, concern the ‡ Weal Publick and general Good of the ſaid Company and Plantation, as namely, the Manner of Government from time to time to be uſed, the Ordering and Diſpoſing of the Lands and Poſſeſſions, and the Settling and Eſtabliſhing of a Trade there, or ſuch like, there ſhall be held and kept, every Year, upon the laſt *Wedneſday,* ſave one, of *Hillary* Term, *Eaſter, Trinity,* and *Michaelmas* Terms, for ever, one great, general, and ſolemn Aſſembly, which four Aſſemblies ſhall be ſtiled and called, *The four Great and General Courts of the Council and Company of Adventurers for Virginia;* † In all and every of which ſaid Great and General Courts, ſo aſſembled, our Will and Pleaſure is, and we do, for Us, our Heirs, and Succeſſors, for ever, Give and grant to the ſaid Treaſurer and Company, and their Succeſſors, for ever, by theſe Preſents, that they, the ſaid Treaſurer and Company, or the greater Number of them, ſo aſſembled, ſhall and may have full Power and Authority, from time to time, and at all times hereafter, to elect and chuſe diſcreet Perſons, to be of our ſaid

---

‡ M. S. *W,* with a Blank after it.   † M. S. *in and every.*

Council

Council for the faid firft Colony in *Virginia,* and to nominate
and appoint fuch Officers, as they fhall think fit and requifite, for
the Government, Managing, Ordering, and Difpatching of the
Affairs of the faid Company; And fhall likewife have full Power
and Authority, to ordain and make fuch Laws and Ordinances,
for the Good and Welfare of the faid Plantation, as to them,
from time to time, fhall be thought requifite and meet: *So always,* as the fame be not contrary to the Laws and Statutes of
this our Realm of *England*; And fhall, in like Manner, * have
Power and Authority, to expulfe, disfranchife, and put, out of
and from their faid Company and Society, for ever, all and every
fuch Perfon and Perfons, as having either promifed, or fubfcribed
their Names, to become Adventurers to the faid Plantation of the
faid firft Colony in *Virginia,* † or having been nominated for Adventurers, in thefe or any other our Letters Patents, or having
been otherwife admitted and nominated to be of the faid Company, have neverthelefs, either not put in any Adventure at all,
for and towards the faid Plantation, or elfe have refufed and neglected, or fhall refufe and neglect, to bring in his or their Adventure, by Word or Writing promifed, within fix Months after
the fame fhall be fo payable and due.

IX. AND whereas the Failing and not Payment of fuch Monies, as have been promifed in Adventure for the Advancement
of the faid Plantation, hath been often by Experience found, to
be dangerous and prejudicial to the fame, and much to have hindered the Progrefs and Proceeding of the faid Plantation, and for
that it feemeth unto Us a thing reafonable, that fuch Perfons, as
by their Hand Writing have engaged themfelves for the Payment
of their Adventures, and afterwards neglecting their Faith and
Promife, fhould be compelled to make good and keep the fame;
Therefore our Will and Pleafure is, that in any Suit or Suits,
commenced or to be commenced, in any of our Courts at *Weftminfter,* or elfewhere, by the faid Treafurer and Company, or
otherwife, againft any fuch Perfons, that our Judges for the time
being, both in our Court of Chancery and at the Common Pleas,
do favour and further the faid Suits, fo far forth as Law and E-
quity will, in any wife, further and permit.

X. AND we do, for Us, our Heirs, and Succeffors, further
GIVE AND GRANT to the faid Treafurer and Company, or their
Succeffors, for ever, that they, the faid Treafurer and Company,
or the greater Part of them, for the time being, fo in a full and
general Court affembled, as aforefaid, fhall and may, from time
to time, and at all times for ever hereafter, elect, choofe, and
admit into their Company and Society, any Perfon or Perfons,
as well Strangers ‡ and Aliens, born in any Part beyond the Seas
wherefoever, being in Amity with us, as our natural Leige-Sub-
jects, born in any our Realms and Dominions; And that all fuch
Perfons, fo elected, chofen, and admitted to be of the faid Company, as aforefaid, fhall thereupon be taken, reputed, and held,

* M. S. *have and Authority.*   † M. S. *of.*   ‡ M. S. *as.*

and

and ſhall be, free Members of the ſaid Company, and ſhall have, hold, and enjoy all and ſingular Freedoms, Liberties, Franchiſes, Privileges, Immunities, Benefits, Profits, and Commodities, whatſoever, to the ſaid Company in any Sort belonging or appertaining, as fully, freely, and amply, as any other Adventurers, now being, or which hereafter at any time ſhall be of the ſaid Company, hath, have, ſhall, may, might, or ought to have and enjoy the ſame, to all Intents and Purpoſes whatſoever.

XI. A N D we do further, of our eſpecial Grace, certain Knowledge, and mere Motion, for Us, our Heirs, and Succeſſors, G I V E A N D G R A N T unto the ſaid Treaſurer and Company, and their Succeſſors, for ever, by theſe Preſents, that it ſhall be lawful and free, for them and their Aſſigns, at all and every time and times hereafter, out of any our Realms and Dominions whatſoever, to take, lead, carry, and tranſport, in and into the ſaid Voyage, and for and towards the ſaid Plantation of our ſaid firſt Colony in *Virginia*, all ſuch and ſo many of our loving Subjects, or any other Strangers, that will become our loving Subjects and live under our Allegiance, as ſhall willingly accompany them in the ſaid Voyages and Plantation ; With Shipping, Armour, Weapons, Ordinance, Munition, Powder, Shot, Victuals, and all Manner of Merchandiſes and Wares, and all Manner of Cloathing, Implements, Furniture, Beaſts, Cattle, Horſes, Mares and all other things neceſſary for the ſaid Plantation, and for their Uſe and Defence, and for Trade with the People there, and in paſſing and returning to and from, without paying or yielding any Subſidy, Cuſtom, or Impoſition, either inward or outward, or any other Duty, to Us, our Heirs, or Succeſſors, for the ſame, for the Space of ſeven Years from the Date of theſe Preſents.

XII. A N D we do further, for Us, our Heirs, and Succeſſors, G I V E A N D G R A N T to the ſaid Treaſurer and Company, and their Succeſſors, for ever, by theſe Preſents, that the ſaid Treaſurer of that Company, or his Deputy, for the time being, or any two other of the ſaid Council for the ſaid firſt Colony in *Virginia*, for the time being, or any two other at all times hereafter, and from time to time, have full Power and Authority, to miniſter and give the Oath and Oaths of Supremacy and Allegiance, or either of them, to all and every Perſon and Perſons, which ſhall, at any time or times hereafter, go or paſs to the ſaid Colony in *Virginia :*

XIII. A N D further, that it ſhall be lawful likewiſe for the ſaid Treaſurer, or his Deputy, for the time being, or any two or others of our ſaid Council for the ſaid firſt Colony in *Virginia*, for the time being, from time to time, and at all times hereafter, to miniſter ſuch a formal Oath, as by their Diſcretion ſhall be reaſonably deviſed, as well unto any Perſon or Perſons, employed in, for, or touching the ſaid Plantation, for their honeſt, faithful, and juſt Diſcharge of their Service, in all ſuch Matters, as ſhall be committed unto them for the Good and Benefit of the ſaid Company, Colony, and Plantation; As alſo, unto ſuch other Perſon or Perſons, as the ſaid Treaſurer, or his Deputy, with
two

two others of the said Council, shall think meet, for the Examination or clearing of the Truth, in any Cause whatsoever concerning the said Plantation, or any Business, from thence proceeding, or thereunto belonging.

XIV. And furthermore, whereas we have been certified, that divers lewd and ill-disposed Persons, both Sailers, Soldiers, Artificers, Husbandmen, Labourers, and others, having received Wages, * Apparel, and other Entertainment from the said Company, or having contracted and agreed with the said Company, to go, or to serve, or to be employed in the said Plantation of the said first Colony in *Virginia,* have afterwards, either withdrawn, hid, or concealed themselves, or have refused to go thither, after they have been so entertained and agreed withal; And that divers and sundry Persons also, which have been sent and employed in the said Plantation of the said first Colony in *Virginia,* at and upon the Charge of the said Company, and having there misbehaved themselves by Mutinies, Sedition, or other notorious Misdemeanors, or having been employed or sent abroad, by the Governor of *Virginia* or his Deputy, with some Ship or Pinnace, for our Provision of the said Colony, or for some Discovery, or other Business and Affairs, concerning the same, have from thence most treacherously, either come back again and returned into our Realm of *England,* by Stealth, or without Licence of our Governor of our said Colony in *Virginia* for the time being, or have been sent hither, as Misdoers and Offenders; And that many also of those Persons, after their Return from thence, having been questioned by our said Council here, for such their Misbehaviors and Offences, by their insolent and contemptuous Carriage in the Presence of our said Council, have shewed little Respect and Reverence, either to the Place, or Authority, in which we have placed and appointed them; And others, for the colouring of their Lewdness and Misdemeanors committed in *Virginia,* have endeavoured, by most vile and slanderous Reports, made and divulged, as well of the Country of *Virginia,* as also of the Government and Estate of the said Plantation and Colony, as much as in them lay, to bring the said Voyage and Plantation into Disgrace and Contempt; By Means whereof, not only the Adventurers and Planters, already engaged in the said Plantation, have been exceedingly abused and hindered, and a great Number of other our loving and well-disposed Subjects, otherwise well-affected, and enclined to join and adventure in so noble, christian, and worthy an Action, have been discouraged from the same, but also the utter Overthrow and Ruin of the said Enterprise hath been greatly endangered, which cannot miscarry without some Dishonour to Us and our Kingdom;

XV. Now, forasmuch as it appeareth unto us, that these Insolences, Misdemeanors, and Abuses, not to be tolerated in any civil Government, have, for the most part, grown and proceeded, in regard our said Council have not any direct Power and

---

* M. S. *Appell an other.*

Authority, by any expreſs Words in our former Letters Patents, to correct and chaſtiſe ſuch Offenders; We therefore, for the more ſpeedy Reformation of ſo great and enormous Abuſes and Miſdemeanors, heretofore practiſed and committed, and for the preventing of the like hereafter, do, by theſe Preſents, for Us, our Heirs, and Succeſſors, GIVE AND GRANT to the ſaid Treaſurer and Company, and their Succeſſors, for ever, that it ſhall and may be lawful for our ſaid Council for the ſaid firſt Colony in *Virginia*, or any two of them (whereof the ſaid Treaſurer, or his Deputy, for the time being, to be always one) by Warrant under their Hands, to ſend for, or to cauſe to be apprehended, all and every ſuch Perſon and Perſons, who ſhall be noted, or accuſed, or found, at any time or times hereafter, to offend, or miſbehave themſelves, in any the Offences before mentioned and expreſſed; And upon the Examination of any ſuch Offender or Offenders, and juſt Proof made by Oath, taken before the ſaid Council, of any ſuch notorious Miſdemeanors by them committed, as aforeſaid; And alſo upon any inſolent, and contemptuous, or indecent Carriage and Miſbehaviour, to or againſt our ſaid Council, ſhewed or uſed by any ſuch Perſon or Perſons, ſo called, convented, and appearing before them, as aforeſaid; That in all ſuch Caſes, they, our ſaid Council, or any two of them, for the time being, ſhall and may have full Power and Authority, either here to bind them over with good Sureties for their good Behaviour, and further therein to proceed, to all Intents and Purpoſes, as it is uſed, in other like Caſes, within our Realm of *England*; Or elſe, at their Diſcretions, to remand and ſend them back, the ſaid Offenders, or any of them, unto the ſaid Colony in *Virginia*, there to be proceeded againſt and puniſhed, as the Governor, Deputy, or Council there, for the time being, ſhall think meet; or otherwiſe, according to ſuch Laws and Ordinances, as are and ſhall be in Uſe there, for the Well-ordering and good Government of the ſaid Colony.

XVI. AND for the more effectual Advancing of the ſaid Plantation, we do further, for Us, our Heirs, and Succeſſors, of our eſpecial Grace and Favour, by Virtue of our Prerogative Royal, and by the Aſſent and Conſent of the Lords and others of our Privy Council, GIVE and GRANT, unto the ſaid Treaſurer and Company, full Power and Authority, free Leave, Liberty, and Licence, to ſet forth, erect, and publiſh, one or more Lottery or Lotteries, to have Continuance, and to endure and be held, for the Space of our whole Year, next after the Opening of the ſame; And after the End and Expiration of the ſaid Term, the ſaid Lottery or Lotteries to continue and be further kept, during our Will and Pleaſure only, and not otherwiſe. And yet nevertheleſs, we are contented and pleaſed, for the Good and Welfare of the ſaid Plantation, that the ſaid Treaſurer and Company ſhall, for the Diſpatch and Finiſhing of the ſaid Lottery or Lotteries, have ſix Months Warning after the ſaid Year ended, before our Will and Pleaſure ſhall, for and on that Behalf, be conſtrued, deemed, and adjudged, to be in any wiſe altered and determined.

XVII.

XVII. AND our further Will and Pleasure is, that the said Lottery and Lotteries shall and may be opened and held, within our City of *London*, or in any other City or Town, or elsewhere, within this our Realm of *England*, with such Prizes, Articles, Conditions, and Limitations, as to them, the said Treasurer and Company, in their Discretions, shall seem convenient:

XVIII. AND that it shall and may be lawful, to and for the said Treasurer and Company, to elect and choose Receivers, Auditors, Surveyors, Commissioners, or any other Officers whatsoever, at their Will and Pleasure, for the better marshalling, disposing, guiding, and governing of the said Lottery and Lotteries; And that it shall likewise be lawful, to and for the said Treasurer and any two of the said Council, to minister to all and every such Person, so elected and chosen for Officers, as aforesaid, one or more Oaths, for their good Behaviour, just and true Dealing, in and about the said Lottery or Lotteries, to the Intent and Purpose, that none of our loving Subjects, putting in their Names, or otherwise adventuring in the said general Lottery or Lotteries, may be, in any wise, defrauded and deceived of their said Monies, or evil and indirectly dealt withal in their said Adventures.

XIX. AND we further GRANT, in Manner and Form aforesaid, that it shall and may be lawful, to and for the said Treasurer and Company, under the Seal of our said Council for the Plantation, to publish, or to cause and procure to be published, by Proclamation or otherwise (the said Proclamation to be made in their Name, by Virtue of these Presents) the said Lottery or Lotteries, in all Cities, Towns, Burroughs,   and other Places, within our said Realm of *England*; And we Will and Command all ‡ Mayors, Justices of Peace, Sherifs, Bailiffs, Constables, and other Officers and loving Subjects, whatsoever, that, in no wise, they hinder or delay the Progress and Proceedings of the said Lottery or Lotteries, but be therein, touching the Premises, aiding and assisting, by all honest, good, and lawful Means and Endeavours.

XX. AND further, our Will and Pleasure is, that in all Questions and Doubts, that shall arise, upon any Difficulty † of Construction or Interpretation of any thing, contained in these, or any other our former Letters Patents, the same shall be taken and interpreted, in most ample and beneficial Manner for the said Treasurer and Company, and their Successors, and every Member thereof.

XXI. AND lastly, we do, by these Presents, RATIFY AND CONFIRM unto the said Treasurer and Company, and their Successors, for ever, all and all Manner of Privileges, Franchises, Liberties, Immunities, Preheminences, Profits, and Commodities, whatsoever, granted unto them in any our former Letters Patents, and not in these Presents revoked, altered, changed, or abridged. ALTHOUGH express Mention of the true Yearly Value or Certainty of the Premises, or any of them, or of any

---

‡ M. S. *Mayor.*   † M. S. *or.*

other Gift or Grant, by Us or any of our Progenitors or Predeceffors, to the aforefaid Treafurer and Company heretofore made,
in thefe Prefents is not made; Or any Statute, Act, Ordinance,
Provifion, Proclamation, or Reftraint, to the contrary thereof
heretofore made, ordained, or provided, or any other Matter,
Caufe, or thing, whatfoever, to the contrary, in any wife, notwithftanding.

IN WITNESS whereof we have caufed thefe our Letters to
be made Patents. Witnefs Ourfelf, at *Weftminfter*, the twelfth
Day of *March*, in the ninth Year of our Reign of *England*,.
France, and *Ireland*, and of *Scotland* the five and fortieth.

Nº. IV.

*An Ordinance and Conftitution of the Treafurer, Council, and
Company in* England, *for a Council of State and General
Affembly.* Dated July 24, 1621.

I. TO all People, to whom thefe Prefents fhall come, be
feen, or heard, The Treafurer, Council, and Com-
pany of Adventurers and Planters for the City of *London* for the
firft Colony of *Virginia*, fend Greeting. KNOW YE, that we,
the faid Treafurer, Council, and Company, taking into our careful Confideration the prefent State of the faid Colony of *Virginia*, and intending, by the Divine Affiftance, to fettle fuch a
Form of Government there, as may be to the greateft Benefit
and Comfort of the People, and whereby all Injuftice, Grievances, and Oppreffion may be prevented and kept off as much
as poffible from the faid Colony, have thought fit to make our
Entrance, by ordering and eftablifhing fuch Supreme Councils, as
may not only be affifting to the Governor for the time being, in
the Adminiftration of Juftice, and the Executing of other Duties to this Office belonging, but alfo, by their vigilant Care
and Prudence, may provide, as well for a Remedy of all Inconveniences, growing from time to time, as alfo for advancing of
Increafe, Strength, Stability, and Profperity of the faid Colony:

II. WE therefore, the faid Treafurer, Council, and Compa-
ny, * by Authority directed to us from his Majefty under the
Great Seal, upon mature Deliberation, do hereby order and
declare, that, from hence forward, there fhall be TWO SUPREME
COUNCILS in *Virginia*, for the better Government of the faid
Colony aforefaid.

III. THE one of which Councils, to be called THE COUN-
CIL OF STATE (and whofe Office fhall chiefly be affifting, with
their Care, Advice, and Circumfpection, to the faid Governor)
fhall be chofen, nominated, placed, and difplaced, from time to

* Vide Sect. XIV. and XXIII. of the fecond Charter, and Sect. VIII.
of the third.

time,

time, by Us, the faid Treasurer, Council, and Company, and
our Succeffors: Which Council of State fhall confift, for the pre-
fent, only of thefe Perfons, as are here inferted, *viz.* Sir *Francis
Wyat*, ‡ Governor of *Virginia*, Captain *Francis Weft*, Sir *George
Yeardley*, Knight, Sir *William Neuce*, Knight Marfhal of *Virginia*,
Mr. *George Sandys*, Treafurer, Mr. *George* † *Thorpe*, Deputy of
the College, Captain *Thomas Neuce*, Deputy for the Company,
Mr. *Pawlet*, Mr. *Leech*, Captain *Nathaniel Powel*, Mr. *Chriftopher Davifon*, Secretary, Doctor *Pots*, Phyfician to the Company,
Mr. *Roger Smith*, Mr. *John Berkeley*, Mr. *John Rolfe*, Mr. *Ralph
Hamer*, Mr. *John* * *Pountis*, Mr. *Michael Lapworth*, Mr. *Harwood*, Mr. *Samuel Macock*. Which faid Counfellors and Council
we earneftly pray and defire, and in his Majefty's Name ftrictly
charge and command, that (all Factions, Partialities, and finifter
Refpect laid afide) they bend their Care and Endeavours to affift
the faid Governor; firft and principally, in the Advancement of
the Honour and Service of God, and the Enlargement of his
Kingdom amongft the Heathen People; and next, in erecting of
the faid Colony in due Obedience to his Majefty, and all lawful
Authority from his Majefty's Directions; and laftly, in maintain-
ing the faid People in Juftice and *Chriftian* Converfation amongft
themfelves, and in Strength and Ability to withftand their Enemies. And this Council, to be always, or for the moft Part, refiding about or near the Governor.

IV. The other Council, more generally to be called by the
Governor, once Yearly, and no § oftener, but for ‖ very extraordinary and important Occafions, fhall confift, ** for the prefent,
of the faid Council of State, and of two Burgeffes out of every
Town, Hundred, or other particular Plantation, to be refpectively chofen by the Inhabitants: Which Council fhall be called
The General Assembly, wherein (as alfo in the faid Council
of State) all Matters fhall be decided, determined, and ordered,
by the greater Part of the Voices then prefent; referving to the
Governor always a Negative Voice. And this General Affembly
fhall have free Power to treat, confult, and conclude, as well of all
emergent Occafions concerning the Publick Weal of the faid Colony and every Part thereof, as alfo to make, ordain, and enact
fuch general Laws and Orders, for the Behoof of the faid Colony,
and the good Government thereof, as fhall, from time to time,
appear neceffary or requifite;

V. Whereas in all other Things, we require the faid General
Affembly, as alfo the faid Council of State, to imitate and follow

---

‡ It is to be noted, that the Governor is always inferted in the old Com-
miffions, as a Part, and the Head of the Council of State.
† M. S. *Thorne*; but as I am perfectly well acquainted with thefe Names
and Perfons, by perufing the ancient Records, I fhall take the Liberty of cor-
recting the Errors of the Tranfcriber.
* M. S. *Downtus*.
§ M. S. *officer*.
‖ M. S. *very and extraordinary important*; which likewife makes Senfe,
taking *extraordinary* adverbially.
** M. S. *for prefent*.

the

the Policy of the Form of Government, Laws, Cuſtoms, and
Manner of Trial, and other Adminiſtration of Juſtice, uſed in the
Realm of *England*, as near as may be, even as ourſelves, by his
Majeſty's Letters Patent, are required.

VI. PROVIDED, that no Law or Ordinance, made in the ſaid
General Aſſembly, ſhall be or continue in Force or Validity,
unleſs the ſame ſhall be ſolemnly ratified and confirmed, in a
General Quarter Court of the ſaid * Company here in *England*,
and ſo ratified, be returned to them under our Seal; It being
our Intent to afford the like Meaſure alſo unto the ſaid Colony,
that after the Government of the ſaid Colony ſhall once have
been well framed, and ſettled accordingly, which is to be done
by Us, as by Authority derived from his Majeſty, and the ſame
ſhall have been ſo by us declared, no Orders of Court afterwards ſhall bind the ſaid Colony, unleſs they be ratified in like
Manner in the General Aſſemblies. IN WITNESS whereof we
have hereunto ſet our Common Seal, the 24th of *July* 1621,
and in the Year of the Reign of our Sovereign Lord, *JAMES*,
King of *England &c.* the **** and of *Scotland* the ****.

---

* M. S. *Court.*

V

14

4428